Organizational Behaviour

This book offers a fresh and comprehensive approach to the essentials that constitute the discipline of organizational behaviour with a strong emphasis on the application of organizational behaviour and performance management in practice.

It concentrates on the development of effective patterns of behaviour, values and attitudes, and relates these issues to effective organization performance in times of organizational and environmental change and turbulence. The book is divided into four parts, providing a clear structure for the study of the subject:

- Part 1: The context of organizational behaviour
- Part 2: The disciplines of organizational behaviour
- Part 3: Organizational behaviour in practice
- Part 4: Organizational behaviour – expertise and application

Organizational Behaviour is packed with references to current topics, practical examples and case studies from large corporations from around the world, including Ryanair, The Body Shop and RBS. This book covers examples of both good and bad practice, making it an interesting and unique introduction to the study of organizational behaviour.

Richard Pettinger is Principal Teaching Fellow and Reader in Management Education at University College London, where he is also Director of the undergraduate Information Management for Business programme. He also continues to consult with organizations in all sectors.

Organizational Behaviour

Performance management in practice

Richard Pettinger

Routledge
Taylor & Francis Group

LONDON AND NEW YORK

First published 2010
by Routledge
2 Park Square, Milton Park, Abingdon, Oxon OX14 4RN

Simultaneously published in the USA and Canada
by Routledge
270 Madison Ave, New York, NY 10016

Routledge is an imprint of the Taylor & Francis Group, an Informa business

Typeset in Times New Roman by
Florence Production Ltd, Stoodleigh, Devon
Printed and bound in Great Britain by
CPI Antony Rowe, Chippenham, Wiltshire

British Library Cataloguing in Publication Data
A catalogue record for this book is available from the British Library

Library of Congress Cataloguing in Publication Data
Pettinger, Richard.
    Organizational behaviour: performance management in practice/
    Richard Pettinger. – 1st ed.
        p. cm.
    Includes bibliographical references and index.
    1. Organizational behavior.   2. Leadership.   3. Industrial management.
    I. Title.
    HD58.7.P49 2009
    658.3 – dc22
                                                        2009034166

ISBN: 978–0–415–48142–7 (hbk)
ISBN: 978–0–415–48143–4 (pbk)
ISBN: 978–0–203–85759–5 (ebk)

To Rebecca

Contents

Boxes

Figures

Tables

Preface

The first part of the twenty-first century has seen unprecedented economic, social, political and cultural upheaval. This, in turn, has affected every aspect of human activity, and above all, organizational and managerial practice.

In particular, the world has witnessed an unprecedented collapse in the banking and financial services industries, and asset values. The world has witnessed the discrediting and disgracing of the political establishment, which in many countries has come to be regarded as almost entirely self-seeking.

Other industries are not immune. Large and world-renowned corporations in the motorcar, pharmaceuticals, retail goods, airline, energy and telecommunications sectors have all faced serious difficulties in the present and recent past; and this means that either they have had to rescue themselves, or else go out of business altogether.

This has occurred on the back of what was widely perceived to be a global and industrial economic boom, bringing hitherto unheard of levels of prosperity to all. The fact that 'all' referred largely to the middle classes of the western world, Far East, Japan, Russia, Australia and New Zealand of course went largely unnoticed.

The common factor binding all of this is: it was all created by humans. Nothing in any of the above happened of its own accord; nor was any of the above certain to happen whatever the actions taken to try to mitigate its effects. So the political and economic turbulence, social upheaval and perceptions of prosperity all came about as the result of decisions taken by those in leadership, directoral, managerial and key positions in government and commercial organizations. All of these were the products of human behaviour.

In the overwhelming majority of cases, the ways in which people behaved (and continue to behave) in political, economic, social, industrial and organizational situations is driven by a combination of expediency, laziness and an incapability and/or unwillingness to learn how things should be done properly. In political and economic organizations and institutions, there has existed a fundamental lack of integrity, coupled with a lack of understanding of what it takes to energize organizations in the pursuit of their stated goals and objectives, and make them successful and effective.

At the core of all organizations are the people who work in them, and for them. This fact remains largely ignored by many top and senior management teams in all institutions; and this is because it is much safer and easier to make pronouncements about 'business models' (whatever these may be), 'organizational models' (whatever these may be) and 'drives for value' (again, whatever these may be). Life is easier and much more straightforward if everything can be reduced to this kind of simplicity.

The world has lived to regret this; and therefore it has to reform itself. Only this time, it has to be done on the basis that those in senior, key and responsible positions do actually know and understand what they are doing. At the heart of this knowledge and understanding lies the discipline of organizational behaviour.

Organizational behaviour encompasses a range of disciplines; and these disciplines include economics, sociology, politics and ethics, as well as more precisely organization and work-based expertise including leadership, motivation, the ability to survive and be effective, and an understanding of how particular decisions are taken and implemented in given sets of circumstances.

None of this is new. Literature concerning all aspects of management and business practice comes regularly to the conclusion that the success or otherwise of organizations is driven by the extent of expertise in the management of the staff, and in the understanding of how organizations actually work. If this is related to the human involvement and active decision-making that has caused the failure of banking and other industries, and the discrediting of the political institutions, then it becomes clear that this part of managerial expertise is critical to institutional success.

This is the basis and context on which the book is founded. Quite simply, what has gone on in the past cannot persist for the future; apart from anything else, the commercial world cannot afford it.

The book is divided into four parts as follows:

Part 1 deals with the context in which organizational behaviour is structured and formed. It refers to the need for a clear understanding of a range of disciplines, including economics, sociology, psychology and anthropology, at least in so far as these are present within organizations. It is also essential to understand the wider environment in which organizations operate, and the pressures present. It is further necessary to understand that this environment is changing; and so organizations and their managers have to have responses available, as well as to be able to take initiatives within this part of the context.

Part 2 deals with the foundations of organizational behaviour, and the disciplines that it is necessary to understand in order to be effective. For convenience, this part is divided up into chapters covering perception; attitudes, values and beliefs; influence, power and authority; organizational politics; technology and working practices; and organizational culture. In practice, none of these exist as isolated or complete disciplines; rather they all interact with each other. However, to study these in overtly 'isolated' chapters does at least reinforce the need for a wide range of overall knowledge and expertise, as well as indicating the range of the discipline.

Part 3 relates the disciplines and context of organizational behaviour to what is required in practice. This part therefore covers leadership; roles and functions; organization and work structures; and human resource management. This is to reinforce the point that, increasingly, all organizations are looking to expertise, rather than (or as well as) to those in charge of their destiny; and to drive home the point also that the position and influence of HR departments, divisions and functions is all too often neglected. In particular, the point is made that effective HR functions make a major contribution to the cost effectiveness of organizations.

Part 4 is concerned with the relationship between effective patterns of behaviour and overarching organizational practice. General management, strategy formulation and implementation, the ordering and structuring of operations, and the creation of effective patterns of behaviour in the workplace are all dependent upon a fundamental understanding of collective and individual human behaviour. Without this, the contention is that no effective strategy, policy, direction, operations or activities are possible.

As stated above, the overall context is that organizations that have failed have done so on the basis of their lack of attention to collective and individual human behaviour. Those in top, senior and key positions have tended to go their own way; those working within organizations have been, and remain, unsure of what they are supposed to do, how or why. Organizational behaviour is therefore a critical managerial discipline, a key foundation of effective and professional – and expert – management practice. This is the context in which this book is to be used.

Richard Pettinger
University College London
March 2010

Acknowledgements

The structure and basis for this book arose from an increasing awareness of the huge pressures that collective and individual human behaviour exert on organization and management practice, activities and effectiveness. The work was carried out against the background of the financial, political and commercial crises of the period 2008–2010, and the conclusions that were clear to everyone at this time – that what had occurred in the finance, banking, political and commercial spheres arose as the direct result of decisions taken by those at the very top of the main organizations and institutions in these sectors. The decisions taken were therefore driven by humanity rather than expertise or rationale; and so it therefore became (and becomes) vitally important to understand the behavioural (human) basis for these decisions. This is so that managers and organization leaders for the future can acknowledge and understand where the pressures lie, and so develop an understanding and awareness in order that the same mistakes are not made again in the future.

As usual, many people gave great and valuable assistance in developing the approach and overall context for this work. I am particularly grateful to Peter Antonioni, Jane Burns Nurse, Peter Clark, Kelvin Cheatle, Frances Kelly, Paul Griseri, Jacek Klich, Brian Murphy and Jia Jia Ye; to Terry Clague, Sarah Enticknap and Nigel Hope at the publishers; and also to Ken Batchelor, Roger and June Cartwright, Mark Genney, Mike Hutton, Anthony Impey, James Pollock and Keith Sanders as always.

Every effort has been made to trace all copyright holders, but if any have been inadvertently overlooked then we will be pleased to make the necessary arrangements at the first opportunity.

Part 1

The context of organizational behaviour

The first part of the book deals with the context in which organizational behaviour has to be understood, and in which the particular disciplines are to be applied.

Chapter 1 draws particular attention to the wide range of disciplines that have to be understood, at least from an operational point of view; and these disciplines include economics, sociology, psychology, anthropology and mathematics. These disciplines form the foundations on which a true understanding of more directly applicable expertise can be applied subsequently: leadership, motivation and the effective structuring and ordering of teams and groups, and patterns of work.

The second chapter deals with organizational behaviour in its environment. This is to underline the point that organizations are flexible, dynamic and living entities, developing and advancing all of the time. Organizations that seek or aim to become steady and orderly actually become inert. Organizations have additionally to be able to exist in the context of the locations and markets that they exist in and serve; and in terms of the technology and expertise that they employ.

The other part of this context is change; and this is dealt with in Chapter 3. Organizations have to be capable of responding to changes and pressures in their environment; and they also have to be able to change themselves in order to meet fresh challenges and developments. Organizations have to be capable of accommodating advances in human and technological knowledge, and in harmonizing these to best effect in the pursuit of successful activities.

The overall context is bounded by the need for managerial expertise in integrating all of the lessons into a body of understanding that forms the basis for the study of knowing how people think, behave, act and react in a variety of situations.

1 Introduction

Organizational behaviour is concerned with the study of the behaviour and interaction of people in restricted or organized settings. It involves the understanding of, and prediction of, the behaviour of people, and of the means by which their behaviour is influenced and shaped.

Organizations are bodies or entities created for a stated purpose. They may consist of one or more people. In the case of the sole trader or single operator, he/she needs to build relationships with suppliers, contractors, customers, clients and the community. For those that consist of more than one person, internal as well as external relationships have to be created and maintained. Organizations therefore consist of individuals, groups and relationships. Objectives, structures, systems and processes are then created to give life, direction and order to activities and interactions.

Organizational behaviour is therefore of great concern to anyone who organizes, creates, orders, directs, manages or supervises the activities of others. It is also of concern to those who build relationships between individuals, groups of people, different parts of organizations, and between different organizations themselves because all of these activities are founded on human interaction.

The study of organizational behaviour is therefore concerned with:

- the purposes for which organizations are created;
- the behaviour of individuals, and an understanding of the pressures and influences that cause them to act and react in particular ways;
- the qualities that individuals bring to particular situations;
- the creation of groups – collections of people brought together for given purposes;
- the background and context within which activities take place;
- the energizing of activities;
- the use and combination of resources for productive purposes;
- relationships and interactions with the wider environment and with other organizations and groups;
- the management and ordering of the whole and its parts into productive and effective work relationships.

Organizations exist for the particular purposes for which they were constituted; and in order to deliver these purposes effectively and profitably, strong and enduring patterns of behaviour have to be created and managed.

The context of organizational behaviour

Gratton (2006) states that organizations exist in time; but they exist for a purpose; and that they have a fundamental humanity as well as aims, objectives and priorities.

The factors are all of critical importance in understanding the crucial nature of organizational behaviour in the effective management, direction and ordering of organizations and those who work within them, and in creating the conditions in which organizations and their activities can be developed.

'In time' means that organizations have to be capable of delivering their stated purposes in the present and future, according to the conditions prevailing, and the current needs, wants and demands of markets and societies.

The development of organizations presumes that every process, practice and activity is capable of improvement and advancement; nothing is perfect or finished. This is a self-evident truth; every activity is capable of being delivered more quickly, with greater accuracy, with fewer mistakes and with less wastage. Collectively and individually, people find ways of learning things more quickly, and of developing ever-more effective tools, technology, practices and procedures along the way.

The humanity of organizations has too often been neglected in the past. In many cases, those in top and senior management positions have assumed that either by making strident pronouncements, or creating restrictive and supposedly assured standards and patterns of behaviour, the humanity of organizations can be made predictable. This is not so; anyone seeking any position of influence in organizations needs to know and understand the uncertainties of human behaviour, and from this to learn and understand how to develop their expertise, so that they are able to better achieve their organization and business objectives.

To bring all this together: understanding the ways in which people behave in organizations, what drives their actions and how activities are energized has never been so important. The industrial, financial, banking, political and social crises of the early twenty-first century have all been caused by people in organizations; they have not occurred by chance, or as the result of the forces of nature. The decisions that have driven such diverse organizations as the UK House of Commons, General Motors, the Royal Bank of Scotland and the BBC into crisis, disrepute, extensive financial loss and the point of bankruptcy have all been taken by managers. These decisions have been taken without reference to how people think, believe, behave and react; they have been taken either on the basis of narrow expediency, short-term advantage or self-interest, rather than that of wider society and the environment. In many cases too, these decisions were taken on the basis of an unwillingness or inability to do the work that should have formed their core. These decisions lie at the root of these crises and they show a fundamental lack of understanding of how people behave, and an unwillingness to learn this as part of managerial expertise.

The basis of organizational behaviour

Organizational behaviour is not a natural or absolute science, nor is it a distinctive field of study. It draws on a range of disciplines and is viewed from a variety of perspectives. Rather than provide an absolute or perfect body of knowledge and expertise, each of these offers a different point of view on the whole, so that as complete an understanding as possible may be built up. Consideration of organizational behaviour from each stand-point indicates both the broad context, and also some of the specific areas, of concern.

Moreover, each discipline and perspective is incomplete and imperfect. Each is in itself an ever-developing and enlarging field. However, this at least indicates why a full understanding of organizational behaviour is not yet achieved and the context in which studies in the field are to be seen.

The disciplines of organizational behaviour

The main disciplines that contribute to the study of organizational behaviour are as follows. In summary, they are concerned with the capabilities and potential of people; influences on capabilities; the attitudes and behaviour of people; influences on behaviour; the organizational context; organizational processes and the execution of work; and interaction with the environment.

- **Psychology**: the study and understanding of human personality and behaviour, the traits and characteristics of individuals; their perceptions, attitudes, values, beliefs and motives; their goals and priorities; their capabilities and potential.
- **Sociology**: the study of behaviour in groups; influences on this behaviour; interactions between groups; the extent to which people organize themselves and the ways in which they do this; processes of socialization (the ordering and limiting of individual behaviour by groups and the environment); the creation of norms, rules and regulations.
- **Anthropology**: the study of large groups, nations and cultures; global beliefs, customs, ideas and values; the wider processes of socialization (for example, through religious activities, caste systems, aristocracies, technocracies).
- **Economics**: the study of the ordering, use and distribution of the world's resources; of gathering and using these to best effect in particular situations and in the pursuit of stated aims and objectives.
- **Ethics**: the establishment of absolute standards which relate, above all, to the nature of interpersonal relationships and interactions, including standards of honesty, integrity, probity, value, esteem and respect.
- **Mathematics and statistics**: the need to prove absolutes and facts wherever possible; to give a basis of certainty to particular situations; to provide the means by which logical and demonstrable conclusions from bodies of knowledge and research can be drawn.

Each of these disciplines offers a different point of view and contributes to understanding; none, however, offers the complete picture. The major problem is the inability to arrive at absolute facts and conclusions. This is in direct contrast to the study of physics, mathematics, mechanics, chemistry and biology, each of which is capable of:

- absolute and logical reasoning;
- the combination of components and variables to produce certain and predictable results;
- consistent relationships between variables through time and space that are incapable of being reinterpreted due to differences in nationality or location;
- capability of validation and demonstration through experimentation.

In particular, the validation of human behaviour requires extensive experimentation, and constant reconfirmation, as a condition of the strength of the conclusions drawn.

A single experiment, however wide-ranging, can never 'prove' that people will behave, act and react in certain and assured ways. Even well understood organizational behaviour 'proofs' such as the forming-storming-norming-performing approach to group develop-ment and the motivation theories of Maslow and Herzberg require constant and current validation and re-validation if their strength and integrity are to be maintained.

The development of organizational behaviour

As the result of the sheer volume of work carried out in the field, and as the result of the validation and re-validation referred to above, there is an extensive body of information available. Studying this body of information needs to become a priority of all those who seek or aspire to managerial positions. Learning and understanding the complexities, uncertainties and vagaries of human behaviour ought to be part of the professional discipline of management.

It is necessary to study extensive bodies of information from the field of organizational behaviour because of the fact that it requires this validation and re-validation. Other than mathematics and statistics, none of the component disciplines of organizational behaviour have any certainty or predictability. Especially, people do not behave in consistent or rational ways. Every situation is unique and so it is impossible to recreate the conditions under which one experiment took place in order to repeat it. Rather than controlled experimentation, organizational behaviour investigations rely on observed experiments, case studies, the analysis of documentation and the use of qualitative investigations and questionnaires to provide the information with which they arrive at their conclusions.

Observations and observed experiments are subject to perception and interpretation; the use of the senses; and the ability to take in enough of a particular situation to form a sufficient understanding on which judgements can be made.

Additionally, observed experiments are limited by the ability of researchers to design hypotheses and devise means for testing these in ways that are capable of being validated.

The study of case histories and examples is subject to perception and judgement, except where cause and effects can be directly related – for example, where £10 was made because 10 items were sold at £1 each.

Also, the analysis of documentation is subject to the knowledge, quality and judgement of those who originally produced the documents, as well as being subject to the interpretation of those currently using them. The use of questioning and questionnaires is limited by the capabilities of the researchers to define their purpose, ask the right questions, interpret and analyse the responses and draw conclusions from the information and material gained. Limitations are also produced by situational factors, individual priorities and perspectives. These are continuously being influenced by their environment and can quite legitimately provide a different set of answers to the same questions within moments if their circumstances suddenly change. Their responses are influenced by the ways in which they are questioned. Additionally, the response to written questionnaires is affected by their length; the number of questions; the nature of questions asked; the ways in which these are asked; the length of time required to complete the questionnaire; the length of time at the disposal of the individual; the responses of others if these are known; the language used; the extent of interest of the individual in the material; the visual presentation of the questionnaire (or the interviewer); and the amount of space or time given for each answer.

The response to oral questioning is also influenced by the medium used (face-to-face or telephone); whether it is an individual or group situation; time constraints; attitude of questioner; personality of questioner; importance of subject matter to interviewer and interviewee; extent of mutual respect; appearance, manner, and dress; and speech patterns and emphases on different words.

Responses are also conditioned and limited through the responder not knowing the answer to questions or only knowing a part of it; they may also tell the interviewer what they think they want to hear, or what they think the answer should be; they may lie; they may give no answer; they may give an answer at variance with their own views or understanding because they perceive that this is expected of them; or they may just make something up. Responses are also conditioned by wider situational factors and constraints; matters of confidentiality; the use to which the information is going to be put; or any opportunities or threats that are known or perceived to arise as the result of giving particular answers.

This has all then to be interpreted and analysed by others. Because there is no absolute basis or certainty, reception is subject to the expertise of the receivers and also matters of familiarity, credibility and acceptability – all of which are highly subjective.

The outcomes of organizational behaviour research

The outcomes of organizational behaviour research, with all the uncertainties, inconsistencies and anomalies indicated above, require some form of classification. If it is to be useful and valuable, and contribute to the development of a professional discipline, the classification has to be capable of being understood. Accordingly, the following headings are proposed as a way of looking at some of the major issues which organizations and their managers have to face, and they reflect also some of the major concerns that those who work in organizations legitimately have.

Clearly, some of these classifications are simplistic; this is part of the trouble of studying something that is necessarily uncertain and unpredictable. Neither are the classifications mutually exclusive; there are overlaps between all of them. However, it is necessary to start somewhere, so the classifications used reflect some of the major concerns of those who manage organizations, and also those who carry out professional and occupational duties to the best of their capability.

- **Structures and edifices**: the physical premises of organizations often represent the hierarchical and value structure – for example, top managers on the top floor or away from the noise and bustle of production.
- **Aims and objectives**: where relationships are drawn or inferred between the design of the organization and the purposes for which it was designed.
- **Stability**: where the future of the organization is viewed in terms of its past history, its traditions, long-standing areas of activity, achievements and reputation. This also often includes a community role, the provider of regular and constant employment of the particular locality or with certain skills and expertise.
- **Dominance-dependency**: the general state of relationships between the organization and its employees and also between particular groups. These relationships may be based on each or all of the following:
  - (a) authority: the ability of one group (for example, supervisors) to get others (for example, workers) to carry out work because of their position;

(b) function: the ability of one group to get others to work in particular ways because of their particular expertise;

(c) economic: the ability to persuade people to work because of their need to earn money and support themselves;

(d) social: the ability to persuade people to a particular point view because it is held to be right or important.

Organizational behaviour as a field of professional and managerial expertise

If the context, disciplines, development and outcomes are put together, the result ought to be a body of knowledge and understanding based on the volumes of information available, which is capable of being taught, learned and applied. Each of the headings and short descriptions below represents a summary of the different perspectives on organizational, collective and individual behaviour that is essential for managers to know and understand. Each of the areas requires application in the context in which the manager is working and operating; and each is therefore incapable of detailed or assured prescription. Especially, failure in any of the areas below, whether caused by lack of understanding, misapplication or lack of value placed on the particular area, is certain to cause additional and unnecessary expense, trouble, conflict or disorder in the activities of the organization concerned.

- **Restriction**: the ability to guide, order and organize people in the pursuit of stated purposes (i.e. restrict their freedom to act as they might otherwise choose to do). It refers to the extent and perspective by which rules and procedures are drawn up and applied.
- **Creativity**: the fact of continuous professional development, that individuals (and therefore their organizations) are forever enlarging their knowledge, skills, capabilities and experiences, and that organizations have this ever-increasing fund at their disposal if they so wish. It also includes the approaches used to address issues and solve problems, and the presence, or otherwise, of inventiveness and imagination.
- **Interaction**: the totality of the relationships that exist. Interaction includes relations between, and within, individual groups, departments, divisions and functions; between different positions in the hierarchies; between different types and levels of expertise. It also refers to the interactions between work and non-work, between the people and work, between the organization and other organizations, and the organization in its wider environment.
- **Psychological contract**: the extent to which a psychological bond (as well as a contract of employment) is deemed or perceived to exist between organization and employees. It has implications for wider concerns for individual welfare, loyalty, identity and commitment.
- **Stakeholders**: everyone who has a particular interest in the well-being of the organization. Stakeholders are staff, potential staff, former staff (especially those dependent on the organization for references or a pension), customers, clients, share-holders, other backers, directors, governors, the community and influential figures.
- **Effectiveness**: the need to maximize and optimize resources and to pursue aims and objectives successfully. This is concerned with the tangible – providing goods

and services for sale at a profit and, in public service terms, meeting demands in full – and the intangible – generating levels of expectation, satisfaction and confidence among customers and clients so that they will return in the future.

- **Managerial**: the ability to plan, organize, coordinate and control activities in the pursuit of effective performance. It refers to the ability to get things done through other people, arranging and ordering equipment, processes and materials, and designing work and organizational forms for this purpose.
- **Means and ends**: the relationships between what is done and why, and the ways in which things are done and why. This concerns the nature and standard of the relationship between an organization and its people, managers and staff, and levels of understanding, compliance and acceptance of purposes. It has implications for organizational policies, ethics and integrity. It also normally directly relates behaviour and performance effectiveness.
- **Employment**: the basis of the employment relationship. The main strands of this are hiring people because there is work to be done which they can do, and giving opportunities for progress, enhancement, variety and development (in personal, professional, occupational and economic terms). In the past, some organizations sought to offer lifetime employment, guaranteeing that there would be no lay-offs or redundancies. Others tried to create complete stability and certainty based around permanent technology, skills, output and quality.
- **Conflict**: the adversarial or confrontational view taken of employment relations. It is based on a combination of mistrust, occupational status and personal differentials. It normally implies a proliferation of rules and regulations, administrative processes and the means of institutionalizing and formalizing conflict.
- **Cooperative**: the cooperative perspective takes the view that success and effectiveness are most likely to come about where people are encouraged and directed to work with each other for the good of the organization – and by implication, for the good of each other and themselves. This can only be achieved through the creation of a harmonious environment, equality of opportunity and treatment, clear communications and well understood aims and objectives.
- **Case histories**: lessons learned and conclusions drawn from extensive studies of organizations and situations. These are then used as the basis for evaluating success and failure and may hold (or be perceived to hold) wider lessons for other organizations and situations.

Conclusions

Understanding the behaviour of organizations arises from combining the elements of the sciences or disciplines indicated with a number of more general and overtly subjective assertions. The total picture is incomplete, ever-changing and constantly developing. The drive is therefore towards as complete an understanding as possible rather than absolute enlightenment. This understanding is based on the application of methods of research and inquiry that are capable of contextual evaluation. This also concerns the validation and reliability of results and conclusions, especially when the divergent and conflicting nature of the different perspectives is considered. Ultimately, conclusions and predictions about human, and therefore organizational behaviour, are always subject to measures of uncertainty and interpretation.

2 Organizations and their environment

Introduction

Organizations are created on the basis that more can be achieved by people working in harmony and towards a stated purpose than by individuals acting alone. It is also more efficient and effective to specialize in seeking to serve or fulfil a given set of wants or needs. Resources – technology, expertise, information, finance and property – can then be commanded and ordered for the stated purpose. Activities can be determined, coordinated and controlled.

The result of this is that society is more or less founded on a highly complex and all-pervading network of organizations, each of which serves a given purpose and all of which serve the entire range of purposes required. Organizations affect all aspects of life – economic, social, political, cultural, religious, communal and family. They serve needs and essentials – food, shelter, health, education, water, energy and communications; as well as wants and choices – cola, cinema, football. They serve these needs and wants from before the cradle, through every aspect of life until after the grave (see Box 2.1).

An organization is any body that is constituted for such a given purpose, and which then establishes and conducts activities in pursuit of this. Organizations may be considered from a variety of different points of view. These are:

- legal status and formal regulation;
- primary beneficiaries, those for whom the organization is especially important for some reason;
- approach and attitude to staff;
- psychological contract, or the nature and level of mutual commitment between organization and staff.

Legal status

The main forms are as follows.

- **Sole traders**: in which an individual sets him/herself up as a going concern and puts their own resources into it. People who do this are entitled to receive any profits or surpluses accrued; and are also responsible in full for any losses.
- **Partnership**: in which two or more people establish themselves as a going concern as above.

- **Limited company**: in which the organization is based on the private sale of shares which provides it with a financial and capital base. The company is given its own life and entity in this way and it receives any profits made and is responsible for making good any losses. The liability of shareholders for any losses is limited to the extent of their share ownership.
- **PLC or corporation**: as for a limited company but where shares are offered for sale to the general public on a recognized stock exchange.
- **Friendly or mutual society**: in which the benefits accrued by activities are distributed among members as agreed between them.
- **Cooperative**: usually constituted as a company or partnership in which everyone involved has a stake (financial, physical or psychological).
- **Public bodies and public corporations**: central, regional and local government functions to provide essential public services and ensure adequate infrastructure, transport and communications for the society at large.
- **Quangos**: (quasi autonomous non-governmental organizations), autonomous entities funded by government grant and constituted for a particular purpose.
- **Charities**: funded by donations and other receipts for stated purposes; these funds are then distributed to the areas with which the charity is concerned. Charities must be registered with the charity commissioner in order to carry out activities in this way.

Box 2.1: HBOS and the nature of organizations

Getting 'the nature of organizations' right in each case is vital. Failure to do this results in a lack of clarity on the part of everyone in terms of what they ought to expect from the organization; and in terms of products and services (customers), staff (work patterns and content) and reputation (society at large).

Over the period from the early twenty-first century until the onset of the banking crisis in 2008, HBOS sought to change the perceived certainty of its position in relation to its staff, customers and society. Andy Hornby, the company CEO, decreed that HBOS was to be 'a sales-driven organization'. The result was that staff were required to engage customers in conversations about new products and services that the bank could provide. Customers wishing only to make deposits and withdrawals, and to pay their bills, now found themselves engaged in new and uncertain forms of conversation and interaction.

When the banking crises duly arrived, and it became clear that HBOS was effectively bankrupt, everyone sought answers as to why this had happened. From being a standard retail bank and mortgage provider, the company had generated uncertainty among all of its regular customers through its sales drives. It additionally became clear that those in charge of the company had sought to move it from being a known and understood distinctive UK market player into 'a global organization' (whatever that might have meant). These strategic and operational decisions aside, the organization had sought to move itself from being something that was known and understood to be 'certain', to something else – without, however, taking staff, customers or society at large along with it. When the crisis broke at the bank, it quickly became clear that staff were uncomfortable with their sales roles; customers were uncomfortable with being faced with continuous sales pitches; and the impact on society at large was the destabilization of both this institution and also the banking industry as a whole.

Box 2.2: Stakeholders

The stakeholders of an organization are individuals and groups who have an active, legitimate or passing interest in what the organization does, how it does it and its immediate and lasting effects.

Stakeholders are:

- **Financiers and backers**: those who put their money into the organization and expect a return.
- **Customers and clients**: those who come to do business with the organization, expecting excellent and valuable products and services in return.
- **Suppliers**: those who supply the organization and expect a steady and assured volume of business.
- **Staff**: those who work in the organization and expect security and stability of employment, together with the opportunity for progression and advancement.
- **The immediate locality**: in which the organization exists, and which is expected to make a positive and continuing contribution to overall prosperity.
- **Society**: society expects all its organizations to have a positive and enduring impact on its own security, development and advancement.
- **The media**: who may be expected to commentate both positively and negatively on different aspects and activities.
- **Observers and 'passing stakeholders'**: anyone may be expected to pass an opinion (both well informed and otherwise) as they wish and choose.

It is essential that those responsible for the direction and operations of organizations understand the full range of stakeholders and interests. It is essential that each interest is recognized and served as appropriate. Failure to recognize the full range of interests means that the organization is certain to operate in a measure of isolation. It is certain also that when specific interests do have to be addressed, the organization will be under-prepared. It is additionally the case that while organizations do indeed have primary beneficiaries (see below), ultimately anyone coming into contact with them will have a legitimate interest from their own perspective.

Primary beneficiaries

Primary beneficiaries are those people for whom the organization is especially important or for whom it was constituted. A primary beneficiary approach requires organizations to be looked at as follows.

- **Business organizations**: where the primary beneficiaries are shareholders and staff, and where the benefits accrue from providing products and services required by customers and clients.
- **Utilities**: where the primary beneficiary is society at large. Utilities include gas, electricity, water, transport, post, telecommunications and information service providers.

- **Public service organizations**: where the primary beneficiaries are particular client groups drawn in because of their characteristics. The functions of public service organizations include provision for the homeless, destitute, elderly, disabled, disadvantaged and handicapped. At present, in the UK and other parts of the world, many of these roles are carried out by charities and commercial companies, as well as public service organizations.
- **Cooperatives**: where the primary beneficiaries are all those who work in them. Cooperatives coordinate their business from the point of view of this mutual commitment and identity.
- **Convenience organizations**: where the primary beneficiaries are those who avail themselves of the organization's products and services on the basis of convenience. This includes village and local shops and amenities. One form of this is also to be found in organizations that take a 'just-in-time' approach to the purchase of stocks and raw materials.
- **Institutions**: where the primary beneficiaries are those who avail themselves of the institution's services and facilities or who are sent there (for whatever reason) by society. Examples include schools, colleges and prisons; and again, many of these are presently provided on a commercial basis.
- **Mutual benefit organizations**: where the primary beneficiaries are the members; mutual benefit organizations include trade unions, churches, political parties, clubs, friendly societies and cooperatives.
- **Service organizations**: where the primary beneficiaries are the clients who come to use services for stated reasons, or when they need them on particular occasions. Examples include hospitals, police and fire service; and again, many of these are presently provided on a commercial or partly commercialized basis.
- **Bodies for the regulation of society**: constituted by government and given the means and wherewithal to act in the known and perceived interests of members of the society. The main examples of these are the police, the judiciary and other arms of the law, and also watchdog bodies that regulate areas such as energy and finance.
- **Bodies for the defence of society**: including civil and military defence, national banks (for economic defence and protection) and prison services.
- **Common general organizations**: where the primary beneficiaries are the general public. These include police services and also education, health and social services.

Approach to staff

Organizations may also be viewed from the standpoint from which they regard their staff. They may be viewed as:

- **Unitary**, in which the aims, objectives, hopes, fears, aspirations and ambitions of the individual must be harmonized and integrated with those of the organization – and where necessary, subordinated so that the overall purpose of the organization remains the main driving force.
- **Pluralist**, in which the organization recognizes the divergence and, often, conflicting aims, objectives and drives of the people who work for it. Organizations that take this view normally include opportunities for personal and professional (as well as organizational) fulfilment. The basis is that by recognizing this divergence and attending to all needs organization needs will be satisfied.

Box 2.3: The beneficiaries of the university sector

It has always been perceived, known and understood that the beneficiaries of the university sector have been the students who want to learn, and the staff who want to teach and research. By extrapolation, society at large is also known, believed and perceived to be a beneficiary resulting from implementing what has been taught, learned and delivered.

In recent years, new and different funding regimes, the internationalization of the sector in the UK, specific drives for 'world-class status' (whatever that means) and the initiatives of top and senior managers have caused this believed and perceived certainty to change.

The result is that many institutions in the university and higher education sector have been forced to move away from that which was clear (teaching, learning and research activity) to involvement in overseas ventures, organizational change and restructuring, commercial consultancies and links with a myriad of other institutions.

While the teaching and research effort has remained at the core of everything, the direction, focus and priority has, in many cases, been lost. This direction, priority and focus has been further clouded by:

- following politically motivated incentives and directions, especially the expansion of the number of undergraduate places. This has meant that institutions have had to put on a much greater range of courses in order to be attractive to the new larger numbers;
- internationalization, resulting in a proportion of university resource being spent on overseas attraction and recruitment initiatives;
- producing fee regimes that meet the statutory demands of UK and European Union institutions, and deliver a fully commercialized version of the service to overseas students.

This in turn has led to decisions being taken on a short-term rather than long-term basis. In particular, annual funding cycles are often at variance with the need to deliver education and research programmes which have anything from two- to ten-year delivery cycles.

The result has been that the known and understood primary beneficiaries of the sector and its individual institutions have again found themselves uncertain of what to expect when they either enrol on courses, or become part of research teams and projects.

- **Cooperative, consultative, participative and involved**, in which the organization establishes a psychological and behavioural basis of partnership and involvement based on the value of the contribution that everyone is to make.
- **Confrontational** – an adversarial approach to staff. This is based, at best, on the recognition that harmony of objectives is impossible, leading to the creation of systems and processes for the containment and management of conflict. At worst, it is based on mistrust and coercion, often stemming from a lack of genuine value placed on staff (see Box 2.4).

Box 2.4: 'Our staff are our greatest asset'

'Our staff are our greatest asset' is a phrase to be found in every annual report or organizational commentary. The extent to which this is indeed true (or otherwise) is found in the actions of specific organizations. For example:

- Royal Bank of Scotland used this phrase knowing that they would have to cut up to 20 per cent of their workforce in 2008 and 2009.
- General Motors used this phrase while producing huge volumes of cars that nobody wanted to buy during 2007–9.
- Haringey Council Social Services Department in North London used this phrase in 2006 in its annual statements, two paragraphs before going on to state that staff training and development had had to be cut because of lack of funding.

Of course, there are many organizations that use the phrase very positively. Whatever the attitude, it constitutes a major contribution to the nature and effectiveness of the psychological contract that operates between staff and organization (see below).

- **Paternalist** – an approach to staff based on absolute confidence in the direction taken by those at the top of the organization, but without the involvement of the cooperative approach. The result is that the relationship between the staff and those in charge of the organization becomes akin to that between parents and children. While to many this is very comfortable, it can become a recipe for complacency, whereby the staff, especially, work purely on the basis that 'the top management know best'.

Psychological contract

Organizations may be viewed from the nature of the psychological contract that they engage in with their staff. This is the result of implications and expectations that arise as the result of the given organizational, occupational, professional and personal relationships in specific situations. They vary between all organizations and situations and may be summarized as follows.

- **Coercive**, whereby the relationship between organization and staff, and also organization and customer, is founded on a negative. An example of this is prison – the prisoners are there against their will. It is also present where sections of the community are forced or pressurized into using a monopoly or near-monopoly for an essential commodity or service – examples are electricity, telecommunication, petrol and fuel. It can also be present in institutions such as schools and colleges where the children or students attend because they are required to do so by the society.
- **Alienative**, whereby the relationship between staff and organization is negative. This has traditionally applied to large and sophisticated organizations and especially

to those staff working on production lines and in administrative hierarchies where they have no, or very little, control over the quality and output of work.

- **Remunerative**, whereby the relationship between staff and organization is clearly drawn in terms of money in return for efforts and attendance. It is normally to be found as the dominant feature where there is also a low level of mutual identity between staff and organization.
- **Calculative**, whereby the staff have a low commitment to organization goals and high commitment to current levels of earning and satisfaction. It is again a key feature of the wage–work bargain for production and administrative staff. For those with high levels of professional and technical expertise, the calculative relationship is based on the ability to practise, the need to find an employer and outlet for those skills and individual drives to serve and become expert.
- **Normative**, whereby the individual commitment to organizational purpose is very high. This is found in religious organizations, political parties and trade unions. It is also increasingly found in business organizations where there is a high level of identity either with the organization or with its founder or leader. It is effective as long as the wage–work bargain itself is sound and the organization accepts a range of obligations and responsibilities to ensure that it is maintained.

The psychological contract may be either active or passive. An active psychological contract, or active involvement, is much more likely to mean that there is a committed and involved workforce. A passive psychological contract does not necessarily mean that there is an uncommitted workforce; it does mean that the workforce is much more likely to be pursuing its own interests rather than those of the organization.

Viewing organizations from a variety of positions in these ways indicates the background against which aims and objectives are to be drawn up. It also indicates the source of some of the limitations and constraints that have to be taken into account when considering the capabilities of organizations and the nature and relationship of these with the purposes that are to be pursued.

Organizational goals, aims and objectives

However constituted, and from whatever point of view they are considered, all organizations have purposes – goals, aims and objectives, their reason for being. These provide the essential foundation on which the organization is to be built. Some essential features of aims and objectives should therefore be defined.

- **Clarity**: aims and objectives should be specific and capable of being understood and accepted by all those who are to be engaged in their pursuit.
- **Measurable**: aims and objectives provide the measures against which success and failure are to be evaluated. The clearer the means of measurement, the more accurate the assessment; and the easier it is to establish why something has been successful or why it failed (as well as the fact of the matter).
- **Capability**: organizations combine resources – human, technology, financial and other equipment – to pursue their goals. The purpose is to maximize and optimize usage of those resources. Inadequacy of resources leads to loss of capability. Surfeit of resources leads to waste and profligacy. This may also lead to incapability

caused by a loss of drive or urgency – if too many resources seem to be available, those concerned may feel no need to maximize/optimize performance.

- **Time scales**: these act as a general discipline on the organization as specific performance indicators on groups and individuals.
- **Efficiency and effectiveness**: Drucker (1955) defined these as: efficiency is doing things right; effectiveness is doing the right thing. Efficiency is therefore concerned with performance during the task and attention to best use of resources. Effectiveness is concerned with the end result; and may also be concerned with resources, especially where these constitute the building blocks of the eventual outcome.

Organizational performance

Organizational performance may be classified under the following headings.

- **Steady-state**: the conduct of day-to-day activities, routines and tasks; the creation of structures, systems, rules and procedures to ensure that these continue; the creation of stability and confidence.
- **Innovative**: the drive continuously to improve all aspects of the organization and its work; seeking improvements in efficiency and effectiveness; seeking new products, opportunities and markets; seeking new and better means of staff management, organization and development.
- **Pioneering**: the drive for radically new activities and markets; the drive for radical new technology, its uses and applications; the drive for radically new means and methods of organization, staffing and management.
- **Crisis**: the handling of emergencies, problems and dramas when they occur; the structuring of activities and resources to ensure that there is a balance between being able to meet crises when they do happen or taking steps to ensure that these occur as infrequently as possible; the avoidance of crisis management – lurching from one emergency to another; the recognition and addressing of the likely and actual components of crises in the given situation.
- **Strategic and directional**: concerned with the organization, its purposes, goals and overall aims and objectives; the monitoring, review and evaluation of these and of the activities organized and structured in their pursuit; attention to the success and effectiveness – and profitability – of performance; taking remedial action where required. Strategic and directional performance also includes attention to the nature and mix of steady-state, innovative, pioneering and crisis aspects indicated above.

This can then be related to the different headings under which objectives are classified. In general, these are a combination of:

- **Strategic**: concerned with overall direction of the organization and the focus for all other activities.
- **Operational**: concerned with the effectiveness of day-to-day activities in pursuit of the strategic.
- **Behavioural**: concerned with the human aspects of the organization, management and supervisory style and the aura of general well-being.

- **Ethical**: concerned with particular standards of operation and interaction, the ways in which staff, customers, the community and the environment are treated and the general level of respect in which they are held.
- **Attitudes and values**: the psychological focus of the organization and requirements and expectations placed on staff and customers.
- **Superior and subordinate, or supporting, aims and objectives**: the inter-relationship, harmony and unit of purpose and drive between overall aims and the goals set for departments, divisions, functions and individuals.

Other boundaries

Other boundaries that shape, constrain and limit overall purposes, aims and objectives are as follows.

- Policies, representing the ways in which the organization seeks and determines to operate, and the standards (especially of honesty and integrity) that it sets for itself. These normally refer to:
  - attention to staff and staff relations;
  - attention to customers and customer relations;
  - attention to community and community relations;
  - attention to the environment and waste disposal;
  - standards of image, marketing and public relations;
  - the promotion of equity and equality;
  - the extent of commitment to product and service quality, and customer satisfaction.
- Specific operational constraints; the interaction with suppliers, distributors and customers; any legal constraints; the effects of internal and external pressure groups and vested interests.
- The preferences and drives of shareholders and other stakeholders – especially in terms of the nature of the results required and the deadlines for these.
- The nature of expertise required. Where persons of high professional or technical qualifications are employed, there is often a potential conflict between their commitment to the organization and to their profession or occupation.
- Ethical and social constraints. These are based on the norms, values and standards of the wider society and communities in which activities are to be conducted; the extent to which the organization itself is, or seeks to be, a good citizen.
- The need for discipline, guidance and motivation on the part of staff and the creation of support functions, procedures and processes of supervision and management for these reasons.
- Competitive pressures: the need to compete for business, work and customers; and the need to compete for staff and resources. Competition for staff and resources may have both external and internal constraints.
- Cooperative pressure: the extent of dependency on other bodies and organizations (i.e. suppliers, distributors; also banks and other sources of finance; any other particular expertise required); the extent to which other bodies are allowed to influence the direction and purpose of the particular organization.
- Relationships between means and ends, and the priority that is placed on each; the extent to which people and groups are rewarded for hard work (means) as distinct from effective or productive work (ends); the views taken by the organization of success and failure.

These constitute the main constraints within which organizations have to set their aims and objectives if they are to be effective. It is impossible to work in isolation from these except in the very short-term and where a monopoly on the particular product or service is held.

Limitations

Limitations on effectiveness are as follows.

- The drive for volume of work rather than quality or effectiveness. This is exacerbated where rewards are given for volume rather than quality. This is satisfactory only as long as competitive position can be maintained on the basis of volume and as long as some level of profit is achieved. It is invariably unsatisfactory in the long-term unless accompanied by drives for quality and effectiveness.
- Lack of attention to supposedly non-quantifiable aims and objectives – especially for managers, administrators and support functions.
- Attention becomes focused on length rather than effectiveness of attendance, and volume rather than quality or purpose of work.
- Operational and political influence of interest groups increases at the expense of their productive output.
- Concentration on compliance and conformity rather than effectiveness.
- Compliance is not achieved. This is either because the required attitudes and standards are not recognized or valued, or because those working in the organization place no value on the overall purpose, and so the work is not carried out.

Analysing the environment

Specific analytical approaches

Specific analytical approaches are used to ensure that whatever is envisaged and carried out is kept under regular and constant review as part of the drive by the organization to maximize its outputs, and also in order to be able to see any problems as they become apparent. The process of analysis should be both rigorous and streamlined; the purpose is to highlight issues that are of importance with the purpose of rigorously assessing, evaluating and discussing them. Any particular matters arising can then be prioritized for action. They may be accepted or rejected at their face value. They may also be used as the basis for further research and analysis.

Evaluation of primary beneficiaries

As stated above, primary beneficiaries are those people for whom organizations are especially important or for whom they were constituted. Primary beneficiary analyses and evaluations are therefore undertaken so as to concentrate on the following:

- Who is supposed to benefit from the existence of the organization; who does benefit; and how they benefit?
- Any secondary beneficiaries of the organization (e.g. does the organization make a contribution to society as well as serving its customers?).

- Whom the organization does not serve, and why?
- Any specific good done by the organization alongside its primary purpose.
- Any specific harm done by the organization alongside its primary purpose.
- Its impact on the location in which it exists.
- Its impact on society at large (see Box 2.5).

Box 2.5: Primary and other beneficiaries

The primary beneficiary approach ought to indicate clearly the priorities and direction of the organization and the ends to which resources should be concentrated. However, it is important to note the following.

- **Ultimate beneficiaries**: it is usual to define the ultimate beneficiaries as customers, clients, consumers and end-users of particular products and services. This, however, becomes lost in organizations and situations where there are other powerful, dominant – and therefore ultimate – interests. Political beneficiaries tend to disrupt the effectiveness of public services in the interests of their own position and reputation. Short-term shareholder interests often disrupt the long-term effectiveness of commercially driven organizations.
- **Changing beneficiaries**: this becomes important when organizations change their status for whatever reason. For example, newly privatized public services have suddenly to operate under the financial regimes dictated by the new owners. Companies founded, developed and grown by individuals often lose their identities when they are floated on stock markets or sold on by the founder. Mergers and takeovers mean that staff and customers of the previous organization have to get used to new ways in which they are to be dealt with, and the clarity of this may be lost as the new regime seeks to impose new directions and priorities.
- **Continuing beneficiaries**: this is overwhelmingly the staff interest. It is also essential to recognize the position and influence of a continued family presence through the generations following the foundation and development of an organization by an individual (such as the Sieff family of Marks & Spencer, the Sainsbury family of Sainsbury's supermarkets) and long-term, established and secure shareholder interests.

    It is also essential to recognize that one of the obligations of the continuing beneficiary approach is to provide that which was promised or indicated whenever it is required. From the point of view of the staff, this means ensuring the ability to provide career paths, promotion opportunities, variety development and enhancement in the work, and a pension upon retirement. Organizations that promise or indicate strongly that these aspects will be delivered must either ensure that delivery is indeed made; or if not, must be prepared to lose reputation and loyalty as an employer in consequence.
- **Non-beneficiaries**: this occurs where people do not receive the products and services that they expect from organizations in which they are overtly considered the primary beneficiaries. Of especial present concern in the UK are health, education and social services; a reliable transport infrastructure; and reliability in the quality and delivery of public utilities.

The SPECTACLES approach

Cartwright (2001) takes a detailed approach to assessing the organizational, environmental and operational factors, features and constraints under which activities have to be conducted and decisions taken. Cartwright identified a ten-point approach under the acronym SPECTACLES as follows.

- **Social**: changes in society and societal trends; demographic trends and influences.
- **Political**: political processes and structures; lobbying; the political institutions of the UK and EU; the political institutions and their influence upon any other area in which business is to be conducted; the political pressures brought about as the result of, for example, market regulation, government policy or trading in major power blocks.
- **Economic**: referring especially to sources of finance; stock markets; inflation; interest rates; property prices; government and EU economic policy; local, regional, national and global economies.
- **Cultural**: international and national cultures; regional cultures; local cultures; organizational cultures; cultural clashes; culture changes; cultural pressures on business and organizational activities.
- **Technological**: understanding the technological needs of business; technological pressures; the relationship between technology and work patterns; the opportunities to develop and enhance product and service provision as the result of advancing technology; the need to invest in technology; communications; e-commerce; technology and manufacturing; technology and bio-engineering; technological potential.
- **Aesthetic**: communications; marketing and promotion; image; fashion; organizational body language; public relations.
- **Customer**: consumerism; the importance of analysing customer and client bases; customer needs and wants; customer care; anticipating future customer requirements; customer behaviour.
- **Legal**: sources of law; codes of practice; legal pressures; product and service liability; health and safety; employment law; competition legislation; specific legal pressures; whistle-blowing.
- **Environmental**: responsibilities to the planet; responsibilities to communities; pollution; waste management; genetic engineering; cost benefit analyses; legal pressures.
- **Sectoral**: competition; cartels, monopolies and oligopolies; competitive forces; cooperation and collusion within sectors; differentiation; segmentation.

Cartwright states that his intention is:

> to widen the scope of analysis that needs to be carried out in order to include a more detailed consideration of the environment and culture within which an organization must operate, the customer base, competition within the sector and the aesthetic implications, both physical and behavioural, of the organization and its external operating environment.

The approach requires managers to take a detailed look at every aspect of their operations within their particular environment and niche. Managers need to understand fully the broadest range of environmental constraints within which they have to conduct effective activities. The approach is also much more likely to raise specific, precise, detailed and, often, uncomfortable questions that many people responsible for strategic management and strategy development would rather not have to address.

Above all, the SPECTACLES approach can be used by managers at any organizational level in order to make themselves think more deeply about every issue and constraint present in their own particular domain in order to be able to operate effectively. For those responsible for the strategic management and direction of organizations, the SPECTACLES approach generates a broadness of consideration that, in many cases, is not present at all.

The key benefit of the SPECTACLES approach is to ensure that every aspect of the organization and its environment is addressed. It especially requires that the softer and more nebulous aspects such as culture and aesthetics are considered.

The SPECTACLES approach can then be developed in further detail using:

- SWOT analysis;
- STEP analysis;
- industry structure analysis.

Strengths, weaknesses, opportunities, threats: SWOT analysis

The purpose of conducting a SWOT analysis is to help organizations to learn, to clarify issues, to identify preferred and likely directions, and to conduct a general and quick analysis of their current position.

In SWOT analyses issues are raised, highlighted and categorized under four headings (see Figure 2.1).

- **Strengths**. Things that the organization and its staff are good at, do well and that they are effective at; that they are well known for; that make money; that generate business and reputation; that generate confidence and understanding in the marketplace; that cause customers to come back for repeat business; that cause other organizations to try to learn from them; those matters on which the organization has built its past reputation.
- **Weaknesses**. These are the things that the organization does badly; the things that are ineffective; the things that the organization is notorious for. It also includes consideration of those elements that cause it to make losses; that cause hardships, disputes, grievances and complaints; that should generate business but do not; and the raising and clarification of issues that have caused business to be lost and elements of bad reputation to be gained.
- **Opportunities**. These are the directions which the organization could profitably take for the future that may arise because of strengths or the elimination of weaknesses. This involves a consideration of the environment from the widest and most creative possible standpoint.
- **Threats**. Threats arise from competitors, from strikes and disputes, from resource and revenue losses, from failing to maximize opportunities or to build on successes. They also arise from complacency, organizational and strategic lack of rigour, and from the erosion of margins due, for example, to rising cost levels.

Example: Virgin Cola

Strengths	**Weaknesses**
• Virgin name • Generic product • Profile of Sir Richard Branson • Public confidence in other Virgin offerings • Reputation of Virgin group and name	• Lack of organizational expertise in the soft drinks industry • Lack of cultural familiarity in this specific sector • Possible lack of willingness of staff to work with soft drinks
• Failure of this product may cause questioning of other offerings • Strengths of existing cola brands • Confidence and loyalty of public to existing brands	• Size of generic markets • Developments and advances into soft drinks (and other foodstuffs)
Threats	**Opportunities**

The purpose is to give a quick and highly visual analysis of an organisation, situation, product or service. It then becomes the basis of more detailed analysis and evaluation.

Figure 2.1 SWOT analysis model for Virgin Cola. Note that the venture failed, in spite of the clear and present strengths and opportunities stated (see also Box 2.7)

In general, opportunities and threats reflect the relationship between the external environment and the forces that work in it. Strengths and weaknesses are candid assessments of areas of activity within the organization.

The analysis is carried out in the form of a brainstorming and creative discussion. It is an effective means of gathering and categorizing information; of illustrating and illuminating particular matters; and of generating a great deal of interest in the organization and its activities very quickly. The result of such an exercise should be to provide the basis on which a more detailed analysis can be conducted.

Social, technological, economic, political: STEP analysis

The purpose of STEP analysis (see Figure 2.2) is also to help organizations learn. However, the material that arises from a discussion such as this is likely to be much more concerned with the analysis of the wider context, the organization in its environment and more global concerns.

- **Social**. This is to do with the social systems in place at the workplace, departmental and functional structures, work culture, attitudes, organization and working methods; it also includes both formal and informal aspects of the organization. In external terms, this is the relationship between the organization and its environment as regards the nature and social acceptability of its products and services and the ways in which it does business; consideration is also given to the impact of marketing, promotion and public relations activities; and the general regard with which the organization is held in its markets, communities and the wider environment.

- **Technological**. This relates to the organization's technology and the uses to which it is put, and also its potential uses; to the technology that is potentially available to the organization and others operating in the given sector; to the technological advances that are present or envisaged elsewhere in the sector and the opportunities afforded by these to the organization in question.

- **Economic**. This concerns the financial structure, objectives and constraints placed upon the organization. This relates to both the external (that is, the levels of profit and turnover generated and the extent to which this is viable and able to sustain current and envisaged levels of activity) and the internal financial position (means of financial controls, budgeting systems, budgets and financial management and practices). It also considers the market position, general levels of economic activity, the competition for the offerings made by the organization and the commercial prospects and potential of the products and services offered.

- **Political**. This consists of assessing the internal political systems, sources of power and influence, key individuals, key groups of staff, key departments, key managers and key executives; questions of management style, human resource management and industrial relations issues; general levels of motivation and morale.

Externally, it considers particular factors in the establishment of markets, by-products, vocation, ethics and values. There may also be political and legal constraints placed upon the activities of the organization in question, especially where it is trading in places other than its own indigenous locality. Again, this is a starting point only, and the

Social	**Technological**
• Population • Lifestyle • Spending patterns • Social attitudes and values • Prejudices • Segmentation	• Education, training and expertise • Technological advance and invention • Obsolescence • Potential • Energy
• Legal factors • Sector regulation • Political pressures • Green issues • Governmental stance	• Confidence • Spending patterns • Propensity to spend • Inflation • Fixed and variable costs incurred
Political	**Economic**

Purpose: a quick and highly visual representation of the external pressures present, and their potential for limiting and enhancing proposed activities.

Figure 2.2 STEP analysis model

information thus raised must be further analysed and evaluated. The purpose is to establish in some detail the background against which particular initiatives take place already and may do in the future. It also highlights any wider concerns or issues that may in turn require attention; in particular, it highlights matters over which the organization has no control. Finally, a full STEP analysis will probably consider wider general directions and likely initiatives taken by governments in regard to social, technological, economic and political issues.

Industry structure analysis

Porter identifies five elemental forces of competition.

Rivalry between direct competitors. It is essential to know and understand the nature and extent of rivalry among those organizations currently operating in the field and the implications of this for the future. This may include consideration of the extent of differentiation activity, the prospect of price wars and impacts and implications for profit margins. It may also include questions related to the capacity of the sector (in terms of both existing levels of business and future potential).

The bargaining power of suppliers. This includes the extent to which they may be able to withdraw or flood the market (on the supplier side); the propensity and pressure to buy (on the buyer side); and the opportunities, constraints and threats imposed by the bargaining power of suppliers. Organizations that command rare or exclusive supplies of components, raw materials and information sources are able to impose their own preferred ways of dealing with particular organizations, as well as commanding price levels including premium payments and economic rent. Others on the supply side may use their influence to withdraw particular products, services and components altogether, or else to flood the market. Organizations that flood the market normally do so in the expectation of medium- to long-term dominance in their particular sector (see Figure 2.3).

The bargaining power of buyers. Powerful buyers are able to command the conditions under which they deal with particular products and services. Powerful buyers are able to influence their sectors as follows:

*   volumes of products and services made available;
*   prices and charges for particular products and services;
*   the nature and locations of outlets for the particular products and services;
*   the presentation of particular products and services at the point of sale;
*   price levels, payment methods and charges;
*   competitive influence, in which powerful buyers state to suppliers that they will only take particular volumes of products and services, provided that the suppliers give them terms advantageous to their rivals;
*   the need for some suppliers to have specific buyers in order to be able to distribute their products and services (see Box 2.6).

The extent and nature of actual and potential substitution processes. Substitution includes the potential for offering near alternative products and services; genuine choice to the market; redesigned and reprocessed products and services; and similar products and services that use different (normally more efficient) production and

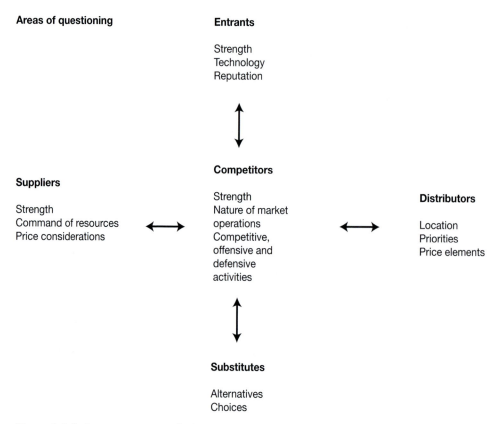

Figure 2.3 Industry structure analysis

distribution methods. The provision of substitutes and alternatives has to be seen in a broader context as follows.

- A high reputation organization operating in different sectors may be able to bring an immediate competitive advantage as the result of its standing elsewhere (whether or not its offerings in the present sector are any better than those of existing providers).
- A key part of providing effective substitutes and alternatives is the ability to change buyer, consumer and supplier perceptions and confidence; and one competitive response by existing players that is always available is to ensure that relations are developed and enhanced with the supply and distribution aspects.
- If there is a serious threat of substitution or alternative provision, organizations presently operating in the particular sector need to analyse accurately the factors that are causing the potential for new entrants to come into the sector. These factors are dealt with extensively elsewhere (see Chapters 3 and 9). However, at the core there is almost invariably a known, believed or perceived dissatisfaction with the nature, level and quality of present provision in the sector, or else an ability to develop the potential of the particular sector more fully.

Box 2.6: The bargaining power of buyers

In 2009, the UK Competition Commission published the latest in a long line of reports into the buying practices of the big UK supermarket chains – Tesco, Sainsbury, Asda, Morrison and Waitrose. The report had been commissioned following widespread complaints from farmers and the other suppliers of fresh and processed food and produce that they were being unfairly squeezed by the bargaining power of the supermarket chains. These complaints had included:

- the ability of the supermarket chains to cancel contracts at 24 hours' notice;
- the ability of the supermarket chains to vary contracts at a moment's notice;
- the inability of suppliers to find alternative outlets for their produce in commercially viable volumes, given the nature of the dominance exerted by the supermarket chains;
- short-term variations in production and requirement volumes on the part of the supermarket chains;
- the constant downward pressure on wholesale prices.

The report again exonerated the supermarket chains of any wrongdoing. However, the report did again draw attention to the responsibility of those in powerful and influential commercial positions to act in everyone's best interests. Supermarkets and others in positions of commercial influence were required to take account of supplier, customer, staff, community and environmental interests as well as ensuring their own long-term commercial viability and shareholder value.

Potential entrants: those who might conceivably come into the market and the effects on the ways in which business is carried out.

Other forces: other competitive forces that increasingly have to be taken into account are as follows.

- The threat of regulation: key areas of present concern include advertising (e.g. the continued pressures on fast food advertising); product quality and description (e.g. plans exist to ensure that all products fully itemize the ingredients or components with which they are made); prices (e.g. the privatized utilities, gas, electricity, water, telecommunications and transport are all subject to scrutiny by government and official regulators); staffing policies and practices (e.g. regulations surrounding employment protection, hours of work and wage levels).
- The threat of withdrawal: the withdrawal of large and dominant organizations may destabilize whole market sectors.
- Threat of re-entry: organizations that have mothballed particular activities, products and services may find new ways of reintroducing these at greatly reduced cost; or at greatly enhanced quality, design, presentation and reputation.

As well as knowing and understanding the nature and strength of the forces present, it is also essential that a fully informed view is taken of the confidence in which the

Box 2.7: Virgin Cola

In all of its markets, the Virgin organization enjoys high levels of customer confidence. This confidence occurs as the direct result of delivering products and services of a known quality and value, and supported by the perceived personal strength and integrity of Richard Branson himself. Virgin Cola was launched in order to take a niche (up to 5 per cent) of the total sales of cola soft drink products. Virgin Cola was deliberately designed to have a slightly distinctive taste which, together with the Virgin branding, would ensure that the specific market targeted was satisfied.

The initial prognosis was excellent. Indeed in blind tastings, Virgin Cola consistently tasted better than Coca-Cola and Pepsi-Cola. This caused:

- Pepsi-Cola and Coca-Cola immediately to panic! This was until they realized that their customers were buying the whole brand and its associations, rather than purely a tasty soft drink;
- Virgin to go into full production, on the basis that the best tasting drink was what the customers wanted.

Virgin Cola turned out to be one of Virgin's very few outright failures. This was because:

- the strengths of the brand were mistaken in this particular case;
- the nature of customer demand was mistaken;
- the fact that the product was the 'best' in its field was not what the customers asked for.

The lesson is therefore that any form of analysis has to be capable of testing and evaluation. It is not enough to itemize the strengths and weaknesses, and take these at face value.

organization is held by its customers and suppliers. Whatever its strengths, bargaining power, sources of advantage and reputation, if either, or both, do not have full confidence, or else events occur which cause this confidence to change, then this affects all dealings with these groups. Additionally, if the strength of the overall position is mistaken, then the whole commercial activity is damaged (see Box 2.7).

Failure

The Virgin example in Box 2.7 indicates how a full organizational and environmental analysis can be carried out, and yet the product or service delivered at the end ultimately fails. Insufficient attention to the organization's strengths and weaknesses, its environment and the forces present, and the position from which competition has to be engaged are certain to result in failure. Otherwise, the key elements that have to be considered if failure is to be avoided are as follows.

- Insufficient attention to the behavioural aspects of operations, above all in creating effective and suitable conditions and support systems as the basis for carrying out the work. This also includes insufficient attention to the need to motivate and value the staff engaged in the work.
- Insufficient attention to the quantifiable performance requirements of management and to the establishment of proper aims and objectives in managerial, administrative and support functions.
- Prioritizing short-term results at the expense of the long-term future together with the over-consumption of resources in this way. This normally occurs because the organization can see easy results if it pursues the short-term. It also occurs because of pressures for demonstrable and immediate success in difficult times.
- Artificial constraints and deadlines, driven by budget systems and reporting relationships, requiring energy and resources to be used in non-productive and often counter-productive activities, rather than as a check on continuous performance.
- Establishment of priorities for reasons other than performance effectiveness and especially for reasons of publicity, kudos, status and the demands of key figures for their own purposes.
- Setting unreasonable deadlines for the achievement of particular objectives.
- Casting plans, aims and objectives as 'tablets of stone' – once they are written they are never to be changed or modified.
- Failure to recognize that which cannot be controlled may nevertheless have great effects on organizational activities. This includes changes in customer demands and expectations; legislative changes; the activities of competitors; loss of sources of supply; change in relationships with distributors; and so on.
- Complacency, often based on a long history of success, continuity and achievement in the past, and which tends to lead to feelings of infallibility and immortality. This leads to loss of commitment to purpose, loss of focus and what constitutes truly effective performance.
- Attention to means rather than ends and the confusion of hard work with productive work. Sheer volume of work therefore becomes the measure of performance rather than the purpose for which it is being conducted.

Systems

The final part of organizational and environmental analysis is to consider the operating systems present. All organizations need systems to make them productive, and to ensure the harmonization of resources necessary for effective work to be carried out.

A system is a collection of interrelated parts and components that form a whole. Typical organization systems are production, communication and electronic data systems. Systems may first be defined as:

- **Closed**: those that are self-contained and self-sufficient, and do not require other interactions to make them work. There are very few systems that are genuinely closed. Some domestic central heating systems are more or less closed. In these cases the components are assembled. The system is switched on and must operate continuously or else break down. Even in these cases they are dependent upon being fed a constant

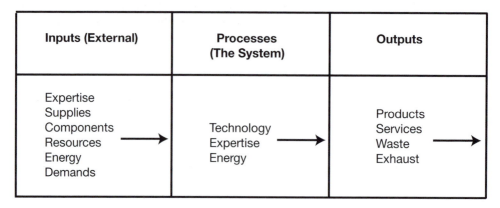

Figure 2.4 An open system (fed by external inputs)

supply of energy to ensure continuity of operation. They are also dependent upon maintenance, both to prevent breakdowns and to make repairs when faults occur.

- **Open**: open systems are those that require constant interaction with their environment to make them work (see Figure 2.4).
- **Formal**: devised and developed by the organization with specific purposes in mind and with the view that effective operations are dependent upon those which are put in place.
- **Informal**: devised by individuals and groups to facilitate their own place and well-being in the organization and to fill those gaps left by the formal approach.
- **Networks**: the combination of the formal with the informal, networks are normally based on human interaction and information exchange (and sometimes information hoarding and trading). Their purpose is to support both the operations of the organization and also to ensure the continuity and stability of the position of individuals and groups.

Inputs (External)	Processes (The System)	Outputs
Raw materials Energy Expertise Components Information Demand Ideas Inventions	Raw materials Energy Expertise Components Information Demand Ideas Inventions	Finished goods Services Waste Exhaust

Figure 2.5 Organization systems

Organization systems may now be shown as follows (see Figure 2.5). They convert human activity, energy, information resources and components of raw materials into products and services, usable information, by-products and waste.

Main systems

Main systems are those devised to ensure that the organization can pursue its core purposes successfully. They are normally the production, service and information systems essential to well-being and success. Systems may be largely:

- human or social, where achievement of the core purpose depends greatly on interactions between people;
- technological, where achievement of the core purpose depends greatly on the output of large volumes of items;
- socio-technical, in which the interaction between the two is critical (see Figure 2.6).

Main systems include the following.

Maintenance systems

These are devised in order to prevent any blockages occurring and to put them right when they do happen. Maintenance systems require attention to both social and technical

Technical System Components	Social System Components
• Materials	• Personal and organizational capabilities
• Apparatus and equipment	
• Energy	• Social needs
• Technology	• Social interactions
• Production and service processes	• Psychological needs
	• Professional needs
• Physical locations	• Training and development
• Process structures	• General relationships
• Equipment maintenance	• Communications and information
• Equipment replacement	• Work patterns
• Supplies	• Work development

Technical System ————————— Social System

Inter-relationship

Socio-technical system

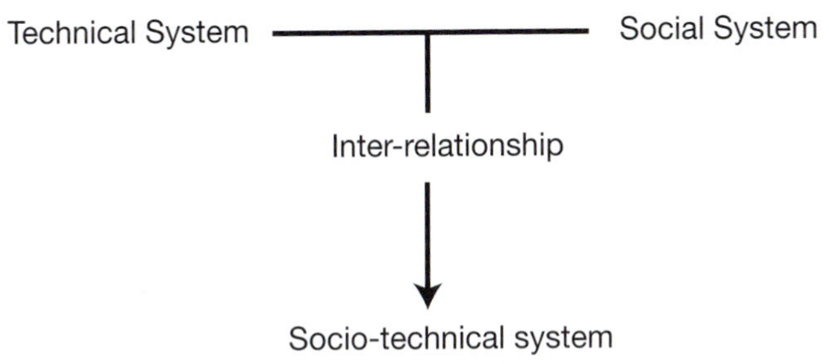

Figure 2.6 Socio-technical systems

aspects. A part of organization and individual development is concerned with maintaining the human resource. This includes attention to morale and commitment, as well as skills, knowledge and expertise.

Crisis systems

These are devised and put in place on the basis that they are seldom to be used – but nevertheless when they are required they can be speedily energized. Emergency systems are clear examples of this, as are systems for the handling of operational input and distribution breakdowns and hiatuses; and in these cases they will normally consist of hot-line arrangements for emergency supplies, activities and distribution.

Managerial systems

At their best these start with the performance of others. They are created to provide a process for evaluation of performance, organization adaptation, coordination of activities and taking decisions.

1 **Evaluation of performance** – the actual performance of the system will be evaluated through constant monitoring and review, and the results achieved analysed to show why successes have been achieved, and where and why any failures have occurred. This will also indicate general areas for attention, capabilities for improvements and progress; it will also include establishing the reasons for success so that these may be built on for the future in other areas.
2 **Adaptation and change** – this is concerned with the future of the organization, the development of structures, attitudes, values, skills, knowledge and expertise for the purpose of achieving aims and objectives and planning for longer-term strategies and directions.
3 **Coordination and control** – this is the harmonization process, the ordering of the disparate and divergent elements, conflict resolution, balancing and ordering of priorities and resources.
4 **Decision-making** – this is attention to the processes by which effective decisions are made and the elements that contribute to this.

For effective performance in each of the processes to take place, a systematic approach is required. This is to ensure that sufficient attention is paid, and examination of each area takes place, on the basis of depth and breadth of knowledge so that, in turn, a full basis of judgement, analysis and assessment is achieved and ensured.

Organizations in their environment

As no organization exists in isolation from its environment, the nature and extent of the relationship and interactions must be considered (see Figure 2.7). Organizations are subject to a variety of economic, legal, social and ethical pressures that they must be capable of accommodating if they are to operate effectively. In some cases, there are strong religious and cultural effects, and local traditions that must be capable of effective harmonization also. More specifically, organizations need access to workforces, suppliers, distributors, customers and clients; and to technology, equipment and financial resources.

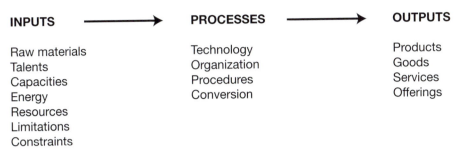

Figure 2.7 Archetype model of the organization and its environment
Source: Katz and Kahn (1978).

Relationships between organizations and their environment may be simply summarized as:

- **Environment domination**: especially overwhelming legal, social and ethical pressures and also those that relate to any strong local histories and traditions.
- **Organization domination**: where the environment is dependent on the organization for the provision of work, goods and services.

This is then to be seen in the context that the best organization–environment relationships are generated where measures of general responsibility are attached to each. If the environmental pressures are too great, or somehow otherwise unacceptable to the organization, it will eventually relocate elsewhere. If the organization takes an expedient or cavalier view of its involvement in a particular area, it will be rejected by those who live there. The picture is further complicated by the fact that all organizations interact with other organizations that are also part of their own environment and they influence these, and are influenced by them.

Contingency approaches

Contingency approaches indicate the context in which effective organizations are devised and designed. Burns and Stalker (1961) defined the contingency approach as 'the most appropriate system for a given set of circumstances'. While this may appear a statement of the obvious, the fact that effective and appropriate organizations cannot be designed in isolation from their situation does at least indicate the important relationship between appropriateness and circumstances.

Divergence and integration

Divergence and integration can be seen at three levels: between organizations and their environment; between different organizations; and within organizations (see Figure 2.8). Some parts of the relationship between organizations and environment are based on the reconciliation of conflicting demands. Other parts are based on a stated or implied mutuality of interest. The problem is therefore to recognize where the mutuality lies and the extent of this as the basis by which the points of conflict can then be addressed. Some factors of this may be distinguished.

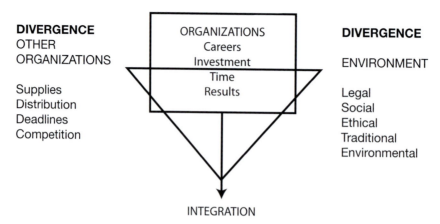

Figure 2.8 Divergence and integration pressures

The more dynamic and diverse the environment, the greater the degree of differentiation and specialization required within organizations to cope with its demands. High degrees of integration are also required (a) to build up effective working relationships with each part of the environment; and (b) to harmonize differing, and often divergent, efforts within the organization itself.

Less dynamic and more stable environments require high degrees of interaction to ensure that the stability is preserved. A major cause of conflict is lack of communications and understanding caused in turn by lack of attention to continuing relationships.

The more dynamic and diverse the environment, the greater the likelihood of misunderstandings and conflict occurring. In these situations, a proportion of organization resources is therefore likely to be required to ensure that these can be tackled effectively when they do arise.

Conclusions

It ought to be clear from everything discussed here that there is clearly no best way to organize. As the environment changes, organizations must change and adapt and, additionally, systems, aims and objectives must be flexible and responsive.

The environment changes in both predictable and unpredictable ways. To an extent it changes in ways that can be controlled and influenced. However, it especially changes in ways that cannot be controlled and influenced. The problem for managers therefore lies in the extent of their understanding of their environment and in their ability to anticipate the unexpected by building systems and responses that are capable of accommodating these pressures. Because of the nature of the relationship with the environment, organizations must spend time on external issues, assessing and understanding the environment, and the changes and turbulence within it. Above all, the environment is dynamic and not static or rigid, allowing for limitless opportunities for change to occur; investment in environmental adaptation and transformation are as essential to success as investments in capital, equipment and staffing. The more complex and turbulent the environment, the more essential this form of investment becomes.

The additional purpose of this chapter has been to summarize and indicate the various forms of organization, the different points of view from which they may be considered and the wider context in which they operate. No organization operates in isolation from, or without reference, to its environment. The environment provides staff, customers, resources, technology and equipment, and also the overall basis for building and developing confidence and expectations – the context in which successful and effective activities take place.

3 Change

Introduction

Current political and economic turbulence, and the globalization of business and competition, has called into question all the hitherto accepted ways of organizing and conducting affairs, making products and delivering services. This has been fuelled by advances in all forms of technology such as production, service, consumer and information. There is a much greater capacity for producing products more quickly, more uniformly and to higher standards of quality and reliability. The result of this has been to transform consumer expectations. With the ever-greater choices afforded by the internationalization of activities no organization, company, industry or sector is immune from these pressures.

It is clear that much of the perceived order and stability of the 1950s and 1960s was brought about by what has turned out to be a global dominance–dependency relationship: the dominance of manufacturing and production by western industrialized nations serving ever-expanding and almost guaranteed markets. The entry of organizations from the Pacific Rim into this area with advanced technology and attention to product quality and reliability has transformed. There are now more organizations from more countries competing for the same markets.

Those responsible for designing organizations have therefore to create the conditions in which change is accepted and embraced when necessary. This consists of fostering attitudes of flexibility, dynamism and responsiveness; seeking structures and cultures that are positive and organic; and developing the human resource to its maximum capacity. It also includes providing space and resources for creative and high-quality individuals and groups to pursue projects and other developments; and to continually develop and improve skills, knowledge, qualities, processes and practices. Innovation, development and change have to be accepted and valued in the future, just as order and steadiness were in the past (see Box 3.1).

The change process

All organizational change takes place as a process; and this process may be summarized as follows: 'Change – from what, to what, when, where, how and why?'

Most organizations and their managers get the 'change from what' right, in at least recognizing that the status quo cannot be maintained or assured. In many cases also, they identify the bits that do need changing, that are inadequate or uncompetitive for some reason.

'Changing to what' is not always as straightforward; nevertheless, this part of the process needs to be clarified at the outset of any organizational approach to change. This is because:

- people will resist change if it is not known or understood to be in their interests; or if it is known and understood that it is not in their interests;
- people will embrace change if it is known and understood that it is in their interests;

Box 3.1: General Motors

When General Motors filed for bankruptcy in 2009, it brought to an end over 100 years of steady-state and assured motor car production. Once the largest manufacturing company in the world, General Motors (GM) had come to the position in which it found itself through a combination of factors as follows:

- inability to control its costs;
- inability to innovate in motor car production;
- continued production of cars that nobody wanted to buy (or not in the volumes necessary);
- inability to recognize and respond to changing environmental concerns;
- inability to respond to changing market demands.

All of these factors may be summarized under the heading of 'inability to change'. In particular, the company failed to recognize the opportunities that each of the above factors presented, namely:

- the opportunity to pioneer and develop a full range of fuel-efficient cars of the type that the market would want to buy;
- inability to change the organization structures and culture to move with the times;
- inability to use the capabilities of the workforce to change and develop existing production and operational processes.

The company's problems had become apparent some months earlier, when it became clear that the recession of the period 2008 onwards was going to mean a sharp reduction in people's willingness and capability to buy new cars. Together with the top management of Ford and Chrysler, the senior GM team flew to Washington to meet with the president and other senior politicians in their own private planes. This action brought the top managers of each of these companies into ridicule – flying in an executive jet to a meeting to ask for government support for the companies was hardly the best way of going about things.

It also caused industry and market analysts to begin to take a real interest in the strengths and weaknesses of the companies themselves. What they found reinforced the image created by the use of the private planes in the above circumstances – that top and senior management were detached, complacent and either unwilling, or unable, to develop their organizations for the future.

- people will resist change on the grounds that the present is certain and assured; but if what is to happen in the future is uncertain, unknown or unassured, they will resist changing from what may be summarized as 'the known to the unknown'.

The 'how, when, where and why' of change represent the key organizational challenges. Each has to be explained and made clear to all concerned so that they do indeed know what is going to be expected of them in the future, and can therefore accept (or reject) what is proposed.

Change and denial

If the process of change, and the objectives that it is supposed to deliver, are not made clear, then people will deny the need. Denial is especially a problem when:

- an organization is profitable, effective and held in high reputation;
- work patterns are steady and assured, and volumes of work demanded are high;
- there is a fundamentally strong organization culture, harmony of behaviour and performance, and levels of commitment are high.

Even in situations where the organization is declining in performance, people will deny the need for change if it is not made clear. So in all cases, it is essential to explain fully and clearly why particular changes are necessary (see Box 3.2).

Changing the status quo

Changing the status quo is a process. It is not enough to destroy the existing order, however desirable that might be, that simply causes chaos. It is also not enough to take the view that dissolving the old order as the first step in changes should be done with a view to seeing what happens next. The process must have a view of 'from and to' in order to be effective. People will not willingly step off the kerb of a pavement if they do not, or cannot, see how far down it is to the road. Much less will they willingly follow major disruptions to any part of their lives, including work, if they cannot see where this is supposed to lead.

The 'change from' part of the process therefore requires the recognition of the behavioural and psychological barriers that will present themselves when the change is first proposed (see Figure 3.1). The 'change to' part is to create knowledge, understanding and acceptance by those involved, and to present the desired result in terms of the benefits, enhancement and enrichments to working life that are to accrue (see Figure 3.2).

Change catalysts

Change catalysts are anything that happens that causes the organization to need or want to change. Examples of change catalysts are as follows:

- actions of a competitor;
- sudden loss of a supplier or customer base;
- sudden gain of a new supplier or new customer bases;
- technological obsolescence;

Box 3.2: Out of Fleet Street and into Wapping

Traditionally, Fleet Street was the centre of the UK national newspaper industry. However, over the past twenty years, new technology has meant that different sorts of premises have been needed for the effective and profitable production of newspapers; and so for many organizations, it became necessary to rebuild rather than refurbish where they worked from and to relocate elsewhere.

When the *Sun* and *Times* newspapers relocated from Fleet Street to Wapping, this was accompanied by major industrial strife. The companies' printers refused to work in the new premises; and so agency staff had to be brought in by bus under police guard. Many journalists also refused to work out of the new premises.

At the same time, the *Financial Times* successfully relocated all of its activities from Fleet Street to the premises next door to those used by the *Sun* and *The Times* in Wapping. It did so with no problems at all.

The difference was in the attitude taken. The owners and top managers of the *Sun* and *The Times* simply stated that this was to happen. They presented a *fait accompli*, reinforcing this with a collective 'take it or leave it attitude'.

The *Financial Times* engaged in full consultation with all their staff, gave assurances to everyone concerned that no jobs would be lost; that any specific difficulties that people might have in getting to the new location would be accommodated for periods of up to one year; and that nobody would lose either their job or their salary, unless they chose to take a voluntary severance.

The Times and *Sun* staff who resisted the move 'denied' that such a change was necessary or possible; and that in particular, the move would be impossible without the support of the staff.

The top management of the *Financial Times* recognized that if they did not explain things fully, their staff also would take the attitude of denial.

In each case of course, the change came about. The effective management of denial in the case of the *Financial Times* meant that it was much easier, more effective and profitable to manage denial by addressing people's concerns, and maintaining as much stability as possible, while undertaking a move that had to be completed for operational reasons.

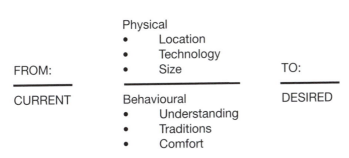

Figure 3.1 Barriers to change. Barriers are classified under the three physical and behavioural classifications, and then the desired state of affairs is classified under the same headings. The actions required to address each barrier in relation to the desired state of affairs can then be defined.

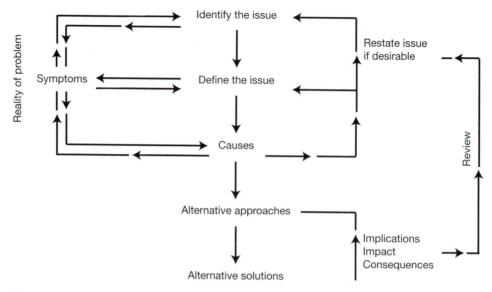

Purpose: to ensure that a rigorous and disciplined approach is recognized and understood as being necessary in all situations.

Points for consideration throughout the process must include: where change is demanded, its context and nature when it is occurring; where it is occurring; why; its impact on the rest of the organization, department or division; the extent to which it can be avoided; the extent to which it can be controlled; the consequences and opportunities of not changing (which is always a choice).

Figure 3.2 Simple change model

- the initiatives of top and senior management;
- the invention or introduction of a radical new product or production process;
- changes in economic circumstances and market strengths;
- changes in the political, legal or social framework.

None of these issues should come as a surprise to top or senior managers. Expert top and senior managers have, as part of their knowledge and understanding, a full awareness of the environment, and how this might change. The best top and senior managers additionally make sure that all their staff are kept informed of the progress of the organization, the changing conditions in which it is operating and what may therefore happen as the result (see Box 3.3).

Change agents

Change agents are those who energize, direct and drive the processes. They include key appointments – people brought in to give particular emphases; outsiders – coming in because the views of the insiders are unacceptable for some reason; distinctive experts – who bring confidence and credibility, understanding and acceptability by virtue of their level of skill or knowledge.

Top and senior managers can, and do, also act as change agents. Those in top and senior positions ought to know and understand where the internal and external drives

Box 3.3: Branded change management programmes

Initiatives such as business process re-engineering (BPR), total quality management (TQM) and six sigma programmes are implemented in response to particular needs for change. Such programmes are delivered by consultants and specialist organizations. Their stated purpose is:

- to change the organization from its present state of being to that which is desired/necessary;
- to provide a basis for activities, including milestones for the measurement of change and development along the way;
- to give a clear focus and priority for the change that is necessary or desirable.

Thus, the clear implication is that BPR will concentrate on the processes of the organization; while TQM will concentrate on the quality of every aspect of organizational practice, and also the quality of the products and services.

These programmes work best when they are used in the particular context demanded by the organization. They are less effective when they are introduced as prescriptions, with little or no regard for how they should be implemented in the particular context of the organization.

Otherwise, the positive benefits are:

- everyone gets used to the idea that change has to take place;
- clear milestones are indeed set and prescribed;
- change does indeed take place.

However, in many cases, such bespoke programmes have negative and adverse effects on the morale of the staff, and on the productivity, output and reputation of the organization. This is because, in many cases also, such programmes are implemented without regard for the particular situation, and without reference to the particular needs, wants and demands of the organization, its staff and other stakeholders.

and pressures are coming from, and how to respond to these. Companies and organizations can, and do, also create project and development groups to design and implement programmes of change from within the organization. This approach has the great advantage of being conducted from the point of view of full knowledge and understanding of the organization itself. The disadvantage is that, with the best will in the world, it cannot take a fully independent view.

Companies and organizations also use externally appointed consultants to devise, implement and drive change processes. As above (see previous Box 3.3), the advantage is that people get used to the idea that something has got to happen; the disadvantage is that what is to happen may not be what the company or organization actually needs (see Box 3.4).

Box 3.4: The use of consultants

British Airways

In 2008, faced with a downturn in passenger numbers, increased competition on its short-haul routes, higher fuel costs and increased airport passenger and landing charges, the top management of British Airways decided to call in McKinsey, the global management consulting practice, to advise on its future direction.

McKinsey duly arrived, and their consultants set to work. After an investigation, McKinsey proposed:

- 400 redundancies, to be taken from the ranks of middle management and supervisory staff;
- concentration of route networks at Terminal 5, and reduction in operations at Gatwick airport (the company's second London hub).

Satisfied with the report, British Airways duly set about implementing the proposals. Short-haul flights were removed from Gatwick and relocated to Heathrow Terminal 5. All those in middle management and supervisory positions were canvassed, and volunteers for redundancy and severance were sought. The canvassing was accompanied by a promise that anyone who applied for voluntary severance or redundancy would receive it. The terms offered were overtly advantageous: up to three year's salary for long service staff in particular was supposed to be very enticing.

At the end of the exercise, 454 staff agreed to take redundancy.

All this happened during the autumn of 2008. In May 2009, British Airways declared a corporate loss of £830 million. It stated the reason for this loss as follows:

- declining passenger numbers;
- increased fuel costs;
- increased airport and landing fees.

The position, stated the company's top management, was only going to get worse. However, the report made no mention of the McKinsey exercise, nor of the savings that it was supposed to have delivered. The overwhelming evidence is therefore that the McKinsey exercise did nothing to tackle the problems which were stated at the outset, but rather simply implemented what McKinsey knew how to deliver.

The key lesson is therefore: any organization using external agents of change needs to ensure that they are fully briefed on what they are to do, and ensure also that when proposals are finally submitted, they are evaluated in full. Otherwise, organizations will simply repeat the British Airways experience above: that what was proposed did nothing to address or ameliorate the underlying and continuing problems.

Drives for change

The need for organizational change is created by the following.

Changes in ownership

These may come about through takeovers, mergers, acquisitions; through the privatization of public services; through changes in the balance of shared ownership. In each case the new owners will normally bring their own views on the present and desired performance of the organization, and this invariably affects many of the other areas indicated below.

Changes in management style

Such changes are driven by a general organizational recognition that the current approach is not right. This is normally accompanied by training developments and familiarization programmes and briefings for all staff. It may also lead to some restructuring of patterns of supervision, allocations of responsibility and divisions of work.

Changes in management style can, and do, occur when new appointments are made. In practice, new managers and supervisors always want to make their own mark on their departments and divisions very quickly, as well as reassuring staff of the continued value of their contribution and their work.

Changes in management style need to be introduced clearly, at the outset of a new manager's appointment. The basis and reasons for these changes also need to be made clear, again, so that staff know and understand what the position is, and so that they can continue to work in the ways required, and in the sure and certain knowledge that they have the full support of the new person (see Box 3.5).

Changes in technology

These are driven by the need to improve product, volume and quality and to maintain and improve the given competitive position. This normally leads to retraining, redeployment, transfers – and also often to redundancies. It also often leads to the redesign and restructuring of the work environment and, again, is likely to affect patterns of supervision, management and work group cohesion. This can be a good thing if it is felt necessary for any reason to break up existing patterns and locations of work. If existing patterns of work are effective and productive, however, breaking them up has to be accompanied by clear explanation so as not to avoid either personal or occupational trauma, loss of staff or loss of morale.

It is also the case that radical shifts in technology can have far-reaching effects on companies, organizations and, indeed, whole sectors. For example:

- using the internet to book holidays and make travel arrangements has fundamentally altered the structure of the travel agency sector;
- using e-mail and teleconferencing networks to keep in touch now means that people can be at work at any hour of the day or night;
- the ability to locate technological centres of excellence means that work can be carried out anywhere in the world where this expertise exists;

Box 3.5: Change in management style

The press office of one of the UK's major political institutions had always been a convivial place to work. Additionally, people always turned up on time, and carried out their work and duties as befitted the effective operation of the press and public relations requirements of a top political institution. The Cabinet minister in charge of the institution attended on a daily basis; and everybody called him by his first name, enjoyed a friendly, open and positive relationship – as well as getting the work done. Whenever there were crises and emergencies (and because of the nature of the work of the institution, these were frequent occurrences) there was no problem ever in getting people to come in early, work late or respond to requests at short notice.

In due course, the minister moved on, and was replaced. The new minister now sought to make his particular mark. He insisted that everybody wore formal dress, including suits for everyone, and ties for the male staff. He insisted that everyone called him by his surname, or 'Minister'. He tried to insist that everyone used formal titles of address when speaking with those of different ranks from themselves.

Within a very few weeks, the work ethic had changed. It now became very difficult to get people to do more than their jobs; in particular, getting people to come in early or stay late was now almost impossible. Staff immediately began putting in for transfers, and within three months, half of them had left.

New staff coming in, unaware of what had gone on before, soon settled into the new routine. Before very long, this became the standard and accepted way of working.

The key lesson is that, whenever a change in management style comes about, it needs to be made clear immediately. In this particular case, new dress codes and modes of address were introduced without this clarity. The result was an upheaval, including the loss of staff, and the need to recruit new staff (who then of course have to be inducted into the ways of working). How much easier it would have been if only the new Minister had felt able to explain why he wanted to make these changes.

It should also be noted that, as stated above, such changes do work through and become effective in their own way. However, this can all be done without the trauma of upheaval or staff loss, again if explanation is made.

- developments in technological capacity mean that a much greater volume of information can now be stored, managed, retrieved, gathered and distributed;
- developments in production capacity, and improvements in production methods, mean that a much greater volume of products and components can now be produced to ever-increasing quality and accuracy standards, as well as in ever-greater volumes (see Box 3.6).

Changes in markets

Changes in markets are driven by current levels of activities in relation to desired or required levels. They may also be driven by the need to seek new outlets for existing activities or new ranges of activities. The likely effects are again retraining and redeployment. There may also be issues of identity to be overcome.

Box 3.6: Procter & Gamble

Procter & Gamble, one of the world's leading producers of soaps, detergents and household goods, discovered a radical new way of producing soap powder. The soap powder itself was of a much higher quality than existing products. It was also produced with a greater concentration of active ingredients, and a lower volume of other ingredients. This meant that:

- less soap powder packaging was required;
- less of the non-active ingredients was required from the supply side;
- different designs of the active ingredients were required from the supply side;
- smaller transport fleets were required to distribute the products in the numbers and volumes required in order to satisfy existing market demand.

On the face of it, Procter & Gamble had discovered a winner! However, it became apparent that there were going to be problems, as follows:

- the lower volumes demanded on the supply side meant that suppliers were now going to receive less income themselves from this customer;
- the reduced requirement for transport meant that some of the lorry fleets now had excess capacity, which they would have to fill from elsewhere;
- those who supplied the packaging would also receive lower volumes of business from Procter & Gamble.

It was also apparent that customers were used to buying soap powders in large boxes; and so their perceptions and attitudes would have to be managed so that they understood they would indeed get a higher quality wash out of a reduced volume of soap powder, delivered in a smaller box.

In operational terms, it therefore became necessary for Procter & Gamble to operate the new production process, and to rebrand the new products, so as to make them distinctive from the existing stock. Additionally, the existing soap powder products would have to continue for the foreseeable future, until such time as customers themselves perceived or believed that it was in their interests to use the new product and thus smaller volumes.

Changes in costs and charges

All organizations ultimately operate at the mercy of changes in costs and charges as follows:

- changes in energy costs;
- changes in staff costs;
- changes in taxation regimes;
- changes in currency values;
- changes in interest rates.

Each of these represent costs and charges that the organization itself has to bear as a condition of opening for business. When changing attitudes, behaviour and perform-ance, these costs and charges represent boundaries within which organizations have to work and be effective. Especially if such costs and charges rise steeply, the organization has to have a series of responses in place so as to be able to address the effects of these increases without damaging productive capacity.

Changes in job and work organization

Changes in job and work organization are driven by the need to improve production and output, and enhance the working environment. This normally means the creation of flexible patterns of work, offering increased levels of responsibility; and broadening, enlarging and enhancing individual jobs. This, in turn, has the purpose of leading to increased identity with the organization, greater levels of commitment, greater levels of volume and quality of output – and better wages and salaries for the staff.

Changes in job and work organization additionally lead to organizations and their top and senior managers considering such activities as:

*   outsourcing;
*   relocation to more advantageous premises (see Box 3.2 above);
*   enabling staff to work from home.

Whatever changes to job and work organization are deemed necessary, it is essential that companies and organizations, and their managers, make clear the basis on which the changes are to be implemented, and the advantages that are to accrue to the staff as well as the organization. For example, while to many people the idea of working from home seems very attractive and advantageous, it can and does lead to isolation and displacement, and a loss of mutual identity between the staff members and the organization.

Changes in structure

These are driven by assessments which conclude that the current structure is not as effective as it might be. This is normally arrived at by identifying blockages – in produc-tion, output, systems and communications – and relating these to structural factors. Restructuring will therefore be designed to ensure that these are removed. Restructuring also covers work practices. It also may include changes in work organization as, for example, with the move from production lines to work groups and self-managed teams (see Box 3.7).

Changes in culture, value, attitudes and beliefs

Changes in culture, values, attitudes and beliefs are driven by the fact that what goes on at present is inappropriate or ineffective. These matters are addressed through major communications, retraining, redeployment, organization and personnel development; and enhanced by other related activities such as the changes in technology structure and work patterns indicated.

Effective changes in culture, values, attitudes and beliefs require careful definitions of where the problems lie. With a production process, this is overtly much more

Box 3.7: Volvo

Faced with the problem of managing the alienation and displacement of their production line workforces, the Volvo car company decided to move away from traditional approaches, towards self-managed teams. Each team would be responsible for operating the whole of the production process. People would not simply do one job and then watch as the production line moved on. Each team was to ensure that every member was fully trained in every aspect of the work; and this was so that all jobs could be rotated and carried out by anyone. Before long, the self-managed team approach came to include quality assurance and customer relations (meaning that any complaints about the finished product from customers or dealers could be referred directly to the production team that had made it).

After the process had been in place for three years, it was evaluated by the company's top management. The immediate finding was that productivity had not significantly improved. However, the cost per unit production had fallen by 30 per cent. There was less wastage and less downtime. Left to themselves, the self-managed teams now organized everything from the basis of their own expert knowledge of what the production process actually entailed. Cleaning and maintenance were carried out when convenient to the self-managed teams, rather than when ordained by the company.

Additionally, the volume of customer complaints fell; and the speed at which they were resolved rose.

straightforward: not enough products are coming off the production line quickly enough or there are too many faults. Defining behavioural and attitudinal changes in the same way is very much harder.

Changing people's attitudes, values and beliefs is very much harder than changing their behaviour or changing the performance targets which they are expected to meet. In many cases, this only comes about as the result of:

- an organizational trauma or crisis, including acute loss of market;
- the departure of a major key figure, and their replacement by somebody else.

The need is therefore to ensure that people have positive and committed attitudes as an integral part of their employment. These attitudes are instilled at induction, and reinforced by collective prevailing attitudes and behaviour, and by the organization's management style (see Chapters 4, 5 and 6).

Obsolescence

This change may be driven by the entry of a new player into the sector who has found radical new ways of operating that are much more effective than the status quo. Others either have to make the same shift, or else reposition their existing activities (or else cease business).

The usual immediate effect is to destabilize the whole sector while all players come to terms with the new ways of working. This form of change has occurred throughout the car and electrical goods industries driven by the Japanese approach and ways of working.

Obsolescence may also be brought about by government action. For example, the sudden placing of legal restrictions or taxation charges on particular products and activities may cause people to turn away from them, leaving the organizations hitherto involved highly at risk.

Obsolescence in one organization also occurs when others come along with substitute products and services. These are then taken up by the customers of the first organization, again leaving it vulnerable.

In each case, obsolescence may come about very suddenly. It may also be due to circumstances over which the organization has little, or no, control.

Managerial drives

These come about as the result of concerns by managers that the status quo will not serve the organization forever. These drives are often hard to accept when the organization is ostensibly going along extremely effectively and profitably; harder still, when they are allied to high levels of motivation, commitment and identity. These drives question and address each of the areas indicated. They come from within the organization rather than outside. They are also likely to come from the point of view of taking preventative action rather than having to respond to crises.

Performance indicators and outputs

The assessment of these by managers leads to drives for change if either the operational or behavioural indicators give cause for concern. In these cases, the causes of each will be assessed and addressed. They, in turn, lead to change programmes that remedy the total performance of the whole organization and the contribution of each department, division and function.

Performance indicators may be divided up as follows.

*   **Strategic**: related to successful and effective performance over the lifetime of an organization.
*   **Operational**: related to the success and profitability of products and services; product mixes and portfolios; productivity and output.
*   **Specific**: including organizational income or profit per member of staff, per customer, per offering, per outlet, per square foot; returns on investment; density/frequency of usage; longevity of usage; speed of response; product durability and longevity of usage; volume and quality targets.
*   **Behavioural**: related to the perceptual and staff management aspects; desired and prevailing attitudes and values; the extent of strikes, disputes, absenteeism, labour turnover and accidents; harmony/discord, cooperation/conflict; the general aura of well-being.
*   **Confidence**: the relationship between the organization and its environment, its backers, its stakeholders, its customers, its communities.
*   **Ethical**: the absolute standards of behaviour and performance that the organization sets for itself and their acceptance in their markets and communities.

These form the basis on which organization performance may be analysed and help to pinpoint its strengths, weaknesses and areas for concern.

Continuous improvement and development

The drive here stems from the recognition that there is no such thing as the perfect organization and that the environment within which it operates is continuously fluctuating and changing. New and improved methods of work and constant attention to the behaviour and functioning of the individuals and groups therefore become a key feature of all effective organizations. The logical conclusion is therefore that everything is subject to potential change and that even if something is seen and known to work extremely effectively, it may still be improved if the right means can be found.

The approach to continuous improvement and development is, therefore, as much attitude and state of mind as operational. As such it needs feeding, supporting and nurturing to ensure that everyone involved adopts the approach. The desired output is a combination of flexibility, dynamism, responsiveness, pro-activity and pioneering leading to enhanced business performance and greater levels of personal identity with, and commitment to, the organization.

These drives stem from a combination of organizational effectiveness and behaviour. They reinforce the point made at the outset that neither can be achieved in isolation from the other. Any change programme that arises must address both – achieving effective results is only possible if the staff are also committed to the chosen direction (see Box 3.8).

Box 3.8: Sony

The original and iconic Sony Walkman was first developed under the guidance and direction of Akio Morita, the company's founder. The Walkman was originally designed so as to be convenient to carry around, while at the same time have the capacity to deliver radio programmes as well as the ability to listen to music cassettes.

The first Walkman products caused everyone to marvel at just how small such items could be made. However, as each new prototype emerged from the company laboratories, Akio Morita threw them into a bucket of water and waited for the bubbles to emerge. Then he would say: 'See – there is still space in this product. It can still be made smaller. Air is escaping from it. Go away and make it smaller.'

Eventually both the size and the quality were satisfactory and acceptable to Akio Morita; and the products started to roll off the production line for distribution to the shops and customers.

The whole approach then became the basis for fundamental reappraisal of what was possible in the electrical goods, music and personal entertainment industries.

This kind of approach is only possible if the following are present:

- the drive and commitment of the leader or director, as above;
- the commitment of the staff to follow the leader and director;
- the willingness to drive for continuous improvement, as above.

Dissatisfaction with the status quo

Whatever the apparent strength of the familiarity, comfort and vested interest barriers, general and overwhelming dissatisfaction has to be changed. This is normally mainly behavioural, although the outputs of high levels of dissatisfaction are likely to be found in poor volumes, quality of products and increasing levels of customer complaints.

Crises and conflicts

Where an organization is perpetually in crisis, radically different ways of working and patterns of behaviour are required and must be sought.

Of course, no organization should be perpetually in crisis or conflict. Organizations that blunder from one crisis or emergency to another at the very least become very expensive to operate, and very demoralizing to work in. Alongside the management of crises, therefore, it is essential that top and senior managers get to grips with why these events are occurring, and why people can do nothing about them until after they have occurred.

Lack of clear direction

Lack of clear direction is nearly always present in failing or under-performing organizations. Everyone involved needs clarity:

- the staff so that they know what they are supposed to do, and how and why they are supposed to do it;
- customers and clients so that they have assurances about products and service quality and value;
- suppliers so that they have confidence in continuing relations with the particular organization;
- financiers and backers so that they know and understand the purposes to which their money and resources are being put.

Where there is a lack of clear direction, the situation is analysed and the clarity of purpose sought and established. This, again, is likely to lead to changes in attitudes, values and beliefs (indeed, it is often likely to fill a void in these). It also normally leads to the establishment of firm absolute standards of behaviour and performance.

Taking control

Organizations and their leaders and managers ought always to be in overall control of direction, activities, resources, processes and purposes. However, from time to time, managers do lose full control over daily activities as they leave departments, divisions and groups to go about their normal range of activities. In times of change it is essential to assert authority and direction; and a key part of this means taking control of the whole process. This in turn means that the position of vested interests, over-mighty departments, divisions, groups and subjects and other lobbies and influences (for example, trade unions and consumer groups) has to be addressed, and where necessary confronted and engaged, so as to ensure that clarity of purpose is not damaged or diluted.

Summary

All drives for organizational change arise from a combination of organizational effectiveness, performance, direction and behaviour. Any effective change programme must therefore address each aspect – achieving sustainable and lasting results is only possible if every part is tackled in full. Reasons for organizational change therefore normally fall into each of these categories to a greater or lesser extent (though the balance will clearly differ in each situation). Each situation is also likely to have present most of the drives indicated above, though again the actual emphasis and mixture of these varies between, and within, organizations.

A summary framework may now be drawn up (see Table 3.1).

The change process

The process by which particular changes are to be achieved arrives from assessment of the components of the framework and elements indicated above. There are certain essentials.

- Organization commitment must be absolute.
- Aims and objectives are to be clearly stated in terms that all affected understand.
- Resources are required for all aspects of the process and each of the activities conducted in its pursuit.
- Continuous monitoring, review and evaluation processes are to be conducted in the name of those responsible for designing and implementing the change programme.
- Recognition of the expectations, hopes, fears and aspirations of all affected will themselves be changed, and these require understanding and satisfaction.
- Recognition that the process itself will generate its own life; that it will bring opportunities and problems that are not apparent at the outset; and that part of the successful management of change lies in assessing these opportunities and problems as they arise and having the capacity to take whatever steps are necessary as the result.
- The process requires leadership and direction, and general and specific responsibilities allocated to everyone.
- Recognition that the unfreezing of the status quo is potentially destabilizing and leads to chaos if it is not a part of the complete process, and targeted.

Table 3.1 Summary framework

Why change:	What are the reasons and the drives; what are the barriers; what are the desired outcomes?
What to change:	Technology, jobs, structure, style, attitudes, values, beliefs, culture.
How to change:	What is the route to be followed between the present and what is required?
When to change:	What is the deadline for implementation and when must interim activities be completed?
Who to change:	Retraining, redeployment, redundancy; job titles and descriptions; areas of responsibility; areas of activity; changing aspirations, expectations, hopes and fears.
What to change to:	Benefits and consequences; advantages and disadvantages; for the organization and for all concerned.

- General organization support is required for all those affected. This is necessary in the form of communications, counselling, empathy based on an understanding of the situation of those involved; and also in providing retraining, redeployment and time off to look for alternatives.
- Recognition that change is not an end in itself and that it will lead to further opportunities.

Changing unsatisfactory attitudes and behaviour

Unsatisfactory attitudes and behaviour generally take the form of being negative or indifferent or not positive enough. Negative attitudes and behaviour especially arise as the result of a lack of clarity of purpose and where the organization has paid insufficient attention to the standards of behaviour, performance and output that are required.

Negative attitudes and behaviour may also arise as the result of the influence of different groups and individuals. This occurs when these groups and individuals have some cause for dissatisfaction and seek to influence others as the result. A form of siege mentality may develop – a negative form of group-think in organizational behaviour terms.

Negative attitudes and behaviour also develop alongside work structuring and organization and the management style that has been devised to support it; and also where this is alienative, based on status differentials, lack of respect and esteem and absence of equality of treatment.

Barriers

The main barriers to change are:

- Prior and current commitments – occurring where people are unwilling to change because they have invested energy and expertise in the status quo and perceive or understand it to be working well and in their own interests.
- Ego-protection – occurring where people are unwilling to admit that there is something wrong with the situation and especially that they have made mistakes or committed themselves to faulty courses of action.
- Value defence – occurring where there is a strong group or individual identity with prevailing values, whether or not these are effective and successful from the organization's point of view.
- Lack of information – this is where people will not change their attitudes because they do not see it as being in their interests to do so because of a lack of information in relation to the imperfections of the status quo and because there is insufficient information made available about the purpose of the required and desired changes.
- Fear – this is, above all, fear of the unknown and engages defensive and protectionist attitudes on the part of those involved.
- Influences of individuals – occurring especially where strong and dominant personalities tell others that the desired change is not required or that it is to be punitive or coercive (or negative or detrimental in some other way). This is reinforced if the particular individual has a history or reputation for having been right about these things in the past.

- Influences of groups – the influences here are similar to those of particular individuals. People have a strong tendency to conform to group think and group norms. This is exacerbated if the group in question has high status or reputation. The group also has influence if the individual has taken a conscious decision to join it – such as a trade union or professional association. In these cases the stated views of the group in relation to a particular situation are perceived to have a high degree of substance and credibility – and again this is enhanced if a group has a history of having been right about such matters in the past.

Drives for change

Changes in attitudes, behaviour and performance will only take place if each of the barriers is addressed effectively. The means of doing this are as follows:

- Addressing prior and current commitments as stepping-stones on the path of progress rather than seeking to deny or destroy them, and recognizing and valuing the level of commitment that individuals have placed on these. If they have been largely motivated by self-interest then means must be found of harmonizing this with the commitment to the organization that is now required.
- Addressing ego-protection from the point of view of ensuring, again, that what has been done was not of the order of fatal or mortal error (unless it was based on vanity, arrogance or incompetence). More positive still, recognition is to be given for the value and effectiveness of whatever was done and achieved in the past; and where this is minimal or lacking, it may still be represented as a stepping stone.
- Addressing values from the point of view of building on the past and present rather than destroying it; this is likely to be most effective where the organization repositions or restates its shared values and other absolute standards of policy and behaviour at the same time, taking active and positive steps to ensure that these are accepted and adopted – and that any sanctions used are given to those who do not, or will not, respond positively.
- Overhauling channels of communication to ensure that what is put out is of quality and value, as well as volume, and to address the basic problem of ignorance that is the barrier here.
- Addressing fear from the twin standpoint that it is a barrier to attitude change and that it can also be used to change attitudes. Fear as a barrier normally constitutes fear of the unknown and is thus largely addressed by the attention to the channels of communication activities indicated above. Fear as a drive for attitude change has to strike the balance between stating on the one hand that the status quo can no longer go on, and on the other that something that is too threatening simply leads to a negative response (normally rejection). This is compounded by the fact that too little emphasis on the fear factor means that people perceive that there is nothing to be fearful of.

Drives and barriers may be represented as a 'Force Field Analysis'. 'Force Field Analysis' involves representing the changes required, and the barriers and restraints as follows (see Figure 3.3).

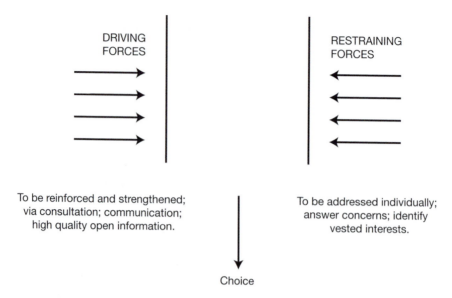

To be reinforced and strengthened;
via consultation; communication;
high quality open information.

Choice

To be addressed individually;
answer concerns; identify
vested interests.

Notes:
The drives and driving forces present in the situation are classified in the left-hand column; and the restraints and barriers in the right-hand column. This then provides an illustration from which people can work, in deciding for example:

- which of the restraints can be negated or overcome through drives;
- which of the restraints can be neutralized or made ineffective;
- where the priorities lie.

Figure 3.3 Force Field Analysis

Other factors in the management of change

Co-opting

This is the process of getting highly influential groups and individuals involved in the change process. Those who defend the status quo and the prevailing attitudes and values are invited to participate in the drive for change, to suggest and devise means by which the changes required can be implemented successfully while at the same time having regard to their own needs (see Box 3.9).

Use of operational changes

Operational changes are also used to affect attitudes by emphasizing and enhancing the opportunities that are to become available to staff as the result. This is part of the process of addressing the fear and ignorance elements. A relationship between the future ways of working and the general interest of those affected is defined. This is likely not to be an end in itself. Opportunities for training, occupational variety and redeployment normally have to be offered alongside operational change if new attitudes are to be formed effectively.

Box 3.9: The co-opting of trade unions and employees' representatives

Over the recent past, as the need for organizational change across all sectors has become apparent, many top and senior managers have found it both necessary and also productive to ensure that trade unions and other employees' representatives are engaged in change processes from the outset.

This sends the following clear messages to the staff who are to be affected:

- their interests are being looked after;
- the company has sufficient confidence in its own proposals to make them public to those who might otherwise be hostile to them.

This form of co-opting is essential in gaining the support and commitment of the staff concerned.

This is reinforced by the fact that many trade unions now work with organizations as joint or social partners. This means that, as well as representing the staff interest, they adopt an active interest in the welfare of the organization (and therefore, of course, the welfare of the staff).

The result, where it works effectively, is a much greater openness and transparency all round; and a much greater responsibility on the part of managers to ensure that any proposals for change are fully thought out before they are made public.

Use of technological change

Changes in all organization technology – operational, production and information – invariably lead to attitude change because of the need to be retrained in order to be able to use the new equipment effectively. The result is the development of new outlooks as well as skills and knowledge, enhancement and proficiency, opening up new horizons, possibilities and potential.

Restructuring

Co-opting, operational and technological change may all lead to, and contribute to, restructuring. The process can also be used to break up resistant groups and departments, as well as addressing operational effectiveness. It is also often possible to redefine relationships with trade unions and professional bodies and associations during restructuring on the grounds that, while the old ways may have been suitable in the past, they are no longer relevant to the new-style organization.

Cooperating with the inevitable

If something is certain to happen, if the decision to change has already been taken, there is no point – and no honesty – in giving any other impression. Indeed, to do so is detrimental to the quality of future relationships. It also contributes to any prevailing negative attitudes. People who are given to understand that they have some say in matters, then subsequently find that this is not so, generate feelings of mistrust and of negativity towards the organization.

Positive attitudes are generated in response to the inevitable by presenting the benefits of the new situation, by dealing with negative aspects in open and straightforward ways, and reinforcing each with necessary activities. Above all, this means attention to communications and the ways in which these are delivered and presented. It also means giving organization support to groups and individuals who are to feel particular effects – especially negative effects such as job loss – in the form of retraining and redeployment where possible. This should always be supported in terms of counselling, help, support and advice. It demonstrates respect and esteem for the staff. It acknowledges their past contribution and is a mark of value. It is also of benefit to those who remain, even if they have not been directly affected by the changes, because it proves the organization's care, concern and respect for all staff.

Letting go

Prevailing attitudes – both positive and negative – are familiar and therefore comfortable. Part of the process of changing attitudes is therefore concerned with generating acceptance of, and comfort with, the new. It may be possible to gain a general acceptance that the new is highly desirable – but the old has still to be left behind, people have still to 'let it go'.

Again, the likelihood of this is greater, the greater the level of direct and active involvement taken by the organization and generated in the people. Again, the value and quality of communications and counselling, attention to groups and individuals, and reinforcement of respect and esteem are critical. Again also, the overall need is to persuade people to adopt and internalize the required attitudes and to let go of the old because it is in their interests to do so, and they will be better served by the new than the old.

Consultation

Consultations will begin to take place at the point at which proposals for change become clear. The purpose is to ensure that initial familiarity with the idea is generated as quickly as possible – a form of ice-breaking.

Subjecting proposals to a wider audience is also likely to ensure that any absolute objections are raised as early as possible. This, in turn, identifies the nature and location (and the likely strength) of potential lobbies and vested interests. It may also draw in responses to real problems that nobody so far concerned had hitherto considered.

Consultation will therefore be as wide as possible, drawing everyone involved (and any representative bodies such as trade unions and professional associations) into the process. It is the first step towards identity, internalization, ownership – and acceptance – by all concerned.

Participation

Genuine participation in the determination of change is unlikely. In most situations this is the key task and responsibility of top managers. Participation in the implementation of change is essential. The process will be much smoother and more effective if what is proposed is accepted and internalized by those directly concerned. These are the direct results of effective participation. Participation in change is also conducted through all the instruments available within the organization – staff meetings, briefing groups, work improvement groups, quality circles and quality assurance groups, any trade unions and other staff representative committees. The role of each is to accept and adopt the change processes, give them life and energy, and ensure that everybody is involved (see Box 3.10).

Facilitation

This is the provision of specialist and directed support to groups and individuals through the facilitation process. It is especially important if there is to be a major restructuring or if redundancies, redeployments and retraining are to take place. Those affected in these ways have special needs and anxieties that must be supported.

Box 3.10: Unfreezing – change – refreezing

The key priority of effective consultation, participation, facilitation and communication is to ensure that the status quo, and the attitudes and behaviour that go with it, are 'unfrozen'. The sheer flood of information, and the means of participation and involvement used, mean that nobody can possibly be in any doubt about what is being proposed and why. As long as the proposals are clear and transparent, and can stand up to scrutiny and questioning, these approaches to change and development are likely to be effective.

Diagrammatically, the process can be represented as follows (see Figure 3.4).

As stated above, these processes are designed to ensure that the present position is 'unfrozen'. This then creates the conditions in which people are prepared to be positively involved in what is required.

The re-freezing does, however, need further consideration. In practice, in the present context, organizations ought not to be seeking to substitute one set of assured comfortable (and often complacent) patterns of behaviour and performance. 'Re-freezing' therefore needs to be the 're-freezing' of attitudes that now embrace change and development all of the time, patterns of behaviour that are positive and committed, and performance levels which are ever-increasing.

UNFREEZING – TRANSFORMING – REFREEZING		
UNFREEZING	**TRANSFORMING**	**REFREEZING**
• consultation • high quality open information • getting people used to the idea	• introduction of new technology, work patterns, products, services, attitudes	• the new becomes the steady-state and familiar • note the danger of becoming rigid or set anew

Figure 3.4 Unfreezing – transforming – refreezing

There may also be problems with 'pockets of resistance'. Individuals and groups that refuse to accept the proposals need special counselling and additional support.

Specific individual problems may also need to be addressed in this way – such as the provision of company transport to enable people to get to a new location that is not on public transport routes.

Organization development

The establishment of programmes of organization development, learning cultures and programmes of continuous development and improvement both creates and reinforces the environment within which changes take place. In these situations participation in the programmes is normally an absolute requirement. Skills and knowledge are therefore changed and developed first. This leads to changes in behaviour, expectations and aspirations; and in turn again, prevailing styles, relationships, attitudes and values are affected.

This is reinforced through the use of quality circles, work improvement groups, briefing groups, and targeted group and staff meetings.

Conclusions

With every change effort and programme there are winners and losers. Attention needs to be paid to the losers as well as to the winners. This is especially important for long-serving employees who came into the organization under one set of circumstances and who are now being required to adapt to others – or even face the fact that their skills, qualities and expertise are no longer required. It should always be remembered that their contribution was valuable in the past and this should form the basis of the attitude adopted towards them for the future – whether or not they are to be kept on.

All change processes and programmes require wholehearted organization commitment supported with adequate levels of resource and time.

Successful change only comes about where managers successfully energize and drive each of the elements indicated. The key issue, therefore, is for organizations to adopt attitudes of flexibility, dynamism, responsiveness and positiveness, and the drive to maximize output and resource usage. Change is a process; it is also a state of mind (just as order and steadiness were in the past).

It therefore requires active involvement and direct and positive participation rather than simple acquiescence; and this should apply to everyone. Hierarchical progressions, steady jobs and administrative functions and their historic output of satisfactory performance and results are all being questioned, and often abolished, in the pursuit of direct contribution to performance, and continued improvement and development.

Above all, the role of managers and supervisors must change from the operation of systems and procedures to the development of expertise, skills, knowledge and qualities in their people. The new manager will be a leader, director, developer and coach of the human resources, and the creator of conditions in which this can be successful. This, above all, is why an understanding of the behaviour of organizations, and those who work in them, is so valuable.

Part 2

The disciplines of organizational behaviour

This part of the book is concerned with breaking down the different aspects of collective and individual behaviour into 'component parts'. In many ways, this is misleading; none of the material covered in this part exists in isolation, nor can it be studied without reference to the other aspects.

Nevertheless, it is necessary to start somewhere! The benefit of taking such an approach also means that the main principles on which a full understanding of human behaviour are founded can be illustrated and developed.

In this context, this part covers:

- perception: how individuals and groups see the world, and how their view of the world is shaped, formed and limited;
- attitudes, values and beliefs: how attitudes, values and beliefs are founded, formed and developed; and referring especially to the need for positive attitudes, values and beliefs within organizations;
- ethics and standards: the need for a strong moral and ethical stance, and basis of integrity; and the need for an effective and understood work ethic;
- motivation: the need to engage people with expertise so that they are both capable and willing to work for the organization;
- communication: the critical nature of effective communications; and the problems that are caused when communications are ineffective or inadequate;
- influence, power and authority: how influence, power and authority are established, maintained and developed; and the nature of responsibility in using influence, power and authority;
- the nature of organizational politics, and the need to be able to survive in order to be effective in work situations;
- the ability to identify sources and causes of conflict, and to take steps to address them effectively;
- the ability to combine individuals into effective teams and groups, relating the human aspects to the nature of work and the technology that is available so that effective and successful (and profitable) activity is delivered;
- the nature of organization culture: the need to create a basis of how things are done in, and within, particular organizations, so that people act and operate with confidence, comfort and a wider understanding, as well as effectively and successfully.

Collectively, these disciplines form the basis for the understanding of individual and collective behaviour. As understanding is developed, it then becomes necessary to look at the ways in which behaviour can be shaped, managed and developed so that the interests of the organization are served, as well as those of the individuals concerned.

4 Perception

Introduction

Perception is the process by which all people form their views of the world. Perception is essential because of the amount of information, signals and cues with which the senses are constantly assailed. The total amount of information is not capable of assimilation because it is constantly changing and developing and because of the constant nature of human activity. A process of some sort is therefore clearly necessary by which this is first limited and then transformed into something that is useful and usable.

The process by which individual perception is developed is both learned and instinctive. Some of it comes from the senses – sight, hearing, touch, taste and smell. Some of it also plainly comes from instinct – one's view of what is edible is clearly coloured by how hungry one is.

That which is learned comes from a combination of civilization and socialization. This gives rise, above all, to moral and ethical codes by which behaviour is regulated. It also gives rise to the formation of norms, expectations, customs and etiquette. It forms the basis for concepts of fashion and desirability and the need for achievement (see Figures 4.1 and 4.2).

The context of perception

Knowing and understanding this part of human behaviour, the effects that it has on organizations and the ways in which they conduct themselves, is vital. This is because, ultimately, nobody can gain or understand the whole picture of anything and so everything is limited by:

* people's overall ability to grasp and understand the environment and context;
* people's ability to know and understand the ways in which the organization is supposed to operate, and the ways in which it does operate;
* knowing and understanding how people act and react in particular situations and in response to specific events and occurrences.

Additionally, the nature of perception gives everyone the following capacities which they can, and do, use for good and ill:

* editing and closure, meaning that they can either see only a part of the full picture; or that they choose to see only a part of the full picture;

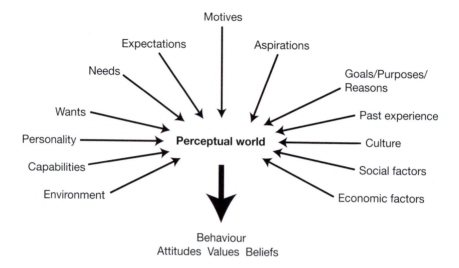

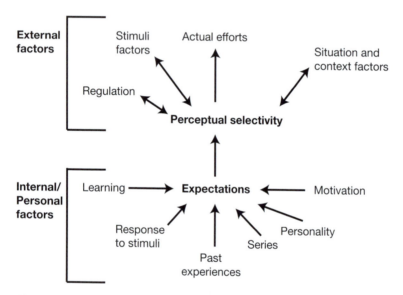

Figure 4.1 Relationships between perception, behaviour, attitudes and values
Source: Huczynski and Buchanan (1993).

• shortcomings in which they either recognize that they do have shortcomings and so take steps to develop their own capacities; or that they use their shortcomings as a foundation for everything that they then do.

Understanding the nature of perception means that necessarily people have to grasp the fact that it is a very complex and uncertain world. Again, the dilemma is whether to welcome this complexity and uncertainty, or to seek some sort of order, certainty and tidiness based on perception (see Box 4.1).

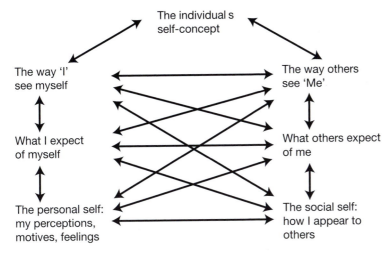

Figure 4.2 The basis of interpersonal perception
Source: C. Rogers (1947).

Box 4.1: Toxic assets

The collective attitudes taken by the banking industry towards the products and services that it offered prior to the crisis of 2007 and beyond were based almost entirely on perception, and the assumptions that came about as a result.

In particular, sub-prime mortgages were offered to those who had bad credit ratings and poor debt histories. The line of reasoning was that by charging high interest rates and placing heavy penalties on defaulters, products could be offered to those in this position. The fact of the heavy penalties, especially, would mean that people would pay up rather than incur these charges.

These products were therefore launched in these markets. Almost immediately, people started to default, and the banks repossessed the properties. The banks then parcelled up these properties into 'bundles of assets', and sold them on to others (who then sold them on to others, who sold them on to others – and so on). The result was that the 'bundles of assets' formed a kind of currency in themselves, to be bought, sold and traded between the different institutions.

The initial valuations of the properties on which the loans had been made were maintained on paper; and some of these properties were valued at the outset as if the full repayment, including interest and other charges, had already been completed.

The crunch came when one or two financial analysts began to evaluate in detail exactly what the bundles of assets were worth. The analysts found that these 'assets' were, in practice, worth only a fraction of what the book values stated. The banks were trading in 'assets', buying and selling them, without knowing and understanding what they were really worth, or knowing and understanding only too well what they were really worth but doing so to keep up the illusion that all was well.

continued . . .

Box 4.1: Toxic assets ... *continued*

None of this would have happened if the key perceptions and assumptions had been even superficially tested in advance, as follows:

- people with bad credit histories and ratings are more likely to default; and they are more likely to default if the charges are high than if they are low;
- the assumed values of the 'bundles of assets' were never tested or confirmed;
- the assets should never have been valued as anything until they were realized (i.e. sold).

The result was, and remains, the creation of a colossal global block of 'toxic assets' (in fact, toxic liabilities) which the banking sector can neither support nor service.

In the shakedown that followed, this led one former risk manager to state that he had indeed tried to warn his top management that the problems would occur; but he had been shouted down (literally – and on many occasions).

Another, a product development manager at Citibank provided a 'What if?' scenario based on 50 per cent default rates; and he was told to go away and change the figures to those based on 5 per cent default rates.

Another section head was moved to describe her own top management as 'bone idle' and 'unwilling to do anything to test the assumptions, and unwilling to let anyone else do so either'.

The result of acting on perceptions and assumptions in these ways, rather than doing the real work that is indicated, has been to destabilize not just individual companies and organizations, but the whole global financial sector.

Neatness and tidiness

There is a perceived relationship between order, neatness and tidiness, and efficiency and effectiveness. There is a legitimacy and an illegitimacy attached to this.

Legitimacy

The legitimacy of neatness and tidiness is based on the following:

- **Overall expectations**: people prefer to do business in places that are neat, tidy and orderly; people prefer to work in organizations, buildings and neighbourhoods that are orderly, neat and tidy. People expect to be met and greeted by others who 'look right' and so are smart, clean and tidy. People expect their colleagues to turn up to work looking smart, neat and tidy; and if the organization has dress codes, or provides uniforms or work overalls, then these too are expected to be worn to particular standards. Effective implementation of these kinds of meeting expectations reinforces organizational product and service branding, and identity. It gives staff, customers and suppliers a known, understood and agreed point of reference. It can also act as a staff motivator (see Box 4.2).

Box 4.2: Eddie Stobart Ltd

When Eddie Stobart Junior became the chief executive of his family's haulage company, he set about transforming all aspects of staff behaviour and performance.

The cornerstone chosen was the context of staff management. Eddie Stobart took the immediate following actions:

- he put all of the staff, including lorry drivers and labourers, on salary rather than hourly and piece rates; and went on to state that any overtime or shift allowances would be consolidated into the salary which was to be among the highest in the haulage industry;
- the provision of uniforms which had to be worn in a particular way. The uniforms for the labouring staff and truck drivers were functional, distinctive and comfortable, and also completely practicable in terms of wearing them comfortably while, at the same time, doing the work effectively.

By doing this, Eddie Stobart brought everybody in the organization on to the same pay scale, regardless of occupation. Everyone now knew what everybody else earned; nobody could therefore complain that they were under-paid relative to others doing the same occupation.

Everyone also now wore uniforms in the Eddie Stobart colours (principally dark green); and because of this design and comfort, people felt proud and positive in themselves when they were dressed for work.

The key lesson is that, from time to time, people's perceptions have to be managed (see also below). Companies and organizations can, and do, take effective actions in managing perceptions; of equal importance is the transparency and integrity with which the actions are taken.

- **Consistency**: people expect consistency in all parts of organizational activities and practice. Marketing and sales campaigns therefore have clear messages and images running through them reinforcing consistency (even though actual presentations may vary). Consistency and understanding of norms, habits and modes of address and interaction reinforce comfort and identity within the workplace. Brand images and logos are designed and implemented so that they deliver messages of consistency over extended periods of time. Product and service standards, quality, prices and charges are expected to remain consistent over extended periods of time also. Once expectations have been established, variations and changes are always noted; and if the organization does wish or intend to vary or change anything, then this has to be actively managed, and clearly explained. This is so that people's perceptions are led in the required direction, rather than left to find their own way individually (see Box 4.3).
- **Cleanliness**: there is a strong perceived relationship between neatness, order and tidiness, and cleanliness. Nobody likes to work in an environment that is known, believed or perceived to be dirty; as well as being harmful to health, it is demeaning and devaluing for those who work there, and ultimately to the organization itself.

Box 4.3: Santander

Over the recent past, Santander, the Spanish banking group, expanded into the UK buying Abbey, Alliance and Leicester, and parts of Bradford & Bingley, the smaller UK banks.

For a time, Santander continued to operate these companies and their activities under their existing company and brand names. Subsequently, however, Santander decided that it would incorporate all of these under its own name using its own distinctive colour scheme (bright red) and identity.

This process was carefully orchestrated. Beginning with news briefings, company spokespersons sought to explain the rationale: that the perceived strength and unity offered by a single and distinctive name would give reassurance to customers at a time when the banking industry was going through a very difficult period.

These news briefings were reinforced with advertisements for each of the companies. The first phase of the advertisements maintained the names of the individual companies but with the Santander byline clearly attached.

The second phase of the advertisement reversed this position: Santander was now the name given prominence, while at the same time maintaining the old British names alongside.

The third phase was to demonstrate the full incorporation of the three British companies into Santander, and to reinforce the perceived strength and identity of the new brand.

The key to the approach was to manage everyone's perceptions at each stage, so that no business confidence was lost at any point.

Illegitimacy

Order, neatness and tidiness become illegitimate concerns when they are used or manipulated. This introduces a key issue (developed in full in Chapter 6) that why things are done is as important as what is done. For example:

- someone who produces excellent work may be criticized for their lack of neatness, tidiness or conformity;
- someone who produces bad work may nevertheless be promoted and rewarded for their conformity and loyalty.

In each of these cases, people need the consistency and understanding referred to above. If conformity is the priority, and everyone knows and understands this, then there is nothing wrong; what is wrong is to ask people for one thing and then when they deliver it, criticize or blame them for something else (see Box 4.4).

Perceptual errors

The sources of error in personal and situational perception include:

- not collecting enough information;
- assuming that enough information has been collected;

Box 4.4: Mark Player

Mark Player worked as a sales representative for one of the UK's large department store chains. Mark was very good at this work; and it was not long before he was promoted to senior sales representative. Further glowing reports followed, and he was promoted to sales manager.

In this new job, Mark developed the workforce, the sales volumes and overall profitability. Over the five-year period in which he was in charge, turnover went up by 300 per cent; and profit margins rose from 5 per cent per annum to 8 per cent per annum. Everyone agreed that he was an outstanding sales manager; and everyone agreed that he would indeed 'go far'.

After he had been in this post for five years, the sales director position became vacant, and Mark duly applied. He was unsuccessful, though the feedback from the interview was very positive. Nevertheless, an outsider was appointed.

After a year, the outsider suddenly left. Mark again applied for the position; and again, despite glowing references, he was turned down.

Shortly after this, the company restructured and reorganized. A further sales directorship now became available. Mark duly applied; and again, while everything was overtly positive, he was turned down.

Upset, angry and frustrated, Mark now approached the company managing director. He asked: 'Everyone thinks that I am good at the job. Everyone says that I should "go far". Why have you not appointed me to a directorship?'

The managing director prevaricated. He tried to couch his response in woolly terms to do with 'experience', 'range of products' and 'company acumen'.

Each time the managing director raised one of these questions, Mark was able to answer in detail that he did have the right attributes and experience.

Finally, the managing director said: 'You should smile more.'

Mark found a sales directorship three month's later with a competitor.

- not collecting the right information; collecting the wrong information;
- assuming that the right information has been collected;
- seeing what we want and expect to see; fitting reality to our view of the world (rather than the reverse);
- looking in others for what we value for, and in, ourselves;
- assuming that the past was always good when making judgements for the future;
- failure to acknowledge and recognize other points of view;
- failure to consider situations and people from the widest possible point of view;
- unrealistic expectations, levels of comfort and satisfaction;
- confusing the unusual and unexpected with the impossible.

The remedies are:

- understand the limitations of personal knowledge and perception; that this is imperfect and that there are gaps;
- decide in advance what knowledge is required of people and situations and set out to collect it from this standpoint;

- structure activities where the gathering of information is important – for example, this should apply to all interviews, research activities, questioning, work organization, use of technology;
- avoid instant judgements about people, however strong and positive, or weak and negative, the first impression may be;
- avoid instant judgements about organizations, whether as customer or employee;
- build expectations on knowledge and understanding rather than halo effects, stereotypes and self-fulfilling prophecies;
- ensure exchanges and availability of good-quality information;
- ensure open relationships that encourage discussion and debate and generate high levels of understanding and knowledge exchange;
- develop self-awareness and understanding among all staff;
- recognize and understand the nature of prevailing attitudes, values and beliefs – and prejudices;
- recognize and understand other strong prevailing influences – especially language, nationality, culture and experience (see Box 4.5).

Box 4.5: The price of friendship?

What is Facebook worth? Its value has fluctuated wildly. Although Facebook had only been founded in 2004, a deal with Microsoft in 2007 seemed to put it at about $15 billion. By the summer of 2008, it was reported that shares were being sold privately at prices implying that Facebook was worth less than $5 billion.

Business fashions come and go. But the uncertainty of the valuations of networking sites such as Facebook and MySpace is not surprising. Their value presumably has something to do with the number of connections that they make possible.

Counting the connections is easy enough. Metcalfe (1980) proposed that the value of a network is proportional to the square of the number of users or devices on it, reasoning that, for example, a single fax machine is useless; a pair of fax machines can make a single connection; five fax machines can connect ten ways. Because each new machine can talk to any of the existing machines, each new one is worth more than the last.

Metcalfe went on to invent the Ethernet standard for computer networking, and became a hi-tech entrepreneur and venture capitalist. Yet, while the maths of his law is indisputable, its economic logic is debatable. This matters because, while Metcalfe can see office law as applying to small Ethernet networks, it has often been uncritically applied to much larger networks.

The problem is that not every connection is equally important. The first telegraph linking Europe and the United States was hugely valuable. The ability to fax to the company next door is not. When Microsoft bought a slice of Facebook, it had about 90 million users; meaning that 4,000 trillion two-way connections were possible, but few will ever be useful.

The economic value of a network also depends critically on the ease with which people can switch to another network. Fifteen years ago it would have been inconceivable for everyone to scrap their fax machines. Yet it is not so hard to imagine

Facebook's users deserting in droves for the next big thing in social networking. And a network that can be abandoned overnight is a network whose value can be destroyed overnight too.

The key lesson therefore is the application of perception: in this particular case, to a very great extent social networking sites are worth whatever people think they are at a given moment in time. Microsoft clearly paid a price that they felt was good value in terms of what they were acquiring; and the owners of Facebook acquired a good price for the particular slice of their company. However, if circumstances change, then the price and value will change also.

Comfort and liking

Comfort and liking occur when elements and features accord and harmonize with each other. Instant rapport is achieved when initial perceptions – strong characteristics, halo effects – coincide, meet expectations and lead to an initially productive relationship. This is developed as people become more familiar and knowledgeable about each other and about situations and circumstances. Discomfort and dislike occur when the elements are in discord. This is usually found in strong and contradictory initial and continuing impressions.

Some illustrations of perception can be seen in Figures 4.3 and 4.4.

Box 4.6: Perceptions and interpretation: two examples

1 Straightforward interpretation:
 A farmer was asked how many animals he had on his farm.

> 'Well,' he replied, 'I have 233 heads and 843 legs. Work it out from that.'

2 Perception and the workplace example:
 An organization's work group members have the following distances to travel to work:

> Henry: 270 miles (2.5 hours)
> Andy: 9 miles (1.5 hours)
> Bert: 3 miles (45 minutes)
> Rebecca: 700 miles (4.5 hours)
> Christine: 80 miles (2.5 hours)
> Alan: 40 miles (3 hours)
> Dave: 120 miles (2 hours)

If the company that they work for organizes a residential course on the premises, requiring them to work late into the evening and starting early in the morning, what differences (if any) should there be in sorting out overnight accommodation?

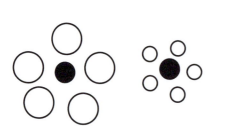

(a)   Which black spot is larger?   (b)   Old lady or young girl?

(c)   Water flowing up and down?

Figure 4.3 Perception: illustrations

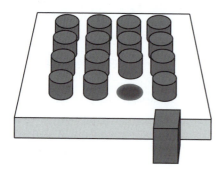

Figure 4.4 Cultural influences on perception

Note: This picture was used to illustrate one of the fundamental drives of management: 'fitting a square peg into a round hole' (i.e. trying to make things fit that otherwise do not fit easily). Ye (2009) found a different perspective. Coming from a different cultural background, she stated that the board of round holes represented standard organizations, and an incompleteness of organizational coverage in the market. However, the square peg rather represented a unique, special and expertly managed company or organization, divided from the mainstream by the thick line in the illustration, and looking for opportunities elsewhere.

Discomfort and dislike

The illustrations and examples in Figures 4.3 and 4.4 indicate some of the contrasting and contradictory images and conundrums that people have to be able to reconcile. This may now be developed further.

As stated above, comfort and liking come about when the characteristics and attitudes of people are assumed – perceived – to be in harmony. For example: it is easy to 'like' someone who is friendly, kind and helpful. It is also easy to 'dislike' someone who is unfriendly, unkind and unhelpful.

However, when relating to someone who is unfriendly, kind and helpful, or friendly, unkind and helpful, discomfort occurs. This is because people do not know where they stand; they do not know whether the contrasting characteristics mean that those who have these complexities of characteristics are 'nice' or otherwise (see Box 4.7).

Box 4.7: Reconciling characteristics: examples

Martin Luther King was one of the great world figures of the twentieth century. He was a person of extraordinary courage and character; and led fundamental deep-lasting and irreversible change across the whole of US society. He was also a womanizer.

Ian Thorne had a wife and two teenage children, a son and a daughter. Ian was a senior civil servant. As the children grew up, it became clear that the daughter was destined for a glittering academic career, followed by a top corporate management position, while the son would become an artisan (probably a carpenter). After a while, however, it became clear to Ian that things were more complex. In particular, the levels of his daughter's achievements started to fall. Finally, she went to see him and said that she was a chronic drug addict. Years later, Ian was sent to prison for ten years for possessing over £1 million worth of cocaine with intent to supply. His defence was that he had only become involved in the illicit drugs trade in order to provide an assured supply for his daughter.

George Rogers died aged 70. He had had a glittering career, having been chief executive of companies in the engineering and financial services sectors; and he had also spent five years as vice chancellor of one of the UK's leading universities. At George's funeral, his eldest son delivered the eulogy. He stated: 'We all salute my father as a wonderful man, and as someone who succeeded at everything that he went into. However, our biggest sadness is that he died of liver failure brought on by chronic alcohol over-use. For the past forty years, as I expect you all know, my father had a very serious drink problem.' Until the son mentioned this, nobody had any idea that this was indeed the case.

The key lesson is that everyone has weaknesses and contradictions. The question arises as to the extent to which they are 'allowable weaknesses', which means that the remaining character and/or achievements take precedence; or that they are 'unallowable weaknesses' which means that the weakness takes precedence over anything that may have been achieved.

To manage these aspects of perception, and to deepen their own understanding, people use the processes of:

- inference;
- halo effect;
- stereotyping, pigeonholing and compartmentalization.

Inference

People infer or make assumptions about others and about things, situations and circumstances based on the information available and their interpretation and analysis of it. Simple forms of this are found in the halo effect and stereotyping.

Halo effect

This is the process by which a person is ascribed a great range of capabilities and expertise as the result of the initial impression of one overwhelming characteristic. As stated above, the person who has a firm handshake is deemed to be decisive. A person with a public school education is deemed to be officer material. The person who can play golf is deemed to be an expert in business.

The converse of this is the horns effect (the halo apparently comes from heaven; the horns therefore clearly originate elsewhere). This is whereby a negative connotation is put on someone or something as the result of one (supposedly) negative characteristic. Thus the person with the soft handshake and lisp is perceived to be soft and indecisive. Anyone who wears fashions from a past era is deemed to be eccentric or old-fashioned (see Box 4.8).

Stereotyping, pigeonholing and compartmentalization

It is a short step from the halo effect to developing a process of stereotyping, pigeon-holing and compartmentalization. This occurs at places of work whereby because of a

---

Box 4.8: The halo effect in practice

Understanding the influence of the halo effect can be illustrated with examples from all walks of life.

Kim Philby was able to act as a Soviet spy for twenty years with ease because nobody in the British establishment believed that anyone with his impeccable credentials could possibly be anything other than a pillar of the aforesaid establishment. Richard Branson is perceived to be dynamic and iconoclastic partly because of the clothes that he wears and the style with which he presents his company in the media. Apples sold at Marks & Spencer must be good because they are shiny and bruise free.

It is also worth drawing attention to the dedication in the book *Recruitment and Selection* by Clive T. Goodworth. This book is dedicated as follows. 'To all those who can spot a good chap as soon as they walk into the room. And to all those who suffer as the result.'

past range of activities, somebody is deemed to be that kind of person for the future. This may both enhance and limit careers, activities and organization progress dependent upon the nature of the compartmentalization. In any case, it gives specific and limited direction. The person who has worked overseas for a multinational corporation for a long time may have difficulty getting a job back at Head Office because they have been pigeonholed as 'an expatriate' and may be perceived to have difficulties should they be required to conform to the Head Office norms and practices.

Self-fulfilling prophecy

Self-fulfilling prophecy occurs when a preconception or prejudgement is made about someone or something. The person making the judgement then picks out further characteristics or attributes that support their view and edits out those that do not fit in. The prejudgement – the prophecy – is therefore fulfilled. For example:

- People enjoy their holidays because they expect to enjoy them.
- People who are used to bad service from a company will not in the future note the occasions when they get good service; they will note the occasions in the future when the service is bad.
- If you are going to meet someone whom you perceived to be strong and assured, you will look for signs of strength and assurance when you do meet them.
- 'If you want people to be trustworthy, trust them. If you want people to accept responsibility, give them responsibility.' (R. Semler, 1992).
- People will behave as they expect those in charge would behave in the same situation. *The Herald of Free Enterprise* sank because the staff perceived that it was important to set sail in spite of the fact that the bow doors were not closed. When the ship turned over the hunt was for scapegoats, not mistakes. (*Brass Tacks*, BBC2: 1989)
- Universities have adopted systems of numbered exam papers. This is so that those who mark the papers see what is actually written rather than what they expect to see written by particular students to whom they can put a name and therefore a set of perceptions and preconceptions.

Perceptual mythology

This occurs where myths are created by people as part of their own processes of limiting and understanding particular situations. A form of rationale emerges, usually spurious (though not always harmful).

Thus, for example, people will say such things as: 'I can tell as soon as someone walks in the door whether they can do this job'; or 'I always ask this question and it never fails'; or 'I never trust people in white shoes/white socks/with moustaches/with tinted glasses' – in order to give themselves some chance of understanding and therefore mapping the person who stands before them.

People also use phrases such as 'in my opinion' and 'in my experience' and 'personally speaking' to try and give some kind of (real or perceived) authority and substance to the myths that they have themselves formed and developed in their way of understanding and perceiving the world around them.

Box 4.9: The real world

'The real world' is a major aspect of perceptual mythology; and the phrase 'in the real world' is used by individuals when they have nothing else to fall back on. For example:

- 'In the real world, you have to act quickly; you cannot afford to think.'
- 'In the real world, profit is the key and the only thing that matters.'
- 'In the real world, you cannot treat people kindly.'
- 'In the real world, it's dog eat dog.'
- 'In the real world, we have to earn a living; public servants don't live in the real world.'

All of this begs the question of what the 'real world' actually is. Additionally, people who use this phrase never then go on to define what the other/unreal worlds actually are.

Personal mapping and constructs

In this process people, situations, activities, images and impressions are being fitted into the perceived map of the world in ways which can be understood, managed and accommodated. The information thus gathered is broken down into constructs or characteristics that may be categorized as follows.

- **Physical**: by which we assume or infer the qualities of the person from their appearance, racial group, beauty, style, dress and other visual images.
- **Behavioural**: whereby we place people according to the way they act and behave or the ways in which we think they will act and behave.
- **Role**: whereby we make assumptions about people because of the variety of roles they assume; the different situations in which they assume these roles; their dominant role or roles; and the trappings that go with them.
- **Psychological**: whereby certain occupations, appearances, manifestations, presentation and images are assumed to be of a higher order of things than others (part of this is also sociological). This reflects the morality, values and ethics of the society of the day, as well as the environment and organization in question.

This part of the perception process aims to build up a picture of the world with which the individual can be comfortable. Comfort is achieved when people and situations are perceived to have complementary characteristics or constructs. Discomfort occurs when characteristics and constructs are contradictory. For example, there is no difficulty placing an individual who is kind and gentle on the perceptual map. There is difficulty, however, in being comfortable with an individual who is both kind and violent.

Closure

Closure exists from two points of view:

- where people see part of a picture, and then assume the rest;
- where people hear a part of a statement, and then assume that they understand the rest (sometimes even, often maddeningly!, completing the sentence on behalf of the first speaker).

Proximity

Proximity is based on the desire to understand and be comfortable with that which is close at hand – to be at ease in the immediate environment. Matters that cause discomfort therefore assume importance, often out of proportion to their actual effect.

Proximity also concerns the tendency to group people or items that are physically close into groups. Those who work in the same office, for example, are a group and if one or two continually raise grievances, the whole may come to be seen as a collection of troublemakers.

Proximity also becomes a staff and operations management issue, when it comes to be known, believed and perceived by the workforce that the closer that they work to head office, the greater their chances of promotion, opportunities and advancement. The converse then becomes known and understood also: that the further people work away from head office, the less their chances of promotion opportunities and advancement.

Intensity

Perception is affected by extremes of heat, cold, light, darkness, noise, silence, colour, taste, touch and smell. People who wish to stand out from the crowd wear bright or other eye-catching colours. People who move from the city to the country notice the contrast between the noise and bustle of the one and the peace and quiet of the other (see Box 4.10).

Box 4.10: Intensity and customer loyalty

Businesses use a variety of different incentives and loyalty schemes in an attempt to keep their existing customers and attract new ones as well. But, with so many similar loyalty schemes in operation, a question arises: 'Which features of a loyalty scheme are most effective at persuading customers to remain loyal to your company's products and services?'

Researchers from two American universities conducted a series of loyalty experiments that involved handing out loyalty cards to hundreds of customers at a local car wash. The customers were told that each time they visited the car wash, they would get their card stamped and when they completed the card, they would receive their next car wash free.

The researchers issued two types of card. One of the loyalty cards required customers to collect eight stamps to claim their free car wash. The other loyalty card required customers to collect ten stamps; however, they were given the first two stamps for free to set them on their way.

Essentially, the required purchases and the rewards were exactly the same for both groups. What was not the same, though, was the number of customers in each group who stayed loyal, completed the card and claimed their free car wash.

In the first group, only 19 per cent of customers made enough purchases to claim their free car wash. However, with those using the second card (who had been given the head start) the purchase rate rose to 34 per cent.

continued . . .

Box 4.10: Intensity and customer loyalty ... *continued*

The effect of giving the customers a head start without actually reducing the required purchases almost doubled the effectiveness of the promotion. The head start also increased the speed of purchases. Customers who were asked to collect ten stamps and given a head start completed their loyalty cards more quickly than those required to collect eight stamps from a standing start.

The researchers suggested two fundamental reasons for this occurrence:

* First, people are generally more willing to commit to tasks that have already been started but that are incomplete, than they are to begin a new task.
* Second, the closer that individuals get towards completing a goal, the more effort they tend to exert to get the task completed.

In this particular case, the intensity of the relationship, and the intensity of customer perception, were both enhanced by the fact of a perceived free gift, and the fact that some progress had already been made towards the goal.

Source: S. Martin (2009) 'For Starters' – *Business Life*.

Attribution

Attribution is the explanation put by individuals on behaviour or activities. Attribution may be:

* rational – 'you burnt your hand because the plate was hot';
* pseudo-rational – 'he is a bully at work because he has a difficult home life';
* empathized – 'in her place I would have done the same thing';
* mythological – 'this was how we always used to do it and it worked then'.

Whether rational or not, attribution gives people a point of reference for their actions and for those of others. It also helps in the attaining of comfort and satisfaction, enabling people to explain – to themselves at least – why they continue to work in particular occupations, ways, situations, or with particular people (see Box 4.11).

Other influences on perception

The following more general influences may also be distinguished.

Repetition

The repetition of a message or an event gives currency, familiarity and validity. This may subsequently become a barrier to change.

Familiarity

This is the outcome of repetition and also of continued exposure and involvement in given situations. The most positive form is comfort; the negative is complacency. It is

Box 4.11: Safe pairs of hands

When looking for people to fill top and senior management jobs and critical executive positions, many organizations are at a loss to know precisely how to go about doing this. They therefore fall back on a kind of parallel or spurious attribution which is nevertheless comfortable, and which (in terms of their own comfort) therefore does the job.

At this level, people resort to the following attributes:

- a safe pair of hands;
- a person of great experience;
- a person of forceful personality;
- a high achiever;
- a person from the right background.

In practice, all of these phrases look and sound positive. All of these phrases are actually empty and meaningless. Nevertheless, such approaches do give organizations the latitude to appoint those whom they choose, often regardless of their true capabilities.

a general bonus, however, in the generation of organizational format (such as for memos, reports and letters). It has great importance in the development of a house style for general communication purposes (see Box 4.12).

Authority, responsibility and position

These relate to the person giving the message. This influences the propensity of the receiver to accept or reject it. The person who understands well the strength or weakness of his/her own position in this regard is always likely to be a more effective communicator than one who does not.

Emotions

Feelings of anger, antagonism, mistrust and disregard emphasize the tendency to reject. At the very least, therefore, any such feelings present or potentially present in a given situation are to be recognized at the outset and at least neutralized where possible.

The greatest of all emotional barriers in organizations is pride. Nobody likes to lose face or to have it made plain that they were wrong. Nor do others wish to be associated with someone who is forced to be seen as defeated, to back down or to climb down from a given position.

Visibility

Much is made of visibility as an instrument of the generation of effective organizational behaviour throughout this book. Visibility is the cornerstone of so much. It is a

Box 4.12: Perceptual dysfunction

As stated above, familiarity comes about as the result of repetition and continued exposure and involvement in given situations. Familiarity is then developed by individuals in terms of their own 'self-familiarity'. In this way, individuals come to have their own view of how they appear to others which may, or may not, be accurate. For example:

- someone who believes themselves to be strong and decisive may be viewed by others as strong and decisive indeed – or as a bully;
- someone who is forever making jokes may indeed be seen by others as being good for morale – or else as a bore and a show-off.

Handy (1986) cited research which stated that:

- 80 per cent of managers and supervisors saw themselves as being open, friendly and approachable;
- the staff who worked for those same managers found 80 pcer cent of them to be cold, stand-offish, distant, inaccessible and unavailable.

The CBI (2006) produced similar findings. A survey conducted among organizations in the City of London found that 80 per cent of managers and supervisors who thought that they were reasonable, fair, honest and cheerful were found to be cold, distant, tyrannical and unfair by their subordinates.

The key lesson is that familiarity, and the assurance that comes from familiarity, needs constant evaluation on the part of everyone concerned.

Source: C.B. Handy (1986) *The Hungry Spirit* – Arrow; CBI (2006) *Staff Management Survey* – Staff Management Association Publications.

prerequisite to effective communication. It greatly helps in the generation of confidence, familiarity and interaction. It underlines levels of honesty, trustworthiness and straightforwardness. It helps develop both professional and personal relationships between those involved. There are therefore both general and specific benefits to be gained from an effective face-to-face relationship.

The converse is also true. Lack of visibility is both a perceptual barrier in itself and also compounds others that are present – such as general feelings of disregard, distrust and dishonesty. Misunderstandings occur least, and are most quickly and easily sorted out, at the face-to-face level. Where this is not present, such misunderstandings invariably take longer to resolve and may quickly become disputes and grievances (see Box 4.13).

First impressions

First impressions count: this is received wisdom and applies everywhere. Yet first impressions are plainly misleading – *prima facie* you must know less about someone after 30 seconds than after 30 minutes.

Box 4.13: The cockroaches

A hospital building in the centre of London had extensive underground passageways. These were subject to flooding during periods of bad weather. As the flood waters rose, so they brought with them debris, flotsam and jetsam from the depths of the London sewers.

The building itself was aged, and started falling into disrepair. After a time, it was found to have cockroaches, not only in the basement but also as high up as the third floor.

One of the medical staff notified the hospital's facilities manager who came to see for herself. She went to the facilities director to order a full cleaning and sterilization of the premises. The facilities director said that he would look into it; and so nothing was done.

This process went on for nearly three years. During one heavy downpour, however, both the facilities manager and the facilities director happened to be present when the underground parts of the building flooded. As usual, the cockroaches and the rest of the rubbish floated to the surface. Now the facilities director saw at first-hand the full scale of the problem and what needed to be done.

The cleaning operation was ordered the following day.

However, the first impression gives an immediate frame of reference to the receiver. The appearance, manner, handshake and initial transaction is the writing on a blank sheet. Before there was nothing, now there is something on which to place measure and assess the other (see Figure 4.5). The impact is therefore very strong. It is essential to recognize this. The consequence of not doing so is that a one-dimensional view of the individual is formed and everything which is contrary to that dimension or which indicates complexities, other dimensions and qualities is edited out.

Expectations

People go into every situation or transaction with a purpose, and the fulfilment of this purpose is their expectation. Expectations are measured in hard material terms, soft behavioural terms and a combination of the two.

- **Hard**: goods for money.
- **Soft**: courtesy, honesty, trustworthiness, value.
- **Combination**: value for money; a combination of the measurable (the money) with the immeasurable (value).

The following approaches to expectation may be distinguished:

- **Expectation as a customer**: of value for money; of utility and reliability of products and services; to be treated with courtesy and accuracy.
- **Expectation as a shareholder or stakeholder**: of the longevity, stability and profitability of the organization; of steady and increasing returns on investment; of strength of positive reputation.

People	Service
• appearance, dress, hair, handshake • voice, eye contact • scent, smell • disposition (positive, negative, smiling, frowning) • establishing common interest/failure to do so • courtesy, manner • age	• friendliness (or lack of) • effectiveness • speed • quality • confidence • value • respect • ambience • appearance
Objects	**Organizations**
• design • colour/colours • weight • shape • size • materials • purpose, usage • price, value, cost	• ambience • welcome • appearance • image and impression • technology • care • respect for others • confidence • trust

Note: This is a useful (but by no means perfect or complete) means of compartmentalizing the cues and signals that are present when coming into any situation or into contact with someone for the first time. There are certain to be contradictions and contra-indications. It is essential to recognize and understand this in order to understand, in turn, the impact and influence of first impressions.

Figure 4.5 First impressions

- **Expectation as a staff member**: to be treated well and fairly; to be paid well and on time; to have prospects for advancement; to have pay and rewards increased; to participate in the success of the organization; to be treated with respect; to receive accurate and up-to-date information.

Fulfilment of expectations is a key feature of the motivation of the individual.

Failure to fulfil expectations is therefore very demoralizing, and changes overall perceptions from positive to negative. Managing people's expectations, and above all managing people's *perceived* expectations, is critical in delivering staff, customer and shareholder satisfaction. In order to do this effectively, it is essential to know and fully understand what the expectations are, why the particular groups hold them, and then take steps to address any changes that are needed.

Perceptual defence mechanisms

People build defences (blocks or refusal to recognize) against people or situations that are personally or culturally unacceptable, unrecognizable, threatening or incapable of assimilation. Perceptual defence normally takes one or more of the following forms.

- Denial – refusal to recognize the evidence of the senses.
- Modification and distortion – accommodating disparate elements in ways which reinforce the comfort of the individual.

- Change in perception – from positive to negative or from negative to positive, often based on a single trait or characteristic becoming apparent which was not previously so.
- Recognition but refusal to change – where people are not prepared to have their view of the world disrupted by a single factor or example. This is often apparent when people define 'the exceptions to the rule' (of which there may be dozens, and no rule in fact).
- Outlets – where the individual seeks an outlet, especially for frustration or anger, away from its cause. For example, browbeating a subordinate offers a sense of relief to someone who has previously been browbeaten themselves by their superior.
- Recognition thresholds – the higher the contentiousness or emotional content of information, the higher the threshold for recognition (i.e. the less likely it is to be perceived readily).

Adaptation

Adaptation is 'perception as a continuous process'. Our view of the world is influenced directly by the circumstances and surroundings in which we find ourselves. Part of the process also relates to priority levels – what is important now; and what is important for life, work, leisure and so on.

Adaptation is therefore the process by which our view of the world and our relationships with it, and within it, and its people and its organizations, establishments and events constantly change. It is based on a combination of expectation and anticipation, knowledge, actions, previous experience and the continuing development of particular situations. It is accentuated by the other perceptual effects indicated above.

Adaptation is positive and negative and a constant process. It is accentuated by priorities, crises and constantly changing circumstances.

For example, an individual who is waiting for a train may become agitated if the train is late, especially if they have to get somewhere else quickly at the other end. When the train finally arrives, it is crowded, dirty and noisy and the person has to stand. They therefore start thinking of alternatives – the car, the coach. The train makes up time on its journey and arrives 20 minutes early. The person has therefore time for food and drink before going on to their appointment. The overall feeling becomes one of satisfaction because the speed of service and time of arrival were the highest priority. The other factors simply contributed to the nature of the situation at the particular point in time.

Conclusions

Perception is the basis on which everyone forms their understanding of the world. People make interpretations of others whom they meet, and places and situations that are encountered, by combining each of the elements indicated to produce their own individual picture which they can then understand and be comfortable with.

Perception is affected by repetition and familiarity. Something or someone who is always present acquires the illusion of permanence. Routines and habits are formed by organizing activities and interactions into regular patterns based on a combination of expectation and near certainty.

Perception is affected by the context in which individuals are placed. There is a great range of responses to the request 'please do this for me'; this depends on who has made the request and under what circumstances – for example, whether it was a manager, subordinate, child, spouse, customer, waiter, barman; and whether the person to whom the request was made was feeling well, ill, good or bad tempered, calm or stressed; and the tone of voice in which the request was made; whether it was a work or social situation; and what had gone on immediately beforehand.

Perception is affected by the characteristics of perceiver and perceived. The greater the knowledge of perception on the part of people and organizations, the greater the mutual understanding likely to be generated; and where problems do arise, the greater the potential for addressing these effectively. Personal characteristics affect the type of characteristics likely to be seen in others, their levels of importance and whether these are, or should be, negative or positive. Those being perceived greatly influence the views of the perceiver through their visibility (appearance, manner, dress, speech); their status and role (either in the given situation or in a wider context). The simplest form of this is a conversation between two people; this becomes much more complex where the conversation is between more than two people, and more complicated still where this is in a new or unknown situation.

5   Attitudes, values and beliefs

Introduction

Attitudes, values and beliefs are the mental, moral and ethical dispositions adopted by individuals to others and the situations and environments in which they find themselves. Attitudes, values and beliefs can be ordered and summarized as follows.

*   **Emotional**: feelings of positivity, negativity, neutrality or indifference; anger, love, hatred, desire, rejection, envy and jealousy; satisfaction and dissatisfaction. Emotional aspects are present in all work as part of the content; working relationships with other people; reactions to the environment; and the demands placed on particular occupations.
*   **Professional**: the nature of identity with the work; the belief in the importance and value of the work; the contribution that the work makes, and is supposed to make; the extent of commitment to the organization; identity with the organization and the expertise delivered.
*   **Social**: contribution to society; disposition towards society, and the component groups; disposition towards neighbours and others in the locality; propensity to use local organizations; propensity to be involved in social activities.
*   **Personal**: religious convictions; political convictions; conduct in society (including work); participation in social institutions and clubs; contribution to the needs and wants of society.
*   **Informational**: the nature and quality of the information present and the importance that it is given. Where this is known or widely understood to be wrong or incomplete, feelings of negativity and frustration arise.
*   **Behavioural**: the tendency to act in particular ways in given situations. This leads to the formation of attitudes where the behaviour required can be demonstrated as important or valuable; and to negative attitudes where the behaviour required is seen as futile or unimportant.

Attitudes, values and beliefs are shaped and influenced by the following.

*   **Past experience**: memories of what happened in the past affect current and future feelings.
*   **Preconception**: impressions formed of something or someone in advance of meeting them, participating, or being involved.
*   **Specific influences**: especially those of peer groups, work groups and key individuals – managers and supervisors. These also include family and social groups; and they may also include religious and political influences.
*   **Prejudices**: which may be harmless (e.g. 'London is the best place in the world') or repugnant (e.g. prejudices against racial, religious or social groups).

Box 5.1: Before going to bed . . .

Peter Scott, a management consultant, was running a residential course. On one of the evenings, there was a late session, and it ran on until 10.00 pm. As the group was breaking up for the night, Peter asked them: 'If you were at home, what would you now be doing?'

Back came the responses, and there was all the usual and expected content: watching the late night news, making a cup of tea or coffee, checking on the children, taking the dog for a quick walk, putting out the cat. Peter asked: 'Why? Why do you do these things?'

Back came the usual responses: the cat needs to go out; I need to make sure that the children are comfortable and settled; I like to see the news before I go to bed.

Peter alighted on the news: Why, he asked, was it necessary for people to watch the news before going to bed? What was the attraction of knowing everything that was going on in the world immediately before 'switching off'?

The discussion developed further. Steering the discussion around the news and watching it last thing at night, Peter observed that several of the course delegates were getting agitated, and one or two were getting angry. Why shouldn't they watch the news last thing at night? What was wrong with watching the news last thing at night? Why were they even discussing it?

Peter found himself having to conduct a full debrief. Concentrating on the response to the news question, it became clear that people used this not particularly to know what was going on in the world, but as a behavioural 'full stop' at the end of the day. Many of the delegates were prepared to admit that they could not even remember what had been on the news by the time they got to bed. Nevertheless, this was how they always behaved; this was how they brought closure to every day. Questioning this (or even denying them the opportunity to watch the news) meant that you were in fact calling into question one of the fundamental behavioural points of reference for people.

- **Organizational identity**: the extent to which people have pride (or otherwise) in working for their organization; the extent to which people value their job, work and contribution; and the extent to which the organization values them, and their contribution.
- **Defence**: once formed, attitudes and values are internalized and become a part of the individual. Any challenge to them is often viewed as a more general threat to the comfort of the individual (see Box 5.1).

Attitudes

As stated above, attitudes are the dispositions adopted by individuals and groups towards others, to their surroundings and society, to their environment and to their organization and occupations. Attitudes are shaped, formed and developed by every influence, activity and institution that people come across in their lives. People form distinctive attitudes towards each of the following:

- their family and friends;
- their occupation, profession and place of work;
- societies and institutions that they come across as they go about their lives;
- companies, organizations, societies and institutions with which they do business;
- individuals, organizations and institutions about which they have plenty of general knowledge (e.g. the Queen, the prime minister, Australia/France/China) but little, if any, direct experience or contact.

In the place of work, attitudes towards the particular organization, and the attitudes held by organizations towards their staff and other stakeholders, are of vital concern. The attitudes of the individuals are shaped by:

- the approach taken by the organization when individuals first apply to work there;
- the recruitment and selection process;
- the basis on which appointments are made;
- the induction and orientation process;
- the initial and continuing attitude and demeanour of colleagues, managers and supervisors;
- the overall management style;
- the culture and climate of the organization;
- the collective prevailing work ethic.

The attitudes held by the organization towards its staff are shaped by:

- the perspective adopted, whether adversarial, consultative, participative, positive or negative (see Chapter 2);
- the nature of rewards on offer, who gets them and for what (e.g. performance, conformity, obedience, loyalty);
- the approach taken to the management of discipline, grievances and disputes;
- the organization's stated priorities (e.g. sales, marketing, production, service delivery, customer satisfaction);
- the organization's actual priorities (ideally the same list as above, in practice it includes self-service and organization politics, the search for favours, patronage and influence).

Shaping and reinforcing the attitudes of people at work is therefore vital to organization staff and group harmony; personal, professional and occupational comfort and confidence; and the generation of involvement and commitment. People's capabilities and expertise have to be harnessed so as to produce a willingness to perform, as well as capability to carry out, their tasks and duties to the best of their abilities (see Box 5.2; Figure 5.1).

Positive and negative attitudes

Attitudes are infectious. Companies, organizations and work groups that have positive attitudes find that new starters and incomers quickly become positive also. Companies, organizations and work groups that have negative attitudes find that new starters and incomers also quickly begin to become negative themselves.

Box 5.2: Capability and willingness

The need to have staff who show commitment and who want to work for the particular organization has caused many managers to concentrate on attitudes rather than expertise when making staff selections. The standpoint is that, as long as people are good at (but not necessarily expert) at their job, high levels of commitment will deliver a much better long-term output than those who are expert but uncommitted, as follows:

Notes

- Levels of high capability but low willingness can be observed at the top end of the football industry (among others), where high-reputation players are engaged on excellent wages – and they then fail to deliver. They have joined the particular club for money only; otherwise, they do not want to be there.
- On the other hand, a fully committed attitude will not carry people through if they do not have at least a fundamental capability for the job. At least one CEO of one of the UK retail banks that failed was fully committed to the job and the organization, working long hours and being actively involved in everything. However, he simply did not have the capability or understanding to do the job effectively.

So, an active decision is required in all cases; it is not possible to make any form of rule that 'a positive attitude will compensate for lack in expertise at all times'. However, it does remain true that for a great many tasks and occupations a willingness to learn is the product of a positive and committed attitude.

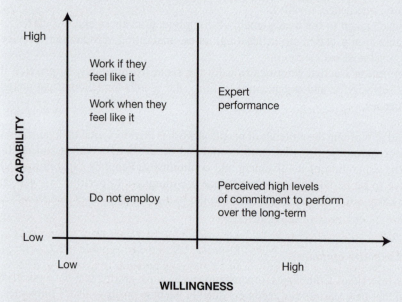

Figure 5.1 The balance between capability and willingness

Box 5.3: Negative attitudes

'You don't have to be mad to work here, but it helps' is an urban myth posted on many an office and factory wall.

As long as that is where it stays, this is fine. However, there are various attitudes which, as stated above, can, and do, become infectious as follows:

- 'I hate it here';
- 'It's boring';
- 'That blasted manager or supervisor' (not always such a polite turn of phrase).

Recognizing that all was not quite right at his organization, one senior general manager of a corporate communications company started joining his staff either at their breaks, or when they went outside for a cigarette. The staff quickly engaged him in conversation and he found that negative attitudes were coming from a small, but influential, group of administrative staff who felt themselves to be seen as 'only the office'. Recognizing that he had been at fault in this matter, he took steps to ensure that they received exactly the same amount of attention as sales, technical and engineering staff, and so was able to both restructure the attitude of this particular group, and also enhance collective organization spirit and commitment.

Clearly, the ideal is to have:

- positive attitudes on the part of all staff, resulting in collective commitment to the work, the customers, the other stakeholders and the organization;
- collective involvement so that, as well as generating high levels of team, group and organization spirit, there is an overall and understood body of commitment that can be called on at any time when necessary.

Additionally, where attitudes are positive, the word quickly gets around that this is a good organization to work for, and that the staff are friendly, kind and decent as well as expert and committed (see Box 5.3).

Values

Values are the absolute standards by which people order their lives. Everyone needs to be aware of their own personal values so that they may deal pragmatically with any situation. This may extend to marked differences between individuals or between an individual and the demands of the organization.

Value conflicts often arise at places of work; anything to which people are required to ascribe must recognize this and, if it is to be effective, must be capable of harmonization with the values of the individual. These values may be summarized as follows:

- **Theoretical**: where everything is ordered, factual and in place.
- **Economic**: making the best practical use of resources; results orientated, the cornerstone of people's standards and costs of living.

- **Aesthetic**: the process of seeing and perceiving beauty; relating that which is positive and desirable or negative and undesirable.
- **Social**: the sharing of emotions with other people.
- **Integrity**: matters of loyalty, honesty, openness, trust, honour, decency; concern for the truth.
- **Political**: the ways and choices concerning the ordering of society and its subsections and strata.
- **Religious and ethical**: the dignity of mankind; the inherent worth of people; the morality – the absolute standards – of human conduct; this includes specific beliefs and requirements of particular religions.
- **Organizational**: the values espoused by the organization, and the ways in which it delivers these and reinforces them.
- **Occupational and professional**: the value placed on the occupation/profession by individuals; and the value placed on the occupation/profession by organizations.

Values have to be capable of acceptance by everyone involved. Values have therefore to be supported by a combination of known and understood organization responsibility, the managerial and supervisory style present, and the procedures and institutions of the organization. It is no use overtly espousing a positive set of values if every managerial procedure and activity is negative. It is no use espousing a collective set of organizational values and work ethics if the organization in practice rewards individual performance in isolation from the total effectiveness of overall performance (see Box 5.4).

Box 5.4: The Financial Services Authority

The banking crisis of 2007 and beyond in the UK was brought about by the actions of individuals working within those organizations. However, the Financial Services Authority was supposed to oversee these actions, and prevent banking and financial institutions from taking unnecessary risks, or becoming involved in markets and activities of which they had no expert knowledge.

Part of the initial inquiry conducted into the failure of the UK banking and financial services system laid the blame firmly at the door of the Financial Services Authority, which had demonstrably failed to discharge its duties, leaving banking and financial services' companies to go about their business as they saw fit. A disease of complacency, sloppiness and indifference was identified, and this prevailed among all the regulatory staff at the Financial Services Authority.

This did not prevent staff from picking up bonuses to the collective value of £20 million in 2009. Defending the decision to award these bonuses, a spokesman for the Financial Services Authority stated: 'For many years, they have tried to do their best. In particular over the past twelve months, they have worked very hard.'

Both the action in awarding the bonuses and also the statement above reflect the lack of value placed on either the work or the organization. On the basis of the story as told above, staff are simply receiving these bonuses for turning up to work.

Shared values

Shared values are a clear set of values or direction offered by an organization to its people, its customers and environment that give a clear sense of identity. The adoption of shared values is central to the generation of high levels of commitment and motivation among those who work in organizations. Recognizing that people bring a diverse range of qualities to an organization is essential. Giving a clear corporate purpose that is both above individual aspirations, and also accommodates them, is a major function of the articulation of shared values. This is also instrumental in structuring particular ethical and moral stances that are taken.

Shared values are affected by:

- past experiences and interactions with the given person, people or situation;
- continuing experiences and interactions;
- perceptions and levels of general understanding;
- presence of, and understanding of, the particular rules, regulations and other limitations with which these are bounded;
- particular mental and physical aspects;
- levels of identity with the others involved and with the situation;
- the extent to which the people/situation are known or unknown;
- aspects of risks and uncertainty;
- levels of active or passive involvement;
- positive aspects – the extent to which something good and productive is certain or expected to come out;
- negative aspects – the extent to which something negative and unproductive is certain or expected to come out;
- any strong or prevailing moral, ethical or social pressures;
- general degrees of comfort – again usually based on levels of knowledge and understanding.

Each of the above elements has an effect, and so has to be taken into account when creating a work ethic to which everyone can subscribe, as well as patterns of behaviour, attendance and performance (see Box 5.5).

Formation of attitudes and values

The elements indicated are adopted by individuals in their own unique ways to form their own distinctive attitudes. The main processes that are involved are:

- Their propensity to accept rather than reject those attitudes and values of the group (including the organization) to which they seek to belong; they have a high degree of potential compliance.
- Their perception of the future relationship as being productive, effective, profitable and harmonious – people do not willingly enter a situation if they have no expectational perception of this; people are more willing and likely to enter situations the greater the likelihood of this being achieved; and people will avoid situations where these elements are neither present nor apparent.

Box 5.5: Creating a positive work ethic

'Teams that play together, work together' is a strap-line or mantra used by outward-bound and physical training and activity centres to try to gain corporate clients. The line of reasoning is: by getting staff to engage in such things as paint-balling activities, long distance walks, orienteering and similar activities, a team spirit can be built.

In isolation, activities like this are never enough to build a genuine and lasting team spirit, *esprit de corps* and collective, positive and harmonious work ethic. This has to be formed in the organization.

The foundations of this are that everyone involved respects and values the contribution of the others, so that they can deliver their part of the activities required in the sure and certain knowledge that everyone else is doing the same.

Forming these collective attitudes and shared values depends crucially on how people are integrated into the organization, and the extent to which this integration is acceptable to:

- the present staff;
- newcomers and incomers.

In many cases, there are introductory rituals and performances that particular work groups do demand of newcomers and incomers. However, they have to be carefully structured so as to provide a basis on which the professional and occupational activities can be developed, and not so that the relationship is destroyed.

Many outward-bound activities also tend to reinforce differences rather than create harmony. For example, when the business studies department of a further education college went for a three-day residential outward-bound break at a centre in Devon, the two top managers present were able to excuse themselves from the orienteering and rock-climbing activities on the grounds that they were 'out of condition'. This simply meant that, while the rest of the staff had a nice time in general, they would rather have been at home, and not participating in an exercise which those in charge had destroyed through their own lack of participation.

- Relating past experience to current and future situations, relationships and environment; positive experiences tend towards the formation of positive attitudes; negative experiences tend towards the formation of negative attitudes.
- Relating present experience to preconceptions and prejudgements about new situations, relationships and organizations.
- Availability and completeness of information; availability includes access and clarity; completeness includes reference to key and critical gaps; and also to the value and usefulness of that which is available.
- The general state of organizational well-being, the general state of the individual, and the relationship and interaction between the two.
- Other pressures, including the views of peers, co-workers, superiors, subordinates, family, friends; and economic, social, legal, moral and ethical pressures. These are likely to include sweeping generalizations, prevailing received wisdom, opinions

and prejudices (opinions formed without full reference to available facts); and again, from the variety of sources indicated.

- Any myths and legends present in the particular group or situation. For example, the statement that 'The person who holds job X or sits in office Y always gets promoted first/never gets promoted at all' puts behavioural and psychological pressures on each situation.

Each part of the process is present in the promotion and development of all attitudes, though the mix varies between particular situations and individuals. The mix also changes as people come into, and go out of, organizations and their groups. Also, by seeking to move, individuals may require (or perceive themselves to require) to change their attitudes in order to stand any chance of being successful. Their attitude may change again, depending on whether or not they were able to make the move, and if they did, whether or not this was successful (see Box 5.6).

Adjustment of attitudes and values

Adjustment is the development of attitudes and values (positive and negative) in a given situation. The processes by which adjustment is achieved are similar to those above.

Box 5.6: 'We always did this at my last place'

When managers (especially new managers) say to their staff 'We did this at my last place', they ought to be given a hearing, and this then ought to form the basis for a useful and productive discussion about what the matter in hand happens to be.

In practice, however, it can be (and often is) a maddening phrase because, said in the wrong way, it gives the impression to the present group of staff that their situation and circumstances do not count. This is very dangerous towards collective and shared values, and can be very destructive. For example, a sales team at one of the UK's leading double-glazing companies was used to working on its own and informing head office of their movements and whereabouts on an informal basis. When a new manager was appointed, he wanted to get everybody to use the oracle diary management system. This would enable everyone (including him) to know where everyone was at any given time. Proposing this, the manager stated: 'This is not to check up on you. It is so that I know where you are at all times. It also makes the scheduling of staff meetings very much easier.' He then went on to say: 'We did this at my last place, and it was very effective.'

Over the next two months, nobody used the system. The manager sent round a reminder, and requested that everybody become familiar with it and install their movements on it within the next six months.

In practice, of course, nothing happened. The system was easy enough to use; however, nobody saw the value of it, either to themselves or to their work. The manager's overall approach had simply ensured that the system would never be implemented (it is also entirely possible that by giving the staff six months to get themselves familiar and get their movements on to the system, he was bowing to the inevitable – that it would indeed never be used).

However, they tend to reinforce what is already present – for example, the perception if the future is well understood; if the availability of information is regarded as satisfactory.

Problems occur when a radical adjustment is either required, or else is to be imposed. The first response to such an adjustment or shift is often simply to shut it out – those affected do not believe the evidence before them.

Adjustment therefore works best where the prevailing attitudes are being developed rather than radically transformed (see Figure 5.2). Where a radical change of attitude is required, it is much better from the point of view of generating effective organizational behaviour and interpersonal and inter-group relations if it is tackled as a major change.

Adjustment in practice

Adjustment in attitudes and values takes place in all working situations. Once people know and understand what adjustments they need to make, the reasons and how quickly, they will normally do so. However, they will only do so if it is demonstrably in their interests. Requiring people to change their attitudes and values therefore requires full and active involvement on the part of managers and supervisors, reinforced by extensive consultation and communication, institutions and procedures that are in regular and effective use.

If all of this is present, staff normally have a good and clear understanding of specific, key and critical developments in their organization, and the implications for their own jobs and work practices and methods. Within the best-run organizations, in many cases, staff will approach their managers and supervisors concerning matters that need adjustment before they are ever raised by the organization.

Positive	Negative
• Equality of opportunity and treatment • Saying what is meant, meaning what is said • Identifying and solving problems • Clarity of purpose • Unity of purpose • Reward for achievement, loyalty and commitment • Openness of management style • Particular standards set at outset • Absolute standards for everyone • High and equal value placed on all staff • Recognition of every contribution • Pride in the organization • Identity with the organization • High levels of esteem and respect for staff • Clarity of communications • Harmony • High-quality information • Open personal relationships • Open operational and professional relationships	• Inequality of opportunity and treatment • Expediency • Victimization, scapegoating • Lack of clarity • Fragmentation of purpose • Rewards based on favouritism and infighting • Remoteness and distance of management style (both physical and psychological) • Standards allowed to emerge • Different standards for different groups, departments, divisions and individuals • Different levels of value placed on different staff groups • Lack of recognition • Lack of pride in the organization • Lack of identity; rejection of identity • Low levels of esteem and respect; variations in levels of esteem and respect according to occupation, department, division and function • Lack of clarity of communications • Hostility • Low-quality information

Figure 5.2 Influences on attitudes at work: summary

Box 5.7: Ryanair

When Michael O'Leary became chief executive of Ryanair, the Irish airline, he declared that the company was now to become a low-cost, mass-passenger carrier. When Ryanair opened up its initial route network, people were pleasantly astonished to find that the fares were as low as £1 per single journey, and anyone who was going to the right place at the right time could, from time to time, get free tickets.

The established airline industry confidently waited for Ryanair to go bankrupt. Top and senior managers at British Airways and others remained completely confident that theirs was the only 'business model' that worked.

However, Ryanair did not go bankrupt. The extreme level of fares caused people who would not otherwise normally travel by air to take an interest, and to begin to take themselves on trips.

Catches were found of course. In many cases, while the outward journey was indeed very cheap, the return fare was much higher. Hidden charges began to emerge. Ryanair charged people extra whether booking online or over the phone; and when they removed the telephone and check-in desk facility altogether, it still cost £5 to check-in online. The route network grew; and while the fares rose, they did not rise to the levels charged hitherto by British Airways, Air France, KLM and other national flag carrying airlines on short-haul routes.

And, of course, the national flag carrying airlines had to make their own adjustments. In particular, they had to bring down their fares on short-haul routes to levels which were at least comparable with those of Ryanair and other low-cost operators (especially easyJet).

This example shows adjustment in practice at each point. When it started out in this form, Ryanair believed it could adjust the whole basis of passenger air travel. It believed it could do this for its own chosen levels of fares and not those charged by the rest of the industry. It caused the rest of the industry to adjust its expectations and ways of working. It caused passengers to adjust their expectations of how to book and what they would have to pay for.

Each of these adjustments contributed (and continues to contribute) to the development of the airline industry, and especially to this form of air travel.

However, if organizational practice is not supported by this level of communication and involvement, adjustment is much harder to achieve. When organizations and their managers try to tell staff that radical changes must take place, and the reasons for these, staff tend to resist (see also Chapters 3 and 17). The result is that adjustments take place more slowly, more grudgingly and with less active involvement. People see threats to their positions rather than the opportunities created by the need for advancement (see Box 5.7).

Beliefs

Beliefs are the certainties of the world. They may be:

- **Absolute**: based on such things as mathematical fact; night following day, mortality and taxation.

- **Near absolute**: based on seasonal changes; the continuous development of knowledge and awareness; continuous technological and social development.
- **Acts and articles of faith**: based on the certainty of God; and often underpinned by religious allegiance and the following and adoption of the teachings of those who pronounce in the name of God; this may also extend to the adoption of social and political creeds.
- **Political beliefs**: based on the dogma and teachings of specific political leaders and thinkers.
- **Other strong ethical and moral standpoints**: relating to honesty, trustworthiness, right and wrong.
- **Strong illusions and perceptions of order, permanence and stability**: often founded on long steady-state factors.
- **Right and wrong**: personal judgements of what is right and what is wrong, and the ways in which right and wrong actions should be undertaken (or not).
- **Moral aspects**: related to right and wrong, but also with wider connotations (e.g. if it is wrong for a man to hit a woman, is it also wrong for a man to be as abusive as he likes towards a woman, though stopping short of hitting her?).

Beliefs are the psychological cornerstone of the lives of people. They provide the foundations and framework upon which people order and structure the rest of their lives. They are internalized to the heart and soul of the individual, providing the basis for other attitudes, values and chosen behaviour.

Everyone needs and wants to believe in something – and this 'something' includes:

- faith and religion, as above;
- political ideologies and systems;
- particular individuals.

People also need to 'believe' in the company or organization for which they work. After all, they give a large proportion of their life to their work, and so they need to know and understand (believe) that what they do is of value, worthwhile and founded on some kind of integrity. They need to have some kind of belief in the overall integrity of the organization, and in the expertise and commitment of its top and senior managers. They need to have some kind of belief in the products and services produced and delivered. They need to have some kind of comfort, security and assurance in their patterns and standards of conduct, behaviour and performance so that they are able to assume that if they, and everyone else, do their jobs properly, then the organization itself is both secure and also profitable.

People also have a strong propensity to 'believe' in the character and integrity of their colleagues, as well as the managers for whom they directly work.

It is immediately clear from this that there are different levels of belief. These levels of belief may be classified as follows.

Faith and conviction

This is where people collectively and individually are convinced to the point of certain knowledge and understanding of the righteousness of everything that they do, say, think and believe. This occurs most strongly in religious and political beliefs; and it is reinforced by the fact that religious and political groups are composed of those who share the same beliefs and convictions.

Faith therefore comes from within, and is reinforced by those with whom people associate. This kind of faith and conviction sets a pattern for life, and has direct influences on what people will, and will not, do.

Right and wrong

Everyone has a sense of right and wrong which they apply as they go about their daily and working lives. Right and wrong is not always absolute, however; what people are prepared and willing to do, and what they are not prepared or willing to do, comes partly from their own beliefs and convictions, and partly also from the following.

- What the law allows and does not allow.
- Levels of personal and collective comfort and discomfort.
- The particular situation in which people find themselves (see Box 5.8).
- Responsibility: people's knowledge and understanding of what is right and wrong is tempered by corporate responsibility. In the name of the organization, and when they know that they will be supported, people will therefore carry out actions that they know to be wrong because the organization has given its assurance and permission.

Box 5.8: Right and wrong (1)

The level of adjustment concerning right and wrong, and some of the factors which limit the absolute nature of right and wrong, can be seen from the following examples.

- A Scottish equal opportunities officer is both comfortable and also happy to engage in sectarian chanting at Celtic versus Rangers football matches.
- People are happy to take paper and pens from their place of work, or to use the office computer to book their holidays, but would not dream of stealing from shops.
- MPs claiming large allowances for second homes and incidental expenses insist that they have worked within the rules.

In these cases, therefore, what is right and wrong is tempered by the situation, circumstances and, by implication, what is permissible and not permissible behaviour. More generally:

- everyone knows that it is wrong to jump the queue at the supermarket, but if we are in a hurry, we will all do it;
- everyone knows that it is wrong to weave in and out of traffic when driving, but again, we all do it in different sets of circumstances.

It is a complex part of human behaviour, and one that needs to be carefully managed in organizations. Otherwise, 'wrong' becomes 'not wrong', and if such behaviour is still not limited, then it becomes 'right'.

Box 5.9: 'We need a victim'

When things go wrong in companies and organizations, the culture and prevailing attitudes and values demand that someone is held accountable, and some visible and discernible action is taken as the result.

In many cases, this has caused companies and organizations to make specific high-profile dismissals and redundancies. For example:

- When the opening of Terminal 5 at Heathrow airport went badly wrong in 2008, British Airways very publicly dismissed two top managers who were associated with the project.
- In order to meet a budget deficit, Kent County Council very publicly reduced the range of courses on offer at its further education colleges, making 300 redundancies.
- When the Royal Bank of Scotland announced its record losses, it very publicly made 14,000 staff redundant.

Whether there is any connection between the ills of the organizations, the budget deficits or the losses and the need for redundancies is never actually made clear. It also means that those who took the decisions to (in these particular cases) implement the Terminal 5 project, expand the range of further education teaching and employ the numbers of staff at Royal Bank of Scotland are never called to account. Neither are the top managers who, in fact, did nothing about the problems until after they had occurred rather than creating conditions in which these issues could not occur in the first place.

- Accountability: people's knowledge and understanding of what is right and wrong is tempered by the ways in which they will be held to account for their actions. If they know that no sanction is forthcoming, they will tend to act in ways that they choose. If they know that they are going to be rewarded for bad, unacceptable, morally wrong or illegal behaviour, then they will nevertheless tend to act in these ways (see Box 5.9).

General expectations

This is where people make assumptions, especially about the certainty and stability of the organizations for which they work. These general expectations and assumptions are something less than utter faith. Nor do they mean that collective and individual assumptions about the organization are always right. However, these assumptions come to be ingrained, especially if people have no reason to question them.

These expectations, and the kinds of belief that they foster, apply to all the major aspects of organizational life:

- management style, attitudes, priorities, demands and expectations;
- pay and rewards, including 'the annual pay rise', and also bonuses, trappings of status and badges of office;

Box 5.10: General expectations

Just how deep people's general expectations actually are (see also Chapter 4) can be seen from the flood of complaints that television companies receive when supposedly assured and predictable programme schedules are disrupted for a reason. For example:

- when soap opera broadcasts are cancelled or shifted in order to accommodate sporting events, there are always complaints;
- when major crises and emergencies occur, news programmes tend also to take over from light entertainment.

In 2008, Shannon Matthews, a nine-year-old girl, vanished from her home and was believed to have been kidnapped. After a three-week search, Shannon was found, and her mother and partner arrested on charges of kidnapping and conspiracy to defraud. On the day that the mother and partner were convicted, the BBC replaced an episode of 'Holby City' with a 'Panorama Special' on the Matthews' kidnapping case.

This programme change brought 19,000 complaints. It was hardly a major issue; but it interrupted and distorted a major general expectation of people's lives.

- interpersonal, inter-group and intra-group relations and patterns of behaviour on which these relations are based (see Box 5.10).

Complacency

Complacency occurs when people come to believe, as absolute fact, in everything that goes on around them. This can, and does, happen from time to time in all organizations. The best organizations take active steps to make sure that their staff do not fall into positions of complacency, and so come to believe in the utter infallibility and immortality of everything that they do (see Box 5.11).

Socialization

Socialization is the process by which individuals are persuaded to behave in ways acceptable to their society, family, social groups and clubs. This also applies to work organizations and their groups, departments, divisions and functions. Effective socialization results in compliance and conformity with the values, beliefs, attitudes, rules and patterns of behaviour required.

For this to occur, the group's attitudes, values, beliefs, behaviour and rules must be capable of being accepted by the individuals who seek to join, or who are required to join. They tend therefore to reflect the prevailing customs of the wider society and to be in harmony with general ethical and social pressures.

On the other hand, socialization should also leave enough space, latitude and freedom for individuals to express themselves in the given setting. Too great restriction leads to frustration. At the other extreme, a lack of clear understanding of these standards leads

Box 5.11: Napoleon

Napoleon Bonaparte was from Corsica. As a young man he joined the French revolutionary army; and by dint of sheer hard work and attention to detail, he rose through the ranks to become chief of staff. Using his military expertise to gain political influence, in 1799 he became first consul and then emperor of France and the expanding French Empire.

On his way up, he paid attention to every detail, as above. He checked every aspect of military equipment and made sure that the routes on which he took his soldiers would have plenty of food and water (provided, of course, they continued to win their battles). When he moved into politics, he adopted the same attitude, attending to every detail of the comfort, equipment and resources that his offices needed and used (he even made sure that his secretaries had adequate supplies of coffee).

In the early nineteenth century, at the height of his powers, however, he started to believe in his own infallibility and immortality. The attention to detail which had served him so effectively now went by the board. He chose to do things 'because it was his destiny', and because he was obviously infallible.

This complacency, and the attitude on which it was based, became the vehicle of his downfall. There is a lesson for all those who do not work hard, adequately, effectively or properly.

to lack of focus and purpose, leaving the individual in a void – and this can be just as harmful and stressful as over-restraint.

Socialization takes place from the moment of birth. It is conducted in the early years by parents and family, schools and colleges, religious institutions, sports and leisure clubs. By the time individuals arrive in work they therefore have been subject to a great variety of pressures and influences. The problem for organizations lies in their ability to build on this and create conditions that are both acceptable to individuals, and which also ensure that productive and effective work can take place (see Figure 5.3).

This problem is greater with mature employees who may arrive at an organization after experience in many others. They will therefore have formed their own ideas about high standards, best practice and optimum ways of working, and this in turn leads to the need for effective orientation at the outset of the new job.

This underlines the importance of adequate and effective induction and orientation programmes. Too many organizations and their managers still neglect this, believing it to be a waste of time, cutting into their other priorities; or else they have simply never learned to see it as an investment, the return on which is a committed and effective employee – and if this is really successful, much of the process is achieved over a relatively short period of time.

Socialization and belonging

In organizations, socialization takes place as the process of getting people to belong and to feel comfortable and assured in the institution so that they become productive in their work. It is essential that socialization is influenced as much as possible by the needs and

Organization	Individual
• Productive effort	• Comfort
• Effective workforce	• Warmth
• Effective individuals	• Belonging
• Effective groups	• Contact
• Continuous development	• Success
• New talents and energies	• Fulfilment
• Work harmony	• Achievement
• Expectations	• Professionalism
• Job proficiency	• Expectations
• Professionalism	• Rewards
• Success	• Training and development
• Value	

The lists represent two sides of the same coin. Organization socialization is designed and devised to bring them together, to match up and harmonize the pressures. Some of these pressures are convergent, others divergent; all must be integrated and interrelated as far as possible.

Figure 5.3 Social needs

wants of the organization. Otherwise, people will form their own habits and norms; and while in some cases these are very positive and productive, in others they are not.

In organizations, therefore, the purpose of socialization is as follows:

• to generate the required attitudes and values;
• to instil the required work ethic – the desired combination of what is to be done, and how it is to be done;
• generating effective and positive inter-group and intra-group relations, as above.

If the organization does not take an active role in this, then people will form their own ways of doing things, as above. This may, or may not, be productive and effective. If effective, clearly this happens by chance; if ineffective, it can lead to serious behavioural problems (see Box 5.12).

Learning

Learning is the process by which skills, knowledge, attitudes and behaviour are formed and developed. It takes place as the result of education, training, socialization and experience. Learning also occurs as the result of conditioning and restriction – whereby the individual is persuaded to adopt, and ultimately accept, guidance, regulation, conformity and compliance in particular situations.

Individuals learn at different rates, times and stages in their lives. Some people acquire new knowledge, skills and qualities easily, while others struggle to learn the very basics of the same things (see Figures 5.4 and 5.5). This is based on a combination of the following.

• The desire and motivation to learn brought about by the individual's own needs and drives, usually in the expectation that this will bring success, rewards, enhanced potential and expertise, marketability; and also increased esteem, respect and status.

Box 5.12: Bullying and victimization

Laura Wright worked in the marketing department of a large multi-product international organization. Because of her capabilities and commitment, and the ways in which she behaved, she rose quickly to be deputy product manager, responsible for the marketing and delivery of a range of frozen foods across the whole of the European Union.

One year, she went on holiday. While she was away, she e-mailed some of her holiday photographs, including a picture of her in a bikini. One of her colleagues now took matters into his own hands, producing a life-size blow up of the bikini photograph and hanging it on the wall. Very quickly, people began to add rude, personal, disgusting and revolting comments.

The marketing director visited the department by chance. He looked for a moment at the picture of Laura on the wall, and then passed on.

On her first day back at work, Laura arrived early at the office in order to catch up on all that she had missed. She entered the office – only to see the life-size picture of her in her bikini on the wall with the comments. Horrified, she reported the matter to the marketing director.

The marketing director did not see what all the fuss was about. He refused to discipline those who had made the comments. The upshot was that Laura took the company to employment tribunal, and came away with £900,000 compensation.

The key lesson is that, if top managers do not see the value of socialization, and of using part of this process to determine what is right and wrong, acceptable and unacceptable, then nobody else will either.

- The quality and suitability of the learning and teaching methods (including the quality of instruction).
- Pressures to learn placed on individuals by others – including organizations – to enable them to acquire the knowledge, skills and qualities required; and also to adopt the attitudes, values and behaviour required in order to be comfortable in the particular situation.
- Specific drives and requirements such as the onus placed on individuals in particular occupations to keep abreast of new developments and initiatives in their field.
- The nature of the individual's attitude and disposition to acquire new skills, knowledge and qualities.

The result is to increase the range, depth and interactions of thoughts, ideas and concepts, as well as skills, knowledge, attitude, behaviour and experience; to increase the ability to organize and reorganize these; and to order them in productive and effective activities (whatever they mean in the particular set of circumstances).

Retention

The ability to retain and internalize that which has been taught and learnt is based on a combination of the following factors.

- The ability to practise and use, and become proficient in, that which has been taught and learnt.

- Its actual value once it has been taught and learnt (as distinct from its perceived or anticipated value before it was learnt).
- The regularity and frequency with which it is to be put to use.
- The rewards that are to accrue as the result.
- The punishments and threats that occur if learning does not take place (this is especially important in the acquisition of attitudes, values and behaviour, and in conforming to rules and standards).

(a)

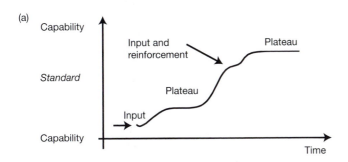

(b)

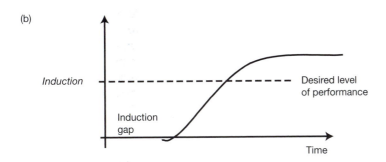

(c)

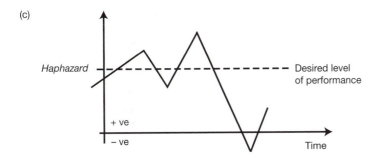

(a) Theoretical, based on rational and ordered input, familiarization, practice and reinforcement.
(b) The theory of induction – time taken at the outset leads to long-term high levels of performance.
(c) The theory of non-induction and non-training, based on trial and error.

Figure 5.4 Learning curves

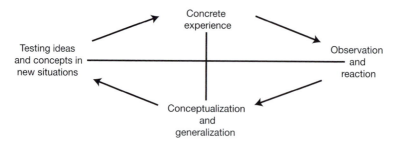

The cycle illustrates the importance of the relationship between behaviour, action and experience. It also emphasizes (testing and experience) the need to reinforce abstract learning with practice and performance.

Figure 5.5 Learning cycle
Source: Kolb (1985).

This is usually called learning reinforcement. Reinforcement may be:

- continuous, in which case the learning is soon internalized;
- intermittent, in which case it is likely to become important from time to time only and may lead to the need for revision, retraining and refresher courses;
- occasional, in which case the learning is likely to have been of general or marginal value only.

More generally still, learning, acquiring and becoming proficient in new skills and qualities normally leads to enhanced feelings of personal confidence and self-respect. It enhances flexibility of attitudes and approaches. It is also increasingly likely that it will bring greater general perceptions of worth and value to the organization.

Feedback

Feedback is essential on all aspects of performance leading to enhanced general levels of understanding, confidence and support. Related specifically to learning, feedback is best when:

- It is positive rather than negative, in that it enhances the general concept of progress to which learning is supposed to contribute. The negative is best as a 'nuclear deterrent' (i.e. it is present, but is never to be used). It is normally to be applied to persistent failure to accept and conform to necessary rules, rather than because of failure to learn skills and knowledge.
- Concentrating on processes as well as results so that the individual both knows their results, and also understands why they have succeeded or failed.
- Delivered as near to the conclusion of the learning as possible and then followed up with opportunities to apply that which has been learned and for this also to be incorporated into the feedback process.
- Continuous in general, so that any problems with what which has been learned will subsequently become apparent, or any later decline in performance can be quickly rectified.

Learning styles

Individuals have preferred learning styles. For some this may be very marked – they can only learn in one particular way and other methods have little effect.

Honey and Mumford (1986) identify four preferred learning styles as follows (Figure 5.6).

1 **Activist**: concentrating on learning by doing and via direct experience, and through considering the results of trial and error so that performance may be improved next time.
2 **Pragmatist**: concentrating on that which is possible and practical, and of direct application to given situations.
3 **Theorist**: concentrating on why things are as they are and investigating theories and concepts that form the background to this.
4 **Reflector**: concentrating on assessing and analysing why things have turned out in particular ways and using this as the basis on which to build understanding.

Honey and Mumford designed a questionnaire, the purpose of which was to identify under which of these four headings the individuals' preferred learning style fell. The results would then be used to ensure that the individual understood why they tended to learn some things better than others; to seek out those activities that were best suited to their preferred learning style; and to develop their lesser and least preferred areas of learning to enhance their total learning capability.

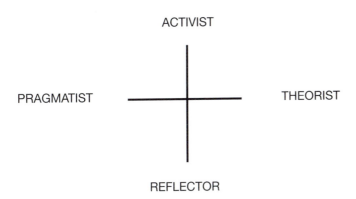

This spectrum was devised by Honey and Mumford to identify the preferred learning style. By completing a questionnaire and plotting the results the respondent would:

(a) identify those activities likely to be most and least beneficial;
(b) identify those areas which needed working on, so that full benefit from all activities could be gained.

Figure 5.6 Preferred learning styles

Other aspects of preferred learning styles may be identified.

- the influence of rewards and outcomes;
- economic factors – career and payment enhancement;
- peer, professional and social group expectations;
- the nature of the material and the means by which it is taught/learned;
- the quality of the teacher;
- time factors.

There are also some absolutes. For example, eventually someone who wishes to know whether they can drive a car will have to sit in a car and drive – however much of a theorist they may be. Similarly, it is not possible to be an effective leader of people if there is no basic understanding of why people behave in different ways in different situations (and different ways in the same situation), however much of a pragmatist they may otherwise be. This underlines the need to broaden the preferred learning style into an individual learning style that can accept effective input and information from as wide a variety of sources and means as possible.

Individual development

Both in organizational terms, and also for the benefit of the individual, the primary purpose of individual development is to enhance skills, knowledge, qualifications and expertise so that a productive and fulfilling life can be lived, both in work and also in society at large. If this is to be achieved, the following must be clear.

- Aims and objectives, and measures of success/failure.
- Positive motivation of both trainers and trainees.
- Rewards must be perceived and available.
- Benefits in terms of personal, professional and organizational performance and objectives must be met.
- It must be capable of reinforcement at the workplace.
- It must be current and relevant.
- It must have organizational and managerial support.
- It must be planned and integrated into the workload of the individual and have priority and importance at the time when it takes place.
- It should be part of a total package and process of continuous learning and development.
- It should be evaluated afterwards by all interested parties, both in the short term and also into the future.

If this is to be achieved, organizations must also consider individual development from the point of view of

- organization requirements, the need and drive for enhanced current and future performance;
- professional and expertise requirements, the need for the individual to enhance and improve their general skills, knowledge and expertise;
- personal drives and preferences.

Other points may usefully be made.

- Individuals must be motivated to learn. This motivation arises from a combination of personal and professional or occupational circumstances, drives and needs and the requirements of the organization.
- Learning and development are part of the general commitment to each other made by organization and individual. The organization is entitled to expect the individual to learn; and the individual is entitled to expect training and development.
- Whatever is learned must be capable of recognition and measurement so that performance standards can be set and identified.
- The better understood the activity, the stronger the motivation and drive to learn. It is often necessary to break complex tasks and practices down into smaller parts to avoid confronting the trainee with too much to grasp at any one time.
- Feedback is essential to reinforce understanding, expertise and commitment. Current or immediate feedback is much better than delayed feedback – the greater the delay, the greater the loss of meaning and impact.

Conclusions

Forming and nurturing the required attitudes and values clearly requires a broad knowledge and understanding of all the factors and elements indicated. If this is to be effective, the following must be present.

- Identification of the required attitudes and values, together with the reasons why these are desirable and ensuring that these are capable of being supported and adopted by all those concerned.
- Taking positive steps to reinforce them in the ways in which the organization and its departments, divisions and functions operate and penalizing any shortfall.
- Recognizing the effects of all training and development activities on attitudes and values, whatever the training and development is overtly concerned with. Attitudes and values are shaped, developed and reinforced by all learning activities, as is the general mutual relationship and commitment between organization and individual.
- It is also necessary to recognize that attitudes, and especially negative attitudes, emerge whether or not they are shaped and influenced by the organization. Where the organization has no influence on attitudes, these are formed by other pressures, especially peer, professional and social groups.
- Positive attitudes help to provide a harmonious and open working environment, and increase general levels of motivation and morale. Negative attitudes tend to reinforce any stresses and strains – poor working relationships, lack of trust and value.
- Attention to workplace attitudes, especially at the induction stage, helps employees to adopt and find the place required of them in their environment. It helps to provide a clear mutual understanding between organization and employee, and is one of the cornerstones of the working environment. Above all, as organizations strive for ever-greater levels of flexibility and responsiveness, building these characteristics as positive and valuable attitudes is essential.

Attitudes and values, as well as skills and knowledge, have to be taught, learned and assimilated. It is therefore essential to know and understand how individual learning and development takes place, and the importance of learning curves, learning cycles, learning styles and the learning process – learning, reinforcement and feedback. Additionally, learning skills and expertise helps to reinforce the attitudes and values desired; and it also helps to eliminate those attitudes and values which are not desired and not acceptable.

Finally, the development of attitudes and values, and the learning that reinforces these, if properly directed, is a major aspect of desiring the collective work ethic, organizational morality and strength of cohesion and identity, that are all essential for enduring effective organizational practice.

6 Ethics

Introduction

Ethics in management is concerned with those parts of organizational, operational, occupational and professional conduct that relate to absolute standards and moral principles. Establishing standards of conduct requires reference to questions of what is right and wrong in absolute terms; the desired ends and outcomes; and the ways and means by which the ends and outcomes are achieved. There are additional factors of:

- the nature of working, professional and personal relationships;
- attention to the quality of working life;
- compliance with the law;
- and working effectively within the constraints of social, cultural and religious customs.

Below are a variety of views and perspectives on the relationship between ethics, business and management.

Sternberg (2006) states:

Business ethics applies ethical reasoning to business situations and activities. It is based on a combination of distributive justice – that is, the issuing of rewards for contribution to organization goals and values; and ordinary common decency – an absolute judgement that is placed on all activities.

Johnson, Scholes and Whittington (2007) state:

Ethical issues concerning business and public sector organizations exist at three levels. At the macro level there are issues about the role of the business in the national and international organization of society. These are largely concerned with addressing the relative virtues of different political/social systems. There are also important issues of international relationships and the role of business on an international scale. At the corporate level the issue is often referred to as corporate social responsibility and is focused on the ethical issues facing individual and corporate entities (both private and public sector) when formulating and implementing strategies. At the individual level the issue concerns the behaviour and actions of individuals within organizations.

Adams, Hamil and Carruthers (1994) identify a series of factors and elements against which the performance of organizations could be measured in ethical terms. These factors are:

- the nature of business; and Adams, Hamil and Carruthers identify contentious industries such as tobacco, alcohol, chemicals, armaments;
- the quality, integrity, availability and use of information;
- participation, consultation, employment relationships, the recognition of trade unions, means and methods of representation;
- relationships with emerging economies and markets;
- connections with governments – especially where these were considered to be undesirable or where the regime in question was considered to be unethical itself;
- marketing and selling initiatives, knowing and understanding where responsibilities truly lie (see Box 6.1).

Box 6.1: Products, prices, charges and responsibilities

In recent years, marketing and selling practices have become contentious issues. For example:

- **Retail**: supermarkets present products such as chocolate, crisps and toys at levels where children can see them and pick them up.
- **Fast food**: the promotions undertaken by McDonald's and other fast food chains are designed specifically to attract children.
- **Financial products**: investments and savings, and even mortgages, have been made attractive to people on overtly advantageous rates, terms and conditions.

These and other practices have provoked debate around the following:

- where the boundaries of marketing and selling truly lie;
- what companies and organizations ought, and ought not, to do when presenting their products and services for sale;
- where the responsibilities of the customers and purchasers truly lie.

On the one hand, the supermarkets, fast food chains and banks state quite clearly that nobody is forced to buy their products and services. On the other hand, the marketing and sales techniques employed, whether advertising presentations, shelf displays or more direct sales methods of the financial services sector, do have a persuasive power all of their own.

It is additionally the case that any company that foregoes the opportunities offered by these marketing and sales techniques is likely to lose sales of market share to those that continue to use them.

So the question then arises: where do the ethical balances of these activities lie? What, if anything, ought to be done about them?

These are major business dilemmas, both for those who manage organizations, and also for those who consume products and services. From this point of view, this is less of an issue for those who sell sweets and fast food. It is much more of a serious ethical, as well as commercial, issue when customers buy financial products and services for the long-term, only to have these ruined by the subsequent actions of those responsible for the direction of companies in the sector.

Ethics and management

Understanding ethics is a key managerial priority. It is therefore essential that organizations and their managers know and understand where the boundaries of organizational business and managerial ethics lie. These boundaries are as follows:

- compliance with the law, as above;
- general approaches and attitudes to staff and customers;
- attitudes to the communities in which they operate;
- attitudes to environmental issues – especially waste disposal and recycling; replanting; the ways and means by which scarce resources are consumed;
- business relationships with suppliers and markets;
- product testing, where this involves the use of animals;
- product testing, where the outcomes are not fully known, understood or evaluated;
- product marketing, using specific 'tags' outside their full context (see Box 6.2).

Further perspectives on the relationship between ethics, business and management include:

> The more successfully the manager does their work, the greater will be the integrity required. For under new technology the impact on the business of decisions, time span and risks will be so serious as to require that each manager put the common good of the enterprise above self-interest. Their impact on the people in the enterprise will be so decisive as to demand that the manager put genuine principles above expediency. And the impact on the economy will be so far reaching that society itself will hold managers responsible. Indeed, the new tasks demand that the manager of tomorrow root every action and decision in the bedrock of principles so that they lead, not only through knowledge, competence and skill, but also through vision, courage, responsibility and integrity.
>
> Drucker (1955)

Payne and Pugh (1970) identified the relationship between the absolute standards of the organization and its 'climate'. They stated that: 'Climate is a total concept applying to the organization as a whole or some definable department or subsystem within it.' It is descriptive of the organization. There are four main aspects of climate:

- degrees of autonomy given to particular individuals, groups, departments, divisions and functions;
- the degree of structure or flexibility imposed on work positions;

Box 6.2: Fairtrade

Many organizations now use the 'Fairtrade' tag, to emphasize the perceived authenticity and integrity of their products.

Fairtrade is an organization that is set up to monitor the relationships between companies and organizations from the west and other parts of the developed world, and their suppliers from the third and emerging worlds.

Fairtrade is supposed to ensure that any supplies, raw materials, crops or commodities bought under their banner are produced by people working in 'acceptable' and 'humane' conditions; and those companies and organizations paying for these crops and commodities pay a 'fair' price.

Any company or organization that meets the Fairtrade guidelines, and has been approved by the Fairtrade organization, may use the Fairtrade stamp on its products, services and packaging.

However, in practice this clouds as many issues as it clarifies. The question of what a fair price is for particular commodities and crops from different parts of the world is largely a matter of perception. When the prices are paid, there is no evidence that any of the money goes to the people who actually do the work; and while in many cases, this does clearly happen, it is equally clear that in other instances this does not happen. It is not clear whether the production methods used are healthy or otherwise, both to those who actually carry out the work, and also those who consume the final products. Finally, the Fairtrade brand makes no reference to the means of transport used, and the conditions under which those who carry out the transport activities (i.e. shipping, lorry and truck driving employees) actually work.

- the reward orientation, in terms of both individual satisfaction and overall organizational achievement;
- the degree of consideration, warmth and support; the human aspects of staff–management relationships.

There is clearly no common agreement on what constitutes an absolute body of knowledge and expertise in the area of business and managerial ethics. Some useful initial conclusions may, however, be drawn as follows:

- it is essential to take a long-term view, as well as having to satisfy immediate interests and demands;
- absolute standards are required relating to organizational policies, aims and objectives;
- common standards of equity, equality, honesty and integrity are required; and if they are not established, they will, *de facto*, emerge anyway;
- there is a relationship between organization standards and integrity, the delivery of performance and the distribution of rewards;
- there are key relationships between means and ends, and actions and motives;
- identifying and establishing where conflicts of interest lie, and the reasons for their existence.

The key areas for attention in this context are:

- survival;
- relationships with employees;
- relationships with suppliers;
- relationships with customers;
- relationships with communities;
- means and ends;
- corporate governance.

Survival

Survival therefore becomes the main ethical duty of the organization, to its staff, customers, communities and other stakeholders. For this to happen over the long term, a long-term view must be taken of all that this means. For business and companies, profits must be made – over the long-term; for public services, this means effectiveness – over the long-term. This is the basis on which confidence and an enduring and continuous positive relationship with customers (or service-users) are built and developed. This is also the only ground on which an effective and satisfactory organization for the staff is to be created.

The key ethical duty, therefore, is to take steps and decisions, and to order the financial and other resources of the organization in ways which are:

- profitable in the long-term;
- effective in the short-term, as well as the long-term;
- having, as priorities, products and services that customers and clients will want to buy.

This implies that producing products and services of quality and integrity are clear ethical duties, as well as mainstream organizational responsibilities.

Short-term views, expediency, the need for triumphs – all detract from this. Especially, there is a serious problem in this area with some public services. For example, the output of education can take 15–20 years to become apparent. Health and social services have similar extreme long-term requirements and commitments. Yet those responsible for their direction (both service chiefs and Cabinet ministers) need to be able to show instant results to be presented before the electorate or before the selection panel for their next job.

This is not wholly confined to services. For example, pressures from bankers and other financial backers in some sectors (especially loan makers) leads to companies being forced, or strongly encouraged, to sell assets during lean periods in order to keep up repayments or show a superficial cash surplus over the immediate period. This happened with the UK construction industry over the early 1990s when there was a great decline in work brought on by recession and general loss of confidence. Short-term cash gain was made through the sale of assets (especially land banks). Long-term survival was threatened because these assets would not be present when any upturn in confidence and activity came about.

However, this again has to be balanced with matters of general confidence and expectation. If backers expect to see a series of short-term positive results then these have to be produced, especially if backing may be withdrawn if these are not forthcoming or do not meet expectations. This implies re-educating backers into the long-term view. It also means seeking out others who are disposed to take the long-term view.

Relationships with employees

The key ethical issue in relationships with employees is the integrity (or lack of) at the core. Whatever the style of HR and employee relations, people need to know and understand its basis, and how they are therefore expected to behave and perform.

Confrontational or adversarial styles of employee relations are always founded on mistrust and reinforced by offensive and defensive positions adopted by the two sides concerning particular issues. The phrase 'the two sides' confirms and underlines this. Resources are consumed in this way to the detriment, both of organization performance and also of resource utilization – those used in these ways cannot be put to better use elsewhere.

Adversarial employee relations are therefore normally unethical at least at the core, even if things work adequately in practice. However, greater or full participation and involvement is only ethical if the point of view adopted is itself honest – if a genuine view of respect and identity is taken. This is made apparent – or not – in the continuity and enduring nature of this relationship. It is underlined by the volume, quality and relevance of information made available to the staff, the means by which problems are addressed and resolved, the prevalence of equality of treatment and opportunity, and the development of staff.

It also refers to the attention to the standards to which employees are to conform, the ways in which procedures are operated and the management approach. It covers all aspects of the standard HR area – recruitment and selection, induction, performance appraisal, pay and reward, promotion and other opportunities for development and advancement. Above all, at its core lies equality of treatment for everyone.

Responsibilities and obligations to staff

Organizations are required to take an active view of their responsibilities and obligations to their staff. Questions of flexibility of work and attendance, the work-life balance, and the wider humanity of employment have all to be addressed.

It is essential to acknowledge the range of pressures and priorities that exist in the lives of everyone, including health, family, social, ethical and religious, as well as those related to work. The outcome of this is understanding and not interference or imposition. It sets the relationship between work organizations and people in context. It indicates areas where stresses and strains are likely to arise. It indicates the relationship between organization and individual priorities, where these coincide and where they diverge. It indicates areas for accommodation and for regulation.

Extreme human concerns and conditions have to be dealt with. This refers to personal crises – serious illness, death, bereavement, divorce, drink and drug problems. The concern is to ensure that the organization gives every possible support to people facing these issues so that a productive and profitable relationship is maintained even through such times. Individuals can, and should, be referred to outside professional support services and agencies for these matters with the full backing of the organization.

Ultimately, however, organizations do not have the right to pry into people's personal affairs. Individuals may be referred for counselling or other expert help and advice if they give their consent unless the matter is adversely affecting their work performance beyond a fair and reasonable extent, or where they constitute a real or potential threat or danger to their colleagues or the activities of the organization.

Problems related to drug or alcohol use or addiction always fall into the latter category and are therefore always a matter of direct concern. Organizations set absolute standards of handling and using equipment, carrying out activities and dealing with the public. Addiction and abuse problems directly affect each of these. The individual is therefore to be removed from these situations and supported through rehabilitation.

It is essential to preserve confidentiality and integrity in all dealings with staff. This is the cornerstone on which all effective staff relationships are built. Where confidences are not kept, where sensitive personal and occupational information becomes public property, the relationship is tainted and often destroyed. Confidentiality also encourages people to be frank, open and honest themselves, and this leads to a genuine understanding of issues much more quickly. It also enables managers and supervisors to address their matters of concern – for example, declines in standards of performance and behaviour – directly and immediately they are observed.

It is essential to respect individuals for the value of their contribution to the organization. If they bring no value, they should not be there in the first place. Ideally, therefore, the fact of their employment (in whatever capacity) equates to high and distinctive value – and where it does not, stress and conflict invariably occur.

This respect extends to all aspects of the working relationship; and includes attention to the current job, future prospects, continuity of working relations, creation of suitable working environments, creation and maintenance of effective occupational and personal relationships, and creation and maintenance of effective management and supervisory styles.

The traditional or adversarial view of this approach to responsibilities and obligations was that it was soft and unproductive, and diverted attention away from production and output. Organizations could not afford to be 'nice' to their employees while there was a job to be done.

The reverse of this is much closer to the truth. The acknowledgement, recognition and understanding of the full nature and range of complexities and conflicting pressures on individuals is the first step towards effective and profitable activities. By engaging in a basis of honesty, confidentiality, trust, support and integrity – rather than coercion, confrontation, dishonesty and duplicity – a long-term positive relationship can be established. The interests of organization and individual are bound up with each other, especially over the long-term. Ultimately, therefore, the interests coincide. A critical part of this approach is concerned with creating the basis on which this can be built (see Box 6.3).

Relationships with suppliers

There used to be a received managerial wisdom, that it was good and effective practice to create 'a multiplicity of suppliers', because this would 'keep suppliers on their toes', and 'keep suppliers loyal'. In practice, companies that adopt this approach actually show no loyalty to suppliers; they simply shop around, taking either the short-term view that they will accept deliveries from the lowest-priced suppliers at the particular moment; or taking the expedient view that particular suppliers may be changed at will.

This especially applies where there is an over-supply of particular commodities, components, and primary and raw materials.

By the same token, companies and organizations may know, believe or perceive themselves to be held to ransom by those who supply rare or highly-sought-after primary resources and components.

Wherever either of these two extremes exists, the relationship has to be managed with integrity if long-term security of purpose and business is to be achieved. Indeed,

---

Box 6.3: Alcan Manufacturing Ltd

Alcan Manufacturing Ltd is a small company producing office furniture, filing cabinets and other industrial and commercial furnishings.

When Ken Lewis took over as chief executive of Alcan, he stated: 'Throughout my managerial career, I have always thought that there must be a better way of doing things than what goes on in most companies and organizations. I could never see the point of people turning up to work to go through a predictable pattern of tasks and then go home.

When I took over here, one quarter of the premises was taken up with offices. I have removed all these and turned the space over to manufacturing. After all, without manufacturing, we have no products, no customers – and therefore no company.

Other than sales, we have turned all of the other duties over to the manufacturing teams. They now have full responsibility for product scheduling, recruitment and selection of new staff, deciding who needs what training and when, even their hours and patterns of work.

The result is that we are getting more and more out of less and less. Our wastage and scrappage rates have declined to the point at which we now have to have our bins emptied only twice a week instead of once a day. Staff turnover last year was 2 per cent only. Staff absenteeism is 2 per cent also. In spite of a decline in turnover, we were able to maintain the targeted profit margin of 4 per cent because of the effective management of costs.'

Dave Hall, one of the manufacturing operatives, stated:

Ultimately, it is not Alcan who pay my wages, but the customers. Once we know what the production targets are, we have a duty to get the products made as quickly as possible and to the standards required, and then to get them shipped out. Everyone in the work group is clear about this; and so everyone pulls their weight.

People are flexible in their working arrangements. If we have a sudden order come in, people have to be prepared to stay 10, 12 or 14 hours a day until the order is delivered. After that, when work is not so tight, we can arrange things so that people do get to take the time off that they deserve. We also set our own pay rises and bonus levels. Then we approach Ken Lewis. He either says: yes, we can have the rise and the bonus; no, we cannot have the rise and the bonus, and these are the reasons.

Everything about the company encourages you to work hard and productively. The result is that we have survived where many others have not.

any business or managerial relationship where there are dominant and dependent partners must be considered from the business requirements, rather than the imbalance of power which exists.

It is also true that those organizations that secure themselves medium- and long-term contracts to supply large public and commercial institutions may take advantage of this security of relationship. For example, those supplying management consultancy services and medical supplies to the UK National Health Service have, in many cases, secured for themselves premium-priced contracts in return for stability and security of supplies. Organizations engaged in public–private partnerships and other forms of contracting out of particular activities normally found in the public service domain have been able to get themselves fully underwritten by the government, in case of changes in the business relationships, or strategic and political directions of particular services. Similarly, those organizations providing subcontracted specialist products and services to industries such as civil and mechanical engineering, building and construction, and information technology have also been able to charge premium rates at the times on which their particular expertise is required.

This has caused many organizations and their managers to take a fresh look at the nature of the desired relationship with the suppliers. At the core of this must be attention to the short-, medium- and long-term organizational and business demands; and also the nature, value and frequency of the supplies required. This is certain to change with technological advance, the opening up of new markets and increased availability of supplies of components, materials and information from different parts of the world (see Box 6.4).

Relationships with customers

This is the basis of the commercial or service provision: the respect and value in which the customers and clients are held. From this springs the drive for product quality, presentation and offering; of public relations and other customer management and service activities; and of handling complaints.

It also impinges on the staff. Where staff know that high standards of customer service and top-quality products are being offered, the relationship between organization and staff is also reinforced. The converse is also true – where these standards are low or falling, or where it is known that poor products and services are being offered, the integrity of the relationship between organization and staff is also compromised.

This affects all production, output and sales activities; especially in terms of attention to product quality, the terms under which it is offered, its uses and availability, and recognition of the levels of satisfaction that are required by the customers. In the long-term, if this is not present, confidence is lost. While it is possible to identify areas where short-term gain has been made without integrity (for example, in the sale of building products, home improvements, life assurance and pensions, poor quality Christmas presents), there is no (or reduced) likelihood of repeat business occurring. This also fails to satisfy either the long-term criteria or the requirement of confidence on the part of the employees; above all, there is no integrity of relationship. This way of conducting business is therefore also unethical.

Attention is additionally required to the marketing activities undertaken and the point of view adopted. Creative and imaginative presentation is highly desirable as long as this underlines, and does not misrepresent, the quality, desirability and image of the

Box 6.4: Managing the supply side in the clothing industry

Over the years, there have been many scandals relating to the supply side in the clothing industry.

The development of a manufacturing base in South-East Asia, India, Pakistan and Central America led many western clothing companies to explore the possibility of having their manufacturing done in these locations. Labour and raw materials were cheap and plentiful; and even taking into account the shipping costs, products could be manufactured and distributed for a fraction of the cost of doing all the work in the home country.

However, it was not long before scandals began to emerge. It became clear that many of the factories making branded clothing for Nike, Adidas and Gap were either using child labour, or else employing adults in conditions little different from slavery. The children and adults were being paid very little; and they were having to work up to 18 hours a day on the production lines. The factory themselves were noisy, dirty and dangerous, and there was no health and safety training or management. Those working on the production lines who got injured were simply sacked and replaced.

The responses of the western companies did not help in many cases. One crew filming a factory in rural India was beaten up and had its cameras destroyed. Another managed by chance to confront the American product manager who happened to be on site at the time. He became abusive, threatening legal action as well as physical retribution. Others still fell back on the fact that they complied with local labour laws in the factory locations (where, in many cases, there were effectively no labour laws).

To date, some of the worst excesses have been cleared up. At the same time, some bad practices still clearly continue to exist. To date also, there has been little effect on the behaviour of consumers, even though they know that many of the products are made under these conditions.

particular product or organization. Again, where integrity is missing, the relationship is invariably short-term and terminated by loss of confidence in the organization and loss of regard for its products and services. This applies to all aspects of marketing – promotion and advertising; packaging and presentation; direct sales and distribution; and marketing and business relationships (see Box 6.5).

Relationships with communities

The complexities of organizational and managerial relationships between companies and public service bodies, and the communities within which they operate, have to be addressed. The factors that have to be considered are as follows.

Communities expect the provision of long-term enduring work and the prosperity that this brings to communities. One of the major problems that was not managed in the UK during the recessions of the 1970s and 1980s, and the job losses that accrued as a result, was the provision of substitute or alternative sources of work, and therefore economic support, for communities at large. This had an enduring social effect on attitudes to work in certain areas of the country. Moreover, there is plenty of evidence

Box 6.5: Customer and client relationships in the City of London

'I was on holiday in Ibiza, and decided to go to a nightclub. And – I couldn't believe my eyes! For there, dancing as if there was no tomorrow, was one of my corporate clients. This person, a man in his fifties, had been a good client until quite recently; but the level of business that we had done had tailed off.

I looked again. He was dancing with a girl young enough to be his granddaughter. Apart from a tiny top and skirt, she was wearing very little indeed.

I picked up my drink and walked over to him. I waved a greeting to him. I then went and sat down. Sure enough, ten minutes later, he came over to see me. He started to explain what he was doing, but I stopped him. Then we cut to the chase; I asked him how business was, and why I had not seen him for quite a few months. He promised to be in touch as soon as he got back to London.

And – of course, he did indeed get in touch! He knew that I knew he was married; and he knew that I knew many of his contacts in the City of London.

Shortly after that, he placed £20 million worth of business with my company, and he has continued to look for new opportunities with us.'

Source: R. Leadbetter (2008) *City Boy* – HarperCollins.

to suggest that this part of the transition process is seldom addressed. For example, the extensive job losses and community deprivations that have occurred in the former East Germany as the result of reunification; and in countries such as Poland, the Czech Republic and Vietnam, as the result of the fall of communist regimes.

Community confidence is founded in general feelings of social well-being that accrue as the result of having particular organizations located in specific communities. This may bring with it particular ethical dilemmas – for example, there is a conflict that has to be addressed in areas where nuclear power stations are located. These stations provide large volumes of high-value and well-paid work to the communities, and this has to be reconciled with continuing concerns and perceptions about radiation pollution.

There are concerns around pollution and environmental damage, especially the disposal of waste and effluent; noise and lighting blight; and the effectiveness of waste and effluent management by organizations. Closely related to this are more general concerns surrounding the health and safety aspects of specific operations that are located in particular areas. Much of this is compounded by a failure to pin down global and corporate responsibilities for particular activities, as well as legislative inadequacies, and a lack of executive powers on the part of statutory executives.

Community disruption is caused, for example, by construction and civil engineering activities, which bring with them 'building blight' for the duration of their activities. They may also leave 'residual blight' if those responsible for drawing up the contract have not ensured that the particular construction or civil engineering firm concerned has been made responsible for the restoration and enduring quality of the broader environment in which the work was carried out.

Exploitation is a key issue when organizations move into particular areas as the result of the cheapness and perceived plentiful supply of labour and other resources. This was a problem that successive governments tried to address in the 1970s and 1980s in the UK through the use of regional aid and other development grants in areas of high unemployment. This is less of a problem now in the UK; however, there are enduring concerns about the wholesomeness and integrity of those organizations that source their manufacturing operations in the poorest parts of the world, purely because labour is cheap, plentiful and unregulated.

Social dominance and dependence come in three main forms:

(a) Where a large organization moves into a particular location and is able to poach staff from others already working there, by virtue of its economic ability to provide substantially superior terms and conditions of employment.

(b) Where large firms are able to insist on specific development activities to the known, believed or perceived detriment of the rest of the economic community. Of specific concern here is the development of out-of-town industrial and retail centres, which are believed to damage or destroy the economic viability of centre-of-town activities.

(c) The economic ability of large organizations to transcend their central responsibilities, by ensuring that they have powerful political and economic support. In these cases, they are able to build and operate what they want from their own point of view and narrow self-interest, rather than what is in the wider interests of the particular community.

Attention to each of these areas is therefore vital in developing effective community relations (see Box 6.6).

Means and ends

Crimes are not annulled by altruistic motives even though they may arouse human sympathy. For example, where a hungry person robs a rich person just so that he can eat, a crime is still committed. Robin Hood was a robber, whether or not he gave the proceeds of his robberies to the poor. The sale of cocaine on the urban streets of Europe and North America is wrong even if it provides the means of economic survival to the people of South America or Central Asia.

This applies to organization practices also. If a manager dismisses an employee to make an example of him, and if the employee did not deserve dismissal, then a wrong act is committed even if it brings the remaining staff into line. If the organization secures its long-term future through gaining a contract by offering a bribe to a major customer, then a wrong act is committed. In each of these cases, in practice, stated ends are very unlikely to be secured anyway because there is no integrity in the relationship. In the first case, the staff will look for other ways of falling out of line (but without risking further dismissals); in the second case, the corruption may come to light and the relationship be called into question or cancelled as a result.

Organizations must recognize and resolve conflicts of interest (as above). The first step lies in acknowledging the legitimacy and certainty of these. From this, steps can be taken to ensure their resolution which benefits the long-term future of all concerned. Conflicts of interest arise between all organization stakeholders; and between individuals within, and between, departments and divisions. These conflicts may be based on divergence of aims and objectives, as well as on general professional and expertise

Box 6.6: Nuclear power stations

The construction of nuclear power stations has always been contentious. It is now widely known and understood that they produce waste which has to be carefully stored for thousands of years; and following the Chernobyl disaster in the Ukraine in 1987, it is well known also that they can be very dangerous.

Those responsible for the construction and operation of nuclear power stations have therefore to be very careful in the management of the communities and locations in which they are to be built and operated. The following have to be accentuated:

- the provision of work and therefore prosperity for the community;
- the job opportunities that exist, and how local people need to go about taking advantage;
- contracting work that is available, together with a determination to use local contractors whenever, and wherever, possible;
- support for local community institutions, including clubs and societies.

The nuclear industry has always paid good wages and salaries relative to others for its unskilled, skilled, engineering and maintenance staff. In this way, the work becomes immediately attractive, transcending any moral philosophical or operational objections that people may otherwise have, especially concerning health and safety.

Doing things in these ways gives a good solid and positive foundation for effective community relations. However, the companies have to continue to meet their obligations also. Absolute attention must be given to the health and safety of the staff, as well as to the power stations themselves; and any failing on this front is certain to result in local trauma, as well as adverse national media coverage. There is also an enduring obligation to continue to provide work for future generations coming from the particular communities so that the strong basis of the mutuality of interest and relationship is continued.

disagreements as to the best interests of the organization (as well as matters of in-fighting and operational and personality clashes).

The ethical approach is bound up in an integrity and visibility of management style and working relationships, and the early recognition of operational, professional and personal problems. These are then addressed when they arise and before they are allowed to fester and become a part of organization folklore. What is to happen as the result of these matters arising can then be transmitted early, and it can be demonstrated why this is in the best interests of the organization (see Box 6.7).

Corporate governance

Corporate governance is the term used to describe the constitution, processes, actions and priorities by which organizations are led, directed and developed. It refers to the policies and practices that are present and in use. However, behind this overtly simple and straightforward assertion lies a complexity of organizational, managerial and ethical issues, and so it is a critical priority for those in top, senior and key positions.

Box 6.7: Right and wrong (2)

Absolute questions of right and wrong transcend all ethical considerations. Everyone has their own sense of what is:

- right;
- wrong;
- neither right, nor wrong.

Organizations, too, develop this facility in their staff in terms of what they:

- reward;
- sanction and punish;
- do not take action about one way or the other.

The structure for right and wrong may be constructed as follows:

- the right thing for the right reasons;
- the right thing for the wrong reasons;
- the wrong thing for the right reasons;
- the wrong thing for the wrong reasons.

However, doing the right thing for the wrong reasons (e.g. flooding a market with good quality products and services at low prices in order to drive out the competition), and doing the wrong thing for the right reasons (e.g. selling drugs to feed your family, or causing a product to fail because you need the capacity for something else) are always contentious; and so a moral compass is needed to ensure that whatever is done in these circumstances is at least justifiable in the circumstances.

Following the collapse of Enron, there was widespread international alarm concerning top management practice in the direction and reporting of company activities and finance. As the result the Sarbanes–Oxley Act came into force; and this required companies to make explicit the following:

- standards of conduct and behaviour;
- managing shareholders' interests;
- managing other stakeholders' interests;
- working within the law;
- setting and maintaining absolute standards of probity, integrity and transparency; and managing dishonesty;
- establishing clarity in rewarding top and senior managers;
- providing clear paper trails as to the use of organizational resources;
- managing the independence of company auditors.

Although enacted in the United States, Sarbanes–Oxley became accepted as the basis for all international corporate governance. A clear statement of duties, as above, requires active involvement and delivery on the part of top management; it is not enough merely to comply passively, or to assume that each of these areas is receiving full attention just because they are prescribed by law (see Box 6.8).

Conclusions

The ethical approach is not altruistic or charitable, but rather a key concept of effective long-term organizational and business performance. The commitment to the staff is absolutely positive. This does not mean any guarantee of lifetime employment. It does mean recognizing obligations and ensuring that staff, in turn, acknowledge their

---

Box 6.8: Corporate social responsibility

Corporate social responsibility (CSR) is the term used to describe the full range of responsibilities and obligations that companies and organizations have to society, and to the communities within which they work; and the position of corporate governance adopted indicates how wider social responsibility is to be accepted, implemented and discharged. CSR is therefore concerned with developing corporate governance and taking into account the following additional aspects:

- reconciling what is right and wrong in absolute terms, with what communities expect, and what the organization demands in practice;
- reconciling organizational and community priorities, expectations and aspirations;
- reconciling obligations to shareholders and backers with obligations to everyone else;
- reconciling the need for productive activity with the ability to manage waste and effluent.

These specific priorities can, and do, change over time. For example:

- School headteachers are responsible for the education of pupils and students within their care; they have also to meet government targets in terms of standards attained and exam performance. At different points in time, therefore, the question arises: which is the priority – are all pupils to be entered for all exams; or are only those pupils who are known to be capable of passing the exams to be entered?
- The top managers of companies have to choose, from time to time, between paying dividends to shareholders, and investing in the future of the business. After a difficult year, the dilemma can arise: whether to make payments to shareholders and backers in order to maintain their confidence and willingness to invest; or whether to ask shareholders to forego their dividends so that limited resources can be invested in the future.

The key lesson is always to look at the complexities of the situation; and so to form the expert basis for judging every situation on its own individual merits. This way, lines of reasoning that are both ethically sound and also demonstrably acting in everyone's interests can be developed.

obligations. These obligations are to develop, participate and be involved; to be flexible, dynamic and responsive. The commitment of the staff to organization, and organization to staff is mutual. This also extends to problem areas – especially the handling of discipline, grievance and dismissal issues, and redundancy and redeployment – and the continuity of this commitment when these matters have to be addressed.

Organizations must structure decision-making processes in ways that consider the range and legitimacy of ethical pressures. This also means understanding where the greater good and the true interests of the organization lie, and adopting realistic steps in the pursuit of this aim. An ethical assessment will consider the position of staff, the nature and interrelationship of activities, product and service ranges, mixes and balances, relationships with the community and the environment (see Figure 6.1).

Organizations are not families, friendly societies or clubs. By setting their own values and standards and relating these to long-term effectiveness they become distinctive. They are almost certain to be at variance from those that are, and would be, held by natural families and clubs. Problems that arise are clouded, therefore, where the organization does indeed perceive itself to be 'a big happy family'. Families are able to forgive prodigal children; organizations may not be able to afford to do so, however, if they are to maintain long-term standards, or if substantial damage has been done to customer relations for example. Organizations exist to provide effective products and services for customers while families and clubs exist to provide comfort, society and warmth. These elements are by-products; they are not the core.

Organizations are not obliged to provide employment at all except in so far as they need the work carrying out. They will select and hire people for this on the basis of capabilities and qualities. They have no obligation to take staff from the ranks of the unemployed (though they may choose to do so). They have no obligation to locate for all eternity in particular areas (though again they may choose to do so).

Organizations that pursue high ethical standards are not religious institutions, nor do they have any obligation to reflect any prevailing local traditions, values, customs, prejudices – or religion.

Japanese organizations setting up in the UK were and remain successful precisely because of this. Rather than trying to integrate their activities with the traditions of their locations they brought very distinctive and positive values with which people who came to work for them were required to identify.

Organizations must distinguish between right and wrong. Lying, cheating, stealing, bribery and corruption are always wrong and can never be ethically justified.

This has to be set in the context of the ways in which business is conducted in certain sectors and parts of the world. If a contract is only to be secured by offering a bribe the relationship is corrupted and based on contempt. If, and when, prevailing views change, the total relationship between organization and customer is likely to be called into question and any scandal or adverse publicity that emerges invariably affects confidence. It is in any case extremely stressful for individuals to have to work in this way or indeed to connive or conspire to any overt wrongdoing (though this may clearly be accommodated if the organization institutionalizes such matters, protects individuals who are caught or accepts responsibility for every outcome).

The ethical approach to organization and managerial activities is adult and assertive; it is not soft, religious or moral. It takes the view that continuous and long-term existence is the main duty of organizations to their staff, customers, suppliers, community and environment.

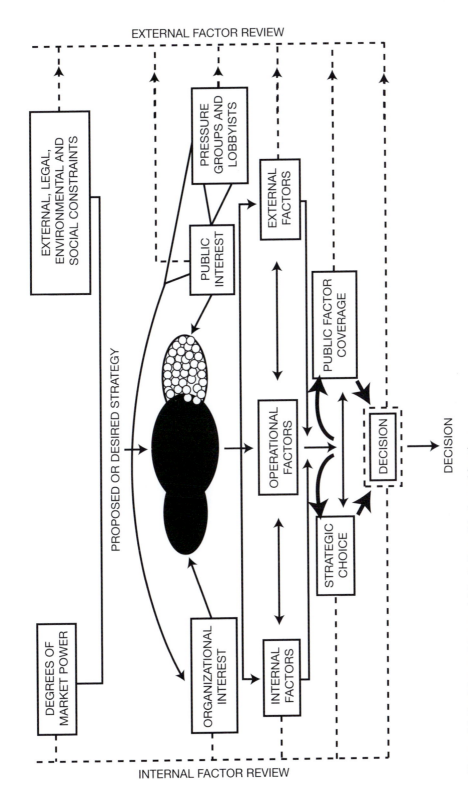

Figure 6.1 Decision-making model including ethical considerations

Above all, this requires a fundamental shift in corporate attitudes away from the short-term or expedient, from the instant approach to returns, from the needs of the influential figures, and from wasteful and inefficient budgeting control and production systems. These are to be replaced by active participation and involvement by all, in each of the areas indicated, in the pursuit of effectiveness and success. It requires placing a value on everyone with whom the organization comes into contact – above all, staff, customers, backers, suppliers and communities. Organizations are only sustainable in the long-term if adequate and continuous investment is made in technology, staff and staff development; research and development into new products and services; and in constantly improving and updating products, services, processes, systems and practices. This, in turn, is made most effective where everything is done with clearly stated aims, objectives, priorities, opportunities and consequences, and where these are understood, adopted and valued by everyone concerned and where there is a clear set of guiding principles present also.

7 Motivation

Introduction

Motivation is a reflection of the reasons why people do things. All behaviour has a purpose (often several). All behaviour is therefore based on choice – people choose to do the things that they do. Sometimes this choice is very restricted (sink or swim for example). Sometimes again, it is constrained by the law (for example, stopping the car when the traffic lights are red). And again, it is constrained by the norms and processes of society – for example, people tend to wear smart clothes to a party where they know that everybody else will be well dressed. In each case, however, there is a choice, though the propensity, encouragement and direction to choose one course of action rather than the other in the examples given is strong, if not overwhelming.

The following key features need to be understood.

- **Goals and ambitions**: these must be present, and both realistic and achievable if satisfaction is eventually to occur. Problems arise when the goals set are too low (leading to feelings of frustration), or too high (leading to constant lack of achievement). They must also be acceptable to the individual concerned – in terms of self-image, self-worth and self-value – so they are likely to be positive and based on the drive for improved levels of comfort, capability and well-being. They must also be acceptable (or at least not unacceptable) to the society and environment in which the individual lives and works, and capable of being harmonized and integrated with them.
- **Recognition**: a critical part of the process of developing self-esteem and self-worth lies in the nature and levels of recognition accorded to the achievement of particular goals. The need for recognition itself therefore becomes a drive. Individuals therefore tend to pursue goals that will be recognized and valued by those whose opinion and judgement is important to them – family, friends, peers and social groups, as well as work organization. Dissatisfaction occurs when this recognition is not forthcoming.
- **Achievement**: the components of achievement are the anticipated and actual rewards that the fulfilment of a particular goal brings. High levels of achievement occur where these overlap completely. High levels also normally occur where real rewards exceed those that are anticipated. Low levels occur where the anticipated rewards are not forthcoming; this devalues the achievement. High or complete achievement is normally seen and perceived as successful. Low achievement or failure to achieve is seen and perceived as a failure.

From this, in turn, other aspects of motivation become apparent.

- **The need for success**: people tend to aim their sights at what they know they can do, or think they can do or think that they may be able to do so that success is forthcoming. Genuine successes, victories and triumphs enhance feelings of self-esteem and self-value; failures diminish these.
- **The need to be recognized and valued by others**: this is a combination of pursuing things that the individual knows or perceives will be valued by those around them (as stated above) and also of seeking out those who will value the achievements for themselves.
- **The need to develop and improve**: this is a positive statement of need. If satisfaction is not forthcoming in one field, individuals are likely to lose interest and find something else to pursue. As well as matters of comfort and well-being, it also includes broadening and deepening experience and variety of life (including working life). It also includes developing new skills, capabilities and interests with the view to pursuing personal potential as far as possible.

These are social and behavioural needs, wants and desires; they are influenced, developed and conditioned by societies and organizations, and groups within them. They are based on more fundamental human needs.

- **The need and instinct for survival**: when an individual is hungry or thirsty, their prime motivation is for food or drink. When an individual is cold, their instinct is to find warmth and shelter. When the life of an individual is under threat (for example, from war or disaster), the instinct is to take actions that preserve life.
- **The need and instinct for society and belonging**: this is a reflection of the need for esteem, warmth and respect. More fundamentally, it is the need to belong, to interact and to have personal contact with those with whom the individual has identity, respect, liking and love. It also includes being drawn to those who have similar hopes, aspirations, interests and ambitions.
- **The need to be in control**: this is the ability to influence the actions and feelings of others; and the ability to influence the environment, to make it comfortable and productive in response to the particular needs, wants and drives. Control is a function of purpose – the organization and arrangement of particular resources (including other people) for given reasons.
- **The need to progress**: this is a reflection of the capacity to develop, to enhance knowledge, skills and capability. It includes:

  (a) economic drives for better standards of living, quality of life and enhanced capacity to make choices;
  (b) social drives to gain status, respect, influence and esteem as the result of enhanced capability and economic advantage;
  (c) personal drives reflecting ambition and the need to maximize/optimize the potential to achieve;
  (d) opportunistic drives, the identification and pursuit of opportunities that may become apparent and attractive to the individual;
  (e) invention and creativity, the ability to see things from various points of view and create the means by which quality of life can be enhanced.

Development, adaptation and creativity are also features of the needs for survival, society and control. They are a reflection of the extent to which the individual is able to influence their ability to survive, belong and control their environment.

Except at the point of life and death, when the instinct for survival is everything, these needs constitute part of the wider process of adaptation and interaction. At given moments therefore, some will be stronger than others – there is no linear progression from one to the next (see Box 7.1).

Major theories of motivation

Achievement motivation theory: D.C. McClelland

Much of the background on which the nature of motivation is based was organized and summarized by D.C. McClelland. Working in the 1950s and 1960s he identified the relationship between personal characteristics, social and general background and achievement.

Box 7.1: Honda UK and changing patterns of work

Honda UK, the car manufacturing company located in Swindon, Wiltshire, had for many years delivered steady and assured patterns of work. The whole operation was based on continuing demand for the company's good-quality, medium-value, middle-of-the-range cars.

One of the first industries to be affected by the economic downturn of 2007 and beyond was the car industry. Honda UK's response was as follows:

- to shut down production for the first six months of 2009;
- to keep everyone on payroll on their basic salary for the period of the shutdown;
- to require people to work an additional three hours per week when manufacturing finally picked up.

The company reinforced this with regular and substantial consultations and communications with all the workforce. Consequently, there was absolutely no doubt on the part of anyone as to the seriousness of the company's position, nor of the actions that needed to be taken.

Before the downturn, the staff were used to steady and assured volumes of work, including overtime. The staff had always been well paid and well looked after.

Now, when the downturn came, the company was able to maintain the commitment of the overwhelming majority of the workforce. This was because there was a fundamental mutuality of interest, and a positive psychological contract. At the point at which the company's survival and viability were at stake, therefore, the expectations of the staff were able to be shifted very quickly and positively.

During the period of the shutdown, the company undertook to ensure that all staff were kept fully abreast of any further developments. Members of staff could visit the premises or speak to any of the management team at any time on any matter at all.

The lesson is that by doing things in these ways, periods of great stress and uncertainty (including the matter of company survival and viability) can be managed effectively. In order to be fully effective, however, it is essential that staff are fully and actively engaged in the process.

Persons with high needs for achievement exhibited the following characteristics:

- task rather than relationship orientation;
- a preference for tasks over which they had sole or overriding control and responsibility;
- the need to identify closely, and be identified closely, with the successful outcomes of their action;
- task balance: this had to be difficult enough on the one hand to be challenging and rewarding; to be capable of demonstrating expertise and good results; and gaining status and recognition from others. On the other hand, it needed to be moderate enough to be capable of successful achievement;
- risk balance: in which the individual seeks to avoid as far as possible the likelihood and consequences of failure;
- the need for feedback on the results achieved to reinforce the knowledge of success and to ensure that successes were validated and publicized;
- the need for progress, variety and opportunity.

Need for achievement is based on a combination of:

- intrinsic motivation – the drives from within the individual;
- extrinsic motivation – the drives, pressures and expectations exerted by the organization, peers and society.

It is also influenced by education, awareness, social and cultural background, and values.

One potential problem was identified in relation to the appointment of high achievers to highly responsible managerial and supervisory positions. Because the higher achievement tended to be task rather than relationship driven, many did not possess (or regard as important) the human relations characteristics necessary to get things done through people.

Rensis Likert: System 4

Likert's contribution to the theories of workplace motivation arose from his work with high-performing managers; that is, managers and supervisors who achieved high levels of productivity, low levels of cost and high levels of employee motivation, participation and involvement at their places of work. The work demonstrated a correlation between this success and the style and structure of the work groups that they created. The groups achieved not only high levels of economic output and therefore wage and salary targets, but were also heavily involved in both group maintenance activities and the design and definition of work patterns. This was underpinned by a supportive style of supervision and the generation of a sense of personal worth, importance and esteem in belonging to the group itself (see Figure 7.1).

The system 4 model arose from this work. He identified four styles or systems of management, as follows:

- **System 1**:
  Exploitative Authoritative, where power and direction come from the top downwards and where there is no participation, consultation or involvement on the part of the workforce. Workforce compliance is thus based on fear. Unfavourable attitudes are

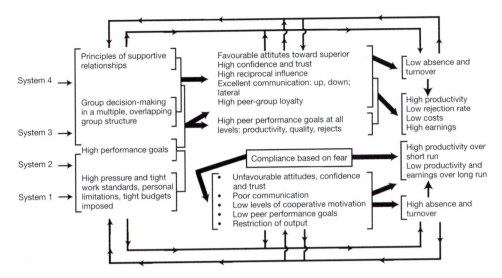

Figure 7.1 System 4
Source: Likert (1961).

generated, there is little confidence and trust, and low levels of motivation to cooperate or generate output above the absolute minimum.

- **System 2**:
  Benevolent Authoritative, which is similar to System 1 but which allows some upward opportunity for consultation and participation in some areas. Again, attitudes tend to be generally unfavourable; confidence, trust and communication are also at low levels.

In both Systems 1 and 2, productivity may be high over the short run when targets can be achieved by a combination of coercion and bonus and overtime payments. However, both productivity and earnings are demonstrably low over the long run; there is also manifestation of high absenteeism and labour turnover.

- **System 3**:
  Consultative, where aims and objectives are set after discussion and consultation with subordinates; where communication is two-way and where teamwork is encouraged at least in some areas. Attitudes towards both superiors and the organization tend to be favourable especially when the organization is working steadily. Productivity tends to be higher, absenteeism and turnover lower. There are also demonstrable reductions in scrap, improvement in product quality, reduction in overall operational costs and higher levels of earning on the part of the workforce.

- **System 4**:
  Participative: in this system three basic concepts have a very important effect on performance. These are the use by the manager of the principle of supportive relationships throughout the work group referred to above; the use of group decision-making and group methods of supervision; and the setting of high performance and very ambitious goals for the department and also for the organization overall.

System 4 was Likert's favoured system. Wherever the principle of supportive relationships is engaged, organizations have a much greater chance of maximizing their returns on investment in staff expertise, and in ensuring continuing high levels of motivation and commitment.

Abraham Maslow: a hierarchy of needs

Abraham Maslow was a behavioural scientist whose researches led him to depict a hierarchy of needs which explained different types and levels of motivation that were important to people at different times. This hierarchy of needs is normally depicted as a pyramid. The hierarchy of needs works from the bottom of the pyramid upwards, showing the most basic needs and motivations at the lowest levels and those created by, or fostered by, civilization and society towards the top of it (see Figure 7.2). The needs are as follows.

1   Physiological – the need for food, drink, air, warmth, sleep and shelter; that is, basic survival needs related to the instinct for self-preservation.
2   Safety and security – that is, protection from danger, threats or deprivation and the need for stability (or relative stability) of environment.
3   Social – that is, a sense of belonging to a society and the groups within it, for example, the family, the organization, the work group. Also included in this level are matters to do with the giving and receiving of friendship; basic status needs within these groups; and the need to participate in social activities.
4   Esteem needs – these are the needs for self-respect, self-esteem, appreciation, recognition and status on the part of both the individual concerned and the society, circle or group in which they interrelate; part of the esteem need is therefore the drive to gain the respect, esteem and appreciation accorded by others.
5   Self-actualization – that is, the need for self-fulfilment, self-realization, personal development, accomplishment, mental, material and social growth, and the development and fulfilment of the creative faculties.

Thus was the hierarchy of needs outlined. Maslow reinforced this by stating that people tended to satisfy their needs systematically. They started with the basic instinctive needs and then moved up the hierarchy. Until one particular group of needs was satisfied, a person's behaviour would be dominated by them. Thus, the hungry or homeless person will look to their needs for self-esteem and society only after their hunger has been satisfied and they have found a place to stay. The other point that Maslow made was that people's motives were constantly being modified as their situation changed, and in relation to their levels of adaptation and other perceptual factors. This was especially true of the self-actualization needs in which having achieved measures of fulfilment and recognition, man nevertheless tended to remain unsatisfied and to wish to progress this further.

Maslow's work was based on general studies of human motivation and as such was not directly related to matters endemic at the workplace. However, matters concerning the last two items on the pyramid, those of self-esteem and self-actualization, have clear implications for the motivation (and self-motivation) of professional, technical and managerial staff in organizations.

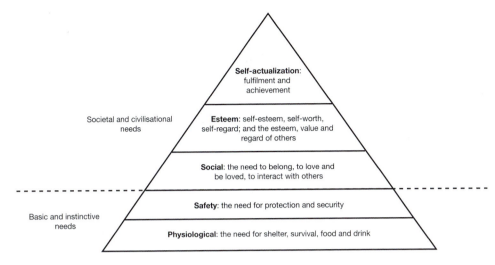

Figure 7.2 A hierarchy of needs
Source: Maslow (1960).

Douglas McGregor: Theory X and Theory Y

McGregor identified two distinctive sets of assumptions made by managers about employees. From this he articulated two extreme attitudes or views and called these Theory X and Theory Y. His thesis was that, in practice, most people would come somewhere between the two except in certain circumstances.

Theory X

This is based on the following premises.

- People dislike work and will avoid it if they can. They would rather be directed than accept any responsibility; indeed, they will avoid authority and responsibility if possible. They have no creativity except when it comes to getting around the rules and procedures of the organization. Above all, they will not use their creativity in the pursuit of the job, or the interests of the organization.
- People must be forced or bribed to put out the right effort. They are motivated mainly by money that remains the overriding reason why they go to work. The main anxiety concerns personal security, which is alleviated by earning money.
- People are inherently lazy and require high degrees of supervision, coercion and control in order to produce adequate output.

Theory Y

This is based on the premise that work is necessary to everyone's psychological growth. People wish only to be interested in work and under the right conditions they will enjoy it. People gain intrinsic fulfilment from it. They are motivated by the desire to achieve and to realize potential, to work to the best of their capabilities and to employ the creativity and ingenuity with which they are endowed in the pursuit of this.

Box 7.2: Footballers' wages

Top professional footballers in the UK and Europe earn very high wages indeed (up to £150,000 per week at 2009 values). Because of their position, they are also very favourably placed to take advantage of high-earning endorsements, advertising and marketing campaigns.

In return for these wages, many of the players do indeed play to the best of their ability at all times. Some, however, are less motivated, as follows:

- the wages are an incentive, not a motivation, and so the job remains the same whatever the individual is paid;
- some players have been demotivated and demoralized by the high levels of wages because they have come to understand that they have been turned into commodities (and therefore dehumanized);
- some players have considered themselves undervalued or unvalued because they are only on three-quarters of what others earn;
- some players have accepted high levels of wages to go to clubs that they would not otherwise have joined; and once installed at the club, they have found (in spite of the wages) that they nevertheless did indeed not want to join the club, and do not want to be there.

There is an assumption on the part of the top end of the football industry as a whole that players are only motivated by money. Rather than concentrating on intrinsic aspects of motivation (e.g. 'We only want people at this Club who want to be here' and then working out contracts of employment from there), everything is directed towards the extrinsic rewards. The result is that the attitudes exhibited in Theory X are overwhelmingly applied, even at the top of this overtly very glamorous industry.

People direct themselves towards given accepted and understood targets; they will seek and accept responsibility and authority; and they will accept the discipline of the organization in the pursuit of this. People will also impose self-discipline on both themselves and their activities.

Whatever the conditions, management was to be responsible for organizing the elements of productive enterprise and its resources in the interests of economic ends. This would be done in ways suitable to the nature of the organization and its workforce in question; either providing a coercive style of management and supervision, or arranging a productive and harmonious environment in which the workforce can, and will, take responsibility for erecting their own efforts and those of their unit towards organizational aims and objectives (see Box 7.2).

Frederick Herzberg: two-factor theory

The research of Herzberg was directed at people in places of work. It was based on questioning people within organizations in different jobs, at different levels, to establish:

(a) those factors that led to extreme dissatisfaction with the job, the environment and the workplace, and

(b) those factors that led to extreme satisfaction with the job, the environment and the workplace.

The factors giving rise to satisfaction he called motivators. Those giving rise to dissatisfaction he called hygiene factors (see Figure 7.3).

The motivators that emerged were: achievement, recognition, the nature of the work itself, level of responsibility, advancement and opportunities for personal growth and development. These factors are all related to the actual content of the work and job responsibilities. These factors, where present in a working situation, led to high levels and degrees of satisfaction on the part of the workforce.

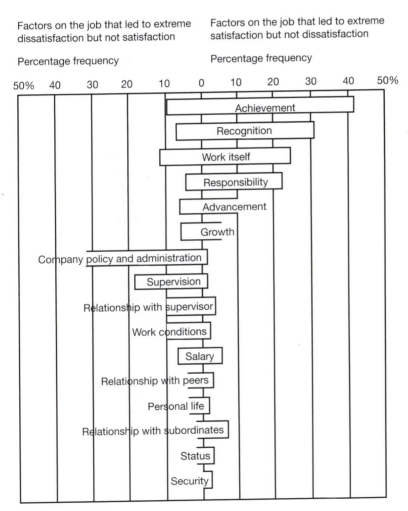

Figure 7.3 Two-factor theory
Source: Herzberg (1960).

The hygiene factors or dissatisfiers that he identified were as follows: company policy and administration; supervision and management style; levels of pay and salary; relationships with peers; relationships with subordinates; status; and security. These are factors that where they are good or adequate will not in themselves make people satisfied; by ensuring that they are indeed adequate, dissatisfaction is removed but satisfaction is not in itself generated. On the other hand, where these aspects were bad, extreme dissatisfaction was experienced by all respondents. Organizations that failed to provide adequate hygiene factors tend to have high levels of conflict, absenteeism and labour turnover and low general morale.

The work of Herzberg encourages concentration on the following.

- Management style, attitude and approach to staff that is based on integrity, honesty and trust, whatever the nature, limitations or technology concerned in the work itself.
- The working environment that is to be comfortable, functional and suitable in human terms, again whatever the operational constraints and limitations may be.
- General factors of status and importance that ensure that every member of staff is respected, believed in, treated equally and given opportunity for change, development and advancement within the organization.
- Effective and professional operational relationships between members of staff that, in turn, promote profitable and successful activities across the entire organization. This includes recognizing the existence of barriers and potential conflicts between departments, divisions and functions and taking steps to provide effective counters to these.
- Administrative support and control processes and mechanisms that are to be designed, both to make life easier for those working at the front line while at the same time providing the necessary management information. This particularly refers to the nature and effectiveness of the roles and functions of corporate headquarters and the relationships between these and the frontline operations indicated.
- The work itself, and how it is divided up. There is particular reference here to those parts of the work that are looked upon with disfavour but which nevertheless must be carried out adequately and effectively (see above).
- Security of tenure. This ensures that people are employed on a continuous basis as far as that is possible. At the same time, steps have to be taken to ensure that there is a steady and open flow of information so that when changes do become necessary the staff concerned are both forewarned and positively responsive.
- Concentration on people's innate drives and ambitions. The purpose here is to make sure that, as far as possible, organizations match what they have to offer to potential staff, and potential staff have enough information to seek out the kinds of organizations that they would like to work for (see Box 7.3).

V. Vroom: expectancy theories

In essence, this approach to motivation draws the relationship between the efforts put into particular activities by individuals, and the nature of the expectations of the rewards that they perceive that they will get from these efforts.

This is clearly centred on the individual. It relates to the ways in which the individual sees or perceives the environment. In particular, it relates to his view of work; his expectations, aspirations, ambitions and desired outcomes from it; and the extent to which these can be satisfied at the workplace or carrying out the occupation in question.

For example, the individual may have no particular regard for the job that he is currently doing but will nevertheless work productively and effectively at it, and be committed to it, because it is a stepping stone in his view to greater things – and these are the expectations that he has of it and which constitute the basis of his efforts and the quality of these efforts. This is compounded, however, by other factors – the actual capacities and aptitudes of the individual concerned on the one hand, and the nature of the work environment on the other. It is also limited by the perceptions and expectations that the commissioner of the work has on the part of the person who is actually carrying it out. There is a distinction to be drawn between the effort put into performance and the effectiveness of that effort – hard work, conscientiously carried out, does not always produce effective activity; the effort has to be directed and targeted. There has also to

---

Box 7.3: Recruitment of expert staff in the central banking sector

For many years, the central banking sector has lamented its inability to attract, recruit and retain highly qualified and expert economists, financiers and analysts. People with these qualities and expertise are essential for the effective operation of the central banking sector. The central banking sector is responsible for the money supply, the relationships between currencies and the maintenance of price stability within, and across, national boundaries.

The problem that the sector always felt that it had was its inability to compete for staff who had this expertise with the commercial banks. This expertise is also highly sought after in the commercial banking sector; and because of their inability to offer the same levels of rewards, the central banks therefore found themselves, in many cases, faced with shortages of expert staff.

Only belatedly did some of the central banks start to look at the problem differently. While the levels of pay and reward on offer in the central banks were not as high as those in the commercial banking sector, nevertheless they were very good. There were also additional and different opportunities in the central banking sector as follows:

- the opportunity to influence national policy;
- the opportunity to work in a distinctive and critical sector;
- the opportunity to gain a distinctive and unique experience;
- the opportunity to move between one central bank and others.

Once these opportunities were crystallized and understood, the process of targeting those with the required expertise became much more straightforward. People could be attracted who wanted these opportunities (and not just money); and the intrinsic rewards on offer in terms of uniqueness, distinctiveness and the particular nature of variety were very high indeed.

The lesson is therefore that if staff cannot be attracted through one line of approach, there is always the possibility of looking at the particular issue from other points of view.

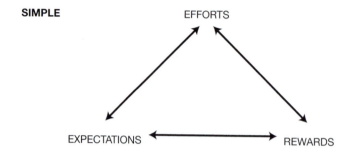

Figure 7.4 Expectancy theory
Source: Luthans (1986).

be a match between the rewards expected and those that are offered – a reward is merely a value judgement placed on something offered in return for effort and if this is not valued by the receiver it has no effect on their motivation (see Figure 7.4).

Consequently there has to be an understanding of the nature of the motives and expectations of the individual, related to an ability to satisfy these on the part of the organization if it is to address effectively the issue of motivation. The approach required is therefore to take both an enlightened and specific view of what constitutes job satisfaction (rather than assuming that it exists, or exists in certain occupations at least); and an understanding of the processes of perception and the nature of reward in relation to the aspirations of those conducting the work.

The components of the expectation–effort–reward mixture are as follows.

- **Personal ambition**: the inner drive to make progress and the rewards that this progress brings with it.
- **Professional ambition**: the drive and desire to make it to the top of the chosen occupation.

- **Situation**: the ability of the situation to provide the rewards expected and anticipated.
- **Performance**: in which individuals gravitate towards those tasks that are seen to produce a greater level of desired rewards.
- **Perception**: understanding that most of the drive comes from within the individual rather than being imposed or directed; the highest levels of individual motivation are achieved in workplaces where the conditions are created that enable this to take place.

Motivation and achievement

An alternative view of the expectation–effort–reward mixture consists of restating this as motivation, achievement and rewards. Drives for particular goals are enhanced by the capability to achieve them and the rewards that are to accrue as the result.

These rewards are a combination of:

- **Economic**: monetary pay for carrying out the job, for special achievement, for responsibility and accountability; monetary pay and rewards expected to continue and improve in line with the relationship between organization and individual, in terms of both current and future occupations and also loyalty and commitment. Economic rewards meet the needs and expectations of individuals, and also reflect the value in which they are held by the organization.
- **Job satisfaction**: intrinsic rewards attained by individuals in terms of the quality of their work, the range and depth of expertise used and the results achieved.
- **Work content**: the relative contribution to the output of the organization as a whole and the feelings of success and achievement that arise from this. As stated elsewhere, operating a small part of the production process or administrative system tends to be limited in its capability to satisfy this part of the requirement for achievement.
- **Job title**: certain job titles give images of prestige as well as a description and summary of what the work is, and the respect and esteem in which it is held by the individual and her peers and social circles.
- **Personal development**: the extent to which the individual's capabilities are being used (or limited in their use); and the extent to which alternative means of achievement and reward may become apparent through the development of both current and new expertise.
- **Status**: the relative mark of value placed on the individual's rank, role, expertise and job by those whose views and opinions they value. This invariably includes those of the particular organization, because of the nature of the continuing relationship between the two. It is also likely to include, again, the views of social and professional circles.
- **Trappings**: these are the outward marks of achievement and success, material and visible benefits by which others can recognize its extent. They include:

  (a) benefits – such as cars (both the fact that a car as been issued and also the value of the car itself); other business technology; business trips; sabbaticals; course and seminar attendance; health care. They are marks of achievement when presented in professional and social circles;

(b) autonomy – the ability of the individual to set their own patterns of work; to come and go as they see fit, to work from home; to attend the place of work at weekends or other quiet periods in order to be able to work without interruptions (as distinct from having to attend during the same time as everyone else); to make work arrangements based on sole individual judgement without reference to higher authorities; to exhibit absolute, professional or technical expertise and judgement;

(c) secretaries, personal assistants and personal departments – normally integral to the nature of the work, they also constitute a trapping in so far as they are an outward representation to the rest of the organization of the value and importance of the individual's work;

(d) accessibility – in many organizations, the inability to get to see someone, either because of their rank or because of their workloads, constitutes a mark of achievement, often perverse (see Box 7.4).

Box 7.4: Scott Adams (1)

'I have always thought I was staffed by idiots but now I'm not so sure. After our last reorganization conference I inadvertently came across the name of my new HR representative. I decided to call her just so that she would know that I knew who she was. I called the company operator to get her number. The conversation went as follows:

Me:	I'd like the number for my HR representative please.
Operator:	I'm sorry, that number is unlisted.
Me:	I don't want her home number, I want her office number.
Operator:	Right. It's unlisted.
Me:	I'm an employee. She's my HR rep. I need to call her.
Operator:	I'm sorry.
Me:	I can't talk to my HR rep?
Operator:	Oh, you can talk to her if she calls you, but I can't give you her number. Sorry (Click).

Undaunted, I walked over to the last rumoured location for HR. I found a locked office at 10.00 o'clock in the morning, and a list of 800 numbers taped to the door.

I copied down the 'If you need assistance' one and went back to the office. I called the number and tried the first option, which led to four more options, the first of which led to three more. I tried the first one again – it disconnected. I called back and tried the 'dial back' option – it disconnected me. Not easily dissuaded, I called every single option. They all disconnected me.

So at my Fortune 50 company, we have HR reps with unlisted office phone numbers and an HR "help"-line that disconnects all callers with no human intervention. In fact, it would seem that there are no humans in HR.'

Source: Scott Adams (1998) *The Joy of Work* – Boxtree.

The Hawthorne Studies

The Hawthorne Studies were carried out between 1924 and 1932. They took their name from the Hawthorne Works of the Western Electrical Company in Chicago where the research was conducted. The original objective was to ascertain the relationships between the physical working environment and operational productivity. However, the main findings were in terms of the social environment of work – membership of groups, both formal and informal; relationships between workers and supervision; relationships between workers and organization; and the degree of attention and interest shown by the organization to its staff.

The work was carried out by George Elton Mayo (1880–1949), an Australian academic. He was Professor of Industrial Research at Harvard Business School, and an authority on industrial fatigue, labour turnover and accidents, and health and safety. He was called in by the Western Electrical Company to advise on the results of a study that had already been carried out by the company into the effects of lighting on productive output and staff morale. One group – the core group – had the lighting levels in which it had to work varied; the other – the control group – had constant lighting levels. The output of both groups rose consistently over the period of the experiment (1924–27). The output of the core group rose whether the lighting levels were increased or diminished. The output of the control group where the lighting levels remained constant also rose.

Four aspects were addressed: employee attitudes; group attitudes; personal factors; and physical conditions. The findings were as follows.

Employee attitudes

Employee attitudes overall were formed on the basis of an assessment of relative satisfaction and dissatisfaction of work, and this, in turn, was based on:

* social organization of the company, both formal and informal, including the formation and membership of cliques and other groups;
* organizational policies and directives;
* the position, work content and status of the individual;
* outside demands and commitments placed on employees.

Group attitudes

* The need to be part of the work group is very strong.
* The pressures to conform to the norms and standards of the group (as distinct from those of the organization) are very strong.
* Attitudes are shaped and influenced by the group – both between members and also in relation to the work.
* These pressures and needs are strong motivators, especially in the ways of working and its organization. The individual is more responsive to peer pressure than organizational and managerial incentives and exhortations.

Personal attitudes

* The motivation to seek out particular types of work, the determination to follow a particular career, to work in particular sectors, occupations, trades, professions and crafts.

- The motivation to apply for specific jobs, with specific employers, to complete the application process and to subject oneself to the recruitment and selection processes.
- The motivation to accept job offers, to accept the salary/occupation/prospects mixes of particular organizations.
- The motivation to turn up for work on the first day.
- The motivation to turn up for work on the second day and to continue turning up on a daily basis; and to start and continue to produce effective and successful work on behalf of the organization.

Physical conditions

- The response to the physical conditions was much more complex. Whenever the lighting levels were adjusted, productivity went up. This too was the case when other changes were made, including the introduction and withdrawal of breaks (productivity even rose when breaks were withdrawn by the experimenters). In the particular case, the conclusion was drawn that those involved were responding to special treatment. They were the centre of attention; they had a good relationship with the researchers; and by being placed in separate accommodation, they felt special and distinctive, with consequent increases in morale and self-worth. So long as they understood the changes in the physical conditions, they were happy.
- Beyond this, the experimenters found that people working in any situation tended to operate in ways that were both comfortable as well as productive.

Both from the findings of the Hawthorne experiments, and also in relation to wider studies of motivation, there are lessons to be drawn which have direct applications for the effective management of people (see Box 7.5).

Box 7.5: Scott Adams (2)

'This incident happened to a former colleague at a bank. Let's call him Bob. Bob was assigned an urgent project with a very high priority which involved designing a new product in a very short period of time. Bob worked 18-hour days for weeks. He treated weekends just like weekdays, only going home to sleep.

The project was completed on time and Bob's boss, who we will call "Satan", was congratulated heartily by the bank's executives.

The next week was time for Bob's performance appraisal.

The appraisal meeting took five minutes. Satan sat Bob down and said: 'Bob, I think you may be a little disappointed with the rating I have given you. Generally speaking, you have been working well. However, there are two problems which need to be addressed. First, I have never seen you go a whole day without unbuttoning your shirt and loosening your tie. Second, and this is more important – you have a habit of stretching out at your desk and kicking your shoes off. Frankly that is offensive. If it weren't for these problems, you would rate as solid "competent". As it is, you are scruffy and I'm afraid that means you are "developing".

Bob is now talking with employment agencies.'

Source: Scott Adams (1998) *The Joy of Work* – Boxtree.

Job and work design

When considering job and work design from the point of view of human behaviour and motivation, it is essential to try to reconcile the organization's often conflicting operational, technical and professional requirements into sets of activities – jobs and occupations – that are effective, productive and satisfying, both from an occupational and personal point of view (see Figure 7.5).

This may be reinforced by the use of job titles, which may be either demeaning and dissatisfying, or else a reflection of status or expertise. It is a key organizational responsibility to address the issues – both positive and also negative – that these matters raise.

It is then necessary to empathize – if those responsible for the design and ordering of work know themselves that what is proposed will be repetitive, boring and dissatisfying, then the likely output is loss of morale.

It is within this context that job enrichment, job rotation, job enlargement and empowerment activities are to be considered. If carried out effectively, motivation and commitment can be generated in any staff or occupational group, whatever the working situation and provided that the behavioural satisfaction aspect is also addressed. It is also to be noted that the converse is true – that where jobs and occupations are not

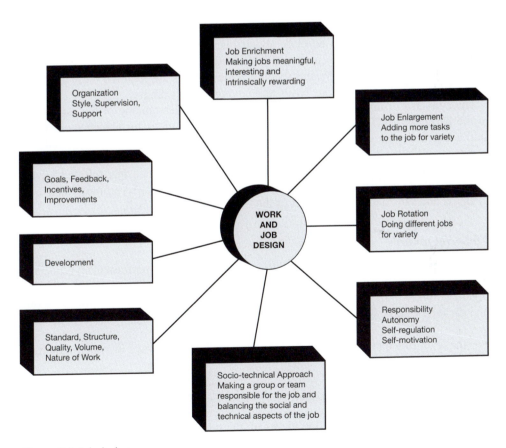

Figure 7.5 Job design

effective, productive and satisfying, demotivation and demoralization occurs whatever the interests inherent in the particular profession may be.

The other prerequisite for effective job and work design is the existence of effective channels of communication, the presence of constant feedback and absolute knowledge of results. The outcome of this is a clarity of purpose both of the occupation in question, and also of the context in which it is carried out.

Rewards

Rewards are a major means by which organizations set and maintain their standards of activity, attitude and behaviour. It is important to establish what they are given for. This covers the area of achievement, success, loyalty and conformity and relates both to individual and team performance.

Each organization sets its own reward mix within these broad boundaries. The relationship between motivation, effort and reward from the organization's point of view is thus clearly indicated. Those working there are shown the pathways to achievement in the particular situation. The opportunity is afforded either to accept or reject these pathways.

Demotivation and disaffection occur when the pathways are not clearly indicated or if the achievements at their end are not then duly rewarded. This also happens in individual cases where they were taken on by the organization or given tasks to do within it on the basis of misunderstandings of what was expected, or what the rewards were to be. It is essential to be clear about this. There is no point, for example, in recruiting or retaining task-oriented staff in situations where rewards are for loyalty and time service (or vice versa). Where specific achievements are required these are to be stated in clear and unambiguous terms and rewarded accordingly.

The converse of this is the requirement for a clear understanding of the aspirations of the particular staff employed. It is no use offering rewards for achievement if the staff concerned value continuity and longevity with rewards based on loyalty – and vice versa.

Any reward must be issued if the person or team concerned has fulfilled all the requirements necessary to achieve it. The reward should be issued promptly and with gladness and satisfaction on the part of the organization to its staff.

Financial rewards

Money – in the form of wages and salary – is the reward for performance, especially and ideally, effective and successful performance. Wages and salaries are paid by organizations to individuals to reward them for bringing their expertise into the situation and for their efforts. The payment made must therefore reflect:

* the level of expertise brought by the individual, and the ways in which they have been required to apply it;
* the quality and intensity of effort;
* the effectiveness of individual performance; and the effectiveness of overall performance;
* the value that the organization places on the presence of the particular expertise;
* the value placed by the individual on their expertise;

Box 7.6: Perceptions and financial rewards

There is a strongly perceived relationship between pay and job importance. A chief executive who declares an annual salary of £20,000 will be widely considered not to have a great deal of responsibility or authority. A marketing officer on £80,000 a year will be generally perceived to have a responsible and high-powered job. This now extends to the individual – if someone perceives themselves to be on 'only £x' it affects their self-esteem and self-worth because it is a statement of limited value. The converse is also true – where people can state that they are on 'good money' this underlines feelings of high value.

- the expectations of the individual for particular levels of reward;
- the anticipation of continuity and improvement in reward levels.

These must then be set in a wider context.

Herzberg makes the point that money is of limited value as a motivator even where pay levels are good, but that it is very demotivating when pay levels are bad and do not meet expectations (see Box 7.6).

Continuity

In conditions of relative stability and permanence, people are more disposed to accept or trade off between current levels of reward and the certainty of continuity. In the UK, over the period from 1945 until the late 1970s, this was virtually explicit in many organizations – that while at no stage would reward levels be particularly high, they would be steady, would gradually improve and would last the whole of the working life and beyond by paying a retirement pension.

In times of turbulence and uncertainty the drives are more complex as follows:

- one drive is for higher immediate rewards as a hedge against the uncertainties of the longer-term future;
- another drive is to negotiate an agreed level of pay and reward in return for assurances over job security;
- there are opportunities to take periods of leave of absence and sabbaticals, again in return for longer-term job security and the prospect of substantial work when the period of turbulence has subsided.

Expectations and obligations

Problems are greatly reduced in the money area where expectations and obligations are clearly set out, understood and accepted by both organizations and individuals at the outset (see Figure 7.6). Problems occur where the individual has not understood the nature of effort required to achieve rewards; and where the organization has not made clear (either through ignorance, accident or deliberately) the levels of effort and commitment that it requires.

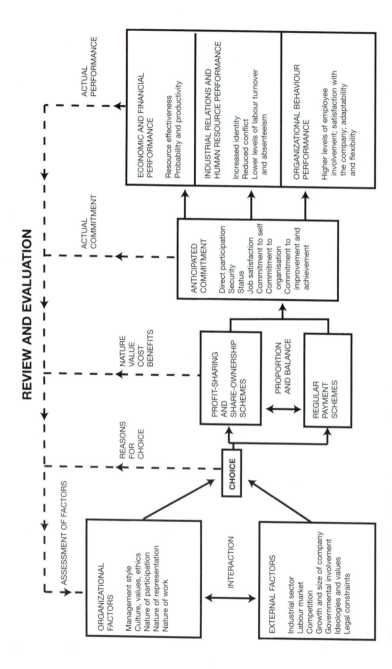

Figure 7.6 The relationship between pay and performance

People in particular organizations have expectations of payment methods. For example, the sales person may expect all or part of their reward to be in the form of bonus or commission because this has worked well for them in the past. They therefore perceive themselves to be able to earn much more through this means than through a simple salary and to control their own earnings level. Operative and clerical staff may expect part of their work to be paid as overtime; this is again perceived to enhance the ability to earn and also underlines the intrinsic feeling of value based on 'you are so important to us, you must stay and work; we cannot possibly allow you to go home yet – and we will pay you extra'. Problems occur in these areas when the facility is introduced, institutionalized, becomes expected and is then withdrawn.

Frustration

Frustration occurs when the relationship between expectation, effort and reward is skewed for reasons outside the individual's control. It is caused by a range of factors.

- The removal of anticipated rewards during the effort phase. For example, an individual may pursue qualifications in the expectation, anticipation – even near certainty – that they will receive job promotion, enhancement and opportunities when they have finished their course. Towards the end of the course, if the organization is taken over, or moves into new fields, or if the individual's superior changes jobs, the reward disappears.
- The cancellation of anticipated rewards through arbitrary (or even rational) action by the organization. To take a similar example, the achievement of qualifications may have led in the past to pay rises – and then there is a change of policy during the course of the individual's studies and the rewards are now no longer available.
- When promised or indicated, opportunities for training and development do not materialize for whatever reason.
- When the intrinsic satisfactions afforded by the job do not meet the wider needs (especially esteem and economic) of the individual. This has occurred in recent years in the UK with public services and occupations such as teaching, nursing and social work.
- When the nature of opportunities afforded and anticipated do not match up based on misperceptions on either part.
- When the individual knows or strongly believes that they are not being offered the opportunities that their talents and qualities merit; and this occurs especially when the individual feels that this is as a result of the perceptions of their superior.
- Where opportunities are simply not available, causing individuals to have to look elsewhere for their future prospects.
- Restriction of the capability to act by rules, regulations and procedures.

Motivation as a process

Each element and factor indicated contributes to the pay and reward process. By the very nature of the continuity of the wage–work bargain, this in itself is a continuous process. As such it requires constant attention and maintenance. If this is not done, people perceive that they are being taken for granted and if this persists, it leads to feelings of being neglected. The process is therefore maintained in ways equivalent to anything else.

- With regularity, consisting of regular and frequent reviews; stated occasions for rises; stated levels or criteria for rises and improvements; and ensuring that these are paid in full on the required dates.
- Rewarding enhanced performance, either because people have developed and enhanced their skills, knowledge and expertise and therefore their value to the organization; or because the organization has had a successful, effective and profitable year. In the latter case especially, there is a current consensus that the staff of organizations should receive their fair share of the rewards that have been generated by their efforts. This applies equally to the best public services and not-for-profit activities, rewarding staff from the proceeds of enhanced effectiveness of performance (for example, the enlargement of jobs or workload that enables the organization to reduce staff levels), or from other efficiencies and savings (for example, in premises charges or through the simplification of procedures).
- Issuing regular symbols of value. Part of this includes praise and recognition. Genuine recognition is enhanced through the use of small, creative, varied and frequent rewards issued to everyone regardless of rank, status or occupation, and based on the total contribution of everyone to organizational performance.
- Ensuring that pay levels are kept up to the organization's own absolute standards and taking remedial action where this has been allowed to slip as soon as possible. Further, it may have been necessary in the past to reduce or depress pay levels for reasons of organization performance; when things get back on track, the staff should be rewarded for their loyalty and commitment over the difficult period.
- Never losing sight of the absolute value of the staff to the organization and their need to be valued of which one of the main manifestations is the nature and level of financial reward over the long-term. (See Table 7.1.)

This constitutes a basis of the relationship between motivation and money. Some general points should now be made. Monetary reward does not make a job more satisfying or interesting except in the very short-term, though it may, and does, lead to

Table 7.1 Payment methods and motivation

Method	Aspects of Motivation
Weekly cash wages	Meets traditions and expectations of industrial and commercial sectors and other parts of society also.
Monthly salary into bank account	May be status attached to being 'salaried'.
Time rate	Encourages attendance for particular periods; overtime may be desired and available outside set times.
Piece rates	Encourages production volume (and possibly also quality and deadline achievement).
Flexitime	Encourages attendance, especially where there is the opportunity for overtime or time off once sufficient time has been accrued.
Commission, bonuses	Relates performance output to payment level.
Profit-related pay	Relates to organization performance and payment levels; difficulties lie where profit levels are outside the control of the staff.
Performance-related pay and merit pay	Relates own performance with payment levels; difficulties lie with setting, assessing and validating performance objectives and targets, especially in unquantifiable areas.

high levels of commitment (again, especially over the short-term) if the individual has an overriding need to earn. Moreover, lack of adequate financial reward for a job that is otherwise very satisfying leads to frustration and stress and the individual struggles to reconcile the conflicting pressures of loving the job but not being able to afford to stay in it.

Attendance and other bonuses and allowances

These have been used in many forms and in a variety of situations over the years. At their best, they reward (or give the perception of rewarding) special efforts and commitments such as working at night, at weekends and over bank and public holidays and away from home.

In many cases otherwise, however, they simply demonstrate the limitations of this approach – and the consequent limitation of money as a motivator if other types of reward and achievement are not present. For example:

- The bank room wiring operations at the Hawthorne Works actively conspired against their organization's bonus system because they perceived that it would be changed to their disadvantage if they demonstrated the full capacity to which they could work.
- CountyCare care homes stated that all unauthorized absence would have to be taken as annual leave. The company reasoned that this would stop people not turning up to work for no good reason. Very quickly, however, people started to ring in sick, and subsequently they did this even for holidays, going to the trouble of getting doctors' notes, and then claiming leave allowances as payment in lieu at the year end.
- In the 1980s and 1990s, the Allied Irish Bank gave an additional week's holiday to every member of staff who took no time off for sickness during the previous year. Once people had had a day's sickness, they therefore would tend to take at least another five working days to ensure that they did not miss out anyway.
- The Batchelor's Food Company undertook a policy which stated that anyone who was more than 10 minutes late for work would lose half a day's pay. The result was that anyone who was more than 10 minutes late – whether at the start of the day or returning after lunch – would simply take the rest of the period off.
- In the early twenty-first century, at the height of the banking crisis, managers and executives nevertheless sought reassurance that their bonuses would be paid. These bonuses had been earned during periods in which trading volumes had shown surpluses, and the organizations themselves had declared operating profits. Now, the demand for the bonus was that it was an integral part of the reward package; effectively, that it should be paid just for turning up to work.

Profit-related pay

The purpose of relating pay to profit is part of the process of targeting the reward package and also the motivation and commitment effort. By combining the two elements, the line of reasoning is that all staff are focused on the greater good of all, and the ending profitability of the organization. Profit-related pay is also perceived to give employees a direct stake in their own future, and it is supposed to help build a positive mutual identity. Profit-related pay also ties wages and salaries to collective and individual performance.

Profit-related elements come in two main forms. The simplest of these is to allocate a percentage, or proportion, or amount from the surplus generated by the organization, and to share this out. For maximum equality, this will be as a percentage of salary to everyone. The other approach is to offer shares and equity in the organization; the employees therefore become investors in their own future.

The relationship between profit, ownership, commitment and pay is a constant theme of the Excellence Studies. In the UK, the Bell–Hanson Report of 1989, researching 113 publicly quoted companies, found that profit-share companies out-performed others by an average of 27 per cent on returns on capital, earnings per share and profit and sales growth.

For best results, the scheme must be believed in, valued and understood by all concerned. The overall purpose of profit-related pay is to reward effort and achievement on the part of the staff. Staff must also clearly understand that this payment will be forthcoming if the organization has a good year; and that it will not be forthcoming if for any reason the organization has difficulties or does not make profits.

Above all, profit-related pay is never to be used as a means of cutting wage and salary bills. Its purpose is to target these and to reward efforts not penalize them. Its general effect is to put up wage and salary bills – and as stated in the text above, this both raises the expectations of the individuals concerned, and is also a quite legitimate means by which the organization can raise its expectations of the individuals.

Conclusions

The standpoint taken is that people work better when highly motivated, there is a direct relationship between quality of performance and levels of motivation, and that volume and quality of work declines when motivation lowers or when demotivation is present. The need to motivate and be motivated is continuous and constant. Some specific conclusions may be drawn.

- Motivation comes partly from within the individual and partly from the particular situation. It is therefore both constant and also subject to continuous adaptation.
- Value, esteem and respect are basic human requirements extending to all places of work and all occupations (and indeed, to every walk of life). The key features of this are the integrity of relationships, levels of knowledge and understanding, general prevailing attitudes (whether positive or negative) and the nature of rewards, including pay.
- All people have expectations based on their understanding of particular situations, and that they will be drawn to or driven from these in anticipation of rewards and outcomes.
- People respond positively to equality and fairness of treatment, and negatively when these are not present.
- People respond positively to variety, development and opportunities when they know or perceive it to be in their interests to do so. They are less likely to respond to genuine opportunities if they do not understand or perceive them as such.
- People respond positively when they know the attitudes, behaviour, values and ways of work that are required; and negatively or less favourably when these are not apparent or not strong.

- People need constant attention to their individual wants and needs and will seek this from many sources, including work. If the work is demotivating, they will seek this attention elsewhere.

The key to positive motivation is the establishment of a high level of mutual trust, commitment and responsibility. The main obligation here lies with the organization. Individuals may be expected to respond positively when these are present. They may not be expected from individuals when the organization is itself uncommitted to this, or where it takes an expedient, confrontational and adversarial view of its staff.

8   Communication

Introduction

Effective communication is based on information:

- the volume that is available;
- its quality;
- the means and media by which it is transmitted and received;
- the use to which it is put;
- its integrity;
- the level of integrity of the wider situation. ˙

Communications and information feed the quality of all human relations in organizations. Good communications underline good relations and enhance the general quality of working life, motivation and morale. Bad and inadequate communications lead to frustration and they enhance feelings of alienation, lack of identity and unity (see Box 8.1).

It is therefore necessary to consider each aspect of the communication process in turn. This is followed by a discussion of the elements that contribute to their quality and effective usage.

Box 8.1: What communication is not

Effective communication is none of the following:

- the passive provision of information, however great the volume and quality;
- all-staff e-mails sent in isolation from what is important to the receivers;
- website links that cannot be fully or regularly accessed;
- meetings and forums that are held without specific purposes or agendas;
- staff consultation and communication exercises in which the results and feedback are ignored.

The key lesson then is the response of the receiver. The purpose of all communications is either to elicit a response, or to transmit information. Anything that lacks a key, sharp or clear purpose is ineffective. In some cases also, this is seen as malicious or toxic (see below).

One-way communication

This is where edicts are issued by organizations to their employees, usually without any regard for their effect. This is invariably due to ignorance. This effect is always dysfunctional. It occurs only in the worst of organizations, with the most alienated of workforce, and the most insular of managements and directorates.

Two-way communication

This is the dialogue process, the engaging in a communication-and-response process, the results of which are understanding, enlightenment, effective action and progress. It takes place in written and non-verbal, as well as oral, formats and constitutes the relationship between any sender and recipient of a communication.

Upward and downward communication

Downward

This is the use of communication hierarchies and structures for communication purposes. Information is cascaded down from directors to senior managers, from senior managers to junior managers and then to supervisors and their staff. This is also the means of promulgation of policies and directives, instructions, employee handbooks, rules and regulations, reports, memoranda, newsletters; and the focus of electronic information systems. Use is made of committees, structures and methods (see Box 8.2).

Upward

The nature, content and volume of upward communication arises from management style. At the extreme, where management is absent or inaccessible, this is limited to formalized channels such as joint consultative committees, joint negotiating committees and the raising of disputes and grievances. At the opposite end of the scale, where managers and supervisors 'walk the job' and have regular continuous contact with their staff, a greater, regular and more accurate use for volume and quality of information is gained.

Channels of communication

These are as follows.

Formal

These are the hierarchies, systems, procedures and committee structures referred to above. This also includes the use and operation of written procedures and policies. It also includes the use of electronic systems.

Informal

These are the ad hoc gatherings that take place between people all the time at every place of work. This includes scribbled notes, post-its, canteen and tea room gatherings.

Box 8.2: Downward communication in the telecommunications industry

One of the largest domestic telecommunications companies engaged in a restructuring programme. At the end of the exercise, staff needed to be briefed on how things were to change, and what their new roles were going to be.

The company decided on a 'communications cascade' method of breaking the news, meaning that top management would agree on the core message; and this would then be transmitted to departmental managers and section heads who, in turn, would brief their staff.

Accordingly, the company's top management gathered at a five-star hotel for a week to decide what the message was, and to agree the content, format and media to be used.

Departmental managers and section heads were briefed at two-star hotels over a weekend. They then took the message back to the rest of their staff, whose briefings were held in regular staff meetings (duration 2–3 hours). Where this was not possible, some sections of the organization held these meetings in church and village halls.

The documentation was then presented to the staff to be taken away and read. These papers were handed to the staff in bright new carrier bags carrying the company logo. Those staff who had them put the papers in their briefcases and discarded the carrier bags. Those who were forced to use the carrier bags turned them inside out so that the company logo could not be seen.

Meeting sometime afterwards, the company's top management wondered what had gone wrong.

The key lesson is that downward communication of this kind has to carry a fundamental integrity. Clearly, where organizational change has been decided and is to be implemented, staff look for a clear sense of purpose, direction and priority. However, the delivery of the message itself has to carry a fundamental integrity – otherwise, the effect is lost. In this case, the means of delivery carried a much stronger message than the communication itself.

Above all, it includes the organizational grapevine – the things that people gossip and chat about and other general discussion sessions.

Edicts and proclamations

From time to time, organizations and their top managers need to make pronouncements on specific issues. In many cases, staff will welcome this – the effective use of edicts and proclamations is to set people's minds at rest, reassure them and tell them clearly of the organizational direction for the future. It is also necessary, from time to time, to use top management pronouncements to convey bad news; and again, if this is carried out with clarity and integrity, people at least know where they stand (see Box 8.3).

Box 8.3: Edicts and proclamations

The strength of any leadership and management style is directly related to the effectiveness of its communications and the communication processes used. As long as there is a clearly known and understood psychological contract (see Chapter 3 above) and as long as the nature and content of communications reflects and supports this, each reinforces the other. For example:

- Virgin: any statement made by Richard Branson on behalf of the Virgin organization is eagerly awaited and listened to with great care by all of the company's staff.
- Body Shop: when the Body Shop was taken over by L'Oreal, one of the gaps that the new owners had to fill was the regular communications that were issued from Anita Roddick, the Body Shop founder.

On the other hand, edicts and proclamations (whatever the organization) have always to carry a fundamental integrity. When this integrity is neither present, known or understood, problems do occur. For example:

- Royal Bank of Scotland: following the company crisis and restructuring in late 2008, business analysts started to become concerned that RBS would have to lose thousands of jobs. This caused the company leadership to issue a statement saying: *'Rumours of job losses have been greatly exaggerated. There are no plans for substantial job losses for the present.'* Two month's later, RBS announced 10,000 job losses; and a further 10,000 job losses were announced later in 2009.

The problems with RBS were compounded by the fact that the 'channel of communication' used was effectively the media. Staff at the company found themselves learning more from the media than from the company itself. In this particular case, therefore, the problems of the company were compounded by the lack of effective communication.

Consultation

Consultative means of communication are used in the implementation of decisions and policies. The purpose is to ensure that those being consulted understand what is required of them and why, and the opportunities and threats of a particular situation (see Figure 8.1). It is also a reflection of the requirement that people have for confidence in those in charge and in the directions that they propose. Effective consultation and the associated processes normally reflect the fact that what is proposed has been well thought out and tested.

Genuine consultation is also the means by which any flaws in decision-making processes or the implementation of particular proposals may nevertheless be raised. However well or thoroughly an issue has been thought through, it must be capable of wide general scrutiny and examination.

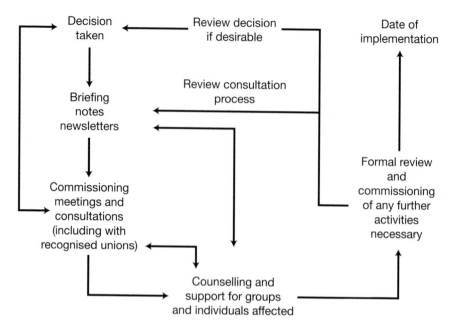

Figure 8.1 Consultation

Genuine consultation and participation require effective and clear decision-making processes that have both to satisfy the openness and cooperation indicated, but without discussing, stifling and analysing everything to the point of inertia. Effective participation must meet the criteria of both effective communication and effective decision-making.

Committees

Committees are constituted for a variety of reasons. From the point of view of communication, the important point is that they should enhance both the quality and value rather than act as a blockage. If this is to happen, the purpose, scheduling of meetings, size, composition, agenda, control and recording must be managed. The ultimate test of the value of any committee is in its output. If this is either not forthcoming or not effective, then alternative means should be found of tackling the issues that the committee or committee system of the organization is supposed to be facing.

Committees have positive and negative uses, and both are quite deliberately engaged by organizations from time to time. Positive uses are:

- monitoring, reviewing and evaluating projects and operations;
- strengthening the institutions of staff management and employee relations;
- managing the liaison between customers, clients and project work;
- information dissemination and discussion.

The negative uses of committees are:

Box 8.4: Royal Commissions

Royal Commissions are constituted by Parliament to carry out a full investigation into specific substantial matters.

That, at least, is their stated purpose. In practice, it is known throughout the political establishment that Royal Commissions are carried out when there is no collective political will to do anything about the matter in hand. On the other hand, the political leadership finds itself unable unilaterally to drop or ignore the particular matter.

The result is a lengthy and expensive piece of work normally resulting in a large and obscure report being presented. By the time the report is presented, events have moved on. Nevertheless, it is perceived by the political establishment that 'honour has been satisfied' by being able to point to the fact that a large volume of work has indeed been carried out and a 'substantial' report produced.

Source: Anthony Jay and Jonathan Lynn (1980)
The Complete Yes Minister – BBC.

- to neutralize particular individuals and groups by giving them something to do that is of little, or no, value;
- avoiding confrontation of problems by 'putting them out to committee';
- giving them a woolly or imprecise remit so that whatever is done is never quite complete;
- using a group or committee to 'neutralize' bad or awkward staff by giving them high-volume, low-value work.

Used effectively, committees can be energized to become a major driving force of organizational progress and advancement. Used negatively, they become an expensive waste of time, and the work carried out becomes worthless (see Box 8.4).

Elements necessary for effective communication

These are as follows.

Clarity of purpose on the part of the sender or initiator

This means addressing the questions of what the message is, why it is being sent; the receivers and their likely reactions and responses; the possible range of reactions and responses; what is to be achieved as the result; and what the barriers to this achievement might be. This is the basis of 'saying what is meant and meaning what is said'.

Integrity of purpose

This is the relationship between what is said and what is meant. This means using clear, concise and unambiguous terms so that there is no doubt about the impact on the receiver. The message is honest and straightforward, subject to as little interpretation and uncertainty as can be achieved by the sender.

Integrity (or lack of it) in communications reinforces the general ways of working of the organization, and also the wider state of mutual trust, respect and esteem held by all concerned for each other.

Specific problems with the integrity of communication arise when:

- there is a lack of understanding of the fundamental importance leading to the issuing of communications;
- there is a known and understood state of ignorance on the part of the receivers, and the communication does nothing to address this;
- the people issuing the communications are known to be dishonest or incomplete in the ways in which they deal with people;
- the language of the message is deliberately obscure;
- the language of the message is deliberately designed to inform people that what they are being told is not the full truth;
- the language of the message is disrespectful, condescending or threatening (see Box 8.5).

Box 8.5: Robert Christie

Robert Christie worked for a merchant bank conducting investment appraisals on major overseas projects.

At short notice he was assigned an urgent project with a very high priority. In particular, the bank required the decision on this project in three months; the process would normally have taken up to a year.

For the whole three months, Robert worked long hours, including weekends. He spent little time at home, and this placed a strain on his domestic and family life. However, the project was completed on time, and the senior partner for whom Robert worked was congratulated for producing a viable proposition in such a short period of time.

Robert then had his performance review with the senior partner (the one who had been congratulated).

The performance review was very short. The senior executive drew attention to the following:

- Robert was scruffy, especially early in the morning and late in the evening;
- in the evenings, Robert was in the habit of bringing fast food into the office, leaving an unpleasant smell;
- Robert was known to have cat-napped on the office floor on at least two occasions in direct contravention of company rules;
- Robert had been spotted with his feet on the desk by one of the senior partners (again, in direct contravention of company rules).

Robert therefore received an adequate and average performance review. He received no credit at all for the work that he had done, nor for the extra effort that he had put in.

The key lesson is that this kind of behaviour on the part of top managers simply destroys any integrity and strength of relationship. If, in any set of circumstances, it is necessary to warn somebody about their dress or demeanour (or habit of bringing food into the office) then this ought to be done as a side issue at least in the first instance. Self-evidently, performance reviews should concentrate on performance; and in circumstances such as this, this is where the emphasis should have been.

It is abundantly clear that there is no integrity whatsoever in the relationship. It is also the case that any employee faced with this kind of review, after putting in a lot of extra effort, will simply tell everyone what had happened.

Integrity of parties and relationships involved

The basis of this is the mutual trust and honesty of the particular relationship, as well as the roles, personalities, work relations and context of communication involved.

Use of language and media

The language and media used should be those most suited to the receivers. The simpler and more direct the language used, the greater the likelihood that the message will be understood on the part of the receiver. The basic rule is: say what needs to be said; write what needs to be written; reinforce what is spoken with simple and direct written documentation. This is particularly important in each of the following cases:

- rules and procedures for staff conduct, behaviour and performance, which must be written in language that everyone can understand, and made accessible to all through media that are readily available to all;
- specific procedures, especially disciplinary, grievance and health and safety, which again must be delivered in clear, concise and direct terms that everyone can understand.
- organizational training and development activities, which have to be carefully targeted at different parts of the workforce.

Visibility

People respond much more positively if they know who is issuing things. This is better still if they have a general and continuous face-to-face relationship based on mutual respect and understanding. This is much more likely where the particular manager or supervisor manages by walking around and demonstrates an active and positive interest in staff and activities (see Box 8.6).

Clarity and unity of overall purpose and direction

Clear communications, therefore, tend to reinforce clarity of both overall purposes and sub-aims and objectives, and also to concentrate the minds of those responsible for the ordering and direction of the organization to the fact that overall purposes and sub-aims and objectives should be clear at the outset (see Box 8.7).

Box 8.6: Gerry Robinson

When Gerry Robinson, the previous head of the Granada organization, undertook a project designed to improve communications at the North Staffordshire NHS Trust, he quickly found that there were dedicated teams of healthcare professionals doing their best to serve their community.

The subject quickly turned to the management of the organization. Two things became immediately apparent:

- the organization had a new chief executive;
- nobody knew what he looked like.

Further investigation led to the discovery that the 'new' chief executive had been in post for nearly a year. The fact that nobody knew what he looked like raised an immediate concern. Accordingly, Gerry Robinson went to find him. Eventually he tracked him down in a large office tucked away in a corner of the management building. Gerry Robinson tackled him about this. Back came the response: 'Oh, the staff don't want to see me. In any case, I am far too busy.'

It took several months of persuasion to get the chief executive to see things differently. It was also true that the staff did not want to see him – because they felt that he had nothing to offer. Only as the result of becoming 'visible', and engaging in professional and substantial discussions about the nature of patient care and the future direction and priorities of the hospital, did it become clear that the staff had plenty to offer to the CEO and vice versa. It also became clear that the communication barriers were causing serious delays in the volume and quality of work carried out and in attending to the overall cleanliness of the hospital.

Box 8.7: Use of language (1): councils get banned jargon list

UK council leaders have compiled a banned list of jargon, bland phrases and clichés. The press release put out by the local government association read as follows.

Words and phrases such as 'taxonomy' and 'predictors of beaconicity' are banned. Clichés such as 'level playing field' and inscrutable terms such as 're-baselining' have also been prohibited. In some cases, clear translations of terms were possible, such as 'measuring' for 'benchmarking'; 'idea' for 'seedbed'; 'delay' for 'slippage'; and 'buy' for 'procure'. Otherwise, no translations were forthcoming for any of the following: mainstreaming; holistic; contestability; synergies; blue-sky thinking; can-do culture; coterminosity; double devolution; arise and scanning; value-added; thinking outside the box; symposium; revenue streams; potentialities; improvement levers; quantum.

The French word 'tranche' meaning 'slice' in English is also banned.

Commenting on this initiative, the chairman of the UK local government association, Barbara Eaton, stated: 'Why do we have to have coterminous stakeholder engagement when we could just "talk to people" instead? All public bodies have a duty, not only to provide value for money to people, but also to tell people what they get for the tax that they pay.'

This was supported by a spokeswoman for the plain English campaign who said: 'This gobbledegook has to go. Jargon has its place within professions but it should not be allowed to leak out to the public as it causes confusion. Churchill and Einstein were both plain speakers and they did OK. Public bodies should follow their lead.'

Being positive

A positive approach to communications reinforces general positive attitudes, values and feelings on the part of all concerned. Language and messages therefore should reflect all the associated elements of encouragement, enhancement, enrichment, satisfaction, achievement, fulfilment, potential, creativity, innovation, progress and improvement.

Each of the above elements only works if they are fully integrated and if they are delivered in the specific context. In particular, there are matters of common courtesy, manners, the extent of genuine and general friendliness of approach between members of an organization. The extent to which these prevail is a reflection of the prevailing mutuality of interest and common purpose. They also contribute to the avoidance of problems and disputes and when these do arise, to their early settlement to the satisfaction of all involved. They also help to engender positive attitudes and values and mutual concern and respect (see Box 8.8).

Box 8.8: Sceptical questioning

Many managers find themselves unable to debate operational problems and issues with their staff without adopting an unpleasant or negative tone.

For example: one manager at a major financial institution ran what he considered to be a 'tight ship'. He was consistently unpleasant to his staff, and made a virtue of this, stating: 'If my staff hear nothing from me, they know that they are doing a good job. If I simply go and ask them for something, they will not tell me. So I make sure that anything that I ask is couched in threatening tones so that they will take notice.'

A survey of the staff within his department found that he was universally loathed on a personal level, as well as disrespected professionally. While it was true that communications were effective up to a point, it also became clear that nobody ever reported problems until after they had occurred and after every step had been taken to resolve them without involving the manager.

True to form, eventually the company promoted the manager away from this situation and to a corporate strategic position. A new manager was appointed who immediately set about improving things. However, two specific immediate issues presented themselves:

- the force of the previous manager's personality had been so strong that staff did not know how to behave in the new (and much more positive) set of circumstances;
- the new manager had to work very hard to convince people that he did indeed intend to be fully participative; and he had to work very hard, in particular, to ensure that people did raise problems, issues and concerns without being asked or threatened.

Non-verbal communication

Non-verbal communication gives an impression of people to others without saying or writing anything. It also reinforces what is being said or written. It also tends to give the real message – the non-verbal message is usually much stronger. The main components that must be understood are as follows.

- **Appearance**: this includes age, gender, hair, face, body shape and size, height, bearing, national and racial characteristics, clothing and accessories. Each of these items and their combined effect has great implications for interviewing, public images, creating impressions, advertising, public relations, salesmanship, presentation, design brand, marque, layout, comfort and familiarity.
- **Manner**: indicating behaviour, emotion, stress, comfort formality/informality, acceptability/unacceptability, respect/disrespect.
- **Expression**: expression, especially facial expression, becomes the focus of attention and that is where people concentrate most of their attention.
- **Eye contact**: regular eye contact demonstrates interest, trust, concern, affection and sympathy. The depth of expression in the eyes generates deeper perception of feelings – anger, sorrow, love, hatred, joy.
- **Pose**: this is either static or active, relaxed, calm, agitated, nervous or stressful. It reinforces the overall impression conveyed. Different parts of the body, especially arms and legs, are used for expression, emphasis, protection and shield.
- **Clothing**: especially in work situations, clothing provides an instant summary of people. A technician is instantly recognized by their overalls; the police and traffic wardens by their distinctive uniforms; and so on. Many organizations whose staff deal regularly and consistently with the public insist either on a dress code or the wearing of a uniform – it helps to reinforce organizational image and the trust and confidence of the public.
- **Touch**: this reinforces a wide range of perceptions. Consider the difference between different people's handshakes and the impressions that these convey. Touching also reinforces role and sex stereotypes – the chairman/chairwoman banging their fist on the desk; the woman meticulously arranging her clothes.
- **Body movement**: this may be purely functional and fulfilling for certain requirements – for example, cleaning the car. Movements may be exaggerated, conveying anger or high emotions; languid, conveying comfort, ease or indolence; or sharp and staccato, conveying forcefulness and emphasis.
- **Position**: this reinforces formality/informality; dominance/dependency; superiority/subordination. People use position to enhance feelings of control and influence. For example, people may face each other across a large desk – this conveys a sense of security and defence to the person whose desk it is and a barrier to be crossed by the other. Chat show hosts sit without tables and ensure that their guests do not have recourse to this prop either. This puts the professional at an advantage and ensures that the guest is sufficiently alien to the environment to be subservient to the host.
- **Props and settings**: props and settings are used to reinforce impressions of luxury and formality. They are designed to ensure that whatever happens does so to the greatest possible advantage of the instigator. They either reinforce or complement perceptions and expectations; or else they contrast perceptions and expectations so that the person coming into the situation is impressed for whatever reason.

- **Discrepancy**: this occurs where the body conveys one message while the spoken or written conveys others.
- **Social factors**: people are conditioned into having preconceived ideas and general expectations of particular situations. For example, people do not generally attend promotion panels or job interviews unshaven or dressed informally. There is no rationale for this other than the expectations of society and the general requirement to conform.
- **The other senses**: other aspects of non-verbal communication include the use of scent and fragrance; the use of colour and coordination of colours; matters of social and ethical importance and expectation; design and use of materials.
- **Listening**: listening is both active and passive. Passive listening may be no more than awareness of background noise; it may also be limited to a general awareness of what is going on. Active listening requires taking a dynamic interest in what is being received. While the message is received through the ears, it is reinforced through eye contact, body movement, pose and through the reception of any non-verbal signals that are given by the speaker.
- **Reinforcement**: non-verbal communication tends to reinforce relative and absolute measures of status, value, importance and achievement; relative and absolute measures of authority, power and influence; confidence and well-being; and psychological barriers.

The priority in designing and delivering effective communications is to ensure that the message, the media used, the language and the non-verbal aspects are in full harmony. People expect consistency; this reinforces their need to know and understand where they stand in all sets of circumstances.

If there is any inconsistency, people will simply believe the stronger signal. This is almost always the non-verbal aspect. For example:

- if somebody delivers a positive set of words and phrases, but is clearly very angry, it is the anger that will be believed and remembered;
- if somebody delivers a positive set of words and phrases, but clearly does not support them, it is the lack of support that will be remembered;
- if somebody makes a promise, but does not make eye contact in delivering that promise, then the promise itself will not be believed.

Barriers and blockages

Barriers and blockages in communication arise either by accident, habit, negligence, design or distance.

Accident

This is where the choice of language, timing or method of communication is wrong with the best of intentions. In such cases, those involved will simply step back from the situation and rectify it as quickly as possible. This is the only sure remedy. The worst thing that can, and does, happen is that the organization rather takes on a defensive position and that a simple misunderstanding quickly becomes a major dispute or dysfunction.

Habit

Companies, organizations and their staff get into corporate habits of delivering specific messages. Over periods of time, these habits can become general and sloppy. People assume that others know what they are talking about. Different departments, divisions and functions deliver what are supposed to be corporate messages in their own particular ways; and so consistency is lost. More insidiously (again) companies, and their managers, can get into the habit of thinking that if their staff hear nothing from them, then they must be doing a good job.

Negligence

This is where barriers and blockages are allowed to arise by default. The organization and its managers perceive that things are at least 'not too bad' or 'going along pretty well'. In such cases, communication dysfunctions are seen as 'one of those things'. Specific problems are ignored or treated with a corporate shrug of the shoulders. From the staff point of view, however, these are the first signs of corporate melees and neglect. If allowed to develop, the overwhelming perception on the part of the staff is that the organization does not care for them, or what happens to them (see Box 8.9).

Design

This is where the barriers and blockages are both created and also used by those within the organization to further their own ends. They are used also to bar the progress of others. In these cases, above all, information becomes a commodity to be bought and sold, to be corrupted, skewed and filtered in the pursuit of the sectoral interest in question. This is endemic throughout the mid to upper echelons of the military, civil and public service institutions, multinational companies and other multi-site organizations with large and complex head office institutions where an active and negative form of realpolitik exists (see Box 8.10).

Box 8.9: Managerial priorities

One of the most telling signs of negligence in communications is where a large volume of information is published which concerns the activities and interests of top management only. What happens in the rest of the organization is not communicated.

The result is that staff get to learn more than they ever thought possible (or indeed wanted to learn) about the comings and goings of top management, conferences attended, overseas trips and exciting new ventures (exciting at least to the top management team). On the other hand, achievements of those working lower down the organization are not highlighted, appraised or made public.

The result of all this is to lead those in lower positions to believe that they exist only to serve the interests of top management. The problem is compounded when top management fail to recognize this as a symptom of corporate malaise, and continue to publish their own deeds and activities regardless.

Box 8.10: Use of language (2): 'Some of our data is missing'

Over the recent past, there has been a lot of publicity given to the large volumes of data that are 'lost in transit'. These 'losses in transit' usually refer to data discs and sticks that have been sent through the post and somehow failed to arrive at their destination. Common explanations (and occurrences) are:

- they were simply lost in the post;
- they were stolen;
- they were inadvertently left by somebody on a train/on a bus/at an airport lounge.

Whatever the explanation, following the losses and the publicity received, it is difficult to believe that organizations continue to send data in these ways without recognizing the possibility of loss.

In particular, one such occurrence was of RAF data containing personal details of senior and critical staff. These details included drug use, criminal records, extra-marital affairs, as well as family details.

There is no suggestion that any of these data were deliberately lost. However, in practice a barrier is being created every time data is transmitted in these ways with the prospect of it failing to arrive.

Distance

Distance in this context is both physical and psychological. The physical barrier also carries psychological overtones. For example, when one is operating at a physical distance from the organizational headquarters, there is a psychological feeling of autonomy also. This is compounded by the presence of over-mighty subjects. The institution therefore generates its own identity. All of this acts as a barrier to effective cross organization communications.

At a more localized level, the psychological distance is compounded or reduced by the presence (or absence) of trappings such as offices, secretaries, forms of address and titles.

Visibility – especially a lack of visibility – compounds any psychological barriers that may also exist. In particular, a lack of visibility on the part of those issuing communications reinforces any feelings of one-wayness in communications that may already exist (see Box 8.11).

Channels of communication

The more filters through which a message must pass, the longer the channel of communication demanded (Figure 8.2).

Communication agenda

This is the frame of reference for the communication in question. This is either direct and precise with the result that the message is clearly and unambiguously understood and

Box 8.11: Mark McCormack and management by ringing around

Mark McCormack, the founder of IMG, the sports star and celebrity public representation group, always fully understood the importance of communication as a critical factor in the success of his organization. In practice, many of his staff worked in different locations across the world as they pursued opportunities for their clients. McCormack himself never forgot this; and he used to make sure that he stayed in touch with all of his key staff at least once a week. If it was not possible to meet with them in person, he would telephone, having a long and detailed conversation about the activities of the specific executive, the opportunities that had presented themselves, and any specific problems encountered.

In this way, Mark McCormack ensured that the problems of distance were addressed and managed effectively without becoming barriers to effectiveness.

received by those concerned. Conversely, it is indirect and imprecise with exactly the same result – except that in this case, those involved assess the other negative and dishonest features of the communication in coming to their conclusions and understanding of it.

Stated or primary agenda

This is the way in which the communication in question is presented. The extent to which this is the real message depends upon the nature and clarity of the message and of the language used in support of it; and the extent to which the organization then gives life and substance to it through the use of resources, the placing of it in the system of priorities and the behavioural encouragements and sanctions with which it is underpinned.

The reverse also exists. If the words used are empty, and if there is no support for what is stated, the primary agenda will be disregarded and those concerned will look for the secondary and hidden agenda that always exists in such cases.

The problem also arises if the organization changes and the initiative in question requires resurrection or rejuvenation. New forms of presentation and language must invariably be found when this occurs.

Secondary agenda

Secondary (and indeed multiple) agenda exist where the primary has no substance. There are many forms to look for and of which to be aware. Individuals put particular items out for a variety of purposes – for example, self-aggrandizement, to be seen to be doing something, to prove that they have done something, because they know that the subject is close to the heart of the patron. In other cases, organizations put out messages that appear frothy and insubstantial, but which will contain somewhere the item or concept that has genuine purpose. The result is that while most of the offering gets ignored, the one crucial item does therefore gain a foothold and familiarity. However, if the item is in any case dishonest or toxic, then the crucial point is deliberately buried in the volume of froth that is otherwise present.

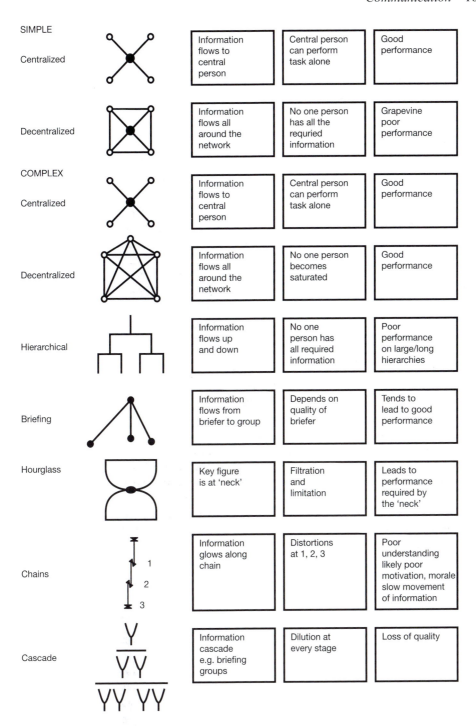

SIMPLE Centralized		Information flows to central person	Central person can perform task alone	Good performance
Decentralized		Information flows all around the network	No one person has all the requried information	Grapevine poor performance
COMPLEX Centralized		Information flows to central person	Central person can perform task alone	Good performance
Decentralized		Information flows all around the network	No one person becomes saturated	Good performance
Hierarchical		Information flows up and down	No one person has all required information	Poor performance on large/long hierarchies
Briefing		Information flows from briefer to group	Depends on quality of briefer	Tends to lead to good performance
Hourglass		Key figure is at 'neck'	Filtration and limitation	Leads to performance required by the 'neck'
Chains		Information glows along chain	Distortions at 1, 2, 3	Poor understanding likely poor motivation, morale slow movement of information
Cascade		Information cascade e.g. briefing groups	Dilution at every stage	Loss of quality

Note the comments in the right-hand column – and especially the fact that very few of the methods used lead to good communication performance.

Figure 8.2 Channels of communication

Hidden agenda

This is the extreme form of the above. It usually takes on some form of intra-organizational collusion or conspiracy. It is often a cause-and-effect type approach – for example, whereby a low pay rise is offered in the knowledge that the staff will strike – and that they can therefore be dismissed. This form also occurs in the field of new technology and new market introduction. New technology is introduced so that the old and those working on it can be divested. New markets are proposed in the knowledge that the sales team will not be able cope and that they too can be dismissed.

A variation occurs when a department takes on a highly prestigious or critical project. Once this is up and running and cannot be cancelled without great losses (including prestige), the particular department pleads for more resources.

This also occurs where a department or individual is given a particular task that they cannot possibly complete in the full knowledge and for the purpose of exposing them as failures. They again become a target for corporate cuts.

In practice, of course, everyone knows what the real agenda is; and so they work out their own responses accordingly. The whole management of agenda and objectives, therefore, becomes a form of corporate game in which those in charge publish a stated agenda or remit, and everyone else knows what is really expected to happen (see Box 8.12).

Organizational toxicity

Organizational toxicity and toxic communications exist in organizations that have acquired malady or disease. Symptoms of toxicity are as follows.

Box 8.12: Stalin and the Russian Revolution

After the Russian Revolution of 1917, the Communists came to power replacing the Imperial family (who were subsequently murdered). The leader of the Communist Party, Lenin, became *de facto* emperor.

Stalin became party secretary. Stalin used this position to amass large volumes of information about all those in key and critical positions. Much of this information was clearly necessary to hold and be available.

However, when Stalin came to power himself in 1923, he used the information that he had gathered in his previous role to further his own advantage and shore up his position as leader. He was now able to bring charges (some genuine, many trumped up) against those who had served the cause faithfully. He also then extended this remit to remove those whom either he simply did not like, or whom he regarded as a threat to his position (this latter, especially, applied to the military officer class who were exterminated wholesale).

In practice, everyone knew what was going on; and in practice also, everyone knew that Stalin would get his own way. However, by using the information available, and by going through some form of official process, Stalin and the Russian authorities were able to give a form of legitimacy to their activities. The process also served to ensure that anyone who did oppose the wishes of Stalin and the Russian Communist authorities knew exactly what they were letting themselves in for.

- **Blame and scapegoat**: the organization finds individuals to carry the can for its corporate failings. Sales departments get the blame for falling profits. Personnel get the blame for disputes and grievances. Individuals are blamed for specific failures (for example, the failure of a particular promotion campaign; the failure of work restructuring). They are often also named in this respect and their failure publicized around the organization.
- **Accusation and back-stabbing**: this is a development of blame and scapegoat. It exists where it is allowed to exist – that is, where the organization either actively encourages, or at least acquiesces in, departments and individuals making accusations and allegations about each other. This is an integral feature of any blame culture.
- **Departmental feuding**: this is where forms of internecine warfare exist between individuals, departments and functions. This is a derivation of both blame and accusation, where both become institutionalized. Again, some organizations either actively encourage this, or at least acquiesce.
- **Meddling**: this is where persons meddle outside their legitimate areas of activity. One of the most extreme forms of this is where top and powerful individuals promise favoured customers that special activities and deals can be done on their behalf and where, as the result, production, sales, marketing, finance and human resource functions are seriously disrupted.
- **Patronage**: meddling also includes the promotion and appointment of family and friends on the basis of kinship and friendship rather than capability. It includes other forms of favouritism and opportunism, and concerns both departments and individuals.
- **Secrets**: this is where information becomes a commodity to be used as a source of influence. Information becomes graded and classified. There emerges a culture of information bartering and exchange at an institutional level; and an over-active and destructive grapevine at an informal level.
- **Corporate self-deception**: this usually occurs in two ways. The first is where an elite is created (or where a group is encouraged or comes to see itself as such). Securing its unassailable excellence, it produces plans, proposals and outputs that must necessarily also be correct and excellent. In many cases, of course, what is proposed does indeed start out as correct and excellent. When things go wrong, there are two courses of action open:

    - to put them right;
    - to persist in the illusion of excellence, and to ignore the problems.

While it is clearly better to address the problems rather than ignore them, many organizations and managers indeed do just that. The result is a form of communication that can (and often does) maintain a veneer of credibility and confidence to the outside world. Within the organization, there are always those who do know what is going on, and this becomes an ever increasing circle (see Box 8.13).

Assertiveness

The 'assertive' approach to communications adopts the point of view that any communication can only be effective if it is well thought out, its effect is understood in advance and the message is delivered clearly and directly to the recipient. Used

Box 8.13: Enron

Enron, the gas and electricity energy trading company, collapsed in 1998 with the then largest losses in corporate history. Before that, Enron and its top managers had managed to maintain a façade of strength and profitability for many years, even though this was founded on a set of illusions.

During its rise in the late 1980s and early 1990s, Enron had become understood to be a beacon of excellence, a model for all companies and business drives for what was then the future. Enron expanded aggressively, buying up energy supplies wholesale and then selling them on to corporate customers for good-value prices but with long-term (and therefore high-priced) contract values.

The company attracted extensive publicity, and became a major sports sponsor (the Dallas Cowboys NFL Football Club played its games at Enron Field) and political sponsor.

However, those with financial responsibilities in the company began to be worried about the amount of liabilities that were not on the balance sheet, but which were nevertheless stacking up and would one day have to be addressed and repaid. This led, in 1994, to one senior manager quietly disposing of his share entitlements. Subsequently, one or two others did the same.

The word now began to get out. Industry watchers and stock market analysts now paid attention to the company, trying to assess where its real strengths lay. It quickly became clear that the customer base served was insufficient and inadequate to service either the company's debts or its fixed costs.

When the company collapsed, it quickly became apparent that corporate self-deception had been practised on a grand scale. The extent of the self-deception had led to top managers engaging in criminal activities to try to hide the extent of the company's liabilities, and also to obtain by deception further financial advances in order to keep the company going on an operational day-to-day basis.

This all took place at a time when the company was, as stated above, being hailed as the future of corporate business. Three weeks before the company collapsed, it declared:

'From the world's best energy company, to the world's best company – this is Enron.'

universally throughout organizations, the approach is the most effective counter to barriers and blockages, misunderstandings and any toxic elements that may be present.

It is necessary to understand the following forms of behaviour and demeanour and their effects on communications, as a prerequisite to understanding the basis on which the assertive approach is effective.

- **Aggressive** – characterized by shouting, swearing, table thumping, arguments (cross-transaction). The matter in hand is lost as the aggressor strives to impose their point of view. Winning the argument becomes everything.
- **Hostile** – where the main emphasis is on the personalization of the matters in hand. Often also characterized by shouting and table thumping, the outcome is normally a personal attack (sometimes in public) on an individual or group.

- **Submissive** – characterized by saying or doing anything that the other party wants so that they will finish the argument or transaction and remove themselves.
- **Inconsistent** – characterized by according people different levels of quality and value, treating different standards for individuals and groups. This also extends to treating the same individual or group in different ways according to mood or the environment for example.
- **Non-assertive** – characterized by the inability of the individual to put their message across. This is either because they are not sure what to put across, or else have not used the correct words or media.

In order to resolve the problems caused by these forms of approach an absolute standard of behaviour demeanour and language is used. This is called assertiveness.

Assertive behaviour, demeanour and communications consist of the following.

- **Language** – clear, simple and direct; easy to understand and respond to on the part of the hearer or receiver; the words used are unambiguous and straightforward; requests and demands are made in a clear and precise manner and with sound reasons.
- **Aims and objectives** – precise and clear; considered in advance; recognizing the effect that the message is likely to have on the recipient.
- **Delivery** – in a clear and steady tone of voice, or where written in a well-presented and easy-to-read format. The use of voice is always either neither too loud nor too soft, and does not involve shouting, threat or abuse.
- **Persistence and determination** – where problems or issues are raised by the recipient, the sender sticks to their message, aims and objectives; they do not become side-tracked; they answer any problems that are raised without diverting from the main purpose.
- **Positive and negative** – the general thrust of the message is always clear and apparent; this does not vary, whether the overall tone is positive or negative. This approach is especially important in handling general staff problems – especially matters concerning grievances and discipline.
- **Face and eyes** – the head is held up. There is plenty of eye contact and steadiness of gaze. The delivery is reinforced with positive movements that relate to what is being said (for example, smiles, laughter, nodding, encouragement; or a straight face when something has gone wrong).
- **Other non-verbal aspects** – the body is upright; hands and arms are open in order to encourage positive response and productive transaction; there is no fidgeting or shuffling; there are no threatening gestures or table thumping; or other displays of other forms of behaviour (see Box 8.14).

Situational factors

Assertive delivery is based on an inherent confidence, belief and knowledge of the situation, and confidence in the people. Openness, clarity, credibility and personal and professional confidence all spring from this.

Any clarity of purpose or delivery is always spoilt through having to operate from a weak position or one which is not fully known or understood. This weakness or lack of clarity leads to other forms of behaviour and communications indicated above.

Box 8.14: Effective use of language

Anyone wishing to become an expert and effective communicator must understand how to use language, and the effects of different approaches on those receiving the communications.

Accentuating the positive

- It is excellent and it is very expensive (rather than it is excellent but it is very expensive).
- He/she is a secretary (rather than he/she is only a secretary).
- You will get to the top if . . . (rather than you will never get to the top unless . . .).

In each of these cases, the positive is accentuated rather than the negative; and the result is that the statement will be received as positive and worthy of attention rather than negative and demoralizing.

Acronyms

If you use acronyms, make sure that everyone knows and understands what they stand for. Everyone has been to meetings where some of those present talk in their own jargon – and it is maddening to have to listen to (especially if nobody present bites the bullet and asks them what on earth they are talking about)!

Over-praising

If you praise people to the skies for delivering mediocre work, or pay them bonuses for doing no more than their regular job, the effect is always demoralizing on those around them. Everyone very quickly comes to learn that this is the new standard for which high praise and high rewards are delivered. Additionally, if there is any perception of unfairness or favouritism, this reinforces the negativity of this form of communication and presentation.

Ambiguity

Those who understand the need for effective communications, and how to deliver them, prepare in advance so as to avoid any ambiguity or misunderstanding. There is little worse than being fully prepared to deliver excellent news to everyone all around; and then to have the whole process go wrong because some of the phrases used were ambiguous or unclear.

The other part of ambiguity is that it is a serious barrier to communication, and can also constitute a form of toxicity (see above). Those who regularly deliver ambiguous messages are deemed to do so not because they have not thought things through sufficiently, but because they have something to hide. Those who continue to deliver ambiguous or unclear messages will come to have a reputation for duplicity (whether or not this is deserved).

Conclusions

This chapter has concentrated on:

*   the importance of communications as a critical factors of effective organizations;
*   the extent and prevalence of barriers to effective communication;
*   means by which the processes of communication may be understood.

The result of this is the ability to produce effective communications capable of being received, accepted and acted upon, or responded to. This is an organizational group and individual issue requiring recognition at all levels and remedial action where communications are poor or ineffective. It reinforces the need for clarity of purpose and language to which constant reference has been made. As many channels as possible or necessary should be used, giving the same message through each so that the message received is complete and not subject to editing, interpretation or distortion. Where communications are not direct, they are indirect and people will search for hidden agenda and meanings.

Organizations are therefore responsible for creating the conditions in which effective communications can exist. Managers and supervisors must be trained in both the content and processes. All staff must be made to understand the importance and value of their contribution and how this is best made. This only happens when there is a high-quality working environment and a suitable general management style is adopted. Effective communications are an integral part of this. More generally, this is the foundation for all effective interpersonal, professional and occupational relationships; and relations between departments, divisions, functions and levels in hierarchies and throughout organizations.

9   Influence, power and authority

Introduction

Influence, power and authority are present in all organizations and these stem from a variety of sources. It is first necessary to distinguish between them.

- **Influence** is where a person, group or organization changes the attitudes, values, behaviour, priorities and activities of others.
- **Power** is the capability to exercise influence in these ways.
- **Authority** is the legitimization of the capability to exercise influence and the relationship by which this is exercised.

Authority is based on recognition and acceptance of the right and ability to restrict the freedom to act, to set boundaries and to encourage or order sets of activities for given reasons. Responsibility and accountability normally come with authority, especially in relation to the results achieved by the given activities and the ways in which these are ordered and conducted. Authority also refers to the establishment and enforcement of rules, regulations and norms.

Authority therefore legitimizes the use of power and influence in organizations. If subordinates believe and accept that they are in junior positions, they legitimize the power and authority of the superiors. Chains of command, reporting relationships, spans of control and organization structures all tend to reinforce the existence and legitimization of authority and hierarchy. Legitimate authority is a feature of many organization roles, and a key to managerial effectiveness. This authority is supported and reinforced through the use of other sources of power and influence.

Authority is therefore a relationship that is recognized by those concerned – involving both exertion on the part of the superior and acceptance by the subordinate (see Box 9.1).

Sources of power and influence

In companies and organizations, managers have to be particularly aware of the following, and to be able to take effective steps to address them when they do arise. This needs to be seen in the context that all organizations, and the individuals who work in them, have power and influence of some sort; and it is a basic human, as well as professional and occupational, need and drive to be able to influence events, people, the environment and their own progression.

Organizations and society, and their institutions, have power and influence over people and other organizations. Personal, professional, occupational and organizational

Box 9.1: Acceptance and rejection of authority

A senior manager working in local government had fallen out with his director. It was known and understood across the entire organization that the two did not get on at all; and as well as having no time for each other on a personal basis, neither respected the other's professional contribution.

Matters came to a head when the senior manager was offered a job in another authority. The reference provided by the director was dreadful, and this led to a confrontation.

The director tried to pull rank, seniority and power of personality to forbid the senior manager from leaving. At the height of the argument, the director shouted: 'I will not accept your resignation! I forbid you from joining this new organization!'

The senior manager replied calmly: 'Well, I am going anyway.'

The director now lost his temper completely. He started to shout and swear, repeatedly using the phrases: 'I will make it my personal business to see that you never ever work again'; and 'I will break you'.

The senior manager calmly walked out and went to join the new authority. This resulted in another problem; that the director now tried to prosecute the senior manager for breach of contract (he was on six months' notice and had left his job at a moment's notice as the result of the row).

The new employer stood by the senior manager, who went on to have a very successful career.

The story spread like wildfire across the whole of the local government sector. It became much talked about at managerial and conference gatherings across the sector. The senior manager was also quite happy to relay his side of the story to anyone who would listen; and this, of course, included his former colleagues.

The result was that the director lost all of his authority. Though he stayed in his position for several years afterwards, it became increasingly difficult for him to exert any influence on the future direction of events and activities.

The lessons are:

- always be certain of the position from which authority is being exerted;
- always be certain of the response;
- know the difference between right and wrong uses of power and authority (see below);
- be aware of the enduring, as well as immediate, effects of the exertion of power and influence;

and

- never lose your temper!

power and influence are therefore constrained, as well as enhanced, by other sources and institutions. In particular, all personal, social and collective behaviour, as well as what happens in organizations, is bounded by legal frameworks and regulatory institutions, as well as more general customs, habits and expectations.

In any situation, as above, people can choose to accept or reject the power and influence of others. It is therefore essential to understand this broader context in the consideration of the main sources of power and influence which are as follows.

- **Physical power**: the power exerted by individuals by reason of their bodily shape, size and strength in relation to others; and by organizations in relation to their financial market or operational size.
- **Traditional power**: whereby the ability to command influence derives from accepted customs and norms. For example, traditional power is present in the hereditary principle whereby the office or position is handed down from parent to child.
- **'Divine Right'** and **'The Natural Order'** should also be considered here. Both have been used in the past to reinforce the position and influence of those in power. Divine right was ascribed to European monarchs over the Middle Ages and beyond – it attributed their position to the will of God so that anybody who took up rebellion against them was also attacking God (see Box 9.2).
- **Expert power**: is based on the expertise held by an individual or group and the demand for this from other parts of society. The power and influence that stems from highly prized expertise is dependent upon the volume and nature of demand,

---

Box 9.2: From parent to child

In today's business environment, many organizations and institutions continue to find ways of ensuring that organizations and occupations remain in the family.

In practice, this is not new. For generations during the period of heavy industrialization, it was usual for parents to be able to find jobs for their sons (and it was invariably sons) in factories and dockyards, and in the coalmines.

Other examples include:

- NewsCorp Inc.: Rupert Murdoch, the founder and chairman of NewsCorp, has ensured that key positions exist for his children within the organization.
- Members of Parliament: take steps in many cases to ensure that when the parent retires, their place is taken by a child (e.g. Anthony and Hilary Benn, Douglas and Tristan Hoyle, Alf and Estelle Morris).

In these ways, a strong tradition and 'natural order' is preserved. The advantage is that it helps to provide a certain familiarity and can, in some cases, build confidence and assurance of the continuity of the organization and institution. On the other hand, whoever takes over from the parent has to be both good at the job, and also committed.

The other side of the coin is as follows: neither Richard Branson nor Anita Roddick found positions in their business empires for their children. In each case, their children were required to make their own way in the world, and to demonstrate that they had their own commitment. Indeed, if the children were to start up their own businesses and to seek backing from their parents' organizations, this would only be forthcoming on exactly the same basis as if it were an independent venture.

the location of the expert and their willingness to use their skill. Expertise comes as professional and technical skills, knowledge, aptitudes, attributes and behaviour. It also includes situational and social knowledge.

Expert power normally carries an economic value; and expertise is hired by organizations according to their own needs and wants. The reverse position is that all those with specific expertise may make this available for sale, rent or hire. It is additionally important to note that expertise can, and does, become obsolete. This places pressure on organizations and individuals to continue the development of their own expertise, skills and knowledge so as to remain both current and also valuable. When expertise does become obsolete, especially in unskilled or semi-skilled occupations, organizations have the clear choice as to:

- making the relevant parts of the workforce redundant, and hiring those with the new expertise and occupational skills required;
- retraining and redeveloping the existing workforce (see Box 9.3).

Box 9.3: Real and perceived expertise

For years, Bernie Madoff was regarded as one of the main sources of authority in the financial services sector. His expertise was highly sought and valued; and people would place investment with him and his organizations in the sure and certain knowledge that they would gain growth far in excess of what was otherwise on offer in the banks and stock markets.

In 2008, Bernie Madoff was indicted for fraud. It became clear that his empire was a sham, built on false promises. It became clear also that his expertise was a sham; he had managed to develop the perception of expertise on the basis of:

- providing demonstrably high returns on investment made with his organization at the early stages of his career;
- generating a very positive public relations campaign around his achievements.

As a result of generating this reputation, he was able to operate unchallenged by financial services authorities and regulators.

In particular, it came to light that when financial services authorities had tried to assess the strength or otherwise of his institutions and practices, Madoff had used his power of personality, rather than expertise, to drive them away.

The lesson is: always be sure that those who say they have expertise do indeed have expertise. Additionally, it is essential to take an active responsibility to ensure that this expertise does not become either tainted or obsolete.

Other sources of power and influence

The other sources of power and influence which organizations and their managers need to be aware of are as follows. The ability to understand and use these sources of power, and to develop capability in their usage, is essential for effective organizational and managerial practice.

- **Referent power**: is based on the degree of attractiveness of the person in the position of power. For example, someone with a high level of desired expertise may not be hired because of other undesired characteristics (for example, they may be scruffy, bad time keepers or hold extreme political views) while, on the other hand, someone with a lower level of expertise may be hired because their wider characteristics or points of reference are considered more suitable. A key priority in building a position of influence is the development of the individual as a point of reference. Effective referent power therefore consists of:
  - the confidence of others to approach the individual in the position of power and authority on any matter whatsoever;
  - the capability of the person in the position of influence and authority to deliver solutions to problems, explain things clearly and generate an effective self-presentation;
  - visibility, so that people can always get hold of the individual at any time, for any reason at all;
  - consistency, meaning that people know and understand that they are going to get evenness and equality of treatment;
  - fairness in dealings with all individuals, groups and problems;
  - integrity: the knowledge that whatever is said or done will be transparent and honest; and, where required, supported by full and accurate explanations, with data to support if required.
- **Charismatic power**: charisma is the effect of one personality on others, the ability to exert influence based on force of personality. It is also the ability to inspire high levels of confidence and identity among other people.
- **Resource power**: this is the ability to influence others both positively and negatively, based on the command of resources.
- **Reward power**: this is the ability to influence behaviour and activities by holding out and offering rewards for compliance and acceptance. The extent of influence exerted in this way is dependent upon the nature and volume of rewards and the extent to which these meet the needs of those over whom influence is sought.
- **Punishment power**: again, the extent of the influence exerted depends upon the nature of the punishment being threatened and whether this is felt to be important by those affected.
- **Reputation and confidence**: organizations and individuals are able in some circumstances to exert influence based on their achievements to date and the respect and esteem in which these are held. Past reputation and influence, and past triumphs and successes are used as the basis for securing future work, for example.
- **Coercive power**: this is the ability to bribe, bully or threaten someone into doing something that they would not otherwise do. It is usually based on physical or economic strength and reinforced by negative and threatening attitudes and

behaviour. It also normally carries dire consequences if the focus of effort does not do that which is required of it.

- **Conformity**: this is where organizations and leaders set distinctive norms, attitudes, values and behaviour standards which those who wish to be a part of the situation are required to accept. This may be imposed formally by the organization in the setting of rules and standards of behaviour and activity, or informally by groups exerting their own autonomous and informal pressures and norms.
- **Position power**: this is where someone is given power and influence according to the position or role held. Military and organizational ranks carry different forms and extents of this depending upon their position in relation to others.
- **Legal/rational power**: this is the limitation, ordering and direction of power and influence in the name of organizations. It is based on the setting of rules, procedures, regulations and norms for each job, role, department, division and sector.

This is an exhaustive list and forms the basis for both understanding the sources of power and authority, and also in developing a position of power, authority and influence.

Those in specific positions have to know and understand where the limits of their power, influence and authority lie. If they make promises, they must be capable of carrying them out. If they establish themselves as a point of reference for any stakeholder, they must be capable of delivering what the particular stakeholders require. They must also have the strength of character to state clearly to any individual or group where the extent of their authority lies and, when required, to be able to hand things on to someone else.

Centres of power in organizations

Each department, division, function and group always has its own power base to a greater or lesser extent (see Figure 9.1).

The position of departments, divisions, functions, groups and individuals is further influenced by:

- The nature of their own function in relation to all the others present, and the nature and extent of the influence that they are able to exert.
- The nature and volume of resources that they command and use, the ways in which resources are allocated and the wider question of availability of resources.
- The nature of inter-group and inter-departmental relations; the extent to which these are positive and cooperative or negative, dysfunctional and divisive.
- The physical size of certain groups and departments, the numbers of people involved and the scale and nature of resources and technology commanded.
- Relations between operating departments and functions, and the organization's top management (invariably the supreme centre of power).
- Elements of group hierarchies. These are often found in sophisticated and diverse decentralized organizations where, for example, the head office and its functions have greater proximity to senior managers and directors, and therefore the physical capability and location to bid for resources, establish priorities, establish personal relationships and get ahead of the more distant activities.
- The extent and nature of the authority vested in given officials, ranks, departments, divisions, groups and individuals; and the extent of autonomy and devolution that goes with this.

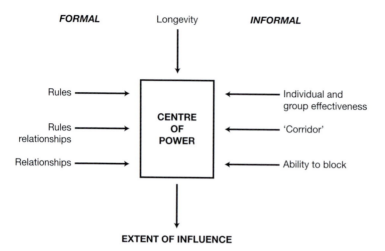

Longevity: people, groups and institutions become behaviourally both strong and influential when they have been in place for a long while. This has implications for needs and demands for change, reorganization and restructuring.

Blocking: this is the power to prevent things from being done. It exists in most situations and is a combination of resource and reward restriction and work prioritization. It is also the ability to call upon other resources and influences to ensure that the blocking process is effective.

Corridor diplomacy: this occurs as a route to be considered around problems when the formal procedures of the organization have been exhausted. Power and influence are used between the parties concerned on an informal basis to try and explore other means of resolving the issue.

Success and failure: a run of successes may lead to an individual or group becoming acknowledged as experts enabling their influence to grow. Conversely, a series of failures is likely to lead to loss of influence, whatever the absolute standard of the expertise present.

Group energy: this is the ability of the group as a whole to influence things, both positive and negative. Especially negative, groups can become very effective in dissipating the energies of those who come to them. For example, those dealing with bureaucracies and who are constantly handed on from one person to the next spend a great deal of energy on this and may well give up altogether if the goal is not important or if some other way of achieving it can be found.

Figure 9.1 Factors relating to the centres of power

- The capabilities of managers and group leaders both in absolute terms – the extent of their managerial expertise – and also in relation to each other.
- Critical factors such as the ability to command, limit, edit and filter information; the command of critical technology or expertise; and the influence of this upon the ways of working of other functions and groups, and of the organization as a whole.
- The structure of the organization and the extent to which certain functions are accorded higher status, importance, influence and authority than others in the formal structuring.
- The priorities of the organization in its dealings with its customers, clients and markets, and also internally in terms of its operational ways of working.
- The culture of the organization as a whole, and of its different functions and groups (if a distinction can be drawn between the two). This includes reference to prevailing

shared values, attitudes and beliefs, and to general levels of motivation, morale, mutual trust and respect; ethical considerations; and any absolute standards of integrity and activity.

- The extent and prevalence of pressure groups and lobbies, and the extent to which organizations feel that it is in their own best interests to extend forms of influence and representation to them (see Box 9.4).

Over-mighty subjects and departments

Over-mighty subjects and over-mighty departments wield great levels of influence and autonomy in certain situations, especially in multi-site and multinational organizations

---

Box 9.4: The children's home

The owners of a large house in a pleasant suburban street sold their house to a children's charity. During the process of buying the property, the children's charity asked for, and received, planning permission to turn the house into a secure unit for disturbed adolescents, many of whom had been abused during their childhood.

When the rest of the neighbourhood got wind of this, there was uproar. This was followed by extensive lobbying of the local council, and supported by full media coverage.

However, the local council refused to budge. The property would be maintained in good condition; and because it was a secure unit, no danger would arise in the community.

Collectively, the community now wrote to their local MP; who in turn wrote to the council asking for full details and an explanation.

The council now reversed the decision to award planning permission, and accordingly, the sale was cancelled.

However, the local MP, instead of being satisfied, now became very angry. He wrote to the council and to the children's charity stating that he had asked for an explanation for information only, not for cancellation; the fact that the venture had been cancelled just as the result of his letter meant that the proposal could not have been very good in the first place. He also called into question the strength and integrity of the planning process and the basis on which change of use of premises was decided.

The key lessons are:

- all organizations have to have a position of response to lobbies and pressure groups;
- lobbies and pressure groups advance a point of view in which they are both interested and also actively involved; and so this has either to be accommodated or else managed effectively;
- additionally, from the point of view of the MP's involvement, it is essential that all organizations and their managers have a defined set of principles on which decisions are taken, and that these can be supported and defended where necessary.

where a large measure of local independence of operation is granted. In these circumstances, there are key issues which organizations have to address as follows:

- the extent and nature of the authority granted to local and regional managers;
- the extent to which patterns of behaviour and absolute standards are to be varied, according to local and regional demands and pressures;
- the nature of reporting relationships between head office and remote and distant locations;
- the maintenance of an overall identity between head office and remote and distant locations.

In these cases, the nature of authority exerted by head office is of paramount importance. This has to be founded on a clear understanding of the particular pressures in locations as above, and reinforced through the expertise of local and regional managers, and how they wield their power and influence.

Clearly, a measure of autonomy is required; clearly also, this has to be delivered in the context and in accordance with the priorities of the organization overall.

Additionally, over-mightiness and over-influence are not confined to remote and distant locations. In many organizations, specific groups and departments are known, believed or perceived to have power, influence and authority in excess of what they actually deliver. The extent of this power and influence may be based on:

- real expertise, and the results delivered;
- patronage and favouritism (see Chapter 11);
- the confidence in which the group and/or its members are held by the organization and its top managers;
- other factors; for example, the over-mighty or over-influential individual or group may deliver excellent PR or media coverage for the organization.

In each of the above cases, this form of power and influence can be either legitimate or illegitimate. Organizations and their managers need to know and understand clearly which it is. They need also to know and understand the basis of the power and influence of the particular group or individual (see Box 9.5).

Power and influence relationships

These relationships exist within, and between, all groups, divisions, departments and functions; and also between the individuals involved. The main features are as follows.

Orders of priority

This refers to the position of each individual group or department in relation to all the others involved. This is often called the pecking order. It is established as a result of a combination of factors – the respect and regard held for the group or individuals by the organization's top management; demands for resources and ability to command these; the extent of its influence on organization output; the extent of its influence on internal ways of working; the size of the group and the nature of the expertise that it wields; its

Box 9.5: Surgical scandals

The children and paediatrics unit at the Alder Hey Hospital, Liverpool, was for many years known to have an especially high mortality rate; meaning that many of the children who went in for operations and medical treatment either died during procedures, or else shortly afterwards.

In spite of the fact that this had been known for years, neither the health authorities nor the patient watchdogs were able to do very much about it. Eventually, however, a public inquiry was undertaken, and the findings that came about were unacceptable from both a professional, surgical and also an organizational point of view.

The public inquiry found that it was widely known in the hospital that procedures in the paediatrics unit were sloppy. Surgical activity was not properly recorded. The cleanliness (or lack of it) of the operating theatres was also a major factor.

The questions were asked: Why did the authorities not do anything about this beforehand? Why was this state of affairs allowed to persist for so long?

Back came the answers: the surgeons and medical teams involved were a very tight-knit group. They used their position to defend collectively any individual accusation of malpractice. If anyone persisted in lines of questioning, the group as a whole simply became unpleasant and aggressive.

When top and senior managers from the health authorities had tried to tackle the problem, this had regularly resulted in shouting matches. The consequence was that 'nobody quite liked to' become involved because they knew that the situation would become unpleasant.

The key lessons are:

- over-mighty and over-influential groups bond together; and use any measures (in this case unpleasantness) that they deem necessary to preserve their position;
- organizations and their top and senior managers have to find their own influence and authority to question over-mighty and over-influential groups and individuals;
- if problems are known or generally understood to be present, they have to be tackled eventually.

physical location; and the nature and quality of its leadership, output and results, both in absolute terms and also in those required and valued by the organization.

Dominance–dependency

This is the extent to which some groups are able to influence, direct and dominate the courses of action of others, and the benefits and consequences that arise as the result (see Figure 9.2).

Ultimately, all those who work in an organization are dependent upon it for rewards and continuity of employment. This involves at least acquiescence and normally, also, acceptance and compliance with its given ways of working. Dominance and dependency are features of all organizational and interpersonal relationships. Dominance–dependency may be entirely one-way (though this happens very rarely in practice). It is much more

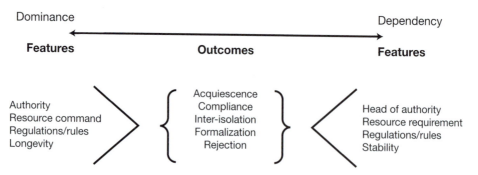

Figure 9.2 The power/relationship spectrum

likely to be more complex – even a slave owner is dependent upon the slaves actually carrying out the work.

It is much more useful therefore to see dominance–dependency as a process in which mutual responsibilities exist. Where groups are dependent upon the continued confidence of top managers for continuity and allocation of resources, the top managers are dependent upon the groups to produce results.

Another way of looking at this is as follows.

- **Acquiescence**: where the people have no particular respect or liking for the organization and its norms, rules, customs and practices, but go along with them because it is in their current interests to do so or where there are no alternatives apparent.
- **Compliance**: a more positive approach than acquiescence, but where the fundamental basis of the relationship remains the same. This normally involves, however, adopting the required patterns of behaviour.
- **Acceptance**: where people adopt the norms, values and standards positively and with some degree of enthusiasm and interest; but again are likely to see that at least part of this is dependent upon their current interests.
- **Formalization**: where conditions are placed on the particular relationships between the organization and its staff – for example, the need to use particular processes, channels of communication and approaches.
- **Institutionalization**: where people adopt the norms, values and standards absolutely and use them as key factors in their life and work patterns. Such an approach is often very effective in progression through the organization, and also gives a structure to wider aspects of life. Institutionalization is also a key feature in the lives of school children; those in the full-time care of health and social services (and prisons); and those who work for long periods of time in large, sophisticated and highly structured organizations.
- **Internalization**: where people adopt the organization's beliefs and where these affect their personal beliefs and value systems; eventually such people come to 'believe in' the organization and all its works.
- **Rejection**: where people reject the organization and everything concerning it. This normally leads at the very least to those concerned having stresses, strains, disputes and grievances. People who reject in this way are either neutralized – for example, given project work that removes both them, and their negative feelings, from the

mainstream activities. This may drive them to change their feelings from negative to positive. If this does not happen, the organization normally rejects them.

How people respond, collectively and individually, to power, influence and authority is a key priority. In particular, the two extremes above are primary concerns as follows:

- Rejection is always certain to lead to conflicts and disputes. Where power, influence and authority are rejected, whether by groups or individuals, there must always be a full investigation. The outcome of such investigations needs to be an understanding of the basis on which influence and authority were rejected; the context in which the position arose; and examination of the authority and influence of the organization's management and supervisory style, and the institutions and procedures that underpin them.
- Internalization, where staff groups and individuals blindly accept everything that the organization says and does as an article of faith, also comes with its own specific responsibilities. Staff who do internalize the values of the organization to this extent, and accept the influence and authority as absolute, have to be managed very carefully (see Box 9.6).

Box 9.6: Oradour-sur-Glane

On 6 June 1944, the D-Day landings took place in Normandy, northern France. The D-Day landings were undertaken by British, American and other allied forces with the purpose of freeing France and western Europe from the Nazi empire.

It quickly became known around northern and western France that the invasion had taken place. Accordingly, the French population in the area now began to rise up against their Nazi overlords. One such uprising took place in the city of Limoges, in western France. However, this uprising was quickly put down. This, however, was not enough for the Nazi authorities.

They determined upon reprisals. Accordingly, a detachment from the Thiegel Battalion under the command of Colonel Joachim Peiper was sent out to the village of Oradour-sur-Glane. There, under the direction of Peiper himself, the soldiers rounded up all the men from the village and shot them. They then herded all the women and children into the village church and set it on fire. Anyone who tried to escape was shot as they ran out. After that, they then set the whole of the rest of the village on fire. Finally they returned to base in Limoges and reported back. The Nazi high command commended them on a job well done, and the commitment especially of Peiper was recognized.

Subsequently, Peiper was tried and hanged as a war criminal. However, Peiper himself and the soldiers involved carried out this atrocity because they had all fully internalized the Nazi way of operations. They had been trained to do a particular job in specific ways, and when this is related to the internalization of the organization's values (in this case, the Nazi Party and SS) this was the performance that could be (and can be) delivered.

The key lesson is therefore that any internalization or commitment on the part of the staff has to be managed from a position of active responsibility. There also has to be a very clear and high moral compass and wider ethical standing to this position; otherwise, people will indeed act as they are directed.

Hierarchy

Organizational hierarchies are normally based on a combination of rank and function and this is reflected in job titles (marketing director; quality manager; production supervisor; personnel assistant). This is normally well understood by those in particular organizations. The process is clouded by job titles such as secretary, officer, executive and controller and again, these have to be understood by those involved.

The hierarchy is a feature of organization design and is composed of structure, job and work allocation, and rules and procedures. It indicates where power and influence lie and its extent and nature. It indicates spans of control, areas of responsibility and accountability, chains of command (the scalar chain) and reporting relationships. As well as a functional and divisional map of the organization, the hierarchy is a representation of the nature and limits of power and influence (see Figures 9.3 and 9.4).

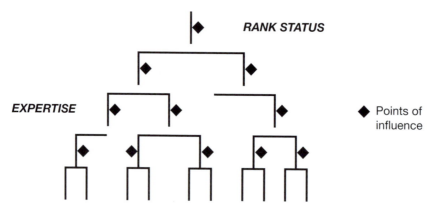

Figure 9.3 Hierarchies

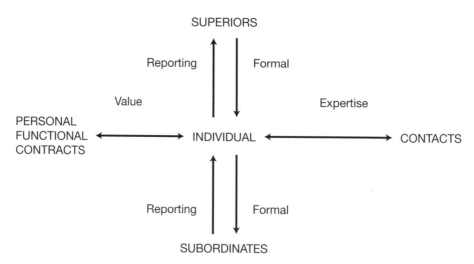

Figure 9.4 Influence relationships: the individual's position in the hierarchy

Status

Status influences the perceptions of power relationships in organizations. It is also a reflection of general perceptions of influence. Status is a reflection of the rank or position of someone (or something) in a particular group. Relative status is based on the interrelationship of each position. Status is based on the importance and value ascribed to the rank by the organization and individuals concerned and by the esteem and respect that accrue as the result of holding the given rank. Status is also based on the ambition, self-esteem and self-worth of the rank holder – the ability to say with pride: 'I hold job X' or 'I work for organization Y'.

Status is therefore both given and taken. It is a feature of both individual and group perception. It is formalized largely by rank and capability. It also has informal features based on personality and integrity. Other individual capabilities, whether critical to group functioning and effectiveness or not, also influence status (see Figure 9.5).

Status is reinforced by the trappings that go with the rank held – personal office, expensive furniture, car, mobile phone, expense account – and by the volume and quality of items such as these.

It is also reinforced by the responsibilities of the rank held – size of budget, numbers of staff, performance requirements. It is also often reinforced by the physical location of those concerned, for example, whether their office is in the 'corridors of power' (that is, the same as that of the top managers). In wider social circles it may also be reinforced by perceptions of glamour or excitement that are assumed to exist in certain occupations – for example, show business, publishing, travel (see Box 9.7).

Friendships

Friendship influences power relationships in organizations where people who have positive feelings for each other also work together. A part of the way of working then becomes the desire to support the friend to ensure that they derive some of the benefits

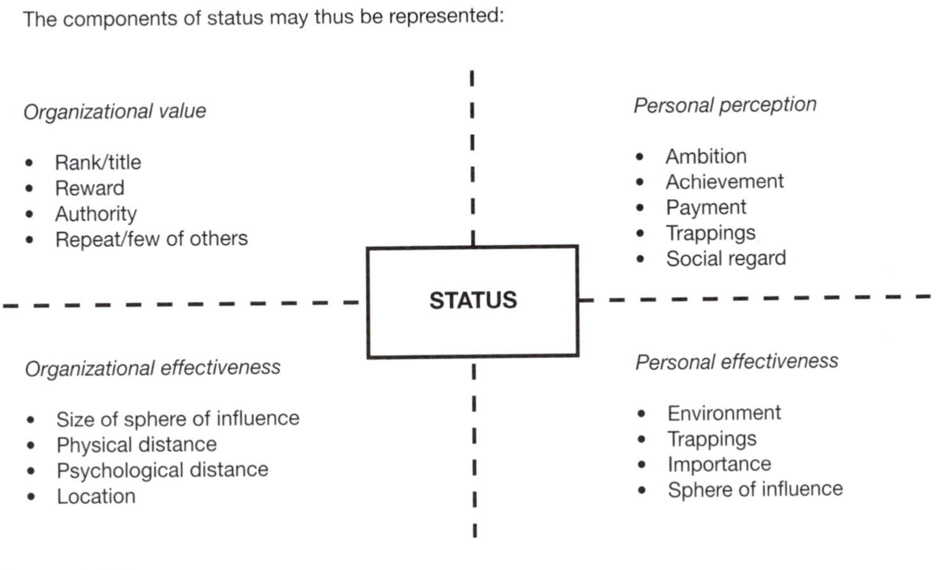

The components of status may thus be represented:

Figure 9.5 Status

Box 9.7: Managing status

As stated above, status arises as a combination of self-perception and the perceptions of others. In some part of their lives, everyone needs recognition and admiration. For many people, the status afforded by holding a particular job, occupation or profession, or working for a particular organization, or holding a particular rank, are quite legitimate aspirations.

On the one hand, therefore, organizations need to recognize this as a legitimate human and professional need, and make clear what trappings of status are available within the organization (and what trappings are not available). Organizations need to make clear how these marks of status are to be achieved and the conditions that individuals must satisfy in order to meet them.

For example:

A small department in one the UK's leading universities wished to appoint a new head of department. None of the internal candidates was thought suitable, and so the position was advertised outside.

There were only three applications and none of these was suitable either. However, shortly afterwards, the department was moved from within its present faculty (division) into another which had a much higher profile.

From within the new faculty, the post was now re-advertised. Now, instead of being called head of department, the post was now called 'director of studies'.

The result was that the university now received sixty applications, the overwhelming majority of them suitable.

In this particular case, therefore, the problem was not the job itself, but the status attached to it. When it had a mundane title, and operated out of a small faculty, nobody was interested. However, the exact same job, but operating out of a large faculty and with a new title, satisfied the overall demands for status and recognition, as well as operational excellence.

that are to accrue from particular courses of action. The use of friendships, of personal contacts, to resolve problems and address issues is a general feature of the informal organization. It represents the ability to use personal influence (referent power) to the organization's advantage.

However, friendships in organizations become corrupted when they are misused or abused in order to gain some kind of personal advantage (see Chapter 11). Particular problems arise as follows:

*   where friendships are manipulated in return for favours;
*   where friendships are used as the basis for seeking or gaining promotions and opportunities;
*   where someone is known to offer friendship and alliance within the organization in return for favours important to themselves.

In practice, this goes on all of the time. It therefore becomes a matter of priority understanding for those in top, senior and critical managerial positions in order to know when they are being asked for their backing for particular ventures and initiatives on the basis of organizational priority and commercial acumen; and when they are being asked for this backing on the basis of the advantage that accrues to a particular individual.

Dislike

The converse is where antagonism exists between people. This is nearly always a barrier to effective organizational activities. It is used to block or hinder the progress of the other individual or group, and is compounded where operational reasons are given for the purpose of satisfying a personal grudge or grievance.

On the other hand, nobody can possibly like everyone with whom they have to work. It is essential that a basis for fully effective professional and occupational cooperation is developed and maintained, however. If this is achieved, any personal antagonism can at least be contained; and it may also be that this dislike is reduced. In general, people have to be capable in work situations of recognizing the value that everyone delivers, whether or not they have any personal affinity.

Dislike is influenced by other personal emotions – of envy, jealousy, hatred and resentment. It is also influenced by organizational and operational matters of expediency, especially where there is the need to find a scapegoat for a failure (see Chapter 11).

Organizational features

Some organizational features are easily seen as power relationships; for example, the supply chain, which is the process by which materials are drawn and combined together to produce finished goods and services. Influence can be exerted by groups that have key tasks to perform in this. By regulating their own output in pursuit of some other course, influence can be brought to bear for the stated purpose. Pressure is exerted to help ensure that the other purpose is satisfied (see Figure 9.6).

For example, a workforce unloading supplies from lorries may deliberately regulate their efforts in order to take a particular length of time. This may be to prove or indicate

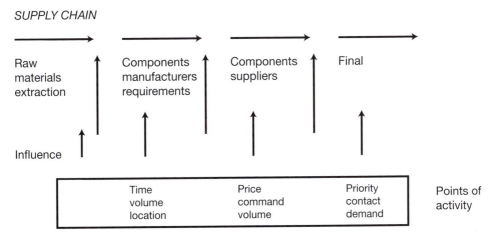

Figure 9.6 The supply chain and points of influence

that the reason that it took so long was because of a shortage of staff; to lobby for extra equipment (for example, cranes, forklift trucks); to seek more money ('We will work faster if you pay us more'); or to act in support of another group further down the chain that they know to be under pressure.

Control mechanisms

The main control mechanisms are as follows.

- **Financial controls**: in which influence resides in the demands for financial information and the ways in which this is presented. It is also present in budgeting and resource allocation activities, and in checks on resource utilization, timescales, progress chasing and checking, and the pressures exerted by those responsible.
- **Staff controls**: including discipline, grievance and disputes mechanisms, the ways in which these are constituted and the approaches taken by those responsible for their handling.
- **Quality controls**: the standards of quality set, the means by which these are achieved and the means by which problems of quality are identified and dealt with. This is likely also to include attention to customer satisfaction (both internal and external) and systems of enquiry and complaints.
- **Work allocation and job descriptions**: these are also sources of influence. This takes the form of requiring people to attend at set times, to produce set volumes (and quality) of output. It is also affected by flexibility of working arrangements and lines on job descriptions that state (usually at the end) 'Anything else that the organization may require you to do'.
- **Factors that affect the health, safety and general well-being**: of those concerned, the means by which these are controlled and the extent and influence of health and safety committees, welfare offices and occupational health professionals. This also influences the design of work environments and workstations. Further, there are legal constraints affecting many aspects of work – for example, extremes of heat and cold; length of time worked without breaks; length of time in front of computer screens – with which organizations must comply. Influence therefore resides in the hands of those who must enforce each of these features.

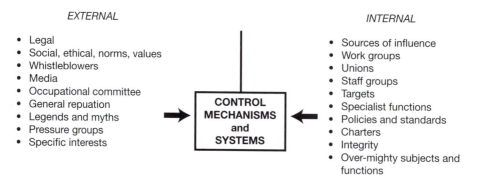

Figure 9.7 Behavioural influences on organization control

- **Ethical controls**: related to general standards of best practice and also to particular features such as equality of treatment. The driving force here (for good or ill) is likely to derive from the organization's stated policy or point of view. Clear direction is given in the best cases. A form of direction emerges in the worst cases or where standards are not set by the approaches taken by individuals and groups to these matters, and the extent to which they are condoned and supported by the organization.
- **Sanctions**: taken against individuals and groups in response to specific unacceptable activities or behaviour, and the ways in which these are applied. The power lies in those who carry out the sanctions and is also found in the relative ability of those affected to resist or combat them. This is, in turn, influenced by the general standpoint that is adopted by the organization. It affects all aspects of organizational performance, either directly or indirectly – general, individual and group behaviour, relationships between superiors and subordinates, and the collective attitude and state of morale. It also affects perceptions of fairness and equality (or otherwise) of treatment (see Box 9.8).

Box 9.8: Kent and Sussex Hospital Trust

Recently, it came to light that ninety-five patients had died as the result of hospital-acquired infections at the hospitals of the Kent and Sussex Hospital Trust. The subsequent investigation, and evaluation of professional practice, found that there was a general sloppiness of professional nursing and surgical practice, and that there was no active management involvement (either on the medical or on the administrative side).

In particular, the hospital itself was filthy. There was no adequate cleaning, nor did anyone take active responsibility to ensure that this was carried out. Additionally, patients were left unwashed for several days at a time in many cases; and neither were soiled sheets and bedding necessarily changed.

This amounted to gross managerial misconduct and, accordingly, the hospital trust's chief executive, Rosemary Ball, was dismissed. A new top manager and senior management team were appointed, and the process of cleaning and reforming practice was undertaken.

Rosemary Ball, however, claimed unfair dismissal. She stated that her practice had indeed been excellent, that it was not her fault if the hospitals were not clean and that she could not be expected to know everything that was going on. The hospital trust had therefore to decide what to do about the unfair dismissal claim.

If the relationship between sanctions and behaviour was fully known, understood and published, the trust would have a very strong position from which to defend itself. However, if this had never been made fully clear, it would be harder to defend the position.

The key lesson is that, where sanctions are stated and when they need to be imposed, everybody needs to be fully clear about what the sanctions are, and the conditions in which they are implemented. In practice, this is:

- a major managerial priority;
- a major managerial failing.

Delegation

Delegation is the allocation of work to subordinates accompanied by the handing down of:

- authority in the given area to carry out the work and to make requests for equipment, materials and information; to act in the name of department, group or superior in the given area;
- control over the process by which the work is to be carried out. This normally involves, in turn, relaxing a part of the process of work supervision. Activities taken in pursuit of the task are normally left entirely to the subordinate.

There is an effect on the wider issues of responsibility and accountability. Overall responsibility, especially to the wider organization, normally remains with the superior. Any problems arising, especially questions of failure or ineffectiveness, therefore remain a matter between the superior and the rest of the organization. However, this is invariably accompanied by discussions between the superior and subordinate. Where such problems do arise, to apportion blame to the subordinate in dealings with the wider organization leads to loss of morale and accusations of scapegoating.

Misuses of power and influence

In organizations the most commonly found misuses of power and influence are as follows.

- **Favouritism**: the ability to influence an individual's career, prospects and advancement by virtue of a personal liking and at the expense of others.
- **Victimization**: the converse of favouritism; the blocking or reduction of the career prospects and advancement.
- **Lack of manners**: calling out rudely to people; abusing and humiliating subordinates in public.
- **Lack of respect**: treating subordinates with contempt; giving individuals dressing downs in public; conducting discipline in public.
- **Bullying and harassment**: overwhelmingly by superiors of subordinates. This is also found in the following forms:

  - racial prejudice and harassment;
  - sexual harassment (especially of female staff by males);
  - bullying of the disabled by the able-bodied;
  - religious manias and persecutions (for example, where a Catholic company bullies the elements of its workforce that are of other religions);
  - personal likes and dislikes – especially where the dislike is based on a perceived threat to the security of the senior's position.

- **Scapegoating**: the need to find someone to blame for the superior's errors (see Box 9.9).
- **Inequality of opportunity**: the setting of a priority order for the advancement of staff based on gender, race or disability elements.

The extent and prevalence of each of these misuses is always fully understood by the staff, at least at an informal level. The presence of each is always extremely damaging to both individual and overall motivation and morale.

Box 9.9: Work experience

John Grist was nineteen years old. Halfway through his university course in business studies, he undertook a period of work experience at the regional offices of a major retail organization.

Immediately, John settled in well. The regular staff of the company quickly became used to his friendly and cooperative attitude and the willingness with which he carried out his duties, and his eagerness to learn.

He was so good that on one occasion he was left in charge of the premises while everyone else was attending a staff meeting. While on reception duty, a delivery arrived. John checked the papers; everything seemed to be in order, and so he signed for it. The delivery, of a large volume of stationery, was left in reception to be taken away when the staff returned from their meeting.

In due course, everyone emerged from the staff meeting, and the assistant branch manager came to find John. He saw the boxes of stationery in reception, and asked aggressively: 'What on earth are these things doing here?'

John replied: 'It is all in order; I checked everything. Everything that is on the delivery note is there. So I signed for it.'

The assistant branch manager said: 'This is the wrong place for this stuff to have been delivered. You should have known this. Now I am going to have to pay overtime for the stuff to be moved. And it is all your fault. Give me the phone.'

The assistant branch manager, in front of John, now phoned head office to request permission for overtime so that the delivery could be moved. In front of John also, he stated: 'The problem is that all this stuff was signed for by a work experience kid. Still, what can you expect? It is not my fault, it is his. And yes – I will have him off the premises by tonight.'

Relationship structures and spheres of influence

The main factors to be understood are as follows.

- The nature of the relationship between all the parties, and whether this is cooperative, competitive or conflicting; based on mutual trust or antagonism; if more than two groups, whether there are alliances or other areas of mutuality between some of them; the personalities involved; whether the groups are permanent or ad hoc; the rules and boundaries within which the relationships take place.
- The nature of the matters in hand and the extent of their importance to each individual and party concerned. For example, the organization's tea person wields great influence over the chief executive if his/her desire for tea is overwhelming and if he/she cannot easily go elsewhere to get it.
- The relationship between the overt, primary or stated agenda and any parallel, secondary or other hidden agenda – either on the part of the groups involved or some of the individual players. For example, trade union officials will often fight the cases that they know that they cannot win because it shows their concern and care for every member whatever their difficulties. Further, the trade union officials

involved have their own career paths to follow and concern for all members is likely to be a key feature and requirement. The official therefore gains a reputation for being prepared to fight any corner, and this, in turn, leads to both their own advancement and also increased membership brought on by feelings of confidence and goodwill generated by the approach.

- Management style of the organization and its tolerance of parallel, secondary and hidden agenda; the recognition of any dominance or dependency exerted in the steps that it takes to minimize and control this; the extent and presence of physical and psychological remoteness and distance.
- The conduct of the relationships. This is likely to be based on:

    - conflict, a power struggle, the need for ascendancy in a particular situation;
    - cooperation, the establishment of areas of mutual interest; harmony – recognition of the need to resolve any issues for the greater good of all; openness – the extent to which each party involved is able (or feels able) to declare its own position completely; expediency – the need to gain a result quickly for some reason;
    - publicity – what others are to make of the outcome of the matter in hand once this is known.

- Isolation is a power relationship because of the physical isolation brought on due to the remoteness of a group from the rest of the organization (for example, an overseas subsidiary) which leads, on the one hand, to the feelings of loss of control and involvement on the part of the main organization; and on the other to feelings of autonomy and independence on the part of the subsidiary. Additionally, psychological isolation is brought on by matters such as resource starvation, denigration and general lack of respect and regard for the work of the group or for its members. This leads to the adoption of a siege mentality on the part of the group affected as they defend themselves from the pressures of the rest of the organization; and also on the part of the organization as it seeks to make fresh inroads into the already beleaguered group.

Group think is also a form of isolation. For example, top managers and directors may create their own view of the organization in its environment without reference to reality or based on an historic perception and reputation. Project groups and think-tanks may also find themselves in this form of isolation if their relationship with the rest of the organization is not carefully nurtured and managed (see Box 9.10).

Spheres of influence

These are created by a combination of formal and informal authority and power. They relate to the nature of activities and operations. They overlap and interact with each other (see Figure 9.8).

Spheres of influence are less easy to define than areas of legitimate, expert and role/ office power. They encompass especially areas of coercive/conformist referent and charismatic power. They also include specific areas of functional and legitimate power – for example, trade union officials have legitimate positions in any areas where they have members and the union is recognized; the human resource function has legitimate areas in any other function that requires their services such as in recruitment selection and handling disciplinaries and grievances.

Box 9.10: Isolation in practice

When the UK MPs' expenses scandal broke in 2009, it quickly became clear that:

- a sizeable minority of MPs had actively used the system of claiming expenses to their own advantage;
- a majority of MPs had simply used the system in all its imperfections;
- a minority of MPs had taken an actively responsible position, claiming only what they had actually spent.

One of the minority was James Mead, a Liberal Democrat. He had first been elected in 2002. When he came to take his seat in Parliament, he had been approached by the House of Commons authorities so that they knew that he understood what his allowances and privileges were. He went on to say: 'I was told what I could claim and how to go about claiming it. I was encouraged to make every claim as high as possible. I was told that this was the norm – that it was expected. I was also told that everyone else was doing it.'

He went on to say that when he found out what was actually going on, he was truly horrified. He tried to raise this with the fees office, and with the Speaker's department also. At first he was met with discouragement, then with outright hostility.

It had first become apparent that there were problems with the fees and expenses system of the House of Commons in 2007. James Mead himself was prepared to speak on the record to anyone who asked him. He went on to say that, as the result of this willingness to be open and transparent, there were now several dozen MPs who would not speak to him; indeed, that they had not spoken to him since he first went on the record in 2007.

Speaking to the BBC and Sky News media television channels in May 2009, Mead remained upbeat about this isolation. However, he did state that this had made it very much more difficult for him to get information from certain sources, and this was because both the fees office and also the Speaker's department had warned everyone else that he was a troublemaker.

Spheres of influence may be defined as 'the psychological territory of the individual or group'. Individuals and groups may have many spheres of influence in an organization. Handy developed the idea as follows.

Ownership of territory is conferred partly by deeds and partly by precedent, squatting or staking a claim. The boundaries of the territory are set out in various ways; physically with screens, offices, separate buildings; procedurally, through committee memberships and circulation lists; socially, through dining groups, informal groupings, carpets and other status signs. Some conclusions may be drawn as follows:

- territory is prized by its inhabitants; they will not willingly relinquish it, nor allow it to get overcrowded;
- some territories are more prized than others;
- trespassing is discouraged; you enter another territory by invitation only;

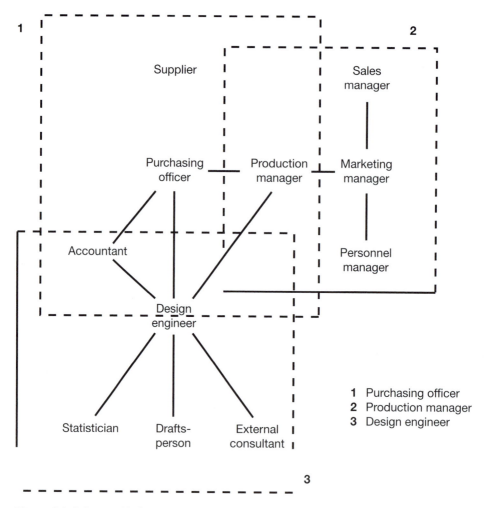

Figure 9.8 Spheres of influence

- one can seek to increase or improve one's own property even to the detriment of the neighbourhood as a whole;
- territory is not to be violated; if so, there will be retaliation and conflict;
- territory is jealously guarded – especially in relationship to its own trappings and status, including office sizes, dining rooms, cars, personal assistants and secretaries;
- territory is always to be improved and enhanced – both in the interests of maintaining the current position and also in order that this may be improved.

Pressures to maintain and increase the sphere of influence depend on a variety of factors. These include the following.

- The confidence, respect and regard in which an individual or group is held. If it is high, those concerned seek to enhance and build on this. If it is low, those concerned are likely to seek other means of gaining influence (for example, through the control of information and functional triumphs).

- Functional expertise, and the extent to which this is prized and valued by the organization. Again, especially if this is low, others sources of influences will tend to be sought.
- The rewards of influence. These are normally better work, increased resources, enhanced reputation and moves up the pecking order. They also include (in some organizations) the ability to influence the direction, activities and operations of the organization – and therefore transform (rather than merely enhance) the prospects of a particular department or individual.
- Attaching oneself to an over-mighty subject or department in the expectation of favours and enhancement.
- Increased status and prestige for those involved. This often leads to increased benefits and pay and increased prospects (especially from within the organization) for those concerned.
- Favouritism on the part of the organization's top managers, driven by real or perceived operational necessity, the top manager's own expertise and familiarity (for example, the director who came up through the ranks of the marketing department is likely to continue to favour marketing), personal friendships, expediency and the availability of a triumph.

Conclusions

The acquisition and use of power is a basic human as well as organizational need. The requirements and ability to control and influence the environment, and to make it comfortable and supportive, are factors in all behaviour. It is necessary to understand the ways in which people seek to do this in organizations, and the effects of this on aims and objectives, performance, behaviour and resource utilization.

How power is used and what type of power is used affects all aspects of performance, as does the means of dividing and allocating responsibility and authority. From this point of view, a key part of the creation, design and structuring of organizations consists of creating patterns of control and influence. This is formalized in hierarchies, reporting relationships, functional and expert activities, and results areas. Space is also created for the operation of communication and information systems, and group and inter-group relationships – both formal and informal.

It is also necessary to pay constant attention to the ways in which power, influence and authority are used and wielded within organizations to ensure that this continues to be legitimate, and to ensure that conflict and organizational politics, which might otherwise arise, are kept under control.

10 Realpolitik

Introduction

Realpolitik is the art of survival in the particular organization and situation. The term was first used by Otto Von Bismarck, the nineteenth-century Prussian chancellor, who defined it as: 'The capability and practice to gain, maintain and develop power and influence, using political systems, and formal and informal networks.'

This requires knowledge and understanding of the ways in which both organization and situation operate, of the different pressures and influences that are brought to bear. It also requires knowledge and understanding of the likely outcome of particular approaches. It is further necessary to adopt particular forms of approach to different individuals based on an understanding of what they are receptive to and what they are likely to reject.

All organizations have their own internal politics – the means by which influence and rewards are gained or lost. The organization itself and those responsible for its governance, direction and performance need to recognize the nature and prevalence of the different forms of political activity. This includes the effects on operations, effectiveness and success. Much of the infighting and competition at different levels and among functions may not be apparent to those at the top. Further, they may not perceive that their activities, those achievements for which they issue rewards and punishments, or the basis on which resources are allocated create strife and dissension elsewhere. They may also hide behind 'the need to consider the wider picture' and the equivalent as reasons and excuses for encouraging and rewarding the activities of lobbies and pressure groups, or of being seen to favour particular departments at the expense of others (see Box 10.1).

Box 10.1: Lloyd's Bank Chairman to step down

In May 2009, the Lloyd's Banking Group (formerly Lloyd's TSB) announced that its chairman, Sir Victor Blank, was to step down the following year.

The Lloyd's Banking Group shareholders no longer had full confidence in Sir Victor's ability to lead the company into the future.

Prior to this announcement, the company had gone through a very difficult period. Late in 2008, the then Lloyd's TSB had taken over HBOS, only to find subsequently that the losses made by HBOS were very much higher than had previously been understood.

Lloyd's TSB had been placed under heavy political pressure to take over HBOS which may well otherwise have gone bankrupt. Lloyd's TSB, under the guidance and direction of Sir Victor Blank, had succumbed to this political pressure, and so the deal was done. The result, however, was to reduce the immediate performance and viability of Lloyd's TSB. This called into question the wisdom and expertise of Sir Victor Blank.

Following the announcement, a statement was made on behalf of the Board of Directors by Lord George Leitch, the deputy chairman, as follows: 'The Board of Lloyd's Banking Group is very sad that Sir Victor Blank has decided to step down. Sir Victor Blank has been a chairman of extraordinary capability and vision. He has led the company very successfully into the new globalized banking era. The Board of Directors was unanimous in wanting Sir Victor Blank to seek re-election as chairman for a further three years.'

Nevertheless, under the pressure from the shareholders as stated above, the Board of Directors accepted Sir Victor Blank's resignation. Clearly, if it had come to a struggle between the shareholders and the Board of Directors, the Board of Directors would have lost.

In this case, 'the wider interest' was (and remains) clearly the viability of the organization. Ultimately, every organization is bigger than any individual; and so any action taken has to be, and has to be seen to be, in the enduring interests of the organization, rather than the immediate interests of an individual, or group who happen to support him (or her).

Organization politics are also often encouraged and used as forms of control by those at the top. They observe the effects of encouraging this form of behaviour in terms of giving some form of direction and focus to the different groups and individuals. They may also observe this behaviour as some form of 'rite of passage' – the opportunity for an individual or group to prove themselves. In absolute terms, however, this only has any form of validity where it is clearly linked to organizational purpose and effectiveness. Success and failure should never be seen merely in terms of the ability to operate and compete within the system (see Box 10.2).

Teams and groups that depend on particular forms and resources, and support for their continued well-being and existence, need to establish relationships with those who hand these out. As well as performance effectiveness, the basis of this is likely to include other matters such as support for the backers in other initiatives, sharing of the profits and merits of success, and distance from any apparent failure.

Individuals need to be able to create physical and psychological space in order to be able to pursue their own aims, and practise and develop their expertise. Ideally, this will all accord with the organization's overall direction; even where this is so, a certain amount of politicking and lobbying is normally required (for example, for new and improved equipment and the opportunity to attend training and development). Where this is less apparent, the individual will in any case seek to ensure that their own aims and objectives are met to a greater or lesser extent, whether or not these comply with those of the organization. Where the organizational and operational situation is very bad, individuals will pursue their own goals to the exclusion of those of the organization (see Box 10.3).

Box 10.2: 'It is the system that is at fault'

The UK political scandal of 2009 had at its core a system of allowances and expenses which Members of Parliament and those working in the House of Lords were allowed to claim. The revelations made about many hundreds of MPs and Members of the House of Lords covered everything from extravagant works carried out on large country homes and luxury flats, to claims of a few pounds (or even a few pence) only – for example, one claim was for 59p for a box of matches; another for £5.00 which had been put into a church collection; another for £10.00 which had been used to purchase 'adult movies'.

The collective defence mounted by all MPs and Members of the House of Lords was that 'it was the system that was at fault'. It became clear that the system of allowances and expenses had been allowed to burgeon, to try to offset periods of pay restraints and self-discipline that MPs had been asked to demonstrate as part of their commitment to managing the public finances and keeping expenditure in control.

Accordingly, the mass of MPs used the system to their own short-term advantage. The longer-term, and enduring, result, however, was a complete destruction of confidence in the strength and integrity of the UK political system and its institutions.

The key lesson is therefore that all systems have to be seen in their wider context. Operating a system in isolation from this context may (as above) deliver short-term advantages to those within it. Anyone doing this, in any organizational situation, does need to be aware of what can, and might, happen when the system itself is found to be at fault.

Box 10.3: Peter Curran

Born in South Africa, Peter Curran, from a very early age, showed signs of exceptional brightness, intelligence and an extraordinary capability to study. From an early age, therefore, he determined to enter academia, and to follow a long, varied and interesting career in that sector.

His early achievements were remarkable, his PhD thesis a ground-breaking piece of research which changed everyone's view of this particular area of expertise.

As the result of this, many of the top universities from all over the world asked him to come and work for them. Accordingly, by the age of 40, Peter had worked in the US, France, Germany, China and Australia, as well as his native South Africa.

At this time, he was approached by one of the UK's leading universities to head up a new department. He would be able to bring his research with him, and had a wide freedom in making the appointments that he chose.

Because he had never worked in the UK, Peter accepted the appointment and set to work. However, it soon became clear that everything was not quite as had been promised during the appointment process. When he tried to make the appointments that he had been promised, these were blocked. When he tried to generate research projects, these also ran into difficulties; and the university found itself unable to support him financially. He came to realize that anything that he wanted to do, he would have to fund for himself from external rather than university sources.

Peter quickly realized that he had made a mistake. Accordingly, he used the reputation that he had built over the years to get back on the global conference circuit. In the countries where he had worked previously, he was well known and celebrated; and when it became clear that he was available to attend conferences and deliver talks, the invitations came flooding in.

It also became clear to everyone in his field of study that the UK appointment was not working out. The job offers from elsewhere in the world started to come in; and after sticking out the UK situation for a very short period of time, he left to join Yale university in the US.

The lesson is that if organizations wish their top, key and expert individuals to pursue organizational goals as well as their own, then the conditions have to be created in which this is possible. Above all, it is no use appointing people on the basis of telling them half a tale, or encouraging them to misconceive the full range of conditions that they are likely to encounter.

Departments, divisions and functions become involved in organization politics, overwhelmingly because of the need to compete for resources and to maintain their own reputation and standing.

Again, this is invariably present to some extent even in the best of organizations. In other cases, competition for both resources and reputation is often based on the distributive principle whereby one succeeds at the expense of others and this becomes the driving force behind departmental success.

Understanding, surviving and operating in the political systems of organizations stem from this. It is very short-term and anyone who tries to take a more rational, long-term and operational view is likely to lose out at the expense of those who know how the political system works and how to succeed within it. Otherwise, the major output of these forms of activity is inter-departmental and inter-individual conflict, together with the prioritization and use of resources in the pursuit of political advantage at the expense of operational effectiveness.

Survival

The first duty of any individual is to survive within the organization setting; it is no use being expert at the job, occupation or profession if the behaviour and practices of the institution make it impossible to work effectively. So, individuals and groups have to survive long enough to become successful and effective operators.

They have therefore to be able to make use of systems, procedures, practices and support mechanisms. With the best will in the world, there is no point in taking an enlightened or ethical view of this if the organization's ways of working will not support it.

People therefore develop their own format for the niches that they occupy and the roles and functions that they carry out, in order to maximize their chances of being effective and successful operators (as distinct from expert in the performance of their expertise or function). In each case this consists of:

- Developing informal, as well as formal, authority, based on networks of friendships, recognition and respect, as well as expertise, status, rank and seniority.
- Developing approaches based on a combination of role, function and personality – adding a personal strand to the professional and operational. This means developing measures of trust, warmth and liking as a part of the professional and operational dealings.
- Developing approaches based on individual influence. This involves recognizing the nature of the influence of the individual and the ability to present it in ways useful to others within the organization.
- Developing networks of professional, personal and individual contacts and using these as means of gaining fresh insights and approaches to issues and problems (see Figure 10.1).
- Developing funds of bargaining chips – equipment, information, resources, expertise – which can be used in trade-offs and for mutual advantage and satisfaction when required.
- Developing sources of information which are of value and can be used (and misused and abused) when necessary (see Box 10.4).
- Developing a clarity of thought around the entire aspects of organization operations and activities. This is based on the one hand on what is important, urgent and of value, and to whom; and on the other on what facilitates progress, and what hinders or blocks it. This also involves recognition of where the true interests of the individual lie and how these can best be served in the situation.

Different forms of each approach are required for each role and function carried out. A different approach may also be required to the same individual or group where there is interaction on more than one basis. For example, a production supervisor may be able to request financial information from the accounts supervisor in one way; while the approach to the same supervisor would vary considerably if they were also the local union lay official representing a grievance on the part of the member of the production team (see Box 10.5).

Personal promotion and advancement

In an ideal world, personal promotion and advancement ought to be based on capability, commitment and expertise. In practice, this does not always happen; and in many organizations, it is necessary for individuals and groups to engage in forms of self-promotion and self-advancement, simply because otherwise top and senior managers will neither recognize nor value their contribution.

These forms of self-promotion and self-advancement are as follows.

- All staff e-mails, celebrating every achievement (and/or every activity that can be presented as an achievement or advancement).

FORMAL

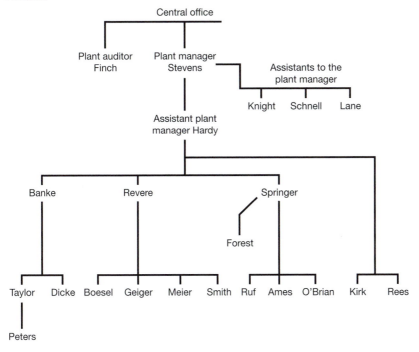

INFORMAL

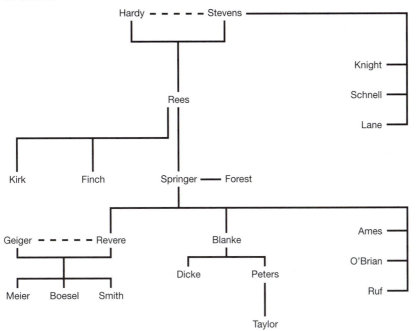

Figure 10.1 Formal and informal organization relationships

Box 10.4: The role and function of the personal assistant

Those who occupy personal assistant roles working for top and senior managers have very little formal authority. However, they have a great deal of informal authority, and so in practice their friendship and favour is sought in many cases, by pushy and ambitious people.

The reason for seeking these friendships is so that those who are ambitious do their best to know and understand what the top and senior managers are thinking, and who they are thinking of promoting to particular positions, and when. Ambitious people use these relationships and forms of friendship also to ensure (or try to ensure) that their name keeps coming up in conversations between the top manager and their PA.

In practice, this goes on everywhere. Everyone knows the rules of the game. In particular, senior secretaries and PAs fully understand that their friendship is being sought, not because they are inherently pleasant or attractive, but because of the benefits that they can deliver to ambitious people.

Box 10.5: Bird's Eye Foods

Over recent years, the production of frozen foods by Bird's Eye (a part of Unilever) has undergone many reorganizations and restructurings. This has resulted in the closure of some production facilities, and the relocation and reorganization of others. In particular, at the facilities in Lancashire and Humberside, these restructurings and reorganizations have been accompanied by extensive industrial unrest.

In one instance, the HR and ER teams responsible for the restructurings and re-organizations came to meet with trade union representatives with a view to presenting a clear, well-ordered, well-structured and, above all, well-costed proposal.

However, on each point, the trade union representatives were able to challenge successfully the assertions made by the HR and ER team. This was because they had used their informal contacts, both from within the organization and also outside, to gain all the information that they needed to make informed judgements about where the proposals were coming from, and what the actual intentions were. In particular, one trade union official had been able to gather extensive financial data about the true costs of redundancies and redeployments, and the installation of new production technology.

As so often happens in cases such as these, the HR and ER team now concentrated on where the information had come from rather than dealing with it on the basis that it was accurate. However, this only reinforced the perception that the reorganization proposals were, in fact, ill thought out and badly costed, and in the end it became impossible to proceed.

The lesson is that all managers (and everyone else for that matter) should enter such situations on the basis that everyone is fully informed. It is also the case that, where people are either badly informed or misinformed, they will eventually find this out, and so will take steps to ensure that they are never again left this vulnerable or exposed in the future.

- Using public meetings to talk up achievements and advancements.
- Attaching oneself to the achievements and advancements of others.
- Making sure that credit is given to groups where necessary, and where this can be used for self as well as group advancement.
- Blaming others and other circumstances for failure.
- Pointing out the failures of others.

There are few, if any, top and senior managers who will admit to recognizing, promoting and rewarding individuals purely on the basis of their self-presentation. However, in practice this goes on in all but the most clearly focussed and tightly disciplined organizations. Depending on the culture of the organization, it is necessary to produce written and verbal reports about progress and achievement to date; and again in practice, many people use this as the opportunity for self-promotion and advancement (see Box 10.6).

Box 10.6: SEB Ltd

SEB Ltd, the electrical goods manufacturer, had a regional sales team for the UK and Ireland, and another regional sales team for western Europe (France, Spain, Italy, Belgium, Netherlands, Luxembourg and Germany). Each was headed by a regional sales manager.

The UK regional sales manager became aware that a German supermarket chain wished to begin to stock SEB products. Accordingly, he made sure that the supermarket chain's branches in the UK and Ireland were well stocked; and he then passed the contact details on to the western European regional sales manager.

The western European regional sales manager quickly came to the same arrangement for the stocking of French, Italian and Spanish supermarkets with SEB goods.

At the quarterly top and senior management meeting, however, a bombshell was dropped. The western European regional sales manager calmly announced that he had managed to secure an exclusive deal for his team to stock and re-stock the UK and Irish branches of the particular supermarket chain. He cited this as a major achievement and ground-breaking initiative, and called on the members of the top and senior management team to congratulate him.

This they duly did; and he was rewarded with a large bonus.

However, it subsequently became clear that he had used his influence on the European mainland to give the overwhelming impression that the UK and Irish markets were being badly served by that sales manager and his team. The top and senior management of SEB were now faced with the dilemma: whether to disrupt what was a very profitable and assured agreement in the interests of fairness; or to do what was right by the UK and Irish sales manager and his team.

Because of operational expediency, the agreement negotiated by the European sales manager was allowed to stand. The UK and Irish sales manager and his team were all given excessive bonuses and a large pay rise.

Spheres of influence

In this particular context, people construct their own spheres of influence in order to give themselves both space and time to be able to operate a stage further on from the capacity to survive. Around this are constructed personal networks and support systems that enable help and assistance to be sought for problem-solving, project work and general support. This includes the formation of pressure groups and special interest groups, and professional and peer group clusters. Each comes to prominence when wider organizational matters demand it, require particular input or threaten its territory or influence. People gravitate towards those that are deemed to be successful and effective, that are suitable and which can be made to work to their advantage; and they gravitate away from those that are deemed to be unsuccessful, ineffective or unsuitable (see Box 10.7).

Patronage

This is where the position, hopes for advancement and influence of an individual or group – the protege – are placed at the disposal of another – the patron. The patron provides encouragement, resources and space so that the protege may prosper and flourish. A form of effort–reward relationship is thus engaged. The protege depends for success on performing the task, acting and behaving in ways acceptable to the patron.

Box 10.7: Self-fulfilling prophecies

As people develop their own spheres of influence, they come to be recognized and judged on a set of perceptions. Those who have good experiences within the particular sphere of influence report these; and so others who come into the sphere of influence do so on the basis of the expectations that they have already heard about.

As the result of one or two good or bad actions, individuals can, and do, come to have an overriding reputation. For example:

- Those who go to work for the Virgin organization do so knowing and understanding the public persona of Richard Branson. They have therefore taken the active decision that they wish to go and work for him, and that it will be fun, rewarding and fulfilling. And so – in many cases – it is!
- Those who go and work on the UK railways do so on the basis that they have had bad experiences on the railways, and have seen extensive adverse media coverage. Their initial perception is therefore that this is a sloppy and uncaring organization; and this is the attitude that they have when they first start work. Network Rail HR staff state that this is one of the major preconceptions that they have to get over during induction programmes.

It is important to restate the importance of understanding what people's perceptions are of particular individuals, and the necessity to manage them, removing any misperceptions and reinforcing the priorities and positives.

Box 10.8: The Blair kitchen cabinet

When he became prime minister in 1997, Tony Blair quickly appointed a close circle of advisers. These were people whom he had known for many years, and in whom he had full confidence. They were also understood to be persons of great capability. The overall standpoint was therefore that Blair and this group of advisers would work out the main elements of policy and present them to the Cabinet and to Parliament for approval and implementation.

However, it quickly became apparent that the relationships themselves were starting to drive activities. For example:

• Derry Irvine, who was appointed as lord chancellor shortly after Blair became prime minister, had been Blair's university tutor.
• Bernie Ecclestone, appointed to advise on industrial and sports management, had made a large donation to the Labour Party, in return for relaxing the rules on tobacco advertising.

The result was that the strength of purpose, policy and direction that had been sought fell quickly into disrepute; and the relationships and the nature of favours sought and delivered became the perceived driving force.

At its best, this is found in mentoring, nurturing and other positive and encouraging relationships, the output of which is both organization and individual development. In other cases, it is at the core of organization and intra-organization power and influence struggles and consists of 'favours for favours' – support and compliance in particular activities in return for rewards and favours when the struggle is over and successfully concluded.

Favouritism

Favouritism is an extreme form of patronage. It occurs where the patron gives advancement or rewards to the protege as the result of some personal quality or attribute.

Favouritism also exists when it is known, understood, believed or perceived that specific groups and individuals can deliver organizational, occupational and personal favours.

It becomes clear that favouritism (and also many forms of patronage) is therefore a tainted and corrupted relationship. The only exception to this is where a genuine mutual confidence and mutuality of interest exist, to the advantage of the organization as a whole as well as the 'favoured' party. Otherwise, it quickly becomes clear that the favours that are known, understood or perceived to be on offer quickly become the driving force of the particular situation (see Box 10.8).

Victimization

The converse of favouritism is victimization and occurs when the patron takes a dislike to the subordinate, again for some personal reason. They are then used as a scapegoat or victim when required. If this is allowed to get out of hand, it is stressful and demoralizing to the individual affected and also to those around them. The worst excesses of this are bullying, harassment, persistent personal attacks (physical and verbal) and the blocking of opportunities and prospects for advancement.

Victimization, and the associated ills of bullying, discrimination and harassment, are illegal as well as morally repugnant. However, each is actively used in particular situations when the bully or victimizer sees some advantage to be gained. This advantage, they imagine, arises from a variety of sources as follows:

- the need to build a reputation as a ferocious, strident or dominant manager;
- the need to put a psychological distance between themselves and everyone else;
- the need to build their own personal mythology and legends;
- following patterns of behaviour that are known, believed or perceived to have worked for others in the past.

In all cases where proven, both the organization and the individuals responsible are found to have broken the law. Compensation is always awarded to the victims, and the organization's reputation suffers as the result (see Box 10.9).

The ability to influence

Both patronage and also general political relationships within organizations depend on the extent to which one party may exert influence over others. The key features of this are:

- dependence;
- uncertainty;
- expectations;
- authority;
- confidence.

Box 10.9: Bedpans

A second-year student nurse was undertaking one of her periods of planned work experience on the wards of a busy urban hospital. The work was heavy and demanding; the wards were under-staffed; nevertheless, the student nurse was enthusiastic and committed. She went about her duties, as organized by the ward sister, methodically and purposefully. Everyone admired her fledgling professionalism; and it would not be long before she was able to speed up. Everyone was confident that she would make an excellent nurse once her studies finished.

One morning, she found herself emptying bedpans. At this point, one of the senior nurses came up to her and appeared to deliberately knock her, causing her to spill the contents of the bedpan on the ward floor. In front of everyone, the senior nurse shouted at the student: 'You stupid, clumsy girl! Now go and clean that up.'

The student nurse did as she was told. When she had finished cleaning it up, she went into the sluice to wash everything up. The senior nurse followed her into the sluice, and proceeded to attack her.

Very distressed, upset and angered by the whole incident, the student nurse reported this to her tutor. However, her tutor laughed, and then stated: 'Oh, we know all about this senior nurse. Everyone who goes on to that ward gets a dose of that treatment. It's a good job she liked you; otherwise she would have made sure that you yourself needed some form of hospital treatment!'

The tutor went on to explain that the senior nurse's reputation had existed for many years. The senior nurse meant nothing by this; she simply saw it as a rite of passage that all students ought to go through.

It was also clear that the hospital authorities knew exactly what was going on, and resolutely refused to do anything about it. Indeed, on several occasions when complaints had been made, it had been made clear to the complainants that if they pursued the matter further, it would damage, if not destroy, their careers.

Dependence

The greater the dependence of a protege on a patron, the greater their susceptibility to being influenced to go in particular directions or to pursue particular projects. However, where dependence is seen as a threat to enduring well-being, people, groups and organizations seek to reduce this, and to enlarge their spheres of influence so that they have other outlets and contacts that they can use.

Uncertainty

Where people are unclear or uncertain about the correctness or otherwise of an action, they will nevertheless tend to carry it out if requested or directed to do so by someone in authority because *their* responsibility for it is thus removed. Also where people are unclear about current activities and behaviour, the greater their propensity to change to something that gives clear guidance or sets firm standards (see Box 10.10).

Expectations

Where the expectations of those in organizations and their groups are well understood, anything that is presented to them in ways that are perceived to meet and satisfy them is more likely to be accepted and complied with. Where expectations are not well understood or where there is a lack of attention to the presentation, acceptance is less certain.

Authority

The greater the authority behind a particular drive or initiative, the more likely it is that it will be accepted. This is true whatever the form of authority – rational, legal, expert or charismatic.

Box 10.10: Paper-making

Paper-making is a dangerous process. The paper production lines are all heavily guarded by physical barriers, making it impossible for anyone to injure themselves, provided that proper procedures are followed.

Removing the guards from the machines is a dismissible offence where proven. However, in one of the mills, there was a serious accident in which an operative lost her hand.

The inquiry quickly turned to how this could have happened. If the machines had been properly guarded, and procedures had been followed, it was impossible for her to have put herself in the position of losing her hand.

The inquiry therefore asked her directly: 'Did you remove the guard?'

'Yes,' she replied, 'I was ordered to do so by the supervisor so as to speed up the production.'

In this case, any uncertainty surrounding the removal of the guard had been overridden by the fact of the supervisor's authority and instruction.

In passing, there is a crucial lesson here: that taking shortcuts may deliver a short-term advantage; and that the moment that something goes wrong with the shortcut, the organization and its staff always lose.

Confidence

Within organizations, everyone needs confidence: confidence that they are doing a good job; confidence that they are acceptable and accepted within the organization; and confidence in superior and subordinate relationships, as well as interactions with their peers. This confidence is based specifically on:

- the organization delivering its part of the wage–work bargain;
- the strength and viability of the psychological contract;
- expectations of colleagues to deliver their part of the job effectively and successfully;
- knowledge and understanding of the management style of the organization;
- knowledge and understanding of where the organization's priorities lie.

Part of this confidence also stems from how individuals understand their position in the organization, in relation to how the organization views their position. This requires clear understanding, based on active rather than passive involvement. A major point of reference for assessing this mutual confidence ought to be the regular performance review or appraisal; in particular, this ought to demonstrate:

- where good work has been done and the rewards on offer;
- any shortcomings and the remedies now required.

This basis then ought to form the position from which confidence is developed, and so performance is further enhanced (see Box 10.11).

Box 10.11: Underwear sales

Stephen Jones was appointed UK sales manager for a major lingerie and underwear manufacturing company. When he started, Stephen was given a clear remit: to increase sales by 15 per cent over the course of his first year in post; and to increase sales by a further 15 per cent during the second year.

Stephen found that he had an excellent team, and he soon became fully integrated. In the first three months, they reached the 15 per cent increased target; and so they set out to revise upwards their aspirations and expectations.

Stephen was placed on a six-month probationary period; and when his performance review came up at the end of this time, he walked confidently along to the sales director's office, together with his already excellent sales performance figures.

The meeting lasted a few minutes only. The sales director said to Stephen: 'I am very sorry indeed that we have taken you on. Clearly, you are not the right appointment for us, and so we have to let you go. We will give you a year's salary by way of compensation; however, you are now leaving at this moment.'

Staggered, Stephen stammered out the sales performance figures (the sales director in any case knew these, as Stephen had kept him regularly informed). However, this was to no avail; and Stephen did indeed leave on the spot.

A few days later, he met up with some of his sales representatives. They told him the real reason why he had been sacked. This was that the sales director had been sales manager two years previously, and the effectiveness of Stephen's performance had now called into question the overall effectiveness (especially lack of it) of the sales director's performance, both at present, and also in his previous job as sales manager. Indeed, the sales director had given the rest of the Board overwhelmingly to understand that Stephen had walked out, and that the compensation was negotiated in order to ensure that Stephen did not take his present customer and client list to a competitor.

Refusals and blockages

Refusing to do something, or blocking something from being done, is a major source of power and influence for many individuals and groups. The main reasons for refusing to deal with someone from elsewhere in the same organization normally fall into one or more of the following categories.

- Disdain – the people, department or activities are seen to have no value. This may be the result of general perceptions. It may also be the result of preconceived ideas and notions. It may have arisen as a matter of historic fact (for example, where previous results have been poor; previous cooperation between those affected was disastrous).
- Lack of clarity – where one or both parties view the activities of the others with suspicion based on a lack of knowledge and understanding.
- Benefits of associations may not be clear – especially where one party perceives the benefits but the other does not.

- The wider picture – whereby associating with one group may cause the feelings of other groups to be influenced, in turn (for example, department X has a relationship with department Z; department X is approached by department Y to open up relationships; department Y is the enemy of department Z; department X therefore takes the whole picture into account before opening up relationships with department Y).
- Dominance–dependence – the extent and nature of the need for the relationship, and the position of the two parties on the dominance–dependence spectrum.
- The potential relationship – the perceptions of the extent to which it can and might be developed to mutual advantage and, above all, in the interests of the blockage. In this case, the onus is clearly on the approacher to indicate the likely benefits to the blocker.
- Lack of trust – the extent to which those involved say what they mean, mean what they say; and the extent to which each can deliver what is promised.

Special relationships

The most important of these are those which exist between the chief executive officer's department and other functions; and between the head office and outlying functions of those organizations that are so designed. Invariably, there is a draw of resources, prestige, status and influence towards the head office (and very often this occurs at the expense of those both physically and psychologically remote from the centre).

Right or wrong, it is a key relationship and those who seek to operate successfully must recognize its extent. Where necessary, this relationship must be nurtured and developed and the interests of the chief executive or head office engaged. Conversely, it is a key part of the chief executive and head office function to recognize the presence and prevalence of this, and to ensure that the relationships between themselves and their more distant functions remain productive, effective and harmonious.

Additionally, special relationships exist between those in the same occupations in different organizations, and those of the same rank or status within organizations, in the form of peer group gatherings and clusters. The purpose is to ensure some kind of mutual strength and support when required; and also to build relationships that can, and do, facilitate operational and departmental activities, in given sets of circumstances.

Confidence and trust

The key feature in the nature of organization politics arises from the level of mutual confidence and trust held by those in particular relations. Where there is no confidence or trust the relationship is corrupted at the outset.

In terms of organization politics, this may be a constraint within which the groups and individuals have to work. In the worst cases it tends to lead to blame scapegoating and negative presentation – the denigration of the efforts of others as well as the promotion of self.

However, confidence and trust are destroyed where one party gives these freely and they are not reciprocated; and where information or resources are given over and then used against the giver. They are affected by the balance of truth – the extent to which communications and interactions take place on an overt or covert basis – above all, the use of direct and indirect language, adherence to deadlines and orders of priority.

In organizations with highly developed political systems, confidence and trust start off at a low level, and both individual and groups will make sure that they are very certain of the integrity of those with whom they are dealing before giving out hostages to fortune, departmental secrets and specific matters concerning their own expertise or trade.

Moral compass

From time to time individuals and groups are called upon to interact with those whose ideologies and values they find repugnant. While in absolute terms it is easy to encourage them not to have any association, in practice this is not always possible.

For example, it may be essential to deal with somebody who is known to be a bully to their staff (or their family) or with someone who is known to take all the glory and credit for success for themselves and to find scapegoats and others to blame for failures.

Additionally, organizations and their managers find their whole integrity called into question when something goes wrong that had plainly only been started in the first place for reasons of expedience or short-term advantage. In particular, the morality of the leadership of failing organizations (as well as their expertise) is always called into question when any, or all, of the following occur:

- decline in productive output while accompanied by redundancies at the operational end;
- rewarding those who work in administrative functions at the expense of those at the frontline;
- awarding bonuses and high pay rises to those at the top of the organization, while asking those at the bottom to take pay freezes;
- cutting costs by concentrating only at the frontline of the organization.

The collective moral compass of the organization clearly takes the strength and integrity of the leadership as its starting point. Where there is no moral strength, the following patterns of behaviour start to emerge.

- Everybody becomes self-seeking and self-serving, operating in isolation from the interests of the organization, or else putting their own interests before those of the organization.
- Resorting to identity with their profession or occupation rather than with the organization (this is an enduring problem for health and education services, where people say: 'I am a surgeon' rather than 'I work for the NHS'; 'I am a teacher' rather than 'I work for my local authority').
- Corrupting systems and procedures so that they serve the interests of individuals rather than the organization.
- Undertaking periods of training and development at the organization's expense for personal rather than occupational and organizational advantage.

It is always the case that people prefer to work for, and do business with, organizations that have demonstrably strong positions of integrity, and clear standards of morality. Where this is not the case, it does not necessarily mean that people will refuse to work for them or do business with them; it is the case that performance will decline over extended periods of time as staff and customer seek alternative employers and outlets (see Box 10.12).

Box 10.12: The Wilkinson Report 1992

Wilkinson (1992) conducted an extensive survey of societies, and produced a report from which some clear conclusions could be drawn:

- the greater the spread between those on the highest earnings and those on the lowest, the greater the level of potential and actual social instability;
- people took their lead from those at the top of organizations and society; and where no clear lead was demonstrable, they acted in ways in which either they felt the leaders of society would act, or set their own standards, norms and values;
- there would always be an organizational and social pecking order, in which some groups would always have greater influence than others; and it was therefore incumbent upon the leaders of organizations and society to ensure that every group was attended to, looked after and given the best possible opportunities.

When Sir Fred Goodwin was dismissed as the chief executive of the Royal Bank of Scotland in July 2007, he was allowed to retire at the age of 50 on a pension of £700,000 per annum. It quickly became clear that:

- he had asked for this himself;
- the other top managers of the Royal Bank of Scotland had approved it;
- the approval had been ratified by the Board of Directors;
- the whole package had been ratified and agreed by the UK Financial Services Authority.

The subsequent treatment of the lowest-paid staff of the Royal Bank of Scotland was less favourable. Many of these were on salaries of between £16,000 and £30,000 per annum with no prospect of advancement and no prospect either of pension until aged 66. In March 2009, nevertheless, the Royal Bank of Scotland declared 10,000 redundancies from among these ranks. And the spread between top and bottom salaries in the particular example is reflected in Wilkinson's assertions about instability.

Ambiguity

Problems of ambiguity arise when spheres of influences, roles and lines of activity are not clearly delineated. This especially occurs where everything else is overtly highly ordered and structured. It also occurs where aims and objectives are not clear and where people therefore tend to operate in a void. In this circumstance groups and individuals use this to extend their boundaries and to build their own empires and to pursue their own aims and objectives.

Problems of ambiguity can, and do, lead to personal and professional conflicts within organizations when (often with the best will) individuals from one domain start inadvertently to encroach on the others' territories. This can, and does, lead to conflicts; and if these conflicts are not resolved, matters then quickly escalate into jockeying for positions of power and influence on the part of those involved. Such problems are easily managed by ensuring that people do understand where the boundaries of their authority lie, and any specific limitations on their freedom to act (see Box 10.13).

Box 10.13: Pioneering – or exceeding your duties?

The oil industry wanted to devise, develop and implement a major management development programme. Accordingly, it invited two departments from within the same business school to tender for the work.

To one of the departments, it quickly became clear that this would not be feasible – it simply did not have the resources. Accordingly, the head of department wrote to the oil industry consortium declining the offer, but at the same time stating that he would be more than happy to help as a facilitator in any way that people wanted.

This left the field clear to the other department. Accordingly, it pitched for the work, producing an outline and specification as it saw fit, and stating a price.

The oil industry consortium were not impressed. Respectfully, they asked the department to go away and rewrite the bid, taking into account certain conditions.

Back came the response: there were to be no changes to the specification, nor to the price stated. The oil industry consortium could take it or leave it. This was the way in which the department carried out its work; this was the way in which the department would organize such a programme. In support of this position, the department pointed to the extensive range of awards that the teaching and research staff had achieved. The oil industry consortium was therefore lucky to be able to attract the attention of the department at all, much less engage it to do some work.

Dumbfounded, the oil industry consortium rejected the bid. It now went back to the first head of department, and asked for advice on using other institutions which would indeed deliver the work required.

The ambiguity and uncertainty arose from a combination of factors: the willingness but inability on the part of one head of department to do the work; and the unwillingness of the other department to do the work on anything but its own terms. When this happens, it is always stressful (and often expensive) to those involved. Such problems can be overcome by delineating people's areas and spheres of influence and the range of activities that they may, or may not, be involved in.

Realpolitik activities

These are normally based on one or more of the following.

- **Alliances with powerful people and groups**: especially with those either in or close to the corridors of power and with others among the upper levels of the organization. People may also seek out junior staff from the chief executive's department and other highly influential functions – personal assistants and secretaries for example – as informal friends, advocates and sources of information (secretaries and personal assistants at all levels have access to both volume and quality of information).
- **Showing quick results**: this is in any case excellent for group morale. It is also often politically necessary to be able to prove to backers that their backing was not misplaced. This can, and does, lead to people seeking short-term rather than long-term advantages; and such problems are compounded when shareholders and

backers do come to expect immediate results as the norm, rather than concentrating on the long-term.

- **IOUs**: this is where a favour given brings with it the expectation of something in return, whether instant or deferred – and that the debtor will be expected to pay up when asked.
- **Information acquisition and manipulation**: as referred to elsewhere, information is a resource. When viewed from this standpoint, it is to be filtered, edited and represented (even misrepresented and corrupted) to ensure that the given interest is best served. Information is also packaged in such headings as 'top secret', 'classified', 'restricted' – again, from the political point of view, this gives it exclusivity and desirability – and therefore value.
- **Battlefields**: in political terms, people tend to avoid pitched battles – because they may lose (and moreover be seen to have lost). The more usual approach adopted is the gradual or incremental – the chipping away at the target, rather than setting out to destroy it in one fell swoop (apart from anything else, the victor of an overt and decisive engagement may be seen as a bully, and the defeated as a victim). The gradualist approach is generally much less noticeable and is therefore not regarded as a threat.

Guerrilla war is also engaged in where one department or group seeks to denigrate the efforts and achievements of others. It consists of sniping, gaining adverse coverage and identifying the weaknesses of others and spotlighting them (one of the most powerful positions of all is that of spotlighter – the light is shone on the particular point desired and the spotlighter remains in the relative darkness and invisibility behind the light).

The language used here is that of military engagement and this reflects accurately the organizational behaviour equivalent. Battles and wars are fought – both to preserve and maintain position, and also to enhance it. Those involved store up memories of victories and defeats so that they may build on successes and take steps to avoid future failures.

Competition for resources

As stated above (see Chapter 9) organizations and their top and senior managers still persist in asking their departments, divisions, functions, managers and supervisors to compete for resources, rather than bidding for them on the basis of what is needed in order to carry out effective and productive work.

Where this exists, those responsible for competing for resources simply learn the rules of the competition rather than referring everything to the needs of the department. Thus for example:

- If managers are more likely to give positive responses early in the morning/last thing in the evening, then this is when approaches will be made to them.
- If resources are approved based on one department's ability to denigrate another, then the focus of the bid will be the denigration itself.
- If resources are required for something that top managers understand, it is much easier to gain acceptance and approval, than if bidding for something that they do not fully understand.

Box 10.14: The world turned upside down

'If the ticketing and the footings are all correct, and if the numbers look alright on a single page of paper, in American industry and commerce you can have $30 million of capital equipment for the asking.

If you ask for a quarter of a million dollars to support a staff development programme, people will look at you as if you are mad. And when I discussed this in public with some of the highest-status and highest-paid managers in America, the chief executive of a Fortune 50 company said to me: "But Tom, that's the American way. With the equipment – you can have what you like because you need it for production. But if you train your staff – they'll leave. It's as simple as that."'

Source: T. Peters (1986) *The World Turned Upside Down* – Channel 4.

In practice, nobody ever gets everything that they ask for all of the time. However, top and senior managers can find out for themselves where resources are required and allocate them accordingly. If they do this in detail, they will also be able to respond effectively to resource bids as and when they arise (see Box 10.14).

Lobbying and presentation

The key to all successful internal political activity lies in the effectiveness of lobbying and presentation. Much of this is implicit and even stated as part of the forms of political strategy indicated above. The rest lies in the ability to recognize those emphases of particular initiatives and activities that are likely to gain a sympathetic hearing and those that are not. The problem then is to find the right channels and media to be used to best advantage, and to combine these to form an effective case that can be well presented. As with all communications, therefore, success comes about as the result of under-standing the requirements of the receivers and choosing the right media, format and language. In political activities, and especially when dealing with senior figures, this invariably includes attention to:

- flattery, vanity and triumphs;
- timescales (often the lobby has only a limited time in which to put across their case);
- the combination of substance and presentation (a fair case well presented invariably succeeds at the expense of a brilliant case poorly presented);
- to the merits and demerits of other lobbies and interest – part of any political process consists of denigrating opposing points of view as well as the sound delivery of one's own case.

Lobbying also involves:

- the engagement of other vested interests and special interest groups who may be persuaded to a particular point of view, either because it is related to their interests, or because they may see an advantage accruing as the result of support, or in return for favours previously given;

- use of statistics and other information supports and emphasizes the case, especially when these can be related to direct and positive statements (for example, 90 per cent of people are in favour of this; by doing this we will double our market share in 12 weeks). These can also be used in less rational and even overtly spurious ways (for example, next door had a 12 per cent pay rise, you are offering us 3 per cent, what is the certain effect of this on our morale?) but which nevertheless may be effective. National politicians engaged in public and media debates are expert at this, as are trade union representatives.

Political language

Within organizations the language always varies. This is because people have their own phrases and summaries to describe what is going on in their own particular situation. All organizations also produce their own definitions of specific activities (for example, performance appraisal at BT is called 'appraisement') and they all also have their own jargon, short forms and shorthand.

All organizations also have their own forms of language which are known, believed and perceived to reinforce the words that are actually being stated. This is so that what is being said can quite legitimately be given a context or an emphasis without crossing any boundaries of rudeness, arrogance, ignorance, or unwarranted praise or flattery; or else to avoid making commitments. Serious problems arise when the language used is transparently dishonest or inadequate. Where such language is used, everyone involved quickly learns and understands the messages that are being given off (see Box 10.15).

Organizational health and well-being

Organizational politics are the barometer of its general state of health and well-being. The indicators of this are:

- Levels of absenteeism, sickness and turnover – the stated reasons why each of these occur and the attitude adopted towards them by the organization at large as well as by individual managers and supervisors. The key features are the nature and extent of procedures to deal with these and the ways in which these are used; the use to which any general and specific information thus gained is put; the volume of time and resources expended on these including the creation of departments and functions for their purpose. Particular figures can indicate both general and specific causes for concern – excess absence or departures from particular areas for example. These are always a general indication of states of morale, confidence and motivation.
- Levels, nature and purposes of meetings – the extent to which people are, in reality, employed to attend meetings (rather than for their substantive purpose) and the effects of this on the rest of the work. The purpose and agenda of meetings is a strong indication of this and is reinforced by the extent to which people need to be seen to be present as distinct from having any real contribution to make.
- The nature of rewards and favours – the reasons for which they are issued. Here the remedy lies directly in the hands of those in overall control. By simply offering rewards

Box 10.15: Political language

Never was the use of political language more clearly designated than by Condoleeza Rice, the US secretary of state at the time of the 2005 Israeli invasion of Lebanon. Speaking to the assembled world media about the crisis, she called on the Israeli government to 'order an urgent ceasefire and withdrawal of its troops'.

It quickly became apparent that what she was telling the Israeli government was that it could do what it liked for the foreseeable future. If she had really meant what she gave the overwhelming impression that she meant, the form of words used would have been: 'an immediate ceasefire and withdrawal'.

Other examples include:

- 'I respect your views', meaning 'I do not respect your views'; 'You are talking rubbish'.
- 'Nothing was done wrong'; 'No mistakes were made' – the use of the passive voice means that the individual is unwilling to associate themselves with whatever has indeed gone wrong.
- 'I was part of a team that . . .', meaning 'Much as I would like to, I am unable to take the full credit for this'.

Each of these phrases has legitimate uses in some circumstances. Whenever they are used, people will always understand the legitimacy or otherwise of their use.

In situations where organizations expect people to go above and beyond the call of duty when they carry out their jobs and occupations, the following phrases are always used as a prelude to sanctions:

- 'He/she has exceeded his/her authority.'
- 'His/her enthusiasm got the better of him/her.'

And, most insidiously of all:

- 'He/she has exceeded his/her duties to the point of treason' (a phrase used by Heinrich Himmler whenever he found it necessary to get rid of particular individuals).

for achievement of aims and objectives rather than because of presentation, lobbying, visibility or sycophancy, a swathe of political battlegrounds may be removed.

- The attitude to failures and mistakes – where this is negative and punitive it encourages those concerned to seek scapegoats and victims. It also develops fear and this, in turn, leads to the construction of barriers and protectors by which people can insulate themselves from failure. Where mistakes are viewed as a learning experience again, much of this is removed. Again, this should be seen from the standpoint of both results and politics. Where the overall political system is positive and healthy, poor performance is likely to be seen as the starting point for learning and development.

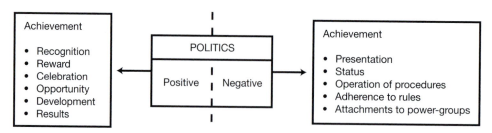

Figure 10.2 Politics and achievement

Where the overall system is unhealthy, this becomes more complicated. Excellent results may be unacceptable politically (for example, where somebody achieves something that nobody else had previously managed). The emphasis may be on presentation rather than achievement and so excellent results, poorly marketed or publicized, may not carry sufficient weight (see Figure 10.2).

- The extent to which departments, divisions, functions and groups continue to serve the purpose for which they were created; the extent to which they are allowed to outlive their usefulness; and what happens to them after they have served their purpose (whether they are destroyed, reconstituted, rejuvenated, made redundant, re-deployed, given other projects, encouraged to seek work as the result of their own initiative and so on). The key factors are the extent to which the organization assumes responsibility for this; and the extent to which the group itself does so – for example, by making itself indispensable, and therefore indestructible; and the extent to which the skills, knowledge and qualities of those involved are transferable elsewhere. For more positive and enlightened organizations, the latter is much less likely to be a problem than the other two.
- The balance of core and peripheral activities; primary and support functions; and the emphasis put on each. Special attention is required for the extent of checking and control functions; the extent of the influence of these; and the extent to which the interaction between these and other functions becomes a part of the ends (rather than the means or processes) of primary functions. Strong indicators of these are highly specialized job titles (for example, clock control supervisor, clock card clerk) or extremely vague job titles (for example, director of corporate affairs). They arise from the notion that 'something needs to be done' but without sufficient attention to what this might be, or why, or how. They may also arise as the result of having to find a niche (and therefore a job) for someone whose previous remit has expired – and again, this often occurs without sufficient attention to the what, why or how.
- The treatment, priority and attention given to vested interests, pressure groups, lobbies, special interests and other pressures, and the reasons why these either succeed or fail (and the reasons why they are perceived or seen to do so). This especially concerns, again, whether they succeed or fail because of the particular merits of the case that they put forward as distinct from their ability to energize powerful forces – for example, influential individuals and the media.
- The extent to which information gathered for one purpose is used for others. For example, at times of performance appraisal, individuals are often asked to state what

their weaknesses are, wherein they think their performance could be improved and what needs for development they may have. In some cases such information may be used to block promotions, restrict openings and opportunities – in the worst cases this may lead even to disciplinary action. This is also true of financial information – when a set of results are reported for one purpose, these may then be taken out of context and used to indicate particular general levels of performance.

Conclusions

The main lesson is to recognize that politics exists in all organizations – all organizations are political systems. Throughout the environment there are various agendas – departments and their managers have secondary and hidden agendas, promoting themselves and their advancement as well as undertaking particular courses of action.

Those responsible for the design and structure of organizations must therefore recognize these components and vagaries of the work environment. In the medium to long term the negative aspects outlined have extremely demoralizing and debilitating effects on everyone concerned and this ultimately includes customers and clients. There is therefore a direct relationship between the state of organizational politics and performance success and effectiveness. Organizations must therefore recognize these activities for what they are and take remedial steps wherever necessary and desirable.

Above all, the nature of political activity within organizations gives a strong indication of its overall integrity, effectiveness and levels of performance. Where the operation of political systems is mainly positive, and where the conversation, gossip and stories are positive and cheerful, this gives a strong indication of the overall strength of the organization, at least at present. Where the political systems and networks are mainly negative, where people are plotting against each other, this is almost invariably a symptom of wider organizational malaise; and an organization that is suffering from lack of leadership, integrity and fundamental strength. Negative organization politics also invariably indicate declining organizational performance.

Finally, where the political climate of the organization is wholly or mainly positive, this takes up very much less energy than where it is negative. Negative behaviour and attitudes, if unmanaged and unchecked, lead to much greater levels of stress and disharmony than those which are positive.

11 Conflict

Introduction

Conflict exists in all situations where individuals and groups are in disagreement with each other for whatever reason. This potential therefore exists everywhere, where two or more people are gathered together – a world without differences and disagreements is inconceivable! Much of the conflict in the world stems from the basic lack of recognition of this, and the inability to address it in ways designed to alleviate its effect or better still, identify the positive and beneficial potential that is inherent in most situations.

In companies and organizations, managers have to be particularly aware of the following, and to be able to take effective steps to address each when they do arise:

- collective and individual power and influence struggles;
- patronage, favouritism, victimization and blame;
- HR, ER and staff management disputes and grievances, and their causes;
- customer and supplier complaints and their effects;
- the purpose and actions of lobbies and vested interests;
- the actions of individuals within the organization (especially those that are ill-considered and also malicious);
- professional differences of opinion;
- personality clashes;
- genuine misunderstandings.

Prima facie, therefore, the potential for conflict exists in all forms of organization. It is essential that all those concerned with conception, direction and ordering of organizations understand its sources and causes, and are able to address these positively (see Figure 11.1).

Levels of conflict

The following levels of conflict may be distinguished:

- argument;
- competition;
- and warfare.

Argument and competition may be either positive, healthy and creative or negative, unhealthy and destructive. Warfare is always destructive. The nature, symptoms and causes must be understood and these then become a focus for management action in striving for productive and harmonious places of work.

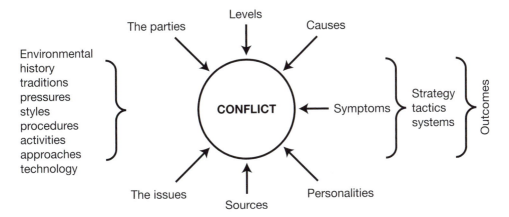

Figure 11.1 The nature and context of conflict in organizations

It is useful therefore at the outset to establish the presence of conflict in organizations (as in all human situations). Conflict may be seen as positive and beneficial, a force capable of being harnessed for the greater good and contributing to organization effectiveness. It is also clearly negative in many forms.

Argument, discussion and debate

This takes place between groups of two or more people and brings about (whether by accident or design) a better-quality, more informed and better balanced view of the matter in hand. Provided that it is positive, the process of argument and debate leads to a better understanding also of the hopes, fears and aspirations of other group members. It also identifies gaps in knowledge and expertise. This can then be remedied, either through training or through the inclusion in the debate of persons with the required expertise. It helps in the process of building mutual confidence and respect. It also encourages individuals to dig into their own resources, expertise and experience and to use these for the benefit of all concerned. It helps to build group identity. It leads to a better quality of decision-making and understanding and acceptance of the reasons why particular directions are chosen.

Argument, discussion and debate become unproductive when they are not structured. People must be clear what they are debating. Otherwise they will inevitably argue about different things. At the very least this leads to group dysfunction and disharmony in the particular situation. The essence is therefore to be able to set out the desired aims and objectives of the discussion and to have available as far as possible all necessary information (see Box 11.1).

Rules for productive and positive argument, discussion and debate

These are as follows.

- Purpose of the debate.
- Clearly stated agenda.

Box 11.1: Change of direction at Marks & Spencer

In 1998, Sir Richard Greenbury took over as chief executive at Marks & Spencer. For many years, he had been the deputy chief executive; and over that period he had formed his own very distinct ideas as to how the company would progress if, and when, he became chief executive.

His immediate actions in taking over were as follows:

- to order a £200 million refurbishment of the company's headquarters in Baker Street, London;
- to introduce a range of products targeted directly at the youth market.

Both were contentious moves. The company had never been known for profligacy in corporate expenditure; and now suddenly this was to change. The company had also never been known for its attention to the youth market: indeed, there was a widespread perception across the UK retail industry that young people 'would not be seen dead' in Marks & Spencer, as this was where their parents shopped.

Both ventures were expensive. In particular, the venture into the youth market failed for exactly the reason and perception stated above: that the youth market had no affinity with Marks & Spencer because this was the store that their parents used. The problem was compounded because now the older generation believed that, as the company was shifting towards the youth market, it was no longer for them; and so they also looked around for other places to shop.

Richard Greenbury left the company in 2004. After his departure, and when the expense of each of the above ventures became apparent, many of the company directors and top managers stated that they knew that the refurbishment was an organizational error, and that the move into the youth market was an operational error. Because of the power of the personality of Richard Greenbury, however, they found themselves unable to state or mount any opposition in practice. This was in spite of the fact that there was plenty of data and information available to back up any assertion that a move into the youth market would not be a good idea. Additionally, the company culture was based on austerity, and so any multi-million pound refurbishment of corporate premises would be badly received.

The lesson is that there was plenty of information available, and plenty of people who (afterwards) were prepared to state their opposition to both ventures. Ultimately, the professional argument and debate did not take place; and this was because the staff involved feared an escalation of debate into warfare with Richard Greenbury. The result was a ten-year slump in company performance (1998 levels of turnover did not return until 2007), because a constructive and substantial debate around two key issues could not, and did not, take place.

Source: J. Bevan (2007) *The Rise and Fall – and Rise Again of Marks & Spencer* – Century.

- Mutual interest of all concerned in the resolution of the matter in hand.
- Commitment to the debate itself and to the matters on the agenda.
- Honesty and openness so that differing views may become public and be heard without prejudice or penalty to the holders.
- A structure for the debate that addresses issues; facts; feelings; values; and which has a clearly understood purpose. This is true of all good discussions. Creative acts such as brainstorming have the clear intent of producing a wide range of ideas in as short a time as possible. The best committees work to an agenda, remit and terms of reference.
- Mutual trust and confidence in the personalities and expertise of those involved.

There are therefore both positive and negative aspects of the argument, debate and discussion process. It is likely to indicate where more serious differences may lie, especially if these indicate persistent clashes between particular individuals; where alliances start to form in the debating chamber which carry on after the debate has finished; and where people adopt contrary positions based on countering the views of someone else in the group.

In these cases argument itself is not going to resolve the problems and it is necessary to look more closely into the situation. Invariably, there will be deeper and underlying conflicts that need to be addressed if the group is to be made effective again.

Transaction analyses

One way of looking at how an argument or debate is progressing, and the likely path that it is going to take, is to study the transactions that are taking place.

'Transactions' in this context are the statements made by one party to the other, and are a combination of:

- what is said;
- how it is said;
- other contextual factors, including aggression, calmness, positiveness and negativity, as well as the actual words used.

For example, a conversational transaction may start with the question: 'Where is my pen?' This question has a range of responses, both in terms of the words used, and also in the tone of voice, for example:

- 'I don't know';
- 'It's on the table';
- 'I haven't had it';
- 'Where you left it';
- 'Am I to always be running around after you?'

The response given, and the tone of voice used, then leads to the development of the transaction. In particular, those participating can choose:

- whether to have a productive discussion;
- whether to use the development of the transaction positively or negatively;
- whether or not to have a row.

Berne (1984) stated that transactions are the function of ego states. 'Ego states' may be classified as:

- nurturing parent, supportive and positive;
- critical parent, aggressive, critical and condescending;
- adult, in which words are used with a clear rationale;
- free child, used in moments of exuberance and indulgence (including self-indulgence);
- adapted child, in which a range of learned and assumed responses are used, relative to the previous statement.

This is represented diagrammatically in Figure 11.2.

Representing transactions in these ways indicates whether or not a particular conversation or debate is likely to escalate, whether it can be kept on a serious, productive and rational footing or whether it is likely to result in a row (as above).

Of particular importance are the following:

- the more that transactions can be kept on an adult–adult basis, the greater the potential for productive debate and argument;
- the adapted child is likely to produce 'acceptable' responses (as in the Marks & Spencer example above, where those involved with Richard Greenbury refused to confront him);
- parent–parent and child–child transactions are likely to result in rows and arguments.

Competition

Competition exists between individuals and groups and within organizations. It also exists between organizations. It is either positive or negative, healthy or unhealthy. At its best, competition sets standards for all to follow – whether within the organization or within the entire sphere within which it operates. On a global scale, the standards of production, quality and managerial practice of certain organizations are held up as models to which the rest of the world should aspire. Some sectors arrange their organizations into league tables, thus shining a competitive light on some aspects of the activities carried out.

The nature of competition may either be:

- closed or distributive, where one party wins at the expense of others;
- open or integrative, where there is scope for everyone to succeed;
- collaborative, where the boundaries of operations of each party can be set to ensure that everyone has a fair share of 'the cake' – i.e. whatever is being competed for. The competitive environment may be dominated by one party or a few large parties who each take what they want from the situation and whatever is left over is to be disputed among the remaining players.

In organizational behaviour terms, competition is more likely to be fruitful and productive if it is open, if the rewards for competing effectively are available to all. Competition is likely to degenerate into conflicts where, for example, competition for influence, resources or accommodation is closed and one party is to succeed at the expense of the others.

Competitive relationships exist best within organizations where attention is positively given to standards, creativity, the nature of the groups and the purpose of creating the situation. The aim is to bring out the best in everyone concerned, to improve performance and efficiency, to set absolute standards for activities and from this to form a base from which improvements can still be made. If these elements and rationale are not present, then organizations should consider alternative means of achieving their purpose. A negative competitive approach is likely to lead to interdepartmental strife, especially where the form of competition is closed (see Box 11.2).

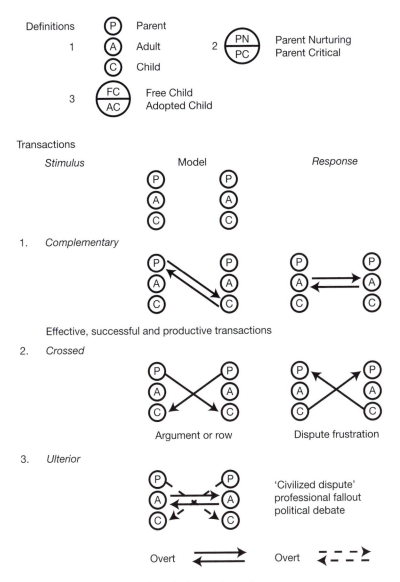

Figure 11.2 Transactional analysis: configurations
Source: E.H. Berne (1984) *Games People Play* – Penguin.

Warfare

Warfare exists where inter-group relations have been allowed to get out of hand, where the main aims and objectives of activities have been lost and where great energies and resources are taken up with fighting the corner, reserving the position and denigrating other departments and functions.

Contextual factors

The contextual factors are:

- personalities;
- groups;
- resources;
- influence.

Personalities

Strident, dominant and powerful personalities have major influences on the extent and prevalence of conflict, and on how particular conflicts turn out. Especially, some strident and powerful personalities will create conflict so as to be able to inflict their own (real and perceived) influence on the situation. If successful, they gain reputation, and the power of their personality is understood to be effective, and also to increase. If this form of behaviour is successful within organizations, ambitious people will develop their own form of personality-based approach to conflict, so that they can progress and advance.

Groups

In many organizations, groups seek to ensure their own position of pre-eminence and influence (see Chapter 9). When conflicts and disputes do arise, the group then seeks to use their position as a lever for getting their own way (whether at the expense of others, or alongside others).

Box 11.2: Who are your competitors?

As stated above, competition exists between, as well as within, organizations. It is also important to recognize the full range and extent of competitive activity. For full understanding, this needs to be viewed at a variety of levels.

At its simplest form, competition is perceived and understood to exist between companies and organizations in the same sector. For example, if you ask anyone: 'Who are the main competitors of McDonald's?' the response will always be Burger King and/or KFC. At a corporate level, this may well be true. At branch/outlet level, it is much more likely to be the case that none of these companies go directly head-to-head with each other, preferring to locate a little way away from their competitors. This is so that the individual outlets have some kind of market assurance, rather than having to compete directly for every sale.

Another way to look at competition is in terms of 'competition for what?'. For example:

- If a customer has £5 in their pocket, they may have to make a choice between buying a meal and having to walk home, or foregoing the meal and paying for public transport. From this point of view, both the fast food outlet and also the public transport provider are competing for the same customer.
- If a customer has £10,000 to spend, they have the opportunity to have a once-in-a-lifetime holiday, to buy a mid-range new car or have improvements made to their home. From this point of view, there exists competition between the holiday provider, the car saleroom and the home improvement organization. In practice, if this particular perspective is adopted, it is not always easy to make judgements about where the true basis of competition lies. It is, however, essential to know and understand that organizations are competing for the disposable income of customers and clients, as well as competing with each other.

Resources

Internal organization warfare is often centred on resource questions and issues. It emerges when departments and individuals perceive that those who have control over resources are susceptible to non-operational approaches. They are also perceived to have their own reasons for issuing resources to particular departments – for example, the availability or potential for triumphs; gaining favour and acceptance as the result (see Box 11.3).

Influence

Competition for power and influence is also apparent. A multiple agenda is normally pursued. Particular groups and individuals present their achievements in the best possible light. This takes various forms and is to ensure that:

- real achievements are recognized;
- achievements are presented in ways acceptable to the sources of power and influence (for example, chief executive officer, top managers, particular shareholders and stakeholders, the community at large);
- the group is receptive to patronage and that there are rewards to be gained by both the patron and those who come within their ambit;
- they are presented as major achievements, the best possible return on resources and expertise put in;
- the department or individual is presented as having high value and expertise themselves, available for higher favours, good jobs; and that they can be relied upon to produce 'the right results';
- the results are attached (where possible or desirable) to questions of organization success (see Box 11.4).

Box 11.3: 'Let's see who wins'

There still persists in some organizations the view that it is 'a good idea' to have different groups of staff competing for resources. Successful competition of this nature is deemed to be 'a mark of staff excellence'; or 'a mark of managerial acumen'.

Where some groups are going to win, and others are clearly going to lose, this form of competition is necessarily negative. Organizations and their top and senior managers ought to be able to apportion resources on the basis of need, operational effectiveness and functional stability and cohesion.

The problem is compounded because:

- those groups that win these forms of conflict gain perceived strength and recognition as the result;
- those groups that lose this kind of competition become resentful; and they will also have to find other ways of gaining resources.

The result is that the time, effort and energy spent on this form of resource competition is very expensive all round for the organization. It damages and dilutes productive efforts, and stores up trouble for the future. It is also an extremely lazy way of managing from the top; rather than taking active steps and doing the hard work to decide where, and why, resources should be allocated, the problem is simply turned over to the staff, and responsibility abdicated.

Box 11.4: 'How much does it cost?'

Anyone wishing to influence top and senior management to their point of view is normally expected to produce reasonably accurate costings, so that those responsible for corporate decisions know and understand the full consequences of what they are letting themselves and the organization in for.

Production of these figures normally falls under one of the following headings:

- accurate, in which everything is costed out as fully as possible, and then presented as a clear statement of what a particular venture, project or idea will cost;
- acceptable, in which a set of figures is produced that is known, believed or perceived to be acceptable at the time that the figures are presented;
- ball-park, in which figures are presented around which there is some kind of understanding or estimate of accuracy;
- false, in which a set of figures is produced that is known and understood to be false, but which may nevertheless be acceptable enough to get the particular venture agreed, commissioned and started.

Figures can therefore be any of the following:

- behaviourally acceptable and factually accurate;
- behaviourally unacceptable and factually accurate;
- behaviourally acceptable and factually inaccurate;
- behaviourally unacceptable and factually inaccurate.

Sources of conflict in organizations

Most organization conflict can be traced back to one or more of the following.

- Competition for resources and the basis on which this is conducted.
- Lack of absolute standards of openness, honesty, trustworthiness and integrity in general organizational behaviour and in dealings between staff, departments, divisions and functions between different grades of staff and between seniors and subordinates; lack of mutual respect.
- Lack of shared values, commitment, enthusiasm, motivation and low morale.
- Unfairness, unevenness and inequality of personal and professional treatment often linked to perceptions (and realities) of favouritism and scapegoating.
- Physical and psychological barriers, especially those between seniors and subordinates, and also those between departments, divisions and functions.
- Inability to meet expectations and fulfil promises; this is always compounded by the use of bureaucratic (mealy-mouthed) words and phrases.
- Expediency and short-termism that interferes with and dilutes the results that would otherwise be achieved.
- The nature of work and its professional, expert and technical context.
- The structure of work, the division and allocation of tasks and jobs.
- People involved, their hopes and fears, aspirations, ambitions, beliefs, attitudes and values.
- Different perceptions of what is right and wrong; differences in attitudes, values and beliefs; different ethical standards.
- Divergence of managerial, professional, technical and commercial objectives; divergence between service demands and budgetary pressures in public services.
- Changes in direction or priorities imposed by leadership and management.
- Known, believed and perceived toxic communications (see Chapter 7).
- Divergence of objectives and priorities between different groups (see Box 11.5).

Symptoms of conflict

Symptoms of conflict include the following.

- Poor communications between groups, individuals and the organization and its components.
- Poor inter-group relationships based on envy, jealousy and anger at the position of others, rather than mutual cooperation and respect. People turn inward to the members of their own group and away from others.
- Deterioration of personal and professional relationships; increases in personality clashes.
- Increases in absenteeism, sickness, labour turnover, time-keeping problems and accidents.
- Proliferation of non-productive, ineffective and untargeted papers and reports, the purpose of which is publicity and promotion of the individuals and the departments that issue them.
- Proliferation of rules and regulations covering especially the most minor of areas of activities.

Box 11.5: Divergence of objectives

In many organizations, the objectives and priorities of management can, and do, diverge from those of staff at the frontline or working in remote locations. A useful classification of this is as follows:

- where management and operational objectives and priorities coincide absolutely;
- where management and operational objectives and priorities coincide to a greater or lesser extent;
- where management and operational objectives and priorities have little overlap;
- where management and operational objectives and priorities do not coincide at all.

Examples of this include:

- NHS managers having to stick within budgets; operational objectives concerned with patient care and hospital and premises cleanliness;
- management objectives concerned with organizational profitability; operational objectives concerned with customer care and quality of service;
- in universities, management objectives concerned with budget management and fund raising; operational objectives concerned with delivering the highest possible quality of teaching and research.

In each of the above cases, there is no reason why management and operational objectives should diverge. In many cases however, these factors do indeed diverge to the point of absolute non-coincidence. Here is an example: when Plessey-Marconi went bankrupt in 1999, all the staff stated that management had no concerns for anything except profit. Clearly, in this particular case, the management concern for profit was misconstrued, misdirected – and above all, greatly mismanaged.

- Proliferation of changes in job title especially 'upwards'. Thus, for example, a supervisor may become a 'section controller'; a financial manger the 'director of corporate resources'.
- Escalation of disputes and grievances arising out of frustration and anger (rather than antagonism at the outset) and leading to personality clashes and antagonism as well as operational decline.
- Proliferation of control functions at the expense of frontline functions.
- Taking sides and ganging up so that when problems are identified, people join or support one side or the other. This happens with long-running disputes and grievances; in these cases the original cause has normally long since been forgotten.
- Informal corridor and washroom gatherings that persistently discuss wrongs, situational and organizational decline.
- The growth of myths and legends via the grapevine; minor events become major events, small problems become crises, a slight disagreement becomes a major row.
- The growth of arbitration – the handing up of organizational disagreements to higher (and sometimes external) authorities for resolutions. The main cause of this is the

need not to be seen to lose, especially as the result of personal efforts. At the point of decision, therefore, the matter is handed on to a different authority to remove the responsibility for the outcome from the parties in dispute.

- The decline in organizational, departmental, group and individual performance. This is often mirrored by increases in customer complaints, relating either to particular individuals and departments or, more seriously, to the organization as a whole.
- Disregard and disrespect for persons in other parts of the organization. This is mostly directed at management, supervision and upper levels by those lower down. It is also to be found among those at higher levels when they speak of employees in disparaging tones – 'the workers' and 'these people' for example.
- Over-attention to the activities of other departments, divisions and functions, together with spurious and pseudo-analysis of the particular situation.
- Non-productive meetings between persons from different departments, divisions and functions based on the needs of individuals to defend their own corner and protect what they have.

These are the outward manifestations of organizational conflict. It is necessary, however, to look more deeply for the causes of conflict rather than treating the symptoms. Otherwise, for example, ever-greater volumes of communication reports and paperwork are fed into systems that are already overloaded, and to people who treat the content with disdain and eventually contempt. In personal relationships and disputes, the temptation is for organizations to take a firm, even hard, line with the warring parties. The normal effect of this is to escalate rather than dampen down the conflict, unless one party or the other can be proven or demonstrated to be wrong, or unless one party or the other can be persuaded to change their mind (see Box 11.6).

Causes of conflict

The main causes of conflict in organizations are as follows.

- Differences between corporate, group and individual aims and objectives, and the inability of the organization to devise systems, practices and environments in which these can be reconciled and harmonized.
- Inter-departmental and inter-group wrangles overwhelmingly concerned either with:
  - **favour and disfavour** – the outcomes of patronage, favouritism and victimization;
  - **competition** – for resources as above;
  - **communications** – especially bad communications and misunderstanding;
  - **integrity** – especially where this is lacking, and where communications and direction are being delivered dishonestly or with duplicity;
  - **territory** – where one group feels that another is treading in an area that is legitimately theirs;
  - **prestige** – where one group feels that another is gaining recognition for efforts and successes that are legitimately theirs;
  - **agenda** – where one group feels that it is being marginalized by the activities of the other;
  - **poaching and theft** – where one group attracts away the staff of the other and perhaps also their technology, equipment, information and prestige.

- The status awarded by the organization to its different departments, divisions, functions, group and individuals. This is to be seen as:

  - formal relations, based on organizational structure and job definition;
  - informal relations, based on corridor influence and possibly also personal relationships;

Box 11.6: The Planning and Finance Committee

The Planning and Finance Committee of a large public institution presented its accounts for the year-end. One of the members of the Committee was Carole Wright. Carole had only just been appointed to the Committee, and was looking forward to her period of service.

Early in the proceedings, Carole queried one of the items in the financial report. Back came the reply from the Committee chair: 'It's alright. Don't worry about this – I will explain it all later in the meeting.'

During the course of the proceedings, Carole questioned three other items (not because they were necessarily right or wrong, but rather because, as a new member, she did not fully understand them). However, the Committee chair, and several of the members, became ever more irritated and exasperated with her interventions. Finally, the proceedings came to an end. The Committee chair prepared to sign off the figures as being a true and fair reflection, as required by law. Carole intervened for one last time: 'Before you sign off the expenses, please could you now explain, as you promised, the questions that I raised.'

The Committee chair now came back angrily: 'You have been nothing but trouble. I cannot think why you were appointed. Kindly shut up and leave these matters to people who know what they are talking about.'

The meeting finished. Carole arranged to meet with the institution's auditors. She raised her concerns with them, explaining that all she had actually wanted was clarification of one or two points.

The auditors were positive and open about her concerns, stating: 'We too share your concerns. We too have tried to get the institution to clarify these matters. They treat us exactly the same. They have worked out exactly the point at which they can represent these finances as "a true and fair reflection", and they go to exactly this point and no further.'

For her own peace of mind, Carole engaged an independent auditor to look over the figures. The independent auditor told her: 'You are quite right to raise these concerns. This institution is effectively bankrupt; and without doubt, unless they do restructure their finances and get a much firmer control, it will have to either seek further sources of funding, or else be bailed out by the public body for which it works.'

The main lesson of this case is that it is possible to shout down conflicting and dissenting voices in the short-term. However, anyone who takes an active interest in things is certain then to go and find out what the truth of the matter is, as far as they are able. Ultimately, whether or not it is possible to shout down contrary voices and opposition, the true strength and realities (or otherwise) of the situation will become apparent.

Table 11.1 Sources of energy in conflict

Sources of energy in conflict
• The personalities involved
• The departments and functions involved
• The agenda of those involved
• The organizational point of view
• The interests of those involved
• The presence and influence of third parties (for example, the CE, trade unions)
• Any absolute organization standards, rules, regulations and practices involved
• Expediency
• Need for triumphs, scapegoats and favours
• Relative necessity and compulsion to win
• Wider perceptions of the dispute
• Wider perceptions of the outcome
• Alliances: the ability to call on outside support

- favoured and unfavoured status, the means by which this is arrived and what this means to those concerned;
- the organizational pecking order and any other means by which prestige and influence are determined.

Conflict arises also, both from the status quo, where people seek to alter their own position; and from changes that the organization seeks to make (see Table 11.1). For example, when an individual or group suddenly loses power, then a void is left which all the others rush to fill. Conversely, an individual or group may suddenly find itself in favour (for many reasons, operational necessity, expediency, the possibility of a triumph for the favour-giver) and the others rush to do it down.

Individual clashes – both professional and personal – lead to conflict if the basis of the relationship is not established and ordered. For example, one individual sees that a point of debate is a personal attack or questioning of their professional judgement – 'a lively discussion' may be regarded by one as the straightforward airing of a point of view, by the other as questioning their expertise and integrity. This is also often the cause of feelings of favouritism leading to clashes between the recipients (perceived or actual) of preferential treatment, and the others around them.

Bullying and scapegoating is also a form of individual clash, causing conflict between bully and bullied. This again may lead to conflict based, either on support for the victim by others, or by others following the leader and setting upon the victim themselves (see Box 11.7).

- Personality clashes also fall into this category. They become seriously disruptive if allowed to proceed unchecked and if steps are not taken to ensure that there is a professional or operational basis on which relationships can be based.
- Groups may be drawn into conflict as the result of a clash between their leaders or between particular individuals. Role relationships have the potential to cause conflict. This is based on the nature of the given roles. For example, trade union officials are certain to come into conflict with organizations in the course of their duties –

Box 11.7: The bully

A small team of management consultants was engaged to assess the strength of operations and activities at one of the UK's major financial institutions. This assessment was to take the form of:

- a questionnaire-based staff survey;
- interviews with managers;
- interviews with a random selection of staff.

This process worked smoothly. However, when the team came to one of the section heads, they were nonplussed when he stated: 'My staff hate and fear me. And this is how I wish to keep it. I bully and victimize them all of the time. I come into work not knowing myself whom I am going to be picking on – and so they don't know either, and so cannot throw a sicky. And I have the highest output of any division in the company, when measured in terms of profitability on activities. Now, what do you say to that, and what are you going to do about it?'

The consultancy team dug further into the matter. They found that everything that the manager said was indeed true. All his staff hated and feared him, and dreaded being the next victim. They also found that his department's profit levels were indeed well in line with the rest of the industry.

The consulting team dug further. They now found the following:

- absenteeism in this department was in fact twice that of the institution overall;
- staff turnover in the department was ten times that of the institution overall;
- in practice, the staff had little personal influence over the profit margins of the department, since a computer program told them when to buy the commodities in which they traded, and when to sell them.

Eventually, the matter came to a head. One junior member of staff took out a grievance against the manager, citing an especially ferocious volley of verbal abuse. At this point, corporate HR at last intervened. They conducted their own investigation into the state of staff relations and morale in the department. They came to the conclusion that this manager should indeed be removed.

The result was that shortly afterwards he was promoted to a position at the institution's head office.

Many of these attitudes clearly persist across all organizations and sectors. There is an uncomfortable truth that one key reason why these attitudes persist is because of the unwillingness of organizations to tackle them unless the problem becomes apparent; and the unwillingness of staff to report them because they are not confident of institutional support in removing the problem and cause of conflict.

they are often representing the interest of members who have some kind of trouble or dispute. Other role relationships that should be considered are:

- **senior/subordinates** – conflicts of judgement, conflicts based on work output, attitudes style;
- **appraiser/appraisee** – where there are differences (often fundamental) over the nature and quality of the appraisee's performance and the action that this may cause to be taken;
- **functional roles** – conflicts between production and sales over quality, volume and availability of output; between purchaser (concerned with cost and quality) and producer (concerned with output); between personnel (concerned with absolute legal and ethical standards) and the departments which call on their services (concerned with solving problems, speed, expediency); between finance (efficiency) and other functions (effectiveness);
- **internal–external** – the priorities and requirements of external roles (shareholder, stakeholder, bank manager, lobbyist, public interest group, community), and reconciling these with the organization's aims and objectives and those of their staff and activities;
- **parallel roles** – clashes occur, for example, where two or more people are competing for one promotion place; or where of two or more people ostensibly carrying out the same job have, or are perceived to have, work of varying degrees of interest, quality, status and prestige.

The parties to the conflict

In any conflict, the parties involved are likely to come from one, or more, of the following groups:

- top and senior management;
- middle and junior managers and supervisors;
- staff and staff groups;
- peer groups, professional clusters and associations, trade unions and staff associations and representatives;
- lobbies and vested interests;
- customers and suppliers, and their representatives;
- specific social lobbies;
- the media;
- the organization's financial interests.

It is essential that all organizations, and their managers, assess and understand in full detail the extent and prevalence of each of these groups, as follows:

- their propensity to engage in conflict;
- the nature of conflict that they are likely to engage in;
- the strength of feeling that they carry, and with which they are supported;
- what it will normally take to reach agreement with them;
- when, where and how they are likely to raise their concerns or seek a fight.

Operational	Behavioural
• Dysfunctional • Dysfunctional • Inefficiency • Squandering of resources • Loss of productive effort • Customer complaints • Customer loss • Loss of confidence • Loss of trust • Loss of morale • Loss of performance	• Loss of face • Wounded pride • Triumphalism • Scapegoating • Humiliation • Loss of faith • Loss of integrity • Loss of morale • Loss of confidence • Loss of trust

Several of these items occur in each column. The purpose is to identify the relationship between behaviour and business performance.

Figure 11.3 Operational and behavioural outputs of conflict

Strategies for the management of conflict

Thus far it is established that the potential for conflict is present in every human situation and organizations are no exception. Indeed, much of what has so far been discussed clearly applies to a variety of areas (for example, families, social groups, Guides, Scouts). Many of these issues present throughout society are emphasized and concentrated by the fact of their being in work organization and compounded by the ways, structures, rules and regulations in which these are constituted.

The first lesson, therefore, lies in the understanding of this. The second lesson is to recognize that, if attention is paid only to the symptoms, overload is placed on the existing systems of the organization as indicated above.

From this, in turn, there derives the need to adopt strategic approaches (rather than operational) to the management and resolution of conflict. This is based on a framework designed at the outset that should:

*   recognize the symptoms of the conflict;
*   recognize the nature and level (or levels) of conflict;
*   recognize and understand the sources of conflict;
*   investigate the root causes of the conflict;
*   establish the range of outcomes possible;
*   establish the desired outcome.

On to this framework can then be built strategies designed to ensure that the desired outcome is to be achieved.

It is clear from this that the symptoms are nothing more than the outward manifestation that something is wrong; and that it is what has brought these to the surface that needs to be addressed. For example, it is no use sending sales and reception staff on customer care courses because of an increase in complaints if the causes of the problems lie within production functions. It is equally useless to train managers and supervisors in the use of disciplinary and grievance procedures without also giving an understanding of what discipline and grievance handling means in terms of a particular organization.

The desired outcome therefore removes the symptoms of the conflict by addressing the causes rather than vice versa.

Structures for the management of conflict

Establishing structures for the management of conflict is the starting point for effective conflict management (see Figure 11.5). The cornerstone of these structures is establishing the following positions:

- **Win:Win** – in which everyone is satisfied with the outcome.
- **Win:Lose/Lose:Win** – in which one party is satisfied but the other is not.
- **Lose:Lose** – in which the conflict escalates into something much more serious.

Clearly, win:win is the ideal outcome. At the other extreme, lose:lose is certain to result in the matter escalating, and organizations and their managers should at least know and understand what they are letting themselves in for should this occur.

In between, the win:lose/lose:win situation does require careful handling. This is because one side has succeeded at the expense of the other. When this happens, there is often resentment, injured feelings, wounded pride, the fact that someone, for whatever reason, has not had their own way. This is certain to result in some comeback at a later date.

The other part of structuring the management of conflict is to ensure that effective means of communication are available when required. These means of communication are as follows:

- the use of joint consultative committees and joint negotiating committees in conjunction with staff representatives, staff associations and recognized trade unions;
- all staff and all stakeholder e-mail circulars;
- regular face-to-face communications with everyone concerned;
- the provision of clear printed information stating why the particular position on the resolution of the conflict has been adopted.

Structuring effective strategies

Effective strategies for the management of conflict clearly vary in content between organizations and situations. In this context, the main lines of approach are as follows.

- Attention to standards of honesty and integrity to ensure that people have a sound understanding of the basis on which the relationship between themselves, their department, division or group and the organization as a whole is established. This is brought about by absolute commitment by the organization and those responsible for its direction and its top managers, and translated into the required management staff by those responsible for the direction and supervision of the rest of the staff.

- Attention to communications to ensure that these meet the needs of receivers and that what is said or written is simple and direct, capable of being understood, honest and straightforward.
- Attention to the hopes, fears, aspirations and expectations of all those who work in the organization. Much of this is based on empathy and mutual identity and commitment – and dissipated by compartmentalizing and differentiating between staff groups.
- Attention to the systems, procedures and practices of the organization and the ways in which these are structured and drawn up and the ways in which they are operated. This especially means attention to equality and fairness of treatment and opportunity; the language and tone of the procedures themselves; and the training and briefing of managers and supervisors in their purposes, emphases and operation. This also normally means the presence of sanctions for those who do not operate these systems with integrity.
- The establishment of organizational purposes common to all those present in the organization, with which they can all identify and which transcend the inherent conflicts of objectives. This is the approach most favoured, for example, by Japanese companies in their operations in Western Europe and North America.
- The establishment of a universal identity and commitment to purpose. In organizational behaviour terms, this involves attention to the outputs of the stated purpose and the benefits and advantages that are to accrue as the result of their achievement. This is the starting point for the establishment of:

  (a) performance-related and profit-related pay schemes, and the generation of the identity, commitment and interest that are the key elements of the best of these;
  (b) briefing groups, work improvement groups and quality circles that reinforce the mutual confidence, commitment and respect of those involved.

- The removal of the barriers that exist between departments and divisions. This involves attention to matters of confidence and respect and to the level, quality and style of communications that impact on and effect operational relationships.
- The establishment of organization conformism based on creation of desired means and methods of participation and consultation, and fused with absolute standards of honesty and integrity. Attention should be given here to:

  (a) the representation of employees and the means by which this is to be achieved;
  (b) their scope and structure;
  (c) the agenda to be followed;
  (d) the rules of engagement – the means by which these are to be operated.

These are the main organizational behaviour approaches required to address and tackle the sources and causes of conflict. They are based on the recognition of its universal potential to exist; the approach in particular organizations clearly varies. They arise from an understanding of the nature of conflict and of the need to recognize rather than attack the symptoms. Energy devoted to dealing with conflict represents energy not spent on more productive activities; time and resources used in understanding and assessing the causes and dealing with these therefore bring their own payback in terms of reduced time, stresses and strains caused by the reality of problems and disputes.

Operational approaches to the management of conflict

The operational approaches used by organizations normally take the following forms.

- Developing rules, procedures and precedents to minimize the emergence of conflict and then, when it does occur, to minimize its undesirable effects.
- Ensuring that communications are effective in minimizing conflict; bad communications may cause conflict or magnify minor disputes to dangerous proportions.
- Separation of sources of potential conflict which may be done geographically, structurally or psychologically (for example, through the creation of psychological distance between functions and ranks).
- Arbitration machinery may be made available as a strategy of last resort.
- Confrontation may be used to try and bring all participants together in an attempt to face them with the consequences of their action.
- Benign neglect: this is the application of the dictum that 'a problem deferred is a problem half solved'. This can normally only be used as a temporary measure while more information is being gathered or a more structured approach is being formulated.
- The use of industrial relations operations for the containment and management of conflict, including consultation, participation, collective bargaining and negotiating structures.

Other means of reconciling workplace conflict

The other means available to reconcile workplace conflict are:

- negotiation;
- conciliation;
- mediation;
- arbitration.

Negotiation

Parties entering into negotiations with a view to resolving conflict need to know and understand the following (see Figure 11.4):

- their precise objectives in taking the conflict down this route;
- what they want from the particular situation;
- the 'bottom-line' of their negotiated position (i.e. the minimum for which they will settle);
- what else they want from the negotiation (e.g. in a negotiation based on a victimization case, one party may want compensation for the victim and the removal of the victimizer);
- the timescales over which the negotiation is to take place;
- what is to happen afterwards if the negotiation is unsuccessful;
- how any agreement is to be drawn up and presented.

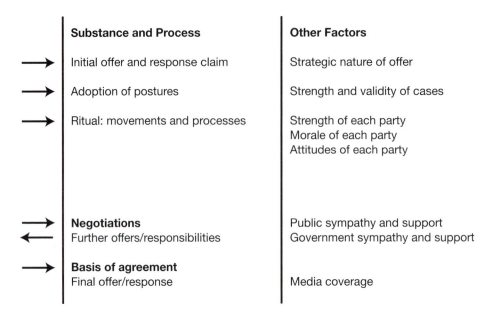

Substance and Process	Other Factors
Initial offer and response claim	Strategic nature of offer
Adoption of postures	Strength and validity of cases
Ritual: movements and processes	Strength of each party Morale of each party Attitudes of each party
Negotiations Further offers/responsibilities	Public sympathy and support Government sympathy and support
Basis of agreement Final offer/response	Media coverage

(a) Steps in the negotiating process

Each of these activities must be undertaken in these circles.
Each of the other factors must be acknowledged and understood.

– –▶ Offer	**Area of agreement**	◀– – Claim
A B	C	D
Low		High
		Staff/ union
Management		

(b) Process operation

The negotiating and collective bargaining process: offers between A and B rejected by staff; between C and D instantly accepted by staff; claims between A and B instantly accepted by management; between C and D rejected by management; B–C is basis for negotiated settlement; normal first offer is around A, which leads to instant rejection; normal first claim is around D, but engages the process.

Figure 11.4 The negotiating process

Conciliation

This is a means whereby employers and employees seek to reach mutually acceptable settlements of their disputes, usually by placing the matter in hand with a neutral and independent third party. Conciliators examine all sides of the case. They analyse areas of agreement and areas of dispute, and present these back to the parties involved. They identify areas where agreement can be made in order to try to effect a reconciliation between the parties.

Mediation

If, for example, conciliation fails two sides may seek a third party to mediate in the dispute. The mediator will put forward their own positive proposals aimed at resolving the matter in hand. The mediator may produce this in the form of a report outlining recommendations for a satisfactory settlement.

The benefit of the mediation and conciliation approach lies in the ability of the third party involved to see the dispute from the detached point of view and to find ways around the behavioural and operational blockages that inevitably exist.

Arbitration

Arbitration differs from conciliation and mediation in that the arbitrator determines the outcome of the dispute by proposing a settlement; in cases that go to arbitration it is normal for both parties to agree to be bound by the findings of the arbitrator at the outset. The usual form of arbitration is open arbitration in which the arbitrator has complete discretion to award whatever he/she sees fit within the given terms of reference and which will provide an effective solution to the problem. The arbitrator also has regard to behavioural matters and the forms of words in which agreements are couched; this is to accommodate the perceptual and behavioural niceties required as indicated above.

Pendulum arbitration is a closed form of arbitration. Again, the arbitrator hears both sides of the dispute. He/she will then, however, decide wholly in favour of one party or the other. Someone therefore always wins (and is seen to win); and someone always loses (and is seen to lose). The concept of pendulum arbitration is based on the idea that faced with the prospect or possibility of losing a dispute each party will wish to resort to resolving the differences without getting into this situation. The approach is widely used by Japanese companies operating in the West. In these companies there are strong cultural pressures on managers not to get into disputes and not to lose them if they do. Again, therefore, there is a pressure to resolve problems rather than to institutionalize them.

Pendulum arbitration normally represents the final solution to any dispute in organizations that use it. There is normally no appeal against the arbitrator's findings. This is clearly stated in the staff handbooks and agreements of the organizations concerned. Those entering into pendulum arbitration agree to be bound by the outcome before the arbitrator hears the case (see Box 11.8).

Conclusions

Understanding the sources and causes of conflict draws away from the hitherto accepted view that organizational strife is caused by troublemakers, trade unions, whistle blowers

Box 11.8: Conflict management options

An alternative approach to this which includes, in different stages, all of the options of negotiating, mediation, conciliation and arbitration, was proposed by Thomas and Kilman. Thomas and Kilman mapped the context and options available on two axes (see Figure 11.5).

- assertiveness: the requirements and ability to achieve an outcome which meets everyone's needs;
- cooperativeness: the requirement and ability to achieve an outcome which meets the specific needs of one party or the other.

Thomas and Kilman stated that each of these options is a valid management strategy in given situations, depending on the outcomes desired and the nature, strength and critical impact of the particular matter in hand. These approaches may also form the basis on which either, or both, parties to the conflict agree to go to conciliation or mediation, or to be bound by arbitration.

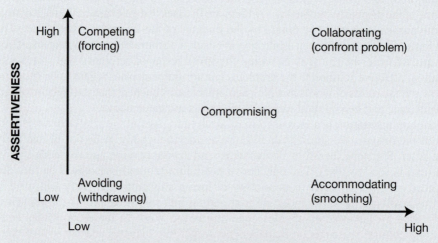

Each of these options can be a valid conflict management strategy, depending on the situation, although each also has its potential disadvantages.

Figure 11.5 Conflict management options

Source: J. Thomas and G. Kilman (2002) *Strategies for the Management of Conflict at Work* – Blackwell.

and other prima donnas or over-mighty subjects or groups. Strategies and systems for the handling and management of conflict clearly institutionalize rather than resolve conflict. They also tend to reinforce (rather than dissolve) more deeply held negative attitudes of mistrust, dishonesty and duplicity.

The current view, therefore, is that conflict is inevitable and that it is potentially present in all human relations and activities – and this includes work. In organizations it is determined by physical layout, physical and psychological distance, inter-group relationships, hierarchies, technology, expertise and by the interaction of individual group and organizational aims and objectives.

Rather than the use of channels, procedures, institutions and forms, the desired approach is to give everyone a common set of values, goals and purposes for being in the organization, that both recognize and transcend the present of conflict and reconcile the differing aims and objectives. Destructive conflict is minimized and resources otherwise used in the operation of staff management and industrial relations systems are released to be put to more positive and productive effect.

12 Teams and groups

Introduction

Workplace teams and groups are gatherings of two or more people that either exist already, or else are drawn together and constituted for a purpose. This purpose is understood and accepted by all those involved; and there is a clear understanding also that the group will serve wider organization requirements, as well as the interests of those involved. It is usual to define workplace teams and groups as follows.

- **Formal**: constituted for a precise purpose. Formal groups normally have rules, regulations and norms that support the pursuit of that purpose. Formal groups also normally have means and methods of preserving and enhancing their expertise. There are also likely to be means and methods that enable people to move in, contribute and move out of a given group.
- **Informal**: where the purpose is less precise but still clearly understood and accepted by all involved. A card school falls into this category, as does a Friday night gathering of friends and colleagues at the bar.
- **Psychological**: viewed from the point of view that membership is dependent upon people interacting with each other; are aware of each other; and perceive themselves to belong.
- **Peer groups**: in which those of the same rank, status, occupation or profession gather together to debate matters of value and interest to themselves.
- **Professional and occupational**: professional and occupational groups draw and bind themselves together in pursuit of a distinctive set of professional and occupational values. This includes membership of professional bodies (e.g. British Medical Association, Chartered Management Institute); and includes also membership of trade unions (e.g. Royal College of Nursing, Transport and General Workers Union).
- **Committees**: all organizations constitute committees, working parties and other meetings for the purpose of addressing problems, issues, procedures and processes.
- **Project groups and teams**: constituted for specific purposes, normally resulting in the delivery of a specific initiative or 'project' after a given period of time.
- **Focus groups**: which are constituted for the purpose of giving responses to a particular question or set of questions.
- **Brainstorming groups**: which are constituted to produce as much information and clarification as possible in a limited period of time on a problem or issue.
- **Other teams and groups**: constituted for specific purposes including client liaison; supplier liaison; work improvement and quality assurance; staff development; joint consultative committees, joint negotiating committees and works' councils (see Box 12.1).

> ## Box 12.1: Elites and super-groups
>
> In organizations, many groups come to be regarded as elites or super-groups. This can arise for a variety of reasons:
>
> - the work for which they were originally constituted is of prime importance and priority, and any results that they produce in the pursuit of this carry high organization value;
> - the members themselves are highly qualified, and if they become effective and cohesive in the first place, they form their own collective view of just how good they are;
> - they form their own exclusivity, engaging others (or not) on the basis of the aspirations of outsiders.
>
> These groups have to be managed carefully and actively. No organization can depend for its existence, viability or solutions to problems, however high their priority, on a single group.
>
> If not managed, the group itself can come to form its own 'bunker mentality'. 'Bunker mentality' is the term ascribed to groups that come to conduct their affairs in isolation from the rest of the world, and produce results which, in the comfort of their own surroundings and company, are 'obviously going to work'.
>
> From this, it is a short step to a complete detachment from reality (as happened for example, during the last days of the Third Reich, when Hitler and his chief advisers and top military staff withdrew from the devastation of Berlin, and instead created their own entirely illusory and comfortable view of the world from the safety of their operational headquarters – their 'bunker').

All organizations have different titles for the teams and groups that they constitute. However, it is essential to realize that each of the above areas has to be addressed in some way or another. From this point of view, organizations and their managers need to know and understand how to constitute effective teams and groups.

From the above, it is possible to identify an initial set of general group characteristics. These are as follows.

- Collective interest in, and commitment to, the stated purpose of the group.
- The ability of each member to communicate with every other member of the group, regardless of rank, status or position within the wider organization.
- The ability to generate a collective identity based on a combination of the circumstances and environment in which members find themselves.
- Shared aims and objectives.

Purpose

Whatever the constitution or structure of the particular group, there needs to be a core purpose, set of targets, aims and objectives, and a pattern of progress. Especially in the creation of new teams and groups, the opportunity for demonstrable early progress and initial successes must be present. Failure to make this available normally leads to immediate demoralization; and members will begin to disassociate themselves from both the group and the work if failures persist and if successes are not forthcoming.

Groups may be constituted formally for specific purposes, or to carry out a continuing remit. For example, a group constituted as a disciplinary panel has a formal set of rules and procedures to which to work, even if it only hears one case. Formal committees have rules and procedures, to underpin their effectiveness in serving a continuing purpose.

Teams and groups may be given a degree of permanence and additional purposes if the delivery of their specific task is seen to lead to other opportunities.

All teams and groups need to be wound up and disbanded when either their purpose is served and there is no prospect of developing this into further effective activities, or when it is clear that they are neither effective nor suitable in carrying out the given purpose.

Membership of work groups gives individuals the following opportunities:

- distinctive work roles within which they can be comfortable and happy and which satisfy their feelings of self-esteem;
- establishing a self-summary and self-concept which can be presented both to others in the work group and also to the world at large;
- contribution to productive, positive, profitable and effective activities. This in itself leads to satisfaction and feelings of personal success and raised levels of self-esteem;
- the ability to fulfil personal aims and ambitions which normally have to harmonized and entwined with those of a particular organization;
- wider feelings of general comfort, familiarity and contribution within the organization.

In practice, people are members of many different groups at places of work. People additionally carry out divergent and sometimes conflicting roles according to membership of specific groups. In some cases, it is not always easy to reconcile work, professional or personal concerns with the demands of specific groups (see Box 12.2).

Group responsibility

The best workplace teams and groups accept responsibility for the work carried out, and the ways in which targets are met. There is therefore responsibility for both processes and also outcomes. While the group is in existence, it is essential to be aware of the nature of responsibility present, and the ways in which it is delivered. For example:

- peer pressure may act as a force for good in ensuring collective commitment to purpose; or it may be used to bully and coerce people into doing things that they would not otherwise do;
- the group may use relationships within the organization in order to gain influence or resources; however, purpose may be tainted if the provider of influence or resources then uses the group to further their own aims and objectives;
- groups may be constituted for a stated purpose; and it then quickly becomes clear that those who constituted the group have done so because they wish for a particular outcome;

Box 12.2: Role conflict in work groups

Publishing

Stefan Ekstrom used to work for an international firm of management consultants. His last assignment was to produce proposals for the restructuring of a large magazine, newspaper and book publishing company. Stefan was then hired as chief executive by the publishing company to implement his own proposals.

The Board of Directors of the publishing company had been perfectly happy with Stefan's proposals. However, now that he, and therefore they, were to be responsible for the implementation of these proposals, he quickly ran into difficulties. In particular, there were two key proposals which were now seen not to fit. These were:

- the divestment of television listings' magazines, which sold well but which Stefan's initial investigations had deemed to be declining;
- the integration of business publications and men's publications into one division.

Stefan's position as CEO quickly became untenable and he was forced to leave after six months.

The role conflicts that ought to have been addressed were as follows:

- Stefan's role as consultant was very different from that of CEO; and specific difficulties were enhanced when it became clear that Stefan actually intended to carry out his proposals.
- The Board of Directors were happy and comfortable in their collective role of engaging and supporting the consultancy initiative; however, it became clear that they had then been expecting to implement the proposals in their own preferred ways rather than having to work in a reconstituted group, which included the person who had originally developed the proposals.

- group members acting together may use the fact of the group to abdicate responsibility for a given set of outcomes (see Box 12.3).

The creation of effective groups

Tuckman (1965) identifies four elements as follows.

- **Forming**: the coming together of the individuals concerned; beginning to learn about each other – personality, strengths, capabilities; assessment of the group purpose; introduction to the tasks, aims and objectives; initial thoughts around rules, norms, ways of working and achieving objectives; initial social and personal interaction; introduction to the group leader/leadership; acquiring and setting resources; constraints, drives and priorities.
- **Storming**: the first creative burst of the group; energizing the activities; gaining initial markers about its capabilities and capacities and those of its members;

creating the first output and results; mutual appraisal and assessment of expertise and process. Initial conflicts tend to become apparent at this stage, together with the need for means for their resolution. Opportunities and diversions may also become apparent. Conflicts between group and personal agenda start to emerge.

- **Norming**: the establishment of norms – the behavioural boundaries within which members are to act and operate; the establishment of rules and codes of conduct that underline and reinforce the standards set by the norms. By doing this, the group provides itself with means of control and the basis of acceptable and unacceptable conduct, performance and activities.

  For rules and norms to be effective they must be clear, understood and accepted by all. They must be capable of doing what they set out to do. They must reinforce the mutuality, confidence and integrity necessary to effective group performance.

- **Performing**: the addressing of matters in hand; attacking the tasks to be carried out; getting results; assessing performance. This includes attention to group effectiveness and cohesion, as well as absolute performance measures – the two are invariably entwined.

Box 12.3: Group responsibility

Handy states that: 'Groups take riskier decisions than the individuals that comprise them would have done if they had been acting independently.' They behave more adventurously.

Fear of non-conformity also contributes to this. When a newcomer joins a group he/she is normally willing and eager to accept its norms and rules. A range of research underlines this.

The Milgram experiments of 1974 were based on the question: 'Would you torture someone else simply because you were told to do so by a person in authority?'

The experiments involved volunteers acting as 'teachers' of those trying to learn word pairs. If the subject got the pairs wrong the 'teacher' administered an electric shock. The shocks increased in intensity, the greater number of mistakes made.

In fact, no electric shocks were administered. However, the volunteer 'teachers' nevertheless pressed the switch that supposedly gave the shocks when directed to do so by someone 'in authority'.

Defiance only occurred when the subject was first encouraged to do so by 'rebellious elements' drawn from among the other group members. Little defiance was exhibited by volunteers working alone.

Philip Zimbardo (Zimbardo et al., 1973) created a simulated prison to observe the impact that the adoption of roles had on individual and group behaviour. The group of volunteers were divided into two sub-groups – prisoners and warders.

Within a very short space of time, each adopted the expected, desired or inferred behaviour of their role. Thus the warders became aggressive, domineering, even bullying and violent. The prisoners at first became cowed and submissive. Later they sought ways of escaping. After thirty-six hours one prisoner left the experiment suffering from a nervous breakdown and three more followed during the next three days. Others promised to forfeit their fees for taking part in the experiment if only they would be released.

There are further elements to be added as follows.

- **Re-forming**: which takes place if, for any reason, the group is ineffective in either processes or task delivery. Re-forming may also take place if it becomes clear that, even for the most positive of reasons, the group is not now right for the purpose originally intended.
- **Rejuvenation**: the process of adding fresh expertise and resources to particular groups once the need is demonstrated. Rejuvenation may take place because of the withdrawal of individual members for some reason (e.g. they leave the organization) and so they are replaced by others. Rejuvenation may also occur as the result of an organization deciding that it needs to re-energize a moribund group.
- **Ending**: all teams and groups ultimately have a finite useful life. Some teams and groups come to an end after the performance of one task (e.g. the disciplinary example as above). Other groups may have a life only for the duration of a particular project or initiative; and others still may lose their legitimacy as the result of organizational, technological and expertise changes.

Owen (1985) identifies the need for groups that have had a long constitution and clear remit to celebrate their achievements and mark the parting of the ways of the members. Owen states that from an organizational point of view, this marks a clear indication that the task is achieved and the work is done; and that from the member's point of view, it marks a parting of the ways as the people involved now go on to new activities.

This is to be seen as a process rather than a linear progression, a series of steps and stages. For example, early successes in the life of the group may be strictly headed under 'performing' but are nevertheless essential to the gaining of mutual confidence, trust and reliance that are integral to effective 'forming'. Regarding this as a process also underlines the need for attention to the behavioural as well as operational aspects (see Box 12.4) – especially group maintenance.

Issues facing work groups

The main issues facing all work groups are as follows.

- Atmosphere and relationships: the nature of relationships; closeness, friendliness, formality and informality.
- Participation: the nature and extent to which participation is to be allowed, restricted and restrained; and the extent to which participation is allowed, restricted and restrained because of clear roles within the group, and also in spite of clear roles within the group.

The priority issue facing all teams and groups at the outset is to ensure that aims and objectives are clarified, and that everyone involved understands and accepts them. Means and methods of communication and decision-making have then to be agreed. It additionally needs to be made clear at the outset how personal and professional conflict and disagreements are to be handled and resolved. The performance of individuals and the group as a whole has to be measured and evaluated.

Box 12.4: Foundation of corporate and collective norms

People seek to belong to peer groups wherever they congregate; this includes in organizational and corporate surroundings. The tendency towards exclusivity exists in open-ended and corporate situations where people come and go. The formation of groups is influenced by the fact that fellow workers have been thrown together from the start in overtly unnatural mixes. At a large cocktail party groups will drift together and apart without constraints but in a company people with different backgrounds and views are forced to work together and form groups. The bigger the company and the wider the range in social attributes of individuals, the better the chances are that there will be numerous groups with tight-knit and defensive norms.

Where both formal and informal norms coexist as they do in companies the informal norms transcend the formal. This leads to what has been called 'shadow organization' in which the apparent management structure is actually superseded in importance by the mesh of group-norm diktats.

Individuals will go to extreme lengths to live up to (or down to) the expectations placed on them by others, even doing things that in other circumstances they recognize as being counter to their own best interests, their characteristics, their normal standards of ethics and behaviour. They can persevere in this behaviour, however, with the easy rationalization that 'everybody else is doing it'.

Norms-imposed habits are lasting. Even when the original members of a group have disappeared and/or when the norms themselves have lost their original purpose there will be strong norm remnants unthinkingly respected by new members. Negative norms cannot be changed unless the norm follower is made aware of their existence because most people respect and go along with the norms quite unconsciously; this is reinforced by pressures to conform.

The nature of the leadership of the group has to be addressed, clarified, understood and agreed. If one person is to be in charge at all times, this must be made clear; and if the leadership is to be rotated, this also must be understood and agreed.

Addressing these issues at the outset provides a strong basis for the development of mutuality of interest and positive and professional working relationships. Attention can then be given to ensuring that the conditions for creating effective work groups are met; and the potential for ineffectiveness is kept to a minimum (see Table 12.1).

Group factors and characteristics

The main factors that affect the cohesion, behaviour and effectiveness of groups are as follows.

Size

The size of the group, including the numbers of people involved and the nature of that involvement. Some authorities have tried to identify optimum size for work groups. This has to be seen in the context of the nature of the task to be carried out –

Table 12.1 Characteristics of effective and ineffective groups

Effective Groups	Ineffective Groups
Informal relaxed atmosphere	Bored or tense atmosphere
Much discussion, high level of participation	Discussion dominated by one or two people
Tasks, aims and objectives clearly understood	Discussion often irrelevant, unstructured and away from the point
Commitment of members of the groups to each other	No common aims, objectives and purposes
Commitment of members of the group to the tasks, aims and objectives	Members do not value each other's contribution nor do they listen to each other
Members respect each other's view's listen to each other	Conflict is allowed to develop into open warfare; it may also be suppressed
Conflict is brought out into the open and dealt with constructively when it arises	Majority voting is the norm; pressure is put on minorities to accept this
Decisions are reached by consensus; voting is only used as a matter of last resort	Consensus is neither sought nor achieved
Ideas are expressed freely and openly; rejection of ideas is not a stigma	Criticism is embarrassing and personal
Leadership is shared as appropriate; is divided according to the nature of the tasks; ultimate responsibility, authority and accountability rests with the designated group leader	Leadership is by diktat and is issued by the group leader only
The group examines its own progress and behaviour	The group avoids any discussion about its behaviour

Source: D. McGregor (1960) *The Human Side of Enterprise*.

if a particular process needs two or fifteen people then this is the optimum size in the circumstances (see Box 12.5).

Leadership of teams and groups

Whatever the size or remit of the particular team or group, those in leadership positions are directly responsible and accountable for creating the conditions, relationships and processes in which work can be produced effectively, and in which those involved are both comfortable and productive.

Morale and satisfaction are monitored through the study of absenteeism, accidents, member turnover and the ability to attract, retain and develop new talent. It is established and developed through a basis of full understanding of the tasks and activities to be carried out and fulfilling the expectations of group members.

Group ideology is normally based around concepts of participation, involvement and recognition of the value of the contribution that each member makes. It is underpinned by norms and rules. Individuals may also choose to belong to a group (or seek to join it) because of the strong and distinctive ideology. Some organizations – for example, Body Shop, Nissan – also attract people because of their strong commitment to the environment or product and service quality.

Team and group spirit must be positive and harmonious, and capable of acceptance by all. Individuals have their own reasons for belonging to groups in addition to professional, occupational and intrinsic membership value; where group spirit is either

Box 12.5: Group size

Creating the right group size requires that a wide range of factors is addressed. There are some absolutes: the size of a tennis doubles team is two; of a rugby team, fifteen. In work situations the technology used may determine that a group size is three, eight, thirty or whatever.

In general terms there is a balance involved between size, contribution and participation – the larger the group, the greater the range of expertise and quality is drawn in, but the lesser the chance of a full participation by individual members.

Larger groups also have a greater risk of splitting into sub-groups (either formal, based on the work, or informal, based on workstation location, friendship, establishment of common bonds and interests). Total group identity may then become diluted. The interaction between the sub-groups becomes a barrier to the progress and achievement of the full group. The sub-groups create their own barriers themselves – especially if these have become constituted around the distinctive expertise of members. If this is in high demand by the rest of the main group, the sub-group establishes its own filter and priority systems based on its preferences and criteria.

On the other hand, smaller groups tend to avoid the sub-grouping effect; they may, however, develop a group identity so strong that it tends to lead to belief in its own infallibility and indispensability.

The size of any group therefore has clear implications, both for their management and leadership and also for participants if these pitfalls are to be avoided.

negative or not present at all, individuals revert to professional and occupational (rather than group or organizational) identity.

Conformity and loyalty are normally expected of individuals who join groups. Conformity and loyalty are at their strongest and most effective where individual aims, objectives and values are capable of being harmonized and integrated with those of the group. Conformity is reinforced by:

- physical identity – including the wearing of uniforms;
- social identity – the use of particular modes of address, manners, and approaches to each other by group members;
- the positive – in which the standards, attitudes and values to which individuals are required to conform are positive;
- regimentation – in which the standards, attitudes and values to which individuals are required to conform are imposed and unvalued.

All teams and groups need to know and understand environmental pressures and changes; and other factors that they cannot control. Groups can, and do, have to be able to operate effectively when resources are reduced, direction and priorities are changed, and results are suddenly required much more quickly than previously envisaged. Groups may also have to work effectively if the leadership is either changed, or if a new leader is imposed.

Group cohesion

Cohesive groups are most likely to be achieved if attention is paid to the division, allocation and structuring of work; the creation of a behaviourally suitable working environment and the installation of a leader or manager who is aware of the pressures and potential problems and acceptable to the rest of the group.

Effective division of work ensures that individual and collective capabilities and expertise are used to greatest effect. It also includes enabling wherever possible people to follow their personal and professional preferences as long as this can be offered to everyone. Unpleasant, mundane and routine tasks are also to be shared out on a basis of equality.

The creation of a suitable environment depends on the availability of technology and equipment, and physical proximity if at all possible. Difference of location is a physical barrier to group identity and therefore effectiveness. This difference may be a matter of yards, or thousands or hundreds of miles.

A productive environment is created only if this is first recognized and then underpinned with adequate and effective methods and systems of communication. If the environment is not managed effectively, those involved will begin to form their own sub-groupings, alternative cultures and unofficial sets of values (see Figure 12.1 and Box 12.6).

Sources of potential group stresses and strains

A key part of the effective leadership and direction of groups and teams is recognizing where things can, and do, go wrong. Those in leadership positions therefore require active and continued attention to the following.

- The nature and mixture of the personalities involved and the nature of activities that are engaged in with the purpose of reconciling these.

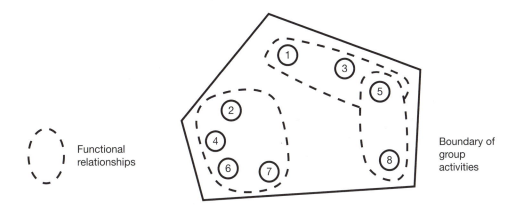

Note key divide between 2467 and 1358
Note relative isolation of 1 and 8

Figure 12.1 Group cohesion: sociogram of an eight-person group

Box 12.6: The whistleblower

In places of work, as with every other walk of life, people have a strong urge and drive to 'belong'. 'Belonging' is not always easy (and can be very stressful and traumatic) when what the group does, and what is acceptable to its members collectively, is unacceptable and wrong to one individual.

Mary Firth worked in a residential home, caring for some of the most vulnerable members of society. The work was very rewarding, the clients (the residents) an absolute delight.

For many years, the place of work was harmonious. Staff delivered expert and effective care, and the residents enjoyed a high degree of comfort and security.

After a while, the assistant manager of the home moved on, and was replaced by Peter Gate.

It became apparent immediately that Peter took a very different attitude. He quickly became impatient with the residents. He ordered changes to the working practices of the rest of the group. He started to limit the amount of freedom that the residents had; and after a while, he started to limit the amount of activities in which they could participate also.

It also quickly became clear that he was both verbally and also physically abusive towards the residents. This became very distressing to the rest of the staff team. The question was: what to do about this?

In fact, the staff team knew what to do about the problem. The key issue was getting the owners of the home to listen to their concerns; and then to take effective action.

The situation persisted for several months, during which Peter's behaviour got very much worse. Eventually, Mary Firth took matters into her own hands.

She called the rest of the staff group together at her home, and told them what she was going to do. She was going to write down everything and submit it to top management, and also to social services and the other care authorities.

The rest of the staff agreed with her in principle; though this agreement was tempered by concerns for how they were all going to be viewed in the future. They also had a serious concern that if Peter was not sacked, working relations would be impossible.

Mary took the bull by the horns and submitted her report. She was summoned to a meeting with one of the company's top managers. Here she went over her concerns, carefully and comprehensively, supporting every assertion with dates, times, places.

The company accepted the report, and Peter was sacked. The immediate response of the rest of the staff group was relief and rejoicing all round.

However, the whole episode had been destabilizing for the staff group, and distressing for the residents. Much of the blame for this now fell on Mary herself. An interim manager was brought in, and her first words to Mary were: 'So, you're the one whose caused all the trouble then?'

Mary left her job shortly afterwards. This was because, while in practice everyone agreed that she had done the right thing, she had nevertheless broken the spirit and cohesion of the work group. It became uncomfortable for the others to work with her, and what she had done had been clearly noted by both the new manager and the organization as a whole.

- The nature and mixture of the expertise and talent that is brought to the group by its different members. This is especially important where some members of the group have expertise that is either rare or else of high price/high value.
- The nature and mix of other and more general strengths and weaknesses that each of those involved brings with them to the group.
- Means and methods of communication, consultation and participation; the availability of good-quality information. Stress and strain is created when these are either inappropriate, inaccurate, dishonest or incomplete.
- The changes in group composition and membership; changes in influence of particular members as the task unfolds; the bringing in of new members; the phasing out of those whose part of the task is done.
- Levels of confidence, trust, respect and regard held by each member of the group in regard to the others and of their position in the group.

Attention must constantly be given to the nature of the working environment, and this includes ergonomic factors, technology, location and design of workstations, and the physical distance/proximity that exists between group members. This also includes extremes of temperature, climate, discomfort, danger and location.

Attention must be given to the form of management style adopted, and its continued suitability to the situation and task in hand. In particular, leadership and management style must be concerned with the suitability of the means of communication, nature of decision-making processes, levels of performance and how these are achieved. It is additionally the case that leadership and management style must be able to operate effectively in relation to matters outside the group's control.

Other symptoms of group and team malfunction are as follows.

- Poor performance in which deadlines are missed, output is sub-standard and customer complaints increase.
- Members decline or reject responsibility for their actions and for the groups itself. They become involved in lobbying and seek to blame others for these shortcomings. The group breaks up into sub-groups and elites are created within the wider group. Individuals claim rewards and bonuses for team efforts. Scapegoating and blame occurs showing destructive criticism and dismissive behaviour towards others, both inside and outside the group.
- Becoming involved in grievances with other group members; increases in the numbers of these; personality and personal clashes; over-spill of professional and expert argument into personal relationships.
- Increases in general levels of grievances, absenteeism and accidents; moves to leave the group.
- Lack of interest in results, activities, plans and proposals of the group.
- The general attitude and demeanour that exists between group members; the general attitude and demeanour of individuals within the group; lack of pride and joy in the group; moves to leave the group again; difficulties in attracting new members to the group.
- The presence of an individual or sub-group that is known, believed or perceived by the rest of the members to be holding them back from greater achievements and successes. It is a very short step from this attitude to the presence of bullying, victimization and harassment.

Box 12.7: Champagne!

Following a particularly successful year's activities, a group of five financial traders took themselves out to celebrate. Each earned a very high salary, and as a result of their activities, each had earned a bonus of well over £1 million.

The venue chosen for the celebration was one of the Spearmint Rhino chain of nightclubs, where the champagne would flow and there would be exotic dancers and all sorts of other hedonistic delights on offer.

In the early hours of the following morning, the police were called to the nightclub and the five were arrested. During the investigation that followed, the following became clear:

- The five had spent £40,000 on champagne and food.
- While the party had started out as raucous and boisterous (with which there was no problem), matters had quickly got out of hand. One of the group had ordered some more champagne, and when this was not immediately delivered, he had thrown an empty bottle at one of the waiters. The club's security staff had then been called, only to be confronted with a full frontal assault from all five members of the group.
- During the course of the evening, one member of the group had torn the clothing of one of the waitresses (this subsequently led to an allegation of serious sexual assault).

The case duly went to court, and the five were convicted of assault, wounding with intent and causing an affray. Each was heavily fined. In passing sentence, the judge stated: 'You thought that because of your status as bankers you could do what you liked. You thought that because you had extraordinary amounts of money that you could do what you liked. You thought that you could treat people waiting on you as serfs.'

The immediate lesson from the case was that there were standards of behaviour which the company for whom they all worked had failed to impose, and so the group assumed that because they had made a fortune, they could indeed do as they pleased.

More generally, all groups need to know and understand where their full range of responsibilities lies, how to conduct themselves and what they need to be accountable for.

Some of these are clearly specific to group activities and functions. Others are more general symptoms that should be considered in the group context as part of the continuing monitoring of its effectiveness. Each gives an inlet for the person concerned with identifying and assessing trouble and potential problems with a view to tackling them (see Box 12.7).

Group development

The creation and formation of effective teams and groups is not an end in itself. To remain effective, cohesion, capabilities and potential must be maintained and developed. This takes the following forms.

- Infusions of talent from outside, bringing in people with distinctive qualities and expertise to give emphases and energy to particular priorities and directions.
- Infusions of new skills, knowledge and qualities from within through the identification of potential from among existing members and having them receive training and development, and targeted work that has the purpose of bringing out the retired expertise.
- Attention to group processes when it is apparent that these are getting in the way of effective task performance; and attention to task performance when it is apparent that this is ineffective.
- Attention to the relationship between team and task. This may involve using a good team to carry out a difficult or demanding task; or using the difficult and demanding task to build good and effective teams. From either standpoint, the results will only be fully effective if the task achievement is within the capabilities of the group. As long as this is so, the rewards of success are likely to contribute greatly to overall group performance, well-being and confidence among members.
- Attention to team roles, both to build on strengths and also to eliminate weaknesses. This is likely to involve reassessing what the requirements and priorities are; reassessing the strengths and weaknesses of each individual; and possibly leading to reallocation or rotation of roles and infusions of new talent, either from within or without.
- Attention to team roles and expertise from the point of view that different qualities, expertise and capability are likely to more or less important at different phases of activity. This may lead to infusions again, or to the buying in of expertise (for example, using consultants) on an 'as-required' basis. It may also involve the recognition that members of the group may need to be divested once they have made their particular contribution; and recognizing also that there will be a time when the group has come to the end of its useful life.

The core of effective group work is the ability to use the talents and expertise of everyone involved to deliver the results required within the constraints and opportunities of group norms; mutuality of interest and respect; and the pressures of the operating and external environment. All aspects of group development must concentrate on these as core issues if enduring high levels of output and productivity, and mutuality of interest, are to be maintained (see Box 12.8).

High-performing teams and groups

The characteristics of high-performing teams and groups may be summarized as follows.

- High levels of autonomy, the ability to self-manage and self-organize. This also includes team responsibility for self-regulation and self-discipline. It encourages the fast and effective resolution of problems and a commitment to dealing with issues before they become problems.
- Clear and unambiguous performance targets, capable of achievement and related to overall organization purpose; understood, accepted and committed to by all concerned.
- Full responsibility for all aspects of production and output process, quality assurance, customer relations and complaints. Issues and problems are identified and addressed

Box 12.8: Faddish approaches to team and group development

'Teams that play together, work together' is a mantra familiar to many managers. This has led the unwary to engage in a variety of team-building exercises including paint-balling, mountaineering, staff nights out and even corporate holidays. These activities are only ever effective if they are structured into a regular programme of events, conducted during working hours, and integrated with hard business, organization, group and individual development activities.

The regional manager of a retail chain decided that a day's cycling would be an excellent team-building activity. Accordingly, all the staff were summoned early one Sunday morning to a starting point. They were required to bring their own bicycle, and to be suitably equipped (including wearing a regulation crash helmet).

Came the day, and everyone duly turned up. It was pouring with rain. Many of the staff had had to hire bicycles (because they did not have their own). 'Not to worry,' said the regional manager. 'We are not going far – only 30 miles.'

In the pouring rain, the staff group set off. Many fell by the wayside very quickly, cold and wet and fed up. Some of those who did do their best to struggle on collapsed of exhaustion; unused to this kind of physical exercise, they were simply not fit enough for the activity. Three members of staff did, however, make it to the finishing line, only to find that the regional manager was not there. He turned up two hours later in his car. He said: 'Oh well, it was one of those things. Still, I think it was an extremely successful team-building activity.'

Of course, the whole episode passed into company folklore and mythology. However, in spite of his statement of 'success', the regional manager never repeated this particular exercise, nor did he try to get any others implemented.

to the particular team so that improvements can be made directly without going through sub-processes and procedures.

- Job titles do not include references to status, differentials or trappings, or other elements of psychological distance.
- Team-based reward systems available and payable to everyone who contributed, based on percentages of salary rather than occupational differentials.
- The open approach – to environment layout (no individual offices, trappings, barriers or other factors of physical and psychological distance); self-commitment for the whole team; open communication systems and high-quality communications; open approaches to problems and issues; open airing of grievances and concerns – these are usually very few in such circumstances, so that when they do arise full attention is paid.
- High-performance teams require autonomy as stated above; and this needs supporting through a 'federal' relationship with the core organization, operating systems and reporting relationships. These relationships are based on monitoring, review and evaluation of production and output targets and other task-based indicators. General management style must be supportive rather than directive, bureaucratic or administrative.

Additional requirements and conditions are as follows.

- Fast and easy access to maintenance and support staff to ensure that equipment breakdowns are repaired as soon as possible and that production levels can be kept as high as possible for as long as possible.
- Full flexibility of work, multi-skilling and interchangeability between task roles. Group roles are assigned to people's behavioural strengths.
- Continuous development of skills, knowledge, qualities, capabilities and expertise; continuous attention to performance quality and output; continuous attention to production, quality, volume and time; continuous attention to high levels of service and satisfaction.
- High levels of involvement, confidence, respect and enthusiasm among group members, both towards each other and towards the work.
- Attention to equipment and technology to ensure that this is suitable and capable of producing that which is required to the stated and expected standards of volume, quality and time.
- Simple, clear and supportive policies and procedures covering organizational rules and regulations, human resource management and discipline, grievance and disputes.
- Continuous monitoring and review to ensure that the intended focus and direction is pursued and that group activities are in accordance with this.

Conclusions

Everybody belongs to groups. To be effective in working situations, it is essential that there is as great a measure of mutual trust, respect, identity, cohesion and clarity of purpose, understood and accepted by all, as is possible in the circumstances. It is also essential that attention is paid to the human values – the shared values – necessary for its effective functioning as a working group.

The critical nature of the relationship between the leader and the group should therefore be apparent. It is essential that the leader establishes both clear patterns of work, and also the environment in which the mutuality of interest and respect can be assured. This is the cornerstone on which cohesion and effectiveness are founded.

Cohesion and effectiveness can then be built on the following:

- mutuality of understanding between the group and its leadership;
- the capability and willingness of each individual member to carry out their task to the best of their capability, and in the context in which the group demands it;
- mutual identity and respect in which all members of the group hold each other;
- the relationship with the group leader, and the willingness to follow his/her instructions;
- understanding of how the task or matters in hand are going to be measured for success or failure;
- understanding and implementing what needs to be done;
- understanding where the responsibility, authority and accountability for actions truly lie;
- understanding the conditions necessary for effective group cohesion and overall performance;

- ensuring that everyone understands the contribution that they need to make in particular situations (see Box 12.9).

If this cohesion does not exist, individual members will only use the group as long as it remains in their interests. Their performance and contribution declines; and they will move on as soon as it becomes apparent that they have no further personal interest, respect or value for the group and its activities.

Effective groups therefore require a combination of early and continued operational successes, together with a mutually enhancing and developing personal and professional respect among the members (see Box 12.10 and Figure 12.2). All group activities that are proposed must be considered from each of these points of view. If something is contemplated or planned in which it is perceived that there is to be a damaging or divisive

---

Box 12.9: British Airways' cabin crew

British Airways' cabin crew deliver a high and clearly defined standard of service on all flights. This is in spite of the fact that, because of different shift patterns and working arrangements, very few individual members of the cabin crew staff work regularly together on an extended basis.

The level of service is therefore dependent upon extensive and continuous staff training. The result is that, by the time anyone goes to work on an airliner, they know and understand their role and the rules by which they are required to abide, and are expert at the tasks to be carried out. As a staff group, BA cabin crew have a very close and strong identity and cohesion.

Once assigned to a flight, the members of staff meet up with their cabin services director. The cabin services director is responsible for all activities on board the airliner, other than flying the plane. The staff arrive three hours before the flight is due to depart. Under the direction of the cabin services director, each member then introduces themselves. Specific tasks and duties are then allocated. The longest-serving member of the cabin staff has first choice; and all duties are allocated and chosen on the basis of relative length of service. This is clearly known and understood by everybody; and anyone who is not happy to work in this way is not allowed to become a member of British Airways' cabin staff.

Once the staff arrive on the airliner, each has a clear set of tasks and duties to perform, both while the plane is on the ground, and subsequently when it is in flight. As stated above, each member of staff has been fully trained and drilled in the conduct of each task and duty, and also in the attitudes and presentation required towards the passengers.

In order for this to be effective, heavy and continuing investment is required in the training and development of all members of cabin crew staff. This is further underpinned by the fact that many of the staff have always dreamed of working as cabin crew, and so the job is something that they had always wanted.

In this part of their activities, British Airways sets the highest possible standards of conduct, behaviour and performance; and this in turn has established, and continues to establish, the norms for customer service and presentation throughout the airline industry of the world.

Box 12.10: Structuring individuals into effective teams

Belbin (1986; 1992; 2002) proposes the means by which the capabilities and characteristics of individuals can be identified, and then harmonized with those with different characteristics and expertise, into effective, productive and eventually high-performing teams.

Belbin isolated individuals' characteristics and capabilities (see Figure 12.2 below).

The value of this approach is to demonstrate the need for a wide range of tasks and activities in all team and group working situations. Whatever the matter in hand, there is a need for creativity; activity; questioning, analysis, evaluation and judgement; attention to detail; and completeness of work.

TYPE	SYMBOL	TYPICAL FEATURES	POSITIVE QUALITIES
Company Worker	CW	Conservative, dutiful, practicable	Organizing ability, practical common-sense, hard-working
Chairman	CH	Calm, self-confident, controlled	A capacity for treating and welcoming all potential contributors on their merits and without prejudice A strong sense of objectives
Shaper	SH	Highly strung, outgoing, dynamic	Drive and readiness to challenge inertia, ineffectiveness, complacency or self-deception
Plant	PL	Individualistic, serious-minded, unorthodox	Genius, imagination, intellect, knowledge
Resource Investigator	RI	Extroverted, enthusiastic, curious, communicative	A capacity for contacting people and exploring anything new An ability to respond to challenge
Monitor-Evaluator	ME	Sober, unemotional, prudent	Judgement, discretion, hard-headedness
Team Worker	TW	Social orientated, rather mild, sensitive	An ability to respond to people and to situations, and to promote team spirit
Completer-Finisher	CF	Painstaking, orderly, conscientious, anxious	A capacity to follow-through Perfection

Figure 12.2 Effective teams
Source: Belbin (1986).

effect on the group, then, where possible, the initiative should be abandoned or repositioned in order to ensure that everybody receives some form of benefit. Where it is not possible to abandon the initiative or proposal, then recognition of the likely effects on group cohesion must be acknowledged and understood. Steps can then be taken to remedy the situation as early as possible, and from the point of view of understanding and pre-planning, rather than surprise.

It is also particularly important that attention is paid to the rewards (both financial and also non-financial) that are available to group members. Ideally, merit, perform-ance and profit-related financial rewards should be paid on the basis of fairness and evenness, and the current prevailing wisdom is that all members should receive an equal percentage of their salary in these cases. Where, for some reason, it becomes neces-sary or right and proper to pay an individual above and beyond the rewards available to the rest of the group, the reasons for this should be made plain to everybody. If these are honest and straightforward, then they will be understood. If they are not, then the leadership and direction of the group is always called into question.

Finally, it is necessary to understand that all groups come to an end. They either outlive their useful life, or the leadership changes, or else the nature of the task and work activities changes to such an extent that the requirement for the group as presently constituted no longer exists. It is essential to manage this end phase, to avoid feelings of loss and deprivation on the part of members. As stated above, many organizations provide wakes and other celebrations at the end of particular group functions, projects or periods of activity. Even if this is not carried out, acknowledgement of the group's contribution must be made formally. This enables everyone involved to recognize for themselves that a particular period of work has come to an end, and to have this publicly acknowledged. They are then able to move on within themselves to the next part of their working life.

13 Influences on the nature of work

Personality, roles and performance

Introduction

Those responsible for the leadership, direction and management of organizations need to know and understand the nature of work, and how the traits and characteristics brought in by individuals relate to the overall effectiveness of collective and individual performance. In this context, the priority is to recognize and understand the following:

- the personality, and personality traits and characteristics, of every individual are different;
- everybody has specific aspirations which they seek to fulfil both from within their work, and also from life outside;
- the relationships between work effectiveness and individual and collective performance lies in harmonizing the characteristics of individuals with what the organization requires.

This forms the basis on which individual jobs (work roles) are devised and implemented from a human point of view. There is little value in having excellent job and work processes (job enlargement, continuous training and development, varied opportunities) if insufficient attention is paid to the nature of the people who are being employed. It is therefore essential to understand the nature of personality, the context of job and work roles, and how these impact on performance.

Personality

Individual personality may be defined as 'the total pattern of traits and characteristics, of thoughts, emotions, attitudes, values, behaviour and beliefs, and attributes and qualities, and their interactions'. Since the strength, presence and interaction of these varies between individuals, each individual is unique. The concept of personality also embraces perception, motivation, aspiration, learning and development. It is therefore necessary to recognize at the outset that human personality is highly complex and that steps must be taken by organizations to understand these characteristics, interactions and complexities exhibited by their people (and those who are potentially their people) if an effective working relationship is to be produced. Some useful distinctions may be made at the outset as follows:

- traits and characteristics;
- qualities, talents and attributes;
- the desire for achievement.

Understanding the nature of personality, and the nature of people's talents, gives a better understanding of how work patterns can be effectively devised, so as to gain the most from individuals, and for individuals, within organizations.

Personality and expectations

Universally, people have expectations. In general, these expectations are for comfort, security and prosperity; for increases in standards of living; and for respect and recognition by those with whom they come into contact, and those whose opinions they value. One key part of understanding the nature of work, and the performance that accrues as the result, is to recognize expectations in these terms, and:

* either to be able to recognize that the organization ought to deliver as many opportunities for progress and advancement as possible;
* or to recognize that if progress and advancement cannot, or will not, be offered, there will be dissatisfaction among the groups of staff as the result.

Traits and characteristics

From an organizational behaviour point of view, the purpose is to identify those traits that are necessary to produce effective activity and harmony of relationship and to seek these among the individuals who come (or who would like to come) and work. The important traits are therefore those that are:

* strong, dominant and frequently exhibited;
* weak and less frequently exhibited;
* overriding, often based on emotional response to particular situations – for example, aggression, shyness, anger, temperament (see Box 13.1).

Traits and characteristics may be perceived as being either positive or negative. One part of understanding personality is therefore to recognize the extent to which specific characteristics are being observed 'because everyone says they are true', the extent to which they are important and valued at the place of work, and the extent to which they are unimportant and/or unvalued at the place of work, when deciding on their relative importance.

Influences on personality

Influences on personality commence at birth. These influences are a combination of the following:

* the overall pattern of life into which the individual settles;
* any traumatic or cataclysmic events that happen along the way (e.g. involvement in a car crash; involvement in other disasters; deprived or abusive home background);
* influences of role models and others whom the individual comes to admire;
* influences of specific institutions, especially educational establishments;
* influences of the social circle and location in which the individual grows up.

Box 13.1: Gordon Brown

During the height of the political crisis of the spring of 2009, Gordon Brown, the then prime minister, brought Peter Mandelson into the Cabinet as minister for work, industry and enterprise.

At the start of their respective careers, Brown and Mandelson had been close friends and allies. After the election of Tony Blair as prime minister in 1997, however, Mandelson became an ardent loyalist and so became distant from Brown.

For many years, Mandelson and Brown had little to do with each other; and Mandelson eventually joined the European Union as one of the UK's commissioners. It was a surprise when he was called back into the UK government by Brown early in 2009.

It additionally became clear that Mandelson had described the personality of Brown as 'insecure and self-conscious' and 'inclined to get very angry when he does not get his own way, or when people raise objections'. When this description became public, Mandelson was asked to defend the comments on the television. He stated: 'These are not criticisms. Everybody has these traits and characteristics. Indeed, Gordon would not be human if he did not have these characteristics.'

The key to understanding this part of personality, therefore, lies in a recognition of the fact that these traits and characteristics do indeed exist, and which of them are to be considered 'overriding'. Part of this is to do with perception: if people think that the overriding characteristics are anger or impatience, then this is what the individual concerned will come to gain a reputation for; if they are recognized as mere facts of being human, then other characteristics will be recognized as overriding.

The two-sided self

The two-sided self is a combination of how individuals see and perceive themselves; and how they are seen and perceived by others. Fundamentally, individuals want to see and perceive themselves as being important, attractive, likeable and giving something of value to the place of work and to society. Serious dysfunction can, and does, arise when individuals perceive and understand that they are important in making a valuable contribution, but others do not see or recognize this, or else they either clearly state or else imply that the individual's contribution is worthless. Or else people may indeed recognize the value and contribution made, but nevertheless draw attention to the other personality attributes and traits exhibited (e.g. vanity, petulance).

The need, therefore, especially in work situations, when assessing somebody's performance, is to recognize the effects that any assessment has on their personality; and from this, recognizing:

- that criticism may have to be delivered in a particular way if it is to be accepted as constructive;
- that criticism is likely to produce a certain response, and so be prepared to handle that particular response;

Box 13.2: David Beckham

By his own admission, from a very early age, David Beckham always loved football. By his own admission also, as a young boy, he was never very good at the game. The turning point came on an occasion at primary school. On this occasion, two teams were being picked; and he was the last to be chosen.

From that day forward, he determined to do something about it. As he started to practise, it quickly became clear that he did indeed have a particular talent for the game. Now the personality characteristic of determination and commitment engaged; and his persistence quickly mean that, even as a young boy, his potential was recognized.

At the age of 12, he joined Manchester United as a schoolboy. His leisure time was spent practising, studying football videos and understanding as much as possible about how the game was played.

The lesson for everyone is that any aptitude has to be supported by personality traits and characteristics that are essential if any potential is to be fulfilled.

- that personality characteristics are affecting someone's performance, and so to use any discussion or appraisal as a means of getting somebody to address particular aspects of their personality.

Understanding and managing the two-sided self is therefore a key area where expert managerial interventions can be made (see Box 13.2).

Emotions

Everyone has the full range of emotions; and everyone brings these from time to time to all situations, including work. It is essential, therefore, to recognize the kinds of workplace situations and activities that are likely to engender emotional responses, and to understand how best to deal with these when they do arise. For example:

- rejection of someone's work is likely to provoke anger and disappointment, and so the reasons for rejection have to be clearly explained;
- rejection of someone for promotion may also provoke anger or disappointment, and so again the reasons have to be explained;
- giving someone notice of redundancy or dismissal may provoke extreme upset or trauma, and so support mechanisms have to be in place for this also.

Defence and offence mechanisms

Everyone has defence mechanisms which they engage when confronting unfamiliar or threatening situations. Common defence mechanisms are:

- aggression;
- anger;

- comparisons (e.g. 'I am not as bad as you', 'I am doing no worse than anyone else', 'Why are you picking on me?').

In general, defence mechanisms are responsive, being engaged only when first confronted. In some cases, defence mechanisms can be 'offensive', and this generally happens when someone thinks they are going to get an aggressive response, and so becomes aggressive before the response has actually been made.

Offence mechanisms become apparent when individuals have problems and issues to address and for which they must take the initiative. Offence mechanisms tend to be much more positive than defence mechanisms; though, as stated above, they can become aggressive when a defensive response is anticipated on the part of those who have now to be involved.

Overall, understanding personality, and its traits and characteristics, is essential if effective work is to be generated, and work relations are to remain positive and harmonious. Understanding personality is also essential for resolving problems, especially when these involve people who are known to be strident or temperamental (see Box 13.3).

Qualities, talents and attributes

Qualities, talents and attributes are the physical and mental capabilities of the individual. All people bring some of their capabilities into all situations. It is the relationship between those that are demanded in the given situation in relation to the range offered by the individual that is important here. For example, a qualified airline pilot who can also

---

Box 13.3: Rodney Ledward

Rodney Ledward was a consultant gynaecologist. When he first qualified, he was held in very high regard, and everyone predicted a glittering career for him.

Before very long, however, it became clear that some of his work was less than precise or accurate; and shortly after this, his female patients started to accuse him of physical and sexual abuse.

These matters came to light more than thirty years after the first allegations had been made, and concerns raised. A group of women whose operations had been botched and bungled now took Rodney Ledward to court. The court case was clear and straightforward: Rodney Ledward's work had indeed been ill-considered, inaccurate and incomplete. Rodney Ledward was struck off the surgeons' register; he retired to Ireland, and died shortly afterwards.

In the fall-out from the case, it became clear that, collectively, Rodney Ledward's colleagues had always had serious concerns about the quality of his work. So had the NHS authorities who employed him. However, for thirty years, as above, they had found themselves unable to do anything about it. This was because he was such an unpleasant personality to deal with. In particular, he had a defence mechanism based on a combination of his own self-esteem, perceived self-status, anger and temper, that rendered him fireproof to any active investigation of the quality of his work.

cook and make tea and coffee is clearly qualified to be a catering assistant – but whether they would want to be so would need careful consideration on the part of both the individual, and also any organization which might be thinking of offering them a job as a catering assistant.

Organizations and their managers have to have a clear view of which qualities, talents and attributes they find acceptable, and those they find unacceptable, and the reasons. They also need to have a clear view of which are the dominant or priority qualities, talents and attributes that they are seeking, and the reasons.

It is also essential to be able to place subordinate attributes in ways that are comfortable and 'assured'. For example, someone who is excellent at their job, always delivers results on time and who is perceived to be attractive may nevertheless attract feelings of envy and jealousy, so preventing them from being appointed to future positions; and this is because subordinate traits (e.g. temperament) or subordinate negative achievements (e.g. they once lost their temper five years ago) attract an unwarranted amount of attention, and this becomes the subordinate attribute on which the negative decision is made (see Box 13.4).

Identification of qualities, talents and attributes by organizations

Organizations identify qualities, talents and attributes in order to fit work to people, and fit people to work. A key part of this is therefore fitting qualities, talents and attributes to roles, and fitting roles to qualities, talents and attributes. So the priority is the identification of qualities, talents and attributes that are deemed necessary to carry out particular sets of activities effectively. This then becomes the basis on which job selection is based.

The process is most likely to be successful when those qualities, talents and attributes are easily observable and identifiable, and can be proven or tested. It is less likely to be successful if they have to be inferred or based on a short conversation or part of an interview.

Expertise

Expertise is a combination of capability and willingness to carry out tasks and activities as directed by the organization, and to the best of the individual's ability. There is additionally a context for expertise: that the organization and staff collectively have confidence in the capabilities of specific individuals is critical to success in particular roles. Someone who is actually excellent at their job will not be valued as such if people do not believe in their excellence. Someone who is clearly excellent at their job nevertheless has to be motivated to carry it out to the best of their ability (see Box 13.5).

The desire for achievement

Desire for achievement is a basic human drive in most societies. The problem lies in the definition of 'achievement'. Achievement means something different to each individual – for example, money, status, power, helping others, a large house, invention and creativity, excellence in a chosen field (social or occupational). For organizations, the problem lies in what they mean by achievement, where the contribution of

Box 13.4: Top and senior appointments

The problem of acceptable and unacceptable, and dominant and subordinate traits and attributes have to be addressed and resolved when making top and senior appointments. As stated elsewhere, this leads many organizations to seek what are effectively parallel attributes as follows:

- 'A safe pair of hands';
- 'Proven track record';
- 'Vast experience'.

This has the following effects:

- it prevents organizations from having to define precisely the dominant and acceptable attributes;
- it prevents organizations from having to define the subordinate and unacceptable attributes.

This effectively gives organizations a free hand in making top and senior appointments. Organizations do not have to define precisely what is meant by 'a safe pair of hands' (safe for what, or safe from what); nor do they have to say what the track record 'proves' or what the experience sought is. The results of such approaches are indeed mixed. For example:

- Andy Hornby was appointed to be chief executive of Boots, in spite of the fact that he presided over the collapse of HBOS. However, his previous experience as deputy chief executive at Asda during a period of commercial success was deemed to override the subsequent problems at HBOS.
- Conversely, a record of success did not prevent Avram Grant from being dismissed as head coach at Chelsea FC in 2007. In spite of the fact that the club came runner up in three of the four competitions for which it had entered, because he was not perceived to be a high-profile character, he was deemed to be a failure.

individuals to that lies and in attracting the right types of individual to ensure that this happens.

Individual desire for achievement is based on:

- economic pressures, the need to support a continuity and quality of life;
- social pressures, exerted by peers, friends, family and relations;
- esteem and value, what the individual regards as important; and what is regarded as important by others;
- status afforded by both self and others to particular achievements;
- respect and self-respect;
- recognition and acknowledgement of achievements;

Box 13.5: Role capability and willingness

Role capability and willingness is addressed through answering the questions: 'Does this individual want to do this job for us?' and from the point of view of the individual: 'Do I want to do this job for this organization?'

This problem is observable in many situations. Reference is made elsewhere to top sports stars who under-perform for their clubs because they have no motivation or commitment; they have joined simply for the money incentive (see Chapter 20 below). Elsewhere:

- One chief executive of a large global pharmaceutical company demanded, and was assured of, a severance package worth £22 million which he would collect if he was dismissed by the Board of Directors.
- One chief executive of one of the world's leading branded clothing companies picked up a severance package of £12 million because he did not deliver his expertise in the ways in which the company demanded or expected.

In each of the above cases, the core of the problem lay in failing to identify accurately the attributes and qualities demanded, and the conditions under which the expertise would have to be delivered. And the expense of failing to address these key issues is therefore plain for all to see!

- association, with particular organizations, groups, expertise and activities;
- individual pressures, the need to live up to (or down to) particular expectations from different parts of society.

The desire for achievement in work situations is based on:

- the nature of the work itself, variety, routines, technical expertise;
- the value of the work to self, the organization, peers, customers, clients and the community;
- willingness to work hard;
- willingness to learn;
- the relative need for development, new opportunities and horizons;
- the need of the individual to demonstrate a range of abilities and qualities;
- the need to be seen as excellent, to be highly thought of in a range of areas;
- the need to complete that which has been commenced; dislike of leaving things unfinished;
- the need for working relationships to be operationally productive and effective as well as friendly;
- time, the need to get things done as quickly as possible; to avoid things being dragged out.

These similarities and overlaps are between the individual desire for achievement and the individual desire for achievement in work situations. The lists above clearly overlap; and because of the amount of time spent at work, professional and occupational achievements are always going to form a part of individual striving for success, as well as those successes demanded by the organization.

The desire for recognition is often fuelled in organizations by self-promotion. If the organization culture recognizes only those people who put themselves forwards, then those with high drives for success and achievements at work will self-promote. This invariably leads to organizational and occupational dysfunction for the following reasons:

- the contribution of those who promote themselves is over-valued;
- the contribution of those who do not promote themselves is under-valued;
- it fuels a culture of 'in sight, in mind'; and a culture of 'out of sight, out of mind';
- the need for self-promotion and the drive for this sort of recognition encourage a culture of patronage and favouritism (see Box 13.6).

Roles

It is necessary to recognize the following context for assigning roles to attributes, and attributes to roles:

- the extent to which roles and the attributes demanded coincide absolutely;
- the extent to which roles and the attributes demanded coincide to some extent;
- the extent to which there is little correlation between roles and attributes.

Box 13.6: Patronage and favouritism

Chris Hume joined a large local government organization. Professionally qualified as a social worker, he set out to make a name for himself through the delivery of high-quality support for his clients, and the effective management of his case load.

For three years he delivered excellent service. The result of this, however, was to simply increase his workload. The average at the council was for each social worker to have fifteen cases; after three years, Chris found that he had fifty cases. He continued to deal with these as effectively as possible.

At this time, by chance, he found himself in conversation with the council's director of social services. The director was quite candid; she stated that she had never heard of Chris nor of his enduringly effective performance. She invited him into the council's head office, where, after a short conversation, she offered him a job on the policy-making side.

Chris accepted, and moved to head office. There he found that the system of patronage and favours worked effectively for anyone who was prepared to engage themselves; and in five years' time, he moved through the ranks, finally gaining an appointment as director of social services at another council. He could not help but note, however, that following his move away from the frontline and into a corporate position, the quality of the service on his old patch rapidly declined. Shortly after he took up his directorate, there was a major scandal, and he wondered if this would have happened if he had remained there.

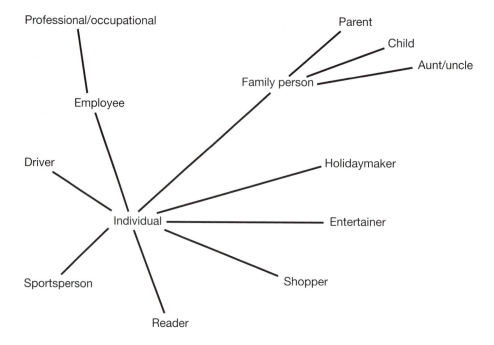

Each role has expectations, pressures, rewards and consequences. There are overlaps and conflicts between each from time to time. To everyone, one will be the most important, and one will be the least important.

Figure 13.1 Individual roles

Roles are combinations of behaviour, activities, expertise, capability and willingness undertaken by individuals in given situations (see Figure 13.1). This is, in turn, set against a backcloth of the variety of expectations that go with each role. The source of these expectations is overwhelmingly a product of the particular community and society in which the individual lives and works.

Role transparency

The question of role transparency has to be addressed because everything has to be collectively acceptable. The first questions to address are therefore:

- the extent to which the role has a stated agenda which is to be carried out;
- the extent to which the role has a hidden agenda which is actually the primary purpose;
- the extent to which the role is permanent or transitional.

This applies from both an organizational point of view, and also in terms of the individual appointed.

From an organizational point of view the priority lies in making as clear as possible the full context, the expertise actually demanded and how the role is to be implemented and developed.

From an individual point of view, the organization's stated demands must meet expectations and perceptions, including any aspects of recognition and value that may be sought.

Problems arise when transparency is either not present, or else not fully understood by both parties. The priorities are therefore to determine at the outset:

- the extent to which capability and expertise are to be restricted (e.g. by reporting relationships);
- the extent to which authority is given, including any specific restrictions;
- the extent to which resources are made available;
- the nature of role development (see below).

If these areas are not clear and transparent, this leads to a combination of frustration, dysfunction and stress; leading in turn to declining performance (see Box 13.7).

Box 13.7: Tom Gibson

After he gained his MBA, Tom Gibson found himself a job with a retail chain as HR executive. Tom fully understood that this was a developmental role for himself; and during his two years at the organization, he set out to learn everything that he could about HR in practice, relating this to the knowledge and understanding that he had gained while on his degree course.

After two years, Tom applied for and was appointed to the position of deputy HR director at a large and prestigious public body. The salary was excellent, and his specific remit was to devise and implement speedy, transparent and effective employee relations procedures within his new institution.

Tom quickly found that this was not the case. In spite of his high salary, he found himself sitting in on extensive disciplinary and grievance activities, taking notes and intervening merely when asked to do so.

Additionally, he found that anything of substance had to go out under the name of the HR director. Anything that he put out under his own name would either not be implemented, or else carried no executive authority.

Effectively, therefore, he was merely a recorder and disseminator of information. The very high salary and job title did not mitigate this.

He therefore determined to move on as quickly as possible. However, he found that prospective employers questioned his actual achievements in his new role, and his authority. When it became clear that neither were present, he found himself being turned down time after time.

It took Tom five years to move on from this role. Over that period, he had thirty interviews; and it was only by chance that the person running the thirty-first interview knew and understood his position entirely (having previously also worked for Tom's director).

The lack of transparency in this case meant that the organization was vastly overpaying for someone who, as stated above, was effectively a recorder and disseminator of information only. It also led to serious frustration (and lack of output) on the part of the individual.

Role sets

People have a great range and variety of roles. Some of these are dominant, some subordinate. Some of these are constant; some are continuous; some are intermittent; some are short-term, others long-term. The total number of roles adopted by the individual constitutes the role set.

It is useful to compartmentalize roles in this way in order to establish a basis for the understanding of the ways in which people behave in the different situations indicated. Often this behaviour is contradictory – the bullying manager for example may also be a loving parent – and it is necessary to be able to understand and explain the reasons (or a set of reasons) for this.

The role is therefore a combination of:

*   who you are;
*   what you know;
*   what you can do;
*   what you want to do;
*   what others want you to do;
*   what others do not want you to do;
*   what you do not want to do;
*   what is important and of value to you;
*   what is not important and of no value to you;
*   economic factors;
*   social factors;
*   who you work for;
*   who works for you;
*   who you associate with;
*   who associates with you;
*   what is expected of you and by whom;
*   what you expect of yourself and why;
*   prospects and progress;
*   situational factors;
*   ethical factors;
*   specific constraints (for example, legal).

Roles differentiate between people, activities, social segments and sectors. Roles vary between work, family, social and community situations.

Role management and development

Role development takes place in the context of:

*   the roles that individuals have to fulfil (see Figure 13.1 above);
*   the balance of role sets, and individual drives.

In practice, most roles have the opportunity for development. This development may be:

- personal, in which the individual uses the occupational role to pursue their own interests and priorities;
- occupational, in which the organization asks for particular priorities and objectives to be fulfilled;
- professional, in which those in occupations such as teaching, nursing and accounting have specific obligations to remain up-to-date with particular developments;
- organizational, in which the individual will be steered by the opportunities offered for promotion and advancement.

This is of particular importance in organization and management development, and in the delivery of effective performance appraisal. Organizations that concentrate on one part only of role development inevitably cause frustration and loss of motivation to their staff. It is therefore essential that the full range of drives for role management and development are recognized, and effective steps taken. Assuming that organizations want the best from their members of staff, this is a point where major and effective interventions can be made.

Role integration

Role integration is the 'juggling act' which individuals have to carry out as they balance the pressures on their lives. Of specific importance are:

- the integration of occupation with economic demands and drives, and specific/ individual demands for recognition and respect;
- the work–life balance, ensuring that either no role becomes too overriding, or else recognizing that where one role does become a heavy priority, there are consequences for others;
- relating personal, professional and occupational drives to other parts of life.

Specific legislation exists to ensure that flexibility of work is offered to those with particular demands on their lives (see Chapter 19); and to ensure that people are protected from occupational stress if the organization and its staff are under heavy pressure (see Chapter 23). However, it is essential to recognize that using legislation to ensure an adequate balance of work and life is often a very long-winded affair; there is a collective organizational and managerial responsibility to ensure that the drives and demands placed on individuals from all parts of their lives are respected and valued, accommodated where possible and supported throughout.

Role hierarchies

For everyone, one role is the most important; and one role is the least important. Within these two extremes, everything else has a place in the individual's priority order. Again it is essential that organizations recognize this; it cannot reasonably be expected that people who hold down part-time cleaning jobs place this at the top of their role priority order. On the other hand, those in top, senior and key positions in organizations cannot be expected to discount every other part of their lives, just because of the critical nature of their job (see Box 13.8).

Box 13.8: Commissioner

Rudi Peeters was a very senior executive at the European Union. Rudi worked up to 100 hours per week most weeks, serving on many committees, and working for different EU directorates.

Rudi had always been a high-flyer. When he graduated, as a great believer in the 'European ideal', he found himself a junior post within the EU bureaucracy, and quickly worked his way up.

Rudi had married young, and he and his wife quickly had two children. All the time that Rudi worked, he did his best to keep up with his children's development; however, in practice, the nature of the job meant that he missed out on things like parents' evenings, school trips, even family holidays.

Twenty years later, Rudi's daughter suddenly announced that she was pregnant. At this point, Rudi's life changed. Having missed out on his own children's growth and development, he now determined that he would be an excellent grandfather.

Overjoyed, Rudi went into work the following week. He announced to everybody, with a huge smile on his face, that he was going to be a grandfather.

Many of the staff were very happy for him. However, his own boss, a commissioner in one of the directorates general, stared at him with a stony face.

It was quickly plain that Rudi's boss had no sympathy with the impending grandparenthood. Relations between the two became frosty; where Rudi's opinion and expertise had been sought, he was now cut out altogether.

Rudi, however, was undeterred. He made a sideways move within the EU, working for someone who shared his joy at grandparenthood. Rudi continued to discharge his duties in the new position, but very much in the context that he was now a grandparent and family man at last.

The lesson is that not all organizations, or managers, are capable of accommodating changes in individuals' role hierarchies. In some cases (as in this one) changes in role hierarchies have to be carefully managed, and it may be that (again as in this case) organizations and their managers are incapable or unwilling to adjust themselves.

Roles within roles

All roles have 'roles within roles'. Thus for example:

- the parent is also a disciplinarian, provider of pocket money, taxi service, cook, washer-person, first-aider, cleaner and gardener;
- managers are also disciplinarians, shoulders to cry on, collective and individual coaches and developers, computer operators, lunch organizers, production and service deliverers, production chasers, financiers and public speakers.

In each of the above cases, the list of roles within roles may be extended to include guardian, teacher, friend, leader, general resource and fountain of authority and wisdom. In many cases also, people in specific positions may become personality, idol, advertisement, star, fountain of confidence and a rock on which to build the foundations of psychological life.

Role clarification

Roles may usefully be clarified under the headings of:

- general categories;
- behavioural constructs;
- trappings and signs;
- trappings and ego.

General categories

- **Family**: mother, father, son, daughter, uncle, aunt, grandparent, niece, nephew, cousin, taxi, cook, teenager, child, consumer, customer, servant, adult.
- **Work**: defined by job title, profession, training, location, hours of work, freedom/ otherwise to operate autonomy/direction, creativity/regimentation.
- **Social**: neighbour, friend, sportsman/sportswoman, gardener, dog walker, taxi (again), organizer, servant, consumer.
- **Community**: American, Japanese, school governor, customer, pillar of community, councillor, elder, organizer.

Roles may be categorized and clarified formally, by title or general understanding; or they may be categorized informally, according to particular status, importance and understanding ascribed by all involved.

Behavioural constructs

Workplace examples of behavioural constructs are as follows.

- **The bully**: either physical or psychological; with particular categories of staff (especially junior); threatening and menacing; abusive and harassing.
- **The braggart**: normally a self-publicist; if boasting on the organization's behalf braggarts normally put themselves in the spotlight also.
- **The barrack room lawyer**: leader of the informal organization and sometimes also an influential figure in the formal, especially if the management involved is weak or insecure.
- **The clown or comedian**: a useful safety valve for the group in which they exist. Clowns attract attention and stories about themselves. The role may be hard to shake off. Clowns are often regarded both as irritants by the organization and also with measures of envy and jealousy.
- **The devil's advocate**: questions and queries everything and is constantly looking for flaws; it is a useful, valuable, even essential role; it is also a major irritant to top managers and those trying to get pet schemes and projects off the ground.
- **The film star**: looks, acts, sounds, plays the part; is always immaculately dressed; has all the relevant trappings; problems arise only when asked to be the part.
- **The eccentric**: eccentrics are accommodated because of qualities and expertise that they also bring; eccentricity is also the means by which a reputation or distinction may be achieved (provided that it is at least perceived to be attached also to results); it is rationalized as being colourful or larger than life.

- **Scoutmaster/scoutmistress**: develops the next generation of talent for the organization; is accommodated as long as this does not threaten the current equilibrium, modus operandi or vested interest.
- **The advocate/lobbyist**: a chaser of causes, some lost and others not; may also be a whiner and whinger; has strong moral and ethical principles, often at variance with those of the organization.
- **The peacemaker**: has a rich supply of oil to pour on troubled waters and consequently often adds pollution to the problems that already exist. The worst form of this is the person who sees no evil, hears no evil and speaks no evil.
- **The scapegoat**: attracts blame for everything that goes wrong in the given situation; may go out of his/her way to do this in order to gain identity (however corrupted or toxic this may be).

How roles are clarified, both formally and also informally, depends on what is of value to the organization, and what individuals seek from their occupations. This issue is compounded when organizations either reward or else sanction individuals for adopting any, or all, of the above roles. For example:

- if organizations are known or understood to reward self-publicity, ambitious people will become self-publicists;
- individuals who cannot make their way through the formal hierarchies of the organization may seek other forms of influence through adopting the position of barrack room lawyer.

More generally, individuals seek some form of recognition and society, and sense of belonging. If they do not get this from one source, they seek others; and each of the above behavioural constructs can, and do, become a vehicle for recognition and esteem. When individuals adopt any, or all, of the above constructs, therefore, there is a core issue that has to be addressed: why they do it, and what they hope or expect to gain from it.

It is therefore a priority that organizations acknowledge and manage these patterns of behaviour. Those in key and influential positions need to know and understand the basis on which they are offering recognition and reward; and if it is on any basis other than the effective and excellent performance of their staff, there are problems that have to be addressed (see Box 13.9).

Trappings and signs

The trappings and signs that define roles are as follows.

- **Dress**: designer labels; colour coordinates; prestige labels (for example Armani and Gucchi); fashion labels (for example Reebok, Nike); dress imitation (of the top management for example); cheap and expensive, special clothing (for example tuxedo).
- **Possessions**: make, model and year of car; domestic hardware and technology; may also include spouse, children, mistress, lover, friends and associates.
- **Fashions and fads**: appearance; self-presentation; job title; also includes dress and possessions and may also include spouse, children, mistress, lover; belonging to the right clubs and associations and groups; taking part in the right activities.

Box 13.9: Role models (1)

Most people identify role models at some point during their careers. Role models are those individuals whose behaviour, performance, appearance and demeanour attract strong feelings of loyalty and identity. Role models can be identified from any part of society, and this includes work.

For example:

- top sports stars are identified as role models because of their perceived glamorous lifestyle, and the fact that they are always in the newspapers;
- managers are adopted as role models by junior staff because of the fact that they have already made it to certain positions.

People who know that they are role models have a critical responsibility to behave in ways acceptable to those who admire them. Of particular concern in the two above examples are the following:

- the sports star who is a major achiever, but who comes subsequently to be recognized as a drug or alcohol abuser, or otherwise a reprobate;
- managers who have a particular following, who subsequently come to be recognized as bullies and braggarts.

- **Technology**: car again; hobbies and interests, make and model of kitchen appliances, television, audio and video, home computer.
- **Titles**: Mr, Mrs, Doctor, Reverend; specific titles such as Your Excellency, Your Grace, Mr President; organizational/functional titles such as Chief Executive, Assistant Manager, Sales Person; professional titles such as Doctor, Surgeon, Actor, Musician.

Trappings and ego

Alongside the above signs are those which individuals adopt and display. For example, those who seek promotion and advancement start to adopt the trappings and signs of those already in the positions sought. Those who wish to be identified with a particular group adopt the trappings and signs of that group. Those who wish to dissociate themselves from particular groups make a point of addressing and displaying themselves in ways that could not possibly be associated.

The elements of title, behaviour and trappings thus combine to indicate the particular role set. They also give off particular perceptions and expectations to those with whom they interact. This is also a part of the wider perceptual process.

Above all, however, it indicates the complexities, issues, inconsistencies and uncertainties that are key and continuous features of human behaviour, and therefore clearly of organization behaviour (see Box 13.10).

Box 13.10: Role models (2)

People who do identify and follow role models need to be certain that the substance matches the trappings and signs. For example:

* One English university (de Montfort) is named after Simone de Montfort, who was responsible for at least a quarter of a million deaths when he put down the Cathar heresy.
* Oliver Cromwell was voted the third greatest English person ever in a BBC poll in 2006, and yet was responsible for the massacre of half a million people in Ireland in the 1650s.
* Tiger Woods, the very great golfer, lost his role-model and iconic status (and also many lucrative endorsements) when it became clear that he was a serial adulterer.

This also reinforces the point (see above) that the substance has to match the impression. If people are appointed on the basis of their decisiveness or assertiveness, they still have to know what they are doing.

Role uncertainties and ambiguities

Role uncertainties and ambiguities arise when there is a lack of clarity as to the precise nature of the role or roles at any given point. They relate to:

* uncertainty about aims and objectives, resulting in uncertainty/lack of clarity as to what constitutes successful and effective performance;
* uncertainty about job/task/occupational boundaries in terms of extent, range and depth of coverage, quality of performance (especially where this is not easily or precisely measured);
* uncertainty about the nature of commitment expected/anticipated/required, including areas of responsibility, authority and accountability;
* uncertainty of expectations arising from misconceptions at the outset; expectations placed on the role by the individual which are not met in the ways anticipated; expectations of others;
* uncertainty of relationships within the group, between groups and across the whole organization;
* uncertainty of prospects, development, enhancement and advancement;
* uncertainty of stability, continuity and confidence.

Each contributes to a lack of clarity of relationship and expectations, and is a source of potential stress and conflict. They may also give rise to clashes, anger, lack of confidence and respect (see Box 13.11).

Incompatibility

Incompatibility arises when an individual is unable to carry out the role. This is normally either because they lack the capability or because they are unable to perform it in the ways required.

Box 13.11: Responsibility and authority

David Stevens was appointed restaurant manager at a large city-centre branch of a fast-food chain. The restaurant was always very busy; and David quickly increased the profits.

After a while, it became clear that he could increase the profits still further if he offered, alongside the existing and prescribed range of products, a combination of salads, smoothie soft drinks, teas and coffees.

Accordingly, he opened a till at the end of the counter serving the drinks, and he installed a salad bar in the centre of the restaurant.

Profits rose instantly. In particular, the new range of products quickly developed to produce 20 per cent of turnover.

Six months later, the regional manager dropped by with a view to congratulating David on his profitability. When he saw the salad bar and the new range of drinks, however, he was horrified. He called David into the office for 'a frank and serious exchange of views'. Company policy forbade the sale of anything other than the defined range of products. David pointed to the revenues from the new range of products, and the popularity in which the restaurant was held.

The regional manager nevertheless forbade David from continuing to sell the salads and drinks.

Here is an example of how role uncertainties and ambiguities can, and do, lead to problems and conflicts. On the one hand, in this example, there is an effective business development; on the other hand, it is not what the particular company is about. In particular also, David had responsibility for delivering profitability from the restaurant; on the other hand again, he was required to do it within the confines of company and organization policy.

One part of this relates to the 'Peter Principle' – promotion to the level of incompetence – whereby someone is given a job or task for which they have no aptitude or capability.

Incompatibility can occur where a supervisor is required by his/her superior to run a highly structured operation and where the staff prefer and are used to a more relaxed and less formal style. Incompatibility may also be an issue where anyone is given any job to do which they are capable of doing, but find difficult or unacceptable either the ways in which it is required to be done, or its context.

Incompatibility comes to be a problem where people are asked to do a job but given no training in advance. This means that they either have to learn on the job, in which case, there is often a large measure of trial and error; or else they do not learn at all, which means that the job is delivered in a haphazard and uncertain way.

Incompatibility is also to be found where values and beliefs are called into question. A supervisor may be required to discipline or dismiss a member of staff and find themselves unable to do so because they believe it to be wrong. If the rest of the group also believe that it is wrong, this will adversely (possibly fatally) affect the supervisor's future relationships with the other group members.

Ultimately, therefore, all staff members have to be comfortable with the roles to which they are assigned; and in specific cases, they must be trained, developed and inducted into what the organization requires.

Overload

This occurs where the individual is required to take on:

* too much work, too many tasks;
* too much responsibility, authority and accountability;
* too much pressure, stress and strain;
* incompatibility, as above.

The result is either that all of the work is unsatisfactory; or that some of the work is effective at the expense of the rest; or that some aspects are not covered at all.

Overload can only be sustained in the short- to medium-term – while the organization is getting through a crisis for example. Continued overload normally leads to loss of performance, loss of achievement and damage to the health of the individual.

Underload

Underload occurs where there is not enough in the role to keep the individual happy and satisfied. This is normally related to feelings of

* undervalue, including where the individual feels that they are being underpaid and under-rewarded; and also where their contribution is not being fully recognized;
* underperformance, where the individual feels that they could be going on to better and higher things;
* not being needed, a lack of confidence in the quality, worth and contribution of the work itself;
* lack of feeling on the part of the organization for the well-being of the staff; on the part of superiors for subordinates;
* loss of self-respect, self-esteem and the esteem and regard of others;
* external and internal pressure, a consciousness on the part of the individual that they are capable of doing far better and of achieving much more; this is compounded when peers, friends, family and acquaintances all believe the same thing.

This may clearly have nothing to do with absolute volumes of work. Indeed, it is most likely to hinge on the individual's perceptions of their own capabilities and potential. People are much more likely to put up with something that does not meet their expectations if they feel that it is a means to an end, a stepping stone on the path of progress. Frustration sets in where these prospects are not present or not apparent.

Stresses and strains

Stresses and strains become apparent where the problems caused by ambiguity, uncertainty, overload and underload become irreconcilable. The symptoms are:

* poor communications, in terms of both volume and quality; lack of accessibility and visibility;
* over-attention to trivia and detail at the expense of the broader picture, aims and objectives;

- over-attention to and over-use of procedures and rules at the expense of issue resolution and problem solving;
- polarization of approach – everything is either very good or very bad;
- poor interpersonal relationships, the presence of tension, friction and irritability;
- withdrawal including absenteeism and sickness;
- the presence of blame, the search for scapegoats;
- loss of volume and quality of performance.

If allowed to go unchecked, the effects of stress and strain invariably include loss of general performance, motivation and morale, and the decline of general working relationships. Individuals within the department withdraw themselves, seeking to ensure that they carry out their tasks satisfactorily; at the same time, they will tend to seek opportunities elsewhere to remove themselves from the current situation. They pursue their own objectives at the expense of, rather than in harmony with, those of the organization (see Box 13.12).

Application

Interaction with, and between, individuals, their personality traits, their aptitudes and the roles that they are required to perform is a critical feature of all organizations, and

---

Box 13.12: Cobra Beer

When Karan Bilimoria founded Cobra Beer, the stated objective was to produce 'the best beer in the world'. Karan Bilimoria set out to analyse all existing products, and to take the best element or ingredient from each, so as to achieve the objective.

After a while, the product was produced to the standard and taste required. It now became necessary to create a marketing and sales structure so that the product could be got out to customers.

A sales manager was hired. The sales manager, Navjot Siddhu, now set to work to create a sales network, marketing campaign and presentation for the beer. Navjot Siddhu worked all hours in order to do this.

The initial marketing campaign was not successful, and it became necessary for Karan Bilimoria and Navjot Siddhu to think about other things. Eventually, no decision was reached. Navjot stated: 'Leave it to me. I will do whatever is necessary to make this product successful.'

Some time later, Karan Bilimoria was on his way out to a restaurant when he saw the office lights still on. Navjot Siddhu was still in the office. Karan called in and said: 'What on earth are you doing here at this late hour? You will die of stress, strain and overwork.'

Navjot replied: 'Yes it is stressful at the moment. But when this is successful, none of us will have the same stress.'

Here, there is an example of having to adjust and re-prioritize roles in order to achieve the desired objective. In the short-term, clearly, this is a very stressful way to behave. However, following Navjot's statement about the outcome, such stress and strain becomes acceptable in certain situations and contexts such as this.

so has to be managed. The main lesson, therefore, lies in understanding the complexity of personality and roles that individuals bring with them to all situations. It is also essential to recognize the pressures that can, and do, arise when individuals have to choose between roles, or switch roles.

Recognition of this means that organizations can then establish the key characteristics and traits that are required, rather than trying and invariably failing to cope with the whole individual. For this to be successful, information must be gathered systematically to ensure that as wide and complete a picture is built up about, and around, the individual in relation to the organizational requirements of them. This is also the context for effective work design and division; creation of structures and cultures; and organizational progress, development and change.

In turn, the effectiveness of all of this is dependent upon the nature of individuals brought into the organization in the first place. The onus is therefore placed on getting the recruitment and selection activities as accurate and informative as possible. This is to ensure as effective and harmonious a match as possible between individual and organization. This is the context in which all recruitment and selection activities should be seen. The purpose is to find someone who can do the job, who will fit into the organization (both the particular niche and the wider internal environment) and who brings potential for the future. This is the basis of an effective, continuous and harmonious working relationship (see Box 13.13).

Personality, roles and performance

People can only do what they are capable of; and they also have to be willing to do it in the given set of circumstances. This is the critical aspect of any attempt to match personality, expertise and role. So it is essential to be as clear as possible about the individual's main characteristics, aptitudes and abilities. The best way to do this is to isolate those capabilities and roles required by the organization, and then set up a series of tests that indicate their presence in the particular individuals.

Box 13.13: Dutton Engineering

Dutton Engineering is a medium-sized sheet metal manufacturing company. Based near Doncaster in south Yorkshire for many years, the company has had a policy of doing as much as possible within the manufacturing teams.

Consequently, all recruitment, selection and development activities are turned over to the manufacturing teams. The teams themselves establish who is to be trained and developed in what and when, what the outcomes are supposed to be and what is to happen if things go wrong. They also choose their own supervisors and team leaders.

Subject to equality of opportunity on the one hand, and the ability to ensure that nobody receives any favours, the great strength of this process is that people are choosing those with whom they want to work, and those for whom they want to work. As long as this is effective, it removes yet another barrier to work efficiency and effectiveness. It also means that the teams have to assess not just what they want doing, but the kinds of personalities that they are able and willing to work with and for.

Forms of test

Each of the following forms of test have their place in particular situations.

- **Physical**: to indicate strength, fitness, physical durability, robustness, ability to stand extremes of heat and cold.
- **Intelligence**: to indicate mental agility, mental dexterity and mental awareness.
- **Verbal reasoning**: to indicate how arguments are presented and developed, how an individual may present or develop a case, sales pitch, negotiating position and so on.
- **Presentation**: to indicate self-presentation, awareness of audience, use of time, structure and a logical order of material, aims and objectives of a situation.
- **Numeracy**: to indicate level of understanding and application or numerical forms, skills in adding, subtracting, multiplying and dividing, use of numeracy technology.
- **Literacy**: to indicate levels of language usage and application, and also particular skills such as spelling and articulation.
- **Skills**: to indicate levels and quality of skills in, for example, typing, shorthand, engineering, presentation.
- **Aptitude**: to indicate the relationship between what the individual can do now as a prediction of what they may be able to achieve in the future.
- **Attainment**: to indicate the depth of knowledge or skill achieved to date in terms of the organization's current and future requirements.
- **Pressure**: to indicate how the individual copes, prioritizes and carries out work when put under some form of pressure (for example, time, interruptions); they may also be developed to indicate how the individual might cope with stress.
- **Work sampling**: to indicate the range and quality of past activities as an indication of current level of competence.
- **Work portfolios**: in which people with distinctive professional and practical aptitudes (e.g. architecture, design) bring and demonstrate examples of what they have done to date.
- **What if?** in which people are given a scenario, and then have to produce an answer; and this indicates both verbal and also professional reasoning.
- **Personality**: to indicate the personality traits of the individual.

For each of these the word 'indicate' is used. None proves a certainty of performance. A typing test that the individual completes successfully proves that they *can* do it; it does not prove that they *will* do it in the work situation; and this applies to each form of testing indicated. Those that are less precise in output – intelligence, aptitude, personality – have to be structured further to provide a correlation between:

(a) the traits and levels identified;
(b) those that are required;
(c) why they are required;
(d) the extent to which past successful holders of the particular job exhibited these;
(e) the extent to which these were key elements of that success.

Testing also does not predict or guarantee performance, or the effort which people will put in. Tests have therefore to be used in combination with each other, in order to assess someone's overall suitability for particular roles. Each test opens up a small part of a personality, and other parts of the individual's expertise (see Box 13.14).

Box 13.14: Big Brother

Big Brother, the Channel 4 reality television series, for many years attracted a large number of applicants who had a burning ambition to be television presenters.

On the face of it, many contestants clearly considered themselves suitable; after all, they were personable, affable, telegenic and by the end of the show, they would be known and loved by the public.

However, those who did get as far as being fledgling television presenters quickly found that there was more to the role. It was essential to be well informed in every aspect of what was being presented. It was also essential to be able to sight-read from an autocue, and to do this while production staff were talking in the earpiece. Television presenting therefore had its own range of expertise and disciplines, which had to be learned and applied while on air.

Consequently, very few of those who have sought to enter television presentation by this route have succeeded. Simple and straightforward though the job may look to the viewers, it is in practice much more complicated; and especially, lack of expertise in presentation skills is clearly and unavoidably observable.

Conclusions

Organizations need to design and structure work, jobs and roles that meet and satisfy the match between people's capabilities and aptitudes as much as possible. They must recognize that this is the basis of productive, effective and successful work, of individual and mutual satisfaction in both occupational and personal terms. They must also recognize the fact that problems are likely to arise and the nature of these when insufficient attention is paid and where there is a lack of full understanding.

Additionally, organizations need to know and understand:

- where people's dominant traits and qualities lie, and how best to fit these to effective work patterns;
- how people are to adopt and perform their roles;
- which roles are acceptable within the organization, and which are unacceptable (see Box 13.15).

Especially, much more attention needs to be paid to selection processes – both for those coming into organizations and for movements within. This means targeting as much as developing the selection process; and this is based on the understanding indicated above, establishing the true nature of the qualities required for successful performance and assessing the extent of these in individuals. Where necessary or desirable, this includes attention to particular attitudes, values and beliefs and to the pressures of the wider environment, as well as distinctive capability and expertise.

Box 13.15: Larger-than-life characters

Many larger-than-life characters, especially at top and in senior positions of organizations, constantly tread the fine line between being 'colourful', and being 'a pain in the neck'.

The problem for all such people, and the organizations that have to accommodate them, lies in knowing and understanding the actual patterns of behaviour, and the ways in which these are perceived by everyone involved.

During the course of his working life, Robert Maxwell moved from war hero, to business founder, to MP, to newspaper owner and finally to criminal. Arriving in the UK in 1940 as a refugee from Nazi Germany, he joined the Royal Air Force, and quickly became decorated for his bravery. After the war, he founded the Pergamon Press, a specialist academic publisher. He was a Labour MP from 1964 to 1979. Following this, he became the proprietor of Mirror Group Newspapers; and from there, things went downhill. He started to use corporate funds for his own personal pleasure; and when it became apparent that he would be discovered, he took his own life.

During the whole of his career, until shortly before his death, he was viewed by the public at large as a larger-than-life and colourful character. This, however, was not the perception of those who had to work with him. On many occasions, those who did work with him found him to be vain, bullying, offensive and overbearing. Several ex-employees subsequently testified to the fact that they had been physically assaulted by him; and many revealed that they had been on the receiving end of extensive and abusive public tongue lashings.

In particular, a junior member of staff working for the Mirror Group's auditors had just produced the company's valuation for one year. The auditor, a man in his early thirties, delivered the figures to Maxwell himself. Maxwell took one look at the figures and standing over the junior auditor, bellowed: 'These figures are unacceptable! Go away and change them – and double the capital value of the company! Get out and don't come back until you have done it!'

The junior auditor did indeed do this. Speaking afterwards, he stated that everything about Maxwell – his personality, the assumption that he would get his own way, and also his physical presence (he was well over 6 feet tall and nearly 20 stone in weight) – caused him to wield power and influence in this way.

14 Technology

Introduction

All organizations use some form of technology and equipment in pursuit of their business and this has a basic and critical impact on the nature, design, structure and conduct of work. Technology also has implications for compartmentalization, functionalization and specialization. Departments and divisions are created around the equipment used – whether for production, communications, information or control. It impacts on the physical environment – particular processes determine the layout and format in which work is conducted and the proximity of individuals and groups to each other. It therefore becomes a factor to be recognized in the creation of supervisory and managerial functions and activities (see Box 14.1).

Box 14.1: Sainsbury's

In recent years, Sainsbury's, the supermarket chain, introduced an automated approach to ensuring that the shelves in each of the branches were fully stocked.

The system looked excellent in its conception. Each time a particular product line stock ran down on the shelves (which would be noted via a combination of bar-codes on the shelves and the goods passing through check-out), a signal would automatically be sent to the managers and supervisors that the product needed re-stocking.

Accordingly, the system was implemented. However, it very quickly ran into difficulties. It became clear that the system did not recognize the fact that customers in practice tend to rummage for the items that they want and leave the shelves untidy. This turned out to be a particular problem in the stocking of foodstuffs with a short shelf-life, bread and cakes and ready-to-eat sandwiches and other foods for immediate consumption. This resulted in many of the stores over-ordering from suppliers; and it became physically impossible to get the fresh products on to the shelves before their best-buy date expired.

The aim was to make the ordering process certain and assured. However, insufficient attention was paid to the crucial nature of supervisory and managerial functions and activities in this particular context – the need to observe the speed at which these products were being sold, rather than to make assumptions from data gathered. Technology can do the work that people ask it to do; it cannot make human or informed judgements.

Box 14.2: Moore's Law

Moore's Law states that the productive capacity of technology doubles every eighteen months. Moore (1988) produced this key finding based on extensive research on the capacity to design and develop micro-chips and the functions that could be placed on them.

However, the 'Law' has clear implications for other technological developments. For example:

- motor car and aero engines now have much greater power, using less fuel, with less waste, and can energize ever-greater loads;
- production technology in all spheres works to a much greater level of accuracy, and again requires less energy to make it do more work;
- information technology means that data can now be transmitted, stored, retrieved and accessed instantly from anywhere in the world, regardless of where the data itself is actually located;
- telephone and communications technology is now fast, accurate and also universally accessible.

Understanding this ought to inform managers of when and where to replace technology; and also to begin to form an understanding about what the next generation of technologies and equipment ought to have.

Again, there is an historic background. Forms of technology and equipment were used in the construction of the great buildings, temples and monuments of the ancient world. Most of this was unmechanized, often requiring armies of people to move heavy blocks of wood and stone into place. Roman war galleys – fighting ships – used slave-driven banks of oars for propulsion and direction and to manoeuvre into fighting positions. In each of these cases a basic technology existed and was exploited – but using human, rather than mechanized energy, to make it effective. In each case also, the task requirements meant that forms of organization were required; and while in many cases the labour was composed of slaves, these nevertheless had to be sufficiently interested, motivated and directed to ensure that the product or output was both effective and of the required quality (see Box 14.2).

The relationship between people and technology

The relationship between people and technology in organizations and organized groups has therefore long been established and recognized. Technology therefore has direct effects on every aspect of organizational and workplace practice: the organization of work; the expertise and skills needed; specific training and development in some instances; and the location of work.

The relationship between technology and organizational behaviour may be considered under the following headings.

- **Approaches to production**: scientific management and its effects on production and behaviour; studies of groups in different working situations; the use of work groups in production.
- **Levels and types of technology**: the effects of the size, scope and scale of operations; the use of production lines; the effects of mechanization and automation on individuals and groups.
- **Information and communications technology**: the ability to gather, store, analyse, retrieve and access data from anywhere in the world; and the ability to be in contact with anyone at any time.
- **Organizational requirements**: the maximization/optimization of production; attention to standardization, quality, speed, reliability and consistency of output.
- **Human and behavioural implications**: work and job variety, development, enrichment and enhancement; and also boredom and alienation; health and safety and occupational health; stresses and strains; job and task division.
- **Integration of technology with a full range of organizational activities**: which requires recognizing the need to provide technology and equipment; the nature of the working environment required; providing accommodation for the staff.

The context of technology usage

Organizational technology consists of:

- hardware – the capital equipment – computers, screens, robots, process machines;
- software – the packages needed to energize and direct the hardware profitably and effectively.

Those responsible for commissioning, acquiring and purchasing technology of any sort need to be aware of the full range of implications. Clear aims and objectives are required in terms of what the technology is supposed to produce (quality and quantity). As above, this then needs directly relating to the volumes of staff required to operate it, and any specific expertise that they may need. Detailed evaluations are required in terms of capacity; continuity of usage; and maintenance and upgrades. Organizations and their managers also need a clear view of how long any technology in use is likely to remain current and competitive, and when it is likely to need replacing. This additionally has to be seen in the context that if one organization in the sector acquires a radical new technology which is going to transform the ways in which business is conducted, then every organization may have to discard what they already have, write off the costs and acquire the new equipment.

Hardware and software are required in the following areas:

- Production technology and equipment: which may be largely manual or mechanized, requiring human expertise, energy and input to make it effective and productive.
- Largely automated, self-driven technology designed to produce products (or components of products) to uniform standards of quality, appearance and performance.
- Support function technology: included computer-aided design, desktop printing and publishing, purchasing, stock room, storage and ordering systems.
- Information systems: for the input, storage, retrieval, output and presentation of data in ways suitable to those using it; and the production of data for purposes of control, monitoring, evaluation and decision making.

- Communication systems: that can support e-mail and internet access as and when required.
- Mobile telephone and telecommunications technology: to ensure that people can be contacted at any time for any reason.
- Specialized: for example, health equipment includes scanners, monitors, emergency equipment, laser technology for surgery and healing, heart, lung, organ and pulse monitoring equipment.
- Bespoke (i.e. specially designed) production, service and information systems.
- Generic: for example, off-the-shelf computerized production and information systems that are of value to a wide range of organizations and activities (see Box 14.3).

Technology development and improvement

As stated above, the capacity of technology generally doubles every eighteen months. However, this does not necessarily mean that it needs to be replaced every eighteen

---

Box 14.3: HR systems

Many organizations now use generic HR systems during their recruitment and selection processes. The stated advantages of these systems are as follows:

- everyone has to produce their application in a standard format, and this enhances equality of treatment and opportunity;
- the data can be accessed at any time by those responsible for the selection processes and making appointments;
- the data gathered is precise, comprehensive and complete enough to enable assessments to be made.

However, serious problems have been found. Many generic systems have been found not to be fully accurate; once a person has logged on to access their own data, they have found that they have been able to access everyone else's also. Such systems require absolute assurance that any data that is inputted, is saved and stored as it has been entered and is not corrupted in any way.

One system for the making of key appointments in public services had an automated referencing system attached to it. This meant that once the data had been inputted, the system automatically contacted named referees to ask for references. However, the generic system requests were sent out from a 'no reply' address, and did not give the contact details to which references should be sent. The result was that at least four universities, and two major urban health authorities, found themselves advertising for posts which they were then unable to fill because no references were received.

Again, automated HR systems give no indication of whether it will be possible to work with the individuals who have applied electronically. The best that can be said for any generic HR system is that it provides a standardized body of data, as above.

months. In many cases, technology remains adequate and effective for long periods of time. Additionally, most technologies have some capacity for upgrade or improvements in operation.

In this context, all technological developments take place with one or more clear purposes, aims and objectives as follows.

- That which is to be used in future supersedes that which was used in the past, either by improving quality or volume of output, or by reducing the time and resources (including human) taken to produce the existing levels.
- That which is to be used in the future has a greater variety of uses and applications than the existing and may lead to the ability to gain entry into new markets and sectors, thus helping to secure the future of the organization.
- The organization itself has an accurate assessment of the nature of the technology required to produce its products to the required volume, quality and deadline and commissions the design and manufacture of the equipment to do this.
- Organizations and the technology that they use must be capable of harmonization with the given culture, values, attitudes, skills and qualities.
- Items of technology must increasingly be capable of integration and interrelationship with each other.

Assessing and evaluating what specific developments and improvements are to achieve requires expert managerial assessment, based on a full understanding of what the organization requires from its technologies, equipment and systems. If necessary, managers need to have access to expert knowledge and information, which can provide advice, and which will then form part of the basis on which they make their judgement (see Box 14.4).

Size and scale of production

The size and scale of production, and the locations in which it is carried out, directly affect the physical construction and layout of organizations. Sizes and scales of production additionally affect the demand for staff and expertise. Whatever is chosen has direct implications for design, layout and structuring of premises.

Woodward (1960) studied the impact of technology and behaviour on each other in a wide range of manufacturing organizations in Essex. From this work there has emerged a widely used classification of sizes and scales of production.

- **Unit**: the production of individual, unique or specialized items. Resources are gathered together to produce these in response to demand and orders. To be successful in this a variety of conditions must exist. The technology and equipment used must be specialized. The expertise available must be both highly specialist in the given field and flexible, adaptable and responsive to individual demands. There must be commitment to quality and attention to the particular demands of customers. Scheduling and patterns of work will be flexible.

  Most unit work is carried out by small organizations. Those who work in them must, in turn, be flexible in their attitude and approach to work. Many people involved in unit production bring with them high levels of technical expertise and this has to be integrated into effective output (see Box 14.5).

Box 14.4: Technology and fashion

Every aspect of organizational activity has its own fashions and fads; and technology is no exception.

The problem is compounded when many organizations offer technological upgrades as a mark of status or importance, rather than because of operational need. This tends to drive patterns of behaviour requiring organizations to change both their technologies and also operating systems because otherwise some members of staff will feel slighted and unvalued.

Over recent years, fashionable and faddish technology upgrades have taken the following forms:

- providing people with Perspex personal computers;
- providing top managers with Blackberries as a mark of status, as well as operational necessity (the problem with this was that when lesser members of staff also got Blackberries, the next generation had come out and so the equipment held by seniors was inferior to that of the juniors, and so a whole new round of upgrades had to take place);
- providing branded goods – in particular there is an enduring problem when deciding whether to give people Apple computers.

Each of these activities feeds the ego (and from this point of view, may indeed be part of fostering an effective working culture). However, unless the full context is understood, it can be a very expensive and dysfunctional way of ensuring that work can be carried out.

Box 14.5: Mass customization in the clothing industry

A combination of unit and mass production exists in the clothing industry. The approaches taken are:

- limited ranges of specific designs superimposed on mass demand items such as T-shirts and jeans;
- the opportunity for individuals to have their own specific design made and superimposed on T-shirts and jeans as above, and also shirts, skirts, trousers and dresses.

This has enabled companies in the industry to expand their range of production at the edges; and as long as the technology used is capable of this kind of setting up, without incurring additional capital costs, it is very effective and profitable. It does however require, on the part of managers and product designers, a commitment to open up their operations in these ways.

- **Mass production**: the design of mass production operations was and remains based on the scientific management principles first developed by Taylor in the late nineteenth century. Work is broken down into simple and progressive operations. Large volumes are standardized and regular output is therefore produced. Automated and computerized production technologies are now widely used for this. The result has been to increase quality, volume, speed and reliability of output (see Box 14.6).

   Mass production requires high and continuing levels of investment in production technology of work premises. It also requires investment in the determination and management of scheduling, storage, marketing, sales and delivery and the organization and training of the workforce. This normally means the employment of a wide range of distinctive, professional or semi-professional functional specialists and experts, and the creation of departments and divisions reflecting this. The contribution of each and their interaction with each other has to be managed and harmonized. Areas of conflict become apparent between the departments and divisions. There is also often the need to reconcile organizational priorities and directions with the demands of individuals to progress and develop their professional and technical expertise and their careers (see Box 14.7).

- **Batch production**: this exists between the unit and mass scales of production. It draws features from each – the specialist quality output and the flexibility and responsiveness of the small producer, combined with the production standardization and larger scales of activities. A batch is therefore a quantity large enough to require substantial technological investment and resourcing. Batch production technology has therefore to be as flexible as the organization requires, enabling it to change production as demand for one kind of product or service ends, and demand for the next batch arrives. Batch production has also to be capable of moving in response to market and consumer demands (see Box 14.8).

- **Flow production**: this is related to mass production in scale, but applies to areas of activity where the output is a continuous stream or flow – such as oil, petrol, chemicals, steel and plastic extrusion. The investment in technology is by far the greatest charge on organizations in these sectors. Input and expertise has to be scheduled in order to ensure a steady and correct flow of raw materials into the production and output processes. The second priority is in the maintenance of the equipment used in order that there are as few breakdowns and stoppages as possible because the other critical level of charge comes from shutting down the processes and then restarting them.

   This gives a general indication of the managerial and organizational behavioural issues that arise as the result of the adoption of particular types and scales of production and the technology used. There are implications for work division and allocation, work patterns, styles and methods of management, and supervision of operations. There are also production and operational pressures on those who actually conduct the organization's primary activities.

Service technology

Service technology exists to ensure that every aspect is delivered to the highest possible quality, precision and accuracy. Service technology consists of:

Box 14.6: Swatch

When the Swiss watch manufacturing industry was restructured and re-formed in the 1970s, a key priority of the industry was to make sure that production was carried out to all of the quality standards and cost advantages that were available in the Far East – but this would be in Switzerland!

Accordingly, extensive investment was made in designing the production technology to absolute standards of quality and product assurance. This was closely related to the design of the watches themselves; whatever the final product was to look like, the workings had to be of the highest possible quality. The outcome of all this was the most cost-effective production facility in the world. Using Swiss technology, on Swiss premises, and Swiss labour on Swiss wages, production was demonstrated to be more cost effective than that achieved by Far Eastern competitors, using Chinese and Japanese premises, with the staff paid on local rates there.

Additionally, by streamlining and shoring the quality of the core components needed to make effective and reliable watches, absolute product assurance could be guaranteed, whether this concerned the industry's cheap or expensive brands.

Box 14.7: Dead-end jobs

An enduring problem with the effective management of mass production jobs has always been how to remove the boredom and alienation (see below).

One of the problems is stereotyping and pigeonholing (see Chapter 4 above). Managers make assumptions about those in particular occupations. In mass production activities, in many cases, the only opportunities for progression from production work is into either supervision or maintenance activities. Over the medium- to long-term, managers and supervisors have therefore to be aware of the following:

- long-term decline in morale, related directly to the repetitive and predictable nature of work;
- psychological detachment, as the staff collectively come to view themselves as being no more than a commodity;
- complacency, as people come to view the assurance and predictability of the work as absolute facts of life.

Where there is little scope for development and advancement, many companies make the wage levels relatively high, so as at least to provide some form of compensation. Others do their best to involve the staff through other means, including social clubs; facilities for children; involvement in the community; and sponsorship of social activities. Some companies do therefore do their best to alleviate the monotony of the work through forms of active involvement in other aspects of life. The problem of motivation and morale where work variety and opportunities are limited remains an enduring priority for all companies and organizations involved in this nature of activities to address.

- the bar-coding of products, and the capacity to read the code and identify every aspect as the result – nature and description; price; date purchased; and any after-sales commitments;
- telephone help-line provision, so that people can get in touch with the supplying organization on any matter whatsoever;
- internet provision, which exists for a variety of purposes in the pursuit of providing excellent customer support – product and service descriptions; ease of access; the provision of e-mail and telephone contacts;
- capability in coordination of different parts or aspects of products and services on offer, especially maintenance, after-sales and upgrade packages (the motor car industry); coordination of different parts of travel arrangements (e.g. flight/crossing, hotel rooms, car hire can now all be coordinated from one point);

Box 14.8: Drinks sachets

In the 1970s, the UK soft drinks industry collectively decided that the glass bottle was obsolete. Research staff at ICI had produced a 'drinks sachet', a soft plastic sleeve that could be made easily in all sizes, and which was now to be the container for all soft drinks. It was to make batch production in the industry very much easier; the only thing that would need to be changed would be the wrapper and branding label. The sachets would be very much lighter than using glass bottles and so less expensive to distribute. The actual production of the sachets would be carried out for a fraction of the cost of producing glass bottles.

Accordingly, the idea was put to the soft drinks companies and bottling plants; and everyone agreed it was a revolutionary step. Soft drinks sachets began to roll of the production lines and into the shops.

It was not long before all the companies started to receive floods of complaints from people who had tried the sachets, and had found them unusable. The moment they were opened they would collapse, spilling the drink. Small children, especially, had great difficulty in using them.

Aghast, ICI and the other production companies went back to the drawing board. The bottle was obsolete; the sachet was unusable; what were they now to do?

At a meeting not long afterwards, someone produced a plastic bottle which they had acquired while on their holidays in Europe. This, it became clear, covered every demand; it was much lighter than glass, while at the same time being sturdy enough to be used exactly in the same way as a glass bottle. Plastic bottles could be produced to any size; and again, the only distinction needed was to produce different labels for the batches of products and brands as they came off the production lines.

The lesson is that something that suits production processes nevertheless has to be seen in its full context. The fact that the sachets made production easier and cheaper did not mean that the products would be of use or value to customers. Had the products been tested under real conditions, the sachet idea would never have got past the drawing board. As it was, it took trial and error, and a chance discovery, to replace effectively a part of the production process that everyone agreed was cumbersome and obsolete.

- complete product and service descriptions, which can be studied in detail by customers at their leisure from their own computer links;
- the provision of e-mail and texting services in terms of general product and service support (e.g. regular reminders are sent out by airline and other travel companies in the run-up to the date of departure, once a booking has been made).

Effectively used, service technology is therefore delivering the following:

- product and service support, as above;
- branding and identity support, delivered through the regular contacts as above;
- confidence enhancement, through the regularity of contacts made;
- product and service assurance, in that the accuracy of the bar-coding technology now delivers full product and sales information, prints it out on customer receipts and stores this information within organization databases.

Effective technology, supported by expertise, is therefore essential in the delivery and development of high-quality customer service; and in developing and enhancing people's expectations of the levels of service that they may expect. Effective use of technology has also enabled organizations in many sectors to radically transform their industries (see Box 14.9).

Speed of service

As well as accuracy, security and assurance, people now expect high-quality service to be delivered instantly. This is especially true for internet and e-mail transactions; people who quite happily queue for several minutes at a branch of the bank, or at a supermarket check-out, become frustrated in a matter of seconds if internet links do not work. This, again, is because people's expectations have been transformed; because some internet and e-mail services can deliver more or less instantly, people expect this from every such provision (see Box 14.10).

Information technology

Information technology, and the systems and expertise that support it, exist in all organizations. The purpose of information technology is to provide an adequate and effective means for:

- storing and retrieving information;
- analysing and evaluating information;
- presenting information in suitable forms to different members of staff;
- presenting information in forms suitable to every organization stakeholder group;
- distributing and disseminating information as required.

Information technology is based on a number of assumptions:

- those requiring information in whatever form have access to the technology necessary to gain this access;

Box 14.9: Low-cost air travel

Ryanair and easyJet, the low-cost airlines, were among the first large organizations to recognize the full range of services and service levels that could be provided by technology. By defining the absolute quality of service that customers would require, and by working back from this, each was able to deliver a service of at least equivalent value to that which was provided by over-the-desk transactions, telephone links and travel agent purchases.

The critical aspects were:

- assurance that once the booking had been made and confirmed, the time, date and destination of the flight were assured;
- any changes that had to be made could be notified to the customers through understood channels (e-mail, telephone and text);
- security of customer details;
- security of financial transactions;
- assurance that each financial transaction stood alone, and that no further charges would be made against the particular booking.

Ryanair and easyJet were able to get people to change their behaviour and expectations in these ways by virtue of the fact that their prices and charges were so much lower than those of the regular airline sector. Had their prices only been marginally lower, nobody would have been interested.

The lesson is that organizations that wish to transform the nature of services on offer and service levels delivered have to do it in the interests of their customers and service-users. The support functions (internet, telephone and text services) have to be fully accurate and secure; and there has to be a behavioural trigger that actively engages the interests of the customers (who are, after all, being asked radically to transform their present patterns of behaviour).

Internally, there is also a critical organization commitment to security of transactions, and currency of website provision. This requires staff with specific expertise to be available at all times. This reflects the absolute nature of organization commitment required.

Box 14.10: McDonald's

Customer service studies carried out by McDonald's produced a definition of 'acceptability' in terms of the speed of customer service required. In the context that, within the time frames, everything had to be delivered as precisely requested by the customers, the McDonald's surveys found the following:

- people were prepared to queue for between 2.5 and 3.5 minutes;
- people expected their order to be delivered in full within 2 minutes of being placed;

- people expected to be able to hand over (real and perceived) high denomination banknotes (£20; £50) and to receive change quickly, accurately and in the denominations convenient to them.

These timings set the standards for fast food, other takeaway services and the coffee bar industries. This case additionally supports the view that, while people are generally prepared to wait for between 5 and 6 minutes for a face-to-face transaction to be completed satisfactorily, this does not apply to all services or in all sets of circumstances.

- information that is fed into the system remains in the state in which it was fed in, and is not corrupted or otherwise damaged in any way;
- information is capable of storage for long periods of time;
- information systems are secure, capable of being accessed only by those with legitimate authority to do so;
- data held is itself secure, again capable of being accessed only by those with legitimate authority to do so;
- the information held must be capable of remaining secure if the specific systems and software are upgraded;
- information systems must be capable of access and operation by the staff concerned; staff therefore require training and briefing in how to operate the systems present.

Technology-based information systems must be capable of integration with other sources and funds of information used within the organization. Particular priorities are:

- paper-based information storage and filing systems;
- the expertise held by individuals in their roles and offices;
- formal and informal information and communication networks (see also Chapter 15);
- sources of primary data – that which is gathered by the organization for stated specific purposes;
- sources of secondary data – that which is available from other organizations and institutions, and used by the organization to inform particular activities, decisions and initiatives;
- sources of general data – gathered from news media and industry and professional associations, providing more general background information.

At the core of the effectiveness of any information system is the capability and willingness of the staff to use it, and to make it effective and productive. Organizations therefore require the following categories of staff in the effective management of information technology:

- professional/expert staff, capable of maintaining, developing and upgrading information systems as and when required; and capable of solving problems when they arise;

- security specialists, capable of producing systems that will ensure that the confidentiality and integrity of the information held; and providing access to specific groups as above;
- operational effectiveness, so that those who need to use particular systems in the course of their duties are effective;
- general awareness, so that staff know where/who to go to for particular sources of data, even though these may be outside their operational remit.

Technology management and organizational behaviour

The need, therefore, is to assess the interaction between organization, technology and expertise in order to be able to draw up effective methods of work that are both satisfactory and challenging to the experts and professionals involved, and also successfully and profitably integrated with the organization's drives and purposes.

It is apparent from all this that there is a range of conflicting pressures that must be considered:

- the scientific management and organization of activities demand the standardization and ordering of work in the interests of efficiency, speed and volume of output;
- outputs of the scale and scope of production dictate that the flow, mass and (to an extent) batch types of activities require technology that is capable of delivering absolute product and service standardization and uniformity;
- professional and technical staff require variety, development and the opportunity to progress and enhance their work and expertise;
- everyone, whatever their occupation, has basic human needs of self-esteem, self-respect and self-worth.

The need is, therefore, to be able to address and reconcile these issues, and to develop and implement effective patterns of work, whatever the technology used and specific task required (see Box 14.11).

Whatever the nature of technology used, and the expertise or staffing that supports it, the following key managerial priorities have to be addressed:

- alienation;
- technological advances;
- workforce management.

Alienation

Alienation is the term used to describe the feelings of:

- Powerlessness – the inability to influence work conditions, work volume, quality, speed and direction.
- Meaninglessness – the inability to recognize the individual contribution made to the total output of work.
- Isolation – which may be either physical or psychological. The physical factors arise from work organization requiring that people are located in ways that allow for little human interaction and feelings of mutual identity and interest. The psychological

Box 14.11: On-line recruitment – again

A major government institution needed to recruit four key HR professionals to head up a major organization development in this area of expertise. It required an expert and experienced practitioner in each of the areas of employee relations; training and development; recruitment and selection; and equal opportunities.

Accordingly, it engaged an executive search agency; and this agency quickly came up with a strong and extensive field of candidates. It found thirty people for consideration for each post, all suitably qualified and experienced.

Then the government department was reorganized, and the positions were no longer required in the format originally stated. However, the government department agreed that it would be a good idea to retain the details of each of the candidates on file, so that when suitable opportunities came up in the future, these people could be easily contacted.

Accordingly, this data was catalogued and stored. Just over a year later, the reconstituted government department came to the conclusion that it did indeed now need this expertise. Accordingly, it contacted all of the people on the database.

The result was pandemonium! Some of the people who had been previously interested, had now moved on; and in two cases, the fresh contact caused serious problems of assurance and confidence with their new employers. A total of nineteen of the candidates had no prior knowledge that they had even been put forward by the agency the previous time, and so were truly staggered to find themselves being contacted. The following problems were also found:

- the classification of expertise by the employment agency hired, and the understanding of this expertise by the government department were very different;
- the presentation by the employment agency of the candidate's data turned out not to be suitable for government department recruitment.

Additionally of course, the data was now well over one year out of date. In any case, therefore, it would all have to be made current before any further action could be taken. Also, once the initial decision not to go ahead had been taken, candidates' details were stored without any form of evaluation. Therefore not until the need arose again did anyone look in detail at the data; and the fact that it was now well over one year out of date, as above, meant that it was in practice useless.

The original exercise had cost the government department £200,000. There was therefore huge pressure on the government department to use the data that they had, rather than admitting to a blunder, and discarding it. It turned out to be a very expensive way of gathering data that was:

- inappropriate and ineffective;
- unsuitable for purpose;
- easily retrieved;
- useless.

factors are influenced by the physical. They also include psychological distance from supervisors, management and the rest of the organization.

- Low feelings of self-esteem and self-worth arising from the lack of value (real or perceived) placed on staff by the organization and its managers.
- Loss of identity with the organization and its work, the inability to say with pride 'I work for organization X'. This is reinforced by the physical and personal commitment made by the individual to the organization in terms of time, skill and effort and which does not bring with it the psychological rewards.
- Lack of prospects, change or advancement for the future – feelings of being stuck or trapped in a situation purely for economic gain.
- General rejection – based on adversarial, managerial and supervisory styles and lack of meaningful communications, participation and involvement. This is increased by physical factors such as poor working conditions and environment.
- Lack of equality – especially where the organization is seen or perceived to differentiate between different types and grades of staff to the benefit of some and detriment of others.

Alienation is a major fundamental cause of conflicts and disputes at places of work. It is potentially present in all work situations. Those who design and construct organizations need to be aware of it in their own particular situations and to take steps to ensure that ideally it can be eliminated or at least kept to a minimum and its effects offset by other advantages (see Box 14.12).

Box 14.12: Alienation and displacement: overseas call centres

The combination of technological advance, and the expertise that went with it, together with the much lower pay rates for staff, caused (and continues to cause) many organizations to look overseas for some service delivery functions.

In particular, this has led to many western organizations locating their customer service facilities in call centres in India, South Africa and central and eastern Europe. This, the line of reasoning goes, means that some 'non-critical' organizational activities can safely be outsourced to such areas in the sure and certain knowledge that an excellent standard and quality of performance will be delivered as cost effectively (cheaply) as possible.

It has since become apparent that this has caused alienation and displacement in the following forms:

- alienation of the staff in the call centres, in that because of the nature of the data that they are processing, it has become apparent to them that the companies for which they are working are indeed getting them on the cheap;
- alienation of customers, who expect customer service as a core activity and priority and not as a peripheral, support function or after-thought;
- alienation and displacement of the organization itself, in that they simply assume that these functions will be delivered to full effectiveness by people working thousands of miles away.

It is also apparent that the alienation and displacement has led to other problems. Over 100 companies working in India have reported security breaches and data leaks from their customer service and call centre facilities. The staff working in these centres and facilities have no specific identity or affinity to the organizations for which they carry out the work. In some cases also, this has led to outright anger when it is clear to the staff in the centres that the people whose accounts they are managing and servicing are spending the same amount on daily groceries as they get paid in a month.

Effects of technological advances

Some further conclusions concerning the effects of technology upon worker morale may now be drawn.

- Pay, at whatever level it is set, does nothing to alleviate any boredom or monotony inherent in the work itself. It may make it more bearable in the short- to medium-term. In many cases also, bonus systems are not within the control of the individual operator. Operators may work to their full capacity, only to see their bonus fail because of factors further down the production process.
- Insecurity, and related to this, the threat of insecurity and job loss used as a coercive management tool to try to bully the work out.
- Poor working conditions, especially those that include extremes of temperature and noise, discomfort, lack of human content and warmth, all contribute to poor morale.
- Low status and esteem are generated through feelings of being 'only a cog in the machine'. This leads to feelings of futility and impotence on the part of the operator. It is from this that feelings of hostility towards the organization start to emerge. This also leads to increases in strikes, grievances and disputes.
- Mental health was identified as a feature by the 'Kornhauser' studies, the results of which were published in 1965. A major conclusion was that basic assembly line work led to job dissatisfaction which, in turn, led to low levels of mental health. This became apparent in the low self-esteem of the workers who also exhibited anxiety, life dissatisfaction and despair, and hostility to others (see Box 14.13).
- Adversarial and confrontational styles of work supervision also contribute to alienation and dissatisfaction. This style of supervision tends to perpetuated, even by those who have been promoted from among the ranks of operators. This is partly because it is all that they know and partly because of the pressure to conform that is exerted by the existing supervisory group. It is also apparent that supervisors themselves become alienated because of pressures from their managers and also because of feelings of hostility towards them from the workers (see Box 14.14).

Managing the work

Managing the work, and ensuring effectiveness of operations in situations where technology is a key feature, requires understanding of the following:

- attention to the work;
- security and integrity;
- the nature of work groups;
- attention to the environment;
- attention to the people.

Box 14.13: Computer screens and call centre work

The Kornhauser research studied the effects of the relationship between technology and work, and collective and individual health, based on production line technology. However, the equivalent is also to be found in information and communications technology operations.

Extensive studies carried out by the UK Health and Safety Executive resulted in operational patterns being prescribed for those working with computer screens. Extensive staring at computer screens is known and understood to be damaging to people's eyesight, and so requiring staff physically to remove themselves alleviates the damage done. It also helps staff to re-focus on the wider aspects of organizational and operational life, rather than spending their whole lives restricted to a single computer.

Call centre work can also be restricting and demoralizing; and again, this relates to the technology, which is a combination of earpieces and computer screen. Organizations that insist on certain volumes of work (see also Chapter 20) can, and do, experience hostility from the staff who manage this situation by telephoning each other and their friends and family. In particular, staff who have to make a volume of cold calls about the organization's products and services on offer experience hostility, anger and often outright abuse from those whom they call up, and this leads to reduced self-esteem and increased dissatisfaction on the part of the members of staff.

Box 14.14: Hospital telephones

Long-stay hospital patients need telephone services to keep in touch with their friends and relations in the outside world; and they also need things to keep them occupied. For many years, hospitals used to provide both patient services and also television screens for these purposes. Patients could make and receive calls at any time; and they could also watch the television if they chose.

Early in the twenty-first century, these services were privatized, and taken over by a company called Patientline, which undertook to deliver high-quality, excellent and individually tailored services.

It quickly became apparent, however, that there was a price to pay for this. Patients were charged a minimum of £3 per telephone call, and £1.50 per half hour of television viewing. It also became clear that the call and programme management regimes were not accurate; people found themselves being charged for calls long after they had finished, and also for calls that they had not made. Additionally, if the technology did not work for any reason, then nevertheless the charges were made.

Very quickly, therefore, people started bringing mobile telephones and laptop computers into hospital for their friends and relatives who were in for long periods of time. This provoked an adversarial management response on the grounds that the wavelengths used by mobile phone and internet technology could disrupt sensitive hospital and medical equipment.

Alongside this, the partnership between and the NHS authorities required that use of the technology was actively promoted. This led to patients with long-term illnesses and conditions being pressurized into buying packages. This, in turn, led to friction between those responsible for medical treatment, nursing and care management of patients and NHS and managers. This, in turn, increased overall organizational friction and inter-group conflict.

The service, and especially the charges, quickly became notorious, and the services themselves were hardly used. Hospitals that permitted mobile phones and laptops simply saw these replace the service. Hospitals that did not permit mobile phones nevertheless found these to be in almost constant use.

The overall feelings of hostility, together with the institutional hostility between groups of staff as above, led to the service going bankrupt in 2007. This forced hospitals to make alternative provisions available.

As well as an adversarial approach to these services, the problem was made worse by the fundamental lack of integrity of what was on offer: overcharging a captive and vulnerable audience for services of poor and uncertain quality.

Attention to the work

Attention to the work has taken a variety of forms.

- job enrichment and enlargement, in which operators have their capabilities extended to include a range of operations. In some cases this has meant becoming responsible (with a group of others) for the entire production process in autonomous work groups;
- job rotation, in which operators are regularly rotated around different work stations and activities making a different contribution to the whole;
- empowerment, in which the operator accepts responsibility for their own supervision of quality control as well as for the work itself;
- flexibility, so that people have the maximum possible opportunity to carry out work in ways in which they see fit, subject only to meeting deadlines;
- the capability of organizations to open the hours that they choose (including round-the-clock working);
- the capability of organizations to locate work where they choose, subject only to the availability of the required technology and the expertise to operate it;
- the productivity drive, in which all the above are harnessed towards ensuring that specific resources are used to maximum and optimum capability.

Attention to the work is a continuous process. Today's adventure becomes tomorrow's steady state and the monotony of the day after. There is a great propensity for development to occur in current production systems because of technological advances and also because the globalization of competition has led to organizations to seek new fields and new ways in which to operate (see Box 14.15).

Security and integrity

All technology, whatever its purpose, needs its own fundamental security and integrity, as follows:

- production technology must be capable of repetitive operations to a universal standard, quality, predictability and assurance;
- information technology must be capable of storage retrieval, evaluation and access to those who need it and who are legitimate users, as above;
- telephone and e-mail communications technology must be capable of securing the calls made and notes sent, and confining them to those who have legitimate access;
- energy technology must be capable of delivering power supplies safely and within tolerances that enable what is being driven to operate effectively.

Security and integrity are therefore functions of design and operation. Those responsible for the commissioning, design and implementation of technologies must ensure that

---

Box 14.15: Attention to the work at Heathrow Terminal 5

When Terminal 5 at Heathrow airport opened in 2008, the technology and the organization and operational structures with which it was integrated were fundamental to effective operations. Patterns of work were devised to ensure that the technology operated effectively at all times.

However, it quickly became clear that this was not nearly enough. In particular:

- the baggage-handling technology had been tested only under 'laboratory conditions'; the testing had taken no account of what really happened in large-volume passenger-handling airports (that several plane loads of passengers can, and do, arrive together, and that luggage has to be handled from the point of view of overload and over-capacity on these occasions);
- the security technology allowing staff to access their car parks, and also their place of work, could only process one individual at a time. As the Terminal employs nearly 9,000 people this was clearly inadequate.

The lesson is therefore that when new ways of operation, new patterns of work and new facilities are introduced, the technology has to be effective in terms that:

- support the work, not restrict it;
- support the activities, not restrict them;
- take account of any environmental factors that have to be accommodated.

security and integrity are present at every stage of operations. Those responsible for their usage must ensure that regular checks are made so that security breaches do not occur.

Flaws in security and integrity of systems come from two main sources:

- design faults;
- human activity.

Design faults can normally be spotted in the early stages of operations. At this point, those responsible for their design need to be called in and asked (or made) to put them right. If it then becomes clear that there are more serious flaws, then these to need to be rectified at as early a stage as possible.

Integrity compromises and security breaches normally occur in human activity. Either by negligence or malevolent action, the following need to be guarded against:

- adding the wrong mixes of ingredients to production lines;
- compromising the accessibility of information systems;
- wide dissemination of personal, financial and other sensitive data;
- passing information on to other parties, including the media.

It is essential that organizations have effective systems management and associated risk management programmes and procedures in place; and that these are implemented and follows (see also Chapter 22). It is essential that where breaches of security and integrity of systems are found, these are repaired immediately; and where necessary, disciplinary action is taken (see Box 14.16).

Box 14.16: Leakage!

Over the period 1997–2009, the UK government admitted that over 300 instances of data loss had occurred. The forms in which these losses had taken place included:

- ministers leaving departmental laptops on the train;
- ministers losing their handbag in which there were memory sticks with secure and sensitive data;
- memory sticks and compact discs lost in the post or in other transit;
- memory sticks and compact discs being accidentally thrown away, only to be retrieved by the refuse disposal authorities.

Nor was this confined to government and public bodies. Over the same period, banks and financial institutions also admitted to losing records concerning many millions of customers.

The lesson is that all organizations need to be absolutely certain of how easily data can be lost, and information and technology systems compromised.

The nature of work groups

The general attraction of autonomous work groups is that they appear to address both the operational and psychological factors. The giving of autonomy in deciding the allocation of work, organization and production, attention to quality and output based on broad performance targets (for example, 'to produce X amount of product Y by deadline Z') leaves the group itself to arrange and determine how these are to be achieved. This involves:

• participation in determining and allocating the work, scheduling of priorities and activities and meeting preferences, and gaining commitment to meeting the targets;
• responsibility in ensuring that the broad targets are met and that stages along the total schedule are reached also;
• responsibility for training and development of all members to ensure that they can carry out all tasks required;
• responsibility for recruitment and selection, so as to ensure that the groups get the staff that they feel are going to work most effectively in the work group (subject to transparency of process and quality of opportunity and treatment);
• esteem, in that a complete output is seen at the end of activities with which the individual member of staff can identify;
• spirit and harmony, in that the contribution of everyone involved can be seen and valued.

For autonomous working groups to be successful, high levels of skill and flexibility are required. Production technology and processes must be structured to meet behavioural as well as operational needs. Individual and group training and development is essential in all aspects of the work. The process is also greatly enhanced if the group is able to participate (or at least be consulted) on the target-setting activities and to set its own means of quality control and assurance.

Attention to the environment

Attention to the work environment is now a vastly wider field. It stems from the recognition that people bring their full range of needs to work with them and that the more of these that are met, the lower the levels of personal dissatisfaction likely to arise. Basic and adequate levels of comfort are required. The opportunity to sit down at the workstation unless this cannot for overriding operational reasons be provided is always to be offered. Temperature is to be controlled and extremes of heat and cold avoided or managed. Pot plants, the radio, pictures on the walls are all allowed and encouraged (and in some cases provided) wherever possible. Good-quality furniture, decor and furnishings in all places of work reinforce the perceptions of value that organizations place on their staff.

The present state of technology additionally means that 'the working environment' can be seen in much broader terms. Subject to deadlines and other targets, and the availability of technology, work can now be carried out at any time of the day or night, and is not confined to standard working patterns. This in turn means that many people do not have to spend long hours commuting to 'a place of work' as previously. Work can now be done at home, in the car, in business centres, hotels and anywhere else where there are computer links. Provided that it is fully resourced and adequately supported, and provided that this does not lead to alienation or displacement, this means that work can now be carried out much more responsively and effectively. Rather than spending up to six hours per day commuting, these periods can now be used to produce effective work.

Clearly, however, there are occasions when people do need to go into 'the place of work'. However, the relationships between attendance and productive output can now be made much more direct. For those occupations, industries, commercial and public service sectors where 'normal' patterns of attendance are required, improvements in technology mean that much greater volumes of work, to increasing levels of quality, with reduced waste and effluent production, ought now to be possible.

Attention to the people

Attention to the people in terms of their relationship with, and use of, technology requires that the following are addressed.

- Setting absolute standards of honesty, integrity, expectations of performance, quality of output, attitudes, values and ethics to which all those coming to work must aspire and conform.
- Recognizing that problems are inherent in all jobs and organizing the work based around a philosophy of fairness and evenness that requires everyone to share in the problem areas and unattractive tasks.
- Recognizing cultural issues, and any barriers to technology usage or specific work patterns.
- Recognizing the need for training, development and awareness in all aspects of technology usage.
- Setting absolute organizational standards for managing the staff. These are based on high levels of integrity, support, equality, training and development. Pay and reward levels tend to be high in return for high-quality work. Pay and reward methods are honest, clear and unambiguous. Communications between organization and staff, and the general information flows, are regular, continuous and open.

Conclusions

It is very difficult to overstate the importance of attention to technology and its effects on organizational behaviour. In all circumstances, it affects organization and work design and structure and therefore working relationships, patterns of supervision, control and management style.

The key lies in the choice and effective usage of technology. This involves attention to volume and quality of production and output, the skills and qualities required to operate it effectively, and the quality of input and operation. Specific equipment must also be capable of harmonization and integration with other technology that exists and is used.

Attention to investment, levels and frequency of investment and attitudes to investment have also to change. The best organizations concentrate on purpose, quality and suitability, as well as cost, durability and returns. Investing in technology and equipment is a consequence of engaging in particular activities. Investing in staff training and development so that technology is used to its maximum and optimum potential is also essential.

As stated above, all technologies advance, change and develop; and so does the expertise required to operate them and make them effective. All organizations must be prepared to adopt, adjust, and even sacrifice, current equipment if and when others in the sector find better ways of doing things and better equipment to use. Again, there are implications for the skills, qualities and expertise required, on the part of:

- those responsible for taking decisions to invest in and introduce specific technologies;
- those responsible for the organization of work patterns and staffing practices;
- those responsible for managing and supervising work groups that have strong and distinctive technological influences on their activities.

So, the impact of technology on organizational behaviour and performance is all-pervasive. This is both direct and indirect. It directly affects the size, nature and design of the environment and premises, the numbers of people required and their capabilities. It is also the focus around which support functions, processes and practices are devised and grouped. It also directly affects the behaviour, motivation and morale of individuals and groups.

15 Culture

Introduction

Organization culture is an amalgam and summary of what is done within an organization, how it is done and why it is done, and the patterns of behaviour and standards of performance adopted. Organization culture is based on:

- the size, structure, complexity and diversity of the organization;
- the work that is carried out;
- collective and individual perceptions, attitudes, values and beliefs;
- the sources of power and influence, and how power and influence is used by individuals, groups and departments;
- the nature and strength of the leadership of the organization;
- proposals and plans for the future, and how these are to be carried out.

Culture reflects the overall feelings towards the organization, and encompasses standards, morale, strengths of feelings and general levels of goodwill (or otherwise) present (see Box 15.1).

The foundations of organization culture

The foundations of organization culture are found in the following:

- **History and tradition**: the origins of the organization; the aims and objectives of the first owners and managers, and their philosophy and values; the value in which these are currently held; the ways in which they have developed (see Box 15.2).
- **Nature of activities**: historical and traditional, and also current and envisaged; this includes reference to the general state of success and effectiveness; the balance of activities – steady-state, innovative, crisis.
- **Technology**: the relationship between technology and the workforce, work design, organization and structure; alienative factors and steps taken to get over these; levels of technological stability and change; levels of expertise, stability and change.
- **Past, present and future**: the importance of the past in relation to current and proposed activities; special pressures (especially struggles and glories) of the past; the extent to which the organization 'is living' in the past, present or future, and the pressures and constraints that are brought about as the result (see Box 15.3).
- **Purposes, priorities and attention**: in relation to performance, staff, customers, the community and environment; and to progress and development.

Box 15.1: Organization culture

Reception flowers

Anyone who enters an organization, or comes into contact with it in any way at all, begins to form an impression of 'what it is like' and 'how things are done'. Thus for example:

- Customers who make complaints or try to get problems resolved find that either their matter is handled quickly and effectively and to their satisfaction; or else there are delays, sometimes blamed on 'computer malfunctions' or 'administrative errors' or 'the person you need to speak to is on holiday'.
- The size and complexity of organization structures clearly have effects on what is done and how; if matters do have to pass through extensive chains of hierarchy or communication, this is likely to hamper progress.
- Reception activities and presentation are also vital in that this forms the first impression or contact that people have with the organization. To many, there is nothing more frustrating than automated telephone answering systems, requiring people to press many buttons and follow links until they can speak to someone.

Peters (1992) states that it is possible to identify a failing organization culture as follows:

- when the flowers in the reception area are either stale or else are removed altogether;
- when staff are suddenly asked to pay for tea, coffee and other refreshments that were hitherto provided free.

Box 15.2: History and tradition as a barrier

Organizations that have a strong history and tradition on which success in the past has been based often find it very difficult to look to the future and move forward. For example:

- During the containerization revolution of the mid twentieth century, it became clear that dock working would have to be radically transformed in order to meet the demands of the new shipping methods. Dockworkers nevertheless refused to accept this, stating that ships had always been unloaded in particular ways, and this would continue forever. There was a very proud tradition of dock working, going back for generations. Whole communities were built on dock working, and this had led to high levels of prosperity.

- Airlines: when the low-cost, short-haul carriers started to operate in western Europe, the traditional national airlines confidently expected them to fail. Airline travel had always been expensive and exclusive; passengers expected to be well looked after by both ground staff and cabin crew. This was the tradition of the airline industry, and so this was the way in which it would always work. As late as 2007, some senior managers at British Airways were still denying the capability of easyJet and Ryanair to exist at all, let alone carry the passengers in the volumes that were actually present.

Box 15.3: Golden ages

In the late twentieth century, Nike, the branded clothing and sports goods company, found itself having to transform from an organization driven by the energy of its founders into something that was much more steady-state and assured for the future.

Accordingly, a number of managers were recruited for new corporate positions; and this was accompanied by the hiring of graduates and others who showed potential for management and executive positions in the future.

The new members of staff quickly adopted a swagger and form of public posture that they thought befitted a high brand and well-known company in this industry. This caused one of the top long-serving managers to state: 'If we are not careful, we will hand over everything that has been achieved so far to a new generation of vain, self-serving – and mediocre – managers who are profiting from a past that they were not a part of.'

- **Size**: and the degrees of formalization and structure that this brings. Larger organizations are much more likely to have a proliferation of divisions, supervisory structures, reporting relationships, rules, processes and procedures tending to cause communication difficulties, interdepartmental rivalries and problems with coordination and control. Large, complex and diverse organizations are therefore likely to have sub-cultures, as well as an overriding culture.
- **Location**: geographical location, the constraints and opportunities afforded through choosing to be, for example, urban centres, edge of town or rural areas. This also includes recognizing and considering prevailing local, national and sectoral traditions and values.
- **Management style**: the stance adopted by the organization in managing and supervising its people; the stance required by the people of managers and supervisors; the general relationships between people and organization and the nature of superior–subordinate relations.
- **Real and perceived success and failure**: companies and organizations always publish their successes, so that people have a clear impression of just how good

they are. The media and others also publish stories of failure, in order to redress the balance and give a more rounded picture.

This is the context of organization culture. A simple way of defining organization culture is: 'The ways in which things are done here'.

If organization strategy is about what is done and why, then culture and behaviour relates to how things are done. There is therefore a clear leadership role in shaping, directing and developing the culture desired.

Other statements about organization culture

Other statements about organization culture reflect either collective prevailing attitudes, or the perception and understanding of specific teams, groups and individuals. From time to time, organization cultures are defined as follows.

- Weak cultures, where everyone works in their own interests rather than those of the organization.
- Divided cultures, where there are many groups and individuals competing for influence and resources.
- Bonus cultures, where the staff do everything in the interests of ensuring that they earn their bonus at the end of the year or period.
- Drinking cultures, where there is a perceived common bond achieved through corporate nights out, socialization and drunkenness.
- Cultures of fear, in which staff either fear for their futures, or else fear their managers and supervisors.
- Cultures of blame, in which it is known that when things do go wrong, scapegoats will be found.
- Cultures of favouritism, in which it is known and understood that the only way to make progress is to curry favour with those in top, senior and influential positions.

The foundations of organization culture therefore indicate where the patterns of behaviour, values and aspirations come from. These foundations are then shaped and formed by external and internal pressures.

External pressures on organization culture

The external pressures on organization culture are:

- reputation;
- confidence and expectations;
- legal pressures;
- professional pressures;
- economic pressures;
- social pressures;
- ethical pressures.

Reputation

Reputation must be seen from all points of view. The organization may go into a given location for commercial advantage but with preconceived ideas or prejudices (which may either be positive or negative). The organization may bring with it a particular reputation (again, positive or negative) and again, either about itself or the sector which it represents and within which it operates. There may be wider questions of prejudice, fear and anxiety to be overcome as the organization tries to live up to, or live down to, its reputation.

Areas that have had bad experiences of multinational activities in the past, for example, may be anxious about the next influx. Unless it is carefully managed, those in the particular area believe and understand that companies that now come in will do so from the point of view of oppression and exploitation.

More generally, reputation has to be managed from the twin points of view of what the company believes its reputation to be and what those external to the company actually think of it. This requires full assessment in all situations (see Box 15.4).

Confidence and expectations

Confidence in the strength and integrity of organization culture arises from how patterns of behaviour and levels of performance at work are delivered.

Confidence is founded in how all stakeholders view these aspects of the organization. For example, if staff confidence in the organization is high, this ought to be reflected in the customers' expectations and the willingness of shareholders and other backers to invest funds.

Confidence is damaged, diluted or destroyed when the perceptions and expectations of one or more groups of stakeholders are not met. For example, staff confidence may remain very high, but if customers start turning away, investors and backers may then become less willing to put resources into the organization; and so, when this becomes apparent, staff confidence also starts to fall.

Box 15.4: The invasion of Iraq

When the UK, US and Allied forces overthrew Saddam Hussein in 2003, they were hailed as liberators by the population. This was exactly what the architects of the invasion, President George W. Bush of the US and Prime Minister Tony Blair of the UK, had expected.

However, in a very short period of time, the forces that now occupied the country came to be seen as oppressors. This was something, above all, that Tony Blair could not understand. For the rest of his tenure as prime minister, whenever questioned about the war, he continued to repeat that Iraq had been liberated from a tyrant. Quite clearly, he did not understand that the Iraqis, above all, could possibly have a different point of view.

The result for one week was to enhance greatly the reputation of the US and UK. After that one week, the reputation of the US and UK plummeted; and it has taken, and continues to take, many years to rebuild.

Legal pressures

All organizations have to work within the laws of their locations. These exert pressure on production methods, waste disposal, health and safety, marketing and selling, contractual arrangement, staff management, human resources, industrial relations and equality, or otherwise, of opportunity and access, community relations, organizational and professional insurance and the reporting of results.

Pressures are compounded when the organization operates in many countries and under diverse legal codes. Balances have to be found in these cases to ensure that, as far as possible, everyone who works for the organization does so on terms that transcend the varying legal constraints. Organizations are therefore obliged to set absolute standards that more than meet particular legal minima. Moreover, the phrase 'we comply with the law' invariably gives the message that 'the only reason that we set these standards is because we have to' and that the organization has therefore been pressured into these standards rather than achieving them because it believes that they are right. It calls into question not just the organization's attitude to the law, but also its wider general attitudes, values and standards.

Professional pressures

The external professional pressure arises from the willingness of people with particular expertise to come and work for the organization, and the ease or difficulty with which such people can be attracted and retained. Especially, if it becomes known, believed or perceived that a particular organization is going through periods of difficulty, this can then be managed in one of two ways:

- acceptance of the fact;
- turning declining performance to the organization's advantage, and supporting recruitment drives and initiatives with a clear vision of the future.

People with high degrees of commitment to their profession, occupation or expertise normally relish challenges; and the culture of an organization can always be strengthened by presenting its present position as being full of opportunities (provided that everything else is in place).

Economic pressures

All organizations have to be capable of existence and effective operation in the economic circumstances in which they find themselves. In this respect, the capabilities and willingness of top and senior managers to take prevailing economic circumstances as boundaries within which they have to work is critical. In particular, managers who simply blame adverse trading conditions for poor or declining performance always give impressions of a negative or inert culture. This then rubs off on to other stakeholders: customers become less willing to do business with the organization; it becomes harder to find backers; and more difficult also to attract and retain good staff.

Social pressures

All organizations have to be capable of operating within the locations in which they find themselves, and in response to the social pressures, customers and habits that are present. Organizations that seek to impose themselves on particular parts of society must understand that they nevertheless have to deliver something that is of benefit in social terms, good products and services; assurance of local employment; and the returns expected by financiers in terms of what the particular location expects. Companies and organizations are also expected to make a wider contribution to society and the locations in which they operate, in terms of support and sponsorship for local groups and institutions, and in undertaking to be as clean and environmentally friendly as possible.

Ethical pressures

Ethical pressures arise from the nature of work carried out and from the standards and customs of the communities in which the organization operates. There are also general ethical pressures on many activities concerned that are covered by the law (see also Chapter 6).

The ideal response of any organization is to put itself beyond reproach so that these pressures are accommodated and leave the way clear to developing productive and harmonious relationships with all concerned.

Examples of ethical pressures are as follows.

- **Activities**: most activities carry some form of commitment and others are imposed on their staff by organizations. For example, medical staff have commitments to their patients; community services staff have commitments to their customers; public servants have commitments to their clients.
- **Sectors**: again, there is a universal commitment not to supply shoddy goods and service, rather to provide products of integrity. Some sectors have additional problems with this – for example, tobacco, alcohol, armaments and medical research.
- **Waste disposal**: the onus is clearly on organizations to make adequate arrangements to clear up any mess made by their processes. Some areas and countries have lower standards for this. Organizations assess the convenience of easier dumping of rubbish and balance this against absolute standards of right and wrong and any loss of reputation that might occur in the future if its waste leads to some form of contamination.
- **Equal opportunities, staff management, employee relations and health and safety**: high standards of practice in each of these areas are marks of respect and care to staff, customers and communities. Their absence or variations in them lead, apart from anything else, to feelings of distrust and loss of confidence and, therefore, to demotivation of the staff.
- **Results reporting**: the pressure here is in the presentation. Ideally, this should be done in ways that can be understood by anyone who has an interest or stake in the organization and, indeed, anyone else who would like to know how it is performing. Again, obfuscation tends to lead to those taking an interest to look for hidden meanings and agenda.

Internal pressures on organization culture

The internal pressures on the organization's culture stem from what is important to the staff; what is important to managers; and the extent to which these factors coincide or diverge. Also of critical importance are the traditions and values of the organization, the extent to which these are effective in present circumstances, and the capability and willingness of staff and management to develop these so that they remain both positive and also correct for the present and evolving operation and activities.

The other internal pressure that must be identified at the outset is the extent to which the prevailing culture and work ethic are positive or negative. If they are negative, the reasons must be established; and steps then taken to address the points of concern. Negative organization culture always puts pressure on resources, resulting in less getting done, more slowly and with greater resource usage. Other internal pressures are as follows.

- The interaction between the desired culture and the organization's structures and systems. Serious misfit between these leads to stress and frustration and also to customer dissatisfaction and staff demotivation.
- The expectations and aspirations of staff, the extent to which these are realistic and can be satisfied within the organization. This becomes a serious issue when the nature of organization changes and prevailing expectations can no longer be accommodated. Problems also arise when the organization makes promises that it cannot keep.
- Management and supervisory style, the extent to which this is supportive, suitable to the purpose and generally acceptable to the staff.
- The qualities and expertise of the staff, the extent to which this divides their loyalties. Many staff groups have professional and trade union memberships, continuous professional development requirements and career expectations, as well as holding down positions and carrying out tasks within organizations. In many cases – and especially when general dissatisfaction is present – people tend to take refuge in their profession or occupation, or their trade union.
- Technology and the extent to which it impacts on the ways in which work is designed, structured and carried out.
- Working customs, traditions and practices including restrictive practices, work divisions, specialization and allocation, unionization and other means of representation; and the attitudes and approaches adopted by both organization and staff towards each other – flexible and cooperative, adversarial, degrees of openness.
- The extent to which continuity of employment is feasible; or conversely, uncertainties around future prospects for work and employment. This includes degrees of flexibility, the extent and prevalence of employee and skills development, learning sub-cultures and the wider attitude of both staff and organization to this. It also affects reward packages.
- Internal approaches and attitudes to the legal and ethical issues indicated, the extent of genuine commitment to equality of opportunity and access for all staff; whether or not different grades have different values placed on them, standards of dealings with staff, customers, communities, suppliers and distributors.
- The presence of pride and commitment in the organization, its work and its reputation; standards of general well-being; the extent of mutual respect.

- Communication methods and systems, the nature of language used, the presence/absence of hidden agenda.
- Physical and psychological distance between functions, departments, divisions and positions in the organization and its hierarchies. Especially, the nature of the psychological distance may be found in an assessment of:

  - the extent to which the objectives of different departments and functions are integrated into an overall direction that is effective for the organization as a whole;
  - the extent to which managerial and operational objectives coincide; coincide to some extent; do not coincide at all.

All of this is underpinned by the nature of working relationships, the management style chosen and adopted, the expertise of individual managers, and the policies that are written, produced and implemented.

The work ethic

At the core of the operational part of organization culture is the prevailing 'work ethic'. This is not always easy to define; it is, however, easy to observe and infer. The work ethic of an organization is founded in a combination of the work that has to be done, the ways in which it is organized, the style of management and supervision, and the willingness and commitment of staff to carry out their tasks. Where the work ethic is very strong, this is a key condition for enduring high levels of performance. Where the work ethic is either weak or divided, the following occur:

- people with professional qualifications identify with their profession rather than their organization;
- departments, teams and groups operate in isolation, and in their own interests rather than those of the organization;
- resource utilization is less than effective.

A key area of intervention in the development of an effective organization culture on the part of top management is to ensure that they know and understand the work ethic required, and then take steps to implement and deliver it.

The cultural web

The cultural web is an alternative way of looking at the internal pressures upon organization culture. People draw heavily on points of reference which are built up over periods of time and which are especially important at internal organizational level. The beliefs and assumptions that comprise this fall within the following boundaries.

- The routine ways in which members of the organization behave towards each other and which link different parts of the organization and comprise 'the way that things are done'. These, at their best, lubricate the working of the organization and may provide distinctive and beneficial organizational competency. However, they can also represent a 'take for granted' attitude about how things should happen that can be extremely difficult to change.

- The rituals of organizational life, including attitudes and approaches to such things as dress codes; how people address their peers, subordinates and superiors; how people are expected to present themselves in the full variety of situations that occur at work; and even who puts the kettle on for tea and coffee breaks (see Box 15.5).
- The effects of training programmes, promotion and assessment point to what is important in the organization; reinforce 'the way we do things round here'; and signal what is actually valued.
- The stories told by members of the organization to each other, to outsiders and to new recruits, embed the present organization in its history and flag up important events and personalities (see Box 15.6).
- The more symbolic aspects of organization such as logos, offices, cars and titles, or the type of language and terminology commonly used.
- The control systems, measures and reward systems emphasize what is actually important and focus attention and activity. Especially where there are different terms and conditions for different categories of staff, this creates a feeling of 'us and them'.
- Power structures are also likely to be associated in so far as the most powerful groupings are likely to be the ones most associated with what is actually valued.
- The formal organization structure and the more informal ways in which the organization works are likely to reflect these power structures and, again, to delineate

Box 15.5: Switching on the kettle

For many years, Peter Godden worked as a horticultural labourer at a large commercial fruit and vegetable outlet. Over this period of time, he was happy and productive; and while he kept himself very much to himself, the other staff who worked there found him very pleasant.

One of his duties was to switch on the kettle for the staff at tea and coffee break times. This was purely operational: he was the nearest to the canteen area. So ten minutes before breaks were due to commence, he would walk into the canteen area and switch on the kettle.

Then suddenly he stopped doing it. Questioned first by managers, and then by the company CEO, he simply stated that he now refused to switch the kettle on; and when asked for an explanation, simply stated: 'It is against my principles.'

Considered to be a critical aspect of organization harmony, Peter was put through the company's disciplinary procedure. At his final point of refusal, the company's CEO literally went down on his knees and begged Peter to start to switch the kettle on again. Peter still refused.

Peter was therefore dismissed for refusing to switch on the kettle. He claimed unfair dismissal at employment tribunal. The case was heard; and the company was found to have acted fairly and reasonably. Peter's case was therefore dismissed.

Commenting on the case afterwards, the tribunal chair stated: 'The real reason for Peter's sudden refusal was the engagement of a new member of staff from a particular family. This family and Peter's have been at war for over a hundred years. From time to time it breaks out into actual fighting. For most of the time, though, they simply ignore each other.'

Box 15.6: Common enemies

Many organizations use the 'stories' approach to generate a collective and positive cohesion. Examples of common enemies are:

- **Football**: in the run up to World Cup final football tournaments, the Italian press is always very negative about the players who are picked, and their capability to win the tournament. On two occasions (1986 and 2006), the Italian team management have been able to generate an effective, collective (and winning) team by getting the players to focus on the hostility of the press as a major driving force.
- **Virgin Atlantic**: when Richard Branson first tried to open up a North Atlantic route for the Virgin Atlantic airline, he ran into organized opposition from British Airways and American Airlines. Dressing himself as a pirate, he entered the British Airways airliner compound at Heathrow and managed to get himself photographed sitting astride one of the Concorde airliners. He therefore got extensive press coverage on the point that the only thing that was preventing him from running his airline was an action of an enemy – British Airways.

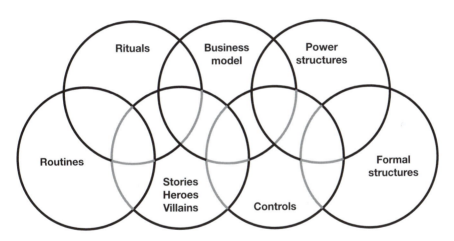

Figure 15.1 A cultural web

important relationships and emphasize required levels of performance (Johnson, Scholes and Whittington, 2006).

Cultural influences

Hofstede (1980, 1996, 2006) carried out studies that identified cultural similarities and difference among the 116,000 staff of IBM located in 40 countries. Hofstede identified basic dimensions of national cultures and the differences in their emphases and importance in the various countries. The four dimensions were:

- **Power–distance** – the extent to which power and influence is distributed across the society; the extent to which this is acceptable to the members of the society; access to sources of power and influence; and the physical and psychological distance that exists between people and the sources of power and influence.
- **Uncertainty avoidance** – the extent to which people prefer order and certainty, or uncertainty and ambiguity; and the extent to which they feel comfortable or threatened by the presence or absence of each.
- **Individualism–collectivism** – the extent to which the individual is expected or expects to take care of themselves; the extent to which a common good is perceived and the tendency and willingness to work towards this.
- **Masculinity–femininity** – the distinction between masculine values – the acquisition of money, wealth, fortune, success, ambition, possessions; and the feminine – sensitivity, care, concern, attention to the needs of others, quality of life; and the value, importance, mix and prevalence of each.
- **Long-term–short-term orientation** – whether the organization was driven by immediate success and results or ending performance and survival.

The studies looked at the extent to which managers and supervisors were encouraged or expected to exercise power and to take it upon themselves to provide order and discipline. In some cases – for example, Spain – this expectation was very high. Relationships between superior and subordinate were based on low levels of mutual trust and low levels of participation and involvement. Employees would accept orders and direction on the understanding that the superior carries full responsibility, authority and accountability.

Elsewhere – for example, Australia and Holland – people expected to be consulted and participate in decision-making. They expected to be kept regularly and fully informed of progress, and had much greater need for general equality and honesty of approach. They would feel free to question superiors about why particular courses of action were necessary rather than simply accepting that they were.

People with a high propensity for uncertainty avoidance – i.e. those who wished for high degrees of certainty – tended to require much greater volumes of rules, regulations and guidance for all aspects of work. They sought stability and conformity, and were intolerant of dissenters. Uncertainty caused stress, strain, conflicts and disputes. Stress could be avoided by working hard, following the company line, and adherence and compliance with required ways of behaviour. Where uncertainty avoidance was lower these forms of stress were less apparent; and there was less attention paid to rules and less emphasis places on conformity and adherence.

The concern here was to establish the relative position of individual achievement in terms of that of the organization, and also the wider contribution to society and the community. For example, in the UK and USA overwhelming emphasis was placed on individual performance and achievement. This has implications for membership of teams and groups and the creation of effective teams and groups in such locations. It also indicates the extent of likelihood of divergence of purpose between the organization and individuals. Where collectivism was higher, there was also a much greater emphasis on harmony, loyalty, support and productive interaction. There was also a much greater attention to organizational performance; and also the position of the organization and its wider environment, and its contribution to society as well as the achievement of its own desired results.

The work considered the value placed on different achievements. Cultures with high degrees of masculinity set great store by the achievement of material possessions and rewards. Those with high degrees of femininity saw success in terms of quality of life, general state of the community, individual and collective well-being, the provision of essential services, the ability to support the whole society and to provide means of social security.

Hofstede's work has been extensively reviewed and criticized. In particular, the ability to define national culture is contentious, especially if this is limited to a few very general characteristics only. The terms in which Hofstede's findings are summarized above reinforce the general limitations in defining culture in this way, and the necessarily sweeping statements that have to be made as a result. However, the work of Hofstede clearly draws attention to the need to understand culture, and to manage within its confines and constraints, whatever the limitations of the particular findings may be.

Dimensions of organization culture

Those responsible for the direction and management of organizations need to know and understand how people act, react and interact, and the overall effectiveness and influence of the total patterns of behaviour on performance.

They need to know therefore where the foundations of the culture of their organization lie; the external and internal pressures; how these interact (the strength of each aspect of the cultural web); and the nature of specific cultural influences.

The outcome of the interaction of each of these areas and pressures ought to be:

- a culture that is strong and inclusive, not weak and divided;
- a culture that is positive and productive, not negative and unproductive;
- a culture which is capable of acceptance by all those in the organization;
- a culture which serves the interests of everyone, and not some groups at the expense of others;
- a culture which embraces change, development and advancement, rather than being rigid and defensive.

There are two further issues which managers have to address as follows:

- cultural displacement;
- organization perception.

Cultural displacement is the extent to which the decisions referred to above cause behavioural and operational problems. It is certain, as stated above, that sub-cultures exist in different departments, divisions, functions and locations; the problem of cultural displacement arises when those sub-cultures are incapable of harmonization within the organization overall. Where cultural displacement arises, top and senior managers have to form a view as to the extent of damage done to overall cohesion, and whether or not it is something that needs to be addressed (see Box 15.7).

Cultural perceptions are a reflection of the ways in which companies and organizations think about themselves, in relation to how others actually see them. As stated above, this needs constant testing and re-testing to ensure that:

- companies that enjoy a high level of reputation do not become complacent;
- companies gain the widest possible perspective on where their shortcomings lie, so that these can be addressed.

Box 15.7: Adversarial employee relations

It is stated elsewhere (see Chapters 2 and 19) that adversarial employee relations are a key perspective which exists as one of the foundations of human resource management.

Clearly, in an ideal world, this would not occur. In practice, however, this may be the best that anyone can hope for, at least in the present situation.

This is because all organizations have to be able to operate from within their present context, rather than constantly starting again from an ideal position.

Where adversarial employee relations do exist, therefore, it is essential that the processes that are present for their management, are made to work as effectively as possible. For example:

When General Motors collapsed in 2009, serious questions arose over the future viability of the company's European operations. In particular, UK regional management and the staff trade unions were extremely concerned about what was now to happen, whether or not the company's two factories at Luton and Liverpool would remain open, and whether or not there would be job losses.

Vauxhall, the UK brand name for General Motors' activities, had always had adversarial staff relations. However, when it became clear that there were problems, the recognized trade unions engaged immediately in consultations and discussions with management so as to try to ensure that activities were indeed kept open, and that as many jobs as possible could be preserved. Additionally, the trade union leaders successfully gained extensive media coverage, to try to influence the outcome of discussions that were taking place around the future of the activities.

These activities – the use of consultation and negotiating procedures, the gaining of external coverage – had always been used to try to influence wider opinion about such things as wage disputes, pay rises and other grievances. Now, the same mechanisms were being used to try to ensure the future of the organization itself.

Other factors in the assessment and development of organization culture

The other factors that have to be addressed at this stage are the extent to which organization culture is:

- designed;
- emergent;
- formal;
- informal.

Designed

Designed cultures are actively shaped by those responsible for organizational direction and results and created in the pursuit of this. This involves setting the standards of attitudes, values, behaviour and belief that everyone is required to subscribe to as a condition of joining the organization. Policies are produced so that everyone knows where they stand, and these are underpinned by extensive induction and orientation programmes and training schemes. Procedures and sanctions are there to ensure that these standards continue to be met. Organizations with very specific cultures are not all things to all people – many, indeed, make a virtue of their particular approach of 'many are called but few are chosen'. High levels of internalization of shared values are required.

Other perceptions emerge from this. Feelings of confidence, trust and respect are created. Individual response to the level of organization commitment that is evident in this approach tends to be high.

Emergent

This is where the culture is formed by the staff (and staff groups) rather than directed by the organization. The result is that people think, believe and act according to the pressures and priorities of their peers and pursue their own agenda. This is clearly fraught with difficulties and dangers – organizations that allow this happen will succeed only if the aims and objectives of the staff coincide absolutely with its own.

It leads to the staff setting their own informal procedures and sanctions, or operating formally in ways that suit their own purposes rather than those of the organization. Individuals and groups, again, are not all things to all people; they may and do reject those who refuse to abide by the norms and values that they have set for themselves.

Formal

Formal cultures exist where there is a high degree of correlation between the institutions, procedures and policies that are in place, and how people think, believe, behave, act and react. As stated above, in some locations and national cultures, people expect a high degree of prescription and stated order and certainty. In such situations where this is not made clear, uncertainty exists; and so this in turn leads to decline in performance.

Formalities are also essential where, for good reasons, specific modes of address and dress are required. In particular these are essential where:

- There is a high degree of inherent danger in not following the formalities. For example, airline pilots have to use precise forms of words in their dealings with air traffic control; they are also required to use precise forms of words in circumstances where there are engine failures. The formalities require that statements made by the pilot and co-pilot are repeated back word for word in all operational matters. This is so that people adhere to absolute standards; and no variation is tolerated.
- In the use of specific tools, technology and equipment, where there are training programmes that have to be gone through in advance of being able to use them; and where there are specific procedures that have to be followed in their operation, and also in their maintenance and cleaning.

Informal

Sub-cultures exist in all organizations. They relate to membership of different groups and vary between these – for example, in the state of openness of dealings between members. Sub-cultures become more destructive when they operate contrary to absolute standards. Forms of this are:

- the canteen culture, whereby the shared values adopted are those of groups that gather away from the work situations and in such places as the washroom or canteen (see Box 15.8);
- elites and cliques; whereby strength and primacy is present in some groups at the expense of others. This leads to over-mightiness. It affects operations when the elites and cliques are able to command resources, carry out projects and gain prestige at the expense of others; to lobby effectively for resources at the expense of others; and to gain favour at the expense of others;
- work regulation, whereby the volume and quality of work is regulated by the group for its own ends rather than those of the organization; when it sets and works to its own targets which are at variance with those of the organization;
- informal norming, whereby individuals are pressurized to adopt the attitudes and values of those around them rather than those of the organization. This occurs most when the organization's own norms are not sufficiently strong or structured to remove the local or group pressure;
- un-led, where people adopt the attitudes and values that they believe to exist among the top management team. The un-led aspect of organization culture normally

---

Box 15.8: Peer pressure

In terms of organization culture, peer pressure is a key factor in the regulation of behaviour. Peer pressure is used in a variety of ways as follows.

- It is used as a force for good, driving production and productive efforts; in these cases, peer pressure energizes everyone towards a common good.
- It is used to regulate productive output, in many cases so that people do not do 'too much', but rather stick to accepted or comfortable group norms.
- It is used for evil when the members of a group gang up on one person for some reason. In these cases, the result is that the individual is victimized, ostracized or ignored. This is always traumatic to the individual, of course. It is also traumatic to the group over the long-term, as other individuals come to realize that they may be next for the treatment. It is in any case morally repugnant; it is also illegal and, where proven, damages against the organization (and sometimes the group members concerned) are unlimited.

Top and senior managers need to know the nature and extent of all peer pressure aspects and activities within their organization. Especially, they need to know and understand where peer pressure is being used for evil so that they can take steps to remedy it immediately.

exists where there is little or no direct connection between the top management team and the rest of the staff.

Archetype cultures

Handy and Harrison (1984; 2004) distinguished the following archetypes:

* power culture;
* people/person culture;
* task culture;
* role culture.

Power culture

This is where the key relationship exists between the person who wields power and influence, and those who work for them. It depends on the figure at the centre, the source of power. Everyone else draws their strength, influence and confidence from this centre and requires its continued support to ensure prosperity and operational viability. The relationship is normally terminated when there is a loss of confidence on the part of the person at the centre of power with those who work for them. Individuals generate power cultures when they attract those who have faith in them and who wish to be involved with them.

The main problem that a power culture must face is that of size. As it grows and diversifies, it becomes difficult for the person at the centre to sustain continued high levels of influence. There is also the problem of permanence, of what happens when the person at the centre of power passes out of the organization. In situations where they have generated the ideas, energy, identity and strength of the situation, a void is left when they leave or die.

The structural form of the power culture may be seen as like a spider's web (see Figure 15.2). The main relationship between the subordinates is with the centre.

People/person culture

People/person culture exists for the people in it – for example, where a group has decided that it is in their own overriding interest to band or form together and produce an organization for their own benefit. This may be found in certain research groups; university departments; family firms; and companies started by groups of friends where the first coming together is generated by the people involved rather than the matter in hand. The key relationship is therefore between people, and what binds them is their intrinsic common interest. Hierarchy and structure may evolve, but these too will be driven by this intrinsic common interest (see Figure 15.3).

Task culture

Task cultures are to be found in project teams, marketing groups and marketing-oriented organizations. The emphases are on getting the job completed, keeping customers and clients satisfied, and responding to and identifying new market opportunities. Such cultures are flexible, adaptable and dynamic. They accommodate movements of staff

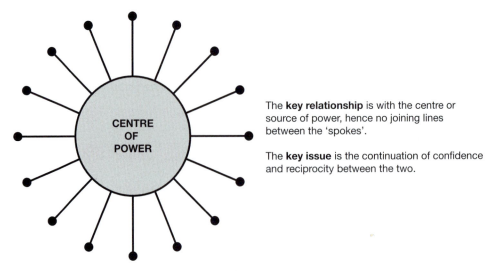

The **key relationship** is with the centre or source of power, hence no joining lines between the 'spokes'.

The **key issue** is the continuation of confidence and reciprocity between the two.

Figure 15.2 Power culture + structure: the wheel

The **key relationship** is between the people; what binds them is their **intrinsic** common interest. Hierarchy and structure may evolve incidentally; they too will be driven by this intrinsic common interest.

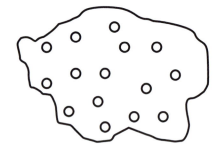

Figure 15.3 People/person culture + structure: the mass

necessary to ensure effective project and development teams and continued innovation; and concurrent human activities such as secondments, project responsibility and short-term contracts. They are driven by customer satisfaction. They operate most effectively in prosperous, dynamic and confident environments and markets. They may also generate opportunities and niche activities in these and create new openings. Their success lies in their continued ability to operate in this way (see Figure 15.4).

Role culture

Role cultures are found where organizations have gained a combination of size, permanence and departmentalization, and where the ordering of activities, preservation of knowledge, experience and stability are both important and present.

The key relationship is based on authority and the superior–subordinate style of relationships. The key purposes are order, stability, permanence and efficiency.

Role cultures operate most effectively where the wider environment is steady and a degree of permanence is envisaged (see Figure 15.5).

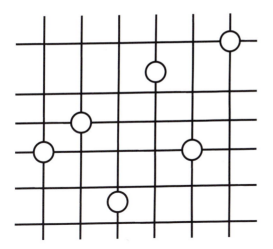

The **key relationship** here is with the task. The form of organization is therefore fluid and elastic.

The **structure** is often also described as a MATRIX or GRID; none of these gives a full configuration – the essence is the dynamics of the form, and the structure necessary to ensure this.

Figure 15.4 Task culture + structure: the net

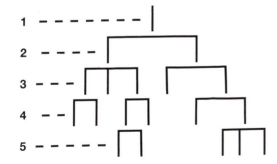

The **key relationship** is based on authority and the superior–subordinate style of relationships.
The **key purposes** are order, stability, permanance and efficiency.

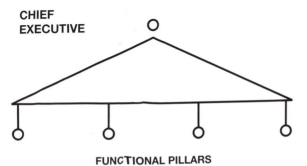

The 'Greek Temple' format delineates function as well as authority.

Figure 15.5 Role culture + structure: the pyramid or temple

Deal and Kennedy (1973; 2001) defined the following archetype cultures:

- tough guy/macho;
- work hard, play hard;
- 'bet your company';
- process-driven.

Tough guy/macho culture

Tough guy/macho culture exists where there is a known and believed fast-moving, high-energy state of activity. Risk taking is high and not always fully informed. Those in senior and key positions are perceived to have a tough attitude. Staff who work in such situations are individualistic rather than team players. The strength of a tough guy/macho culture is that it is understood that things can be done very quickly. However, because of the fast-moving nature, people move on from position to position very quickly; there is therefore a tendency not to learn from mistakes.

Work hard, play hard culture

Work hard, play hard cultures exist in service organizations (including public service). Activities are carried out under great pressure, often with inadequate resources. In work hard, play hard cultures, risk taking is low; everything is concentrated on the steady-state, or the immediate priority. There is pressure placed on people to find quick solutions to problems, and to work through the workload as quickly as possible. The great weakness is therefore that there is a short-term perspective; little consideration (or resource) is given to the longer-term perspective (see Box 15.9).

Box 15.9: Emergency call-outs

Emergency call-outs (often called 999s) are a major feature of the operational lives of the police, fire, ambulance and health services.

999s is also the name given to staff outings. Existing to relieve the extreme professional pressures and conditions under which they work, 999s take the following forms:

- works outings to pubs and nightclubs where staff can get drunk;
- short-term and passionate affairs and sexual liaisons between members of staff;
- clandestine recreational drug usage.

These practices also exist among others working under extreme pressure, for example, financial traders and brokers; commodity buyers and sellers; those working long hours on construction and civil engineering sites.

In each of these cases, the staff work very hard; and so they play hard also. This can, and does, lead to organizational problems from time to time, especially when the above activities either get out of hand or become more widely known.

Work quite hard, play quite hard culture

Less extreme forms of the work hard, play hard culture exist. Work quite hard, play quite hard cultures exist where staff have steady and assured patterns of behaviour, but without the pressures inherent in the professions and occupations indicated above. Thus, for example, those living or working away from home, returning only inter-mittently, may find themselves engaged in a form of parallel lifestyle. People put in long hours while they are at work; and then seek their own forms of release and recreation. This can, and does, lead to gambling; recreational drug use; and alcohol (though this tends towards misuse rather than abuse as above).

'Bet your company' culture

Those who work in 'bet your company' cultures have high degrees of identity with the companies and organizations for which they work. They also have a high degree of professional identity, recognizing that in order to pursue particular professions, they need to work for very specific forms of organization. Because of this identity, in practice, staff can endure long periods of uncertainty and ambiguity, recognizing that this is the nature of the steady-state in which they have to work. Those who work in 'bet your company' cultures dress according to the norms and expectations of the organization itself, and of the rank and status that they hold. 'Bet your company' cultures are founded in the perceived immortality of the particular organization; and so they become vulnerable to short-term economic and market fluctuations.

Process-driven culture

Process-driven cultures exist among large-volume employers. In process-driven cultures, the large volumes of staff work according to rule books and regulations which are clearly understood and provide the basis for all professional activities and patterns of behaviour. Process-driven cultures tend to be cautious and protective of everything that they do. Process-driven cultures tend to be bureaucratic (akin to the role culture above), taking as their priority the need to operate by the set of prescribed rules. In many process-driven cultures, work is both predictable and limited, with restricted opportunities for development. Promotion or relocation to other parts of the organization, and the ability to take advantage of opportunities, is limited by the prescribed set of rules.

Other aspects of organizational culture

The priority of top and senior managers is to know and understand what their dominant culture is, and the opportunities and consequences that arise as a result. Where this concerns large, complex, diverse and multi-location organizations, it is essential to recognize what the dominant culture and values are, what they ought to be and what steps therefore need to be taken in order to address any imbalance or divergence. In this context, other features of organizational cultures may be distinguished.

- **Relationships with the environment**: including the ways in which the organization copes with uncertainty and turbulence; the ways by which the organization seeks to influence the environment; the extent to which it behaves proactively or reactively.

- **History and tradition**: the extent to which the organization's histories and traditions are a barrier or a facilitator of progress; the extent to which the organization values and worships its past histories and traditions; key influences on current activities and beliefs; the position of key interest groups – for example, trade unions.
- **The internal relationship balance**: the mixture and effectiveness of power, status, hierarchy, authority, responsibility, individualism, group cohesion; the general relationship mixture of task/social/development.
- **Rites and rituals**: these are the punctuation marks of organizational behaviour and activities. Rites and rituals include the ways in which achievements are celebrated; how people are greeted when they first start work; the attitudes and actions taken when people leave (e.g. leaving parties, nights out). Rites and rituals also include the collective attitude towards organizational gossip, the sorts of things that are openly talked about, and those that are not.
- **Ritual formalities**: these include pay negotiations; internal and external job application means and methods; disciplinary, grievance and dismissal procedures; rewards; individual, group, departmental and divisional publicity; training and development activities; parties and celebrations; key appointments and dismissals; socialization and integration of people into new roles, activities and responsibilities.
- **Routines and habits**: these are the formal, semi-formal and informal ways of working and interaction that people generate for themselves (or which the organization generates for them) to make comfortable the non-operational aspects of working life. They develop around the absolutes – attendance times, work requirements, authority and reporting relationships – and include regular meetings, regular tasks, forms of address between members of the organization and groups, pay days, holidays and some training and development activities (see Box 15.10).
- **Badges and status symbols**: these are the marks of esteem conferred by organizations on their people. They are a combination of location – near to or away from the corridors of power for example; possessions – cars, technology, personal departments; job titles – reflecting a combination of ability, influence and occupation; and position in the hierarchy pecking order.

The effects of rites, rituals, routines, habits, badges and status symbols all lie in the value that the organization places on them and the value in which they are held by the members of staff. There is no point in offering anything or in undertaking any form of cultural activity if a negligible or negative response is received. In general, therefore, these forms of culture development both anticipate people's expectations and seek to reinforce them and to meet them.

It is essential also to recognize the influence of different aspects of organization design and operation.

- Technology has influence on work arrangements and groupings, physical layout and the nature of the people employed.
- Structure and hierarchy influence personal and professional interactions, personal and professional ambitions and aspirations.
- Rules, regulations and systems influence attitudes and behaviour (positive or negative) depending on how they are drawn up and operated and on their particular focus.

Box 15.10: Changing habits

If it ever becomes necessary to change people's habits and patterns of behaviour for any reason, the areas indicated are those where immediate results can be achieved if they are undertaken with precise objects in mind. For example, one of the UK's top universities set up a new research and teaching facility. Everyone agreed that this was a good idea; top and senior management backed it; and so the facility came to life.

It was immediately successful, and so grew and expanded. However, it now needed premises and accommodation was restricted. Accordingly, it was located in an old building on the edge of the university's campus. Here, internally within the new facility, it quickly became known as a pioneering and creative activity, and all of its outputs were well received by the rest of the university. From an institutional point of view, however, it quickly became forgotten.

This state of affairs persisted for many years. At last, the university found itself able to engage in a building programme; and this included the construction of new facilities, as well as the refurbishment of existing premises. The new teaching and research facility (by now, no longer new) was able to lobby successfully for its own premises in one of the new buildings.

The day for moving in duly came. Everyone was very excited. They moved everything from their old premises, and quickly began to go about the process of settling in.

However, it changed everyone's patterns of behaviour. From being crammed into a messy overcrowded – and old – space, and engaging in a pioneering culture, now people were dispersed across four floors of the new building. Patterns of behaviour changed; interactions became fewer; regular daily direct contact with colleagues was lost.

In time, of course, new patterns of behaviour began to emerge; and these also became familiar, assured and comfortable. However, at the time, the only thing that was seen was the move from old to new premises; and insufficient attention was paid to the disruption to known and understood patterns of behaviour, and to creating new ones, so that the overall effectiveness and success referred to above was not damaged, even in the short term.

- Leadership provides the key point of identity for everyone else, and from which people establish their own perceptions of the organization's general standards.
- Management style influences the general feelings of well-being of everyone else, and sets standards of attitudes and behaviour as well as performance.
- Managerial demands and the ways in which these are made influence attitudes and behaviour also.
- Hierarchical and divisional relations and interactions influence the nature of performance, attention to achievement and the value placed on achievements; this also applies to functional activities.

Where the need for culture change or development is apparent interventions can be made into each or all of these.

Culture development

In practice, organizational culture never stands still. Patterns of behaviour, in particular, are constantly changing, and these have a direct effect on the nature and strength of the organization's culture. Where more serious problems do arise (e.g. weakness, division and sub-cultures), interventions are required in each of the areas indicated. However, when interventions are made, it is essential that there is a direct, stated and clearly understood purpose attached to them, and that the likely and possible range of outcomes has been fully evaluated. For example, as stated above, it is possible to change people's patterns of behaviour by relocating them. However, this is never adequate as an end in itself; alongside the changing patterns of behaviour, there must be organizational and operational objectives that are to be achieved within the context of changing the patterns of behaviour.

Changing from a weak and divided culture to something that is strong and inclusive takes leadership, authority and responsibility; and it has to be accompanied by a sustained, structured and ordered communications campaign so that people are constantly being bombarded with messages about how they are now to behave, and also what the transformation is expected or required to achieve in terms of increased operational effectiveness.

Attention to professional and occupational priorities has also to be delivered in context. It is not enough just to reorganize people's jobs or patterns of work; again, this has to be driven by a full contextual understanding of the relationship between the reorganization and enhanced organizational and operational effectiveness.

Conclusions

Effective organization cultures are positive and designed rather than emergent. They must be capable of gaining commitment to purpose, the ways in which this is pursued and the standards adopted by everyone. Cultures are a summary and reflection of the aims and objectives, and values held. Where neither are apparent, different groups and individuals form their own aims and objectives and adopt their own values; and where these are at variance with overall purpose, or negative in some way, they are dysfunctional and may become destructive.

For this to be effective, a strong mutual sense of loyalty and acceptance between organization and people is essential. Employees exert positive effort on behalf of the organization, making a personal as well as professional or occupational commitment. The reverse of this – the organization's commitment to its people – is also essential. A strong sense of identity towards the organization and its purposes and values is required, and this happens when these are clear and positive. Any commitment made by people to organizations (or anything else) is voluntary and personal – and can be changed or withdrawn. The best organizations produce cultures that are capable of generating this. They create the desire among their people to join, remain with and progress, recognizing their mutuality of interest and the benefits available to everyone.

Part 3

Organizational behaviour in practice

The purpose of Part 3 is to relate and integrate the lessons of Parts 1 and 2 into the foundations of a discipline that is effective in practice.

The critical nature of organizational leadership is dealt with first. This is a critical area of organizational practice; and especially where it is not appropriate or not expert, organizations can, and do, have serious problems. Even where these problems are not apparent, lack of effective leadership means that the organization will always underperform.

This is followed by chapters on the following:

- the nature of roles and functions within organizations: especially relating people's capabilities and aptitudes to desired and demanded work activities, so that a clear fit can be achieved between what the individual can do, and what the organization wants done;
- organization structure and design: so that there is an understanding of the opportunities, consequences, problems and implications of different forms of organizing and compartmentalizing work;
- human resource management and employee relations: so that an understanding is generated of what this particular function ought to be doing within organizations (and in the context that it is very often ineffective, or else uninfluential).

These elements are dealt with in this way because they form the foundations of successful and effective (or unsuccessful and ineffective) organizational practice. Where the leadership is remote, distant or otherwise ineffective, others in the organization tend to follow their own direction. Where roles are not clearly defined, people develop them as they see fit, whether or not this is in the best interests of the organization. Where the organization structure is inappropriate, this leads to delays in production and output, decision-making, and barriers and blockages to communication.

Finally, an effective human resource and employee relations function is of great value to any organization, in removing barriers and blockages to progress, minimizing grievances and disputes, and generating strategic approaches to collective and individual development and improvement.

16 Leadership

Introduction

The context in which leadership expertise is required of managers is as follows:

- it is becoming increasingly essential to be able legitimately to assign responsibility, authority and accountability to those in charge of organizations, and those who head individual departments, divisions and functions;
- it is increasingly difficult, and in some cases impossible, to sustain the expense incurred of having large and complex hierarchical and bureaucratic systems for the coordination and control of organizations.

Employing and assigning those with expertise in leadership, and developing the traits, characteristics and qualities required, is therefore a clear alternative. Employing people with leadership expertise in key and critical positions and functions therefore reduces expense; and it additionally leads to clearer lines of authority and accountability, resulting in increased output, delivered more quickly, and with fewer problems and barriers.

Leadership is therefore the core of all managerial and supervisory activities. This is more clearly observable in some areas than others – political leaders and chief executive officers are self-evidently 'in charge'. However, all those in managerial positions have a leadership function; and all those in leadership positions have managerial responsibilities. These are:

- to give vision and direction;
- to energize;
- to set and enforce absolute standards of behaviour, attitude, presentation and performance.

In this context, the key role and function is having the combination of expertise, commitment and personality required to see things through to completion. It is additionally essential that leaders surround themselves with expertise that they themselves do not have so that any gaps in their own shortcomings are filled.

Definitions and priorities

Definitions

Some useful definitions are as follows.

- A leader is someone who exercises influence over other people (Huczynski and Buchanan, 2004).
- I am the leader now – therefore I must serve (Winston Churchill, 1940).

- Leadership is the lifting of peoples' vision to a higher sight, the raising of their performance to a higher standard, the building of their personality beyond its normal limitations (P.F. Drucker, 2001).
- A leader is: 'cheerleader, enthusiast, nurturer of champions, hero finder, wanderer, dramatist, coach, facilitator and builder' (Peters and Austin, 1986).
- The leader must have infective optimism. The final test of a leader is the feeling you have when you leave their presence after a conference. Have you a feeling of uplift and confidence? (Field Marshal Bernard Montgomery, 1957).
- Leadership is creating a vision to which others can aspire and energizing them to work towards this vision (Anita Roddick, 1992).
- There is a need in all organizations for individual linking pins who will bind groups together and, as members of other groups, represent their groups elsewhere in organizations. Leadership concerns the leaders themselves, the subordinates, and the task in hand (C.B. Handy, 1996).
- Leadership can be described as a dynamic process in a group whereby one individual influences others to contribute voluntarily to the achievement of group tasks in a given situation (G.A. Cole, 1994).

Priorities

In order for leaders to be successful and effective, they have to be able to combine their expertise, authority and character as follows:

- Getting optimum performance from those carrying out the work in whatever terms that is defined.
- Ability to adopt an overview and long-term perspective; and to be able to deliver this alongside attention to detail whenever required (see Box 16.1).

Box 16.1: Nicholas Hayek and Swatch

Nicholas Hayek is the person who saved the Swiss watch industry from total collapse. In the 1960s and 1970s, faced with competition from cheap and accurate watches made in China and Japan, the Swiss watch industry as a whole responded by:

- denying the existence of the competition;
- refusing to believe that anyone else could make watches.

The result was that the industry lost 80 per cent of its market in ten years. Faced with this potential catastrophe, the leaders of the industry turned to Nicholas Hayek, an expert in precision manufacturing.

Nicholas Hayek consolidated the many small companies into one larger one, SMG. He engaged in branding activities for all of the distinctive and well-understood products (e.g. Tissot, Omega). He also introduced a bottom-of-the-range, mass-market product, the Swatch. Venturing into the mass market was a fresh move for the Swiss industry, which had always concentrated on the exclusive brands.

Nicholas Hayek tackled the competition on each of the areas critical to successful and profitable watch manufacturing and sales. These were:

- precision and accuracy;
- branding and design;
- cost and value.

The factories that were established used the very latest manufacturing technology to produce components for watches in all product ranges to at least the same degree of accuracy as the Far Eastern alternatives. The marketing campaigns were reinforced by television advertising, merchandizing presentations in stores and outlets, and association with high-profile sporting events (e.g. for many years, Swatch provided the timings for the winter Olympics).

Nicholas Hayek took a personal and active interest in every aspect of the process, product, service and company development. This led to accusations that he was 'a meddler'. Many of his top managers found that it was only possible to work effectively with him for short periods of time before becoming exasperated by his constant interference.

Responding to the criticism, and defending his position, Nicholas Hayek stated: 'Every chief executive should know and understand every aspect of his or her business. They need to be out among their people and activities, seeing what is going on, and taking an active interest. I do not want mediocre or ordinary executives in my company. Anyone who comes along purely to pick up the salary, and then go home, is not welcome.'

Some of Nicholas Hayek's response states clearly his strategic, operational and leadership position. Some of it clearly does not; it is a defence mechanism. However, the example does illustrate:

- the need for active involvement;
- the need to know as much as possible about the business in question.

It is also much better for leaders to be criticized for meddling, and then have to back off, than to be criticized for remoteness, distance and aloofness – and ignorance.

Other areas of enduring priority are concerned with ensuring continuity, development and improvement in those carrying out the work; monitoring and evaluating both the work and those involved; taking remedial action where necessary. It is essential to relate the skills and capacities of all those involved to the work itself. This is a key part of motivating and encouraging the staff, and promoting positive, harmonious and productive working relations.

There is also a concern in seeking continuous improvement in all aspects of the work environment; and providing opportunities for continuous development and enhancement for everyone involved.

Leadership in practice

Leaders are expected to deliver and achieve what they set out to do; or else to provide a clear explanation as to why this was not possible, and what they now intend to do as a result. Leaders have specific responsibilities and accountability, in the following areas.

- **Results**. Results are measured in terms of what was intended, and the actual outcomes; how and why these were achieved; how they were viewed at the time and subsequently by posterity; and whether this represented a good, bad or indifferent return on the resources and energy expended in their pursuit.
- **Inspiration**. In order to achieve success, leaders must be able to motivate, inspire and energize. In order that people follow, and resources are attracted to their cause, this is normally translated into a simple, direct and positive statement of where the leader is going and how and why this is to be achieved and the benefits that this is to bring to others as a result. They must be capable of inspiring others – it is no use having a good idea if people do not recognize it as such.
- **Hard work**. For all this to occur leaders must have great stores of energy, enthusiasm, dedication, zeal and commitment. They have to inspire and energize people and resources in pursuit of the desired ends. They also set the standards for their followers – in normal circumstances, hard work cannot be expected of others if the leader is not also prepared to put this in.
- **Honesty**. People follow leaders, either because they believe in them or because it is in their interest to do so (or for a combination of the two). Leaders who fail to deliver are normally rejected or supplanted. Leaders who say one thing and mean another will not be trusted and people continue to work for them only until they can find something else.
- **Responsibility, authority and accountability**. Leaders accept their own part in triumphs and successes, and also disasters and failures (see Box 16.2).

Handy (1996; 2004) states that the practice of leadership consists of the following:

- **Ambition**: ambition to progress and develop the company as far as possible, to introduce new products and services, as well as personal drive.
- **Enthusiasm**: it is no use expecting others to be enthusiastic and committed, if the leader is not.
- **Cheerleading**: taking every opportunity to get out into the public domain and doing everything possible to gain recognition for the company and its products and services.
- **Advocacy**: doing everything possible, both among the staff and also the wider public, to get the company's products and services accepted. Advocacy also means doing whatever is necessary to advance every positive aspect of the company's activities.
- **Defender**: when things go wrong, and when crises do occur, all leaders need to be prepared, capable and willing to address problems, and respond to concerns, in public and with expertise.
- **Developer and coach**: the need to ensure that top and senior management teams are as expert, integrated and committed as possible; and also to ensure that there is a ready supply of fresh talent coming through.

- **Activist**: the need for active involvement in every aspect of the organization's operations; and the need to lead by example (see Box 16.3).

Traits and characteristics

There have been a great many studies of leaders, directors and managers from all walks of life and all parts of history. By studying a range of leaders and managers from a variety of situations and backgrounds – for example, sport, politics, the military, exploration, religion and business – it is possible to infer and draw conclusions as to what the basis for their success or otherwise was and what the reasons and causes of

---

Box 16.2: Accountability

Many people in leadership positions are happy to accept the responsibility and authority, but not the accountability. In practice, this means that they are perfectly prepared to take the credit for when things go right, but not the blame for when things go wrong.

Gianluca Vialli, a former manager of Chelsea Football Club, stated: 'If the team does well, this is a collective effort. If a team does badly, this is the manager's responsibility – my responsibility.'

This attitude was almost impossible to find following the escalation of the banking crisis, and the *de facto* bankruptcy of many of the banks and financial institutions. In particular, when facing scrutiny from the House of Commons' Public Accounts Committee, the outgoing chairmen and chief executives of HBOS and the Royal Bank of Scotland pointedly refused to accept any accountability for what had gone wrong.

This attitude was also present when the Lockheed company collapsed some years previously. The company had produced uncompetitive, average and mediocre aeroplanes and helicopters, based on obsolete designs; and when they failed to sell any of these, the company collapsed. Evaluating what had gone wrong, the leadership of the company (and no names were even mentioned) stated: 'We have looked at everything and we have examined everything; and we came to the conclusion that we did nothing wrong.'

Box 16.3: Leadership

Peters and Austin (1985) identified a long and comprehensive list of factors present in a 'leader'; and they contrasted this with the mirror attributes of the 'non-leader' (see Table 16.1 below). Peters and Austin state: 'You now know more about leaders and leadership than all the combined graduate business schools in America. You also know whether you have a leader or a non-leader in your manager's office.'

Source: from Peters and Austin, *A Passion for Excellence: The Leadership Difference* – Harper and Row (1986).

this were. Their contribution can be assessed and analysed together with the other elements and factors present.

Attempts to identify the traits and characteristics present in successful leaders are largely inconclusive in that none identify all the attributes necessary to lead, direct or manage in all situations. However, the following are more or less universal.

Table 16.1 Factors present in a leader

Leader	Non-Leader
• Carries water for people	• Presides over the mess
• Open door problem-solver, advice giver, cheerleader	• Invisible, gives orders to staff, expects them to be carried out
• Comfortable with people in their workplaces	• Uncomfortable with people
• No reserved parking place, dining room or lift	• Reserved parking place and dining table
• Manages by walking about	• Invisible
• Arrives early, stays late	• In late, usually leaves on time
• Common touch	• Strained with 'inferior' groups of staff
• Good listener	• Good talker
• Available	• Hard to reach
• Fair	• Unfair
• Decisive	• Uses committees
• Humble	• Arrogant
• Tough, confronts nasty problems	• Elusive, the 'artful dodger'
• Persistent	• Vacillates
• Simplifies	• Complicates
• Tolerant	• Intolerant
• Knows people's names	• Doesn't know people's names
• Has strong convictions	• Sways with the wind
• Trusts people	• Trusts only words and numbers on paper
• Delegates whole important jobs	• Keeps all final decisions
• Spends as little time as possible with outside directors	• Spends a lot of time massaging outside directors
• Wants anonymity for himself, publicity for the company	• Wants publicity for himself
• Often takes the blame	• Looks for scapegoats
• Gives credit to others	• Takes credit
• Gives honest, frequent feedback	• Amasses information
• Knows when and how to discipline people	• Ducks unpleasant tasks
• Has respect for all people	• Has contempt for all people
• Knows the business and the kind of people who make it tick	• Knows the business only in terms of what it can do for him/her
• Honest under pressure	• Equivocation
• Looks for controls to abolish	• Looks for new controls and procedures
• Prefers discussion rather than written reports	• Prefers long reports
• Straightforward	• Tricky, manipulative
• Openness	• Secrecy
• As little paperwork as possible	• As much paperwork as possible
• Promotes from within	• Looks outside the organization
• Keeps his/her promises	• Doesn't keep his/her promises
• Plain office and facilities	• Lavish office, expensive facilities
• Organization is top of the agenda	• Self is top of the agenda
• Sees mistakes as learning opportunities and the opportunity to develop	• Sees mistakes as punishable offences and the means of scapegoating

- **Communication** – the ability to communicate with all people with whom the leader comes into contact regularly, continuously and in ways and language in which those on the receiving end will both be able to understand and to respond to.
- **Decision-making** – the ability to take the right decisions in given situations, to take responsibility and be accountable for them and to understand the consequences of particular courses of action. Part of this involves being able to take an overview or strategic view of particular situations, to see the longer-term and to take a wider general perspective. This is sometimes called 'the helicopter view'.
- **Commitment** – to both matters in hand and also the wider aspects of the organization as a whole. This includes an inherent willingness to draw on personal, as well as professional, energies and to bring qualities of enthusiasm, drive and ambition to the particular situation.
- **Concern for staff** – respecting, trusting and committing oneself to them; developing them, understanding them and their aspirations and reconciling these with the matters in hand. Staff should be treated on a basis of equality and confidence.
- **Quality** – a commitment to the quality of product or service so that, whatever the matter in hand, customers receive high value and high satisfaction, and the staff involved receive recognition for their effort.
- **Values** – leaders bring a given *set of values* with which others will identify, and to which they will commit themselves. These values are founded in the personal integrity, and the establishment of high absolute standards of conduct and performance required and demanded. Values are then additionally developed and enhanced through levels of respect accorded to all members of staff.

Leadership types

The following different types of leader may be distinguished.

- The traditional leader, whose position is assured by birth and heredity. Examples of this are the kings and queens of England (and of other places in the world). It may also be found in family businesses, whereby child succeeds parent as the chief executive or chair when the latter retires.
- The known leader, whose position is secured by the fact that everybody understands this, at least in general. Kings and queens are examples again. Priests are known to be leaders of their congregations. Aristocrats are known to be masters and mistresses of their own domains. It is known also that they will be succeeded by one from their own estate when they die or move on.
- The appointed leader, whose position is legitimized by virtue of the fact that they have gone through a selection, assessment and appointment process in accordance with the wishes and demands of the organization and the expectations of those who will now be working for them. This invariably carries a defined and formalized managerial role in organizations.
- The bureaucratic leader, whose position is legitimized by the rank that they hold. This is especially true of military structures and is reinforced by the job titles used and their known position in the hierarchy – corporal, captain, major, general. It is also to be found in more complex and sophisticated, commercial and public organization structures. This also normally implies managerial responsibilities.

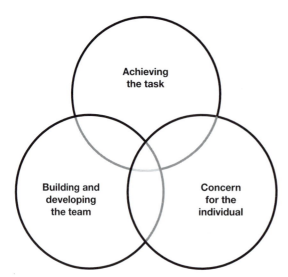

Figure 16.1 Leadership functions model

- The functional or expert leader, whose position is secured by virtue of their expertise. This form of leadership is likely to be related to particular issues – for example, the industrial relations officer may be a junior functionary who, however, becomes the acknowledged leader, director and problem-solver wherever industrial relations problems arise, and whatever the rank or status of other people involved.
- The informal leader, whose position is carried out by virtue of their personality, charisma, expertise or command of resources, but whose position is not formally legitimized by rank, appointment or tradition. This position may also be arrived at by virtue of some other activity for which they are particularly responsible – for example, local trade union representative.
- The charismatic leader, whose position is secured by the sheer force of their personality. Many great world leaders (good or evil) have (or had) this – Napoleon, Adolf Hitler, Winston Churchill, Margaret Thatcher, John F. Kennedy. In the business world, charismatic leaders include Richard Branson (Virgin), Anita Roddick (Body Shop) and Michael O'Leary (Ryanair) (see Box 16.4).

In this way, people come to know and understand – and therefore have confidence in – what the organization leadership is about, and how the individual in the particular position at the time goes about discharging it.

It takes work; and whatever style, identity and charisma is developed needs to be consistent. As long as this is related to expertise, people will have confidence, as well as identity and assurance.

Leadership styles

The rationale for studying management styles is that employees will work better for managers who use particular styles of leadership than they will for others who employ different styles (see Table 16.2 and Figure 16.2).

Box 16.4: Charisma is made not born

Everyone who aspires to, or reaches, a leadership position must have an identity and resonance with their public which is capable of acceptance. This requires hard work.

People state about those in leadership positions that 'they are born leaders'. However, what has happened is that those in leadership positions who are deemed to be successful and effective have identified traits in their personalities. They have then worked on these traits and characteristics to build a positive identity. For example:

Adolf Hitler, who is universally perceived to have been 'a born leader', had his identity, personality and ambition built by two expert public presenters, Josef Goebbels and Leni Riefenstahl. Riefenstahl, in particular, was a Hollywood film director, who understood that anyone aspiring to a position of political leadership needed a very distinctive kind of presentation.

Riefenstahl accordingly filmed Hitler making speeches (often in front of groups of no more than twenty or thirty) and then cut in the words with either split-screen or grainy images that gave the impression that the crowds were very much bigger than in actual fact; and in some of the early speeches and presentations of Adolf Hitler, she cut the speeches with pictures of crowds taken at sporting events.

It was therefore the presentation, as well as the content, which gave Hitler the identity, and enabled the Nazis to emerge from the chaos of post-World War I Germany as a serious political force.

Those in any leadership position have to adopt their own particular approach to building an identity. In particular, people in organizations need to recognize those in charge, and to have their own impression of what the person is like, and what they are doing for them and for the organization. Those in top positions have therefore to take their own characteristics and build them in terms, and in the context, of what is available. This may mean:

- a cheerful disposition;
- an open-door policy (at least at particular times of the week);
- e-mail access;
- engaging in tours of the premises;
- establishing a mode of address (e.g. is the leader going to be 'Mr/Mrs/Ms'; is it all to be first name terms; or what).

There are caveats, however. Any management style must be supported by mutual trust, respect and confidence existing between manager and subordinates. If these qualities are not present then no style is effective. There must be a clarity of purpose and direction in the first place – and this must come from the organization.

Participation can only genuinely exist if this clarity exists also – it cannot exist in a void. Leadership and management styles must also be suitable and effective in terms of cultural and environmental pressures, as well as personal, professional and occupational acceptability.

These factors are interrelated (see Figure 16.2). Account must also be taken of the fact that where leadership style is to be truly democratic, the decisions and wishes of

Table 16.2 Leadership and management styles

Autocratic (benevolent or tyrannical)	Consultative/ participative	Democratic/ participative
1 Leader makes all final decisions for the group. 2 Close supervision. 3 Individual member's interests subordinate to those of the organization. 4 Subordinates treated without regard for their views. 5 Great demands placed on staff. 6 Questioning discouraged. 7 Conformist/coercive environment.	1 Leader makes decisions after consultation with group. 2 Total communication between leader and members. 3 Leader is supportive and developmental. 4 Leader is accessible and discursive. 5 Questioning approach encouraged. 6 Ways of working largely unspecified. 7 Leader retains responsibility and accountability for results.	1 Decisions made by the group – by consultation or vote. Voting based on the principles of one person, one vote; majority rules. 2 All members bound by the group decision and support it. 3 All members may contribute to discussion. 4 Development of coalitions and cliques. 5 Leadership role is assumed by chair.

the group must be accommodated, whatever is decided and whether this is 'right' or 'wrong' in terms of the demands of the work and the pressures of the wider environment (see Box 16.5).

Blake and Mouton (1986): the managerial grid

The managerial grid is a configuration of management styles based on the matching of two dimensions of managerial concern – those of 'concern for people' and 'concern for production/output'. Each of these dimensions is plotted on a 9-point graph scale and an assessment made of the managerial style according to where they come out on each (see Figure 16.3). Thus, a low score (1–1) on each axis reflects poverty in managerial style; a high score (9–9) on each reflects a high degree of balance, concern and commitment in each area. The implication from this is that an adequate, effective and successful managerial style is in place.

The 9–9 score is indicated as the ideal by Blake and Mouton; and this reflects a desired position of equal concern for people and task, and the need for continuous improvement.

The managerial grid also implies that the best fit is along the diagonal line – concern for the task and concern for the people should be grown alongside each other rather than the one emphasized at the expense of the other.

The information on which the position on the grid is based is drawn from structured questionnaires that are issued to all managers and supervisors in the organization section, unit or department to be assessed and also to all their staff.

Contingency approaches

Contingency and 'best fit' theories of leadership take account of the interaction and interrelation between the organization and its environment. This includes the recognition,

Box 16.5: Richard Charkin and Bloomsbury Publishing Ltd

Some time after he was appointed CEO of Bloomsbury Publishing Ltd, Richard Charkin attended the executive development programme at Harvard University.

There he joined top, senior and aspiring managers from all walks of life, many nationalities, and companies and organizations of all sizes from a wide variety of industries, commercial and public services sectors.

Shortly after the programme started, all those attending were required to take a personality test. The purpose of this test was:

- to define the traits of each individual;
- to map these traits against those held by others who had taken the programme;
- to map these traits against those held to be required of effective top and senior managers.

When the results came back, each person on the programme was told what their traits had come out as; and how they compared against previous findings. Richard Charkin stated:

'When the results came back, I was quite pleased to find that I demonstrated some of the traits at least recognized as being essential for effectiveness as a CEO or top manager. However, in the discussions that followed, it became clear that neither the majority of people on my programme, nor the majority of people who had ever attended the course, exhibited those traits required to be effective as a top manager. The majority of traits exhibited were those required to be a junior or middle ranking US navy officer. Junior and middle ranking US navy officers require an assured environment, and a certain and predictable set of responses to operational situations.

So it became clear to me that companies and organizations were identifying potential leaders from among the ranks of those who sought predictable situations and assured responses, when the demands of industry, commerce and public services are that future leaders are able to cope with change, uncertainty, turmoil and chaos.'

Source: R. Charkin (2009) *So You Want to be a CEO?* – Creative Content.

and accommodating of, those elements that cannot be controlled. It also includes recognizing that those elements that can be controlled and influenced must be addressed in ways that vary in different situations – that the correct approach in one case is not a prescription to be applied to others. There is a constant interaction between the leader's job and the work to be done; and between this and the general operations of the organization in question. There is also the requirement to vary the leadership style according to the changing nature of the situation.

Fiedler (1961) used the contingency approach to identify situations where directive and prescriptive styles of leadership and management worked effectively. Directive and prescriptive styles could be engaged where the overall situation was very favourable to the leader; where the leader was liked, respected and trusted by the group. Tasks needed to be clearly understood, easy to follow and well defined. The leader needed to have a high degree of influence over group members in terms of reward and punishment. Additionally, the leader enjoyed unqualified support from the organization.

Directive and prescriptive styles of leadership and management were also effective from the point of view of achieving results, where the situation was unfavourable to the leader. Where leaders were disliked, distrusted and disrespected by the group, where

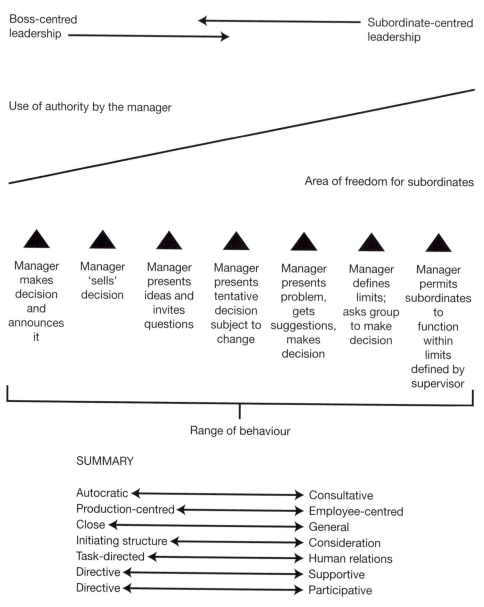

(a) LEADERSHIP CONTINUUM

Boss-centred leadership ⟶   ⟵ Subordinate-centred leadership

Use of authority by the manager

Area of freedom for subordinates

| Manager makes decision and announces it | Manager 'sells' decision | Manager presents ideas and invites questions | Manager presents tentative decision subject to change | Manager presents problem, gets suggestions, makes decision | Manager defines limits; asks group to make decision | Manager permits subordinates to function within limits defined by supervisor |

Range of behaviour

SUMMARY

Autocratic ⟷ Consultative
Production-centred ⟷ Employee-centred
Close ⟷ General
Initiating structure ⟷ Consideration
Task-directed ⟷ Human relations
Directive ⟷ Supportive
Directive ⟷ Participative

Figure 16.2 Leadership spectrum

(b) THE LEADER IN THE ENVIRONMENT

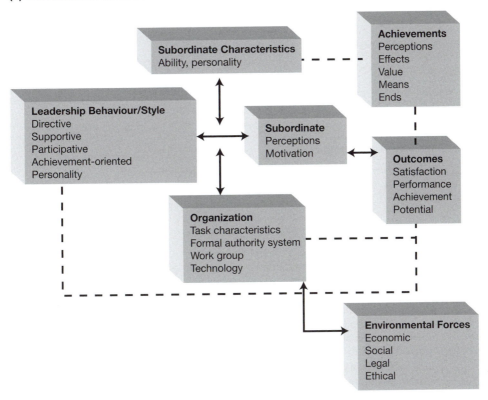

Figure 16.2 Leadership spectrum ... *continued*

they had low degrees of influence over rewards and punishments, and where the leader did not always enjoy the full backing of the organization, concentration on tasks and outputs, together with a knowledge and understanding of the nature of leadership, meant that standard and understood levels of achievement were possible.

Reddin (1968) developed the contingency approach by identifying dimensions of:

* appropriateness and effectiveness;
* inappropriateness and ineffectiveness;

in relation to the organization, nature and composition of work groups, products and services, and environmental pressures. Reddin presented a spectrum of leadership and management behaviour as follows (see Figure 16.4).

Appropriate, effective

* **Bureaucrat**: low concern for both task and relationships; appropriate in situations where rules and procedures are important.

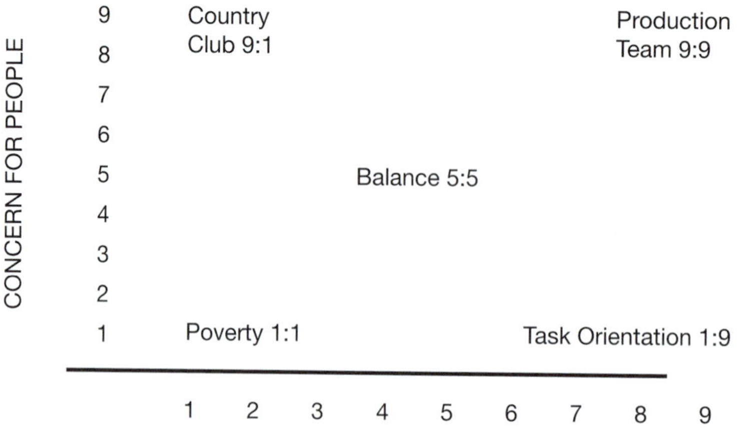

```
9     Country                          Production
8     Club 9:1                         Team 9:9
7
6
5                   Balance 5:5
4
3
2
1     Poverty 1:1              Task Orientation 1:9

         1    2    3    4    5    6    7    8    9
```

CONCERN FOR PEOPLE

Other styles identified are:

- **9–1**: the country club – production is incidental; concern for the staff and people is everything; the group exists largely to support itself.
- **1–9**: task orientation – production is everything; concern for the staff is subordinated to production and effectiveness. Staff management mainly takes the form of planning and control activities in support of production and output. Organizational activity and priority is concerned only with output.
- **5–5**: balance – a medium degree of expertise, commitment and concern in both areas; this is likely to produce adequate or satisfactory performance from groups that are reasonably well satisfied with working relations.

Figure 16.3 The managerial grid

- **Benevolent autocrat**: high concern for task, low concern for relationships; appropriate in task cultures.
- **Developer**: high concern for relationships and low concern for tasks; appropriate where the acquiescence cooperation and commitment of the people is paramount.
- **Executive**: high concern for task, high concern for relationships; appropriate where the achievement of high standards is dependent on high levels of motivation and commitment.

Inappropriate, ineffective

- **Deserter**: low concern for both task and relationships; the manager lacks involvement and is either passive or negative.
- **Autocrat**: high concern for task, low concern for relationships; the manager is coercive, confrontational, adversarial, lacking confidence in others.
- **Missionary**: high concern for relationships, low concern for task; the manager's position is dependent on preserving harmony and there is often a high potential for conflict.

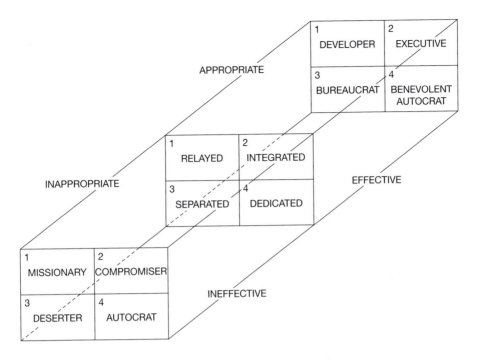

Purpose: The middle set of boxes identifies the four archetype leaders of Reddin's theory. These archetypes may then be translated into APPROPRIATE EFFECTIVE or INAPPROPRIATE INEFFECTIVE personal types.

Figure 16.4 W. Reddin: leadership and management behaviour

- **Compromiser**: high concern for both tasks and relationships; manager is a poor decision maker, expedient, concerned only with the short-term.

The contingency and best-fit approaches to leadership draw attention to the specific requirement and priority to be effective in the given organization, environment and present and evolving set of circumstances, as well as drawing attention to the critical need for an effective style. The question therefore arises as to whether or not individual leaders are capable of varying their style in response to demands; or whether it is necessary to have leaders with particular styles at which they are expert, according to the precise nature of circumstances and demands (see Box 16.6).

The consequence is that leadership is therefore in turn itself becoming more specialized and compartmentalized. In this context, it is usual to identify different types of leader, and the balance of their expertise and effectiveness, as follows:

- **Pioneer**: pioneers and pioneering leaders establish and create new products, services, brands, ventures and markets. Pioneers have a clear vision of what is possible, and through their commitment, energy, enthusiasm and ambition, they use their expertise to create and energize whatever is proposed, and see it into existence, effectiveness and profitability. Pioneers may, however, become ineffective once a particular venture is established, secured and viable.

> **Box 16.6: Stelios Haji-ioannou**
>
> In early 2005, Stelios Haji-ioannou, the founder of easyJet, stated that he was to step down from his position of chief executive of the company. He pointed to the facts of his own strengths and weaknesses as the reason for doing so.
>
> His strengths especially, he stated, were in the foundation of new companies and instituting, creating, energizing and implementing new ventures, not in running the daily affairs of established businesses.
>
> Accordingly, easyJet hired a top management team with the full range of corporate experience and expertise; and the new chief executive, Andy Harrison, arrived with the full backing, support and confidence of the London Stock Exchange.
>
> This reinforced a major prevailing view that, whatever their expertise and commitment, most leaders are at their best and most effective in a limited set of circumstances; and that in many cases, if they do move away from what they are best at, then their influence and effectiveness become diluted. This in turn can, and does, lead to a wider loss of confidence in everything that they do.

- **Transformational**: transformational leaders undertake major initiatives and ventures on behalf of organizations that require 'transforming' in some way. Often appointed purely to see the particular initiative through, transformational leaders must be able to assimilate and become authoritative, comfortable and familiar in a new organizational setting very quickly and effectively.
- **Second in command**: all organizations need a 'second in command', a deputy CEO; someone to take the place of the overall leader whenever they are not present for any reason, and someone to act as a sounding board, confidant, reflector and analyst at top organizational levels. The second in command has to have their own strength of character and expertise in order to be able to debate, argue – and disagree when necessary – with persons more senior than themselves; and additionally to deliver their own expertise in ways credible and acceptable to powerful and expert personalities (see Box 16.7).
- **Corporate**: corporate leaders are appointed to serve the interests of primary and dominant stakeholders; and this normally means the shareholders and their representatives. Problems arise when the returns to shareholders are not made for some reason. Problems additionally arise when someone who has been successful in one industry or company, and is engaged on that basis, subsequently encounters problems in the new organization.
- **Strategic**: strategic leaders are engaged because of their capability in seeing and envisioning the direction that a company or organization ought to take over the medium- to long-term. The key need for strategic leaders is the ability to engage the quality and standing of expertise required to translate the vision and strategy into action and achievement.
- **Operational**: operational leaders are those who provide clear leadership and direction to those who work for them, when working to a clear remit given to them by the organization. The best operational leaders do not normally make fully effective pioneers or creators. Indeed, to be effective in a chair or CEO role, corporate leaders

normally have to have been given a clear remit or set of targets or directions by those who appointed them, especially shareholders.

- **Problem-solver and crisis leader**: problem solvers and crisis leaders are appointed to get an organization out of a mess. Problems and crises may relate to stock market, product or service performance; or to scandals, negligence or incompetence. The key here is the ability to master the brief; and additionally to be able to address and resolve the particular problem, while at the same time restoring morale and reputation. The organization has to be left strengthened by the actions of the leader in this context; it is no use solving one problem but leaving others.

Leadership roles

The main leadership roles are as follows.

- **Figurehead**: in which the leader acts as the human face of the department, division or organization to the rest of the world. For senior managers, politicians, public figures and other charismatic leaders, this is straightforward, and the effect is often enhanced by stage management and presentation techniques.

  At departmental, divisional and functional level, managers and supervisors act as the figurehead in dealings with others. This requires attention both to merits of

---

Box 16.7: From number two to number one

There are sufficient examples of where an excellent deputy has not made the transition successfully to the top job, to draw attention to the differences between the two.

The person in charge is ultimately accountable to all stakeholders, and responsible for delivering the results desired and demanded. This is very different from acting as a sounding board during the process of ensuring that the results are delivered; or ensuring that conditions are being met for entering into a specific venture, or range of products and services.

The person in charge is the figurehead and point of identity of the company or organization; and the deputy is not. Anyone who moves up from second to first has to create an identity and focus for themselves, in exactly the same way as someone who would have been appointed from outside the organization.

Many deputies use their elevation and new position to introduce pet schemes, projects and ventures, which they have nurtured under the previous regime, but which have so far been rejected. Such schemes and ventures require the same degree of rigour and evaluation as under the previous regime.

Many former deputies fail to appoint their own adequate deputy; and this results in not having the capabilities and character close by as confidant, sounding board and evaluator that the new number one used to provide so effectively.

Many former deputies know, believe or perceive that they are themselves on trial, under pressure to deliver early and high-profile results. Everything then becomes concentrated on producing a triumph, whether or not this is in the longer-term best interests of the organization and its stakeholders.

particular cases or arguments, and the effectiveness of presentation and delivery. The key to being an effective departmental or divisional figurehead is extensive preparation, and the development of high-quality communication skills.

- **Ambassador**: in which leaders act as advocate, cheerleader and problem solver on the part of their department, division, organization and staff. Again, for high profile public leaders this is straightforward.

  Every high profile public figure playing this role requires expert briefing and preparation, as well as sound knowledge and understanding of the particular situation into which they are going. This must also apply to organization, departmental and divisional supervisors and managers when they have to carry out these functions.

- **Servant**: this view of leadership and management is based on the premise that the manager is the ultimate supporter or servant of staff, product and service output and quality, and markets, customers and clients (see Figure 16.5).

- **Maintenance**: this role requires:

  - daily maintenance – attending to problems and issues as they arise;
  - preventative maintenance – continuous improvement of the work, working environment, and procedures and practices; and attending to staff development also;
  - breakdown maintenance – handling crises, blow-ups and storms in a quick and effective manner.

- **Role model**: leaders, managers and supervisors set the style, standards, attitudes and behaviour for those who work for them. If leaders show qualities of commitment, enthusiasm, energy and honesty, these may be expected and are likely to arise in subordinates.

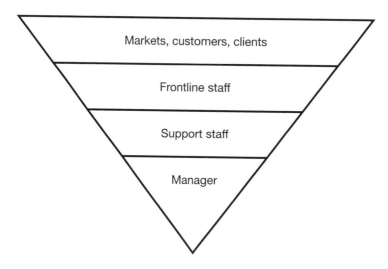

The manager or supervisor is placed at the bottom point, *prima facie* supporting and serving the workforce rather than sitting on top of it.

Figure 16.5 The inverse pyramid

- **Ringmaster**: in their own particular sphere, all managers and supervisors are ringmasters. This is quite apart from any particular knowledge or aptitude for the task in hand.
- **Chief architect of corporate purpose**: designing the immediate and long-term future of the organization, based on an expertise and understanding of what the markets need, want and demand; and designing the organization frameworks and institutions necessary to achieve this.
- **Creator of confidence**: combining personality with energy, enthusiasm, ambition and expertise so that all stakeholders know and understand that the organization and its direction and viability are in safe and expert hands.

The role elements indicated here are essential to successful and effective leadership and direction at whatever level. To be an effective leader there is an overwhelming responsibility placed upon the individual to adopt these roles and the responsibilities inherent within them. It is also incumbent upon the person concerned to develop any of the qualities required in which they are not proficient (see Box 16.8).

Measures of success and failure

The performance of those in leadership positions is assessed in simple terms against whether they delivered what they set out to achieve, or not, and the reasons. The broader approach to the assessment of performance of those in leadership positions relates to the key questions of confidence and complexity.

Confidence

Those who appoint others to leadership and managerial positions are normally confident at the outset that they have got the right person for the job; and following appointment, the development of mutual confidence is essential. Once those in leadership and managerial positions have lost the confidence of the people who appointed them, they normally leave.

For example, the chair of a publicly quoted company must maintain the confidence of the world's stock markets. If they do not, the share price falls. If this continues and the share price continues to fall whatever the activities and directions proposed by the CE in question, they will normally leave. This may also occur as the result of a bad set of company figures, either for a period or on a more continuous and long-term basis.

Confidence may also be lost among other backers and stakeholders. The leader in question may lose the respect and regard of the staff – as the result of some dishonest, expedient or unjustifiably punitive action, for example.

They may lose the confidence of the markets in which business is conducted. This occurs, for example, if a product is launched during their tenure that subsequently fails commercially, has a bad image or which it becomes apparent is unsafe or dangerous.

The converse of this is 'leaving a void'. This is where confidence and identity of the organization with the leader are fully integrated. Any question of the leader departing is therefore viewed with great alarm. For example, commentaries on the Virgin Group always include questions of 'What happens to the organization if anything happens to Richard Branson?'

Confidence is only maintained through honesty and integrity. Where the leader (of anything) is caught lying the clear, instant and unambiguous message given out is that

Box 16.8: Peter Nicholl on leadership

Peter Nicholl is a New Zealander who spent the whole of his career in the central banking sector. He rose to the position of assistant governor and then deputy governor of the Reserve Bank of New Zealand. In these positions, he was responsible for radical transformation at the Reserve Bank of New Zealand; and the work that he did there became a beacon of expert practice which came to have influence across the whole of the central banking sector.

When the former Yugoslavia collapsed in 1990, it fragmented into its traditional component states and ethnic divides. For the next five years, there were wars across the whole of the Balkan region as each of the states and ethnic groups sought to establish their own stability, viability and identity.

One of the states to emerge was Bosnia-Herzegovina. As stability returned to the region at last, all of the newly formed and independent states now required the full range of public institutions.

Bosnia-Herzegovina established its own central bank. Unable to find somebody with suitable expertise, identity or drive from within their own community, politicians of Bosnia-Herzegovina turned to the central banking sector at large for advice. The result was that Peter Nicholl, a New Zealander, was appointed as the first governor of the Bank of Bosnia-Herzegovina.

The initial response to his appointment was hostile. Accordingly, he had to work very hard to gain immediate acceptance; and on this foundation he built his own credibility.

His first action was to immerse himself in the cultural, social and political history, customs, priorities and aspirations of Bosnia-Herzegovina and its people. He quickly gained an understanding of how the country worked, and where any problems might foreseeably arise.

He gained an early triumph in dealings with the World Bank and International Monetary Fund. Officials from these bodies came into the country with a view to proposing a standard restructuring of the financial institutions. Peter Nicholl rejected these interventions, stating to his own new masters and people that what was being proposed was useless and unworkable, and without any understanding of how the country actually operated. This reinforced the confidence in which he was held by the political establishment in Bosnia-Herzegovina, and demonstrated that he had their interests and those of the nation as his priority.

Speaking of his experience, Peter Nicholl identified the characteristics necessary for leadership success, as follows:

- thriving on challenges, at the same time as identifying those challenges that need to be tackled, and those issues that ought to be ignored or dealt with differently;
- capability in recognizing, and putting into managerial forms, priorities that institutions face;
- willingness to tackle specific issues, including crises and emergencies;
- the ability to establish good working relationships with key stakeholders.

In order to do this, Peter Nicholl stated that the following was necessary:

- the ability to establish your own authority;
- the ability to demonstrate that you can indeed cope with change;
- the ability to deal with all stakeholders on their own terms;
- attention to internal processes, as well as external presentation;
- the ability to choose and develop good staff, to reward their initiative, while at the same time dealing with poor or inadequate performance.

Recognizing that this range and complexity of capabilities and expertise needed is essential; and anyone who does not have them, and yet who aspires to a top position, needs to know where their strengths and weaknesses lie, and to take steps to build on their strengths and develop those qualities that they do not yet have in full.

Source: P. Nicholl (2005) *Leadership and Direction in the Central Banking Sector* – Central Banking Publications.

'he/she is a liar'. Any subsequent dealing or transaction with this particular individual is therefore invariably prefixed by questions of the extent to which they may be trusted. It is in turn exacerbated during briefings for those who are to be involved with them along the lines of 'don't believe a word they say' and 'get something in writing and get their signature'.

Complexity

Measures of success and failure will also address the question of what else was achieved during the particular period of office. The direction taken may have opened up a great range of subsequent opportunities and a part of this measurement will relate to the extent to which these were exploited.

This is also to be seen in the complexity indicated. The hard targets may be achieved, for example, but only at the expense of the soft – the destruction of staff relations, motivation and morale. Conversely a superbly integrated and supportive group may be built but one that never actually produces anything of substance. The targets that were set may turn out to have been immeasurable, hopelessly optimistic or conversely far too easy. In the latter case in particular it is both easy and dangerous to indulge in an entirely false sense of success.

The legitimacy of the objectives and performance targets must also be generally and constantly questioned. To return to the hard examples quoted above – increases in output, profit and cost effectiveness by x per cent should always be treated with scepticism. They assume that the basis on which the percentage is calculated is legitimate and valid. They assume that this constitutes the best use of organization resources. They assume (this especially applies to public services) that adequate and effective activity levels can be maintained.

It should be clear from this that the setting of organization performance targets is a process capable of rationalization and founded on the understanding of general organization requirements. In the particular context of leadership, it should be clear also that ultimate responsibility for the success/failure in achieving these targets rests with the leader.

It is also clear that leaders are made and not born. People can be trained in each of the qualities and elements indicated so that (as with anything else) they may first understand, then apply, then reinforce and finally become expert in these activities indicated. This is understood to be on the same basis as aptitude for anything else, however. Not everyone has the qualities or potential necessary in the first place. There is nothing contentious in this – not everyone has the qualities or potential to be a great chef, racing driver, nurse or labourer and in this respect leadership is no different.

Conclusions

In business, commercial and public service sector organizations, leadership is that part of management that provides the vision, direction and energy that gives life to policy, strategy and operations. It provides everyone involved – above all, the staff, but this also applies to suppliers, customers and community groups – with a point of identity and focus, a personification of the organization with which they themselves are involved, and with which they are dealing. Problems always occur when the leader, for whatever reason, is either unwilling or else unable to accept the full responsibilities of the position. These problems are compounded when it becomes known, believed or perceived that the leader is acting without integrity, and is seeking to blame either circumstances or else other people for organizational, strategic and operational shortcomings. In these cases, staff only remain in employment as long as they believe it is in their interests to do so; and this invariably leads to the early loss of good and high-quality staff. Problems also arise when leaders accept their responsibilities to one group of stakeholders, in preference to others – this is a serious problem in large public and multinational corporations when senior managers discharge their responsibilities to shareholders, political interests and the drives of boards of directors and governors, at the expense of staff, suppliers, customers and clients.

Those who aspire to leadership positions must therefore be prepared to accept that there are certain qualities that go with the job – above all, enthusiasm, ambition, clarity of purpose, energy and direction – and must be prepared to develop these as the condition of employment in these positions. It is also important to recognize that this part of management development cannot be achieved except through a period of long-term prioritized intensive and demanding training, supported with periods of further education either at a university or conducted through the private sector. It is impossible to develop leaders purely on the basis of single or isolated short periods of training, unsupported by activities at the workplace.

Moreover, it must be stressed again that the best practitioners of a particular trade, profession or occupation do not necessarily make the best leaders and managers of groups of these staff; assessment for leadership and management potential must be carried out on the basis of the ability to observe the fledgling qualities required, rather than existing professional and technical expertise.

It is clear that this part of management development is going to become very much more important in the future. Organizations are certain to value much more highly the all-round capabilities and willingness to accept responsibility from those whom they place in top positions. In the medium- to long-term, the ability to satisfy dominant shareholder or political interests is certain not to be enough.

17 Organization and management development

Introduction

Organization development (OD) is the generic term given to strategic approaches and initiatives for improving organizational effectiveness through emphases on the capabilities, capacities, qualities and motivation of those who carry out the work. These are supported through harmonizing and integrating individual and collective training and development within all departmental, divisional and functional operations and activities.

OD depends on the development of staff and management for commercial, industrial and public service success and effectiveness. It follows from this that there are roles for change mechanisms, change agents, change catalysts and key appointments with key qualities, as well as training and development expertise and activity, in order to take the organization in the preferred directions.

For this to be fully effective, OD approaches need to understand and address four key areas for collective and individual development (see Figure 17.1).

The need for a strategic approach

The OD process is aimed at changing, forming and developing performance culture, values, attitudes and beliefs in positive and constructive ways, as well as paying specific attention to the enhancement of skills, knowledge and technological proficiency.

The precise nature of OD varies between organizations that adopt the approach. In general, the key values and qualities reflect:

- a measure of conformity and the willingness of the staff to go down the paths indicated;
- obsession with product and service quality;
- strong customer, client and supplier orientation;
- universal identity with the organization at large on the part of all staff;
- setting a moral or value-led example and taking an active pride in the organization and its work on the part of all concerned;
- designing, implementing and supporting the required management and supervisory style;
- higher output per member of staff;
- accuracy in prioritizing those activities that contribute directly to organization profitability and effectiveness;
- the capacity to develop fully flexible skills, knowledge, attitudes and behaviour;
- a much more open and cohesive culture and *esprit de corps*;
- the institutionalization of both collective and individual development.

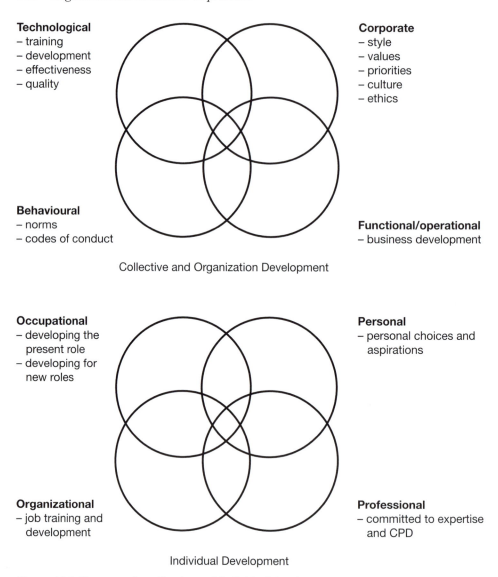

Technological
– training
– development
– effectiveness
– quality

Corporate
– style
– values
– priorities
– culture
– ethics

Behavioural
– norms
– codes of conduct

Functional/operational
– business development

Collective and Organization Development

Occupational
– developing the
  present role
– developing for
  new roles

Personal
– personal choices and
  aspirations

Organizational
– job training and
  development

Professional
– committed to expertise
  and CPD

Individual Development

Figure 17.1 Key areas for collective and individual development

The OD process requires expertise and commitment in all of the component parts of collective and individual development – performance assessment, management and appraisal; problem raising and acknowledgement; access to information; resourcing and implementing individual and collective development activities, including project work and secondments; integrating monitoring, review and evaluation as strategic, as well as operational, commitment.

The OD process is therefore strategic, requiring that organizations place staff at the core of what they set out to do. One way of looking at this is to use a revision of the 7S model (see Figure 17.2) and then build on the skills, knowledge, expertise and experience demanded of proficiency in each of the other areas indicated.

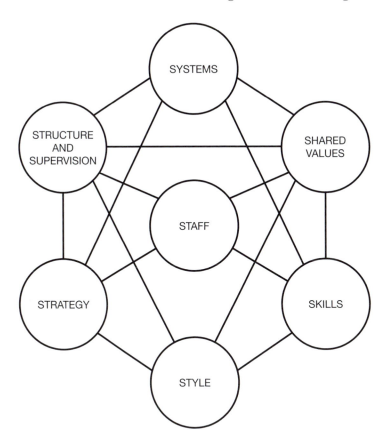

Purpose: a configuration of organisation, pattern and design that reflects the essential attributes that must be addressed in the establishment and development of an excellent organisation.

Figure 17.2 The 7S model developed to put staff at the core
Source: Peters and Waterman (1982).

Key outputs of the 7S approach to OD

If staff commitment is fully developed, it is possible to establish some key outputs and expectations that can be achieved as a result of the investment made. These are as follows:

*   The development of positive and collective culture, attitudes, values, beliefs and ethics.
*   The generation of commitment to the organization on the part of everybody concerned through active staff engagement.
*   Coping with change and uncertainty in products, services, technology, markets and the environment.
*   The management and development of the systems needed to make the organization as efficient and effective as possible.

In summary, a working environment and organization culture are created whereby each of these issues is positively addressed. Problems are recognized early, and because of the fundamental openness of the approach, everyone's interest is engaged in resolving them.

Communications

One part of the nature of any activities established has therefore to consider how people behave, and how they are expected to carry out their tasks and duties, as well as what is actually required. The only way to do this is to place effective and comprehensive communication systems at the heart of any strategic approach to OD.

This is because all messages depend on complete clarity of purpose and objectives, regularly communicated to the staff. A critical part of OD is therefore concerned with ensuring that adequate and effective communication processes are in place, and maintaining and developing these as required.

There is a clear implication for integration and harmonization of all standards and practices, so that everyone knows and understands that they are being treated fairly, equally and solely on the basis of what they do and how they do it.

It is additionally essential that communications, and the development of a positive and cohesive culture, are key managerial and supervisory responsibilities. This in turn requires attention to management training and development (see below) in which attention is given to the creation of the desired work and team ethic.

The development effort therefore is to ensure that everyone indeed understands 'how things are done' as well as what is done and why. The process must result in collective attitudes and values that are:

- designed and defined by the organization's top managers, rather than allowed to emerge as the result of a collective inertia;
- positive, not negative, so that the fundamental approach is to what can be achieved rather than to the barriers to achievement (see Box 17.1);

Box 17.1: 'The enemy is out there'

'A friend once told the story of a boy that he coached to play baseball who, after dropping three catches, marched into the dug-out. "No-one can catch a ball out there", he said.

There is in each of us a propensity to find someone or something outside ourselves to blame when things go wrong. Some organizations elevate this propensity to a commandment: "Thou shalt always find someone else to blame." Marketing blames manufacturing, manufacturing blames engineering, engineering blames marketing. For many companies, "the enemy" has become Far Eastern competition, trade unions, government regulation, or customers who have taken their requirements elsewhere. "The enemy is out there", however, is almost always an incomplete story. "Out there" and "in here" are usually part of a single system. The remedy lies in the organization's own hands.'

Source: P. Senge (1994) *The Fifth Discipline* – Century Business.

- strong not weak, so that everyone has full confidence that how, when, why and where they do something is fully integrated with the organization's position, attitudes and values;
- positively acceptable and capable of compliance rather than nebulous and incapable of rejection (see Box 17.2).

Collective and individual employee development therefore concentrates on:

- instilling the required and desired attitudes and values, and generating understanding of the reasons for these in relation to essential business and service performance;
- underpinning these with the corporate approach to induction, initial and continuous job training, and the delivery of the core programme;
- supporting everything through a clearly understood, accepted, positive and open staff management style (again, whether autocratic, participative or democratic).

No stated or overt culture development survives an adversarial or dishonest management style or general organization ethos where what is stated is unsupported or gone against in practice and delivery (see Box 17.3).

Generation of commitment

One key feature, therefore, is the generation of collective and individual commitment to purpose, and to carrying out activities and expertise to the best of everyone's abilities in the name of the organization. Generating collective and individual commitment to the approach requires:

- the integration of organizational goals with personal expectations. This means a long-term and enduring commitment to professional, occupational and personal development, as well as organization priorities;
- creating a structure of reporting relationships that provides space and encouragement for collective and individual development, rather than restrictions and restraints;
- open, participative and involving functioning of the organization with full access to information;
- fundamental equality of opportunity, normally based on a single set of rules and regulations (rather than those that vary according to status, occupation or expertise);
- mutual openness, respect, value, trust, consideration and support among different levels and occupations;
- the open recognition and discussion of conflict with the emphasis on identifying and resolving issues rather than institutionalizing them;
- managerial behaviour and styles of leadership and supervision based on visibility, openness, honesty and integrity;
- recognizing individual, as well as collective, needs and expectations; and recognizing and valuing every individual contribution;
- implementing systems of pay and reward that are known, believed and perceived to be based on fairness and equality rather than status and influence;
- investing in the quality of the general working and learning environment;
- providing opportunities for personal, occupational and professional variety, enhancement and career progression, as well as organization success, profitability and effectiveness;

Box 17.2: Acceptance and rejection

Strong positive cultures are not all things to all people and this means that some will reject them. For example:

*   **Nursing**: the micro-culture on some NHS hospital wards is so all-pervasive that the staff effectively develop their own total lifestyle based around patterns of work. In particular, social events are organized so that they work together and can rest and play together. Dominated by the siege mentality existing across the NHS at present, and reflected in individual hospitals and wards, the problem facing individuals is whether to adopt the total lifestyle or seek work elsewhere.
*   **Japanese manufacturing**: the macro-culture of many Japanese car and electrical goods organizations operating in the west demands that staff attend out-of-hours functions as part of the work commitment. Again, the pressure to comply is very strong and not always acceptable.

In both cases, there is a cultural discord between how things are done at work, and personal priorities in the rest of life. They are not always easily capable of reconciliation.

Box 17.3: Tait's Greetings Cards

Tait's Greetings Cards Ltd produces cards for all occasions – birthdays, Christmas, celebrations, births, marriages and deaths. It also produces high-quality stationery and postcards under licence to branded providers. The company employs sixty people in a small village. Of these, thirty are production staff, twenty work in sales and there are ten management and administration staff.

Alistair Tait is the company's chairman and chief executive. On organization and employee development he states:

> We have no training policy or strategy. All that we insist on is that staff do 30 days' training per annum. As long as at least one event is directly work-related, they can do whatever they like with the rest. We chose 30 days because that is about the usual commitment of a day-release college course which staff can do if they want. We wanted to give everyone the same opportunity.
>
> If people want to do this during the day, that's fine by us. If they want to go to evening classes, that's fine by us to. We give them work time off in lieu. So if the evening class is two hours, then they get two hours off on one day.
>
> In my 17 years in charge, we have had no complaints. The whole approach costs us about 3% of payroll. The only slight intake of breath I ever had was about 9 years ago, when my secretary suddenly announced that she wanted to do a HGV driving course. I let her go, and she left us shortly afterwards to work as lorry driver. However, she rejoined us three years ago and is now our transport manager. And she still makes at least one run per week.

Source: London Chamber of Commerce and Industry (2001).

- generating a positive *esprit de corps* – a team spirit – that gives high levels of feelings of pride, identity and acceptance by the organization, and feelings of loyalty, mutuality, trust and security.

A key feature of OD is therefore the level of attention paid to the general environment in which work is carried out. If this is effective, then the required basis for the development of the other activities is assured (see Box 17.4).

Box 17.4: Resources

To be fully effective in their jobs, everyone has to be adequately resourced. This does not mean indulging people, providing them with the very latest gadgets or giving them huge acres of office space. It does mean ensuring that they have the tools, technology and wherewithal to do everything that is demanded of them. It also requires integrating patterns of work to ensure that no single element dominates working life so that particular targets and priorities cannot easily be met.

BIFX PLC is a financial services company specializing in the transfer of funds overseas from the UK, and in receiving funds from elsewhere in the world to be converted into Sterling. BIFX serves both corporate and also individual clients.

The company established an on-line transaction service. This was made immediately attractive to customers by offering a full 1 per cent of each currency above the standard transaction value, so as to persuade people to consider the on-line service, and then ideally use it.

It quickly became clear, however, that one part of the resource was missing. While it was indeed possible to use the on-line service at any time of the day or night, customer support services and telephone help-lines only worked normal office hours (that is, Monday–Friday, 9.00 am–5.00 pm).

Accordingly, the company quickly ran into some difficulties. In particular, a large capital transfer which had been booked at a specific exchange rate to be transferred to Hong Kong had first to be withdrawn, then re-presented, when there was a lock-up on the computer system at the receiving end. By the time the transaction was presented the following day, the exchange rate had dropped two cents.

Accordingly, the transferers contacted BIFX. BIFX were profusely apologetic; however, they went on to state that, as the system was in its teething stages, there would be no compensation. Only when the transferer's corporate lawyers sent a stern letter did BIFX change their minds.

The lesson is that full commitment means – full commitment! However any product or service is delivered, it is essential that every aspect that could conceivably be required is included. In this case, there is a clear emphasis on the organization's desire to shift as much of its business as possible on to computer systems and networks. For this to be effective, there has to be physical back-up and support. Otherwise, a further set of flaws is developed. All that this means is that customer service staff receive volumes of complaints from different sources; the problem of complaints is not actually addressed or resolved.

Coping with change and uncertainty

The OD approach to change and uncertainty takes the view that both are inevitable and that they are best overcome by instilling attitudes, values, standards and expertise capable of accommodating and responding to this. This is in contrast to those organizations that go through business process re-engineering and other restructuring and re-sizing programmes as a response to profits warnings, budget cuts, stock market, media and government pressures (see Box 17.5).

In the management of change, OD concentrates on the following.

Primary beneficiaries

So long as these remain customers and clients, the development effort is directed at their service and levels of satisfaction and quality that are as certain as possible to retain them and generate the capability to offer further products and services in the future.

In pursuit of this staff training has to concentrate on the following.

- Speed, flexibility and quality of response together with the development of attitudes of responsibility and autonomy.
- Technological proficiency and capability so that equipment in use at present is maximized and optimized, and that future innovations and consequent changes in expertise are accepted and implemented quickly when required.
- The ability to solve problems and address complaints whenever they arise (see Box 17.6).

Box 17.5: Body Shop (1)

Body Shop, the organic cosmetics company, was founded by Gordon and Anita Roddick in 1976. At the outset, both the concept (using organic produce to make cosmetics) and also the distinctive ethical approach (paying western prices for third world crops) were either ignored altogether or dismissed as unworkable commercially.

However, the company grew steadily over periods of recession and high unemployment, at exactly the same time that people were having to look hard at non-essential expenditure.

The collective overriding ethic was, and remains, to: 'do right by everybody – staff, suppliers, customers, communities and shareholders'. This collective ethic came to be widely understood early in the development of the company. The result of this was to ensure a steady stream of potentially high-quality and committed staff. The company has had a staff waiting list since 1978.

The other main problem to be faced was managing media and stock market expectations. The company consistently produced lower net margins than the rest of the cosmetics and department store sector. However, by making clear the long-term strategy and its foundations in OD, sectoral confidence and support were assured at times when more traditional organizations suffered from profits warnings and loss of confidence.

Box 17.6: Staff as primary beneficiary

Organizations that adopt this approach have to place genuine intrinsic and extrinsic value on their staff. This may be summarized as a commitment to 'high-quality work and high levels of commitment and motivation in return for high and enduring levels of reward'. Thus, for example:

- Body Shop do not pay more than many retail organizations. However, they do offer greater professional and occupational development opportunities, as well as work away from the organization in the community.
- Sanyo UK pay approximately 130 per cent of what is on offer at Phillips, Ferguson and Bush, and other indigenous electrical goods manufacturers. This is in return for full flexibility of working and requirements to develop. The company also points proudly to a staff absenteeism rate of 0.5 per cent (the equivalent of every member of staff taking an average of one day's sick leave only per annum).

Other beneficiaries

This refers especially to shareholders, suppliers and communities.

Potential problems with shareholders' representatives arise when the benefits of OD do not become immediately apparent, and those responsible come under pressure to drop it, dilute it or reduce the desired levels of investment. Certainly shareholders, and their representatives, need educating in the costs and benefits of the approach because the financial aim is to optimize long-term security, and therefore owner value, and not short-term attractiveness.

Suppliers may also need to be convinced of the approach especially if they are used to dealing in orderly and familiar ways with bureaucratic and traditional functionaries. Emphasis is therefore required on the long-term potential for the relationship, and the value and importance of enduring quality, service and mutuality of interest as well as billing arrangements.

A spin-off of successful and enduring OD is the value of 'corporate citizenship'. All communities prefer to have known, believed and perceived good employers in their area (see Box 17.7).

Barriers to change

Genuinely strategic and fully integrated OD approaches have as one of their key advantages the capability to address barriers to change effectively. This is because the desired culture, attitudes and values are wholly positive and committed, and so anything that is seen as an obstacle to progress simply becomes a challenge.

It is, however, essential to recognize and understand that, even in cases where there is a positive and collective commitment to progress, barriers to change can, and do, become problems. For example:

- resource shortages can, and do, mean that what is required cannot be easily or effectively implemented;

- staff and expertise shortages mean that, while commitment and cohesion are fully effective, both the volume and quality of expertise may not be present;
- problems and issues may be wrongly addressed, misunderstood or misdiagnosed, again even in the most open and cohesive of organizations.

Each of the above factors has additionally to be related to the speed at which change and development are required. For example, it may be possible to effect change over a

---

Box 17.7: Change and uncertainty in the airline industry

When the credit crunch began to bite in 2007, it quickly became apparent to the airline industry as a whole that companies would have to face the following problems:

- rising take-off and landing fees and other 'slot' charges (relating to terminal usage, passenger and baggage loading and unloading);
- declining passenger numbers;
- rising operational costs;
- uncertainty over fuel charges.

One of the world's major national flag-carrying airlines realized early that they would indeed have problems with each of these aspects; and so they called in one of the world's top-brand management consultancies.

The management consultancy did its usual examination of the organization; and subsequently presented a report. This report stated:

- the company did indeed have problems;
- the present structures and culture of the company would have to be broken up.

In particular, everyone involved with the company was now going to have to learn to 'cope with ambiguity'. When questioned mildly about what this might mean, the consultants were unable to answer, except in terms that it was 'a volatile market' and 'uncertain operating conditions'.

The consultants offered no mechanisms, prescriptions or guidance for how 'uncertainty and ambiguity' might be addressed; nor did they offer further support should the company choose to implement the recommendations.

The lesson here is that such an untargeted and unfinished approach to coping with change and uncertainty does nothing to address the problems and issues. It simply adds to the uncertainty and ambiguity. While it remains true that the key managerial discipline is 'coping with change and uncertainty', it is essential that those involved are given a clear set of boundaries in which to operate, and some rules and guidelines. Otherwise, something that is known, understood and familiar to all is replaced by something that is unknown, unfamiliar and misunderstood – and this leads to stress, anxiety and above all loss of performance (especially, as in this case, when increase in performance is actually essential).

Box 17.8: Ford UK

Over the period since 1975, Ford UK has consistently spent approximately 5 per cent of payroll costs on staff training and development. However, because it did not address organizational priorities and was not strategically targeted, monitored, reviewed or evaluated, output at the factories rose very slowly (to a maximum 62 cars per member of staff, per annum in 2006, compared to Nissan UK's 135 cars per annum, per member of staff also in 2006). Structural and organizational problems were never addressed. Institutional problems of racism and cultural and social barriers tended to be enhanced by the individual attention given to training rather than the collective attitudes and values that were more likely to emerge if an overall collective, orderly and strategic approach had been taken.

period of a year, when what is required is the same change over a period of a month; or it may be that capability and proficiency in using new technology is demanded immediately but it will take three months to train staff and make them familiar with its workings.

In the most committed of organizations and workforces, these apparent impasses simply become the next set of problems to be solved. People start to look at alternatives, propose solutions, seek different routes to the same destination. However, to be able to do this effectively, full institutional support, and adequate resources, as above, are essential in all cases (see Box 17.8).

Conflict

Effective OD approaches have as a priority that every potential conflict is brought out into the open and dealt with early. One of the key conditions is therefore that people are able, willing and confident to raise problems and issues, whenever they arise, and whatever they might be, as follows:

- work problems and issues, conflicts of priorities and activities;
- conflicts between, and within, groups;
- professional debates and discussions;
- serious problems such as bullying, victimization and harassment.

Creating the conditions whereby anything can be raised and resolved early means that everyone has to have trust in the managerial and supervisory response when such matters come to light. It is therefore essential that those in managerial and supervisory positions are fully trained, willing and able to deal with anything that does arise.

Here also, it is essential that the required standards of conduct and behaviour are fully integrated with the problem or issue itself. This requires in turn:

- staff raising problems and issues knowing that they will get a full, fair and respectful hearing;
- managers and supervisors understanding that staff members will not raise such matters unless they feel that these things are important.

Problems arise with this approach (and this therefore becomes an OD need) when any, or all, of the following become apparent:

- the problem or issue is unacceptable to management or to the organization as a whole;
- the way in which problems and issues are raised does not bring about any sort of a response;
- managers and supervisors use the overt openness of ability to raise problems either to assert themselves, or to denigrate the staff, or both (see Box 17.9).

Box 17.9: Carter's Cleaning Services Ltd

Carter's Cleaning Services Ltd (CCSL) is a nationwide provider of contract cleaning services and commercial premises. For many years, CCSL took a collective attitude to clients that, rather than driving down costs and prices (as was common with the rest of the industry), it would rather offer a high-quality and assured service in return for high fees and charges.

For many years this worked very effectively, and the company bucked many of the trends in the contract cleaning sector.

The company employed a sales team of fifteen. Led by a sales manager, the sales team went around regularly to existing clients, servicing contracts and ensuring that the high standards promised were delivered; and they also made regular cold calls on potential new customers.

The team and its manager built up a fully open, integrated and involved way of working over many years. After a while, however, the sales manager moved on, and she was replaced by David Main, a young, pushy and very successful member of the team.

Everyone expected the present situation to continue and evolve. At one of the early meetings, therefore, Julie Scott felt able to raise a serious problem concerning her workload. It concerned a cluster of her clients in south Wales with whom it would be very difficult now to maintain contact, as there were extensive roadworks on the motorway network around the area. Accordingly, she raised the question, and asked for everyone's input into how best to resolve this matter.

David Main cut in immediately. He stated: 'This is rubbish! We cannot have hold-ups just because the motorways are blocked. Otherwise nothing will ever get done. If it is necessary, you will simply have to get up at 4.00 am in the morning so that you beat the rush hour. If it is necessary, you will find a multi-storey car park and walk around your patch. If you take a taxi, I will need to see receipts and other details, including why it was impossible for you to walk around, or drive around your patch under your own steam.'

Julie started to argue in the forthright and open manner that the previous sales manager had always encouraged. Quickly, however, David Main shouted her down. He said: 'You will now shut up!'

When the rest of the team voiced their support for Julie, David Main gathered up his papers and stormed out of the room. His parting shot was: 'You will do this my way because I say so! I am now in charge!'

The key lesson, as stated above, is managerial and supervisory capability and willingness to get problems and issues out into the open. This capability and willingness has to be part of the process and, as in this case, must be capable of being sustained throughout any staff changes. In this case, as a result of the above conversation, any developmental approach to the management of conflict is now clearly destroyed.

Management development

Management development is concerned with three distinctive activities.

- The development of managers and supervisors.
- The development of all staff through the activities of managers and supervisors.
- The development of overall organizational capability (see above).

Any discussion of management development has to start from the premise that the skills, qualities and expertise required of good and effective managers can be taught, learned and applied. The vast range of management courses, activities, expertise and qualifications would tend to support this view at least to an extent (see Box 17.10).

Box 17.10: Rosabeth Moss Kanter and common sense

The alternative view offered most often is that management is 'common sense' and that therefore anyone can do it. The evidence is to the contrary.

Promotion paths

The traditional approach in much of the western world was to promote the best professional or operative into the position of manager. Thus, the best teacher became head teacher; the best plumber, plumbing manager; the best footballer, football manager. This last illustrates the point most graphically. Very few of the world's top football players have enjoyed long-term managerial success once they have stopped playing. Those who have gained real managerial success are those who learned the trade, partly as the result of not being able to achieve maximum excellence on the field of play.

Figureheads

Others point to the success of individuals such as Richard Branson and the Roddicks. In practice, both of these explicitly acknowledged their own shortcomings; and they went to a lot of trouble to surround themselves with the highest-quality available expertise to compensate for this.

continued . . .

Box 17.10: Rosabeth Moss Kanter and common sense ... *continued*

Rosabeth Moss Kanter when interviewed by Tom Mangold on this point was asked explicitly: 'Is this not just common sense?'

To which she replied: 'Sense, yes. The evidence supports it. Common? Not if you consider all the failures, problems and sheer waste that occurs as the result of bad management decisions.'

Source: Rosabeth Moss Kanter (1998) *Business Matters* – BBC.

In practice, management development concentrates on the identification of the skills, qualities, attitudes, behaviour and proficiency required of present and future generations of managers. It is also essential that management development processes and activities address the required and desired levels of integrity and openness demanded by the organization, its staff and other stakeholders. Management development must also address giving those on developmental paths the broadest possible range of experience and understanding.

In this context, management development addresses the following:

- organization development and managing change (as above);
- behaviour, attitudes, skills, knowledge, expertise and technological proficiency development (as above);
- product, service and operational advancement and improvement;
- delivering this expertise in its environment;
- integrating managerial expertise with organization and environmental pressures, opportunities and constraints;
- increasingly, managing across cultures and in transforming occupations, professions, industries and sectors.

The body of expertise

As stated above (see Chapter 1), there is no distinctive body of managerial expertise that must be acquired in advance of receiving a managerial appointment, or practising as a manager. However, it is possible to isolate specific qualities and attributes that are certain to be required of those who seek or aspire to become successful managers. The body of expertise may be broken down as follows.

- **Behaviour**: integrity, equity, respect and value; respecting and valuing the opinions and capabilities of others; openness, honesty; transparency; visibility.
- **Attitudes**: positive, enthusiastic, dynamic; concerned; flexible and responsive.
- **Skills**: in developing the next generation of managers; in identifying and developing skills, qualities and aptitudes of all. Specific skills development is also required in the areas of leadership, decision-making, delegation, performance measurement. In the specific case of employee and organization development, a part of management development must consist of identifying and engaging in organization, departmental, divisional, collective, group and individual development activities.

- **Knowledge**: keeping abreast of developments; reading; awareness; lessons from everywhere (see Box 17.11).
- **Expertise**: establishing targets and priorities; planning; organizing; motivating; measuring performance; communication; integration; accepting responsibility, authority and accountability.
- **Technological proficiency**: understanding the capacity of technology; understanding its use, value and application; maximizing and optimizing output; scheduling maintenance; developing expertise in its usage; supporting those who use it.

It is important to understand that all of this can be developed – and this includes the behavioural qualities of integrity, respect and value. This is of especial importance to those who have been in organizations for a long time where these qualities are not apparent.

Otherwise, the concern for all managers is to be able to take an enlightened and responsible view of each of these, and to identify their own strengths and weaknesses. Both require building on strengths in order to become expert; the weaknesses in order to become at least proficient.

Sources of expertise

Organizations need to take a strategic or collective view of their own pool of managerial expertise for the same reasons. Managerial audits (needs analyses and appraisal)

Box 17.11: Knowledge and understanding

A key feature of management knowledge is a full understanding of the environment in which managerial work takes place. For example:

- it is not necessary for managers to be able to type, file or make bookings if they have secretaries to do this. However, they must understand the pressures, constraints and volumes of work that secretaries have to undertake in these areas;
- it is not necessary for hospital managers to be expert doctors, surgeons or nurses. However, they must have a full understanding of the organizational and operational pressures and constraints of the professional staff under their direction (failure to ensure that senior and middle NHS managers do indeed have this full understanding of clinical and nursing practice is a major cause of NHS underperformance at the beginning of the twenty-first century).

There may also be cultural pressures that have to be accommodated. For example, many sales executives need, behaviourally and culturally, to work for someone who already has a proven track record as a sales executive. The view is therefore taken that the best sales executives should be promoted into the managerial position. This must be accompanied by thorough and rigorous management training if the move is to be effective from everybody's point of view.

identify areas of overall strength and weakness. A view can then be formed of what should be developed internally, and what needs to be brought in from outside (see Box 17.12).

Buying in expertise is of greatest value when directors and senior managers come to a strategic and supportable view that the development of management now requires fresh talent and expertise; and that this will give those presently in the organization a positive and effective surge of energy. If this conclusion is genuinely arrived at, it must be publicly stated. The justification is then clear to all and the reasons understandable – even if there is some short-term disgruntlement and turnover.

Developing expertise in-house demonstrates commitment to existing staff and their capabilities, determination and motivation. This should never be ignored or forgotten whatever the need for fresh talent and impetus. Most people understand this once it is explained to them provided that it is clear that their own value and worth is being recognized also (see Box 17.13).

Box 17.12: Grow your own or buy in?

To develop your own staff or to engage fresh talent from external sources is another issue on which easy or universal answers are sought – and for which no rules exist. The principle is a balance of giving every possible opportunity to develop and enhance existing expertise, with the need for fresh blood, ideas and talents coming in from outside to prevent introversion.

There are problems with each. Too much emphasis on internal development leaves organizations vulnerable to the inability to accept ideas from elsewhere. Known or perceived over-emphasis on buying in from outside leads to feelings of frustration on the part of those who believe, rightly or wrongly, that they should be given their chance.

Box 17.13: 'Never be afraid to apply'

When she was appointed CEO of Sandals Inc., Elaine Vaughan was asked what particular qualities she thought she had brought to the job. After all, she had no managerial qualifications, nor had she been to university.

However, since the age of 16, she had worked in and around the travel industry; and she had used this opportunity to learn everything that there was to know about how it worked, what was profitable, what customers and clients sought. For a time, she had run her own ticketing agency, selling last-minute cut-price deals to long-haul air travellers. She had then joined Sandals as a senior secretary, working especially for the chief executive and marketing and sales directors.

There had then been a sudden turnover of top management staff. The marketing director had left, quickly followed by the sales director and then the CEO. So, as she was organizing the interviews for possible replacements with the company chairman, she suddenly spoke up and said: 'Please may I have a go?'

She and the chairman sat down. They discussed the position, and the knowledge, skills and expertise that would be required to drive the company forward for the foreseeable future. In the end the chairman recognized that she was indeed a strong candidate. The company formally interviewed Elaine and one other candidate before offering her the position which she accepted.

Supporting her appointment, the chairman went on to state in detail that the range of expertise, knowledge, understanding, attention to detail, market and operating awareness all made her an eminently suitable candidate. Indeed, the only sticking point was the fact that she had never held a top or senior position before. On that basis, both the chairman and also Elaine were of one view: 'Never be afraid to apply. If you think you can do the job, make this clear and back your own judgement.'

Management qualifications

As yet, there exists no statutory minimum management qualification. This does not prevent an ever-increasing number of organizations and those who aspire to managerial positions from undertaking a wide variety of nationally recognized qualifications as follows.

- HND/C and undergraduate business studies courses; and an increasing number of more traditional courses with a business or management element (e.g. civil engineering with management; construction management; information management).
- NEBSM/CMS and foundation courses in professional practice: similar in coverage to much that is taught in universities and colleges of higher and further education though the approach is certain to differ. This is because such courses are normally pitched at those (with and without previously acquired academic or vocational qualifications) who already have several years' work experience. People take these courses as the result of their own drives and ambitions, those of the organization, or as one result of performance appraisal and needs analysis.
- DMS and diploma courses in professional and occupational expertise: these courses are invariably pitched at either those who have done a foundation course as above; or at those in professional occupations (e.g. marketing, technology, teaching, nursing) who now wish to enhance their professional employability or (with DMS) look for opportunities to go into management.
- Undergraduate programmes in business and management: either 'pure', or else related to other disciplines at the same level (e.g. French with management, information management and business).
- MBA and other Masters/postgraduate level qualifications: normally offered to those who already have substantial occupational experience, at least a diploma, and preferably undergraduate qualifications also. Best value is served by those wishing to acquire a substantial body of organizational, economic, behavioural, functional and environmental knowledge as a precursor to advancement into senior positions.
- Doctorate: attained by those with a combination of high-quality managerial experience and substantial academic achievement, as the result of extensive research and write-up of a major problem or issue.

- The vocational qualification route: those who prefer may undertake management development by attaining a set of work-based competencies and having these accredited through the production of a written portfolio of experience, evidence and workplace testing and observation.

The process of gaining formal qualifications and having expertise and achievement credited and recognized serves as:

- an accepted and understood level of achievement;
- a behavioural and perceptual benchmark of progress and opportunity;
- a springboard for the next step;
- a measure of value, respect and worth.

Additionally, all management qualifications are now available on open, distance and flexible bases as well as traditional teaching, so that they are much more open to everyone than in the past. They can also be much more closely harmonized with organization and collective development, as well as individual enhancement. Many of these (especially certificate, diploma and Masters) bring project and secondment opportunities with them (see Box 17.14).

Organizational and environmental expertise

Managerial expertise, whether supported by qualifications or not, is required by all organizations whatever their size, location, sector or remit. A key management development problem remains ensuring that this expertise is used successfully and effectively in any given set of circumstances. Those who have managerial expertise therefore require environmental knowledge, understanding and capability as much as those who have worked in the particular situation for years who nevertheless still need to develop managerial capability (see Figure 17.3).

Fully effective performance is only possible in the shaded area. If there is a high level of both managerial and environmental expertise, there is a sound basis and high expectation of effective performance. If there is a low level of either, this means that:

- those with managerial expertise have no knowledge or understanding of how it should be applied in the particular organization, environment or situation;
- those with environmental expertise have no knowledge or understanding of what it takes to manage activities (though they will clearly understand how to carry them out, and what the pressures and constraints are).

Whichever the gap, those involved are much more likely to be successful if they are:

- prepared to learn and be receptive;
- supported by their organization;
- open to suggestions and ideas from elsewhere rather than only being prepared to stick to what they know (see Box 17.15);
- prepared to modify their own preconceptions and, where necessary, change their own attitudes and behaviour.

Box 17.14: The technology and management initiative

In 2004, faced with a shortage of those with genuine technology expertise (as well as managerial knowledge and understanding), a consortium of the UK's leading employers got together in order to lobby the government about this matter.

The result was that the UK Learning and Skills Council established a body known as E-Skills UK. This body would be responsible for coordinating and driving the integration of technology education with business and management proficiency. The result was a number of initiatives as follows:

- The opening of a venture called 'Computer clubs for girls', to address the fact that girls and young women were not going into technology-oriented careers. This was so successful that the venture was changed to 'Computer clubs for everyone' in 2010.
- The development of a range of undergraduate education under the heading of 'Information technology management for business'. Adopted by many of the UK's universities, this venture sought to work closely with industry in the development of a substantial and high-quality teaching and learning programme, whose graduates would find themselves very quickly in responsible positions in companies and organizations.
- A revision of the 14–19 age range provision in business management and technology, including general improvements to business and technology curricula, and the creation of a series of Diploma programmes to address the problems.

The purpose here was to ensure that the vocational, pre-professional and professional qualifications were both delivered to the highest possible standards of academic excellence, and additionally related to the crucial corporate aspect of practicability and application. This in turn reinforces the assertion that expert management practice, and the skills and expertise demanded as a consequence, can be taught and learned.

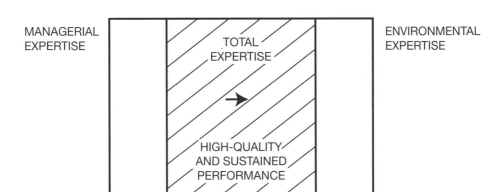

Figure 17.3 The environmental–managerial expertise mix

Box 17.15: Managerial openness

A survey conducted of managerial attitudes found that:

- 76 per cent of managers surveyed believed themselves open, approachable and sympathetic to ideas and suggestions from elsewhere;
- 74 per cent of the staff of managers surveyed stated that their managers were aloof, inaccessible and unreceptive to ideas and suggestions from elsewhere.

Clearly, there is some overlap! The core problem arises from ensuring that attention to managerial or environmental learning and development has a high priority both while it is being achieved and also afterwards. Those in the situation require a mechanism which automatically asks the question *why* when rejection or a blinkered view is being offered. Another survey found that 90 per cent of managers and supervisors who adopted an adversarial, aggressive, confrontational or absentee management style did so either because it was how they had been treated themselves in junior positions; or because it was perceived or understood that this was the way to behave; or because they perceived or understood that this was the style to adopt if they wished to make further progress.

Source: C.B. Handy (1995) *Understanding Organizations* – Penguin.

Core managerial expertise can then be applied to the particular organization, situation and environment as follows.

- Developing this expertise in ways acceptable and applicable to those working in the environment and the pressures and constraints present.
- Developing behaviour, attitudes and values in ways which contribute to the positive development of the organizational and operating culture.
- Developing a state of visibility and access that promotes mutual confidence without being intrusive.
- Builds on past positive experiences that professional, functional and operational staff have had with managers and supervisors.
- Rescuing past negative experiences that professional, functional and operational staff have had with managers.
- Maximizing the opportunities for staff, production and service development that arise as a result.

Management development and product and service enhancement

The contribution of management development to product and service enhancement arises only as the result of understanding the nature of the working environment and the products and services delivered. The contribution then becomes:

- identifying, addressing and removing barriers to effective product and service performance;
- gaining staff commitment to new approaches through demonstrating the benefits and addressing any problems or issues inherent;
- consulting with a view to gaining active involvement and participation;
- addressing key staff priorities including pressures of work, periods of overload and under-load;
- ensuring that the jobs that nobody wants to do are either subcontracted are else shared around equally;
- setting and reinforcing absolute standards of behaviour and performance that apply to everyone regardless of profession, status, occupation, length of service or hours of work; and developing problem-solving capability and routes of access for staff so that when these issues occur, they are raised, dealt with and nipped in the bud (see Box 17.16).

This part of management development is therefore concerned with creating the conditions in which effective and sustainable high-quality product and service delivery are possible. In directly operational and functional matters, effective development is concerned with knowing the jobs, tasks and outputs required, observing and analysing them to ensure that the present effective steady-state is maintained and to see where improvements can be made. These can then be discussed with the staff concerned and either implemented if truly practicable, or else killed off if those carrying out the activities come up with overwhelming operational reasons as to why they are bad ideas.

Management development must be concerned with understanding and improving customer, supplier and community relations. This involves creating the conditions in which all contacts with each of these groups are dealt with as a priority, and addressing specific issues, especially complaints, from the point of view of finding out what truly

---

Box 17.16: 'I must be seen to be impartial'

In the overwhelming majority of cases, managers who use the phrase 'I must be seen to be impartial' when confronted with serious behavioural problems are understood to be avoiding the issue. Overtly, the word 'impartial' implies 'fair' or 'equitable'. The whole phrase implies: 'I would love to help but I cannot.' In practice, therefore, this means that the issue will not be confronted.

If an employee makes an allegation about a colleague, the manager must develop a format that allows the employee to state their case and the alleged offender to respond on a basis of fairness and equality. This must be conducted face-to-face with each.

Once the two sides are heard, then the required action becomes apparent. Above all, if malicious and false allegations are being made, these are dealt with severely and may lead to disciplinary action or dismissal if proven.

Dealing with anything raised quickly in this way normally means that such incidents are kept to a minimum. Where it is known or believed that the manager 'must be seen to be impartial', there are widely held perceptions that nothing will be done.

went wrong and why, and putting them right in ways that satisfy those who first raised them. If staffing or internal issues then become apparent they can be addressed separately.

Management development must be concerned with the operational details of the particular domain. This means knowing and understanding the following.

- **Tasks, occupations and work**: required and desired outputs, and the expertise and conditions necessary for these to be achieved; problem areas and blockages, and what causes these; deadlines and priorities.
- **Technology**: the influence of this on work patterns and behaviour (especially alienation); the consequences of breakdown or inability to recruit the required expertise.
- **Information**: availability and accessibility; quality, volume and value; contribution of information availability to effective, positive and productive decision-making and activities.
- **Organization**: formal structures and reporting relationships; cultural and behavioural issues that these may raise; the nature and expectations of those present (see Box 17.17).
- **Primary activities**: establishing aims, objectives and priorities; coordinating activities; integrating staff; communication and decision-making processes; planning for the present and future.

Box 17.17: Towards flexible and open organizations: MMRC

MMRC was a small but highly expert and profitable London advertising agency. It employed fifty staff on strictly traditional lines and reporting relationships. Everyone had clear job descriptions. From the most positive point of view, it was a role culture.

The company was taken over by a large firm, JWT. The new owners immediately destroyed the prevailing structure, culture and reporting relations. They brought in open-plan accommodation, hot-desking and fully portable technology and a flat operating structure.

Within six months all of the fifty MMRC staff had left. The senior partner at JWT commissioned a firm of consultants to contact the former staff and find out why. The key reasons given were as follows.

- The role culture had grown up over many years and was orderly and familiar. People had expectations and knew what could be achieved, and under what circumstances.
- The role culture was destroyed, and the hot-desking introduced, without consultation, and by people who were self-evidently working to a prescription rather than with genuine understanding.
- Existing staff were given no idea of what was expected of them. It was clear to them that the new owners did not understand *how* the work was carried out, or the constraints and opportunities of the existing ways of working, technology or structure and culture.

- **Key factors**: motivating staff; addressing individual and group needs, including development needs; knowing and understanding when and where to go for help when required; accepting and using power, influence, responsibility, authority and accountability; understanding the priorities, demands and constraints of the particular situation.

Self-development

The increasing professionalization of management requires that those in these positions take an active and personal commitment to their own development. The rewards for expert managers are now extremely high. In return for these, it is increasingly necessary to demonstrate and be able to engage genuine capability in the areas of leadership; decision-making; strategic awareness and strategy design; market knowledge; organizational behaviour; and understanding people. The conflicting and divergent interests of organization stakeholders have to be balanced and accommodated. High and increasing value products and services must be delivered to ever more demanding customer and client groups. Self-development therefore requires a commitment to:

- read widely about all organizations, industries and sectors, to learn from their managerial practice and approaches;
- meet with other managers at cluster groups and professional body gatherings;
- engage in continuous professional development and enhancement activities, whether at the behest of professional bodies, or self-directed;
- search constantly for areas where both individual management practice and also organization capability and output can be improved.

Of particular value are 'back to the floor' and 'action learning' approaches. More generally, managers must be prepared to go into other organizations at any time with a view to picking up ideas. They must be willing to try things out against their own self-generated and preset criteria. Some ideas and initiatives will succeed – others will fail or fall short of full success. So long as there was a genuine pre-evaluation of what was intended, failure and success can both be used as part of the learning process. This approach also tends towards instilling attitudes of self-development in the rest of the staff.

Succession and transformation

The role of management development in succession and transformation is:

- to ensure that there is a steady flow of ever-improving expertise and quality available to organizations to secure a future;
- to identify potential capability and motivation in existing staff and to develop it for the present and future;
- to recognize succession in its broadest terms.

This means addressing it from the point of view of:

- having a fund of staff to promote when required;
- having a fund of expertise and understanding as the organization goes through its own succession and transformation from one set of occupations, activities, markets,

products and services to the next, including the ways in which these are delivered as well as what is delivered;

- taking a broader view of succession and transformation so that expertise and commitment are both available should they be required;
- looking for derived opportunities, especially those that present themselves as the result of following one path of activities.

Traditionally, succession simply meant training the next generation of staff for supervisory, managerial and senior functional positions. Now it is essential that this includes attention to attitudes and behaviour so that qualities of positiveness, flexibility and willingness are instilled and developed. Clear lines of progression through hierarchical organization structures are much less prevalent and subject to restructuring in any case. However, succession opportunities are, in practice, at least as widely available in terms of:

- rotation and progression through departments, divisions, functions, locations, projects and centres of activities;
- moving into a new job and being given the space, opportunity, resources and support to develop it in new ways;
- identifying potential in existing situations and ranges of activity.

Succession, therefore, becomes broadened into progression and transformation. It is dependent on a positive view of the opportunities presently available, as well as those apparent for the future. Organizations that reflect and encourage this approach are certain to get much more out of their staff so long as they commit themselves to offering enhanced salaries and other rewards (which were always the key drives of those on structured promotion paths).

Conclusions

Effective organization and management development depend on organizations recognizing the enhanced contribution and value that expert managerial staff deliver, as well as the derived benefits of generating motivation, commitment and capability in present occupations. It is fully dependent also on attending to the full range of behaviour, attitudes, skills, knowledge, expertise and technological proficiency, and respecting personal, professional and occupational, as well as organizational, drives.

Effective organization and management development has a knock-on effect on attitudes to training across the rest of the organization. Professional, occupational, technological and 'unskilled' staff are much more likely to be given opportunities if these are available to those for whom they work. This enhances collective, group and organization development.

Highly developed and expert managers and staff are also much more likely to understand and value the importance of induction, core programmes and initial job training. As stated below (see Chapter 19) these make major contributions to establishing the required levels of attitudes and behaviour, as well as performance, at the outset, and in subsequently reinforcing these. Conducted effectively, management development is therefore all-pervasive, making a positive contribution to every aspect of performance.

18 Organization structure and design

Introduction

Organization structures reflect the aims and objectives, the size and complexity of the undertaking, the nature of the expertise to be used, the preferred management and supervisory style and the means of coordination and control. Whatever arises as the result must be flexible, dynamic and responsive to market and environment conditions and pressures. It must provide effective and suitable channels of communication and decision-making processes; and provide also for the creation of professional and productive relationships between individuals and groups. Departments, divisions and functions are created as required to pursue aims and objectives, together with the means and methods by which they are coordinated and harmonized.

Structure also creates a combination of permanence and order. This is required to provide continuity for the organization itself, and to generate the required levels of confidence and expectation in customers. It is also necessary to provide staff with (as far as possible) a settled and orderly working life; and so means must be found. Means must also be found of ensuring the permanence and continuity of the organization itself as people join or leave.

The need for continuity is especially important for the following reasons:

- suppliers expect clear points of reference for any enquiries that they need to make in their transactions, and these need to be steady and assured, as staff come and go;
- customers expect clear points of reference in any dealings with the organization; especially, they expect to be able to make complaints and get speedy and effective responses. No customer wishes to be told: 'I am sorry, we cannot deal with your issue; this is because individual x has left'; they need and expect satisfaction whoever happens to be in the particular position;
- backers expect that the fundamental integrity and effectiveness of the organization will continue, whoever is in charge, and whichever individuals hold particular positions of responsibility, or carry out particular duties and operations.

Purpose

Organizations are designed and structured in order to:

- ensure efficiency and effectiveness of activities in accordance with the organization's stated targets;

- divide and allocate work, responsibility and authority;
- establish working relationships and operating mechanisms;
- establish patterns of management and supervision;
- establish the means by which work is to be controlled;
- establish the means of retaining experience, knowledge and expertise;
- indicate areas of responsibility, authority and accountability;
- meet the expectations of those involved;
- provide the basis of a fair and equitable reward system.

Organizations therefore need functional and operational divisions. However, the means by which these functions and divisions are made effective depends on the nature of relationships within the organization. Structure is therefore a system of relationships, as well as a one-dimensional presentation on an organization chart.

General factors

The general factors affecting organization structure are as follows:

- The nature of work to be carried out and the implications of this – unit, batch, mass and flow scales of production and service delivery. Each brings clear indications of the types of organization required as do the commercial and public service equivalents; job definitions, volumes of production, storage of components, raw materials and finished goods; the means of distribution – both inwards and outwards; the type of support functions and control mechanisms.
- Technology and equipment; the expertise, premises and environment needed to use it effectively; its maintenance; its useful life cycle; its replacement and the effect of new equipment on existing structures and work methods.
- The desired culture and style of the organization and all that this means – it affects the general approach to organization management; nature and spans of control; the attitudes and values that are established; reporting relationships between superiors and subordinates and across functions; staff relationships.
- The location of the organization; its relationships with its local communities; any strong local traditions – for example, of unionization (or not); particular ways of working; specific activities, skills and expertise.
- The size and diversity of the organization, including the nature of activities and operations at different locations, and the extent to which work structures, technology and operational priorities vary.
- Aims and objectives strategy; flexibility, dynamism, responsiveness, or rigidity and conformity in relation to staff, customers and the community; customer and supplier relations; stakeholder relations.

Organization structure has therefore to be capable of a combination of:

- providing order, certainty and points of reference for all stakeholders;
- accommodating production, service and information technology, and delivering the products and services demanded by customers and clients;
- providing the basis for every aspect of organizational relationships.

Additionally, it is comforting for people to know that they work in a 'structure'. People know, believe and perceive that the 'structure' provides the foundation of the organization's enduring effectiveness and success. It provides comfort and assurance in the form of steady-state and assured patterns of work; pay and rewards; and a long-term basis for prosperity and advancement (see Box 18.1).

Structural forms

People like to see structural forms and this is because organization structures give an impression of permanence and certainty. The key structural forms are:

* organization charts;
* the building in which they work.

In terms of organization charts, people like to be able to identify their position in relation to everyone else in the organization. An organization chart gives a clear impression and perception of seniority, power and influence, authority, responsibility and accountability. Organization charts indicate career paths. Organization charts additionally identify individuals in particular positions; and these become points of contact. People in different positions also become points of reference; for example, a marketing executive who aspires to be marketing director can look at the capabilities,

---

Box 18.1: Restructuring

In recent years, many organizations have gone through extensive restructuring programmes. These programmes have turned out to be traumatic in many instances, both for the organization as a whole, and also for specific groups of staff and individuals.

The reason for this is because the illusion of permanence and order is challenged. What was hitherto assured and comfortable is no longer to exist.

When restructuring is to occur, this ought to provide the starting point for those responsible. If one key barrier for the effective management of change is the shift from certainty to uncertainty (see Chapter 3), then from the point of view of changing structure, the 'new order' has to be presented in terms that people can understand. They can then begin to get used to the idea, and begin to envisage themselves in the new structure. They can also begin to see where new opportunities are likely to come from; and also, if it is the case, any consequences or negative aspects of the new structure.

In particular, this last point is a key issue. In many cases, organizations and their top and senior managers are unwilling to make clear the new order and structure; and this is because they fear a backlash from their staff. In particular, they worry that good staff will leave; and that they will be left with bad staff.

In practice, this is a wrong attitude and approach. It is essential that everyone knows and understands where they are to slot into the new order. And while it is a comfortable position to hold, that good staff will leave if they do know what is to happen, in practice of course, good staff leave whenever they see opportunities outside, whatever the state of the present structure or order.

Box 18.2: The top floor

Many organizations locate their top and senior management on the top floor of their premises. The rationale for this is that, by being away from the hurly-burly of daily activity, top and senior managers and executives are able to think, plan and execute decisions effectively, without having to face the stress of everything else that is going on.

In practice, this works effectively in many cases. However, there is also a tendency to detachment – the physical removal from what is going on tends to lead to perceptions that 'all is well' unless notified differently.

Elsewhere, other top and senior managers take the opposing view: that they should be located among their staff, so as to avoid any prospect of detachment, and so as to be able to identify problems and issues immediately these arise.

In practice, this does not always work perfectly either. Staff feel themselves constrained and inhibited by the presence of the top or senior manager.

The key lesson is therefore that no structure or location is an end in itself. Whatever the organization chart, whatever the physical location of particular persons, management practice has to be suitable to the overall purpose demanded.

qualities, experience and qualifications of the person presently in that post, and so set out to gain the equivalent as they pursue their ambitions.

In terms of buildings, there are perceptions and implications of power, influence, authority and status, as well as expertise, when specific individuals are related to the positions that they hold, and the location from which they work. In some cases, therefore, seeking a position that requires a specific location additionally becomes important. Or, conversely, people who suddenly find themselves in a particular location may try to use this fact as a stepping stone to greater opportunities (see Box 18.2).

Tall structures

Tall structures mean that there are many different levels or ranks within the total. There is a long hierarchical and psychological distance between top and bottom. Tall structures bring with them complex reporting relationships, operating and support systems, and promotion and career paths, and differentiated job titles. Spans of control (see Figures 18.1 and 18.2) tend to be small. The proportion of staff with some form of supervisory responsibility tends to be high in relation to the whole organization.

Tall structures are attractive especially to individuals trying to identify a career path. An organization with many levels of hierarchy gives the overwhelming perception that people can work their way through the hierarchy, and so arrive at top and senior positions.

However, a major problem with tall structures is the tendency for communications barriers and blockages to exist. Unless the communication systems and networks transcend the compartmentalization, anything that is required to go through several different levels of hierarchy is likely to get delayed at least, if not blocked or lost altogether. Those responsible for the direction and operation of tall structures must know

1. Simple

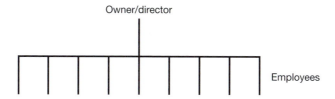

2. Line and staff

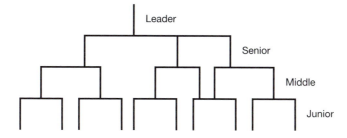

3. Functional

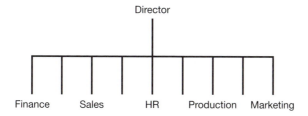

4. Divisional

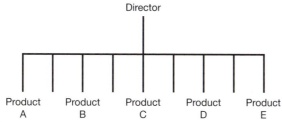

5. Dispersed

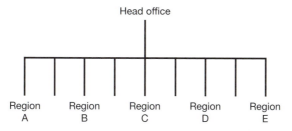

Figure 18.1 Organization structures

and understand this as a more or less universal fact of organizational life, and ensure that management and supervisory style and practice can, and does, get over this problem.

Flat structures

Flat structures mean that there are few different levels or ranks within the total. Jobs tend to be concentrated at lower levels. There is a short hierarchical distance between top and bottom; this may reduce the psychological distance or it may not. Lower-level jobs often carry responsibilities of quality control, volume and deadline targets. Spans of control tend to be large. The proportion of staff with some form of supervisory

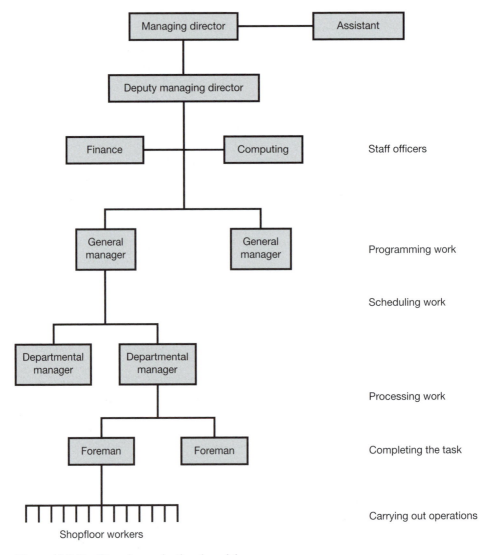

Figure 18.2 Traditional organizational model

responsibility (other than for their own work) tends to be small in relation to the whole organization. Career paths by promotion are limited; but this may be replaced by the opportunity for functional and expertise development, and the involvement in a variety of different projects. Reward structures may not be as apparent as those offered alongside progress through a tall hierarchy. Reporting relationships tend to be simpler and more direct. There is a reduced likelihood of distortion and barriers to communications in a flat structure than in a tall one simply because there are fewer channels for messages to pass through.

Centralization and decentralization

Centralized structures

Centralization is generally an authority relationship between those in overall control of the organization and the rest of its staff. The tighter the control exerted at the centre, the greater the degree of centralization. An organization may therefore operate in a wide range of activities and locations, the majority of the staff may work away from these locations and the majority of work carried out in them also; however, top management may still retain tight control over the ways in which activities are conducted.

The great advantage of centralization is that top management remain fully aware of the operational, as well as strategic, issues and concerns. However, this has to be an active awareness; it is no use simply insisting that all decisions are taken at the centre, without reference to what is actually going on in the operating environment. Organizations that operate centralized structures have therefore to ensure that all managers, including top and senior executives, get out among the staff, operations and activities as often as possible, so that they fully know and understand what it is that they are taking decisions upon.

Conversely, the great disadvantage is that decisions do get taken out of context. Managers who do not get out and about when working in a centralized structure have therefore to take decisions on the basis of their own best guesses or perceptions, or related to how the situation was the last time they did go out and see for themselves. Additionally, managers who do not go out and see for themselves can find themselves placed in precarious positions when particular contextual, environmental or operational factors become apparent (see Box 18.3).

Decentralization

The converse is to delegate or decentralize. The role and function of the centre is therefore to maintain a watching brief, to monitor and evaluate progress and to concern itself with strategic rather than operational issues. The operations themselves are designed and allocated in accordance with overall aims and objectives, and the departments, divisions and functions given the necessary resources and authority to achieve them.

The advantages of decentralization are:

- the speeding up of operational decisions enabling these to be taken at the point at which they are required, rather than having to refer every matter (or a high proportion) back to head office;

Box 18.3: Peter Walker

Peter Walker was a sales representative for a fertilizer company. He had a large country patch; and working from home, he sold fertilizer products directly to farmers, horticulturalists and garden centres. The company had also developed a range of retail garden and fertilizer products, and these Peter Walker sold to retail chains such as Homebase and the larger supermarket branches.

Peter Walker's results were always good. He was largely left to operate on his own, calling in at head office only three or four times a year. His figures were among the best in the sales team. However, the sales manager never came out to see him, or to go with him on visits.

After working for several years in this way, the sales director changed. The sales director now insisted that all sales managers went out with their representatives, to see how they did the job, as well as what they did. The sales director then announced that he would be accompanying representatives on visits; and one of the first representatives he chose was Peter Walker.

Initially, they had some difficulty fixing up a time to meet. This was because it became clear that Peter had 'other commitments' – taking his children to the dentist; collecting his wife from her university course; visiting his father (which he always did once a week). Finally, the sales director set out of his own accord, with the view to meeting Peter at a Homebase branch where he was making a visit.

The sales director turned up at the Homebase branch; however, Peter was not there. In the end the sales director called Peter on his mobile, only to find that he was in fact at home mowing the lawn. When he asked Peter for an explanation, the reply was: 'Oh, I have known this shop for years. I managed to do everything with a quick phone call. They have agreed to take an increased range of our goods. And so – here I am at home!'

The sales director turned up at Peter's home shortly afterwards and proceeded to berate him for his conduct, behaviour and performance. Peter calmly replied: 'My figures are excellent. I have always worked this way. All my clients are now taking more products from the company this year than last. So, I do not see what the problem is.'

The key lesson is that centralized structures do allow individuals to operate in their own ways in circumstances such as these. The key problem is that all staff have nevertheless to be managed and supervised, whatever the context of operations and activities. As stated above, it is essential that managers working in centralized structures do get out and see things for themselves; however, where this has changed from a position of remoteness to a position of involvement, the process has to be managed also. In this particular case, the sales director needed to have briefed Peter Walker on exactly what he expected to see; and the discussion then could have gone on to how to do the job, as well as what to do.

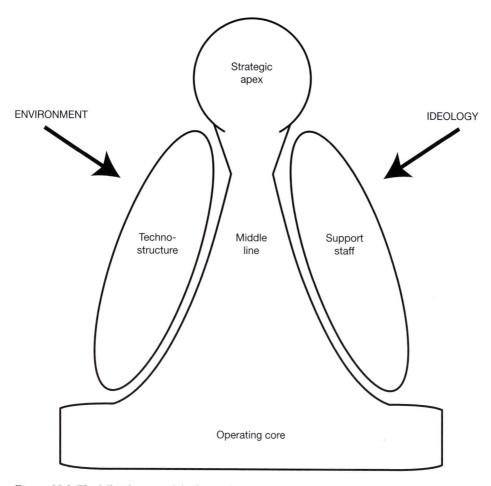

Figure 18.3 The Mintzberg model of organizations

- it enables local management to respond to local conditions and demands, and to build up a local reputation for the overall organization;
- it contributes to organization and staff development through ensuring that problems and issues are dealt with at the point at which they arise. This helps and enables organizations to identify and develop potential for the future;
- by the same token it also contributes to staff motivation and morale. The exercising of responsibility and authority, and the opportunities for development are more likely to filter through to all staff levels in a decentralized organization;
- it enables organizations to get their structures and systems right. Reporting relationships between functions and the centre still have to be designed for effectiveness; activities have to be planned and coordinated;
- consistency of treatment for both staff and customers has to be ensured across all functions and locations. However great the level of autonomy afforded to departments, divisions and functions also, they have still to be contributing to the greater good of the whole organization; they are not personal or professional fiefdoms;

- it encourages organizations to continually assess the well of its talent, its strength and depth. This is, above all, at managerial and supervisory levels; the greater the decentralization, the more likely this is to be important at all levels. It is also essential in the identification and development of professional and other forms of expertise.

The role and function of head office

Head offices in all but the simplest structures have the responsibility for planning, coordinating and controlling the functions of the rest of the organization; of translating strategy into operations; and of monitoring, reviewing and evaluating performance from all points of view – volume, quality, standards and satisfaction.

Whether a relative centralized or decentralized form of organization is adopted, it is essential never to lose sight of this key range of activities. The problem lies in how they should be carried out and not in what should be done.

In large, complex and sophisticated organizations – public, private and multinational – the head office is likely to be physically distant from the main areas of operations and this brings problems of communications systems and reporting relationships. Equally important, however, is the problem of psychological distance and remoteness. This occurs when the head office itself becomes a complex and sophisticated entity. This often leads to conflict between personal and organizational objectives, in-fighting and concentrations of resources on head office functions rather than operational effectiveness. This is exacerbated when jobs at head office are, or are perceived to be, better careers and more likely to lead to personal opportunities than those in the field. In many cases, the head office becomes so remote that it loses any understanding of the reality of activities. Cocooned by the resources that it commands for its own functions, it tries to preserve the illusion of excellence and dynamism often in the face of overwhelming evidence to the contrary (see Box 18.4).

Holding companies

Holding companies are dealt with here as they are a form of combination of centralization and decentralization.

Normally, overall policies, standards of conduct and expectations of performance are set by the holding company centrally. The actual delivery of conduct, behaviour and performance is then decentralized to local and regional chief executives (see Figure 18.4).

It is also the case that some of the companies held may themselves become assets, to be sold off when market conditions dictate. When this is being considered, it is essential to recognize why the company was bought in the first place, and what circumstances have now changed which make it a worthwhile sale.

Holding company structures work best in general when there are clear connections between all of the companies. These connections may be:

- cross-subsidy, meaning that any company that is going through a lean time can be supported by those that are doing well;
- branding, so that whatever is produced or delivered by the individual companies is capable of carrying the overall company logo, brand or identity;

Box 18.4: Head Office as cost

As stated above, for operational reasons, many organizations continue to need large and sophisticated head offices.

Whatever the nature of the organization, its size or complexity, it is essential to view head office as a cost. It is true that in some cases, this cost can be offset by a combination of:

- location, especially where it is located in an important or prestigious place, or close to suppliers, collaborators and others with whom it does business;
- presentation, especially where the appearance of head office can be used in marketing and other activities.

However, this cost has to be managed. A recent survey of the National Westminster building in Bishopsgate, London, UK, found that on any given occasion it was up to three quarters empty. In pure operational terms, therefore, the company was paying four times the going rate for head office functions to be carried out.

Clearly, matters are not as simple as this. However, it is essential to know and understand the full extent of the costs that have to be borne.

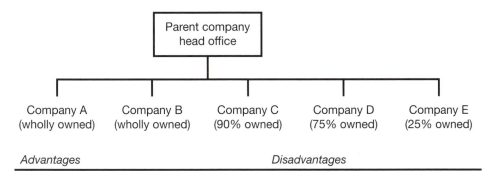

Advantages	Disadvantages
• Low central overheads • Offsetting of individual business losses • Availability of cheaper finance for individual businesses • Spreading of risk for holding company • Ease of divestment for holding company • Facilitates decentralization	• Risk for individual business of divestment by holding company • Unavailability of skills at group level to assist individual businesses • Lack of synergy • Difficulties of centralized control

Figure 18.4 Holding company structure

- points in the supply and distribution chain, whereby, for example, companies buy up key suppliers of raw materials, technology and information, and/or buy up retail distribution and transport companies.

The holding company structure is therefore expected to provide collective strength to all of the companies involved, as well as the autonomy for the individual companies to act as they see fit in the delivery of their specific products, services and responsibilities.

Spans of control

'Spans of control' refers to the number of subordinates who report directly to a single superior, and for whose work that person is responsible.

Spans of control are defined in a broad to narrow spectrum. The narrower the span, the greater the number of supervisors required by the organization in total. A workforce of forty, with spans of control of four (one supervisor per four staff), needs ten supervisors. The same workforce with a span of control of ten only needs four supervisors. If the principle is then developed as a hierarchy, it can be seen that, in the first case, additional staff will be needed to supervise the supervisors (see Figure 18.5).

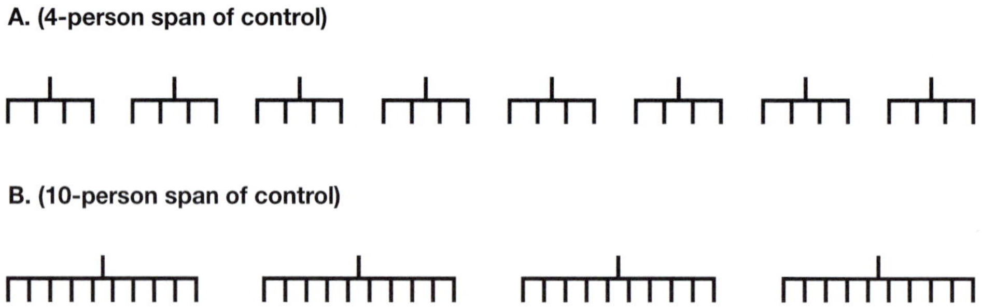

A. (4-person span of control)

B. (10-person span of control)

Figure 18.5 Spans of control: 1

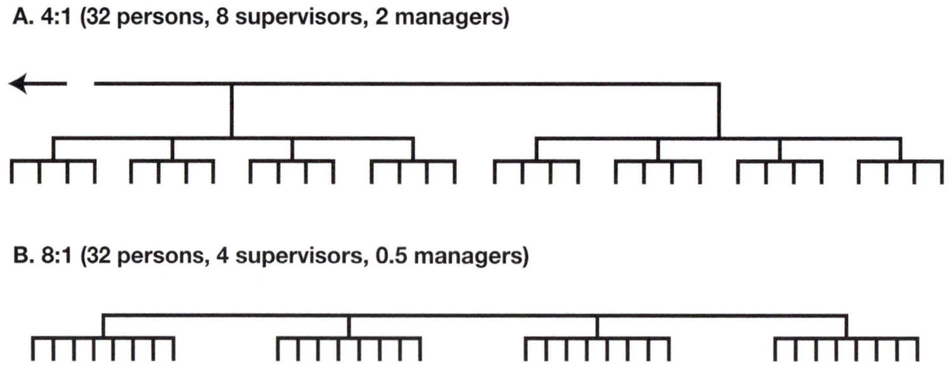

A. 4:1 (32 persons, 8 supervisors, 2 managers)

B. 8:1 (32 persons, 4 supervisors, 0.5 managers)

Figure 18.6 Spans of control: 2

If this principle is followed in larger organizations, layers of management and hierarchy can be removed by increasing spans of control. An organization of 4,000 staff would remove about 800 managers and supervisors by changing its spans of control from 4 to 1 to 8 to 1 (see Figure 18.6).

The matter does require additional consideration, however. Narrow spans of control normally mean a tighter cohesion and closure working relationship between supervisor and group. They also give greater promotion opportunities. There are more jobs, more levels and more ways of moving up through the organization, and this may be a driving force for those within it and one of their key expectations.

On the other hand, the complex structures thus created tend to act as barriers and blockages to communications – the greater the number of levels that messages have to pass through, the more likely they are to become distorted and corrupted.

On the face of it there is, therefore, a trade off between the effectiveness of the organization and the satisfaction of staff expectations through the availability of promotion channels. Assuming that the effectiveness of the organization is paramount, means are to be sought to enable expectations to be set and met in ways that contribute to this. The absolute effectiveness of the promotion channels is therefore to be measured in this way and, where necessary, different means of meeting staff expectations have to be found (see Box 18.5).

Structure and operational factors

As stated above, whatever the organization structure, it has to be capable of providing an effective basis and environment for successful operations to be carried out. It is therefore essential to pay attention to the following operational factors:

- the ability of management to produce results with spans of a certain size;
- the ability of the subordinates to produce results within these spans; in general, the greater the level of expertise held, the less direct supervision is required;
- the expectations of relative autonomy of the subordinates; for example, professional and highly trained staff expect to be left alone to carry out tasks as they see fit; while other types (for example, retail cashiers) need the ability to call on the supervisor whenever problems, such as difficulties with customers, arise;
- the expectations of the organization and the nature and degree of supervision necessary to meet these, or the ability of the staff concerned to meet these without close supervision;
- specific responsibilities of supervisors that are present in some situations, which give the supervisor a direct reason for being there other than to monitor the work that is being carried out. The most common examples are related to safety – for example, on construction sites and in oil refineries; and in shops and supermarkets to handle customers, queries and complaints;
- the nature of the work itself, the similarity or diversity of the tasks and functions, its simplicity or complexity;
- the location of the work, whether it is concentrated in one place or in several different parts of one building or site, or whether it is geographically diverse. Sub-spans are normally created where the location is diversified, even if ultimate responsibility remains with one individual and boundaries of autonomy are ascribed to one person and group in the particular location;

Box 18.5: Promotions and opportunities

It is essential that all organizations make clear the opportunities that are, and are not, available to their staff. Individuals joining organizations with the perceptions that they will be able to gain promotion through the ranks to management invariably become disappointed if, in practice, this is not the case.

It is also the case that, where such opportunities for promotion do not exist, intrinsic rewards have to be made available. Such rewards are as follows:

- the opportunity to move around between different departments, divisions, functions and locations;
- the opportunity to engage in project work;
- the opportunity for secondments;
- the opportunity to develop individual interests, as long as these coincide with those of the organization;
- the opportunity to earn increased levels of extrinsic rewards (i.e. pay, increments and enhancements) in order to meet the expectations that would otherwise be satisfied if there were a taller structure in place.

The advantage of clarifying promotion paths (and especially their limitations) is that it forces organizations to look at how they can reward effective staff without being able to offer progression. Part of this means offering adequate and increasing salaries as above. Part also concerns ensuring that the widest range of opportunities is identified, and made open to as many staff as possible.

It is additionally the case that organizations should make clear what they cannot offer. Some organizations tend to obfuscate or prevaricate on this; however, in practice staff quickly find out what their prospects are. Organizations that are frightened of losing key, expert and effective staff if they do tell the full truth therefore lose them anyway.

- the extent of necessity and ability to coordinate the work of each group with all the others in the organization; to coordinate and harmonize the work of the individuals in the group and to relate this again to the demands of the organization;
- the organization's own perspective – the extent to which it believes that close supervision, direct control and constant monitoring are necessary and desirable (see Box 18.6).

Hierarchies

Spans of control create hierarchies. These reflect the level, quality and expertise of those involved and also the degree of supervision and responsibility of those in particular positions. These are underpinned by job titles that indicate both levels of position held in hierarchy and also the nature and mix of expertise and responsibility.

Hierarchies are a familiar feature of all aspects of life. To turn a previous example around, if someone complains at the supermarket checkout and satisfaction is not

Box 18.6: Cost control

Many organizations that are disposed towards outsourcing such (apparently) peripheral functions as safety, security, catering and customer service do so from the point of view of controlling costs. The line of reasoning is that, instead of employing their own staff, a contract can be agreed with a specialist provider for a fixed fee, thus making this part of the organization's operations predictable and assured.

Cost control, however, is not an end in itself. When the contract provider arrives to open for business, whatever is done has to reflect the overall organization ethos and work ethic. No organization wants to have its reputation destroyed by any, or all, of the following:

- surly or rude safety and security staff;
- cleaners who do not do the job properly;
- customer service staff who have no feeling or affinity with the needs, wants and demands of the customers whom they are supposed to be serving.

So, on the one hand, one form of control is exerted. On the other, whenever an arrangement like this is entered into, other forms of control have to be conceded in return for paying a fixed fee.

forthcoming from the cashier, the person then asks to see the supervisor. If there is still no satisfaction then the manager will be called for; to be followed, if necessary, by a letter or approach to the chief executive. At each point therefore the approach is to the next person up the hierarchy in the hope/expectation that they will be able to resolve the matter in hand.

Hierarchies form the organizational basis of all but the smallest organizations. Commercial institutions have ranks and hierarchies, both to define occupations and also to define seniority. Public institutions have hierarchies for the ordering and management of services – national, military, civil and social – and also as points of reference for those who need to use them.

Hierarchies tend to be formed or to emerge in all organizations for these purposes, and because it is a familiar structural form. From an organizational behaviour point of view, it also acts as the means of separating and defining the activities of departments, divisions, groups, functions and individuals, so that they in turn can be coordinated for the purposes of efficient and effective working (see Box 18.7).

Mechanistic and organic structures

Burns and Stalker (1956) identified distinctive variations in the components of organization structure. These were affected by the nature of the work, the technology used, the rate and nature of change taking place, the stability or volatility of markets, and the nature and expertise of the staff. Their conclusion was that there were two distinctive forms of management system – mechanistic and organic.

Box 18.7: 'My position in the hierarchy'

Hierarchies act as points of reference for organizations and their suppliers, customers and clients as above. Hierarchies have the additional function of serving the human needs of the individuals who work in them. Individuals are therefore able to define themselves, and give a frame of reference, to everyone with whom they come into contact, through the use of their job title. For example:

- teacher (schools);
- lecturer (university);
- nurse (hospital);
- crew member (Disney);
- associate partner (Ernst & Young);
- pilot (airlines).

Each of the examples above, and indeed every job title, conveys a perception and impression to other people. Others then begin to understand what the job entails, and also the extent (or lack) of power, status, influence, authority and expertise.

This process is also important in role clarification. For example, Shirley Jones carries out all of the following roles:

- she is known as Dr Jones at the organization where she is director of research;
- she is also known as

  - Shirl or SJ at the hockey club for whom she plays at the weekends;
  - Shirley to her mother and father;
  - Ms Jones at the children's charity for whom she manages the accounts;
  - Mrs Jones at the school where her children are being educated;
  - Blinkey to her husband;
  - Jonesy to her staff at work when they talk about her behind her back.

In each of her roles, therefore, Shirley Jones has a very different position in the hierarchy in the particular set of circumstances; and the descriptions above illustrate the ways in which these vary.

Mechanistic systems

Mechanistic systems work as machines, and their effectiveness depends on steady and assured inputs of energy resources, raw materials and expertise (see Figure 18.7). Mechanistic systems are only capable of operation in the steady-state. Where re-positioning or redesign is required, this becomes traumatic, both to those involved, and also to the system itself.

Mechanistic systems have the following specific properties:

- Degree of specialization: very high with specialized divisions and differentiation of tasks based on precise job descriptions and pursued on an operational rather than strategic basis.

- Degree of standardization: very high with work methods prescribed and ordered.
- Orientation of members: operational, attention to means and processes.
- Conflict resolution: by the superior, and using procedures and channels.
- Obligations: precisely defined, written in to each role.
- Authority: based on hierarchy, reporting relationships, strictly delineated limitations; includes the setting of work standards and targets.
- Communication: also based on hierarchy; patterns and interactions tend to be vertical; the content of communications tends towards instructions, directions and orders.
- Loyalty: is to the organization, based on obedience to superiors.
- Status: from job title and the job held in the organization.

Organic systems

Organic systems have a much greater flexibility than mechanistic systems (see Figure 18.8). Organic systems are capable of development and modification. Organic systems are able to respond to changes in demands upon them much more easily. Organic systems have the following properties:

- Degree of specialization: low, little specialization, few boundaries and divisions, low differentiation, no restrictive practices, work pursued on task and strategic basis.

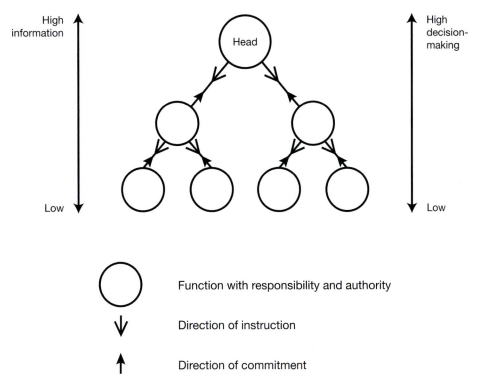

Figure 18.7 Organization structures: mechanistic
Source: Burns and Stalker (1956).

- Degree of standardization: low, individual, interactive.
- Orientation of members: towards aims and objectives, achievement, customer and personal satisfaction.
- Conflict resolution: through interaction, discussion and debate.
- Obligations: to task, output and satisfaction.
- Authority: based on expertise, networks, availability and accessibility.
- Communication: based on strategic and operational need rather than hierarchy; lateral as well as vertical; content is based on advice, information, illumination and enlightenment.
- Loyalty: to task and group as well as organization.
- Status: from personal contribution, results and achievements.

The key feature of any system is its capability to turn what is put into it into outputs that are valuable and desirable. Such outputs may be:

- products and services;
- waste and effluent;
- information presentations;
- bureaucracy management (see below).

The more mechanized a system is, and the greater the predictability of the outputs required, the more mechanistic it is. For example:

- production lines working to the maximum available quality and speed of output cannot easily be re-jigged to improve quality and output;
- information systems that deliver information in predictable and assured, but limited, ways cannot easily be redesigned to change or improve (indeed it is normal for new software to be purchased).

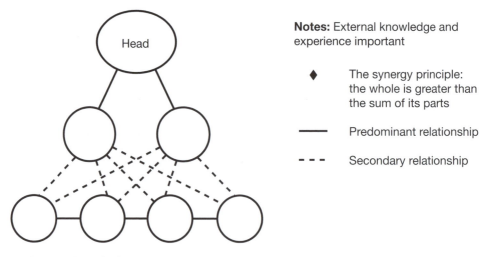

Figure 18.8 Organization structures: organic/organismic
Source: Burns and Stalker (1956).

On the other hand, too great flexibility with the system can lead to uncertainty as to its true capacities and effectiveness.

Burns and Stalker favoured neither one system nor the other. They did state that whatever system or structure was used, it had to be suitable for the purpose, and designed in advance of implementation, rather than being added to as things went on.

Reporting relationships

In line structures reporting relationships are made clear. However, reporting relationships become clouded where operational and functional activities are carried out across locations, departments and divisions. This also leads to questions of workload priority where, for example, an urgent job is required for one department and an important one for another.

Forms of rank, status and authority may also impact. For example, the chief executive officer may want a general request dealt with, the production manager an important request and the finance assistant an urgent request.

Service relationships

Service relationships exist outside the line, functional, authority, control and reporting relationships indicated. Service departments gain and maintain their reason for being through the quality and value of the general contribution that they make to the work of others. There is no absolute obligation on the part of the rest of the organization to avail itself of these services.

Service functions therefore gain an understanding of the requirements of the rest of the organization for their activities. What is provided is a combination of service expertise, presented in ways useful to the receiving departments. This is enhanced and developed by making specific requests for the service in question in order to gain information or solve problems.

Core and peripheral organizations

Core and peripheral forms of structure are based on a total reappraisal of objectives and activities with the view to establishing where the strategic core lies, what is needed to sustain this and where, when and why additional support and resources are required.

The essential is the core. The rest is the peripheral and may be seen as a shamrock or propeller (see Figure 18.9). This may be viewed in the following ways.

'Core and peripheral' organizational structures indicate many opportunities for organizations to engage expertise as cost effectively as possible. Rather than retaining expertise on the payroll, in spite of the fact that it is only used on limited occasions throughout the year, many different approaches are available. In particular, for specialist or non-standard activities, organizations have to manage the twin pressures of being as cost effective as possible, while at the same time having access to the particular specialisms whenever necessary.

Of particular concern are the following.

• Professional and technical services and expertise, drawn in to solve problems; designed and improved work methods and practices; manage, change and act as catalysts and agents for change. All of these functions are conducted by outsiders

(a) *The Shamrock model*

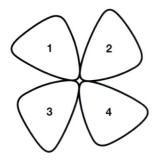

1. The core
2. Specialists
3. Seasonal staff
4. Staff on retainers for pressures
   and emergencies

(b) *The propeller model*

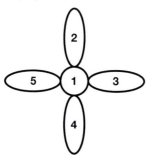

1. The core
2. Specialists
3. Subcontractors
4. Research and development
5. Seasonal staff

Figure 18.9 Core and peripheral forms of structure

on a contracted basis and the areas include marketing, public relations, human resource management, industrial relations, supplies, research and development, process and operations management and distribution.

- Sub-contracting of services such as facilities and environment management, maintenance, catering, cleaning and security. These are distinctive expertises in their own right, and therefore best left to expert organizations.

  This form of sub-contracting is now very highly developed across all sectors and all parts of the world as organizations seek to concentrate on their own expertise and minimize areas of non-contributory activity.

- Operational pressures, in which staff are retained to be available at peaks (daily, periodical or seasonal) and otherwise not present. This has contributed both to the increase in part-time, flexible and core hours patterns of employment; and also to the retention of the services of workforce agencies, which specialize in providing particular volumes of expertise in this way.

- Outworking (often home working), in which staff work at alternative locations including home, avoiding the need for expensive and extensive facilities. This also enables those involved to combine work with other activities – parenting, study, working for other organizations.

  In return for this, people are often paid retainers or premiums to ensure their continued obligation, commitment and loyalty. They may be well paid, even overpaid to compensate for periods when there is no work. They may be retained on regular and distinctive patterns of employment – normally short-time or part-time.

The benefits lie in the need and ability to maximize resources and optimize staff utilization. Rather than structuring the workforce to be available generally, the requirement for expertise and nature of operations is worked out in advance and the organization structured from this point of view. All activities that are to be carried out on a steady-state daily basis are integrated into the core. The rest are contracted or retained in one of the forms indicated (see Box 18.8).

Box 18.8: Outsourcing

In the name of cost cutting (or cost assurance as above) and structure simplifications, organizations in most sectors have been drawn towards the outsourcing of particular activities. The result is that many organizations that used to have everything structured in and on the payroll now outsource such diverse functions as:

- sourcing of raw materials;
- manufacture of components;
- sales and distribution;
- transport;
- catering, cleaning and security (as above);
- customer service functions (as above);
- as well as some more general corporate functions such as HR, finance and accounts.

As stated above, the driving forces are cost cutting and the giving over of these services to specialist providers. However, it is essential that organizations do not abdicate their responsibilities at the same time as they hand over the contract. Outsource providers have to be capable of delivering the required quality and volume of services and activities; and so fair contract prices have to be negotiated. No organization wants to be in the position of losing the whole provision simply because it tried to drive down the contract price. Many large, powerful and dominant organizations have indeed lived to regret this, for example:

- British Airways found itself without catering services when it tried to drive down the prices that it would pay to its catering provider;
- BT lost its outsourced HR function when it tried to drive down the price paid to Accentua which had been hitherto responsible for delivering it;
- GM found itself without components for many weeks, because the outsource provider could not work to the contract value that GM had imposed on it;
- overseas call centre staff have given bad service because they have no conception of what is important to the customers who ring them up.

Each of these instances has led to contract prices having to be renegotiated, as well as the loss of production, service, customers and clients as the result of the venture being ill thought out.

Federations

Federations tend to be regularized over extended periods of time, and come to be known as partnerships or conglomerates that deal in a complete range of products or services for particular customers and clients (see Figure 18.10). For example:

- Coca-Cola uses a large range of transport and distribution companies, but the relationship is more or less assured over the long-term;
- McDonald's uses its own transport and distribution companies, but these are franchised out to individuals;
- smaller companies and organizations call on the services of accounting, marketing, sales and HR people for one or two days per month; and these too are assured relationships that exist over long periods of time.

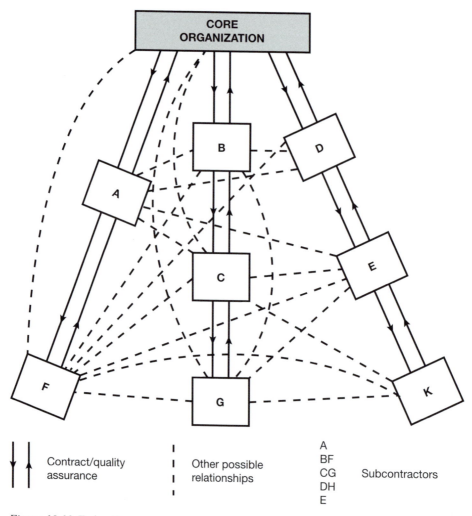

Figure 18.10 Federation

The main problem with federations lies in integrating, coordinating and controlling the relationships and activities required at each stage. The critical factors are ensuring mutuality of interest, continuity of general relationship, confidence and profitability. In particular, the reporting relationship between all those involved has to be structured and coordinated so that:

- mutual confidence and interest are maintained;
- specific problems and issues are raised early and dealt with quickly.

Operationally, the main problem that exists within federations is meeting over-arching performance targets. These performance targets are stated in terms of quality, value, volume and deadlines as usual.

Table 18.1 Principles of organization structure: a summary

	Operational constraints		Key features	
	Environment	*Internal*	*Structure*	*Activities*
Simple structure	Simple/dynamic Hostile	Small Young Simple tasks CEO control	Direction + Strategy	Direct supervision
Technocracy	Simple/static Conformist	Old Large Regulated tasks Technocrat control	Technostructure	Standardization of work
Professional bureaucracy	Complex/static	Complex systems Professional control	Operational expertise Professional practice	Standardization of skills
Divisionalized bureaucracy	Simple/static Diversity Hostile	Old Very large Divisible tasks Middle-line control	Autonomy Reporting relationships	Standardization of outputs Sophisticated supervision
Ad hocracy	Complex/ dynamic Committed	Often young Complex tasks Expert control Middle-aged	Operational Expertise	Mutual adjustment
Missionary	Simple/static Committed	Often 'enclaves' Simple systems Ideological control	Ideology Standards	Policy, norms Standards
Network organization	Dynamic Committed	Young Reformed	Operational expertise Technostructure	Networking

Source: Based on Mintzberg (1979), Johnson and Scholes.

In a single organization, none of this represents a problem; in a federation, it can, from time to time, be necessary to try to insist that another organization (one over which the others have no control) re-prioritizes its own activities so as to meet the demands of the particular federation.

Bureaucracy

Bureaucracy means 'government by office'. The basis of the concept lies in the need to give organizations their own life, permanence and stability and to retain the fund of expertise and precedent that is built up over the period of existence, rather than being dependent on the personal knowledge of individuals. It also prescribes areas of authority and expertise and formalizes the ways in which these are divided.

Every activity is therefore broken down into jobs, offices or positions. Each is formally described and its position in relation to the rest is determined and established. Each is given its own combination of expertise and authority, and its position in the organization's hierarchy. The whole is then circumscribed by rules and regulations, indicating the relationship between each position, the bounds within which the office holder is to operate and the wider general standards by which people are to act and behave.

Bureaucracy therefore has the following characteristics:

- **Specialization**: each position has a clearly defined sphere of competence and activity.
- **Hierarchy**: a firmly ordered system of supervision and subordination in which lower offices accept direction from those higher up.
- **Rules**: the organization follows general rules which are more or less stable, more or less comprehensive and which can be learned by everyone.
- **Impersonality**: impersonality is the spirit in which the ideal functionary conducts business. Everyone is subject to equality of treatment. The official has no partiality or favouritism, either for subordinates or for customers.
- **Appointments**: people are selected for offices on the basis of their expertise and qualifications. They are appointed and not elected or brought into the organization as a matter of favour.
- **Full-time**: officials are employed on a full-time basis and this is reflected in the nature and volume of work.
- **Careers**: the job constitutes part of a career path. There are systems of promotion based on a combination of seniority and achievement.
- **Separation**: bureaucracy separates official and functional activity as something distinct from private life. Wages and salaries are paid in return for the work. The obligation is placed on the organization to provide all necessary equipment and facilities.
- **Permanence**: the expertise of the organization is retained in a system of files so that achievements, precedent and previous activities can be referred to. For each recorded transaction a copy or note is kept for the files.

The approach offers guidelines and patterns for the organization and distribution of work and the structuring of organizations (see Table 18.1 above). It also ensures impersonality and permanence above the particular contributions of individuals. Bureaucracies in this form have sprung up all over the world, and in all sectors and industries. Many people believe that this is the only suitable structural form for large and sophisticated organizations; and that, in any case, the principles of retention and impersonality need to apply to all organizations, however small (see Box 18.9).

Problems of bureaucracy

The main problem lies in the maze of offices and functions created, and their interactions and relationships. At worst, this leads to proliferation of papers, systems, databases and procedures that govern every aspect of work and which, in turn, require monitoring and supervision.

From an internal point of view, this causes chains of command and communication to become clogged up and overloaded. Matters have often to be referred through several tiers for decision and then handed back to the originator.

Comprehensive sets of rules invariably do not cover every eventuality. The more they set out to do this, the more likely anomalies and contradictions are to occur. This leads to the need to refer matters again for decision, and again leads to delays and frustration.

Bureaucracies tend towards tall hierarchical structures and top-heaviness. Too many offices are either procedural or non-productive. Pressure is exerted on those who do work at the front line, both from customers and clients, and also from the higher ranks supervising them.

Bureaucracies are stable and permanent – and the converse of this is inertia. They tend to greatest efficiency and effectiveness when working in a stable work environment with

---

Box 18.9: Priorities of bureaucracy

As stated above, a key priority of bureaucracy is to retain all the knowledge and information that the organization possesses.

Apart from anything else, there is a legal duty to do so. Organizations have to be able to produce specific data upon request; and organizations can, and do, from time to time find themselves having to justify a particular position, especially when they find themselves either potentially or actually in front of the courts.

When this does happen, the courts take a very dim view of organizations that cannot, or do not, produce information required for the particular case. This has led on occasions to the following:

- organizations being fined for failing to produce adequate financial data;
- organizations being fined for failing to produce adequate HR data when faced with complaints about staff management.

Indeed, one of the problems with the UK banking crisis of 2008 onwards was the inability to look at the complete and comprehensive data stating the basis on which the individual organizations concerned had valued both themselves and also the assets against which they were making loans. Effective bureaucracy would have ensured that none of this arose; and adequate management of that bureaucracy would have led to the problems being much more clearly and openly identified much earlier on.

relatively permanent operations, technology and markets. Long-established bureaucracies are often themselves barriers to change and development (whatever the feelings of the jobholders within them) when these become necessary.

Bureaucracies are not customer-friendly. They work best in this respect when the demands of the customer are regular and universal. Problems again arise when this is not the case and when individual sets of circumstances have to be taken into account. Again, this causes frustration if decisions are not readily available (see Box 18.10).

Rules and regulations

Rules and regulations are created to support structures and practices, to establish general standards of behaviour and to provide boundaries for operations, activities and functions.

The simpler the rules, the more likely they are to be understood, accepted and followed. The drive is therefore away from long and complex manuals designed to cover every eventuality (this is in any case impossible) and towards much shorter, crisper and clearer guidelines that set general and absolute standards.

The benefits of the simple approach lie in the ability of all concerned to take a flexible and judgmental view of problems and situations as they arise. Energies are not spent on searching exhaustively for precedent, or in interrupting different clauses according to the point of view adopted. The onus is placed on managers and supervisors to set standards of fairness and equality – this has to be done anyway, whatever the complexity or otherwise of the rulebook. The position adopted is in the exercising of judgement and

---

Box 18.10: The trouble with bureaucracy!

Mark Lawton broke his leg. He was taken by ambulance to his local hospital, where he was quickly assessed, given pain killers and made ready for an operation.

He gave his full details to the triage nurse who quickly assessed his condition from a specialist point of view. All went well; the leg was set, and he was discharged.

He was required to return for a check-up a week later. The hospital quickly found the fact that he was indeed due for an appointment; however, they could not find his notes. He therefore filled in the same questionnaire with the same triage nurse; and again, he was treated well and effectively.

As the leg healed up, the time came for the plaster to be taken off. At this point again, the hospital failed to find his notes. However, from Mark's point of view, this was no problem; the leg was now healed, the plaster came off, and again he went on his way.

However, he needed physiotherapy. Accordingly, he turned up at the hospital as arranged, only to find that, once again, they had no record of his injury. The physiotherapist was therefore unable to prescribe a specific treatment for the injury, since she did not know precisely what the actual problem was.

This occurred at a large regional hospital in south-eastern England. However, the problems of loss of notes are endemic throughout the UK NHS. Clearly, it is possible to document anything at any time; the bigger problems are retention and access when required by those who need them.

Box 18.11: The organizational work ethic

A combination of structure, centralization/decentralization and the rules that underpin all of this give a clear indication of what the organizational work ethic actually is. For example:

- if the structure demands regular reporting through the hierarchy, then this becomes the driving force of how work is carried out;
- if the rules and regulations demand conformity rather than performance, then this becomes the priority here.

Whatever happens in an organization is therefore shaped and informed by the structure, hierarchies and rules that exist. These may either be seen as constraints within which effective work has to be carried out as well as made possible; or they can be seen as boundaries that shape and direct the ways in which work has to be carried out from a positive point of view.

There is therefore no reason why any structure or bureaucracy need be a brake on progress. Certainly, they give direction and order; and from this, it is the ways in which organizations and their top and senior managers decide that things have to be done that become the priority.

dealing directly with problems, however, rather than in searching out and administering the appropriate rule or clause.

The organization itself must have some degree of permanence in order that confidence in it can be generated on the part of both customers and staff. The relationships that are built on that permanence are always based on a combination of expectations, continuity and satisfaction – and this is only achieved if the organization is flexible and progressive enough to develop itself and its staff to ensure that this happens. Structure therefore becomes a basis for their development, just as a house, for example, becomes the basis of personal comfort and satisfaction to the owner or user – the structure is stable, the opportunities and usage afforded are almost infinitely variable. What is required therefore is a genuine understanding and realization of the purpose of structure and the opportunities afforded by an adequately and effectively structured organization. Functions, ranks, hierarchies, bureaucracy and relations are not ends in themselves nor are they per se required. They are components to be combined and used in ways suitable to, and supportive of, the stated purposes (see Box 18.11).

Conclusions

Organizations are designed for particular purposes and circumstances and when these change the structure should move on also. The concept of organization structure has come full circle – from the position of having a structure and seeking uses for it, to having a purpose and seeking the means and order for pursuing it effectively.

Related to this is the expense of carrying sophisticated support functions, hierarchies and administrative superstructures. It is also often very difficult to coordinate and harmonize these with the organization's main purposes. They tend to generate lives of their own – aims and objectives, results areas, systems and reporting relationships – which are both time and resource consumptive, often out of all proportion to the actual purpose served or envisaged.

It is clearly necessary that organizations retain their permanence and their knowledge and expertise, in spite of the comings and goings of the staff. It is also necessary to coordinate and control activities, operations and resources. Most of the principles indicated therefore remain sound. However, the creation of bureaucracies, human structures and pyramids, ranks and hierarchies, administrative systems and reporting relationships in the pursuit of permanence and order is not conducive to effective performance, clarity of purpose or optimum resource usage.

19 Human resource management and employee relations

Introduction

Human resource management (HRM) and employee relations (ER) ought to be at the centre of any strategic approach to developing effective and sustainable patterns of behaviour and performance. This is because HRM is fundamentally concerned with the establishment and development of the processes and procedures that are to underpin the ways in which everyone is to conduct themselves collectively. HRM also has critical operational roles in each of the following:

- attracting and retaining the right staff;
- motivating and rewarding them;
- providing opportunities for development and advancement;
- resolving individual and collective disputes and grievances;
- ensuring (as far as possible) employment assurance, protection and security;
- providing a healthy and safe place of work.

The foundation of this lies in the structures, procedures and practices which the organization provides to ensure that people work to the highest possible standards in the context in which that is demanded.

It is usual to begin by recognizing:

- limitations to effective HR practice;
- organizational and managerial perspectives on HR;

Limitations to effective HR practice

The key limitations to effective HRM are:

- uncertainty and unpredictability;
- discomfort;
- lack of management training and development;
- lack of value placed by top and senior management.

Uncertainty and unpredictability

Nobody ever knows quite how people are going to act and react in any situation. The demands of personal, as well as occupational and managerial, comfort mean that, on the one hand, people do seek certainty and predictability wherever possible.

There is therefore an immediate conflict to be resolved: how to make certain that which cannot be made certain! This conflict, and all the complexities inherent, causes many managers (at all levels) to fall back on received wisdom rather than learning and applying what is actually demanded (see Box 19.1).

Discomfort

Facing up to people in an organized setting, when responses cannot be predicted, is discomfiting. This discomfort is compounded when it is known that what has to be faced is contentious or disadvantageous to one or more parties.

The human response is therefore to adopt one or more of the following positions:

- withdrawal, which includes simply avoiding people and/or contentious issues;
- return to the comfort zone, meaning that unpleasant or contentious issues are dealt with through the comfort of the computer and the e-mail network rather than the discomfort of having to face people directly;
- adoption of a strident, aloof, distant or aggressive manner to head off any assertive response (see also Chapters 10 and 11).

The need is to recognize that HRM and ER cannot be made 'comfortable', and to learn and understand the ways in which people act and behave in organizations as a condition of effective HR and ER practice (see Box 19.2).

Box 19.1: HRM and received wisdom

The complexity of having to address people and their concerns at organizational and occupational levels, as well as on a human basis, causes managers at all levels to fall back on one or more of the following.

- Myths, legends and illusions: e.g. 'When I was young this is how we were treated; it never did my generation any harm, and so this is how I treat people'.
- In charge: e.g. 'I'm in charge and so you do what I say because I say so' or 'I'm in charge; I can do what I like'.
- Phoney rationale: e.g. 'I have earned the right to order you about through my own previous efforts'.
- Unpleasantness and unpredictability: e.g. 'If my staff do not know how I am going to react, they will not come and bother me'.

Each is a commonplace managerial attitude. Each simply leads to HR and ER problems, especially when attached to a defensive, and often strident, manner which people who practise the above attitudes normally adopt.

The result in all cases is that the organization incurs unnecessary expense. In extreme cases, such attitudes lead to accusations of bullying, victimization, discrimination and harassment and these are both expensive and also traumatic to resolve, and can be very damaging to the organization's reputation both as employer and also provider of goods and services.

> **Box 19.2: NHS recruitment**
>
> The recruitment of junior doctors into hospital positions was always seen as messy, time-consuming and expensive by the service's managerial authorities. Accordingly, it was decided to commission an on-line recruitment process which would resolve all of this, and make certain the recruitment process.
>
> Accordingly, rather than applying for posts in writing, junior doctors were required to complete an on-line application form. All the usual details were asked for; and when the applications were picked up, the different healthcare authorities and trusts would be able to view them all, and make their selections and choices from the data provided on-line. However, it quickly became apparent that this attempt to make things 'comfortable' simply produced a fresh set of problems. Junior doctors were assigned to posts without any reference to where they particularly wished to live and work, nor the expertise and specialisms which they wished to develop. In extreme cases, the result was that some junior doctors working in the south-west of England were required to relocate to the north-east; others who had managed to make clear that they wanted to work in a particular region were nevertheless required to commute up to 150 miles to work in each direction.
>
> The system quickly fell into disrepute. Despite assurances that it would nevertheless be fixed, it was cancelled after two years of operation.
>
> The key lesson is that no part of HRM or ER can be made comfortable or assured. There are some aspects of management practice which require active personal, as well as professional, involvement, and there is nothing that can be substituted for this.

Managerial training and development

Great strides in the areas of effective HR and ER practice can be made by ensuring that all those in managerial positions at any level are trained and developed. This must include the context as well as the activities and processes of HR and ER. If this is effective, then many of the 'initiatives' that are undertaken to try to make HR practice comfortable and predictable would have much more impact. They would also greatly reinforce every aspect of any organizational activity, especially overall viability and profitability (see Box 19.3).

Lack of value

It remains true that in many organizations, effective HR practice remains undervalued or unvalued. This is because HR deals with everything that is intangible, amorphous, uncertain and unpredictable concerning the organization – the skills, knowledge, attitudes, values, behaviour and performance of the staff. This is itself uncertain and awkward; and when staffing problems and issues do arise, other managers simply want them resolved as soon as possible. While this is indeed the correct idea, however, the actual resolution is not always easy or clear, and this is where the problem lies. Other managers then turn to someone (HR) to resolve these matters.

This, however, is not valued because the outputs of HR are neither tangible nor easily capable of quantification. Financial returns, sales, production and service activities can

Box 19.3: Semco

'When I took over Semco from my father, it was a traditional company in every respect with a pyramid structure and a rule for every contingency. Today our factory workers sometimes set their own production quotas and even come in their own time to meet them without prodding from management or overtime pay. They help redesign the products, they make and formulate the marketing plans. Their bosses for their part can run our business units with extraordinary freedom determining business strategy without interference from the top brass. They even set their own salaries with no strings. Then again everyone will know what they are since all financial information at Semco is openly discussed. Our workers have unlimited access to our books. To show we are serious about this, Semco with the labour unions that represent our workers developed a course to teach everyone, including messengers and cleaning people, to read balance sheets and cash flow statements.

We don't have receptionists. We don't think that they are necessary. We don't have secretaries either, or personal assistants. We don't believe in cluttering the payroll with ungratifying dead-end jobs. Everyone at Semco, even top managers, fetches guests, stands over photocopiers, sends faxes, types letters and uses the phone. We have stripped away the unnecessary perks and privileges that feed the ego but hurt the balance sheet and distract everyone from the crucial corporate tasks of making, selling, billing and collecting.

One sales manager sits in the reception area reading newspapers hour after hour, not even making a pretence of looking busy. Most modern managers would not tolerate it. But when a Semco pump on an oil tanker on the other side of the world fails and millions of gallons of oil are about to spill into the sea he springs into action. He knows everything there is to know about our pumps and how to fix them. That's when he earns his salary. No one cares if he doesn't look busy the rest of the time.

We are not the only company to experiment with participative management. It has become a fad. But so many efforts at workplace democracy are just so much hot air.

The rewards have already been substantial. We have taken a company that was moribund and made it thrive chiefly by refusing to squander our greatest resource, our people. Semco has grown sixteen-fold despite withering recessions, staggering inflation and chaotic national economic policy. Productivity has increased nearly twenty-fold. Profits have risen ten-fold. And we have had periods of up to fourteen months in which not one worker has left us. We have a backlog of more than 2,000 job applications, hundreds from people who state that they would take any job just to be at Semco. In a pole of recent college graduates conducted by a leading Brazilian magazine, 25% of the men and 13% of the women said Semco was the company at which they most wanted to work.

Not long ago the wife of one of our workers came to see a member of our human resources staff. She was puzzled about her husband's behaviour. He was not his usual grumpy autocratic self. The woman was worried. What, she wondered, were we doing to her husband? We realised that as Semco had changed for the better, he had too.'

Source: Ricardo Semler (1993) *Maverick* – Century; Ricardo Semler (2003) *The Seven Day Weekend* – Century.

all be quantified and therefore presented simply; HR activities cannot. Additionally, if an organization is running smoothly, the perception can arise that no HR expertise is required. The consequence is that HR is seen either as a cost, or else as a form of necessary evil – and both of these attitudes demonstrate a lack of value.

Perspectives

It is now necessary to look at the perspectives of HR. The perspectives of HR reflect the prevailing attitudes held by organizations and their managers to their staff, and form the basis of the relations between staff, managers and the organization as a whole. They also form the foundations of effective HR and ER practice. These perspectives are as follows (see also Chapter 2 above).

- Unitary, which assumes that the objectives of all involved are the same or compatible, and concerned only with the well-being of the organization and its products, services, clients and customers.
- Pluralist, which admits a variety of objectives, not all compatible, among the staff. In the recognition that conflict is therefore present, rules, procedures and systems have to be established to manage it and limit the extent and prevalence as far as possible. This is the approach taken especially in many public services, local governments and large and complex industrial and commercial companies.
- The radical perspective, which is the view that commercial and industrial harmony is impossible until the staff control the means of production and benefit from the generation of wealth. Until very recently, this was a cornerstone of the philosophy of many trade unions and socialist activists in industry, commerce and public services. Some variations on this perspective have been created from an organizational and managerial point of view, especially through staff share ownership and share incentive schemes.
- The adversarial perspective, which institutionalizes conflict as the foundation on which staff are to be dealt with on a regularized basis. Inherent in this perspective is an attitude of mistrust, divergence, irreconcilable aims and objectives. The effective management of adversarial HR and ER requires extensive procedures, institutions, consultative negotiating and bargaining structures to be effective at all times.
- Conformity, where the diversity of staff and technology is integrated through setting absolute standards of behavioural and operational approaches, and reinforcing these through simple, direct, understood and accepted procedures and activities.
- Consensus, where the way of working is devised as a genuine partnership between the organization, its staff and their representatives.
- Paternalist, in which the organization accepts responsibilities for providing staff comfort and support in return for known, understood and assured ways of working, including flexible responses when pressure on the organization is heavy.

Whichever perspective is adopted, it is essential that this is designed rather than emergent, and cohesive rather than fragmented. This means that there needs to be a fundamental collective knowledge, understanding and acceptance of how HRM and ER are conducted, and that the institutions of HR need to be capable of effective operation in that context (see Box 19.4).

Box 19.4: Effective HR and ER

The received wisdom is that 'the best perspective' is either consensus, conformist or unitary (see above) in which everyone is either fully involved in all aspects of the organization and its activities, or else they agree to suborn their own individual interests in the pursuit of the greater good. In practice, this is not always possible, and so what is present has to be made to work as well as possible. For example:

British Airways

The fundamental relationship between British Airways and the British Airline Pilots' Association (BALPA – the pilots' trade union) and Unite (the trade union which represents the sales staff and cabin crew) is adversarial. Yet, it works effectively to a greater extent. This is because the company knows and understands that if their treatment of these groups of staff is not effective, they will simply take out a grievance or resort to strike action. Similarly, the staff involved know and understand that when they do take out a dispute or grievance, they can have a critical effect on the business. Every effort is therefore made to ensure that the relationships are kept perfect, with the interests of the company at the forefront as far as possible, and as often as possible.

When things do go wrong, the effects on the business are very damaging. Some years ago, a dispute blew up over the summer rostering of sales staff and ticketing staff. For some reason, rosters had been published without reference to staff holidays, and the chosen and flexible patterns of work of individuals. It was the beginning of the summer, one of the company's busiest periods.

Matters came to a head when two members of staff failed to show up for work, leading to ticketing desks having to be closed. Queues of passengers quickly built up, and this caused planes to be delayed, and some passengers to miss their flights. One of the shift supervisors tried to chase up the absent members of staff, only to be told that they were on pre-arranged and pre-agreed annual leave. The shift supervisor then contacted their HR representative who ordered the sales staff to clear the backlog.

The rest of the sales and ticketing staff walked out. Frantically, the HR representative tried to get hold of the HR director, and eventually contacted him on his mobile phone. The HR director was enjoying corporate hospitality at the British Grand Prix at Silverstone, and refused to return to sort the matter out.

The strike lasted less than two days. However, the disruption to the service, the compensation that had to be paid and the fact that some of the planes were now in the wrong place and could not easily fulfil their own individual schedules cost the company approximately £30 million.

The lesson is that whatever form of HR and ER is in place, it has to be made to work for the good of the company or organization at all times. As stated above, a fundamentally adversarial relationship can be made to work where required; however, it is essential to recognize that when things do go wrong (especially in the above context) it is both expensive and also damaging to the organization.

The principle of equality

Whatever the size, complexity, location or activities of the organization, all staff must be treated equally and fairly. As well as being a legal requirement, this is a fundamental prerequisite for the creation of organization and operational effectiveness. Managers and organizations must first overcome the tendency to compartmentalize people by race, gender, religion, marital status, disability, age, location and postal address, non-essential qualifications, school background, club membership, hobby or interest. They must take the opposite standpoint: isolating the qualities essential and desirable to carry out a job. They must view people in terms of their potential as staff members, as contributors to the success and prosperity of the organization, and of their capability and willingness to carry out their work. Without this, no equality of treatment or opportunity can exist.

There is also a question of basic human decency that requires that all people be treated the same. This is a social, as well as organizational, concern. For organizations, all activities, management styles, policies, practices and procedures, publications, advertisements, job and work descriptions and person specifications are written in ways that reinforce this.

The purpose is to ensure that people are employed and treated on their operational capabilities and willingness alone. Anyone, including managers, adopting negative approaches or attitudes to equality of opportunities is certain to damage the interests of the organization over long periods of time.

Diversity

Diversity was introduced in Chapter 15 and forms an additional drive for the effective, equal and fair treatment of all staff. In the context of HR and ER, those from diverse backgrounds and with a range of differences are certain to influence the ways in which things are done, and how people behave towards each other.

It is the case that work patterns and workforce behaviour have to be capable of accommodating all differences. These differences include:

*   flexible and non-standard patterns of work and attendance;
*   religious convictions and commitments;
*   family commitments;
*   people with disabilities.

The only test is whether somebody is capable and willing to do the job, as above.

Failure to manage diversity can lead to work patterns being created in order to accommodate prejudices and preconceptions; and this is both dangerous and illegal. Examples of specific problems include:

*   people of one social group refusing to work with those from other social groups;
*   people from one ethnic group refusing to work with those from other ethnic groups;
*   people with one set of religious beliefs refusing to work with those who have different beliefs;
*   people with one set of political beliefs refusing to work with those who have other beliefs.

There is no reason for any organization to accommodate this form of prejudice-based conduct. A key priority is to integrate people from diverse backgrounds into a strong, cohesive and productive workforce; and so the overriding work ethic and organization culture must be strong and positive enough to transcend these kinds of differences. Integration of everyone, regardless of differences, also reinforces the key message that the work is the priority. Successful companies and organizations (in which success is measured in terms of long-term viability, and as employer of choice) have fewer disputes around diversity issues than those that either struggle or fail (see IPD 2008).

It is also the case that any form of discrimination on grounds other than capability and willingness to work is damaging to both morale and performance. Companies and organizations that are known to favour one group over others find themselves engaged in an endless round of disputes and grievances, which (as stated above) are expensive and time consuming to manage. Companies and organizations that are known to discriminate on these grounds have great difficulty in attracting and retaining expert and excellent members of staff. Companies and organizations that refuse to take actions to remedy such attitudes find themselves being removed from preferred contractor lists, gaining adverse media coverage and in some cases face prosecutions brought about by the equal opportunities' authorities.

A fundamental commitment to equality and fairness of treatment is therefore essential as the basis for establishing effective and crucial HR and ER activities in the areas of:

- attracting and retaining staff;
- staff training and development;
- pay and rewards;
- employee relations.

Attracting and retaining staff

The ability to attract, recruit and retain staff is based on a variety of factors, including:

- the relative attraction of the organization and the work offered; the organization's wider reputation, together with perceptions formed by more general contacts with it – for example, through media coverage or as a customer;
- the location of the organization, which refers both to the place of work, and also to ease and convenience of transport and access;
- the relative value and worth of the occupation, both to the individual and also to the organization;
- the relative general perceptions in which the organization and the work are held.

Assessment of these factors indicates the overall attractiveness, or otherwise, of the organization and the work. This has then to be related to the rewards on offer as follows:

- the material rewards, including salary/pay/wages and other benefits;
- the intrinsic rewards, including responsibility, autonomy, opportunities for progress and development;
- reflection of personal value, including status, esteem, rank and job title;
- recognition factors on the part of the individual, the organization and society at large;

- the fit between the particular occupation and the management style with which the work is directed;
- the fit between the work required and the individuals who are to carry it out.

This is clearly therefore complex. It needs to be based on good levels of expert knowledge of each of the factors indicated above. Full assessment of these factors will indicate why people want to carry out their occupation for the particular organization, and the advantages and barriers present (see Box 19.5).

Staff planning

Staff planning is a dynamic and continuous process in which all managers need to be involved. This is because of the increasing complexity of organizational structures. It is also because of the increasing demands placed on organization resources in order to maximize and optimize returns on investment. Of particular concern are the following:

- employment legislation;
- the availability of required expertise;
- the integration of technology with staff and their expertise;
- staff turnover patterns;
- structure of the workforce;
- the changing nature of labour markets;
- imbalances between the expertise available and what the organization demands.

The key elements involved are as follows:

- work analysis to order jobs and occupations in ways that are productive, rewarding and fulfilling;
- assessing the staff mix in terms of age; length of service; jobs held; promotion and career paths;
- matching the supply and demand of staff and their expertise;
- future projections for staff;
- the management of specific problems, including absenteeism and turnover; sickness and accident rates;
- staff and HR problems, especially setting standards of behaviour and performance, and implementing the procedures to ensure that standards remain high and acceptable;
- the management of serious problems, especially bullying, victimization, discrimination, harassment, vandalism, violence, theft and fraud;
- HR and ER information systems, ensuring that data is both accurate and comprehensive, and also that it complies with legal requirements.

With each of these elements, there is a corporate HR and general management responsibility to ensure that every aspect is addressed (see Table 19.1).

Fitting the work to the people; fitting the people to the work

The process of fitting the work to people, and fitting people to work is abbreviated to FWP–FPW.

Box 19.5: B&Q

B&Q, the home products and DIY retailer, took an early and critical step in recognizing the potential that existed in a diverse and imaginatively structured workforce.

For many years, the company had difficulties in attracting and retaining 'the right staff' to work in its retail premises and warehouses. The company therefore took the step of targeting those who fell into the age range 50 and over. This was based on a full evaluation of human expectations and aspirations in that particular age range. The key findings were:

* people of that age range knew what they were letting themselves in for;
* people in that age range knew and understood the nature of the work, and that this was what they wanted to do;
* people wished to fit their working hours with the other demands that they had to face.

B&Q also found that:

* people wanted a sense of identity with the products and services;
* people wanted a sense of belonging and involvement;
* people wanted to be a part of delivering a service that was of demonstrable value to the customers.

From identifying the specific requirements of a well-defined workforce, B&Q moved quickly on to use this knowledge as a form of organization development. The HR strategy for the retail aspects of the company's operations started to focus on everything that was of value to the group of staff employed. This included the human, as well as the operational, aspects of the work. Consequently, managers were trained to ensure that places of work were friendly, positive, open and welcoming. The company provided extensive job training, product knowledge, materials handling, health and safety, customer service training, and job rotation and work development within the environment of the particular stores and warehouses.

Targeting this niche of the workforce was immediately effective. Staff turnover and absenteeism dropped, and productivity rose. B&Q gained a reputation for excellent and effective service delivery, and for its helpful and friendly staff.

There also arose the question of whether the targeting of the particular sector of the workforce was itself discriminatory. B&Q countered this by stating that, in fact, anyone was free to apply for jobs at any of their stores when vacancies arose; and that they would be judged solely on their capability and willingness to do the job. The company went on to state that attracting people in the particular age range, and concentrating on developing patterns of work and a managerial style that suited them, had nevertheless transformed the standards by which the service was delivered, and the management style and context of work. Whoever came now to work for the organization would be working in the new environment and with the new attitudes, values and management style that now prevailed.

Table 19.1 Human resource management summary

Area of Work	Strategy and Direction	Personnel Operations
Work design and structuring	Principles, approaches, departmentalization, organization structure	Job descriptions, work patterns, work structuring
Staff planning	Systems appraisal, design commissioning	Systems usage
Recruitment and selection	Standpoint (grow your own, buy in from outside)	Training of recruiters and selectors, recruitment and selection activities
Induction	Policy, content, priority	Delivery
Use of agencies and external sources of staff	Principles, circumstances	Contacts and commissions
Performance appraisal	Purpose, systems, design, principles, aims and objectives	Systems implementation, training of appraisers and appraisees
Pay and rewards	Policy, levels, mix of pay and benefits, package design	Assimilate individual staff to policy
Occupational health	Policy, content, design of package	Operation of package in conjunction with functional departments
Equality	Standards, policy, content, context, ethics	Policy operation, monitoring of standards, remedial actions
Industrial relations	Standpoints (conflict, conformist), representation	Negotiations, consultation, participation, staff communications
Discipline	Policy, procedure, practice, design, standpoint	Implementation of policy and procedure, support for staff, training of all staff
Grievance	Policy, procedure	Implementation of policy and procedure, training of all staff
Training and development	Priority and resources	Activities, opportunities, accessibility
Dismissal	Standards of conduct, examples of gross misconduct	Operation of disciplinary procedures, procedures, operation of dismissal procedures, support and advice

Human Resource Management is divided into strategic and directional activities; and personnel activities. The role and function is:

- policy, advisory, consultative, supporting, a point of reference;
- personnel practitioner;
- establisher of policy content;
- establishing standards of best practice;
- creator of personnel activities;
- monitor/evaluator of personnel activities.

This approach requires a full understanding of the critical behaviour, attitudes, skills, knowledge, expertise and technological proficiency required of all staff. On the part of managers, this requires the ability to:

- match staff and potential staff with potential job and work requirements;
- understanding the professional and occupational demands of those with these capabilities;
- recognizing the strengths and shortcomings of the present working environment in terms of attracting and retaining staff;
- understanding the aspects of work that are boring, dirty, dangerous or stressful and therefore likely to put people off.

A full understanding of the FWP–FPW balance provides a sound base on which to address each of the following:

- **Job and work descriptions**: parcelling up tasks into occupations and patterns of work.
- **Person specifications**: the behaviour, attitudes, skills, knowledge, expertise and technological proficiency required and asked for in job-holders, and in those who come to work in the organization at large.
- **Methods of selection**: identifying how the critical behaviours, attitudes, skills, knowledge, expertise and technological proficiency aspects are to be tested in individuals for capability and willingness.
- **Induction**: establishing, maintaining and developing standards of behaviour and performance at the outset of employment as a foundation for an enduring and effective working relationship.
- **Collective and individual development**: recognizing and addressing those areas where expertise and capability are either not present, or else in need of improvement.
- **Career management and development**: in which the organization acknowledges the aspirations of those who come to work for it, and takes steps to make available such prospects and opportunities as it can.
- **Work patterns**: reflecting the demands for maximizing and optimizing returns on investment in technology and expertise and in ensuring that products, services and service levels are delivered to customers and clients when they need them.
- **Pay and rewards**: recognizing that any fit between work and people has to be rewarded adequately and in ways that are transparent, equitable and fair (see Figure 19.1).

Maintenance factors in HRM

The maintenance factors in HRM are as follows:

- induction;
- performance measurement and appraisal;
- job and work development;
- occupational health.

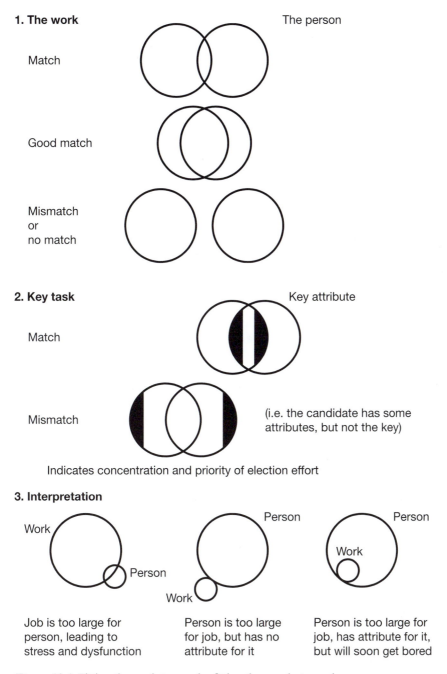

Figure 19.1 Fitting the work to people: fitting the people to work

Induction

The purpose of induction is to get the new member of staff to be as productive as possible, as quickly as possible. This consists of matching the organization's needs with those of the individual as follows.

Viewing the FWP–FPW process in this way enables the following to be made clear:

- the match of skills and capabilities with work demands;
- the extent to which jobs are under-loaded, adequate or overloaded;
- the extent to which jobs and tasks are likely to become meaningful and fulfilling, or boring and alienating;
- the need for precise job descriptions in terms of describing accurately the tasks; identifying areas where shortcomings may be apparent; and using these to target the desired sections of the workforce;
- recognizing that there may be wider problems in terms of how work is parcelled up; management style; the nature of rewards, and the basis on which they are delivered.
- Setting the attitudes and standards of behaviour required; ensuring that employees know what is expected of them, and that they can conform to these expectations and requirements (see Chapter 5).
- Job training and familiarization, mainly to do with ways of working required by the organization and ensuring that these are matched with the new employee's expertise.
- Introductions to the new team, work colleagues, managers and supervisors, and other key contacts as the result of gaining confidence, understanding, mutuality of interest and personal comfort.
- Familiarization with the environment, premises, ways of working and specific obligations on the part of the employer.

Commitment is vital. Many organizations go to a lot of trouble to ensure that the process is adequately and effectively completed, recognizing the returns on excellent and well resourced induction programmes.

It is, however, essential to recognize the problems that can, and do, arise if induction is not effectively carried out (see Chapter 5). Failing to recognize the importance of the employment process leads to uncertainty and discomfort on the part of the staff, lack of immediate familiarization with managers and key colleagues and, in some cases, the new employee making mistakes in their dealings with customers and clients, or in the management of production processes and IT.

Performance measurement and appraisal

Performance measurement and appraisal are conducted for the organization's departments, divisions, groups and individuals. To be effective, performance appraisal and measurement must be conducted as follows:

- preset and pre-agreed timescales in which formal reviews will take place;
- preset and pre-agreed aims and objectives, priorities, performance targets and deadlines for achievement;

- a structure of regularized reviews, combined with a continual and participative working relationship;
- concentration on a combination of measurement and evaluation, recording achievements and setting targets and objectives for the future.

Organizations that conduct effective performance appraisal and measurement find that because of the fully participative nature, much greater staff engagement is achieved.

It follows therefore that there is a necessary body of skills and knowledge required of the manager in the conduct of effective performance appraisal and management. It follows also that there is a required organizational commitment to ensure that the process is an operational management priority, and the results of any appraisal are recorded and, where necessary, acted on (see Box 19.6).

Job and work development

Job and work development takes place on all fronts as follows:

- the development of work expertise so that tasks and occupations are carried out at ever-higher levels;

Box 19.6: John Hargreaves

John Hargreaves was a taxation manager for the Prudential insurance company. John Hargreaves was engaged to make sure that all of the company's dealings with the taxation and revenue authorities were strong, accurate and comprehensive.

John Hargreaves was set specific targets, one of which was to ensure that the company had no problems or comebacks in its dealings with the taxation and revenue authorities. At the end of his first year in post, there were no problems reported, and accordingly the company gave John Hargreaves an excellent performance review and awarded him a bonus.

At the end of the second year, John Hargreaves spotted some discrepancies in the company's dealings with the revenue authorities. He notified these to the company's top management. He was told not to worry about these; and again, he was awarded a bonus.

At the end of the following year, John Hargreaves found the same discrepancies in the company's dealings with the revenue authorities. This time, the company sacked him.

John Hargreaves took the company to employment tribunal; and he won £300,000 in compensation. In a statement made after the case, he declared that he had done no more than agree performance targets, and strive to meet them. It was the results of his meeting in relation to the performance targets that had offended the company.

Clearly, one lesson is that no organization or its managers should ask employees to participate in, connive at or ignore irregularities.

More generally, however, it is essential that companies abide by the consequences, as well as the opportunities, of setting performance targets and then asking individuals to meet them.

- development of attitudes and behaviour so that an ever-greater commitment is engaged between staff and organization;
- development of inter- and intra-group relations so that there is an ever-greater harmony of activities within the organization;
- development of information patterns so that staff are kept as well informed as possible about developments within the organization.

Within this context, it is essential that managers recognize that all staff have their own aspirations in relation to their job, occupation and place of work (see Chapter 8).

For some occupations, job and work development involves job rotation, enrichment and enlargement in which people are trained and developed in an ever-increasing range of tasks and expertise. For other staff, there are development opportunities in project work and secondments. Others still will take further and higher education courses and engage in technical training and activities, and continuous professional development (see Box 19.7).

Occupational health

Organizations are increasingly assuming responsibility for the good health of their staff and taking positive steps and making interventions that are designed to ensure the following:

Box 19.7: Ernst & Young

Ernst & Young, the global/international management consulting firm, requires all of its staff to spend 10 per cent of their working time on 'developmental activities'.

These developmental activities take, with very few exceptions, a fully open and flexible form. Thus, staff can find themselves engaged in:

- prospecting in new markets and locations;
- developing relationships with schools, colleges and universities;
- evaluating present areas of activity for business development;
- engaging in pilot and pioneering activities with particular clients to see if new markets can be developed.

The stated purpose is to ensure that the organization and its staff 'do not stand still'. The benefits to the organization are that the staff, and therefore the collective and individual expertise, are continuously developing. There is also a marketing and public relations advantage, in that this form of encouragement means that positive responses are likely to be forthcoming when clients approach the company with new proposals and initiatives.

Finally, all staff and organizations need the opportunity to progress (see Chapter 8). To limit people's ambitions, or to pigeonhole them into an assured state of activities for the long-term, is both collectively damaging to morale, and individually demotivating.

- the prevention of accidents and illnesses in so far as is reasonably practicable;
- remedial action when work-based accidents and illnesses do occur;
- the management of known and understood occupational illnesses and injuries (e.g. stress; repetitive strain injuries);
- the provision of training and briefing in occupations and tasks that require specific procedures to be adopted;
- compliance with health and safety legislation;
- compliance with specific workplace regulations;
- compliance with specific sectoral regulations.

It is clearly right that organizations take an active interest in the health and welfare of their staff. It is clearly right also that staff are trained and developed in any task or activity that could otherwise conceivably cause illness or injury.

Most organizations support the occupational health effort with official channels of reference to healthcare and occupational health professionals. This is so that, when illnesses and injuries do occur, the organization can gain a swift and expert response, and again use this as the basis for taking remedial action (see Box 19.8).

Employee relations

It is usual to define employee relations as: 'A system for the regulation of workplace practice and behaviour' (Donovan, 1967).

It is additionally usual to define a broad framework for ER as a relationship between:

- government, which legislates for ER and workplace practice;
- employers, in discharging their enduring responsibilities to staff and in conducting and developing their relationships with the staff in accordance with the provisions of the law and the demands of the business;
- employees and their representatives, including trade unions, in ensuring that required standards of behaviour, probity and performance are carried out within the constraints of the particular situation.

Government has an additional influence as a major employer of high volumes of staff with a great range of expertise. Government is therefore extremely well placed to take actions through its own institutions to set the standard, tone and 'aura' of ER.

ER developments

Many organizations have actively re-drawn the relationship between staff management practices and ER in terms of integration with, and contribution to, continuing organizational performance. As well as being concerned with employee terms and conditions, and the state of the working environment, many organizations now consult and negotiate with staff representatives and recognized trade unions on a much wider range of issues including:

- productivity and service delivery issues;
- new product, service and market development;
- organizational operating expenses and how to manage these;

Box 19.8: 'For cod's sake'

'For cod's sake' was the headline run by the national press when it became clear that the health of some elderly people living in warden-assisted accommodation in Norwich was being put at risk by a friendly neighbour.

This neighbour had for several months been going out and buying fish and chips for his less able neighbours. The fish and chip shop was a five-minute walk away from the warden-assisted accommodation. Everyone in the accommodation looked forward to their regular treat. However, one of the wardens felt that there could be a health and safety risk and duly informed the local council's Health and Safety Department who decided to ban it. The reasons given were as follows:

- the food might get cold;
- people could get food poisoning;
- people could choke on the food.

Defending its position the council's Health and Safety Department pointed to food regulations which stated that all hot food brought into this kind of environment must be delivered in appropriately insulated regulation containers in order that the temperature at point of consumption is maintained at a sufficiently high level.

This story is an excellent illustration of the two extremes of the effective management of occupational and organizational health:

- on the one hand, clearly standards and practices have to be set, maintained and followed;
- on the other hand, they have to be tempered with a sense of what is fair and reasonable in the circumstances.

Managers therefore need to know and understand where the boundaries truly lie, and the effects of their actions in:

- ensuring the safe and healthy management of their premises;
- concentration on the letter of the law, rather than the context in which it is being applied.

Source: Daily Express, 28 May 2009.

- the design and implementation of technology changes and upgrades, together with the staff training and development necessary;
- the opening up of new markets, products, services and locations.

This represents a shift away from traditional approaches to ER. Many organizations that had traditional and adversarial approaches to ER now seek more inclusive and participative approaches for the future.

However, it remains true that a substantial part of organizational ER practice is concerned with resolving problems, disputes, grievances and disciplinary issues. These issues arise as the result of any, or all, of the following:

- genuine misunderstandings;
- negligence;
- personal, professional and occupational clashes;
- determination to engage in conflict.

Historically, these matters used to be resolved through reference to lengthy and complicated procedures (and, in many cases, this is still the case). The provision of procedures, together with ensuring adequate representation, remains a statutory duty. However, many organizations and their managers have come to know and understand that if matters can be resolved without recourse to formal procedures, it is much more productive and less stressful for all concerned. This, in turn, has led to a much greater emphasis on management development and training in the field of ER as follows:

- problem-solving and resolution;
- disputes and grievances management;
- correct ways to conduct disciplinary and grievance hearings;
- the context of ER, including the costs involved;
- the management of conflict, including recognition and understanding of how people are likely to behave when any conflict is finally resolved;
- redundancy management;
- restructuring, redeployment and seeking alternatives to redundancies and lay-offs.

This is underpinned by organizations producing comprehensive staff handbooks, in which all duties and obligations are clearly set out. Such staff handbooks have to be made accessible to all staff so that everyone knows the standards of attitude, behaviour and performance required, and the responses that the organization and its managers can, and will, take if these standards are not met.

Problems facing HR and ER

The pursuit of effective strategic and operational HR and ER requires that some fundamental problems and issues are addressed. These are:

- isolation;
- lack of value;
- lack of authority.

It is additionally usual to look at the position of HR in organizations as follows:

- the HR effort is fully integrated with all other activities and operations;
- the HR effort is integrated to an extent with activities and operations;
- there is little or no integration between HR and other activities and operations.

Isolation

The isolation of HR occurs when the function operates without any integration with the rest of the organization. The result is that HR policies and procedures are published but not followed (or only followed by accident). Managers and staff make reference to HR policies and procedures only when they need to, normally when a problem has arisen and become serious.

The result is that HR find themselves having to investigate very quickly matters of which they have no prior knowledge or understanding. They have to find ways of using such events to try to convince managers and staff (and their representatives) that HR advice based on expert knowledge and understanding of the field are both worthwhile, and also effective in business and operational terms.

Such involvement ought then to be used as a lever to try to become more centrally involved. However, in practice it does not always work easily; and it can and does take years in many organizations for HR to gain a substantial and influential position.

Lack of value

The second problem or barrier is the lack of value placed on HR and ER expertise. Where this is the case, HR finds itself in one of the following positions:

- where it is overtly unvalued, the top HR person is of lesser rank and status than those in charge of other functional departments (e.g. there is a marketing director but an HR manager);
- where it is overtly under-staffed, and so demonstrably unable to cope with any volume of HR work demanded;
- where it is overtly, adequately or even over-staffed, but confined to publishing policies and procedures rather than implementing them;
- wherever there are serious HR and ER problems, directors and managers make reference to outside agencies and consultancies directly rather than to HR in the first instance.

The result in each case is that the perception of lack of value is reinforced. For expanded periods of time, if such activities are allowed to persist, HR expertise is lost from the organization altogether.

Lack of authority

Lack of authority occurs where HR find themselves without the same influence in matters of their own domain as other functional areas. Thus, for example, marketing decisions are finalized and implemented by marketing; and the ultimate authority on manufacturing and sales will be the directors of those functions. On the other hand, on employment and staffing matters, HR's authority is not final in this way; and this means that other functional heads are able to implement HR initiatives either in their own ways or else not at all.

Where any of these problems occur, the result is to reduce the ability of HR to make an effective contribution. Where the problems are allowed to persist, the isolation and lack of value and authority become very expensive, because the organization is effectively employing people not to use their expertise.

A strategic decision is therefore required in relation to the nature, competition, remit and influence of HR activities, so that this part of the organization makes a fully effective contribution (see Box 19.9).

> **Box 19.9: The new job**
>
> After many years of working in industry, Nicholas Holmes joined the University Business School as a lecturer. He quickly found that he loved the work, especially the involvement with students, and the opportunity to be involved on projects of interest and value with people from all over the world.
>
> After he had been in post for two years, Nicholas approached his head of department with a view to discussing his progress.
>
> 'Oh, it's fine', the head of department stated. 'You are doing fine.'
>
> The head of department then made it very clear that the conversation was at an end.
>
> Nicholas's performance was not discussed further for another nine years. This was in spite of the fact that HR sent regular round-robin e-mails asking people to arrange their annual appraisals, agree targets and sign forms.
>
> Finally, the head of department moved on. Now a veteran of twelve years' service, Nicholas went and asked the new head of department for an appraisal.
>
> Nicholas and the new head of department followed the internet links to Nicholas's own personnel records. These records stated that he had been given excellent ratings for each of the past eleven years.
>
> This example demonstrates what happens when HR has no influence or authority. Individuals (managers and staff) take it upon themselves to follow HR procedures in their own ways.
>
> It additionally needs to be noted that this can be very dangerous. If, in this particular case, a problem had arisen with Nicholas Holmes, it would have been very difficult to do anything about him, in terms of performance at least, because of his excellent ratings.

Conclusions

The purpose here has been to review the issues present when seeking to manage and develop the staff in terms of what HRM and ER actually demand.

Staff, especially, respond positively when they know and understand they are being treated equally, fairly and reasonably; and they know and understand also when they are not being treated equally, fairly and reasonably. Each of the areas covered ought to be an integral part of all organizational managerial practice.

To fail to understand value and implement these aspects of HRM and ER eventually leads to problems. If the HR and ER effort is not valued, recognized or given influence, organizations find themselves having to pay to resolve staffing problems once they have occurred, rather than having the institutions and practices in place that prevent them from occurring in the first place.

It is therefore essential that organizations and their top and senior managers take an informed, positive and strategic view of what they want their HR function to deliver, and then provide the resources to ensure that it makes this contribution as fully and as effectively as possible. To fail to do this is very expensive as above. To fail to do this also means that it is increasingly likely that organizations will lose any reputation that they may have of being a good employer.

Part 4

Organizational behaviour – expertise and application

The overall purpose of Part 4 is to draw the direct relationship between effective management practice, and an understanding of organizational behaviour, in the full range of work situations.

Throughout the book, the position adopted is that nothing can be achieved without reference to creating effective patterns of behaviour. In this context, the relationship between expertise in OB and its application is drawn as follows:

*   **general management**: the need for a professional approach; the need to engage human commitment as a key to delivering the results required;
*   **strategy**: the need to understand that what is determined and prioritized can only be implemented as a result of the human effort;
*   **operations**: the need to ensure that the specific aspects of quality, safety, security and integrity are present and delivered at all times;
*   **workplace behaviour**: drawing the direct relationship between specific patterns of behaviour, and levels of organizational performance;
*   **stress**: recognizing the effects that adverse patterns of behaviour and management styles have upon individuals, groups and organizations;
*   **looking to the future**: in which the lessons are drawn together, so as to provide a foundation for the future management of organizations.

Again, the view is taken that it is impossible to deliver effective general management, strategy, direction or operational performance without engaging the expertise of those present. The converse of this is that it is very easy to create the conditions in which effective performance is not possible, or where it is certain to fall short of full success.

Finally, for the future, it is essential to recognize and understand that repetition of past mistakes, or continuing leadership and managerial practice based on status or influence rather than expertise, is certain to lead to the mistakes of the past being repeated.

20 The nature of general management

Introduction

Any study of organizational behaviour is only fully effective if it contributes to the expertise of managers in all sectors, organizations and activities. Whatever their precise remit, at the core of managerial expertise is knowing and understanding how all their key stakeholders will think, behave, act and react to given sets of circumstances. The purpose of this chapter is therefore to introduce the application of organizational behaviour and its different 'components' as a crucial part of the managerial expertise demanded (see Box 20.1).

The professionalization of management

At present, anyone can be a manager. There is no recognized entry qualification, body of knowledge or self-regulating management organization. There is no formal oversight of those who practise the expertise of management; and no system of self-discipline. There is no formal requirement for continuous professional development (CPD), and no personal commitment demanded of those who wish to continue to practise.

Having said that, clearly many managers do take a thoroughly professional attitude to their work, putting in a great deal of personal as well as occupational commitment. They spend their own time visiting other companies and organizations, picking up lessons, attending conferences and CPD events, reading management journals, delving into books on all parts of the subject. They make it their business to know and understand every aspect of their own organization's activities, so that they can assess the critical contribution required of their own sphere of activities, and how it integrates with the whole. They therefore build up what is *de facto* a professional expertise both overall and in the crucial areas of:

- achieving things through people;
- making a profit;
- integrity;
- their dealings with stakeholders.

Achieving things through people

In practice, everything that an organization does is delivered through its people, and their expertise and commitment. It is a crucial principle of effective, successful and profitable management; and so to know and understand how people behave, act and react is a major part of managerial expertise.

Box 20.1: Professions

The 'classical' professions are medicine, law, the priesthood and the army. The following properties were held to distinguish these from the rest of society.

- **Distinctive expertise**: not available elsewhere in society or in its individual members.
- **Distinctive body of knowledge**: required by all those who aspire to practise in the profession.
- **Entry barriers**: in the form of examinations, time serving, learning from experts.
- **Formal qualifications**: given as the result of acquiring the body of knowledge and clearing the entry barriers.
- **High status**: professions are at the top of the occupational tree.
- **Distinctive morality**: for medicine, the commitment to keep people alive as long as possible; for law, a commitment to represent the client's best interests; for the church, a commitment to godliness and to serve the congregation's best interests; for the army, to fight within stated rules of law.
- **High value**: professions make a distinctive and positive contribution to both the organizations and individual members of the society.
- **Self-regulating**: professions set their own rules, codes of conduct, standards of performance and qualifications.
- **Self-disciplining**: professions establish their own bodies for dealing with problems, complaints and allegations of malpractice.
- **Unlimited reward levels**: according to preferred levels of charges and the demands of society.
- **Life membership**: dismissal at the behest of the profession; ceasing to work for one employer does not constitute loss of profession.
- **Personal commitment**: to high standards of practice and morality; commitment to deliver the best possible in all circumstances.
- **Self-discipline**: commitment to personal standards of behaviour in the pursuit of professional excellence.
- **Continuous development**: of knowledge and skills; a commitment to keep abreast of all developments and initiatives in the field.
- **Governance**: by institutions established by the profession itself.

Notes

In absolute terms 'management' falls short in most areas. Formal qualifications are not a prerequisite to practice (though they are highly desirable and ever more sought after). Discipline and regulation of managers is still overwhelmingly a matter for organizations and not management institutions. There is some influence over reward levels and training and development. Measures of status and value are uneven. Management institutions act as focal points for debate; and they also have a lobbying function. They do not act as regulators.

There is a clear drive towards the professionalization of management. This is based on attention to expertise, knowledge and qualifications; and the relationship between these and the value added to organizations by expert managers.

In 1995, Charles Handy proposed that all business school graduates should be required to take the equivalent of the Hippocratic Oath, thus committing themselves to best practice and high standards and quality of performance.

If management is viewed in this way, it is a highly professional activity and one that demands a set body of expertise and a large measure of commitment on the part of its practitioners.

In traditional terms, management falls short of the full status of profession in that the elements outlined here do not constitute yet a formal entry barrier (in medicine, the law, the clergy and the military, it is essential to have the stated qualifications before being allowed to practise).

Box 20.2: 'They don't want it'

One of the most insidious statements made by organizations and managers is the assertion that staff do not want responsibility, involvement, advancement and growth. This is a mark of disrespect; and it is normally reinforced by the fact that the organization then becomes self-serving to some groups of staff but not others.

It is, in any case, simply not true. Any group of people given the choice between being bored, alienated and disaffected, or not, will take the latter always.

This extends to all places of work. The idea that 'they don't want it' was perversely reinforced by the Affluent Worker studies of the 1950s and 1960s. These identified widespread and enduring alienation among the workforce, and the value of earnings accrued at work in the pursuit of out-of-work activities.

Because of the alienation of the staff at work, staff sought their own fulfilment through out-of-work activities.

There is a key and enduring lesson from this attitude: the Affluent Worker studies took place, among others, in the UK car companies. All of these companies have had production and operational difficulties; and the largest, General Motors, is effectively bankrupt and trying frantically to restructure and develop for itself a viable position for the future.

It is therefore essential to establish and implement clear standards of behaviour and performance, a work ethic and discipline, patterns of communication and inter-action, a style of leadership to which everyone can respond positively; and collective involvement and participation requiring everyone's commitment to organizational purpose (see Box 20.2).

The results that the organization produces in terms of

- effective, desirable and sought-after products and services;
- financial returns;
- provision of work and employment;
- contribution to the community and the environment;

are all achieved by people. It is therefore necessary to know and understand the expectations of these and other stakeholder groups, and what it takes to satisfy them. It is also necessary to know and understand what causes the behaviour and attitudes of each of these groups to change and how to respond to what is, after all, their (collective and individual) human behaviour.

In this context, achieving things through people requires attention to each of the following areas:

- making a profit;
- establishing performance targets;
- understanding customer and supplier behaviour;
- understanding shareholder and financial demands;
- decision-making.

Making a profit

All organizations of any size, and in every sector, need to make a profit. Part of this 'profit' is a surplus of income over expenditure; and this surplus can be measured in a variety of ways as follows:

- immediate and short-term;
- medium to long-term;
- over the lifetime of the organization.

It can also be looked at from the point of view of:

- surplus per member of staff;
- surplus per location (for multi-site organizations);
- surplus per item of product or service;
- surplus per product/service cluster.

From a purely financial point of view, therefore, there are immediate decisions to be taken: which of these measures are to be used to assess 'profit'? Why have these measures been chosen (and not others)? What are you going to include (and not include) in the calculations against which you are going to measure the surplus; and why? (see Box 20.3).

So there is an immediate and critical decision to be taken. Once the position is determined, it then needs to be explained clearly and openly to everyone. If for any reason this is not acceptable or possible, then the whole question of the financial structure becomes uncertain. This is because:

- backers need to know and understand what they are backing;
- customers need to have full confidence in the long-term viability of the organization as a provider of products and services;
- the staff need assurance about the duration of their jobs and careers.

The communities in which organizations exist and operate also need these assurances. Communities need to know that organizations are going to be active, vibrant and

Box 20.3: Off-balance sheet

It is completely legitimate and perfectly legal for organizations and their managers to decide which costs they are going to offset against any profitability and viability, and which they are not. Accounting and reporting conventions simply require that these costs and liabilities are made clear, that the reasons for not accounting for them at this stage are explained and that some provision is made somewhere for them to be addressed at some stage.

In this way it is possible (and legitimate again) to report what is often called 'an operating profit' – surpluses made on steady-state activities.

The problem arises when off-balance sheet items become 'out of sight and therefore out of mind'. Everything becomes driven by the operating profit. No attempt is made to address the off-balance sheet liabilities and costs. Eventually considering and even acknowledging these costs and liabilities become uncomfortable, and therefore unacceptable. They are therefore ignored in the (forlorn) hope that they will go away.

positive for a long period of time. Communities are not well served if they are littered with closed and run-down business premises and empty shops.

The other parts of profit

As stated above, the financial measure is one part of profit. The other parts are:

- reputation;
- integrity;
- confidence.

Reputation

No organization can remain viable without at least some kind of positive reputation; and this must cover each of the following areas to some extent:

- reputation as an employer;
- reputation for quality and availability of products and services;
- reputation for customer relations;
- reputation for supplier assurance and management;
- reputation for financial profitability and viability.

Clearly, these elements are interrelated. For example, product and service quality is going to suffer if the company gains a reputation as a bad employer; and this in turn affects financial performance (see Box. 20.4).

It is much easier to lose a good reputation than to build one. To build a good reputation takes years; to lose a good reputation can take place overnight. It is therefore essential that all managers do commit to the 'professionalism' required to achieve excellent products and services, supported by excellent service. All managers additionally

Box 20.4: The Virgin approach to reputation management

Richard Branson, the founder and executive chairman of the Virgin organization, has a clear and unequivocal position on the structure on which his organization builds its reputation (and therefore its viability and financial profitability). This structure is based on an order of priority of stakeholders which states that:

- staff come first because without good staff it is not possible to deliver the best-quality products and services or customer service;
- customers come second because the presence of expert and committed staff delivering excellent service is what causes customers to come back again and again;
- if each of these first two are in place, the financial position will follow.

The lesson is not necessarily to copy the Virgin approach; it is to have a position as clear and straightforward as possible and to have this known and understood by all.

Source: R. Branson (1990) *Losing My Virginity* – Virgin.

need to know and understand where reputation may be damaged or destroyed and to have in place:

- a clear response to crises when these do occur (see Chapter 23);
- the capability to assess any situation very quickly, and the expertise to determine and deliver the correct response;
- the personal, as well as expert, presence to face any critics in person and to recognize and address their concerns to remedy things where necessary (or to explain clearly why no remedy is required).

Integrity

Pettinger (1998) describes integrity as a management skill. The contention is that it is a fact of human behaviour that everyone from time to time dissembles or prevaricates, and feels uncomfortable about facing difficult people and situations. In particular sets of circumstances, therefore, people are strongly disposed to lying, not telling the truth in full, losing their temper, pulling rank and finding injury to their pride as a major crisis.

Each of these compromises integrity. So from a professional point of view, managers need to commit themselves not to doing any of these things under any circumstances whatsoever. In practice, including managerial situations, these things will happen. When they do, it is essential that they are acknowledged and put right as soon as possible. To fail to do so simply means that the individual concerned quickly becomes known as one who lacks integrity (see Box 20.5).

Integrity is therefore a skill which has to be learned and applied. Lack of integrity affects personal, professional and organizational reputation, and is certain also to change

Box 20.5: Some commentaries on integrity

- *'He is a great president but a complete sleaze-ball otherwise.'* Commentator on Bill Clinton, 1997 – Fox News.
- *'He is a sweetie and I would not trust him as far as I could throw him.'* Aide to Tony Blair on his accession as Labour Party leader.
- *'He became involved in the cocaine industry to support his family.'* Francisco Escobar on his late brother Pablo (at that time world's largest cocaine dealer).

Frith (2008) states that it is acceptable to tell 'a white lie' in certain circumstances whereby to tell the truth would be either hurtful, harmful or else otherwise unacceptable or discomforting to the others affected; though the 'white lie' must not itself be capable of discovery. Thus, for example, it does become acceptable, in some circumstances, to say to someone that: 'I left my mobile phone in the office over the weekend and so this is why I am only getting back to you now'; or 'I had no computer connection these last few days and so many apologies for the delay in replying'; or 'I got held up on my way into work because the train was late' – as long as the 'white lie' cannot possibly be discovered or do real harm.

overall credibility. Working relations become fractious, and the ability to get things done is compromised when people do not know whether they are being told the truth or the whole truth.

So it is essential to accept integrity as a key part of professional development. Crucially it adds to the viability and confidence of the organization; and when it is not present, it dilutes the whole organizational effort.

Confidence

In their dealings with any organization people need confidence. Specifically:

- staff need to have confidence in the fundamental viability of the organization structures, finances, products and services;
- customers and clients need to have confidence in the quality of the products and services delivered;
- suppliers need to have confidence that they will get paid for the supplies that they do deliver, and that this will occur on a regular and continuing basis;
- backers need to have the confidence that they will get their money back, and the returns that they expect.

Confidence in an organization is founded in what is known, believed and perceived about it, how it conducts its affairs, the products and services that it delivers, its reputation as an employer and its reputation for providing financial profits (see Box 20.6).

People need to have confidence in the organizations that employ them and with which they do business. People need to be certain (in many cases, they need to believe) that they can go to any organization or public service institution, and they will get the products

Box 20.6: Northern Rock

People need to have confidence in the organizations with which they deal and do business. Nothing illustrated this as clearly as the Northern Rock crisis of July 2007.

The Northern Rock was (and remains) a small regional retail bank located in north-east England. In July 2007, it published a short report stating that it was unable to meet its short- and medium-term liabilities and was therefore seeking funds from other sources. This might eventually lead to a take-over.

The regional media in north-east England got hold of the story. The immediate result was that some customers began to withdraw their funds and close their accounts. Some corporate shareholders sold their shares in order to invest elsewhere.

The national media then ran the story. Now the result was a mass panic. The government tried to issue statements confirming that everyone's savings were safe, that nobody would lose money.

This was to no avail. The government statements were thought to be half-hearted. It then became clear that people's savings were guaranteed only up to £25,000. Over the weekend of 14 August 2007, hundreds of people formed queues outside the bank's branches, desperately hoping to withdraw their money before the organization collapsed.

The government moved first to guarantee the survival of the bank (which it took into public ownership). However, the damage was done. Confidence was lost. The top and senior management team was dismissed. Additionally, confidence in the whole banking sector was now called into question (as it turned out with good reason).

The key lesson is to know and understand the full range of consequences when confidence is lost. What might otherwise have seemed to be a normal statement (seeking funds elsewhere, a possible takeover) was very quickly seen in the context that: 'there must be something wrong with this organization', rather than as a steady-state or mainstream business activity.

and services that they seek, to the quality that they expect and at the times when they need and want them. People need to be able to go to not-for-profit organizations and charities, having the confidence that any donation or transaction is going to support the remit or purposes stated by the organization.

Profit has therefore to be seen in its full context. The narrow drive for surplus of income over expenditure cannot take place without reference to the other aspects; and these are all highly contextual issues requiring expertise in how people think, behave, believe and react in practice.

Achieving performance

Achieving performance in the pursuit of profit, success and effectiveness is critical. The problem with all performance management lies in how to structure individual performance so that the desired total output is achieved.

Again, the key question is why? This stems from the overall purpose and remit of the organization and the customers, clients and end-users that it serves. In detail, this means tackling the question 'Why?' as follows:

- Why does the organization serve these customers and clients?
- Why does it (or seek to) do this volume of business and not other volumes?
- Why does it operate in these locations and not others?
- Why does it sell or provide the particular range of products and services and not others?
- Why does it employ these present staff in terms of numbers, expertise, capability and willingness?

Having addressed and answered the questions, attention has then to turn to the outputs as follows:

- How much money does the organization have to make (or in the case of a public service organization, what is the budget that has to be followed)?
- Why is this the right figure? Is the organization capable of making the return (or sticking to budgets); if so, why; if not, why not? Is this return available easily, or only if a particular set of market conditions prevail?

It therefore becomes clear very quickly that assessing the desired and optimum levels of performance, and then creating the conditions in which these levels become feasible and 'right', is both complex and demanding.

This, in turn, causes companies and organizations to go to one or more of the following:

- establishing levels of performance that are satisfactory (Simon, 1962);
- establishing targets that are one-dimensional, clearly understood and therefore supposedly easy to measure;
- taking last year's figures as being perfect, and adding a percentage to them;
- couching targets and desired achievements in the blandest of terms possible (e.g. 'We will seek to optimize our returns on investment'; 'We will aim to be the highest performer in our sector').

The best that can be said for any of these approaches is that good to high performance in terms of achieving organizational potential is feasible where the rest of the behavioural pressures are strong, inclusive, cohesive and positive. Otherwise, performance is at best a range of achievements in disparate parts. More usually performance declines; because there is no clear purpose or overall target, remedies tend to be narrow, piecemeal – and wrong.

The key to performance management is to be able to get to grips with each of the above questions in detail. It is necessary to recognize that much of this concerns the ways in which the organization collectively, and all of its component parts, behave and inter-react together. If it were simply a question of harmonizing technology, information, raw materials and resources, and matching them with expertise, organizational and managerial life would indeed be much simpler.

The driving force behind this need for overall clarity is that once it is achieved, however hard that may be, the nature of the performance required from the component parts of the organization – departments, divisions, functions, frontline and support activities – becomes clear also.

For example, it is much easier to set viable performance targets for HR when the nature of expertise demanded is clear; and it is much easier to set sales targets if the volumes and quality of business have been determined in advance. The converse of this is also true: it is much harder to set clear targets in these and all areas if there is no clarity or understanding about the overall purpose of the organization.

Performance as a process

The other key aspect of achieving performance is to see it as a process, rather than purely as a set of targets. It is true that both overall and also 'milestone' targets have to be set. However, the process of performance establishment and management has to be seen as a combination of individual and collective professional and occupational commitment; and supportive, directive and sometimes prescriptive management style. Again, this is only effective if there is a full clarity of purpose, and an open and strong management style (see Chapters 9 and 16). The process requires the engagement of individuals and groups, and this is only effective if there is overall, as well as individual, clarity of purpose (see Box 20.7).

Box 20.7: Mars, Marathon and Snickers

The Mars chocolate company required its marketing and sales staff to assess the brand names of some of its most well-known products.

A project team was duly constituted, and everyone looked forward to a speedy resolution. However, as well as having different brand names, the products themselves served different markets in different parts of the world. Accordingly, the project team quickly ran into difficulties. The first meeting broke up without agreement, and everyone promised to seek guidance from their own particular locations, and to carry out additional research into what their markets specifically wanted in terms of benefit from the products on offer.

Three months later the project team met and, again, broke up without resolution. Again, however, they agreed to meet in three months' time; and now, this would be in a different location (in order that those from the remote parts did not have to make the same journey on regular occasions).

This series of meetings went on for eighteen months. At last the product director became impatient. As the seventh meeting of the group was breaking up, he asked for a progress report. Back came the response: 'We are making good progress but we still have not reached agreement.'

The product director ordered the group back together and told them not to break up until agreement had been reached. Agreement was reached later the same day.

The lesson is that the project itself, while it had a clear purpose at the outset, quickly became a more or less social situation, in which the task remit was incidental. This happens to many project teams, groups and committees. It also emphasizes the need for effective performance management in every aspect of the organization's activities.

Performance in context

Performance has to be seen in context. At its simplest, this means:

- those who want 30 per cent returns on investment must operate in sectors where these returns are possible;
- companies that wish to be in submarine/nuclear power/groceries/IT must be prepared to take the returns that are on offer in their chosen sector.

By exception, excellent and effective companies do transform the possibilities that are available in particular sectors through their own excellence, vision and imagination (see Chapters 3 and 17). Companies that seek to revitalize their sectors do have to commit themselves as organizations in every aspect of their activities. The process of transforming performance levels and expectations is likely to take many years (Semler, 2003). It is also certain to mean that people will have to leave their familiarity and comfort zones (occupationally at least) and be prepared, capable and willing to find new ways of addressing the work that has to be done.

In any case, the context of performance changes all the time. Favourable conditions may allow for annual targets to be met in eight months; and as long as this has been the subject of constant review and appraisal (see Chapter 19), this then becomes the new starting point for the next phase of activities. Unfavourable conditions may mean that targets established are simply not capable of being achieved; and again, as long as the process is in place, there will be no problem revising them in the light of the new set of circumstances.

Issues arise in both cases. Where desired performance is either not clarified or the subject of agreement it becomes a temptation to take things easy when conditions are favourable, and to panic when problems arise.

Especially if the performance management process is not fully effective, the lack of attention to performance bonuses becomes a further element in creating the divide between managers and the rest of the staff (see Chapter 12).

The ability to establish and deliver specific levels of overall and individual performance therefore depends on managerial capability. This capability must be founded in the fullest possible understanding of:

- what is required overall;
- what is required of each individual;
- how the individual performance is to be integrated with the whole;
- how to operate a continuous process of performance, development and review (see also Chapter 19).

It follows from all of the above that a complexity of measures is needed. Some of these measures are going to be subjective, imprecise and requiring agreement between manager and employee, and/or between members of work teams and groups. Attention is required to how things are done, as well as what is done, so as to avoid doing the wrong things for the right reasons (see Chapter 6). For example:

- the sales teams of power and energy companies meeting their targets, only for the companies to have to pay out both fines and compensation because of mis-selling by representatives;

- hospital managers cutting back on cleaning activities in order to stay within budget, only to have patients becoming ill through hospital-acquired infections.

If no attention is paid to the context, targets are set in isolation. On the day that they are set, targets may well be relevant; over the period within which they are to be achieved, they are certain to require some form of modification. Additionally, if they are not integrated and monitored on a continuous basis:

- staff will slavishly follow them in order to get good performance reviews (including bonuses);
- the organization will never learn and progress;
- managers again are to be seen to be operating in ways detached from the core business of the organization.

Customers and suppliers

The keys to the effective management of customers and suppliers are maintaining their confidence and meeting their expectations.

Customers

Customer confidence and expectations are based on the continued supply of goods and services at the quality, volume and locations demanded; and at the prices and charges expected and anticipated.

Customers also expect continuity of service and enhancements and developments in the quality and variety of goods and services on offer. Customers' perceptions have to be managed if there are material changes to what is being made available for use or consumption. Except in the case of largely captive markets (e.g. transport, energy), radical changes to pricing structures have to be carefully managed and clearly explained. This is because of the following.

- If prices rise steeply without explanation, customers are likely to at least look for alternative sources of satisfaction. Or they may not, in any case, be able to afford the new charges; and so either the customer base diminishes, or new customers have to be sought from other sectors, and their expectations have to be engaged and managed.
- If prices fall steeply, this can, and does, lead to perceptions that the quality and value have also fallen. It may be possible to attract new customers in; and when this does happen, some companies can, and do, become very successful. If managed effectively, it can lead to overall confidence being raised (see Box 20.8).

Suppliers

Suppliers' confidence and expectations are founded in:

- regularity of contracts (or understanding the value of the contract if it is a single effort);
- mutuality of interest and advantage;

> ### Box 20.8: Waitrose and value lines
>
> Waitrose, the supermarket company which is part of the John Lewis partnership, took the hitherto unheard-of step of introducing a value line into its food product ranges. There was immediate concern. Waitrose was always seen as a top-quality supermarket chain, operating in areas that the mass providers (Tesco, Sainsbury, Asda) did not and serving customers who valued what Waitrose had to offer.
>
> Clearly, the new initiative had to be carefully managed. The packaging and presentation of the new range of products clearly set them apart from the main range of goods, but without giving any impression of cheapness or tackiness.
>
> The intention was to develop the existing customer base, as well as attract those who would not normally shop at the company. It also quickly became clear that the volume and quality of the value lines would not be compromised (as, for example, with some of the other supermarket chains, which offered much cheaper products but with quality and volume reduced also).
>
> The result was to introduce a new and fresh range of products into the company. These products were to be of value to the existing customer base as above; and so the overall quality and reputation of the company itself was not compromised.

- recognition of responsibilities to each other;
- the establishment of a working relationship designed especially to ensure that any problems are dealt with as soon as possible;
- the availability of a process for exploiting any prospects of business development.

In recent years, large and powerful companies have seen fit to engage in the following practices (see also Chapter 9):

- playing off one supplier against the others so that prices and contract values are driven down;
- unilateral cancellation of contracts, often at very short notice (see Marks & Spencer example in Chapter 6);
- contracting out to suppliers (usually overseas) purely to drive down costs (see Chapter 6);
- delaying payments for deliveries of goods and services.

The best that can be said for any of these is that it may be necessary to do them as a one-off in order to get the organization out of a crisis (or looming crisis). Otherwise, the practices are unethical (see Chapter 6) and an abuse of corporate power, and will always be recognized as such. The results are:

- the suppliers will urgently seek other outlets for their goods and services;
- the suppliers will tolerate such activities only as long as they have to, and as long as they are dependent on the large and powerful organizations;
- the suppliers will put up their charges to companies and organizations that are known and understood to take an expedient view of the supply side;
- the supplier will go out of business (see Box 20.9).

Box 20.9: Collapse of a key supplier: General Motors

In 1998, General Motors, the US car giant, closed its component manufacturing arm. It contracted with a supplier formed from its previous manufacturing arm to supply all small parts that it would need to continue its manufacturing operations. This would remove a substantial part of payroll investment and technology write-downs from its balance sheet.

The new supplier was called ASSET. ASSET would also be free to contract with GM's retail divisions to provide components for maintenance, and it would also be able to seek work elsewhere.

Once the contract was established, it worked well for a while. In 2004, however, faced with rising energy costs and downturns in demand, GM unilaterally cut its contract prices to ASSET.

ASSET continued to supply at the reduced margins. In 2005, GM cut its prices again; and the same happened in 2006. In early 2007, ASSET filed for bankruptcy protection.

All production stopped for nine days. The result was that GM now had none of the components needed to assemble the cars.

GM's top and senior management were astonished. They had never considered that this would be the effect of constant cost cutting. Nor had they ever considered the scenario that now came to pass: that there would be no production.

It now became necessary for GM to refinance ASSET in order to bring it out of bankruptcy, and to get the components back into production.

There were more lasting results, however, as follows.

- The episode brought into sharp focus a wider corporate malaise, founded on a detached and uninvolved management. It transpired that none of the top fifty senior executives had ever left the office to find out why sales of cars were falling, or to try to establish what the reasons for this might be.
- The episode caused all stakeholders to examine in detail the overall strength of the company. The result of this examination was devastating also. By the end of 2008, the company as an entity was no longer viable; it was only its size and history that kept it in existence.
- The incoming US president, Barack Obama, stated that GM would not be allowed to fail but that there would be changes. The top management team was replaced. There were to be thousands of lay-offs. The production of future models must be more environmentally friendly from the point of view of both the manufacturing process and also the engine emissions.

The main lesson is to understand what can happen when the remedies for declining performance are simply guessed at, or where a simple, rather than comprehensive, approach is taken.

The financial interests

As stated above, one crucial part of general management is to ensure that companies and organizations make a profit or stay within budget; and one part of the profit is generating a financial surplus. This surplus is required for the purposes of:

- paying returns to shareholders and backers;
- paying for future investment in the advancement and development of the organization;
- providing for contingencies, crises and emergencies;
- generating an inherent value, strength and confidence in the company and its products and services as the result of 'sound finances'.

Sound finances

The constitution of 'sound finances' varies between organizations and changes with circumstances. There is therefore a very strong perception around the known, understood and expected financial structure and instruments of particular organizations.

The 'perfect financial position' is where:

- a commercial organization is financed purely through capital and retained profits; and it generates profits at the upper end of the sectoral norm as a result of the sales of its goods and services;
- if it is a public service body, it delivers top-quality services within budget; requiring budget increases only to meet any service development and enhancement, technological improvements and staffing pay rises.

However, in practice, it is not so straightforward. All organizations require overdrafts, short-term finance and lines of credit from time to time in order to get them over market changes and rises in costs of fuel, energy and other commodities. Organizations need to be able to invest in technological upgrades and product and service development when the market demands; and this is not always predictable and so can, and does, lead to requests for further share capital and loan finance.

Expectations

Expectations in the financial sphere of organizations have to be managed and met. For example, if a backer demands or expects 15 per cent return on investment per annum, then they need to be given figures and projections as to how this is to be achieved; and they need also to be given a list of things that could happen that might cause this percentage to vary (up and down). They then clearly know and understand what they are backing (see Box 20.10).

Decision-making

The other key part of professional and expert executive and managerial practice is the capability to take effective decisions; to know and understand the opportunities and consequences that are brought about as the result; and to support and justify the lines of reasoning when arriving at a particular choice.

Box 20.10: Shareholder expectations

Shareholders and their representatives have a clear duty to take an active interest in the reality of their expectations. It is a dereliction of duty simply to take a company's word that the projected returns will occur without investigating fully how ventures are to be achieved, and to establish what can conceivably go wrong.

Where a merger or venture is proposed, it is usual for the value of shares in both organizations to rise. This is because the one company is perceived to be expanding and growing. The shares of the other company are now in demand and so this pushes up the price. If the shares of both companies stay high, it is usually a reflection of actual confidence in the venture, once people have started to do a proper evaluation.

If the shares of the company taking over then fall, it is because people are having second thoughts, and some shareholders are getting out and taking a short-term profit with them.

If the shares then continue to fall, this is overwhelmingly because insufficient attention was paid at the outset to the key behavioural issues of re-forming culture, addressing staff issues and anomalies in pay and other terms and conditions, and integrating the social, professional, occupational and technological differences present.

So this reinforces the key point made earlier that expectations have to be known, understood and managed (Chapter 4). Especially with finances, people need to know and understand what is possible, and the things that change the possibilities and expectations along the way.

The standard basis for decision-making and the processes involved are as follows.

Decisions are taken at all levels – strategic and policy; operational, divisional and departmental; managerial and supervisory; and individual. Whatever the level, there are certain fundamental considerations to be considered if the process is to be effective and successful. There are also different stages that have to be understood and followed (see Figure 20.1).

Problem or issue definition

This is the starting point of the process. Once this is defined, the likely effects and consequences of particular courses of action can begin to be understood. Failure to do this may lead to considerable waste of time, effort and resource.

Process determination

Much of this depends on culture, structure, environmental and other pressures on the organization or department involved. It also depends on ways of working and the personalities and groups involved. There may also be key groups – staff, customers, vested interests, pressure groups – who must be consulted on particular matters. Not to do this, in spite of the fact that the decision may be 'right', is likely to minimize, or even nullify, the whole effect.

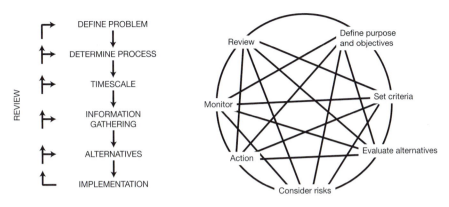

1. PROGRESSION

REVIEW

DEFINE PROBLEM

↓

DETERMINE PROCESS

↓

TIMESCALE

↓

INFORMATION GATHERING

↓

ALTERNATIVES

↓

IMPLEMENTATION

2. PROCESS

Review

Define purpose and objectives

Monitor

Set criteria

Action

Evaluate alternatives

Consider risks

Purpose: to draw the distinction between the two elements of progress and process. The former is a schematic approach; the latter is that from which the former arises, and which refines it into its final format. Effective and successful decision-making requires the confidence that is generated by continued operation of the process.

Figure 20.1 Decision-making: model and process

Timescale

Time is involved heavily in process determination. There is also a trade-off between the quality and volume of information that can be gathered and the time available to do this. The longer the timescale, the better the chance of gaining adequate information, and considering it and evaluating it effectively. However, this also increases the cost of the eventual course of action. On the other hand, a quick decision may involve hidden extras at the implementation stage if insufficient time has been spent on the background.

Information gathering

Very few decisions are taken with perfect information; conversely, decisions made without any information are pure guesswork. Both quality and volume of information are required; and means for the understanding, evaluation and review of that which is gathered are also essential.

The alternatives

The result of the process is that alternative courses of action become apparent. At the very least there is always the choice of doing nothing.

Implementation

This is the point of action. It arises as the result of working through each of the previous elements. The choice made affects future courses of action; as well as the choice, the reasons for which it was made should be understood.

This is an attempt to provide a rationale for courses of action that often have to be taken in ways that are not fully logical. Part of the purpose is therefore to recognize where the non-rational elements lie and, in recognizing these, how they can best be accommodated. It is not a prescription for providing perfect decisions. It is, rather, the means by which opportunities and consequences of following particular courses of action may be understood, assessed and evaluated.

Decision-making: other factors

Risk and uncertainty

Uncertainty occurs where no information exists. This in itself underlines the need to gain as much knowledge and understanding as possible in advance of choosing a particular course of action. However, there is an element of risk in all decision taking. This is reduced by the quality and volume of information available, and the accuracy of its evaluation.

Participation and consultation

This is necessary where a wide measure of support from among the workforce, community or public at large is required. The purpose here is to generate understanding and acceptance of courses of action.

It may also be necessary to consider:

* legal constraints, affecting all aspects of business and organization practice;
* public interest, public pressure, lobby and special interest groups;
* economic, social and political groups – including consumer groups, environmental lobbies, local and public authorities, public agencies and statutory bodies, industrial lobbies and staff representative bodies;
* committees and other formally constituted boards.

Organizational adjustment

This is where the process is limited or constrained, based on each of the factors indicated. The normal result is that the organization alters, adjusts or limits its activities in some way. Sufficient time and resource must be set aside to deal with these if what is proposed is to be supported and accepted.

Effective decisions are therefore arrived at through a combination of the preferred and chosen direction, together with recognizing and accommodating a means which this chosen direction can be made successful. A large part of the consultation, participation, staff and public communication processes are directed at generating understanding and acceptance of particular courses of action. Organizations must accept that everyone is much more likely to follow a course of action if this is understood. If they do not understand what they are being asked to do, people tend either to reject the matter outright, or else view it with suspicion and uncertainty.

Such approaches make decision-making appear rational, based on choices made in the best interests of the organization and its stakeholders. However, there is a broader context that must be known and understood.

The components of this context are:

- decision-making as a process not an event;
- the range of reasons for which decisions are taken.

All decisions have to reflect the context in which they are taken; and this context is constantly changing. Once a course of action is chosen and implemented, attention is required to subsequent developments in the organization and the environment; and the chosen course of action is then modified, steered and re-directed as appropriate.

It is a particular sign of weakness to take a decision and then stick to it when circumstances change. If circumstances change and the decision is not varied or modified, those responsible (and accountable) need to be able to state clearly why not; and if necessary to justify and defend their course of action. They may indeed be right, and they need to be able to explain why in terms that are understood by everyone. If a course of action that was chosen that was right in one set of circumstances subsequently becomes wrong because of changes and developments, then those responsible need to have:

- the capability to change course;
- the expertise to re-evaluate the circumstances and choose what is now right;
- the ability to explain the changes clearly again;
- in some circumstances, the personal courage to admit that they were wrong.

The other part of decision-making is that one choice leads to another. A decision-making process is, in practice, a series or pattern of decisions, each interrelated. Part of this continuous process defines the ability to reconcile divergent (and sometimes conflicting) interests, pressures and demands.

Another part is ensuring that the crucial corporate priorities of delivering products and services on time, to volume and quality are not lost. Another part is taking decisions for the long-term, as well as the short-term; concentrating on enduring, as well as immediate, viability.

The final part of the process requires that responses are in place when crises and emergencies arise. The effectiveness of crisis response lies in the strength of environmental knowledge and expertise, the effectiveness of risk management and risk assessment and prevention processes, the cohesion of corporate culture and the collective expertise of the top and senior management team. When a crisis does occur, there is then both the expertise and also the process in place necessary to prepare and implement effective responses (see Box 20.11).

Conclusions

The purpose of this chapter has been to summarize the nature of professional general management with particular reference to the need for the greatest possible range of understanding and expertise.

Any manager wishing to be effective in the long-term must understand the key components of professional practice, in so far as they are understood at present:

- attention to, and understanding of, what it takes to achieve things through people;
- knowledge and understanding of performance, and how this ought to be delivered in its fullest possible context;

Box 20.11: Reasons why decisions are taken

As stated above, decisions ought to be taken in the interests of the organization's profitability, effectiveness and viability, and in the interests of securing all of its stakeholders' demands.

The full range of reasons needs to be considered and evaluated also; and this includes attention to the following.

- Reasons of expediency: to be seen to be doing something.
- Serving one group of stakeholders at the expense of others (this normally applies, especially, to the financial interest being served at the expense of the staff).
- Reasons of triumph, prestige and vanity.
- The excitement of being involved in corporate adventures (this is a serious concern when considering moving into new and unknown markets).
- The need for a success, which is often a serious pressure on the top management, but which must be delivered nevertheless in terms of what is best for the organization.
- Responding to things that have been generated as the result of media interest or adverse press coverage.

It is also the case that, when decisions are taken and are then demonstrated to be wrong, there is pressure to cancel them. In many cases, the biggest barrier to cancellation is the vanity and pride of those who took the decisions in the first place. This reinforces the point made above (see Chapter 10), that one of the greatest injuries that can be done to anyone is to their personal pride.

- understanding the nature of 'profit', and the full context of what this means;
- the ability to understand the demands of all stakeholders and to manage them;
- the ability to crystallize and integrate all the pressures through the taking of effective decisions, and developing the opportunities that arise as the result.

The nature of expert general management is therefore founded in a clear understanding of organizational, environmental, occupational and behavioural pressures, and in the ability of the individual to integrate these into effective expert practice.

21 Strategy

Introduction

Strategy is supposed to be the rationale for the existence of organizations, and to reflect, define and develop the ways in which products and services are delivered. However, there are major behavioural and perceptual pressures which have to be addressed as follows.

- Strategy and policy are devised in response to the assessment and evaluation of the present position, status and strength of the organization; and the known, believed and understood state of the markets in which operations are carried out, and the wider business environment.
- The issues involved in devising strategy and policy depend, in part at least, on the pressures exerted by powerful and influential stakeholders, the rates of return that backers demand, and the nature and expertise of the staff (see Box 21.1).
- The development of strategy and policy requires evaluation and understanding of what the market is likely to be able to sustain, as well as the overall capability of the organization to fulfil specific needs and wants.
- The evaluation of strategy involves establishing parameters based on what the organization sets out to achieve and why; the extent to which it achieves these purposes; and the nature of the managerial response to opportunities and pitfalls.

Therefore, a clearly articulated, accurate and understood strategy is at the hub of all successful commercial and public activities; where success is not forthcoming, it is often where this clarity of purpose is also not present. This clarity additionally gives a standpoint for the need and capability to manage resources effectively and efficiently; and this continues to be intensified by requirements for greater accountability in both public and private sectors, and also not-for-profit activities (see Box 21.2).

The development of strategy, policy and direction

Corporate strategy is the outcome of a series and pattern of decisions that determine the organization's aims, objectives and goals; that produce the plans and policies required to ensure that these are achieved; that define the business in which the organization is to operate; how it intends to conduct this business and what its relations with its markets, customers, staff, stakeholders and environment will be (see Box 21.3).

Box 21.1: What strategy is not

The aim of all industrial, commercial and public service sector organizational strategies, policies, purposes and directions should be: 'long-term existence in a competitive and turbulent world'.

Anything that does not contribute to this should not be contemplated. Strategy therefore is not:

- a product of focus groups, contemplating what would happen in a hypothetical or imperfectly modelled set of circumstances;
- a statement of blandness or general intention that binds nobody to anything;
- blue-sky thinking or any other meaningless phrase that gives an impression of competence in the first place, but is subsequently unable to withstand detailed scrutiny;
- a licence to spend backers and shareholders' money on untargeted and unevaluated corporate adventures;
- about prestige, triumphalism, vanity or image – except where these factors can also be translated into successful, profitable and enduring activities.

These approaches invariably lead to the avoidance of the real issues of matching opportunities with resources; accepting the consequences of particular choices; concentration on one group of stakeholders at the expense of others; determining to satisfy all groups of stakeholders as far as possible; and above all, ensuring that everything is driven by the required and desired volumes and quality of product and service delivery.

Box 21.2: Charity shops

As the recession of the twenty-first century began to bite, the biggest and most influential UK charities, including Oxfam, War On Want, Help the Aged, Red Cross and RSPCA, experienced an immediate downturn in donations. Each of these institutions relies on individual and corporate donations to ensure that they can carry out the work for which they are constituted.

Accordingly, the charities made representations to the government for any possible advantages that were going. They sought additional tax breaks, removal of bank loan and overdraft fees, and government subsidies where possible.

However, it was not long before they all began to notice an upturn in revenues taken through the shops that they operated (and continue to operate). This came about as the result of people losing confidence in their own individual finances, and so shopping around for the best possible value in terms of the products and services that they sought.

In March 2009, the Red Cross reported a 41 per cent increase in turnover for the previous twelve months relative to the period before. It quickly became apparent that this was also the experience of the other major charities. They were also able to take advantage of falling television and internet advertising charges; and this in turn, reinforced their capability to get their name and brand in front of people, both in terms of seeking further donations, and also in terms of persuading them into their shops.

So, collectively, a clear response to the demands and pressures of the recession began to emerge. This was, however, entirely driven by perceptions:

- the perception that customers had less money and so would spend it more carefully;
- the perception that charity shops offer a source of satisfaction in terms of the products and services delivered;
- developing the perception that these organizations and their shops delivered reliable and assured quality of goods.

The lesson is therefore that in the development and implementation of strategy, attention to the behavioural and perceptual issues is vital. It is no use having excellent goods and services on offer if people do not know that they are there, and if people do not believe that they are good value.

Organizational policies

Organizational policies are based on the choices made within the overall strategic view. They are based upon a continuous appraisal of current and potential markets and spheres of activity; the ability to acquire, mobilize and harmonize resources for the attainment of the given aims, objectives and goals; and the actual means of conduct, including philosophical and ethical standpoints and the meeting of wider social expectations.

Effective strategy development requires that the following are understood and assessed in detail.

- The level of finance and capital required in order for the operation to be established and maintained successfully.
- The levels of income, surplus and profit that the organization needs to make and wishes to make.
- The structure of the organization that is appropriate for those operations to be carried out.
- The management style that is to be adopted and the style of leadership, direction and supervision.
- The priorities that are to be placed on each of the operations; the markets and sectors in which business is to be conducted.
- The timescales involved, especially where these are long-term, and therefore difficult to predict).

Box 21.3: The internet revolution

The inability to attract, retain and serve customers on an enduringly commercial basis is a fundamental, invariably fatal, weakness of the vast majority of internet companies at present. Overwhelmingly, the vast amounts of capital drawn into internet company start-ups were driven by:

- fashionability and faddishness, based on extensive media coverage and public relations activity surrounding what was perceived to be 'a new generation' of entrepreneurs;
- the perceived technological supremacy of the internet, and its infallibility as a commercial medium;
- environmental pull – in which those who were known, believed or perceived not to be at 'the cutting edge' of technology were deemed to be obsolete or boring;
- nobody considered the customer, consumer, client or end-user aspect in any detail;
- nobody considered how the levels of investment made in internet organizations was to generate returns, or where and when these would arrive.

The problem was also compounded by the attitude adopted by many of the new venturers and entrepreneurs when their companies ceased to trade. One virtual shoe retailer stated: 'It was a lovely place to work, and we still can't think of anything we have done wrong.'

Another, a virtual cookery and recipe production company stated: 'We assumed that further investment funds would be forthcoming on exactly the same basis as they had been before.'

Those organizations that have succeeded in using the internet as their hub of activities are the ones that have concentrated on the enduring commercial drives in this context. Amazon, the online retailer, continues to sustain business viability through high-volume, low-profit-margin approaches to sales. Google, the search engine company, makes its profits through its ability to sell advertising space alongside search results. Supermarket and department store chains generate internet sales largely as the result of customer familiarity with their products and services, gained over many years of traditional retail shopping.

Internal strategies and policies

Effective and successful organization strategy is dependent upon integrated and complementary internal policies as follows.

- **Financial, investment, budgeting and resourcing strategies**: concerned with both the underwriting and stability of the organization, and also the maintenance of its daily activities.
- **Human resource strategies**: designed to match the workforce and its capabilities with the operational requirements of the organization; related policies on ensuring

the supply of labour; effective labour relations; and the maintenance and development of the resource overall.

- **Marketing strategies**: designed to ensure that the organization's products and services are presented in such ways as to give them the best possible impact and prospects of success on the chosen markets.
- **Capital resource and equipment strategies**: to ensure the continued ability to produce the required value and quality of output to the standards required by the markets; and to be able to replace and update these resources in a planned and ordered fashion (i.e. including research and development and commissioning of new products and offerings).
- **Communication and information strategies**: both for the organization's staff and its customers/clients, designed to disseminate the right quantity and quality of information in ways acceptable to all.

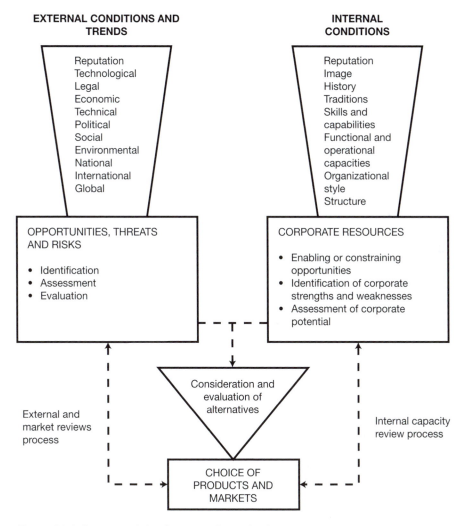

Figure 21.1 Sources and development of organization strategy

- **Organization, maintenance, development and change strategies**: for the purpose of ensuring that a dynamic and proactive environment is fostered; a flexible and responsive workforce; and an environment of continuous improvement and innovation.
- **Ethical factors**: including establishing overall standards of attitude and behaviour; absolute standards in dealings with customers, suppliers and the community; specific approaches to the environment, corporate citizenship; the nature and quality of leadership.
- **Subjective elements**: reflecting collective and individual preferences and priorities; also acknowledging matters of expediency and organizational politics, including the need for triumphs and the pursuit of individual whims and fancies.

In each of the above areas, there are strong behavioural drives. Specific decisions are required in terms of:

- what organizations will, and will not, do;
- how organizations are prepared to conduct their affairs, and how organizations are not prepared to conduct their affairs;
- the absolute standards by which top and senior management conduct the business of the organization;
- the establishment of specific organization forms, structure and culture so that activities and operations may be conducted effectively.

In order to give life to organization strategy, therefore, people and their expertise are essential. The complexity of approach, and the attention to behaviour as well as performance, are of paramount importance in creating, producing and delivering effective products and services (see Box 21.4).

Box 21.4: Ten signs that you work for a failing organization

Peters (1982) and Clark and Pettinger (2009) state that there are ten obvious signs that an organization is failing. These are:

- removal of flowers from reception;
- removal of free newspapers and journals;
- removal of free tea and coffee provision (you now have to pay);
- expenses claims are delayed;
- premises' cleaning contracts are renegotiated;
- cleaning services are now only delivered twice a week;
- bonuses are paid to top managers only;
- pay rises are staged and not paid in full;
- pay for those in top management positions goes up more quickly than for those at the frontline;
- top and senior managers negotiate advantageous share options for themselves.

Each of these points addresses the absence of the factors itemized above, as follows:

- the flowers are part of the general presentation and PR of the organization, and so act as part of marketing;
- the free newspapers and journals are a tiny, but important, part of staff reward practices;
- the need for clean premises reflects a detachment and distancing of attitudes on the part of top and senior managers;
- it becomes widely known and understood that top and senior managers are only interested in their own reward packages, and not the enduring good of the organization.

When it is implemented, each of these activities is therefore damaging to collective moral and can, and does, lead to stress and grievances.

In normal circumstances, additionally, each of the above represents a tiny fraction of the organization's total cost base.

Source: T. Peters (1992) *Liberation Management* – Pan; P. Clark and R. Pettinger (2009) *Foundations of Management* – UCL.

Core and peripheral activities

Core activities

Core activities reflect primary purpose and may be assessed in terms of:

- **volume of activity**: what most people do, or what most resources are tied up in;
- **profit and income**: where most of the money comes from;
- **image and identity**: that which gives the organization its position, status and prominence in the sphere in which it operates.

Peripheral activities

These are the other activities in which the undertaking gets involved. They must not be at the expense of the main or core activities, nor should they be a drain on resources. Rather, they should enhance the core activities, or reflect niche or segment opportunities that exist as the result of the core business. Such activities will nevertheless be essential, expected and extremely profitable. A hospital is not 'in business' to sell food, sweets, newspapers, books, cards, fruit and flowers; nevertheless, it is essential for a variety of operational and social reasons that these activities be undertaken. Similarly, a car company will invariably make additional parts for the replacement, service and spares sectors; these simply require some form of repackaging or 'differentiation' to generate additional business in an obvious and profitable area of activity.

Box 21.5: Strategies for failure

While it is impossible to predict with absolute accuracy where success and failure are likely to occur – especially if a rigorous approach is not taken – it is possible to indicate likely causes of failure. The usual way of expressing this is as follows.

- **Increased price/standard value**: risks loss of market share, especially where lower-price, undifferentiated alternatives are available to the same quality and value.
- **High and increasing prices/low value**: this is unlikely to be sustainable in the long-term in anything but a monopoly situation. Where perceived quality and value for money are not forthcoming, customers and clients will change from using such organizations if they have any choice in the matter at all.
- **Low value/standard price**: in these cases, customers and clients perceive that they are over-paying for a reduced or basic level of benefit and satisfaction. Especially where there is no cost advantage possible, organizations finding themselves in this position are at immediate risk either from others which improve quality and value levels, or from those which reduce prices in order to reflect existing levels of quality and value.

Any strategic approach that is based on each of these is sustainable only as long as there is a relatively captive medium- to long-term customer and client base. For example, petrol retailing manages to secure medium- to long-term advantages under the heading of 'increased price standard value' simply because their product is such a fundamental commodity of the present state of civilization. Some privatized health and social care organizations are able to sustain themselves under 'increased price/low value' and 'low value/standard price' because of the political drive to place clients of these organizations; and because the activities are underwritten to some extent by government policy and willingness to pay. Nevertheless, serious disadvantage is certain to be reached if there is ever a political drive to improve the quality and value aspects.

In recent years, as the result of the internet revolution, a further indicator of likely failure has become apparent:

- **Standard price/low convenience**: in which customers and clients are required to search for products and services on the internet. Even assuming that the correct company website can be found, problems are often compounded by the fact that while this is technologically brilliant, it is customer and end-user unfriendly. It is also increasingly apparent, at least in commercial-consumer transactions, that it is essential that the virtual presence is reinforced by help-lines, or increasingly, an access to a physical presence alongside.

Strategic approaches

All effective organization strategies must have the following components.

- **Performance targets**, in whatever terms these are to be measured (e.g. income, volume, quality, but set against measurable, understandable and achievable targets).
- **Deadlines that are achievable**, that have been worked out in advance and that represent a balance between commitment, resources and contingencies.
- **Contingencies** built in, to cover the unlikely, and the emergency.
- Consideration of the **long-term effectiveness** of the organization.
- Consideration of the organization's **products and services** in terms of value and quality, and utility to customers, clients, consumers and end-users.

All effective organization strategies must have additionally a core foundation or generic position on which to base these considerations, performance targets and deadlines.

Generic strategies

All organizations must have a clear, understood and accepted core foundation or generic strategy. The generic strategy reflects the basis on which all activities are to take place. The generic strategy consists of the following:

- a grand strategy, stating the overall aims, objectives and goals of the organization, and giving a clear impression of how these are to be achieved;
- a detailed organizational strategy, covering the volume and quality of product and service delivery;
- sub-strategies, relating to marketing, sales, HR and financial aspects, as above.

It is usual to define the generic strategy from one of three core positions as follows:

- cost leadership/advantage;
- focus/niche service and specialization;
- brand advantage and differentiation.

Porter (1981, 1985) identifies three generic positions from which all effective and profitable activities arise. These are:

- **Cost leadership**: the drive to be the lowest-cost operator in the field. This enables the absolute ability to compete on price where necessary. Where this is not necessary, higher levels of profit are achieved in both absolute terms and also in relation to competitors. To be a cost leader, investment is required in 'state of the art' production technology and high-quality staff. Cost leadership organizations are lean in form, with small hierarchies, large spans of control, operative autonomy, simple procedures, and excellent salaries and terms and conditions of employment. The drive for cost leadership and cost advantage is essential in any strategic approach that seeks mass market/mass volume products and services for which price is the overriding benefit to customers; and public services and utilities delivery (see Box 21.6).

Box 21.6: Ryanair

Everything about the Ryanair activity reinforces the fact (and belief and perception) that what is on offer is cheap, good value and cannot be beaten on price or cost by any competitor. This is reinforced by:

- the streamlining of the airliner fleet, so as to be able to standardize maintenance and repair schedules and patterns, and the buying of spares in bulk; and also so as to be able to standardize and make predictable the patterns of behaviour required by the on-board crews;
- the advertising looks cheap, and as such defies the perceived demands of all normal presentations, which are otherwise supposed to look glossy, assuring, comfortable and luxurious;
- the fares themselves, which are so low as to force people to take notice;
- the costs and charges which are added on to the fares, and which (up to 2009) have become a combination of talking point, general grumble and myth and legend surrounding the company.

Through attention to each of the above, Ryanair is able to establish, maintain, deliver and develop the overwhelming perception, and in many cases of course, reality, that it is indeed a cheap, reliable and effective service. This has resulted (also in 2009) in the company becoming the largest volume passenger carrier in the world, carrying 59 million passengers.

- **Focus**: concentrating on a niche and taking steps to be indispensable. The purpose is to establish a long-term and concentrated business relationship with distinctive customers, based on product confidence, high levels of quality, utter reliability and the ability to produce and deliver the volumes of product required by customers when required. Investment is necessary in product technology and staff expertise. It is necessary to understand the nature of the market and its perceptions and expectations. It is also necessary to recognize the duration of the market, where developments are likely to come from and the extent to which these developments can continue to be satisfied (see Box 21.7).
- **Differentiation**: offering homogeneous products on the basis of creating a strong image or identity. Investment is required in marketing; advertising; brand development, strength and loyalty; and outlets and distribution. Returns are generated over the medium- to long-term as the result of cost awareness, identity, loyalty and repeat purchase. In practice, all organizations, products and services have some form of branding or identity created for them. This branding and identity is created through the use of consistent advertising, presentation, public relations, and company and product and service logos. The overall purpose is to create specific impressions of quality; value for money; comfort; assurance of product and service reliability; and confidence in the organization and the products and services. In order to be fully effective, all differentiation, branding and presentation have to satisfy the behavioural and perceptual needs, wants and demands of customers and clients (see Box 21.8).

Box 21.7: Architectural practice

Architecture is one of the most uncertain professions in the commercial environment of the UK in the twenty-first century. So many building methods, techniques and materials have become standardized that many construction and civil engineering project managers no longer require the services of architects. Many in the profession have therefore had to enlarge their expertise, in order to remain viable and effective in the niches that they serve.

The result is that many architectural practices now include the following services as part of their business proposition:

- building consultancy services;
- project management services;
- sales and marketing activities;
- entering into partnerships with building and construction firms.

This is in order to satisfy the niches that continue to take advantage of what is, after all, a highly specialized and expert profession. At the core of this, twin perceptions have to be managed:

- architecture professionals have had to recognize that producing beautiful buildings is no longer an end in itself; rather, all buildings have to be delivered in terms of what is agreed with the clients, and also to satisfy economic demands;
- building and construction firms have also learnt that those with specific expertise in design can, and do, have a great contribution to make in the wider conception, construction and delivery of the building in terms of space usage and an environmental feature once it is constructed.

Porter argues that the common factor in all successful strategies is clarity and that this stems from adopting *one* of these positions. Organizations that fail to do this do not necessarily fail themselves; they do, however, fail to maximize and optimize resources. They lay themselves open to loss of competitive position from those who do have this clarity. They tend towards a proliferation of management systems and processes that dilute effective efforts. It is essential that where this happens, organizations take whatever steps they can in order to clarify as much as possible (see Box 21.9).

Outcomes

Outcomes should be pre-evaluated in terms of the following (see Figure 21.2).

- **Best**: what is the greatest level of success that we can possibly gain by following this course of action?
- **Worst**: what is the worst level of failure that can be achieved (if that is the right word) if everything that can go wrong does go wrong?

Box 21.8: Customer needs and wants: the Packard approach

Packard (1958) sought to define the relationship between product, presentation, image, and customer and consumer motivation. The conclusions were that the most successful marketing of products and services arose when both the product, and also its presentation, engaged one or more of the following responses among customers, clients, consumers and end-users.

- **Emotional security, comfort and confidence**: related to bulk purchases of food; safety features in cars; domestic security; and insurance.
- **Reinsurance of worth**: purchases must make customers feel good. This means that customers have to be satisfied with the products and services on offer; and their use of the products and services must also be respected and valued by others around them.
- **Ego gratification**: anything that is sold to gratify the ego must meet the subjective demands of luxury, exclusivity and immortality. Products and services sold to gratify the ego include expensive luxury cars, exclusive holidays and vanity publishing.
- **Creativity**: products and services sold to feed the creativity need put a critical value on the contribution of the customer or end-user to make the product effective. For example, cake mixes that required the addition of eggs were found to be more successful than those that simply required the addition of water, because there was a greater input on the part of the user or consumer.
- **Love objects**: this aspect may be summarized as: 'cuddly toy', 'dear little child' or 'sweet/cute little animal'. Andrex, the major suppliers of toilet tissue to the UK retail sector, has used Labrador puppies as the central feature of its commercials since the 1970s. Children are used extensively in television commercials in the pursuit of engendering this sense of love and warmth; and this extends to the marketing of washing powder, grocery shopping, fast food, cars, holidays, central heating and double-glazing.
- **Power**: the power of the product or offering is reflected in the user of it. Nearly all automobile advertising and marketing is on the basis of power, performance and speed as well as security. Power and strength are also strongly related to cigarette marketing, especially in Formula 1 motor racing, and also the sponsorship of cricket, rugby league, sailing and power-boat racing.
- **Traditions and roots**: this is relating 'the good old days' to the modern era. For example, food promotions use phrases such as: 'just as good as mother used to make'; Rolls Royce cars maintain the traditions of fittings and furnishings, and the reliability and exclusivity on which their original reputation was built. Politicians exploit perceptions and visions of golden ages with calls for 'returns to traditional values' and 'back to basics' because there is a very strong perception of 'the good old days' and association with historical success, order, stability and prosperity.
- **Immortality**: this is related to security, ego gratification and traditions and roots. Maintaining the illusion of immortality is an essential prerequisite of the effective marketing of housing, life assurance, other insurances, loans and other financial products.

People buy products and services for the value, benefits and satisfaction delivered; and the work of Packard sought to indicate that maximizing the chances of delivering benefits and satisfaction required targeting at least one of the above points. It is additionally the case that, by using a managerial approach to marketing and product and service presentation using the above criteria, it was easier to target the subjective (rather than perceived or pseudo-rational) needs of customers, consumers, clients and end-users.

Source: Vance Packard (1958) *The Hidden Persuaders* – Penguin.

Box 21.9: Something else

In practice, only one organization, product or service can be the cost leader in any sector; and only one organization, product or service can be the brand leader in any sector. So other organizations in those sectors have to have 'something else' in order to give themselves the clearest possible core foundation or generic strategy.

Examples of 'something else' are as follows:

- **Second and subsequent positions**: it is possible for organizations to operate effectively in markets on the basis that they have a clear cost advantage or brand advantage in terms of everyone else except the leader. It is essential to recognize that the second and subsequent positions do dilute the ability to achieve full potential because of the clear understanding that the cost or brand leader has achieved. Thus, for example, Pepsi-Cola and supermarket own brand colas generate very effective returns, even though the brand leader is Coca-Cola; easyJet is able to operate an extensive and comprehensive route network and flight schedule, carrying 32 million passengers per annum, even though the clear cost leader is Ryanair.
- **Convenience**: this is reflected in ease of contact or access, especially at times convenient to particular customers. Such activities are likely to be dependent on high volumes of customers, each spending a relatively low amount (e.g. corner shops, public houses, restaurants).
- **Confidence**: in which the core foundation or generic position is founded on personal, occupational or professional confidence. Confidence is likely to be the core foundation or generic position for such diverse activities as travel agency services; specialist building and civil engineering contracting; specialist software design and installation; specialist unit or batch manufacturing activities; specialist management consultancy services.

In each of these cases, a distinctive identity and clarity has to be delivered according to where the strengths of the organization lie. In each of these cases also, the particular strength must reflect a value placed by the customers and clients, and for which they are prepared to pay.

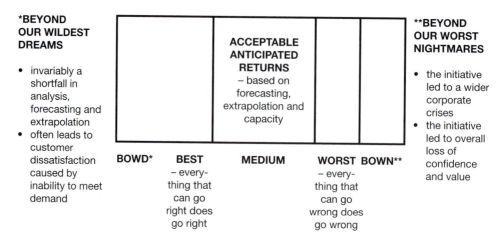

Figure 21.2 Pre-evaluation of strategy, policy and direction

- **In between**: a range of outcomes under the general heading of 'medium' or 'acceptable'.

In particular, the level of bare acceptability of the outcome of a particular strategy should be assessed at the stage of devising strategy. Outcomes should be extrapolated from each of these positions to try to envisage the following stage of the organization's activities and the wider implications for the short-, medium- and long-term (see Box 21.10).

Strategy development

Whatever the core foundation or generic position chosen, strategy is a continuous process, and therefore has to be capable of constant development. This is because no organization, or its products and services, stands still; and also because organizations compete with each other for the disposable income of customers and clients. Organizations have therefore to be able to determine, adopt and implement any, or all, of the following at different points in their existence.

Growth strategies

Growth strategies include growing and developing organizational size, and the range of products and services, in order to ensure long-term profitability and viability. Some organizations additionally choose growth through targeting their existing customers and clients, and trying to persuade them to take more products and services. Organizations seek growth through:

- mergers, acquisitions and takeovers;
- moves into new markets and locations, and opening up new premises;
- acquiring new technology which can produce the same volume of products and services at greater speeds or to greater quality;

Box 21.10: Arthur Andersen

Arthur Andersen was a major accountancy practice and management consulting firm. Over a period of nearly fifty years, Arthur Andersen had built up a very positive international reputation, noted for its capabilities both in dealing with organizational financial problems, and also in addressing and resolving a wide range of commercial issues and corporate problems.

All this came to a sudden halt in 1998. Arthur Andersen were the auditors of Enron; and when Enron collapsed, it became apparent that Arthur Andersen had signed off Enron's accounts in the full knowledge and understanding that there were things that were wrong.

Nevertheless, Arthur Andersen had ratified these accounts. When it became clear that the collapse of Enron was due to fraud as well as mismanagement and incompetence, clients quickly dropped Arthur Andersen.

The result was catastrophic for the firm. It was forced to drop the Arthur Andersen name, which had now become a by-word for complacency and ineptitude. The company was forced to re-brand itself as 'Accenture', and from there to engage in an active client management programme to ensure that further business was not lost.

On the company's own admission, it took nearly four years to rebuild the reputation. In vain did top and senior managers and partners try to justify or defend their position; quite simply, nobody wanted to hear.

Hitherto loyal and long-term clients no longer wished to be associated with the name; and only when the name and several key personnel changed did the clients start to come back to the rebranded firm.

- taking on new expertise so as to be able to diversify into those areas in which the new staff have knowledge and understanding.

In particular, a very important pressure for growth comes from financiers and backers. There is a widespread perception among fund-holders that organizations and their product and service volumes ought to grow. The pressure for growth, diversification and the opening up of new markets and locations can therefore be overwhelming; and in practice, many organizations are encouraged (and sometimes forced) down the growth route.

Growth has to be evaluated in exactly the same way as any other organizational or managerial initiative. In particular, if there is a financial pressure to grow, and yet it is the opinion of top and senior managers that growth is not appropriate in the circumstances, this can lead to serious conflict at the highest levels of companies and organizations.

Retrenchment

Retrenchment is where companies and organizations identify the most profitable core of their activities. They then take steps to ensure that this core is shored up, and that it remains profitable, even if other lines of activity, products and services have to be discontinued.

One part of retrenchment concerns top and senior managers' knowledge and understanding of the worst conditions under which the organization can remain viable. If, and when, things do become difficult, it is then essential that top and senior managers communicate to the rest of the staff why retrenchment is being implemented, what the implications are for those engaged on other activities and where the organization sees itself going in the longer-term.

Diversification

Diversification exists in any, or all, of the following circumstances:

* diversification into new products or services;
* diversification into new markets and locations;
* diversification into new ranges of activities.

Diversification is widely perceived to be positive, and something which all organizations ought to consider. The key to successful diversification, however, lies in the ability to build the same levels of confidence in the new activities as there are in the present range.

If diversification is not fully thought out before implementation, this can lead to serious problems. If diversification is fully though out, and given a sound behavioural, as well as strategic, base on which to develop, then success is much more likely to follow (see Box 21.11).

Other strategic approaches

Other strategic approaches which organizations have to be capable of implementing if, and when, required are as follows:

* **Market domination**: in which the terms of market domination must be clearly set out in advance so that everyone knows and understands whether the basis is market domination by sales volume; market domination by income; market domination by physical presence; market domination by size of workforce (i.e. the company is to become the largest local employer); market domination by brand awareness (e.g. as with Coca-Cola, McDonald's).
* **Incremental strategies**: in which organizations take slow steps forward, cautiously developing new products and services, and carefully testing markets before full implementation. On the face of it, this sounds slow and steady; it can cause organizations to lose out if a more adventurous firm is prepared to take the plunge.

Measurement and evaluation

Measurement and evaluation are carried out against the preset aims and objectives of the particular strategy; quantifiable where possible, areas of particular success or shortfall will be apparent, contributing to the organization's expertise in the field and ensuring further improvement in the strategic and planning processes for the future.

Beyond this, evaluation is both a continuous process, and the subject of more formalized regular reviews at required and appropriate intervals, thus setting a framework against which the strategy is to be judged.

Box 21.11: Diversification

When any organization diversifies, what they go into is not nearly as important as the line of reasoning that supports the decision. As stated in the text, diversification presumes growth, and this is therefore deemed to be positive.

Where the line of reasoning is supported by full market and customer understanding, the chances of success are very much higher than if diversification is based on assumptions alone. For example, the Easy group of companies has been very successful with easyJet. This led to assumptions that the basic company identity and business values could be applied to a range of other activities. The consequence of this has been that the company has opened internet cafes, cinemas, car hire and a cruise operation, all of which have had only limited success. The reason for this is that the company position of good value and centralized services and convenient access (and the distinctive orange colour scheme) was never supported with the specific market analysis that stated that customers would change from their existing providers to the Easy group if they were to open businesses in these sectors.

The following can then be assessed.

- The extent to which the strategy is identifiable, clearly understood by all concerned, in specific and positive terms; the extent to which it is unique and specifically designed for its given purpose.
- Its consistency with the organization's capabilities, resources and aspirations; and the aspirations of those who work in it.
- The levels of risk and uncertainty being undertaken, in relation to the opportunities identified.
- The contribution that the proposed strategy is to make to the organization as a whole over the long-term.
- Market responses and responsiveness; degrees of market captivity or choice.
- The effects – positive and adverse – of dominant stakeholders, driving and restraining forces, and product, service and project champions.

These questions can be answered as part of both the continuous evaluation and the regular review process.

Implementation of strategy

The determination of strategy is therefore a combination of the identification of the opportunities and risks afforded by the environment; the capabilities, actual and potential, of the organization, its leaders and top management; and issues of ethical and social responsibility. Turning this into reality requires that the following issues are addressed:

- Key tasks must be established and prioritized, effective decision-making processes drawn up and systems for monitoring and evaluation of strategic process devised.

- Work and workforce must be divided and structured to a combination of functional and hierarchical aspects, designed to ensure the effective completion of the tasks in hand; this must include relevant and necessary committee, project coordination, working-party and steering-group activities (see Figure 21.3).
- Information and other management systems must be designed and installed; control and constraint systems must be a part of this, to include financial, human resource, production, output and sales reporting data.
- Tasks and actions to be carried out must be scheduled and prioritized in such a way as to be achieved to given deadlines. As well as establishing a background for precise work methods and ways of working, scheduling provides the basis for setting standards against which short- and medium-term performance can be measured.
- The required technology must be made available, and staff trained to use it.
- Maintenance and repair schedules must be agreed and integrated with other activities.
- Research and development, improvement and enhancement schedules must be incorporated with the other activities. This includes making financial, technological and staff resources available as a key part of organization product and service development.

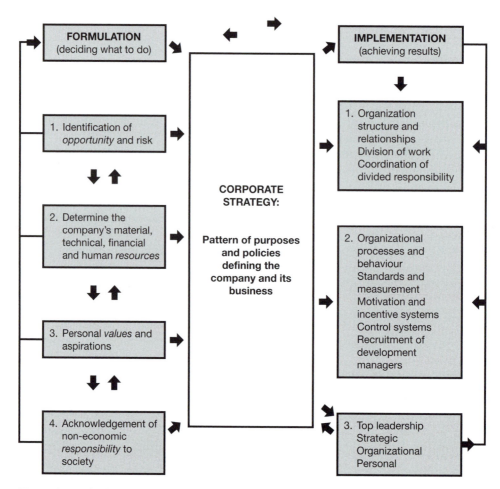

Figure 21.3 The implementation of strategy

- Monitoring, review and evaluation mechanisms and procedures, attending to *hard* aspects of market responses, sales figures and product and service usage; and *soft* aspects of meeting customer, client, consumer and end-user satisfaction and expectations.
- The measurement of actual performance against forecasted, projected or budgeted activities.
- Staff management and human resource polices must be assessed for effectiveness and quality; the extent and prevalence of conflict, communication blockages, disputes and grievances; the effectiveness of pay and reward systems; the application of rulebooks and specific procedures.
- Financial returns must be assessed in line with projections and forecasts. A key feature of strategy implementation is the ability to compare overall returns, costs of sales, product and service delivery, with projections; and to gauge the effects of unforeseen circumstances on particular activities.

Other factors in strategic management

The other factors in strategic management of which all organizations and their managers must be aware are as follows:

- investment appraisal;
- risk.

Investment appraisal

Investment appraisal is the process by which new ventures, initiatives, projects, products and services are evaluated in terms of their commercial viability, the resources that it will take to develop them and get them to market, and the returns that may be expected.

Overtly, this is a straightforward and rational process. However, it is in practice limited by the commitment and expertise of those responsible for taking decisions about investments and ventures; and about personal, as well as professional and occupational, choices. Decisions are therefore taken on the following bases:

- what is good for the company and organization;
- the reflection of a clear development of products, services and markets.

Decisions are also often taken so as to satisfy the following:

- excitement and adventures;
- the need for prestige and triumphs;
- feeding the vanity of top and senior managers;
- media coverage.

In practice, therefore, there is a range of complexities that have to be addressed when decisions are being considered to invest in the organization's future. It is especially essential that organizations and their managers do not get carried away with themselves, and find themselves giving life to something that has, in practice, been inadequately thought through in advance (see Box 21.12).

Box 21.12: Irrational exuberance

'Irrational exuberance' is the name given to the behavioural process out of which arises a form of certainty or absolute assurance that what is being proposed is:

- the next big thing;
- certain to work.

Those involved quickly come to the conclusion that 'nothing can possibly go wrong'. Those involved in the decision quickly create a bandwagon effect; and as the idea gains wider publicity and acceptance, everyone gets swept along. And then people come to believe in something which is still no more than an idea, untested and untried. For example:

- everyone came to believe that the *Titanic* was unsinkable, to the point that the necessity for any lifeboats on board was seriously questioned;
- everybody came to believe that the 2012 London Olympics would be a success;
- everybody came to believe that the price of houses and private property would rise for evermore.

In practice, of course, things are different. Ships sink; the commissioning of large national projects represents the start of hard work, not an end in itself; and the price of anything rises or falls according to demand and the constraints placed on that demand. In each of these cases, however, long-term assurance and confidence was badly damaged when the irrational exuberance became tempered with a dose of behavioural, financial and operational realities.

Other behavioural aspects of investment appraisal

The behavioural aspects of investment appraisal are otherwise founded on:

- making familiar and comfortable the proposed venture or initiative;
- generating collective and individual confidence in the proposed venture;
- generating perceived mutuality of interest with other stakeholders;
- demonstrating willingness to operate within stated economic, social and perceptual barriers (this normally translates as 'this venture will come in on time, to quality, within cost and to the satisfaction of all concerned').

Collective and individual confidence on the part of those proposing the venture is essential. No investment is going to be successful if some key figures are unconvinced or wavering. Where there are waverers, their concerns need to be addressed. Once this is done, such persons should either be convinced of the veracity and integrity of what is proposed, or else removed from the situation. The initiative can then be placed in the hands of those who have faith and are prepared to champion it and see it through.

Confidence levels in ventures can, and do, change. Especially if a key figure leaves or problems hitherto unknown or unconsidered arise, the management of what is envisaged is likely to require restructuring and re-energizing.

Collective confidence is always called into question when the organization is led into a particular venture or direction by a key, dominant, powerful figure or group. The concerns – legitimate or otherwise – of waiverers and doubters are not considered but overridden. Where the dominant figure or group has absolute faith that they have got their position right, they must be able to defend this. They need to be able to respond to concerns and to address questions without having to resort to forcing their position upon everyone else. Where the dominant interests are forcing through their own particular point of view for their own ends, ventures normally enjoy some kind of fleeting positive response and identity, followed by immediate high profile – and then rapid – decline (see Box 21.13).

Risk

Those responsible for strategic management and direction of organizations have to know and understand the risks involved in every aspect of their activities. This is so that:

* they have a full understanding of everything that can possibly or conceivably go wrong;
* they can engage all the staff in an active approach to risk minimization.

Attention to the management and assessment of risk in all sectors has increased in recent years. The key driving forces of this increase in attention have been:

* high-profile corporate failure (for example, GM, RBS) in which it has become clear that trouble and failure would have been minimized, if not avoided altogether, if a full understanding of the risks present in what these organizations set out to do had been fully assessed;
* increased managerial understating of the problems and issues present in all activities.

It is usual to draw the distinction between risk and uncertainty. Risk is inherent in any situation that is partly but not fully known or understood and can therefore be insured against, while in the unknown, there is no point of reference and therefore this cannot be insured against.

It is clear that those who fail to assess or analyse risk do so from a largely subjective point of view. This subjective point of view may be summarized as:

* endless assessment of risk leading to inertia, lack of progress and missed opportunities;
* a lack of will to look at the downside of what may be superficially a strong or attractive proposition;
* a lack of understanding of how risk management ought to be carried out;
* a lack of expertise in assessing the organization, the environment, products, services or customer behaviour;
* complacency and smugness, operating in the sure and certain belief that 'whatever happens in the rest of the world cannot possibly happen here'.

Box 21.13: The Private Finance Initiative (PFI)

The Private Finance Initiative (PFI) was a government capital financial instrument designed to gain support for the public finances from commercial organizations in the development of capital projects and infrastructure in the UK. Originally conceived in the 1980s, one of the earliest examples was the Channel Tunnel (which now operates fully and effectively, but which arrived several years late and many times over budget (see Chapter 12)).

Nevertheless, PFI was, and continues to be, used to generate funding for a wide range of capital projects deemed essential for the development of the UK transport, energy, telecommunications and technology infrastructure.

The 'thinking' behind the conception of PFI was as follows:

- getting private finance to underwrite these ventures would remove these capital projects from the deficit side of public finances;
- private finance and commercial organizations would deliver the ventures to better value anyway, because, as commercial organizations, they managed finances better than the public sector;
- everything would be subject to 'the disciplines of the market', and this too would drive down costs and drive up quality and value.

In practice, none of these things has happened. PFI projects continue to deliver public ventures more expensively, less comprehensively, later and less effectively than where the public services are directly involved. Additionally, it is now the case that the organizations that have built and implemented these ventures are entitled to returns on their capital, and this continues to place an additional burden on public finance.

Most importantly of all, the perceptions surrounding market forces, market disciplines and the presumption that commercial organizations operated better than those in the public sector were never tested. This has meant in practice that the government departments that have commissioned PFI projects are liable in full for projects and ventures of which they have little conception, and over which they have no control.

Behavioural approaches to risk assessment

Effective strategic management and strategy implementation require that risk assessment becomes an organizational and managerial priority. It is essential that a full assessment is carried out, in order to establish:

- those things that are certain to happen;
- those things that could conceivably happen, and the probability of their occurrence;
- those things that cannot possibly happen (and when arriving at the conclusion that something cannot possibly happen, the basis for the assertion needs to be made absolutely clear at the time).

The priority, therefore, is to get everybody committed to the matter in hand, in the full knowledge and understanding of what can possibly and conceivably go wrong. Particular points of attention need to be production and service delivery difficulties; customer and client dissatisfaction; loss of a key supplier; financial overruns; and time overruns. This needs to be followed by staff capability and willingness; and the integration of anything else that is required (e.g. marketing and sales campaigns) so that everything is harmonized to ensure the best possible chance of whatever is proposed being successful and effective.

This has then to be underpinned by clear standards of overall integrity and probity. It is essential that things do not go wrong because of any, or all, of the following:

- negligence or complacency;
- loss of impetus;
- lack of staff capability or willingness to become involved;
- resources drying up;
- criminal activity, especially theft and fraud;
- accidents and disasters.

Organizations and their managers therefore need to look at some specific areas as follows:

- workforce capacity and potential;
- technology capacity and potential;
- market capacity for the new products or services;
- the speed at which the new product or service is required, and the reasons;
- the quality and effectiveness of decision-making processes;
- the nature of environmental expertise, including, especially, the ability to scan the horizon for likely difficulties and crises.

Organizations and their managers can then at least know and understand what they are letting themselves in for, and the nature of commitment required (see Box 21.14).

The 'What if?' approach

A key approach to developing the widest possible awareness of risk is to use the 'What if?' method. The 'What if?' approach can be used in a variety of ways as follows:

- **Events**: what if there is a strike while work is in progress? What if there is an equipment failure? What if one of the suppliers goes bankrupt? What if we lose a key market?
- **People and staff**: what if one of the key players pulls out or loses confidence? What if particular individuals change their jobs and move on?
- **Past history**: what if a soft currency on which we depend halves in value? What if it doubles in value? What if there is a war or revolution in Russia/Thailand/Indonesia/Germany/wherever we are conducting our activities?
- **The unheard of and unthought of**: what if interest rates in the UK are 0.5 per cent/20 per cent/anything in between, both this year, this time next year and in five

years' time? What if the dollar or euro halves, doubles, quadruples in value? What if the price of oil drops to $10 a barrel/rises to $500 a barrel?

- **The totally unthinkable**: what if there is a technological revolution that enables ships, airlines, houses to be built and fitted out in a week? What if the stock market halves/doubles its index in three months?
- **Crime**: what if our key employees are found to have committed fraud? What if we lose a whole team of employees to a competitor?

Box 21.14: Excuses for failure

Strategic failure is normally put down to one or more of the following, at least at corporate level:

- fluctuations in interest rates, inflation, retail prices index, currency values and other economic factors that 'simply could not be predicted or foreseen';
- currency collapses or surges making whatever is proposed too expensive to complete;
- turbulence in the global economy;
- war zones and political instability;
- disease epidemics;
- changes in consumer demand and confidence;
- the actions of competitors;
- political interference, especially from foreign governments which, it is widely stated, 'protect their own industries at the expense of those from overseas, and effectively shut out outsiders';
- the promulgation of news media stories about perceived unfair and unethical trading practices;
- resorting to public relations coaching and the use of phrases such as 'projected synergies did not take place', 'productivitization failed to occur', 'economies of scale were not achieved'.

In practice, of course, these are excuses not reasons. Each and every one of the above can, and should, be foreseen. The fact that they are not covered in the news media for several days or weeks at a time does not mean that they have gone away. For example:

In 1999, a Bird Flu epidemic was widely predicted. This was an especially virulent strain of the virus, and was predicted to cause up to 100 million deaths. More than a decade later, the Bird Flu epidemic has still not arrived. Nevertheless, it has not gone away; and if (when) it does arrive, those who are prepared will find themselves at an advantage.

In 2009–10, there was a Swine Flu epidemic. This started in Mexico, and rapidly spread to many parts of the world. Reactions were mixed, ranging from complacency and indifference; panic, including the closure of schools, hospitals and some office premises; cancellation of international conferences.

Clearly, there is still much to do in developing risk management as an organizational, behavioural and managerial expertise.

- **Random events**: what if we have a good/bad summer/winter? What if an Australian competitor opens up in our market? What if there are especially serious transport and distribution problems?

By feeding all of these elements into the discussions, the following occurs:

- everyone becomes much more aware of the problems that might conceivably be faced;
- this forms the basis for developing real knowledge, understanding and expertise in the area;
- expectations can be adjusted in the light of real analysis (rather than, for example, getting swept along by irrational exuberance (see above)).

It is essential to have organizational and managerial discussions along these lines in order to ensure that everyone involved has at least thought of the range of alternative and diverse outcomes possible in particular circumstances; and to be aware of all the things that can, and do, go wrong (see Box 21.15).

Conclusions

The approach outlined in this chapter is designed to ensure that those involved in the design, conception and implementation of strategy understand the full range of factors that have to be taken into account. Each of these factors needs full expert and professional evaluation in the particular situation, and the context of the organization itself.

It is also clear that strategic management is not simply concerned with conceiving, designing and implementing initiatives. A great range of behavioural pressures has to be taken into account, especially in the management of products and services, assessing the nature of investments and evaluating the risks present or potentially present.

These activities are not ends in themselves. The key to successful strategy lies in how all the information indicated above is evaluated and used in particular situations, how accurately the position of the organization is assessed and the responses to particular

Box 21.15: Burberry

At the turn of the twenty-first century, faced with declining revenues and reputation, Burberry, the exclusive goods and clothing company, took the decision to seek broader appeal. Burberry would now target the business market, as well as seeking new niches among the young and fashion conscious.

Burberry knew and understood the risks. In particular, the company knew that if it lost its identity with the exclusive markets and customers that they presently served, they were likely not to attract the wider niches at all. However, the extensive research and evaluation carried out seemed to indicate that if the market could be expanded, then this would provide additional appeal to the present exclusive niches rather than diluting the brand.

events that are generated. Organizations and their top managers must be able to understand, assess and evaluate the full range of factors present in their own situations so that strategy can be devised, implemented and developed effectively. In particular, this requires translation into effective activity based on a clear core foundation or generic position, and the ability to implement and develop it within the context of the prevailing market and environmental conditions; and knowing and understanding all the pitfalls that could possibly occur.

22 Operations management

Introduction

The effectiveness of the operations of all organizations is governed by the ways in which, at corporate level, each of the following are integrated:

- corporate priorities and attitudes;
- the strength of organization culture and cohesion of the workforce;
- the quality of the working environment;
- the order of priorities of activities.

Corporate and collective attitude

The primary purpose of organizations and their managers is to set the course and order the priorities of the organization. From an operations point of view, in order to follow courses of action that meet the priorities, the ways in which relationships are ordered have to be suitable for the purposes in hand, and capable of being accepted and acceptable to all those doing the work.

This, in turn, means that whatever the circumstances, there must be clear lines of communication; a mutual understanding of what is being done, and how and why; and a transparency of decision-making processes.

Strength of culture

The conditions for effective and productive activities are founded in the strength and suitability of organization culture; the ways in which this translates as a foundation for team and group working; and the working relationships between different departments, divisions, functions and work groups. While different organizations have their own levels of involvement, and work within their context as effectively as possible (see also Chapter 14), the aim overall has always to be a combination of clarity and unity of purpose, and harmonization of activities in pursuit of effective output; and this is much more easily achieved where there is a strong and cohesion culture and work ethic.

This additionally forms the context for structuring and delivering the quality of activities, operations, products and services. This, in turn, is dependent upon:

- quality of the working environment;
- quality of products, services and service delivery.

Quality of the working environment

The quality of the working environment reflects the organization's true attitude to the staff carrying out their tasks as follows.

- Activities that are fully resourced, comfortable and suitable for their purposes, with the right levels of staffing and current and effective technology, are those which self-evidently have the greatest chance of implementing successful activities. However, the style, culture and priorities still have to be clear, understood and acceptable.
- Places that are under-resourced, dirty, too hot or too cold, can, and do, in the short-term lead to a pioneering attitude, especially when a new venture or project is being implemented. However, leaving people and premises in these conditions for the long-term leads to demotivation, demoralization and loss of credibility in terms of the work that is being produced.
- Places that are over-resourced, with luxury furniture, thick carpets, expensive works of art and state-of-the-art or fashionable technology which is always being upgraded, give off a combined sense of vanity, profligacy and complacency. It is very difficult to get continuous productive work out of anyone in these conditions because the overall perception is one of absolute assurance and organizational invincibility and immortality; and so, therefore, the collective attitudes become that nobody actually needs to do any work at all (see Box 22.1).

Quality of products, services and service delivery

The UK Association for Project and Management (2009) defines quality as: 'Meeting customers' needs; and meeting the needs of every other stakeholder'. Within this definition, there is a range of key considerations as follows.

Box 22.1: Body Shop (2)

Body Shop always had, and continues to have, a strong unified culture, a distinctive leadership, a clear management style and priorities, and a good quality of working environment.

Yet, the need for effective operations management still remains strong.

On one occasion, Anita Roddick, the company founder, was visiting one of the shops. The place was immaculate, and Anita Roddick stated her appreciation.

She then moved on to speak to the staff. She asked one member of staff what it was like to work in this establishment. The member of staff replied: 'Oh, I am here to save the world.'

Anita Roddick had then to explain that in fact the primary purpose was to sell cosmetics. Back came the rejoinder from the member of staff: 'Oh, but how can we then save the world?'

The key lesson is that the primary purpose must not be forgotten, even in a strong, positive and (perceived) highly ethical culture. If the organization – any organization – has a clear and distinctive operational standpoint, the priorities that keep it viable and effective must always be reinforced.

- products and services have to do what is expected of them by customers;
- products and services must meet customers' expectations in terms of access, cost/price, maintenance, upgrades and availability of customer and client information;
- products and services must be supported by levels of customer and client service that are also expected by those who use them (see Box 22.2).

Box 22.2: Service levels

One Saturday morning, the chief executive office of one of the UK's largest energy companies popped into the local branch of his bank. There was only one cashier on duty; however, there were only two people in front of him.

So, he decided to wait. And waited. And waited; and waited, while the cashier dealt patiently and politely with a series of small issues from the other customers. After nearly half an hour, the CEO arrived at the till. He said in passing to the cashier: 'Why do you take so much time and trouble to sort out these problems? These could easily be resolved by calling a call centre.'

The cashier replied: 'Oh, but people like to come in here. They do not understand why they should call a call centre. They don't necessarily know where the call centre is located, or how much notice a voice at the other end of the phone is actually taking of them.'

The CEO complemented the cashier on the level of service provided; and he went on his way.

When he returned to the office, he ordered a review of the customer service activities at his own organization. After all, his organization had recently tried to move all of its customer service operations to a telephone help-line.

The results of the customer service review duly arrived. There were two key conclusions:

- from a purely operational point of view, based on costs and benefits, the value of the call centre services was unproven;
- from a customer relations' point of view, the results were clear: customers did not like them, had no wish to use them and given any choice in the matter would rather go to a known, understood and fixed point of service so that they could speak to someone directly.

The CEO reflected; and in the end the organization did nothing to change this. However, it had given him cause for reflection; after all, the move to customer service call centres had been undertaken on the grounds of a combination of efficiency, cost effectiveness and convenience to the organization. Little attention had been paid, however, to the needs and wants of the customers.

The lesson is that no part of the delivery of products, services or customer service can be made simple or predictable. It is also the case (see Chapter 8), that it can lead to customers and customer service being marginalized in the pursuit of a perceived organizational efficiency. The wider questions of customer perception, and the value that customers placed on the service, were not actively considered.

Scales of production and service delivery

As stated above (Chapter 19), scales of production and service delivery are defined by:

- the nature of product and service output;
- the size and nature of markets served;
- the volumes of products and services made available;
- the mix between technology and expertise.

Choosing the scale of production is limited (or enhanced) by the following:

- the resources available, the demand for products and services, and the ability to produce and deliver what is required in the locations where customers and clients are present;
- the supplies of raw materials, technology, information and components, in order to be able to produce and deliver in the volumes and locations chosen and demanded.

Successful organizations find themselves under pressure to expand. This pressure comes from a perception that, because the products and services are in high demand from the present customer and client base, there is therefore a universal and insatiable demand for these products and services everywhere.

This perception is used by top and senior managers to do one, or more, of the following:

- use production capability to its fullest potential, alongside a marketing effort to get the products and services into new markets, sectors and locations; and each of the potential sectors is fully tested and evaluated before being entered;
- using the perception of universal demand as a lever to get shareholder and top management backing for exciting new forays into the unknown;
- taking the perception at face value, and acting on the assumptions rather than testing them. This may indeed lead to success; it is much more likely to end in failure (see Box 22.3).

Scales of production and productive capacity have therefore to be managed. This part of operations management requires an expert contextual approach and understanding so that:

- the good work done with the core market and successful products and services is not undone purely in the name of growth;
- the crucial importance of the core market is not neglected or under-valued;
- the crucial importance of making sure that any expansion is self-sustaining (and not underwritten or subsidized by the core market, except in the short-term).

The quality of the working environment, the nature and scale of product and service outputs that the organization undertakes, have then to be structured and enhanced (and in many cases, limited) by the following:

- health and safety;
- security;

Box 22.3: Taking English lemonade into France

The White Water lemonade company was, and remains, a very successful manufacturer and distributor of soft drinks. As well as producing its own range of products, it also operates under licence, manufacturing soft drinks for sale under supermarket own brand names. Recently, it was awarded a large contract to produce and deliver under licence the full range of Coca-Cola products.

This made it possible for all of the production activities to be expanded. Because of the company's location in south-eastern England, attention was turned to the continental markets.

No particular problems were foreseen. After all, people on the continent were as partial to soft drinks as anyone else. With the licence from Coca-Cola, a commercially viable productive effort would now be highly feasible.

Accordingly, calculations were made; and these calculations indeed proved that it would be possible to distribute large volumes of soft drinks to the major continental supermarket chains. Transport and distribution costs were included, and it was felt that White Water's products would be highly competitive with some of the alternatives on continental supermarket shelves, many of which appeared to be very highly priced.

At this point, fortunately, some common sense began to kick in. It quickly became apparent that the French, Belgian, Dutch and German supermarket chains had all the supplies that they needed. They therefore had no incentive to take deliveries from a new supplier; and the perceived prestige of being a licensee for Coca-Cola also carried no weight – most of the soft drinks companies that already supplied the continental supermarkets were also licensees to either Coca-Cola or PepsiCo. It became clear that White Water was not going to be able to compete on price or reliability; to get a foothold in the market, they were going to have to change the perceptions of both the supermarket chains and also the customers. Accordingly, White Water turned their attention northwards; and indeed became a very effective supplier of an increased range and volume of their products elsewhere in the UK.

The lesson is that productive capability and quality are not ends in themselves. It is essential to find markets that will take the additional output, not just those that are capable of taking the additional output.

- the technology–work balance;
- time factors and timescales;
- the nature and levels of performance demanded;
- management and supervisory style;
- the creation of an effective work ethic.

Health and safety

The creation of a healthy and safe working environment is entirely dependent upon the organization's actual attitude to health and safety. Organizations' stated attitudes to health and safety are more or less universal: 'In so far as is reasonably practicable, to ensure the safest possible working environment'.

This is additionally a legal as well as a moral and operational (and profitable) duty. The actual attitude is then delivered by the real attention paid to safety, policies and procedures, their implementation, and the responses to accidents, injuries and illnesses.

Health at work

By concentrating on safety, many organizations and their top and senior managers become blinded to the problems of health. Yet professional and occupational health issues (in all types of jobs and work) exist in all organizations; and so everyone needs to have a clearly defined approach to:

*   stress and physical injuries such as repetitive strain injury (see also Chapter 24 below);
*   drug and alcohol misuse and abuse by staff;
*   mental health issues, which can, and do, occur in all forms of work (see Chapter 16 – 'Affluent Workers');
*   role overload and under-load;
*   the value of the work delivered and its consequences for health and well-being (see below);
*   health problems brought on by bullying, victimization, discrimination and harassment (in which many people have received large amounts of compensation, but which have otherwise completely wrecked their lives).

Organizational attitudes to such a fundamental issue as creating a healthy and safe working environment form a key measure of the overall standpoint adopted towards the business as a whole, and to the actual relations with the staff, customers and suppliers (see Box 22.4).

Safety

Except for genuinely unforeseen accidents and emergencies, there are steps that all organizations can, and ought, to take to maximize the safety of their staff, and the inherent safety of the working environment.

If substances hazardous to health are being used, staff can be trained in their handling and operation. If extreme conditions of heat and cold are necessary for production and operational purposes, patterns of work can be structured so that there is no long-term damage to people's health or well-being.

In all activities where specialist machinery, equipment and technology are to be used, staff need to be adequately and effectively trained; and in many cases, specified and statutory periods of re-training and refresher courses are also prescribed.

More generally, it is also essential that premises, technology and equipment are kept as clean and tidy as possible. This minimizes the chances of people accidentally injuring themselves by falling over something that should not have been there in the first place.

Again, the organization's actual attitude to its operations is reflected in the attention which it pays to all matters of health and safety in the given context. When accidents and injuries do occur, they are always disruptive to the particular operations where the mishap occurred, and in many cases they become long and drawn out when any legal proceedings are incurred, and costly for the organization as a whole (see Box 22.5).

Box 22.4: Call centres – again

The stated purpose in outsourcing anything is as follows:

- to be able to concentrate on the core business;
- to put peripheral activities out to those who specialize in them;
- to reduce costs;
- to substitute staff costs for a contract cost;
- to improve the payroll as a percentage of capital employed ratio in the eyes of shareholders and backers.

From this can be extrapolated the following:

- the core business does not consist of anything that is outsourced;
- there are costs which can, and ought, to be cut or at least managed effectively;
- there are specific services which can be delivered more effectively by a different organization.

However, organizations that outsource customer service functions to call centres in practice project the following attitudes:

- a lack of value placed on customer service, causing dissatisfaction on the part of customer bases served;
- a lack of value placed on the activities of those who deliver these functions;
- a lack of value placed on the quality of working life, especially in those centres where the work is centred entirely upon volume delivery of calls served.

From this, the following can also be extrapolated:

- managing services that can be outsourced is otherwise a nuisance;
- organizations take an expedient, rather than operational, view of what they outsource;
- organizations are quite prepared to hand on these functions to others so that they do not themselves have to bother.

Clearly, this is not always the case. Many outsource relationships work extremely effectively and productively over the long-term. However, where call centres have been engaged as a matter of expediency rather than operational effectiveness, the lesson is that invariably there is a direct relationship between the organization's overall attitudes to staff, customers and its products and services; and, by implication, to its shareholders and backers. Where work is mundane and repetitive, organizations take the view of off-loading it altogether, rather than addressing the health issues that are implicit. In these cases, the driving force of the organization is therefore likely to be to maximize shareholder value, and raising the share price to its highest level possible. Any analysis based on attention to factors concerning the health and well-being of staff ought, however, to come to the conclusion that maximizing and optimizing long-term shareholder value is certain to fail. This is because the conditions in which long-term shareholder value can be created simply do not exist where organizations are unwilling to address the operational problems that arise as a consequence.

Box 22.5: Food processing

One summer, David Tagg, a university student, took a casual job at the local food factory. This factory was a major producer of processed foods and ready meals, both under its own brand and also for supermarkets to be sold under their names.

Standards of hygiene and cleanliness were exemplary. The machines used to produce and mix the ingredients, cook the foods, and then freeze, dehydrate or dry them out were all exemplary. Regular cleaning days were prescribed in any case; and all machinery had to be thoroughly cleaned when batches of production came to an end.

However, safety was more of an issue. The factory nurse regularly found herself treating those who had slipped and fallen on wet floors, or on pieces of meat and vegetable produce that had not been cleared up.

Much more serious was to come, however. During one of the prescribed machinery cleaning periods, David Tagg was assigned to clean a meat hopper. This meat hopper was like a giant food mixer, mixing ingredients on an industrial (rather than domestic) scale.

David Tagg put his arm into the machine to clean it thoroughly. He accidentally bump-started the machine. His arm was taken off to the shoulder.

David Tagg was rushed to hospital, and made a full physical recovery. However, he had lost his arm; and this in itself was totally traumatic, changing his life and his state of mind forever.

The company admitted liability and paid many thousands of pounds in compensation. Furthermore, a subsequent inspection of all of the company's machinery found that everything was susceptible to being accidentally bump-started. This now meant that the company had to completely rewire all of its machinery so that this could not possibly happen again in the future. All staff had then to be trained in the process that required them to isolate and disconnect all machinery before cleaning.

The particular accident cost the company £500,000 in total. In spite of the fact that it continued to hold a high reputation for product delivery, supermarket chains, in particular, now began to look elsewhere for their sources of supply. Two years later, the factory was sold on to a competitor, and the brand name was lost forever.

Security

The security, or otherwise, of operations directly affects their overall effectiveness and success, viability and profitability. This means that production lines, information systems, website and telephone service points all have to be made reliable and secure to the point at which:

- every item that comes off the production lines replicates exactly the previous one and the next one;
- every transaction over website or telephone line keeps all data secure;
- every transaction or piece of information in a database can be retrieved in exactly the same form in which it was originally stored;

- every production line, database or website is only accessible to those who have express permission.

This nature and level of security is essential as one key aspect of securing long-term customer, staff and supplier confidence. If people in any of these groups come to know, believe or perceive that products are variable, or that their data is not secure, they will cease doing business with the organization and go elsewhere.

Security is therefore additionally a key feature of all complex business relationships. The absolute level of security demanded by all stakeholders has to be capable of being sustained in all of the following circumstances:

- when subcontractors, consultants and outsource providers are used;
- when work is delivered in many different locations;
- when postal and delivery services are used;
- when internet services are used;
- when contract staff (e.g. temporary staff) are used internally in the organization itself.

So the organization and all aspects of its activities and operations have to be made as secure as possible in order to protect itself from any loss of confidence that will arise if people know or perceive that security is not absolute. In serious cases of data loss or breaches of information security, organizations are liable to civil and criminal prosecutions. Where product and service designs are stolen, or patents compromised, organizations can be faced with heavy commercial losses as competitors and alternatives take their share of the market.

Physical security

Physical security is a key issue in many sets of circumstances. Physical security means that people have to be protected from:

- toxic fumes, chemical leaks and all hazardous materials;
- extremes of heat and cold;
- the threat of physical violence and assault, both from other members of staff and also from the wider public.

Clearly, these eventualities are more likely to occur in some situations than others. These eventualities are much more likely to occur where hazardous substances are in wide and essential use (e.g. in production processes); and where the organization gives wide access to the public as a key part of delivering its remit (e.g. public services' facilities, shops and transport). This, in turn, has led many organizations to reinforce the need for physical security as a key operational factor, through the use of:

- security staff and security cameras;
- always prosecuting those from outside the organization who assault their staff;
- always prosecuting those from within the organization who assault their colleagues or vandalize production lines or security systems.

Again, attention to each of these areas reinforces the overall attitude to operations, and to the wider value placed on the staff who deliver them. It also reinforces wider feelings of physical and psychological safety, security and assurance that are essential if staff are to feel confident and comfortable in carrying out their tasks and duties (see Box 22.6).

The technology–work balance

The technology–work balance has to be assessed for the following reasons:

- the size and scale of technology used has clear implications for the location, size and structure of premises (e.g. portable technology means that work can be carried out anywhere; heavy production line technology means that large and secure premises are required);
- the nature of work demanded and the volumes of staff to do it (fitting roles to people–fitting people to roles – see Chapter 14 above);
- the capability to standardize all outputs, both product and service delivery, and also communications and information.

These elements lie at the core of making the technology–work balance as effective as possible in given situations. The technology–work balance has clear implications for the enduring viability of organization structures and managerial effectiveness. The technology–work balance drives all manner and patterns of working relations, both between peers and within occupational groups; and also in relation to management and supervision.

The key, therefore, is to understand the major influences that the technology–work balance exerts on operations. These influences are:

- interest in the work;
- boredom and alienation;
- making some aspects predictable and assured, so that those involved can concentrate on the uncertain and unpredictable tasks;
- using technology to improve overall performance.

Each of the above points represents an area for active management involvement. The enduring problem with those responsible for organization output, and product and service delivery and performance, is that because technology can make the products and services themselves more or less assured, everything can therefore be certain and predictable. Such an attitude either does not recognize, or does not value, the human effort and contribution necessary.

Or else those with this attitude do indeed recognize the problem. They therefore outsource the activities in question so as to pass the problems on to someone else (see also above). However, they then fail to recognize that the outsource provider will have these problems, and that this may affect the quality of the outsource provision. This results in the products, services or functions being delivered unreliably or unevenly, but with the additional problem of not being in direct control.

Therefore, balancing work and technology requires active attention to those areas best carried out by people, and those areas that can be effectively mechanized. It is

Box 22.6: Nurses at work and not so easyJet

In a survey carried out by the Royal College of Nursing (RCN) in 2009, 70 per cent of staff had either been physically assaulted or else threatened with physical violence; and everyone asked knew someone who had been assaulted or threatened with physical violence. This has caused the overwhelming majority of hospitals to employ their own security staff, and to have as much of the premises as possible placed under the surveillance of security cameras. The NHS as an institution states that it will always prosecute members of the public who assault its staff.

However, clearly the problem continues to escalate; the RCN 2009 survey stated, as one of its conclusions, that incidents of either actual or threatened violence had more than quadrupled since 2005.

This situation is not confined to the NHS; situations like this are common in many other occupations. For example:

- those working for social security, in direct contact with the public, in many cases deal with their clients from behind a reinforced glass screen; and again, the premises are protected by security guards and surveillance;
- many people working in retail find themselves threatened when particular products are not available or when, for whatever reason, they cannot find what they want;
- those who sell tickets to the general public for whatever reason (e.g. transport, theatre, cinema, entertainment) regularly complain of physical threats and intimidation.

Another example of intimidation, and at times physical abuse, towards staff is the airline industry. EasyJet, the low-cost, short-haul UK airline, has its own series on television, called 'Airline'. For the making of this series, easyJet allows a television production company unlimited access to every aspect of its operations. The result is that easyJet staff are actually filmed being threatened, intimidated and harassed by members of the public for a variety of reasons. This is demonstrably stressful and traumatic to the easyJet staff, even though, in the majority of cases, the fault lies with the member of the travelling public who has invariably:

- arrived late;
- forgotten their essential documentation (passport, check-in papers);
- brought too much luggage and so has to pay a surcharge.

All of the above represents a contextual change in the operating environment; for whatever reason, social patterns of behaviour have developed to the point at which this behaviour is both expected and also has to be dealt with when it does occur.

However, this does nothing to attract people to the particular professions. In particular, there is an acute shortage of nurses and of people willing to work on social security desks. More generally, any organization that gains a reputation for placing its staff in vulnerable positions is certain to have attraction and retention difficulties.

Source: Royal College of Nursing (2009) *The State of the Nursing Profession* – RCN; CIPD (2008) *Security at Work* – CIPD Publications; ITV (2000–7) *Airline* – Talkback Productions.

additionally essential to recognize (see Chapter 18 above) that technology will only do what it is designed, structured or programmed for; it will not take decisions, make judgements or come to conclusions (see Box 22.7).

Box 22.7: What technology will – and will not – do

In the early years of the twenty-first century, it was widely predicted that, because of the availability of the internet, retail centres of the world would quickly become wastelands. While indeed some changes in buying and consumption habits have changed, and the internet has indeed grown as a medium for commercial activity, the nature and range of retail activities have not changed.

In particular, for some products and services, the internet does not deliver some of the key behavioural buying aspects:

- the ability to touch the product and try it on before buying it;
- the ability to get a feel for the particular product so as to be able to make the comparison between brochure or internet presentations and the physical fact of the product on offer;
- the internet always takes a few days at least to deliver what some customers want immediately.

There must additionally be some clear reason for people to change their retail habits in favour of using the internet. The transaction must be as secure as handing over money and receiving change from a till. The product quality, and level of customer support service, must at least match that on offer at retail premises. The brand offering internet services must carry the same strength as those using physical retail outlets. Any product or service offers available at retail outlets must also be available on the internet.

In addition, there must be some clear perceived advantage of price or convenience that the internet provider can meet. So, for example, Amazon has managed to succeed, in spite of the fact that it now takes at least 2–3 days to receive the products, by offering the following:

- reductions on prices compared to mainstream retail which are of such an order as to make this a valuable proposition;
- absolute reliability and assurance of delivery: Amazon supports this proposition by ensuring that there is access to customer service teams at any time of the day or night; and undertakes to remedy any breach of security, especially in loss of personal data and (via its service provider, PayPal) making good any financial loss.

The lesson is therefore that, in order to be fully effective, the technologically driven provision has to be fully supported by a 'human' service effort that is capable of attending to the needs of everyone involved, and is accessible when people need it.

Time factors and timescales

All activities and operations take place in the context of:

- the time in which they are demanded;
- the time necessary to produce and deliver the products and services;
- the time necessary to conceive, design and deliver new ventures, new products and services and projects;
- the technology that is available and the speed at which it operates.

The management of time is a key feature of operations management, as illustrated by the following two examples.

- 'You cannot make a baby in one month by working nine times as hard' (Russian proverb).
- Matalan and Primark, and other good value clothing and garment companies, reduced the speed of clothes availability from one year to 24 hours by developing software that could scan designs as they came off the fashion catwalks and reproduce them immediately so that everyone could have the latest fashions.

Between these two extremes, all organizations have their own particular context for the management of time. Time has therefore to be seen in the context of the particular operations, and what is feasible, practicable – and deliverable and profitable.

In general, it is usual to break the organizational context of time into:

- steady-state, reflecting the time necessary to conduct the mainstream affairs of the organization;
- developmental, reflecting the time taken to get new products and services to market;
- maintenance, which can either be planned (in which case equipment and technology is taken out of service on pre-arranged times for assessment and scrutiny); or responsive (in which case, maintenance is only remedial);
- overtime, in which staff are required to work extra in the interests of the organization;
- downtime, in which there is nothing immediate or urgent to do;
- contingencies, crises and emergencies, in which time has to be taken to resolve something immediately.

It is essential to have a collective organizational view on the composition of each; and this varies between, and within, organizations, occupations, departments, divisions and functions. Unless the work is precisely deadlined, or predictable (i.e. it is driven by production or service technology), there has to be some leeway for all operations and activities; in practice, nothing can be precisely timed. It is essential to know and understand the sort of contingencies, crises and emergencies that can, and do, blow up; and where these come to be known, believed and perceived to happen on a regular basis, they need to be in-built into steady-state activities as far as possible.

Legal and statutory limitations

It is also essential to ensure that operations are carried out within the legal, statutory and regulatory constraints that affect many jobs, professions and occupations. Especially, the following have to be noted and in-built:

- the need to provide a break of at least 30 minutes after 6 hours' continuous work;
- the need to recognize and be able to accommodate the UK maximum 48-hour working week.

Specific jobs and occupations have particular constraints, for example:

- haulage, in which drivers have to be off the road for particular periods of time after a certain number of hours of driving;
- those who work with computer screens, who must be given breaks after a certain number of hours of constant attention to the screen.

Other jobs, occupations and professions have their own rules and regulations, and these have to be accommodated also, often in spite of the consequences to the business (see Box 22.8).

Box 22.8: Airline pilots

In practice, airliners are driven by technology, especially when cruising; and their emergency systems are almost entirely technology-driven. However, international regulations require that every airliner has two qualified pilots on duty at all times.

This can, and does, lead to operational problems. For example, if an airliner is delayed then this impacts on the pilot's stated maximum working hours; and in the case of extreme delays, this can result in the pilot not being allowed to work by law. One such incident occurred as follows.

There had already been a delay on a short-haul flight operated by one of the major low-cost carriers. Eventually, a pilot came on board, and at last the passengers collectively looked forward to getting off.

However, they were quickly disappointed. The pilot announced over the intercom: 'I am sorry, but we will not be able to depart for one hour. This is because I have been delayed on my last flight, and so I am required by international law to have a break of at least seven hours between undertaking my next batch of duties. There is nothing that I can do about this. We just have to wait.'

The effect of this delay would be to ruin the schedule for the particular plane for the rest of the day (and possibly the following day also). Nevertheless, the statute said that this must happen; and so operationally, the company had to be able to accept and accommodate it. The company was therefore certain to receive angry letters complaining about the quality of the service, claims for compensation and tales of holidays cut short, missed connections and the passengers' collective inability to get where they wanted to be, and when.

The lesson is that all organizations have to be capable of operating within the time constraints imposed on them; and to accept it as a consequence of being in the particular industry or sector, whatever difficulties this may bring about from time to time.

Time pressures

In practice, all organizations find themselves under pressure to do things quickly, immediately, instantly and urgently from time to time. The need, therefore, is to create patterns of behaviour and a collective work ethic that is:

* capable of generating a willingness to respond;
* knowing and understanding the particular time pressures and constraints, and institutionalizing them as far as possible.

This aspect of time management ought to be structured so that it does not take advantage of the collective staff goodwill except in crises and emergencies. This aspect ought also to recognize the contribution that staff do make when under pressure.

It is also to know and understand where the genuine time immoveables lie. The immoveables are:

* statutes and regulations as above;
* the speed of technology-based production and service delivery;
* the speed at which people are capable of working, and willing to work.

Other factors that affect the speed at which things are done include the ways in which communications and information systems work, and the length of time that it takes to gain authorization for particular activities, especially from top and senior management. All of this has then to be bounded by a corporate attitude to time which acknowledges and addresses how operations are to be structured so as to be effective within the constraints present (see Box 22.9).

Box 22.9: Junior doctors

For many years in the UK NHS, it has been custom and practice for junior doctors on their first and second placements to be required to work any hours demanded. In 1994, the European Union, as part of the Acquired Working Rights Directive, prescribed a maximum period of weekly employment for junior doctors as 48 hours per week.

The UK authorities appealed against this. When the appeal failed, they undertook to produce a schedule that would manage the transition from unlimited to a maximum 48 hours per week 'in context'; and, in accordance with the constitution of the European Union, this was agreed.

However, by 2006, little or no progress had been made. A guidance existed that 'in as many cases as possible, no junior doctor ought to work more than 72 hours per week on average'; however, in practice also, this was rarely enforced. It also became clear that any junior doctor who insisted on the right to time off would compromise the quality of the reference needed in order to gain their next post and subsequent promotion.

continued . . .

Box 22.9: Junior doctors ... continued

In 2009, the European Union again reviewed the situation and now insisted that the UK enforce the 48-hour maximum working week. Again, the UK authorities asked for more time; and again, in practice this was granted.

The practice of allowing junior doctors to work in these ways is clearly detrimental to health (see also Chapter 24, Box 24.1). It has also led, in at least one case at a major London teaching hospital, to an incident where when one junior doctor was told to cancel a day's leave, he was also told that if he did not do this, the hospital would notify his wife that he was having an affair with a colleague (it was not true).

What has happened (and continues to happen) in this case is that the authorities have sought to remove the time constraint, rather than manage within it. This has led, and continues to lead, to health, stress and relationship problems on the part of those affected. More crucially for the service, however, the failure to address the operational problems rather than the time constraint has meant that, even at a time of high and rising unemployment, the UK NHS continues to experience great difficulties in attracting and retaining key categories of staff.

Crises and emergencies

All organizations face crises and emergencies from time to time. As well as accidents and disasters, crises and emergencies can be brought on by:

- sudden downturns in markets;
- loss of key contracts;
- cost increases in raw materials and energy;
- breakdowns in production lines;
- computer and information service crashes.

Failure to recognize that crises do occur leads to a collective complacency and false sense of security. So, whatever the size and nature of the organization, and its line of activities, crisis management procedures need to be in place.

If there is a positive and inclusive work ethic, crisis management procedures are much easier and quicker to implement when problems do arise. The whole staff team become actively engaged in addressing the particular problem; and it is much more likely that staff will be engaged more quickly if they feel valued (see Box 22.10).

Levels of performance

In general, it is usual to define performance as being:

- excellent;
- adequate or satisfactory;
- unsatisfactory;
- unacceptable.

Box 22.10: Honda UK: working together in a crisis

During 2008, Honda UK suffered a 40 per cent loss of sales. By the end of 2008, those in charge of the company had to decide what to do in order to meet the crisis. A key problem was that production had continued at normal levels and that there was now a large stockpile of cars waiting to be sold.

Honda UK had always enjoyed an effective and harmonious relationship with its staff. Regular consultations meant that all staff were aware that there were going to be problems and that these would have to be addressed quickly and effectively.

The solution decided and agreed upon by all was:

- to shut down all production for six months;
- to continue to pay staff three quarters of their basic salary;
- to ask the staff to work an extra three hours per week for the next six months when production restarted;
- to take a 3 per cent pay cut only when they returned to work.

There were a few dissenting voices; but the solution found overwhelming support. It also took only two days to agree.

The main lesson is that crises such as this occur in all industries and sectors as above. It is also true that the company's management could have imposed the solution on the staff. To gain people's active agreement very quickly, however, required that all of the conditions were in place so that a speedy resolution could indeed be found.

In operational terms, the problem lies in coming to a definition, clearly understood and accepted by all, of what each of the above means. This causes organizations to concentrate either on one clear measure, often to the exclusion of all others (e.g. the share price/value must rise by at least 15 per cent this year); and so the consequence is that no clear structure is ever delivered for the definition of targets or the integration of activities in pursuit of what are bound to be complex sets of objectives.

Performance has to be structured and organized in terms of:

- what people are capable of delivering;
- what people think they are capable of delivering;
- the need to meet overall organization aims and objectives and priorities; and departmental, divisional and functional objectives that contribute to the overall effort.

The key to effective operational performance management lies in establishing particular targets, aims and objectives, and being able to justify and, if necessary, defend why the particular priorities have been set. Adopting this approach means that there is a much greater basis for staff acceptance overall; and if the staff are not happy with the targets, at least they will understand why these targets have been set.

A combination of clarity of approach and integration of individual and departmental targets with overall priorities means that there is a clear context for establishing whatever performance, demands and drives are required. In particular, this gives a clear basis for a collective understanding of why such targets as:

- a 15 per cent sales increase over the coming quarter;
- a 15 per cent enhancement in share value over the coming period;
- a 30 per cent reduction in wastage rates;
- a 10 per cent reduction in overtime;

are to be implemented. Failure to provide this explanation and context means that staff work in isolation; and again, this means they will tend to find those parts of operations and activities that best suit their own individual purposes rather than contributing to the whole (see Box 22.11).

Management and supervisory style

As stated above (see Chapters 3 and 18), all organizations *de facto* choose their management and supervisory style; and this style may be consultative; adversarial; participative; distant; and hierarchical.

At the core of effectiveness are the reasons for which the particular management style was chosen. This immediately begs the questions: was the management style chosen? Is it the preferred management style (or is it the one that the organization is lumbered with)? Does it work and is it effective?

The answers to the questions identify the extent to which activities and operations are likely to be managed effectively. These answers additionally indicate and imply where problems are likely to occur.

If the management style chosen is adversarial, and everyone knows and understands this, there are certain to be fewer problems than if an organization says that it is inclusive but actually is not. If an organization says that it is inclusive and is indeed so, then deviations (in the form of individual managers adopting an adversarial approach) can be spotted early and remedied.

It is next essential to consider the extent to which management is integrated with operations or remains remote.

Whether remoteness or integration is chosen is not nearly as important as why, and how, it is integrated (or not) with the operational activities and performance demanded. So if performance can be monitored and evaluated on the basis of time-framed output reports and other key aspects such as breakdowns, computer crashes and customer complaints can be handled on an automated basis, there need be few problems. The only need for active management involvement in such situations comes when things occur that are outside the remit or authority of those responsible for output and production.

Fully integrated management styles depend on visibility, presence and active involvement in production and operational activities. Especially, this enables problems to be raised and addressed early, long before they become crises.

Problems

The problems that occur with management style in the effective delivery of sustained and successful operations are as follows.

Box 22.11: The place of incentives

The use of incentives to drive operational performance has never been clearly understood. In the past, organizations and their management used to use incentive pay (in the form of attendance payments, shift premiums and productivity bonuses) to ensure that satisfactory levels of performance at least were achieved.

More recently, individuals in some sectors (e.g. banking and finance, energy, engineering, the political establishment, and top and senior management) have been able to command and earn incentives for delivering particular aspects of performance.

The enduring problem, in all sectors, is the clarity of the context in which the incentives are designed and structured, and are to be delivered. For example: the incoming chief executive of a major international financial institution was given what was called 'a major incentive package' if he turned around the institution from the point of bankruptcy, and returned it to profit. However, upon closer scrutiny, the performance measure on which he would be assessed was related solely to increases in the share price.

Defending the position, the chairman of the company's remuneration committee stated: 'We are in crisis. We have to turn the company around; and we have to increase the share value by nearly 1,000 per cent in order to restore shareholder confidence. If we do that, the company will be generating £9 billion of turnover per annum. We are going to pay the chief executive an incentive of £9 million. A reward of 0.001 per cent does not therefore seem excessive.'

Superficially clear and uncontroversial, the line of reasoning is actually entirely false. It focuses on one key measure only; and gives no indication or guidance as to how the measure is to be achieved. In particular, it makes no reference to the size and scale of operations envisaged; for example, if the organization were to ditch all of its retail customers and concentrate on its small, but specialized, niche of investment banking and the share price then rose by the amount stated, would this constitute success?

So the place of incentives in operational performance management has to be carefully assessed. On the one hand, 'bonuses' are paid for simply turning up to work and producing no more than satisfactory performance. So too is delivering a high-volume incentive based on a line of reasoning that supports the value of the incentive itself only. And in neither case is the context in which the performance is required, nor the clarity that ought to be present, addressed in any way.

- Where management is not integrated and becomes remote and detached. This means that decisions are taken on the basis of perception rather than knowledge and understanding. It means that assumptions are made about production and output in terms of capacity, efficiency and potential. It also means that operational issues are not brought to the attention of those who are in the position to address and remedy them effectively (see Box 22.12).
- Where management is fully involved and integrated, this can lead to meddling; micro-management; standing over the shoulder and watching; discomfort on the part of staff. Over-involvement can, and does, lead to charges of favouritism and

Box 22.12: Leakages in the travel industry

For many years, there have been known and understood 'leakages' in the travel industry. These 'leakages' refer to breakages of duty free goods, and shortcomings in the quality of the ingredients in the kitchens which are used to prepare meals for passengers on flights, ferry crossings and cruises.

From this, it is a short step to ensuring that the 'leakages' do actually occur. Boxes of duty free goods are 'accidentally' dropped; some of the bottles break; the whole box is written off (and the crew take home with them any of the contents that are found miraculously not to have broken). Prime cuts of meat are found to have been 'contaminated'; and again, those that are subsequently found not to have been contaminated go home with the crew.

The top and senior management of companies in these sectors knew and understood in general what was going on. In most cases, they were quite happy for it to continue; it gave the crew a sort of unofficial reward, and the loss could be consolidated into the ticket prices charged to the customers.

Matters came to a head at one of the UK cross-Channel ferry companies, however, when it became clear that the levels of leakage and breakage were far higher than had been perceived. A full assessment was carried out; and it became clear that goods to the value of at least £1,000 per day were 'leaking'. Faced with the true extent of the problem, management were now forced to act. Practices were tightened up; supervision was made more active; and in a very short period of time the level of loss subsided to a fraction of what it had been before.

The key lesson is the need for involvement, whatever the management style. The subsidiary lesson is that, when it is known, believed, perceived or understood that 'a problem does occur', it is essential that those in authority get to the heart of the matter as quickly as possible. Otherwise, in practice what happens is that something is only addressed when it is actively brought to the organization's notice.

victimization, especially where one person is continually on the right or wrong end of the manager's or supervisor's attention.

- Problems also occur where one style is stated or intended, and the other is what actually happens. So when remoteness is stated, but managers and supervisors are actually fully involved, what effectively happens is that everything becomes either permitted or sanctioned by managers even if staff are supposed to self-manage their operations and activities.
- Where managers are supposed to be fully involved but are actually remote, this becomes the basis for staff groups and individuals becoming self-serving. In these cases, the phenomenon of management by exception occurs: that the only time managers are contacted is when their influence and authority are needed to solve problems. The practice of remoteness in these situations also leads to complacency in which both managers and the work groups come to believe that they are doing a good job all of the time. Additionally, remoteness (whether by accident or design) leads to favouritism and victimization based on perception and prejudice.

The outcome in each case is a form of dysfunction which may be summarized as: 'Managers do not know and understand what the staff are doing; and the staff do not know or understand why management are behaving in these ways' (see Box 22.13).

The work ethic

It is essential that all organizations and their work groups adopt a 'work ethic'. The work ethic is composed of the following:

- collective and individual attitudes, values and beliefs;
- the mutual respect in which everyone involved holds everyone else;
- the nature and value of the work;
- the appropriateness of management style (see above, and also Chapter 17).

The work ethic must be capable of acceptance by all. Those who reject it need to be convinced otherwise; and if this does not happen they need to be steered in the direction of other employment (see Box 22.14).

The work ethic is developed, enhanced, limited and modified as the organization itself progresses, advances and ages. As the composition of groups, departments, divisions and functions changes, the work ethic itself changes. This therefore needs to be monitored in order to ensure that it continues to serve the organization's purposes, aims and objectives.

It is additionally essential to note that a strong, positive and cohesive work ethic brings its own responsibilities and accountabilities. For example, the Nazi Gestapo and the soldiers of Pol Pot all had a very strong and inclusive work ethic, though the purpose was revolting and repugnant. The staff at Royal Bank of Scotland, HBOS and other

---

Box 22.13: Operational myths and legends

The two enduring operational myths and legends are:

- management are useless;
- you cannot get good staff.

Such phrases roll off the lips of everyone who finds themselves caught up in managerial and operational dysfunction. The result is the development of a mutual antagonism; and this in turn leads to grievances and disputes – not because there is anything wrong with the operations themselves, but rather because the management style has been allowed to drift.

These problems are easily remedied; but they have to be recognized as having their source and cause in how the management style has been allowed to drift. The management style needs restating as a set of principles and practices, reinforced by events (especially staff meetings and performance appraisal). It then needs relating to operational practices, and restating to the staff involved so that they know now who is going to be around and when, and what they may legitimately expect when they are present.

Box 22.14: The new head of department

For many years, a particular work group had a very strong and cohesive collective work ethic. The work group leader was fully involved; and her main duties as leader were to lobby, advocate and cheerlead on behalf of the group with external bodies and authorities.

After a while, she left and was replaced by a new person. This person, a man in his late forties, came with 'an impressive track record'. His expertise was overtly clearly compatible with that of the work group. However, his work ethic was not. Individually, his work ethic was based on a combination of structure, status, hierarchy and order – none of which had been present until now.

The result was that a fundamentally inappropriate management style was created in that:

- it was hierarchical where this was not valued or expected (or demanded);
- it was involved, but on the basis of rank and status rather than productive output;
- it was known, believed and perceived to favour what the head of department found to be right rather than the objectives of the group.

Detachment quickly followed. The core team re-established their own work ethic, to reflect what they had always held to be important and of value. The team did its best to operate in isolation from the head of department.

The consequence was that the productive effort continued to enjoy high respect and value, and to be in demand; however, the team found itself starved of resources. One or two people drifted off and left; and eventually, the few remaining members became nothing more than a 'rump' of what had been hitherto a highly cohesive and productive team.

The lesson is that the overall effectiveness of the work ethic is dependent upon appropriateness of leadership and management style. However cohesive or productive a particular group may be in any organizational situation, this can be damaged or destroyed when one key feature of it is changed.

UK banks all had (many still have) a very strong work ethic, though this was self-serving at the expense of the customers' interests.

All this points to the demand for active top and senior management involvement in the ways in which operations are structured and carried out rather than confining themselves to knowledge of the activities in isolation.

The value of the work

The value of work carried out is also a key element in defining the work ethic. This value is composed of:

- the financial and other extrinsic rewards;
- intrinsic rewards in terms of development, advancement and fulfilment;

- the perceptions of others;
- the overall respect in which the work is held;
- any pride, or otherwise, in working for the organization and with particular colleagues.

In summary, therefore, the work itself has to be capable of delivering value to the organization, the staff and other stakeholders; and it has to be capable of being understood as a mark of value in wider society (see Box 22.15).

The value delivered by the work changes over time and according to circumstances. For example:

- the value delivered by an office cleaner may not be apparent until the offices are not cleaned;
- as the result of the 2008 banking crisis, the status of banking has changed (see Box 22.11);
- as the result of the 2009 UK political expenses scandal, the status of the political establishment changed.

Box 22.15: Sidelines

'It's a poorly kept secret in the City of London that many people run their own business sidelines, often just to alleviate the sheer boredom of financial trading.

For bright people doing dry-day jobs, the sideline is often the only thing that really persuades them to go into work.

A great friend of mine found himself on the wrong end of his company's corporate lawyers. They discovered that he was running an online art dealing business alongside his main job, and the lawyers told him to shut the website down immediately.

My friend's supervisor commiserated with him. He pointed out to her that everyone was doing it. She told him to wait a while before opening up again.

In practice, everyone knows that it is going on. And it goes on because the work is so boring, the pressure so great, that it is one thing that they can do to have some control and to keep themselves sane.

And when you look at it like this, it is no wonder that City institutions fare so badly. And this is quite apart from the fact that anyone who works in the financial institution is automatically assumed to be a crook.

In a situation such as this, there is no work ethic. There is only the incentive. The work itself is clearly not valued by anyone involved, except as a means to an end. Any organization that finds such activities going on needs to question its entire collective work ethic. Incentives clearly do not work; so something else is needed. A start, of course, will be when managers and supervisors of such companies finally get themselves out and among their staff to see where the problems really lie. In this case, the corporate lawyers could have done worse than suggest this to management rather than merely picking on the illicit sideline when it was discovered.'

Source: City Girl (2009) 'Life in the Square Mile' – *The London Paper*.

These changes go on in all organizations, occupations and sectors; and again they reinforce the need for effective management involvement. The restructuring, reordering and repositioning of staff, activities and operations are easily and neatly drawn up in a boardroom or project team. The active involvement is demanded so that the effects of the restructuring, reordering and repositioning are clearly and universally known and understood, and that the overall work ethic is not damaged (see Box 22.16).

Conclusions

The nature of organizational operations reflects the core purposes, priorities, aims and objectives served; and successful, effective and profitable organizational performance is entirely dependent on the strength and integrity of operational activities and their management.

Operations management therefore brings together so much of the behavioural aspects of managerial expertise. The enduring effectiveness of operational activities and their management is dependent upon those in top, senior and key positions becoming, and remaining, actively involved in every aspect of organizational practice. They must know and understand where problems and issues are likely to occur; and from this, have the capability to address and resolve these as early as possible.

They must know and understand, above all, the need to create, maintain and develop an effective pattern of operational activities. These activities have to be supported by addressing effectively the complexities of performance management, and creating a cohesive set of departmental, divisional and functional activities that contribute to the organization as a whole. Above all, they must create and develop a management and supervisory style and a work ethic that are mutually inclusive, and which strengthen each other.

Box 22.16: Mathematics teaching

For many years, there has been known and understood to be a problem with mathematics teaching in schools. It is widely believed and perceived that standards have fallen and grades have risen – the latter especially in return for mediocre work or in spite of a fundamental lack of understanding.

Rather than addressing the problem of why mathematics teaching had become so difficult, political decisions were taken to make the attainment of qualifications in the subject much easier. These decisions were taken in isolation from the realities of school operational practice, and in isolation also from the demands for absolute levels of mathematical knowledge and understanding, and the ability to apply it in a variety of situations. Both the value of the work and the work ethic of mathematics teachers therefore collapsed. Taking mathematics as a subject now became purely a means to an end; and this, in turn, became a mark of great disrespect to those who were to teach the subject and showed the low value set on them and their work.

The key lesson is therefore that if the work is to be valued, and a work ethic to be maintained, the context for structuring and delivering the work has to be made adequate and not superficial. It also requires active involvement as above, rather than remote imposition.

23 The nature of workplace behaviour

Introduction

Understanding the nature of workplace behaviour is vital to organizational productivity, performance and viability. The key issue faced by organizations and their managers in pursuit of this is therefore creating the conditions in which the collective behaviour is:

- positive and inclusive, rather than negative and alienative;
- supportive, rather than unsupportive;
- aspiring to common goals, rather than using the organization solely for individual purposes.

This ought to be a major concern of top and senior managers. The need to establish the nature of behaviour that is required to generate the overall performance that the organization demands has first of all to be capable of creating a positive, supportive and inclusive environment. Failure to do this means that the organization is always going to be facing dilemmas of where collective and individual interests truly coincide.

As stated above (see Chapter 17) there are completely legitimate self-interests that have to be addressed and accommodated. No organization is going to survive if it concentrates solely on what is good for itself alone. However, getting the right balance, and allowing staff the freedom to pursue legitimate self-interest, is essential. This is because no organization can sustain untargeted self-interest, even when they take overtly excellent, positive and targeted collective decisions (see Box 23.1).

The changing nature of work

The changing nature of work brings pressures on organizations, management styles, practices and priorities, and the operating environment. These pressures are:

- productivity;
- cost effectiveness;
- security and stability.

Productivity

Over the past twenty years, technological innovation and the professionalization of management have had the clearly stated priority of making companies and organizations more productive. Yet the experience, in many cases, has been that less gets done, more slowly, at greater cost. At the core of this is the fact that the drive for productivity and the actions taken are opposing, rather than integrating, forces (see Box 23.2).

Box 23.1: British Airways and baggage handling at Terminal 5

At the point of commissioning Terminal 5, those responsible for the future direction of British Airways clearly understood that there would have to be a suitable baggage handling system. This system had to be capable of carrying baggage to the capacity demanded of the planes, route networks and passenger volumes.

Thus far there was no problem. However, implementation ultimately came down to two choices. The first choice was to extend and develop the existing system in use at Terminal 4 and elsewhere at Heathrow Airport, and also at other British Airways' hubs around the UK. The second choice was to introduce a brand new system, clearly state of the art, but untried and untested. The first would cost hundreds of thousands of pounds; the second would cost £31 million.

The project manager responsible for the implementation of the system, and the operations director, chose the new state-of-the-art system. Implementation would transform baggage processing and management, and the airline would become a beacon of excellent practice in this critical area of operations recognized throughout the industry.

Clearly, it was in British Airways' best interests to have something that worked fully and effectively as above. Clearly also, the recognition that would inevitably follow if the system was implemented successfully was in the interests of the project manager and operations director.

So at the point of decision, there was a legitimate choice to be made in which both the organization as a whole, and also the individuals directly involved, would quite legitimately benefit.

When the system was implemented, there were extensive teething troubles. Particular reference was made to the fact that the system was only tested under perfect conditions, and that there was insufficient staff training and briefing to ensure that it worked well from the outset. To date, the system is widely held to be efficient and effective, though it works more slowly than previous systems, with longer lead and delivery times for baggage than were envisaged.

Box 23.2: Meetings, bloody meetings!

Meetings, bloody meetings is a film that was made in 1984 by Video Arts. Staring John Cleese and Prunella Scales, its purpose is to drive home the message that time spent in meetings is expensive, and so it therefore had better be made productive.

The opening scene takes place in bed! It is late at night; and Cleese and his wife (played by Prunella Scales) have gone to bed. While Scales tries to get to sleep, Cleese now settles down to do his day's work, stating:

'I spend so much time at work at meetings, and at meetings to decide when the next meeting is to be held that I do not have time to do my job.'

Many managers spend a total of 16 hours per week in meetings (CIM, 2006). This is certain to impact on productivity. If, and when, it becomes necessary to extend the working time into early mornings, late evenings and weekends, it is also certain to impact on the work–life balance and to create personal, professional and occupational stress. Overall collective and individual effectiveness and productivity are therefore adversely affected in everything but the short-term.

Technology

The time was when every manager had a secretary whose job and purpose it was to organize the working day, arrange meetings and appointments, type letters and memoranda, and support the overall managerial effort (see also Chapter 14). Now, everyone has a computer; and so, as well as being an expert manager, they are now an excellent secretary and fully effective computer operator.

On average managers spend 2–3 hours per day on answering e-mails (CIM, 2006); and when this is added to the meetings load (see above), it leaves very little time to be fully effective at the crucial corporate tasks of achieving targets, delivering performance, creating effective teams and groups, and developing a positive organization culture.

The immediate result is to put stress and strain on the manager's time and energy. The longer-term outcome is a detachment between managers and managed. This is invariably reinforced by staff recognition of the fact that it is impossible to get to see managers; and so they start to communicate by e-mail or voice-mail; and this adds to the stress and detachment.

So a collective commitment is required with a view to creating patterns of behaviour that enhance rather than dilute performance, that diminish rather than create stress.

The simple steps to take are:

- ensuring that meetings are targeted and effectively chaired with agenda published in advance;
- ensuring that e-mail communications do not become the *de facto* management style, but rather support it;
- ensuring that people's priorities are operational rather than responsive (see Box 23.3).

Presenteeism

Presenteeism is the practice of turning up to work and keeping busy. Presentees are those who always turn up to work, never take time off, are self-evidently busy – and that is it! In practice, of course, many people who do work in these ways deliver enduring and effective performance.

It is also the case, however, that many people who do work in these ways deliver untargeted, undirected and ineffective performance.

The best that can be said for any presentee is that the sheer volume of work that they get through may contribute in some way to the overall priorities of the organization.

In practice also, organizations owe it to staff who show this kind of commitment to ensure that their efforts are targeted, that they are steered in paths that do indeed address targets and priorities, and that they are given the support, resources and facilities to be fully effective (see Box 23.4).

Box 23.3: Long hours cultures

In recent years, many organizations have gained reputations among their staff and managers for encouraging long hours business cultures. In particular, a large corporate telecommunications company placed great strain on its staff and managers by insisting on a long hours culture. The company reinforced this by assessing high levels of collective and individual performance purely on the number of hours worked; whether people could be reached and contacted at weekends and while on holiday; and whether they took their full annual leave allowance. Indeed some individuals and groups of staff got paid performance bonuses on this basis.

Defending the practice, and responding to criticism from commentators, trade unions and professional groups, the company stated that anyone who was putting in the long hours was 'clearly loyal to the company, clearly working hard, and was clearly, therefore, very productive and effective'.

The statement is 'clearly' capable of being criticized at each point. However, it does illustrate a clear dilemma that exists for many organizations and their managers – how to maximize and optimize commitment and output, while at the same time trying to concentrate on organizational and operational priorities. In this case, the company concentrated on collective and individual output as an assumption of the result of long hours attendance. Additionally, all the while the company presumed that the output was (and remained) effective and targeted; in practice too, this is common in many organizations where the culture and management style make it very difficult to be precise about workloads and targets. They therefore fall back on assumptions about productivity; and one of the easiest assumptions is to measure the number of hours worked, and from this extrapolate the productivity as both extensive and also effective.

Box 23.4: Bawden Care Homes Ltd

Bawden Care Homes Ltd provide good-quality secure accommodation for delinquent and disturbed children and adolescents. At one of the homes, a secure unit in south London, a new care manager, Mary Ward, was appointed.

Mary came from the local government sector. She came with excellent references for hard work, total involvement, and commitment to service and the children in her care.

Mary's first action upon arrival was to instigate a full review of the staffing arrangements. She changed everyone's shift patterns without consultation; and many of the staff, including long-service staff, quickly became frustrated and left for other jobs.

From its previous excellent reputation, this particular home now became known as a place of work to be avoided. Mary now found herself relying on expensive agency staff; and she found herself in attendance at all hours. Managers were normally supposed to work 'office hours', and to do some infill at holiday times and at weekends, and the home would then be left in charge of professional team leaders overnight and at other non-standard times including regular weekend working.

In the end, Mary found herself attending every day. Because of staff shortages, she also started working nights and weekends. She had a bed installed in her office so that she could grab some sleep where possible.

After eighteen months, Mary collapsed at work. She was taken to hospital; and subsequently signed off sick for six months with nervous exhaustion and stress. During this period she terminated her employment. After a period of one year on extended sick leave, she started to look for other jobs.

Bawdens were asked to provide a reference for her for a care home management job back in the public sector. Bawdens made reference to Mary's 'total dedication, work commitment far above the call of duty, and her overriding concern for the children and young people in her care'. It made no reference to her presenteeism, to the fact that she changed the care home in her charge from one where everybody was happy and productive to one where nobody wanted to work. In particular, the reference passed no comment on the fact that she had gone into the home, created a mess and then worked herself into the ground clearing up the chaos that she herself had created.

So productivity has to be delivered in its own context. Beyond this, it is a combination of:

- capability and expertise;
- willingness and commitment;
- targets and priorities.

It is only possible to deliver effective and productive output if the staff are engaged and motivated; if there is adequate technology in place; and if there is organizational and managerial support.

So to get effective work out of teams, groups and individuals, each of the above must be in place, and each must be capable of acceptance and integration within the overall purpose of the organization.

To generate maximum and optimum productivity is therefore clearly complex, requiring an expertise on the part of top and senior managers in each of the above areas. It also requires their capability in creating, structuring and delivering in each of these areas so that the conditions for maximum and optimum productivity are present.

It follows from this that the only thing that ought to be in question is the capability of the individual employee. Yet it is all too often the case that capability is present, together with an inherent willingness to perform; and that personal involvement is something that (see Chapter 15) people do indeed seek. The critical area of managerial attention is therefore in creating the patterns of behaviour and working environment in which productive effort can indeed take place (see Box 23.5).

Patterns of work

Patterns of work are influenced by:

- the physical environment, technology, size of premises and overall layout;
- the number, status, expertise and mix of employees;
- the demands on technology of the employee.

Box 23.5: Management support

Nothing can succeed without management support. The best sort of management support is that which is available on tap, but which does not intrude until required to do so, provided there is an effective, comprehensive and open mutual reporting relationship.

All too often, however, management support takes one or more of the following forms:

- demanding frequent progress reports to explain why people do not have enough time to meet deadlines;
- demanding explanations of how, and why, particular activities are not working as well as they are supposed to be (or in relation to a competitor);
- demanding budget cuts and detailed reporting;
- micro-managing – becoming involved in every aspect and detail of activities and operations;
- never being able to access those in authority when required.

In theory, the role of management is to create the conditions in which effective and productive activity can take place. In practice, all too often, managers create the conditions in which it is impossible for effective and productive activities to take place. The result is that procedures and reporting relationships become the driving rather than supporting force; and the result is that the productive effort is diluted and damaged – and, in some cases, destroyed.

Patterns of work are also influenced by the employees themselves as they seek to make things comfortable and assured – and of course productive – in the premises and environment in which they have to work.

Within these confines, employees go on and make the working environment in their own image; and this includes the nature of furnishings, trapping and decorations, as well as the tools, equipment, technology and other resources that they need to do their jobs.

This is then overlaid by the ways in which everyone, collectively and individually, behaves towards each other, towards the work and towards the organization.

The outcomes are patterns of work which ought to satisfy:

- the demands of the organization;
- the demands of professional, expert and occupational practice;
- the culture of the organization;
- the humanity of the organization and its people.

Those responsible for creating and implementing patterns of work need to know and understand this from the point of view of absolute expertise in the field. If any of the above are not present or effective, then people will find ways to create them. Especially where work is dehumanized, or de-skilled to the point of endless repetition, people will subvert the environment in order to make this part of their lives bearable. For example:

- Retail banking staff working on the counters of branches who were given sales targets to meet simply got their family and friends to fill in forms for 'financial products' (insurance policies, deposit accounts, short-term loans) that they had no intention of taking out. During the cooling off period, their family and friends would simply ring up within the time frame and cancel the policy. The practice nevertheless satisfied the banks' insistence on these sales efforts; and in some cases, the staff were paid bonuses and commissions on this basis.
- Call centre staff working on piece rates (having to make a certain number of calls per time period) would have a large volume of numbers that they could call (including each other's mobile and landline numbers) in order to catch up and meet the numbers demanded. This led at least one company to put all of its call centre staff on salaries and radically review the pattern of work demanded.
- All sectors have their own equivalent. Factory production staff find ways of sabotaging production lines just in order to make life bearable, to get away from the noise and repetitive nature of the work. It is also well documented (Goldthorpe and Lockwood, 1961) that from time to time the workforce and their trade union representatives, together with factory managers and shift supervisors, would engineer strikes of between two and five days, also just to give everyone a break.

Other examples include:

- Those working on food processing production lines and responsible for removing 'alien bodies' (packaging and dirt), instead adding 'alien bodies' and then seeing where the customer complaints actually came from, and how long they took to come in.
- Those working in chemical factories adding compounds and ingredients to the exact point that the process will reject them and shutdown might occur. The result is that, in many cases, the process does indeed have to be shut down and the equipment fully cleaned; and again, this breaks the monotony (see Box 23.6).

People also expect a certain amount of autonomy in their patterns of work. They expect some influence in how they go about organizing the structure of their daily and weekly working lives. This is not confined to the professional, technological and managerial classes; for many years Volvo, BMW and Volkswagen were the most productive car companies in the world in terms of speed and cost effectiveness of unit output, and this was because the production teams took full responsibility for work organization, task allocation and quality control without losing any of the collective cohesion of the organization overall. By contrast, one of the main complaints from NHS nurses and other medical professions is that they simply do not have enough time to spend with patients because of staff shortages and other operational pressures.

Flexible patterns of work

As stated above (see Chapters 13, 14 and 19), 'flexibility' is a collective attitude and corporate state of mind. The basis for any 'flexible' approach to patterns of work lies in the corporate will to make it happen.

The issue of flexibility becomes especially important when looking to structure and design workplace patterns of behaviour because of the following:

Box 23.6: Mars Chocolate

For some time, one of the main chocolate processing plants at the Mars Chocolate company ran at very high temperatures. The problem was the cooling system itself; it had been unreliable for many years and when it broke down the factory manager experienced great difficulty in getting parts. Repeated requests for parts and an overhaul of the system were met with promises but no action on the part of the suppliers. Eventually, patterns of work had to be created that would enable production to carry on in the very high temperatures, while at the same time preserving the humanity of the working relationship. The result was that staff had to go into the production area in temperatures of up to 55 degrees centigrade, and work in the area for no more than 15 minutes. They would then come out and spend a further 15 minutes cooling off, and drinking water.

This pattern of work persisted for many months. Eventually, the regional manager came to inspect the premises. Then he saw how production was being carried out. He called a maintenance crew over and said: 'Get the factory manager's desk up here. The factory manager is now going to be working in this production facility until the cooling system is fixed.'

The cooling system was fixed in 24 hours to the satisfaction of everyone.

The main lesson is the need to create patterns of work that suit everyone. It remains true that, in many cases, unless managers are forced to recognize the fact of the unacceptable pattern of work (and in this case, actually become involved in it), then nothing is done about it. People adapt to the environment rather than solving the problem.

- it directly addresses the question of work–life balance; and social considerations, as well as sheer humanity, mean that those organizations that do get this right will always enjoy a better reputation (as employers at least) than those that do not;
- the generation of a flexible attitude and culture in the context of organizational priorities means that production, output, motivation and morale are certain to be much higher;
- UK legislation requires that flexible attendance patterns are made available to all those with dependent relatives and children under the age of 16; and this legislation places the onus on the employer to state why flexible working is operationally costly, ineffective or inappropriate (rather than asking the employee to make the case for flexible working).

To organizations and their managers, therefore, there is both the incentive of ensuring overall effectiveness and profitability, and also the sanction of the law, as drivers towards greater flexibility.

Opposition to flexible working

Those opposed to flexible working raise the following objections:

- it encourages people to come and go as they please;
- it encourages divisions and inequalities in the workforce;

- 'if one person gets flexible working, everyone else will want it';
- how is it possible to control productivity, output or value when people cannot be contacted or made to attend?

Managers in such an environment or culture, especially, state that they have no idea what their staff are doing (Handy, 2006).

Clearly, there are some critical boundaries and conditions which have to be established. These boundaries include:

- attendance when the demands of the business dictate;
- meeting production and service delivery deadlines;
- equality and fairness;
- supervision and control.

Attendance

Attendance itself can only be flexible up to a point. If a shop is open from 8.00 am to 8.00 pm, then clearly check-out and customer service staff have to be present at these times (or on shifts within these hours). Flexibility arises from how they discharge their duties, the attitudes exhibited, the amount of autonomy that they have in their dealings with their customers and any additional responsibilities that the organization may choose to place upon them.

Additionally, if organizations do require their staff to attend regular and complete hours, then they have only to make the case from a sustainable and robust business point of view. No organization is forced to do anything that is operationally detrimental (see Box 23.7).

Deadlines

Deadlines have to be met whatever the state of flexibility. Flexibility comes in the form of how deadlines are met, and how the work is delivered on time. For example, schoolteachers and university lecturers have to be present when they have classes to give. The flexibility comes in the form of how they structure their material, when and where they prepare it, where they do their marking and other tasks and duties, how they go about establishing contact with their students. Each of these elements can be fully prescribed by the organization, or left totally to the discretion of the individual teacher or lecturer. So the prescribed timetable and schedule contains as much or as little flexibility as the organization chooses (see Box 23.8).

Equality and fairness

Equality and fairness are corporate and managerial attitudes and states of mind. Therefore, if equality and fairness are not present in the first place, then any approach to flexible working is going to be functional rather than attitudinal. The result is that some groups and individuals are able to lobby successfully for flexible working, the freedom and autonomy to tackle their jobs as they see fit, while others are not. This reinforces the divides (rather than the cohesion) that are certain to exist already. This, in turn, results in grievances and disputes which are costly and counter-productive. In many cases,

Box 23.7: Otikon

Otikon is a Danish company which produces high-quality audio products for the hard of hearing, and also hearing and listening devices for the mobile phone industry.

The company embraces fully flexible patterns of work – in which everybody has to attend full and regular hours at their designated place of work.

The company's main premises in Copenhagen, Denmark, is laid out around a central staircase. All the offices are open plan. Nobody is assigned a permanent desk.

Explaining the philosophy behind this, the company CEO, Lars Olind, stated:

> We want this organization to be creative, fun and profitable. You cannot have creativity in isolation. Creative and productive activity in this industry results from the coming together of two or more people. We have therefore created the conditions in which people come together all the time – on the staircase, in the offices, and as a result of having to move around because they do not have their own desks. We also have a free restaurant where people can take their lunch, go for coffee – and again, meet with colleagues.
>
> Once projects are defined, people are free to choose those activities on which they work. People who do not have projects are free to get involved in any aspect of the organization's activities. They are also free to start up their own projects.
>
> Everything is evaluated from the point of view of progress. If projects are cancelled, this does not matter, as long as the company learns from the activities.
>
> So we have fully flexible working – and it is a pattern of fully flexible working in which everyone is actively involved with everyone else on a daily basis.

Since Lars Olind took over as chief executive, the company has doubled its revenues and opened activities in twelve different countries.

Box 23.8: Semco and Carrefour

In 1998, during the football World Cup of that year, Semco, the Brazilian white goods manufacturer, was awarded a very high-value contract to refurbish all of the specialist freezer and refrigeration equipment for the Brazilian subsidiary of Carrefour, the French supermarket chain. The work was commissioned early in the summer of that year and was scheduled to take place during the third weekend of July (the date of the World Cup final).

Nobody at this stage considered the football. In so far as it mattered, the French had a good team but were inconsistent. Brazil did indeed have some good individuals, but by common consent they were not a patch on the great Brazilian teams of the past.

And then – the unthinkable happened! The weekend of the contract delivery duly arrived, and France were to play Brazil in the World Cup final. What on earth was Semco to do?

'In the end,' said Ricardo Semler, the company CEO, 'we turned the whole thing over to the staff. The only stipulations were that the work had to be done, and had to be completed by the Monday morning. And so what happened was that each work group organized themselves as they saw fit so that they could fit in both the work and the football. If we had tried to order them to work, or told them when to work, we would have failed. By doing it this way, we made sure that everyone's needs were satisfied.'

The work was duly delivered on time, to quality and budget.

In passing, France won the football; and the Brazilians duly drowned their sorrows.

This is an extreme form of flexibility; it nevertheless illustrates what can be done if tight and absolute organization deadlines are integrated fully with every requirement of the staff.

Source: R. Semler (2003) *The Seven Day Weekend* – Century.

because of the legal constraints (see above) it results in top and senior managers either having to back down, resulting in loss of face, or else stamping their foot and ordering people to work as directed by virtue of pulling rank, which is always counter-productive.

If there are reasons why some individuals and groups can be given (real and perceived) greater autonomy and flexibility, then these reasons need to be clearly explained and understood by all. If this cannot be done, then the practice, rather than the attitude, of flexible working will be made available to those groups that are able to lobby to best effect. This, in turn, leads to groups and individuals learning how to lobby rather than getting on with the job.

Control

The relationship between flexible working and control lies in a combination of management style and attitude, operational priorities and the collective approach to control overall.

None of this need be a barrier to flexible and effective working within whatever confines the organization chooses to impose, in order to satisfy its own demands for management information and overall integrity of working relationships.

The key question again therefore is: why? Why do the organization and its managers need to control specific aspects of operational life? The answers to the question, and the ways in which they are delivered, lie in where the organization's priorities truly lie. If there are established powerful and influential administrative systems and processes, then the organization 'fit' demands that detailed time sheets and work records are kept.

These in themselves are not barriers to flexible working; indeed, they may serve as drivers of progress and output, and the figures from each used to enhance productivity.

So the key is what the organizations and their managers think is important to control, and the attitude with which this priority is delivered (see Box 23.7 above). The controls that are in place ought to provide a framework and set of boundaries within which people can be as flexible as operationally necessary or desirable in the pursuit of their jobs, tasks and priorities.

There are therefore clear answers to the questions that those who would approach the practice of flexible working ask. Once the answers are given and made clear, they pose no threat to either flexibility or operational effectiveness (see Box 23.9).

Locations of work

Locating work and activities used to be so easy! If a production process added weight to the final output, work was located near the markets; if the process lost weight in respect of the final product, work was located at the source of raw materials. Offices and white collar jobs were located in city, town and regional hubs, and people would either live close by or else commute to work each day. Each community and region was served and supported by energy, transport, telecommunications, health and education services, with professionals in these sectors either living in the community or else, again, travelling to work (see Box 23.10).

Technology

The universal availability of production, telecommunications, IT and portable equipment means that work can now be carried out anywhere in the world at any time. Companies and organizations, and their top and senior managers, now choose the location of work on the basis of their own evaluation of where the best places are; and this evaluation includes:

Box 23.9: Nissan UK

Nissan UK introduced a principle of fully flexible working when they first opened their factory in the north-east of England. The grounding for this was full staff training for all; and this included paying for people to travel to visit the parent company in Japan.

The results were:

- On the one hand, the job of everyone was enlarged and enriched to the point where everyone could do every task and every job in their own particular sphere. In particular, production staff were to become responsible for their own quality assurance; and this included handling customer complaints and queries. Any car that was subsequently found to have faults or teething troubles was referred back to the production crew who had built it.
- On the other hand, fully comprehensive training and flexibility meant that the staff were required to do any job that was demanded in the interests of keeping production levels as high as possible. Staff were to be paid excellent salaries relative to the rest of the sector. As far as possible, the company offered life-time employment and a pension scheme that was open to everyone.

Immediately before the crisis of 2007 onwards, the Nissan UK factory was producing 133 cars per member of staff, the highest output of any car factory in the world.

- choosing locations where labour is cheap and plentiful;
- choosing locations where labour is expert;
- choosing to locate in known and understood centres of particular activities;
- choosing to have people working from home, from the car and from business centre premises (often rented by the hour/day/week).

Box 23.10: Sheerness Steel

One of the first companies in the UK to break the pattern of location was Sheerness Steel. Located in the Isle of Sheppey on the north coast of Kent, the steelworks had come to prominence as a specialist supplier of particular steels to the Royal Navy, London Dockyards and railways infrastructure. As these markets declined, so did the company's fortunes.

At the point of collapse, the company was transformed by a new management team. Every single cost was assessed, and reduced or removed if it was not essential to the supply and delivery of top-quality steel products. Staff salaries were enhanced in return for fully flexible working. When it opposed the changes, the staff trade union was de-recognized. The number of accidents (endemic in the iron and steel sector) was cut by 90 per cent, again based on staff training and strict adherence to procedures.

All this had to be done while at the same time searching for new markets and outlets for the steel products. Sheerness Steel was no longer near its markets; and raw materials had to be brought in by sea.

Nevertheless, the result was that for ten years Sheerness Steel was the most profitable steel company in the European economic area. Only when it was taken over by NuCorp did it falter and fail; and this was because the new owners reverted to tradition by reducing staff involvement and cutting back on the training and development effort. NuCorp began a process of asset stripping and cutting production.

The result was that the company closed down altogether. In the aftermath of the closure, it became clear that one of the 'assets' that had been stripped was the company pension scheme, which had been sold on to a finance house. Legal action against the company on the part of pension scheme's trustees and members ensued, and was finally settled in favour of the staff.

The main lesson is that it is possible to establish effective operations away from traditional locations if every other part of the organization and work structure are effective. It demonstrates by implication the need to know and understand the full context of working; and to commit as part of the organizational investment to ensuring that every aspect is maintained.

In passing also, it is a lesson in the behavioural aspects of takeovers. NuCorp bought the company because they thought it was profitable; but they never understood the basis on which that profitability was assured. When they did not understand it, they sold off the assets; and when they found that the company was no longer productive, they closed it down (in spite of the fact that it was their own actions that had made it unproductive). It is finally the case that organizations can be held to account for present and past actions – the pension scheme case referred to above took many years to resolve, running on long after NuCorp ever wished to have any involvement.

In one way, these approaches to choosing the location of work is not new.

- Banking and financial services were always established in capital cities and other known and understood commercial centres of the world.
- The nuclear power industry had normally to be located at coastal or river sites because of the vast quantities of water required for cooling processes.

Technology and transport networks and infrastructure have broadened the choices available. This has resulted in companies and organizations locating their activities in known and understood centres of excellence, for example:

- India (financial services, including call centre facilities);
- Vietnam, Central America (clothing and textiles);
- Mexico (plastic products, including toys – 90 per cent of Mattel's production takes place in Mexico);
- China (precision manufacturing);
- China, Indonesia, Malaysia (mass manufacturing);
- India, Pakistan (sports goods).

There is therefore as much choice of location as top and senior managers would wish for. This choice may be made on the basis of:

- evaluation of information and arrival at a position that can be supported and justified;
- acting as a vehicle for opening up new opportunities and activities;
- acting as a vehicle for diversification;
- responding to shareholder and peer pressures;
- engaging in vanity projects and activities;
- corporate excitement and adventures;
- hammering down the costs of labour and raw materials;
- the presence of large and available pools of labour and expertise.

Top and senior managers take decisions to locate on any, or all, of these bases. The key to effective location (and relocation) is the strength of argument and support for the decision that is brought to bear. The key to effective choice of location is the line of reasoning produced, and the extent to which it can be supported and justified (see Box 23.11).

Responsibility and accountability for decisions on location are essential. The costs of researching and identifying a presence in particular places are always high. The

Box 23.11: Volkswagen in Leipzig

Volkswagen, the German car manufacturing company, had its main manufacturing activities near the Rhine river in western Germany. Effective and productive though the activities were, the company was faced with a gradual decline in productivity, and increases in unit manufacturing costs.

The company therefore decided to build from scratch a state-of-the-art manufacturing facility in Leipzig in eastern Germany. The decision was driven by the fact that there was a large pool of highly trained and qualified labour, and a tradition of engineering activities in the area (these had closed down following the collapse of the communist regime in the former East Germany).

The factory was designed as a single entity. Manufacturing was placed at the centre. Those with office jobs and other professional functions (sales, marketing) had their offices looking out over the manufacturing facility, so that nobody ever forgot that the primary purpose was to make, deliver and sell medium-range, good-quality cars.

The location was critical for a variety of other reasons. These included:

- the ability to open up new markets in central and eastern Europe;
- the ability to take advantage of the large pool of experts and available labour;
- a restatement of the culture of the company, integrating all activities with the crucial priority of car manufacture.

In addition, there was a social aspect to this location: the need to provide work and social, as well as economic, support to the particular location.

As well as satisfying the economic priority, the project therefore delivered additional benefits. The project was, in particular, designed to restate the company's culture and priorities, as well as providing work in a deprived area.

propensity for things to go wrong is high also. Top and senior managers need to be able to evaluate particular proposals, and then support and back their judgement based on their expertise in the given field. Especially, it is no use choosing to go into a particular location, finding difficulties, and then blaming the local staff/culture/technology/market for the results. It is also no use blaming shareholder pressure or regulatory and other legal restrictions – top and senior managers are appointed to act in everyone's best interests, and not to slavishly follow what others think or do (see Box 23.12).

Staff

The location of work gives everyone involved a certain freedom of choice in how, when and where to organize work and carry out tasks; and it gives organizations, in particular, a certain amount of choice about the provision and use of technology, premises and equipment (see above).

Also, as stated above, it crucially means that work can, subject to consultation and agreement, be carried out any time and anywhere. This can be extremely effective in terms of resource utilization. It can also cause stress and overload; and it is a matter of record (ACAS, 2007; Cooper, 2002) that while short-term advantages can, and do, accrue, the longer-term effects are declining performance, burn-out and, in some cases, serious illness.

The capability to create these kinds of work patterns therefore comes with corporate responsibility to ensure that, as a priority, effectiveness is indeed enhanced without creating the conditions at the same time where people are effectively always at work.

Box 23.12: Portsmouth Football Club

In March 2010, Portsmouth Football Club entered administration, effectively bankrupt. The final straw was a bill from HM Revenue and Customs for £3 million in unpaid taxes.

The problems had arisen over the period since 2005, when the club had been promoted into the English Premier League. On the one hand this was a pinnacle of success; on the other, however, the club now had to find top-class players and pay very high wages and salaries.

Rather than doing this in terms of assured income, the club borrowed money against the security of future income from television rights and performance success. This seemed to have been the right thing to do when in 2008 the club won the FA Cup.

However, this attracted prestige rather than income, and the need to borrow to stay competitive grew ever greater. In the months before the administration, it became clear that the position was going to be untenable. When the club did finally enter administration, however, the only explanation provided was that 'this is football, and this is what everyone does'.

It is also essential that staff working in non-standard ways and remote locations do not become displaced or forgotten. This requires distinctive forms of supervision, including a physical presence and support, that may have to be created so that those who spend long periods of time away from the premises remain fully effective (see Box 23.13).

Conclusions

Creating, maintaining and developing effective patterns of behaviour at work is therefore a crucial corporate and managerial task. Foundations of these patterns of behaviour lie in the nature of work, the locations chosen, the technology used and the mix of occupations and patterns of attendance.

It is clear that the core of the expertise required lies in understanding how factors concerning technology, location and patterns of work influence the strength and cohesion of the behaviour and performance of the staff. It is also the case that every aspect has to be considered on its own merits in its own particular situation; to try to prescribe or order specific patterns of work is ineffective.

Organizational and managerial expertise in this respect is therefore essential. This has to be based on a full understanding and evaluation of what is required in each situation, and how to make what is available work to best advantage. Sheer hard and expert work, and how it is applied, are crucial to ensuring that this part of the management of organizations is successful, effective – and profitable. In particular, the following are clear:

- those organizations that do effectively evaluate their particular situation, and create the conditions in which effective patterns of behaviour at work can be developed, are much more likely to succeed than those that do not;
- where insufficient attention is given to this aspect, the conditions for business failure are created.

Box 23.13: Managing by ringing around

If a key tenet in the strength of managerial and staff cohesion is managing by walking around (see Chapter 16), then, where people are working in remote locations or 'on the hoof', an equivalent has to be found. This means that managers and supervisors have to be prepared to re-prioritize their schedules so that they can meet up with their remote staff when possible. It also means having a regular system of managing by ringing around.

Managing by ringing around was a critical management tool used by Arnold Weinstock at GEC. Arnold Weinstock would schedule weekly telephone calls with each senior and key figure with whom he had not met physically, and they would discuss in detail the work that had taken place during the week. Weinstock would examine in detail everything from production schedules and targets, to any staff issues (including grievances and disputes). He expected detailed answers to all the questions posed; and managers who could not provide these detailed answers were given short periods of time only to bring themselves up to speed.

These weekly phone calls became part of the company's myths and folklore. Crucially, however, it ensured that regional and remote activities that were carried out were fully integrated into the overall purpose of the company. The approach also ensured that both human and professional relationships were maintained and developed.

24 Stress and its management

Introduction

Organizational, occupational, collective and individual stress and its management are primary, strategic and operational concerns for all organizations and their managers. This is because of the direct relationship between decency and humanity, good employment practice and successful business. Stress additionally places a cost burden on organizations in all locations and sectors. There is a professional, occupational, social and human price among those who work in stressful situations or suffer from stress-related injuries and illnesses (see Box 24.1).

The need for attention to organizational and occupational stress is reinforced in the UK and EU by legislation that requires an increasingly active responsibility for the health and well-being of employees. This legislation includes specific attention to stress. The costs of settling individual and collective cases and situations where stress has been demonstrated or proven are therefore very high. In such cases, the costs that organizations have to bear are as follows.

- The cost of having staff off sick for stress-related injuries and illnesses.
- The cost of paying compensation to those who can demonstrate and prove that their lives have been damaged or ruined as the result of stress at work.
- Loss of output; declining performance, in which less gets done, more slowly and for fewer customers and clients, at ever-increasing cost.
- Costs in reputation and, invariably, business losses as the result of publicity surrounding specific media coverage in cases of accident, disaster, bullying, victimization, harassment and discrimination. These costs include customers taking business elsewhere where able to do so because no one likes to be associated or do business with this kind of organization. Such organizations experience increased difficulties in recruiting and retaining high-quality, expert staff, because nobody with any choice in the matter wishes to work for such a concern.
- Organization and managerial costs involved in investing and defending individual and collective complaints of stress, and in remedying and resolving these.
- Costs involved in having to manage, address and resolve related issues, for example where staff have turned to drink and drugs as a relief from stress.
- Wider humanitarian concerns, which bring costs with them also; known, believed and perceived stress-related illnesses and injuries cause general damage to workplace and human morale and motivation.

It is clear therefore that high levels of stress can, and do, exist in many companies and organizations. The potential for the existence of stress is also high, whatever the nature of work, size and structure of the organization.

The context of workplace stress

Some stresses are physical, such as Repetitive Strain Injuries (RSIs) and back injuries, and therefore much easier to address, managerially, medically and culturally. Problems are compounded because injuries caused by physical stress give rise to psychological problems in sufferers. Other causes of stress are psychological and behavioural, and therefore much less capable of observation and quantification.

Box 24.1: Junior doctors – again

Jim White, a junior doctor at a large city hospital in south-west England, got out of bed, and got dressed, preparing to go on to the wards. He was very tired. He had already worked over 90 hours in the previous six days; now he was looking forward to this final shift, before he would have two days off.

Just as he was about to leave his room, there was a knock on the door. It was a member of the hospital's HR team. She came into the room, sat down and then said to Jim: 'You know why I am here?'

'No,' replied Jim.

'I am here as you were told last night. I need to investigate the incident.'

'What incident?'

'The incident last night.'

'What incident last night?'

'The incident where you went naked on to the wards, and proceeded to try to do your rounds. We need an explanation of this.'

Flabbergasted, Jim himself sat down. He said: 'Well, of course I did not go on to the wards naked. I did not go on to the wards at all last night. I have been in here, trying to get some sleep.'

However, footage from the hospital's security cameras, and statements of many eye witnesses, did indeed confirm that Jim had been on to the wards with no clothes on at all. He himself had no memory of this.

Jim had simply worked to the point of exhaustion. He now found himself having to defend actions that he could not recall, let alone explain.

This is a true story, documented in the HR archives of the particular city hospital. It demonstrates the exceptional stress under which some people are required to operate. Particularly in the case of junior doctors, there are, in practice, no maximum hours. This is in spite of UK and EU legislation which states that anyone in any job can only be required to work a maximum of 48 hours per week; any additional duties must be agreed with individual employees.

In practice also, for junior doctors in particular, and also many other healthcare and social services professionals, there are enormous institutional and cultural pressures to work very many more hours. Organizations in these sectors exert pressures on staff to work long hours, often threatening them with the prospect of bad references or even falsified accusations of bad working practices.

It also helps to explain why these (and other) professions and occupations have such difficulty in recruiting and retaining staff, especially when it is understood that these occupations are some of the most worthwhile in the world.

Stress also has a very strong subjective element. Some individuals take in their stride what others find extremely stressful. Some people find difficult parts of work more stressful than others, for example some nurses find having to do paperwork to be an opportunity to sit down away from hospital ward pressures, while others resent it because it interferes with the ward work.

Some people complain of stress when, while it is known and understood that the particular working environment is very pressurized, this is nevertheless simply the norm for the particular occupation or organization. Those who do complain consequently come to be badly thought of, and so the individual pressure is compounded.

A major cause of individual stress is being on the receiving end of bullying, victimization, discrimination and harassment (see below). These activities are morally repugnant and an affront to basic humanity. They are endemic in all organizations, industrial, commercial and public service sectors across the western world and Far East. People who suffer these forms of treatment always experience stress and trauma, often leading to irreparable damage to their lives. It is therefore essential that organizations and their managers create the conditions in which these forms of activity cannot and do not take place; and that where they are discovered, effective sanctions are meted out to the perpetrators (see Box 24.2).

Box 24.2: High and mighty

Paul Way was director of policy and research at a major government institution. Still only 40, he had arrived at this position as the result of choosing a career in central government, and of sheer hard work. On his way up through the ranks, he had done whatever it had taken to get him his next promotion and advancement; and now, at last, he had the position to which he had always aspired.

Shortly after his appointment, he was called to a policy meeting. This was a critical event, and how it went would provide an early indication to other top government officials of Paul's capabilities.

Paul set off for his meeting. On the way out, he told his assistant, Robert Errin, that under no circumstances was he to be disturbed.

Some time after he had left, Robert received a phone call from Paul's wife stating that one of his children had been involved in a serious accident. The child was in hospital and nobody was sure whether or not she would live.

Robert went along to the meeting and managed to convince Paul to come out. He gave Paul a mobile phone link to his wife and the hospital and in a terse phone call, Paul assessed the overall situation with his family. Everything was clearly very distressing and uncertain. At last, Paul came off the phone and returned it to Robert. Then Paul said: 'What the hell did you bring me out of this meeting for? Don't you know that I'm in front of some of the most important people in the country? Couldn't this have waited?'

Robert began to explain. However, Paul cut him short with: 'Oh, shut up and clear off!' Then Paul hit Robert hard across the jaw, sending him spinning to the ground.

This is an illustration of what can, and does, happen when many different sources of stress are brought together. In this case:

- Paul has the stress of his new job, of the need to impress, and of his family situation;
- Robert has the stress of working for a new boss, and having to interrupt an important meeting.

In this particular case, the investigation that followed found that 'stress' was indeed to blame! No action was taken against Paul. However, Robert was forced to move on, though with an enhanced pay deal in his new job.

Overall responsibilities

Effective stress management brings direct obligations and responsibilities, and these also have a cost. Organizations and their managers are going to be increasingly required to invest time, financial resources and expertise in creating a quality of working life and environment that acknowledges the potential for stress. This requires recognizing where the potential for physical and psychological stress lies, and taking active steps in workplace, occupation and work design so that it is eliminated as far as possible, or else kept to a minimum. If this is not possible, organizations and their managers must be prepared to accept that they will face problems of absenteeism, illness, injury and burnout as a result (see Box 24.3).

It is also essential to create managerial and supervisory styles which ensure that problems and issues are raised and dealt with early, rather than being allowed to fester (which is in itself stressful). The fundamental approach has to be based on openness, honesty and integrity. It is essential that a mutual respect and value between staff and managers is created and developed – and this is vital, and possible, regardless of whether the organization is hierarchical, bureaucratic, authoritarian, participative or democratic.

A general climate of mutual confidence is also required. This enables all those involved to talk openly about problems and issues so that they can be raised at whatever stage they become apparent, and from whatever source. This includes providing the capacity and willingness to address serious problems – especially those raised by 'whistle-blowers' (see Box 24.4).

An active management engagement is required in recognizing the institutional sources, causes and potential for individual and collective conflict. This means acknowledging that the potential for conflict exists in all human situations, and this includes places of work. Managers are increasingly required to assess their own organizations, those employed, and desired and required ways of working, from the point of view of recognizing the potential for conflict in the particular situation; and creating and developing the conditions in which this can be kept to a minimum, and resolved quickly when it does begin to break out (see Box 24.5).

The primary responsibility is therefore to understand the extent and prevalence of stress within organizations, and in particular occupations and professions. While it is clearly understood to be more of a problem in some sectors, occupations and professions, it should be understood as having the potential for – and indeed existing – across all

Box 24.3: Softies

Many organizations and their managers still do not recognize stress as being anything other than an excuse to malinger, or for employees being work-shy. In many cases, managers and supervisors with this attitude reinforce their dealings with staff in stress-related matters with phrases such as:

- 'We had to work much harder than this in my day, and it never did us any harm.'
- 'Anyone who takes time off due to stress is clearly soft and unworthy of a job in this place.'
- 'The present generation are wet and weedy.'

One such manager was Jim Cantalupo who, for many years, was chief executive of McDonald's. Jim Cantalupo regularly worked 75-hour weeks, and he expected to be able to contact all of the company's corporate management team at any time of the day or night.

At the time, McDonald's was a very successful organization, going from strength to strength, opening ten new franchises per week, and with average annual growth in turnover of 15 per cent, and profit growth of 7 per cent. However, Jim Cantalupo kept up the pressure on his top and senior managers.

Jim Cantalupo died in harness from a heart attack, aged 55. The post-mortem indicated that, while he had not led a particularly healthy life overall, the overwhelming reason for the heart attack was a prolonged case of occupational stress.

Box 24.4: Whistleblowers

Paul Moore was sacked from his job as director of risk management at HBOS.

In the months prior to his dismissal, Paul Moore had repeatedly warned the top and senior management of HBOS, the UK retail banking company, that the 'invest- ments' and loans that they were making were not being properly assessed or evaluated for security and strength. Paul Moore acknowledged that each time such an investment or loan was made, the short-term asset value of the bank did indeed rise. However, in the long-term, these positions could not be sustained, and the true and enduring value was actually unknown, uncertain – and certain to fall at some stage.

Repeatedly, Paul Moore's concerns were brushed aside on the grounds that he was 'worrying too much'. Eventually, Paul Moore raised the concerns once too often; and he was dismissed by the Board of Directors.

When it became apparent that HBOS was indeed in serious financial trouble, Paul Moore went public. HBOS tried to dismiss his allegations as those of 'an embittered ex-employee'. However, the matter would not go away; and as the banking crisis deepened, Paul Moore felt increasingly able to give full details about the warnings that he had tried to make, the responses that he had received, and the consequences for the bank.

It therefore became clear that Paul Moore was an excellent and overtly effective director of risk management. However, the banking industry as a whole continues to shun him and his expertise.

Paul Moore has effectively created for himself the stress of taking on the entire UK banking industry, purely in the name of clarifying a particular position of wrongdoing and negligence.

All forms of whistleblowing carry an equivalent form of stress. In recent times, there have been cases of vandalism, violence, theft and fraud, as well as the most appalling examples of child neglect and cruelty, that have only come to light when someone has finally been able to pluck up the courage to tell all. Even where something is plainly wrong, it takes great coverage (and stress) to go public, knowing that a substantial case is going to have to be made against the might of an organization and its managers and resources.

Box 24.5: Examples of stress at work

The need to recognize and address the relationship between particular occupation, professional and work patterns, and stress and strain, is present in all industries and occupations. For example:

- **Hospitals**: it is impossible for anyone to deliver sustained and effective long-term performance if they are working a prescribed working week of 72 hours (6×12 hour shifts as with UK junior hospital doctors). Indeed, some junior hospital doctors in the UK effectively work, or are on-call, the full 168 hours per week (see also above, Box 24.1).
- **Financial services**: financial services and investment management in Japan also adopt these 'long hours' cultures. Some big banks require that all their staff arrive before the local senior manager or chief executive and do not leave until he (and it is invariably a he) does. Hundreds of staff consequently find themselves sleeping at the office for several days at a time.
- **Football**: professional footballers in Italy do not work to the same degree of pressure. However, their week is fully and comprehensively structured. As well as prescribed hours of training, they are told what to eat and when; and they are also told how much sleep they are to have, and when to take it. Indeed, their only genuinely free time is between the end of matches at approximately 5.00 pm on Sundays, and bedtime that evening. Every other hour of the week is organized on behalf of the players by the clubs. Serious stress is caused if, for any reason, the players are not allowed out at this time (e.g. as the result of a breach of club discipline). This is in spite of the fact that extremely high salary levels are paid (up to 200,000 euros per week in many instances).

sectors, industries and national and social cultures. It is essential that organizations, managers and individuals understand the costs attached to stress, and the benefits of understanding, recognizing and addressing it successfully and effectively.

Understanding stress

Stress is placed on anything that is given special emphasis or significance, especially where this leads to, or involves, psychological, emotional and physical strain or tension. A part of it is therefore subjective, in that different reactions are produced in different individuals by the same set of circumstances.

Stress is caused by a combined physical and psychological response to stimuli (stressors) that occur or are encountered during the course of living, as well as work. There is a clear negative connotation, in that the physical and psychological responses create adverse (rather than positive) feelings.

Further detail can be added as follows.

- Cooper (2002) summarizes stress as: 'everything that deprives the person of purpose and zest, that leaves him with negative feelings about himself, with anxieties, tensions, a sense of lostness, emptiness and futility'.
- Fontana (1989; 2001) draws the meaning of the word from the Latin *stringere*, meaning 'to draw tight', and from the French word *destresse*, meaning 'to be placed under narrowness or oppression'.
- Statt (1994; 2006) draws attention to the physical response:

    the human body is biologically programmed to react to challenges from the environment by mobilizing its resources. We can either confront the challenge and fight it or get away from it as fast as possible. The choice in other words is 'fight or flight', whichever we deem to be more appropriate in the situation. If our brain perceives an imminent challenge, the message it passes to our autonomic nervous system results immediately in the hormones adrenaline and noradrenaline being released into the bloodstream where they speed up our reflexes, raise the level of blood sugar and increase our blood pressure and heart rate. The digestive system closes down allowing the blood used in the normal process of digesting food to be re-routed to the muscles and lungs. Endorphins are released into the bloodstream which reduce pain and sensitivity to bruising and injury. Cortisone is released from the adrenal glands into the bloodstream which slows the body's immune system. Finally, the blood vessels constrict while the blood thickens, flows more slowly, and coagulates more quickly. The sum of these changes is to prepare us to deal with a short-term emergency situation. Stress occurs when these physiological reactions cannot deal with the environmental challenge.

In summary, it is essential that organizations and their managers recognize and understand the potential for stress, the costs involved and the negative effects on productive output (and therefore profits). There is a collective and individual responsibility to ensure that workplace stress is kept to a minimum, and active steps taken to do everything possible to remove the causes and outputs, as far as is reasonably practicable.

Stress and work

In spite of the fact that stress is an individual reaction, it is important to recognize that certain organizational, occupational, environmental and managerial conditions are much more likely to produce foreseeable and more or less predictable adverse human reactions. Key concerns are:

- attention to work and occupational conditions and environment;
- specific problems, including RSI, and the extent and prevalence of bullying, victimization, discrimination and harassment;
- role conflicts;
- organization structure and culture;
- workplace relationships.

Work and occupational conditions and the environment

Arnold (1997) identified five key elements relating to job stress as follows:

- making decisions;
- constant monitoring of devices or materials;
- repeated exchange of information with others;
- unpleasant physical conditions;
- performing unstructured, rather than structured, tasks.

The greater the extent to which any job, profession or occupation possesses each of these elements, the higher the general level of stress. While it is possible to reduce or minimize the effects of stress where one or two of these conditions are prevalent, it is not easy where all five are present. To these may be added the following:

- resources, expertise and other staff and equipment shortages;
- uncertainty of tenure;
- adversarial or dishonest managerial and supervisory styles and approaches;
- lack of known, believed and perceived adequate intrinsic and extrinsic rewards.

It is likely that some of these will also be present to an extent in most occupations. However, it is the extent and mix of each that causes occupational stress. Problems are compounded when those in known or believed stressful situations and occupations understand that they are being overloaded with work when others elsewhere in the particular organization are not.

This may or may not be true. It does indicate the prime importance of an open and visible managerial style as a prerequisite to the effective recognition and acceptance of stress caused by problems at work. If it is impossible to raise or observe such matters, it is extremely hard for there to be any effective subsequent action.

Specific areas for attention

Organizations and their managers need to know and understand the specific areas where effective interventions can and need to be made, in order to reduce and minimize the presence of stress and its adverse consequences. These areas are:

- bullying, victimization, harassment and discrimination;
- organizational and occupational roles;
- cultural and occupational factors;
- working relations.

Bullying, victimization, harassment and discrimination

Stress is caused when bullying, victimization, harassment and discrimination occur and are allowed to persist unchecked. It is also a serious problem when an individual comes across an aspect of organizational or occupational malpractice and feels powerless to do anything about it. Each of these stems from the illegitimate use of power by individuals, groups or the organization as a whole based on:

- position, rank and status;
- resource command and control;
- physical power, strength and size.

The most common outputs are:

- sexual harassment, overwhelmingly of female staff by males;
- threatening behavioural and/or physical violence towards an individual or group;
- refusal to employ or promote people on the grounds of their age, race, ethnic origin, gender or disability;
- refusal to appoint or promote people on the grounds of victimization or scapegoating;
- threatening attitudes and behaviour towards subordinates by seniors involving the misuse and abuse of disciplinary and poor performance procedures; and in many cases, this is compounded by adversarial general attitudes that may be summarized as: 'If you do not do this work or want this job, there are millions out there who do'.

As stated elsewhere (see Chapters 14 and 18) all forms of bullying, victimization, discrimination and harassment are morally repugnant, and also illegal. They also cause great stress to those on the receiving end. They additionally cause damage to reputation and performance to those organizations that allow these actions to persist.

It is also certain that, once an allegation is made, others will emerge from the shadows. It therefore does not take long in many cases for an organization to be known as an institution where these forms of behaviour are allowed to persist.

Roles

Roles are combinations of behaviour and activities undertaken by people in different sets of circumstances. Everyone performs a great variety of roles during their lives (see Chapter 14). If the role diagram in Chapter 14 is adjusted to put the occupation at the centre, it comes out as follows (Figure 24.1).

So, for example, managers can, and will, find themselves in the position of having to reconcile the different roles as follows:

- driving results and performance from those who are otherwise considered as friends;
- disciplining someone who considers the manager to be a friend and confidant;

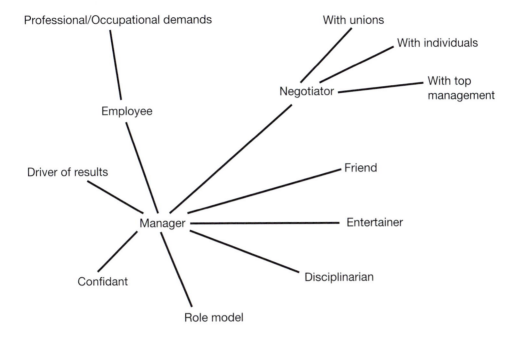

Each role has expectations, pressures, rewards and consequences.
There are overlaps between each and measures of honesty, discord and conflict.

Figure 24.1 Individual roles

- entertaining and cheerleading for the staff, while at the same time driving them for results;
- negotiating with top management with consequences for those regarded as friends, as well as employees.

In practice, everyone is required to adopt different roles at work; and so the above is an example that can be applied to all occupations, organizations and situations.

More generally, stress is always caused where there are role uncertainties and ambiguities, role overlap (especially between work and non-work), role incompatibility, role conflict and role overload and under-load.

Cultural and occupational factors

Organization culture is the summary of attitudes, values, beliefs and activities carried out (see Chapter 15). Culture is reinforced by the stated and actual purposes, priorities and attention given to performance, staff, customers, suppliers, the community and the environment; and to progress and development. The collective and prevailing attitudes taken to each of these groups and activities can either enhance or minimize stress; and this is especially true when the required or demanded attitudes and approaches are unknown or uncertain. It is therefore incumbent upon all managers to ensure that staff are adequately trained and briefed in each of these activities, and in their dealings with

Box 24.6: The Japanese government emergency response

The inadequacy of the Japanese government in responding quickly to crises and emergencies became apparent at the time of the Japanese Airlines disaster of 1987 and the Kobe earthquake of 1992. There was a direct conflict between the need to respond quickly, the capability to do this, and the perceived political drives of Cabinet ministers and senior public officials. The need to respond quickly was driven by the fact that, in each case, a speedy response would save lives. The capability was present – but it was not Japanese. It was American.

US military personnel stationed in Japan and trained in disaster management and rescue missions were on both occasions capable and available. They were not called on because of the perceived loss of face that would arise if the government, by implication, was seen to be unable to respond to its own crises and emergencies.

Considerable stress was therefore caused all round. US military personnel were required to stand by and watch people die or become seriously ill. Those involved in the crises and their relatives would have accepted help from anywhere. Senior Japanese political and public figures acknowledged the problems, but because of their own cultural pressures they were nevertheless required to tackle them in their own ways.

This is not a judgement on what was done, why or how. It does, however, illustrate the extensive potential for cultural differences and working relations, and the resulting clashes that can lead to stress. In particular, the criteria for performance were not fully understood by anyone except the Japanese government themselves; and the stress that was already present was compounded by their distinctive approaches to the groups that were otherwise capable and very willing to help.

each of these groups, so that this part of stress management is effectively undertaken (see Box 24.6).

Also, as stated in Chapter 14, creating an effective and positive culture, and one in which the presence and potential of stress can be acknowledged and managed, is dependent on:

- the extent to which dominant values, attitudes and beliefs advocated by the organization are capable of universal acceptance;
- the nature of the philosophy of the organization, especially whether this is precise, positive and stated, or allowed to emerge unstructured and undirected;
- the ways in which norms and patterns of behaviour are developed, and the reasons for these; and again, whether they are positive and engaging, or negative and coercive;
- the climate of the organization, which is conveyed by the environment, the physical layout, the ways in which participants interact and relationships between different levels in the hierarchy.

Stress in working relations is caused where there is a lack of fundamental identity or cohesion from any of these points of view. In these cases, staff groups retreat into themselves. Their loyalties become tainted and divided. Professional and expert groups with high influence and status identify with each other rather than their organization, and this leads to the formation of *canteen* cultures and *bunker* mentalities (see Box 24.7).

Working relations

Effective working relations are based on a fundamental openness and transparency of organizational and managerial approach and style. This is reinforced by a strong, positive, designed and cohesive organization culture capable of universal acceptance. The extent to which this openness and transparency can be delivered in practice, in the context of organization size, complexity and diversity, has a direct impact on the presence or otherwise of workplace and occupational stress. In particular, if there is no real openness or transparency, and there is also a confrontational or adversarial management and supervisory style, there is great potential for stress and conflict in all occupational areas.

Box 24.7: Canteen cultures

In practice, most work groups have their own 'canteen cultures' – patterns of behaviour, and attitudes towards each other, that both reinforce their collective identity, and provide comfort within the working situation. Canteen cultures can, and do, become a major cause of stress to particular individuals when, for whatever reason, they are not accepted. For example, Peter Harvey spent ten years at the SAS. He was very successful, an effective leader and battle tactician. He rose to the rank of colonel.

Subsequently, he left the service, and was quickly recruited to head up a specialist unit working for HM Customs and Excise, dealing with serious cross-border crimes. His military knowledge, plus his acute strategic and tactical awareness, would make him an ideal candidate. When he arrived to take up his position, he quickly found that the Customs and Excise staff had different ideas. In particular, they were resentful of the fact that it was an outsider rather than one of their own who was brought in to head them up.

More generally, Peter's appointment was felt to be a clear indication of the fact that the staff in the team were perceived to be useless, ineffective and unable to prevent serious crimes taking place.

Peter Harvey did his best. However, he was unable to break the very strong cohesion that the team now exhibited. The team built their canteen culture around 'the common enemy'; and 'the common enemy' was now seen as:

- HM Customs and Excise;
- Peter Harvey himself;
- the world at large that had imposed this person and these attitudes upon them.

Additionally, Peter was used to issuing orders and having them instantly obeyed; he had, after all, worked for many years in a military situation, under extreme operating conditions, and nothing else would do. He saw the problem of serious crime as being exactly the same and immediately failed to understand why the Customs and Excise staff did not take the same attitude.

In the end the appointment failed. The overall stress was too great for anyone involved to bear; and Peter, in particular, found it impossible to break into the canteen culture once it had been formed.

The relationship between specific occupations and stress

Some occupations are inherently more stressful than others; and some organizations are much more stressful places in which to work than others. It is useful to illustrate the kind of jobs that, all things being equal, are more and less stressful than others (see Table 24.1).

It is clear that many of these are generic job titles, rather than specific occupational descriptions. However, they do indicate the inherent extent and potential for stress when individuals and groups with different expertise are employed. The nature of work, and the context in which it is required to be carried out, can therefore be addressed from a much greater level of general understanding, and as a precursor to developing specific remedies.

The relationship between specific situations and stress

Individuals and groups who find themselves in specific situations experience varying degrees of stress. While acknowledging that people do respond differently to different events and situations, the following should be understood as giving rise to personal, professional and occupational stress where present (see Table 24.2).

Table 24.1 Occupational stress scale

Miner	8.3	Farmer	4.8
Police	7.7	Armed Forces	4.7
Construction worker	7.5	Vet	4.5
Journalist	7.5	Civil servant	4.4
Pilot (civil)	7.5	Accountant	4.3
Prison officer	7.5	Engineer	4.3
Advertising	7.3	Estate agent	4.3
Dentist	7.3	Hairdresser	4.3
Actor	7.2	Local government officer	4.3
Politician	7.0	Secretary	4.3
Doctor	6.8	Solicitor	4.3
Tax collector	6.8	Artist, designer	4.0
Film producer	6.5	Architect	4.0
Nurse, midwife	6.5	Chiropodist	4.0
Fireman	6.3	Optician	4.0
Musician	6.3	Planner	4.0
Teacher	6.2	Postman	4.0
Personnel	6.0	Statistician	4.0
Social worker	6.0	Lab technician	3.8
Manager (commercial)	5.8	Banker	3.7
Marketing (export)	5.8	Computing	3.7
Press officer	5.8	Occupational therapist	3.7
Professional footballer	5.8	Linguist	3.7
Salesperson, shop assistant	5.7	Beauty therapist	3.5
Stockbroker	5.5	Priest	3.5
Bus driver	5.4	Astronomer	3.4
Psychologist	5.2	Nursery nurse	3.3
Publishing	5.0	Museum worker	2.8
Diplomat	4.8	Librarian	2.0

Note: This list does not include any reference to building or fishing; collectively, the building and fishing industries have the highest per capita mortality rate of all.
Source: Statt (1994; 2006).

Table 24.2 Life events and stress scale

Life events and stress scale	
Events	*Stress rating*
Death of husband or wife Divorce or marital separation Jail term Death of close family member Personal injury or illness Marriage Loss of job Bankruptcy Moving house	**Very high**
Marital reconciliation Retirement Serious illness of family member Pregnancy Sex difficulties New child Change of job Money problems Death of close friend	**High**
Family arguments Big mortgage or loan Legal action over debt Change in responsibilities at work Son or daughter leaving home Trouble with in-laws Outstanding personal achievement Wife begins or stops work Start or finish of school Change in living conditions Revision of personal habits Trouble with boss	**Moderate**
Change in work hours or conditions Change in schools Change in recreation Change in church activities Change in social activities Small mortgage or loan Change in sleeping habits Change in contact with family Change in eating habits Holidays Christmas Minor violations of the law	**Low**

Note: Many of the above events are much more closely related to life than job, profession and occupation. However, there are some distinctive aspects directly related to work which have to be recognized. Most crucially of all, however, the life events referred to in the list almost universally impinge upon people's ability to carry out their job.

Source: Adapted from Holmes and Rahe (2006).

Understanding occupational stress

It is apparent from social history studies that a great deal of life and occupational stress existed for centuries before it became acknowledged as such. For example:

- under the feudal system, serfs lived or died at the whim of their landlords;
- the price of failure in military campaigns, for footsoldiers at least, was normally death;
- the first factories of the Industrial Revolution offered a form of Hobson's choice – to work and live in the dreadful urban conditions of the eighteenth and nineteenth centuries, or not to work (and therefore live) at all.

Shell shock

The first clear and more or less precise identification of stress as an occupational factor and hazard arose during the First World War (1914–18). A direct relationship was identified between prolonged exposure to military engagement and the resulting loss of sight, hearing, orientation and reason. This was defined as 'shell shock'. It was often accompanied by physical loss of strength and sickness, and compounded by revulsion at the conditions in the trenches (see Box 25.8).

Scientific management

Also at the beginning of the twentieth century, the first stress-related problems with production line factory work were identified. F.W. Taylor and the Scientific Management School designed factory work so that it consisted of a simple series of repetitive tasks in which individuals would soon become expert and proficient. They reasoned

---

Box 24.8: David Walker

David Walker died in a psychiatric institution at Nairn, Scotland, in June 2001 aged 103. He volunteered for service at the outbreak of World War I, and was assigned as a messenger and dispatch rider.

He saw active service in Flanders and on the Somme. He had his first attack of shell shock in 1916. He was placed in a rehabilitation hospital for four months, and then returned to active service at Vimy.

After the war, he found work as a labourer, and then as a clerk. In 1923, however, he suffered a complete physical and mental breakdown. He was committed to the psychiatric institution where he remained until his death. The stress and trauma that he had suffered made him unable to function in any other part of society, or indeed to support himself.

This is a very extreme example of what can happen as a response to stress; however, the fact that this form of extreme reaction can and does happen needs to be clearly understood.

that, so long as enduringly high levels of wages were paid, this form of work would be satisfactory and desirable. However, they failed to realize the levels of stress generated by the excessive noise and dust, extremes of heat and cold, and physical monotony of the work. Moreover, because there was no other challenge or content to the work, production line staff began to suffer psychological, as well as physical, health problems.

Affluent workers

Understanding and acknowledging the effects of stress was further developed by the 'Affluent Worker' studies of the 1950s. These studies were carried out in the UK at car engineering and chemical factories. They identified high collective stress levels in production staff. This was reinforced by a lack of identity between workers and the company, and any social interaction at the place of work. The concept of workplace and workforce alienation was born – a lack of any interest or commitment on the part of staff to company, or vice versa – except for the wage–work bargain. This level of stress was only sustainable so long as wages remained high, quality and volume of output remained low, and was not subject to managerial pressure. It was reinforced from time to time with 'safety-valving' – in which staff, trade unions and managers effectively conspired to engineer strikes of several days or even weeks' duration in order to reduce stress levels and give everyone a break from the situation (see also Chapter 18).

The other contribution of scientific management and 'Affluent Worker' studies was to make clear that stress was suffered by everyone placed in bad working conditions and required to work to patterns over which they had little or no control. This has become a substantial contribution to the understanding of stress in overtly high-value, professional and expert occupations also, and provides a key point for organizational and managerial intervention. It also makes clear that role under-load can be just as stressful as role overload.

Police studies

A further contribution to overall understanding was made by the United States Police Service studies of the 1970s. These addressed general levels of stress, as well as the specific issues of conformity, belonging and identity. They were carried out in New York City, Ohio and California. A key finding was the pressure to conform to, or at least connive at, criminal activities, and to take rewards from them.

Extreme stress was caused to many individuals. Almost everyone had originally come into the service to serve the community. Yet here they were, being pressured by their peers to become involved in exactly those activities that they were supposed to be stamping out. Many members of staff were driven out of the service altogether, while many others retired on health grounds (see Box 24.9).

Personality types

In the 1970s and 1980s, key medical research was linking behaviour (including organizational behaviour and the behaviour of individuals at work) with stress, and identified heart disease as a major output of extensive endurance of high levels of stress. These studies identified two personality types which they called Type A and Type B (see also Chapter 12).

Box 24.9: The London riots of 2009

In 2009, there was a weekend of demonstrations against the largest nations of the world. Representatives of these nations (the G20) had gathered in London to address the economic, political and financial crises that presently existed.

The Metropolitan Police gathered in force to ensure that the demonstrations were kept under control, and that violence was kept to a minimum. However, this was only partially successful; there were many arrests, and one person died – a person who was on his way home after work and who got caught in the trouble.

Attempting to explain what had happened, senior police figures pointed to:

- the heightened stress and tension of the situation;
- the consequent heightened stress levels of the police force members on duty;
- the collective uncertainty and anxiety of the crowds.

While this does not excuse any wrongful or extreme behaviour, the stress of a situation, and the collective pressures both on the police and from the crowds, does at least partially explain it. So a collective tension can, and does happen, even where people are going about legitimate and lawful business; and this is not confined to covert or criminal activities (see above).

Type As were identified as being action- and results-oriented, and in a hurry to complete work and move on to the next task. Type As tended to work faster and harder than Type Bs.

Type Bs were identified as being calm and unruffled. They rarely demonstrated high levels of emotion even in a crisis or emergency.

However, it is important to note that:

- Type As tended towards work and occupational overload. They were much more likely to take on too much work. They exhibited greater signs of stress. They were much more likely to experience conflict and to become side-tracked into non-essential tasks and activities. While they overtly worked harder than Type Bs, they were not necessarily as effective. Also, it became apparent that effort alone did not always bring additional rewards or promotions. Other opportunities for Type As were also limited, except in terms of expanding and extending their existing job or position.
- Type Bs tended to reach the most senior positions in organizations. This was because they were calmer, and more ordered and strategic in approach. They did not confuse action and energy expenditure with effectiveness. They were also to be found much less prone to loss of reputation through open engagement in conflict; or more seriously, occupational and other health problems such as coronary heart disease.

The studies also found that Type A managers were much more likely to smoke, and to have higher blood pressure and cholesterol levels, than Type Bs.

However, it is clear that both types have advantages and shortcomings. Type As tend to excel at tasks that have to be completed under time and resource pressures, and to become impatient with those who block them or hold them up. They exhibit ambition, drive, enthusiasm and commitment. They also clearly expect and anticipate promotions, advancements and rewards, whether or not these are forthcoming (see Figure 24.2).

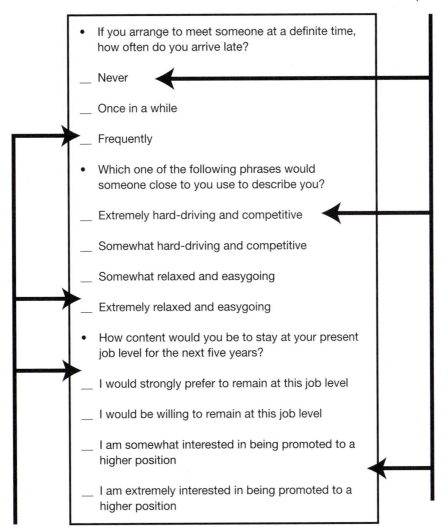

These responses typify the *Type A* behaviour pattern

- If you arrange to meet someone at a definite time, how often do you arrive late?

__ Never

__ Once in a while

__ Frequently

- Which one of the following phrases would someone close to you use to describe you?

__ Extremely hard-driving and competitive

__ Somewhat hard-driving and competitive

__ Somewhat relaxed and easygoing

__ Extremely relaxed and easygoing

- How content would you be to stay at your present job level for the next five years?

__ I would strongly prefer to remain at this job level

__ I would be willing to remain at this job level

__ I am somewhat interested in being promoted to a higher position

__ I am extremely interested in being promoted to a higher position

These responses typify the *Type B* behaviour pattern

Figure 24.2 Measuring the Type A and Type B behaviour patterns: an example

Type Bs tend to excel where a more considered approach is required. This especially means attention to the quality of results and output – the right answer at the deadline, not just any answer. Also in spite of the stated ambition drive, Type Bs tend to make it to the very top, even though Type As change their jobs much more frequently.

Personality type and conflict

As stated above Type As are much more likely to experience and become involved in conflict (see Figure 24.3).

Other research (Baron, 1987) conducted in the food industry again found that Type As were much more likely to engage in conflicts with subordinates and peers. There was, however, little difference when it came to engaging in open conflict with superiors.

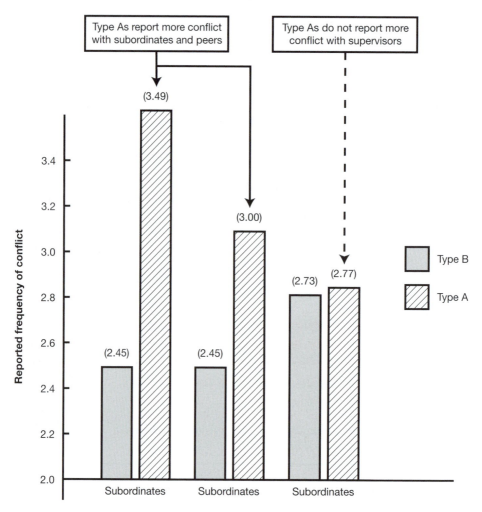

Figure 24.3 Conflict and the Type A behaviour pattern
Source: J. Greenberg and R.A. Baron (2007).

This indicates the following.

- The need for organizations, and their managers, to pay attention to personality, as well as profession and occupation, in the management of groups. Problems clearly arise when individuals are seen only as highly active, extremely busy or high achievers in terms of their output volume alone. It is necessary to attend to ways of working so that the high levels of commitment, energy and capability brought by Type As result in excellent performance output without the attendant conflict-induced stress (see Box 24.10).
- Organizations and their managers need to understand fully the costs and benefits of allowing these ways of working to continue. In terms of individual output, the contribution of Type As is very high. In terms of stress and conflict caused in dealings with others, much of the effectiveness of this contribution is likely to be dissipated in paying for organizational and managerial time, effort and resources

---

Box 24.10: Getting to the very top

Understanding personality types helps to explain why so many high-achieving and self-evidently excellent, professional and occupational performers do not make good directors, and where the organizational and managerial interventions required to get over this should actually be made.

This is a problem in public services, and in industry and commerce. It indicates that subject teaching and learning in the areas of personality, understanding, management and self-understanding are required for the effective transformation of excellent, professional and occupational achievers into top managers. The present finding is that, because these subjects are not addressed, such persons (especially Type As) tend therefore to rely on the qualities that have got them so far to get them on further still. It is also likely that Type Bs are much more receptive to the fact that the skills, qualities and expertise that have got them so far will no longer be adequate if there is to be further progress. This has direct implications for training and development for top jobs in:

- public professions such as nursing, teaching and social services work, where frontline work requires the energy, commitment, enthusiasm and dynamism of Type As; but managing, ordering and directing these professions requires the calm and considered strategy approach of Type Bs. Failure to recognize and understand this means that there are always going to be skills and experience gaps if Type As are promoted;
- industrial and commercial professions such as sales and marketing where again the frontline is highly results-oriented and driven; and again where the strategic approach is required, shortfalls become apparent.

In these cases, the problem is compounded because higher pay and reward levels are almost universally given to managers rather than those at the frontline. Therefore, anyone who needs, or wants, increased recognition and rewards is pressurized into applying for jobs that they are likely not to be able to do.

required for the resolution of disputes and grievances in the wake of the progress of the high achiever.

• It also implies an ethical responsibility to ensure that conditions are created so that Type As can work effectively at their profession, occupation or expertise by setting collective standards of attitude, behaviour and performance to which everyone can conform. These are then reinforced with effective performance appraisal which identifies organization and occupational development needs so that Type As are enhanced by directing their energies into productive and effective output only.

These studies are a major contribution to understanding stress at work in that they relate behaviour, drives, personality and occupation. Specific management interventions are also clearly indicated.

Other studies

Other studies have tended to concentrate on different aspects of stress management. At both macro and micro levels, they have looked at how to reduce stress levels in working environments and also at the human and economic costs incurred.

Goodness of fit

Furnham and Schaeffer (1984) proposed the concept of 'goodness of fit' between individuals, their organization and their occupation. This reinforced the subjectivity of stress – the fact that one person's stress is another's interest, stimulus or indifference. The key is to ensure that individual professions and occupations provide the 'right amount' of stimulation, creativity, drive, reward, challenge and progress. Where these are out of harmony with each other, symptoms of stress such as frustration, conflict, dispute and other behavioural and attitudinal problems are likely to occur. This again reinforces the need for the understanding of stress as a key aspect of management knowledge and expertise.

Karoushi

Tubbs (1993) identified Karoushi or 'stress death' during studies of patterns of work in large corporations in Japan. The original hypothesis was that the sheer physical and psychological demands of working long hours every day meant that people were dying of exhaustion.

Tubbs found, however, that the killer – the last straw – was stress. People who worked these hours felt that they had to. They had no control over their working lives or the demands placed on them by their employers. Many depended on the overtime to make ends meet, to provide for wives and children, and to ensure social standing. It was these pressures that caused death, not the long hours themselves.

Costs

The costs of stress to employers, as well as employees, have never been fully or completely calculated. However, many estimates have been made. UK government statistics show a variety of stress-related illnesses, and the estimates of the costs incurred vary between £1.7 billion and £15 billion per annum. Japanese government and research departments have identified the cultural pressures, as above, that lead to many thousands in professional occupations quite literally working themselves to death.

Both the UK and Japan also recognize the relationship between work-related stress and other social issues, especially alcoholism and family breakdown, and the health and social care costs accrued as the result. Elsewhere, a survey by Canada Health Monitor (2000) found that 25 per cent of workers reported stress, psychological or emotional problems arising from work (as opposed to 9 per cent who said that they suffered from workplace injury, and 9 per cent also who said they suffered from illness brought on by bad working conditions, noise, dust, heat and cold). It is estimated that the cost of stress to Canadian industry, commerce and public services was in the order of $300 million per annum.

Conclusions

It is clear that key contributions to understanding what stress is, and its effects on people at work, have been made from many different sources. The body of knowledge and experience on which effective stress management is based addresses the outputs, costs and consequences, as well as understanding the physical, behavioural and psychological aspects. It is essential that managers take time to understand and become aware of the subject from the broadest possible point of view. Then, whether or not the problem is institutionally recognized, at least individual managers (and also those who work for them) have a much greater understanding of what is likely to occur in their own domain, and can begin to take effective steps to address the issues (see Box 24.11).

Box 24.11: The UK Health and Safety Executive

The UK Health and Safety Executive makes the following statement on organizational and occupational stress:

> By the term work-related stress, we mean the process that arises where work demands of various types and combinations exceed the person's capacity and capability to cope. It is a significant cause of illness and disease and is known to be linked with high levels of sickness absence, staff turnover and other indicators of organizational under-performance – including human error.
>
> For some, the way to deal with work-related stress is to diagnose, treat and rehabilitate people who experience it. For others, it is economically and morally preferable to assess and repair the failed work system or organization. This action reduces the risk of future failure, and the likelihood of future work-related ill health. This approach focuses attention on the antecedents of work-related stress in the design and management of work – but recognizes that interventions at the individual level have a part to play.
>
> Recent statistics confirm that work-related stress is widespread in the UK working population and is not confined to particular sectors or high-risk jobs or industries. That is why a universal and managerial approach is necessary to tackle it.

25 Managing for the future

Introduction

The primary concerns of management have always been as follows:

- making the best use of scarce resources;
- coping with change and uncertainty, and responding to change in the environment;
- establishing and delivering performance targets;
- achieving things through people;
- attending to the needs of all stakeholders.

On the one hand, therefore, nothing much changes. On the other hand, however, effective and expert managers are going to need a much greater understanding of what is actually constituted and included in the above. Effective managers are going to be required to lead and direct change; and cope with the demands and pressures of the operating and wider environment. Effective managers are going to have to create the conditions in which effective staff performance is both possible and also achievable. Effective managers are going to have to develop a body of professional expertise, especially in the field of human behaviour, that enables them to understand why particular pressures are being applied, and how best to respond to them.

This is certain to apply to all managers, whatever their level of responsibility, seniority or occupational position. Organizations can no longer afford the expense of large and sophisticated bureaucratic and administrative structures; and the consequence is that long-term effectiveness, profitability and viability are only possible if a fully professional and expert approach is adopted universally (see Box 25.1).

Clarity of purpose and direction

The aim of all organizations is a required long-term effectiveness and profitable existence in a turbulent and competitive world. Lack of expertise in strategic management and organizational behaviour has meant that this has all too often become lost in the pursuit of short-term gain, or satisfaction of the financial interest alone. In these cases, this clarity has been replaced with:

- The hiring of high-branded consultancies, leading in many cases to a hype in the share price in the short-term in spite of the fact that the consultant's remit and prescription had not yet been agreed.
- The use of parallel communications, using management speak and professional babble to give an impression of direction and clarity (see Box 25.2).

Box 25.1: General Motors

When General Motors went bankrupt in 2009, it quickly became clear that, on an individual basis, everyone involved in the company (including top and senior management) fully understood the basic problems. These were:

- declining sales;
- a strong range of middle market products;
- an ageing range of small cars which had not been replaced or updated;
- maintenance of brands such as Chevrolet as icons rather than profitable business propositions.

It had also been clear for many years that the nature of mass car production would have to change in order to accommodate specific environmental pressures, especially pollution and the need to make fuel-efficient engines capable of travelling long distances on limited volumes of petrol.

However, the organizational bureaucracy, and the dissipation of responsibility and authority that went with this, meant that none of these issues had been addressed at the time of the bankruptcy.

The company asked for, and received, a bale-out from the US government. Speaking at the time, President Obama stated: 'General Motors is a national icon, a national treasure. It will not be allowed to fail.'

From one point of view, therefore, the company had nothing to worry about. However, a collective management expertise, combined with organizational capability to respond, would have prevented the problem from arising in the first place.

Box 25.2: Language incompetency

Speaking in 2006, Tessa Jowell, the UK Cabinet minister responsible for the delivery of the 2012 Olympic project, stated:

When New Labour first came to power in 1997, we had very little collective experience between us. So, we took advice. We were told to use words like 'stakeholder', 'sea change', and 'step change', so that we would appear competent. We had to convince the public very quickly that their faith in us was not misplaced. We were trying to make sure that this confidence would be maintained and developed so that we would have time to get to grips with what really needed doing.

This problem is not confined to the political arena. Managers, including top and senior executives, find a language all of their own to get over the perceived short-comings in substance that would otherwise be associated with them. For example:

continued . . .

> **Box 25.2: Language incompetency ... *continued***
>
> - 'The wholesale capital markets' was a phrase used at the time of the UK banking crisis to describe the fact that capital values were uncertain. The reason why they were uncertain was because nobody had taken the trouble to find out their true value.
> - 'We are well placed to seek opportunities wherever they arise' is used to explain the fact that organizations have spare capacity. However, at second reading, the phrase can easily be translated as: 'We have not got a clue what to do.'
>
> The use of parallel communications such as these is only acceptable if managers understand that now they must be translated into clear, direct and transparent phrases and followed up with action. In each of the cases quoted, none of this was apparent; each of the cases quoted turned out to be a symptom of a longer-term malaise and decline rather than a prompt for action.

Dominant stakeholder drives

In industry and commerce, this refers to the desired priorities of shareholders' representatives, other financial interests, backers and powerful and influential figures who drive their organizations into their own preferred core business. In public services the dominant stakeholder is government, which sets performance priorities and targets according to political need; there is a divergence here from the majority stakeholder – the public – the one high quality enduring good value public services. In the not-for-profit sector, many large charities now take the view that in order to provide the best possible service for their client groups, it is necessary to engage in fully commercialized fundraising activities; in these cases the core business becomes the conducting of marketing campaigns.

Balance of primary and support functions in terms of resources consumption; what the organization values and rewards in terms of output and what it does not; the effectiveness of administration bureaucracy; and in many cases the domination of administration and bureaucracy. In extreme cases the 'core business' of organizations dominated by their support functions is effectively to provide career patterns for individuals within them (see Box 25.3).

Clearly, the dominant stakeholder group varies between, and within, organizations. The ability of particular stakeholder groups to dominate any situation is dependent upon:

- the nature of the resources that they command;
- the nature of any expertise that they have;
- their physical size.

It is then incumbent upon managers to recognize the extent and prevalence of this domination, and to work out:

Box 25.3: Lehman Brothers head took home $300 million!

Arriving at the US Congressional inquiry into the collapse of Lehman Brothers in particular, and the banking crisis in general, Richard Fuld, the senior partner, confirmed that he had received $300 million in salary and bonuses over the eight years prior to the bank's collapse. Richard Fuld's defence was as follows: 'We had a pay reward and compensation committee at the bank that spent a tremendous amount of time making sure that the interests of the executives and the employees were aligned with those of the shareholders.'

Richard Fuld went on to say that he took full responsibility for the decisions taken and for the actions that were implemented. These he defended as 'prudent and appropriate' based on information available at the time.

Responding to Mr Fuld, the inquiry chairman, Henry Waxman, stated that the credit crisis threatened the entire US economy and would have serious implications for global trading. It would be essential, stated Mr Waxman, to identify what went wrong so that it could be put right for the future.

The lesson is clear: neither the interests of shareholders, nor those of the staff and executives, were served by the Lehman Brothers bankruptcy. And at no point is the word 'customer' even mentioned!

- whether to accept the domination;
- whether to try to stand up to the domination in the wider interests of the organization;
- whether to walk away from the situation.

In many cases, the dominant stakeholder interest is of paramount importance to the organization. A large and committed backer, or a large and expert group of staff, is a great and enduring asset when their interests are aligned. Managers have therefore to be able to understand the nature of those interests, and then to ensure that they do indeed remain aligned (see Box 25.4).

Economic and social demands and pressures

It is essential that the macro environment is continuously analysed and evaluated. This is so that as broad a view as possible of likely and potential, and unlikely, change is always kept fully in mind. Organizations and managers that do this are much less likely to suffer from foreseeable if unlikely events such as:

- The energy crash in California 2000–1.
- The stock market crash of 2008, and the uncertainties that followed.
- The possibility of a 'swine flu' epidemic from 2009 onwards.
- The financial crisis that threatens parts of the UK and much of Western Europe and North America.
- The funding crisis facing the UK NHS and healthcare and public services elsewhere in the western world.

> **Box 25.4: 'The grinning schoolgirl'**
>
> Some years ago, LastMinute.com merged with Thomas Cook. LastMinute.com had been founded as an internet-based travel agency and gift company. Both LastMinute.com and its founders, Brent Hoberman and Martha Lane Fox, had gained a high and enduring profile.
>
> LastMinute.com's business premise was to serve those who suddenly found themselves wanting to get away somewhere at short notice, or to make gift purchases at a late stage.
>
> LastMinute.com quickly built up a small volume of business. However, the sheer business volumes were not enough to sustain the capital base of the company; and it was subsequently bought out by Thomas Cook, the travel agency firm. The combination of Thomas Cook's physical presence in shopping centres, together with LastMinute.com's internet presence, would ensure that all angles in the travel industry, as it was developing, were now covered.
>
> One of the conditions placed on the merger was the removal of Brent Hoberman and Martha Lane Fox from executive positions. Especially in the case of Martha Lane Fox, city analysts were unsure of her business pedigree, and one stated: 'In the new organization, we need people of gravitas. We do not need a grinning schoolgirl; she brings no credibility to the City and its institutions.'
>
> Martha Lane Fox was forced to step down. The sheer lack of morality of the position adopted in the City, as quoted above, and the fact that, on an individual basis, nobody could be found to agree with it, did not prevent it from holding collective sway. Additionally, the Board of the newly merged organization found itself unable to stand up to this attitude and so Martha Lane Fox duly left.

Organizations and industries worst affected by those events are those that become so used to their environmental conditions that they come to regard these as certainties; and these organizations and industries consequently have no response when things do change. The consequence in turn is that assumptions, forecasts and projections then take on a life of their own, based on historic stability, and the perceived 'certainty' of the sector's durability (see Box 25.5).

Investment

As stated above (see Chapter 21), investment is supposed to be one of those aspects of organizational management practice which is more or less both rational and also assured.

It is essential not to hold this view! This is because, while calculations do indeed demonstrate where particular financial pressures come from and how they arise, they do not themselves make the decisions.

Managers make decisions! Managers take all of the data that is available to them, assess and evaluate it, and then pursue one or more of the following courses of action:

- take the decision based purely on the financial figures and projections available;
- assess and evaluate the context in which the figures and projections were produced before taking the decision;

Box 25.5: Setanta Sports

Setanta Sports was an Irish broadcasting company, serving the 'pay-per-view' and other specialized niches in the sports broadcasting sector. In early 2009, it became clear that the company was facing a financial crisis. This crisis was based on declining numbers of viewers, especially in the 'pay-per-view' sector. Founded in 2002, the company had quickly established itself as a niche provider, covering:

- boxing promotions;
- football matches in the UK, Scotland, Holland, Belgium, Germany, Italy and Spain;
- cricket, especially the Indian Premier League (IPL);
- one-off events, especially specific cycling, motorcar and wrestling promotions.

In establishing itself, Setanta targeted the 'quasi-public' markets, especially public house and bar broadcasting. It also considered itself to be serving mass, or near mass, markets with UK Premier League football and the Indian IPL cricket.

However, it found itself unable to respond to either competition or events. Sky, the major commercial broadcaster in the UK, took whatever steps were necessary to ensure that it continued to cover all of the top football matches. Setanta was left therefore with lesser games of limited interest; and the revenues from the continental market were also insufficient to maintain this as a viable commercial operation.

Because of security concerns, amid political volatility in the region, the IPL had to be relocated from India to South Africa for the 2009 series. This again led to declining revenues; while the games were very well attended, the pay-per-view fees were considered by many to be too high. Additionally, the South African broadcasting networks managed to gain live coverage rights within the country.

This led, in turn, to Setanta defaulting on a payment to the UK Football Association. Efforts to restructure the company, and to meet its obligations, ran into difficulties; and the company was forced to restructure extensively as a niche provider. Finally, the company ceased trading in June 2009.

On the one hand, Setanta had clearly evaluated its markets, arriving at an accurate conclusion of the charges that could be raised. On the other hand, insufficient attention was paid to market development; there was rather an assumption that the market would remain stable for the long-term future. Consequently, the company found itself unable to respond to events, while maintaining its revenues.

Additionally, at the time of any financial difficulty, peripheral products and non-essential services such as those provided by Setanta are the first to be cut or cancelled by customers and clients. The wider lesson is that it is essential for all organizations and their managers to know and understand how people think, behave and react when circumstances change.

- reduce or modify what is proposed or intended;
- expand and enlarge what is proposed or intended.

At the point of decision (see Chapter 22) managers have to be able to state clearly what they have done, why they have done it and how it is to be implemented. This additionally gives licence to managers to do any, or all, of the following:

- decide to do something because they want to;
- decide to do something for reasons of prestige or vanity;
- decide to do something in the interests of one group of stakeholders at the expense of others;
- decide to do something because they are powerful or senior enough to be able to impose their will.

For the future, decision-making processes have to be improved. If organizational resources are going to be placed in particular ventures, initiatives and developments, there has to be a much greater transparency of justification in terms of how the organization's best interests are being served. A much more active, responsible and accountable managerial expertise in this area is essential for effective investment management.

Investment in production, service and information technology must be undertaken on the basis that it may be necessary to discard it overnight in order to remain competitive and effective, because new equipment is now available to competitors. Appraising potential investment in technology therefore requires that as full a projection as possible is available, as to whether competitive activities around price, quality, output and retention of market share would be sustainable should alternative technology suddenly become available. A key part of the management of investment in industrial, commercial and public service situations is therefore certain to require a continuous and active 'what if . . .' approach – so that answers to questions such as:

- What if this technology becomes obsolete overnight?
- What if we have to replace a particular system at short notice?
- What if a competitor gains access to technology that can produce the particular product or service in a quarter of the time?

are always kept at the forefront.

Greater expertise in forecasting a projection is required overall. This applies especially in those sectors that operate under mega-project conditions, where the true costs and returns on activities may not be realized for many years. Several current and recent high-profile examples of this in the UK must cause a radical re-think of how projections and forecasts are carried out.

This also applies to investment in production, service and public sector technology by individual organizations and departments. This requires a much greater projected understanding of density and frequency of usage, speed and convenience of product and service, and quality enhancement and insurance, as key elements of assessing returns on investment.

Mutuality of interest and confidence between the core stakeholders – financiers, backers, venturers, contractors, political interests, suppliers, subcontractors, clients and end-users must be ensured as far as possible. Ideally, this should also extend to peripheral stakeholders – lobbies, vested interests, social and pressure groups, and the media. If this is not possible among the core group, serious consideration ought to be given to the enduring viability of what is proposed, because it is unlikely that results can be achieved where there is not full confidence or mutuality of interest; and this becomes all the more certain where there is a known, believed or perceived conflict of interest.

Investment in technology projects and expertise has therefore to be viewed as a sunk cost from a managerial point of view – one on which there may not be any direct or apparent returns. This flies in the face of the widespread current behavioural need to make simple the calculation of return on investment. It should be apparent that, despite preaching perfection, this is not possible in absolute managerial terms. Moreover, the return on investment is in every case the subject of personal and professional evaluation and these judgements may quite legitimately vary.

Investment in expertise is dependent at the outset on whether staff are valued as assets or liabilities, and the basis on which this is calculated. This also varies in each case; and is likely to vary within organizations according to:

- The nature of relative and absolute expertise of particular staff in different functions.
- The ease, or otherwise, with which they can be replaced or transformed through retraining and redeployment.
- Specific industrial, commercial and public service advantages (and liabilities) that they bring. This is particularly true of highly capable and well-known key figures in industry and commerce (e.g. Michael O'Leary at Ryanair; Alex Ferguson at Manchester United). It also applies to public services (e.g. Magdi Yacoub, Robert Winston, in health services; Peter Hall in town planning).

This is clearly a double-edged sword; individuals remain assets as long as they deliver their expertise in ways compatible with the priorities of their organization, and there may be a loss of confidence on the part of key backers and stock markets should such a figure suddenly move on.

On the other hand, no organization should be dependent upon an individual, however great their expertise, for their future survival (see Box 25.6).

Mergers and takeovers

All this is reinforced when considering the enduring managerial responsibilities to mergers and takeovers. Investment in mergers and takeovers requires managerial attention to the reasons behind the findings of two surveys carried out in 1996 and 1998 by the Institute of Management and Industrial Society; and these findings were reinforced by subsequent studies in 2004 and 2008 by the American Management Association. The findings were consistent in all the studies: they found that 87 per cent of such ventures do not work at all or fully in the long-term. The reasons for this were found to be exactly those considered elsewhere:

- lack of attention to behavioural and cultural aspects;
- an assumption that these would simply fall into place once the financial deal was completed;

> ## Box 25.6: The replacement of critical figures
>
> EasyJet was founded by Stelios Haji-ioannou. EasyJet was one of the early entrants into the low-cost/good value short-haul air travel industry. Together with Ryanair, the fares charged radically transformed this sector.
>
> Having established the airline, Stelios now turned to other ventures to see if the low-cost/good value approach could be applied elsewhere. As the result, easyJet quickly became 'the Easy group of companies'. With varying degrees of success, Stelios opened:
>
> - Easy cinemas;
> - Easy car hire;
> - Easy internet cafes;
> - Easy bus transport;
> - Easy cruise.
>
> It then became apparent to Stelios himself that his interest lay in pioneering, creating and developing new business ventures, and not in the day-to-day strategic and operational management of them. Accordingly, he went to his backers and proposed that his role be changed.
>
> He would remain as non-executive chairman, taking an active part in business evaluation, but otherwise leaving the executive demands to professional top and senior managers. These top and senior managers would be brought in, and given executive authority to conduct the day-to-day business, and to develop a strategy for the future.
>
> Blessed is the person who knows their own limitations! However, this approach has also brought one major benefit: it will be much easier to replace Stelios when he finally leaves the organization altogether, than if he had retained executive authority and active business involvement. Those organizations where key and dominant figures retain active involvement find it much harder to replace the key figure when they finally leave; for example, it is going to be very much harder to replace Michael O'Leary at Ryanair or Alex Ferguson at Manchester United when the time does finally come for them to go.

- an unwillingness to consider staffing, departmental, divisional and functional structures in the new organization post-merger;
- a willingness to blame staff and trade union intransigence for unwillingness to cooperate;
- a lack of commitment even to address such fundamental issues as different job titles, use of technology, reporting relationship structures;
- an unwillingness to decide on the management style, the nature of supervision and overall organization culture, once the merger had been completed.

Each of the above aspects is more or less unnoticeable when they are in place and working well. However, it is apparent to anyone that the source of all staff dissatisfaction and demotivation in collective morale, arises when any, or all, of the above are either not in place, or else not effective. Additionally, the lack of cultural fit, uncertainties in job roles and accountability, and lack of certainty in managerial and supervisory styles and relationships, regularly give rise to collective and individual disputes and grievances (see Box 25.7).

Box 25.7: Mega universities

A merger was proposed between University College London and Imperial College London. At the time, the two institutions enjoyed very high global, as well as national, reputation. The teaching, academic and research performances of each of the institutions was excellent and internationally renowned. To put the two institutions together would therefore create a mega university with extensive global influence. It would become a world leader in teaching, learning and research.

The merger was to be paid for by (using the precise term) 'flogging off' large swathes of property. In particular, both the institutions were located in central London, where property prices were always high; and Imperial had premises in the Kent countryside which would be ripe for selling off for development. So nothing could possibly go wrong; everyone would benefit and success was assured.

It quickly became clear that this was not quite the case. Staff at both institutions began to raise questions about such diverse issues as:

- funding regimes for particular teaching and research programmes;
- staffing authority;
- different research priorities and targets;
- management and administrative structures;
- academic, teaching and research structures.

It quickly became clear that none of these matters had been thought through. There was also the matter of the constitution of the two institutions; UCL was (and remains) a humanist foundation, while Imperial was (and remains) a Christian foundation.

The final nail in the coffin of the idea came when substantial and comprehensive data were produced to demonstrate that those organizations in the university sector that carried the greatest global weight were small, specialized and focused, and not large, multi-functional agglomerates. Particular emphasis was given to the position of Harvard, the Massachusetts Institute of Technology, Stanford and Yale universities in the US, all of which were (and remain) much smaller than either UCL or Imperial, let alone a merged organization.

The main lessons arise from the fact that nobody involved in proposing and developing the merger idea had thought seriously of any of the above. They had simply seen the blueprint for a merged organization. The fact was that there would be a windfall from property sales, and from this it had been assumed that everything else would work out. The barriers in this case were entirely behavioural, arising from the fact that, apart from both being London universities, there was no structural, cultural or operational fit whatsoever.

Staff management

Effective staff management in the future is certain to be based on the development of management styles based on openness and access to information, and basic honesty and integrity. This is to apply whatever the leadership and management style chosen – autocratic, participative, democratic, hands-on, hands-off or consultative. For there is no reason why any organization should have an emergent rather than a designed management style, whatever the sector or nature of activity. There is quite sufficient management literature, training, expertise (together with examples of good and bad practice) around, to ensure that all those responsible for the design and direction of an organization establish this from their own particular point of view.

Once this is established, then it is possible to address the key elements of the working relationship, wage–work bargain and quality of working life and environment to establish:

- what organizations and their managers require of their staff, why, when, where and how often;
- what staff require of their managers and organizations, why, when, where and how often;
- whether this is practicable, feasible or possible in the particular sets of circumstances.

Whether managers continue to organize staff and workforce structures on traditional or current lines, or whether they adopt more flexible patterns of approach, effective operations are dependent upon the following.

- Integrity of working relations including management and staff hierarchies and, above all, paying attention to the human as well as operational problems brought about through working flexible hours away from the organization location for extended periods, working from home or being on call. This applies as equally to those following regular patterns of attendance.
- Physical means of supervision, e.g. clocking in or logging on, should be universally applied or else not used at all. This applies to factory and production staff as well as those in administrative and support functions. Those who work from home or in the field should never be made to log on or ring in if this does not also apply to their office or location-based colleagues.
- Drawing as closely as possible the relationship between output and rewards; and this applies to all levels of staff. In particular, it requires a detailed assessment of the relationship between the rewards on offer for top and senior executives, and the ways in which their performance is to be assessed. More generally, this applies to all professions, occupations and job categories; and it ought to be targeted towards a much greater understanding of what constitutes profitable and effective activity.
- Paying people for their flexibility and willingness, as well as their expertise. Where it is necessary for staff to work unsocial hours (e.g. financial services and other direct personal sales), or where they are expected to be fully responsive at short notice (e.g. supply teaching, agency nursing, social care, ferry and airline crew replacements), this must be recognized and premium rates paid; many organizations also pay retainers for this.

- Managing by walking around, managing by ringing around and any other means available for ensuring that continuity and visibility of relationship are maintained. Those who work in the field should be called into the office upon a regular basis; and part of the time spent on these occasions must include the opportunity for social interaction. This is both a consequence and responsibility of organizing activities along these lines.
- Balance of primary and support activities: there is an ever-increasing managerial need to look very hard at support functions in terms of overall cost, resource utilization and consumption, contribution to operational effectiveness. This does not mean that administration and support are no longer necessary. It does mean that organization systems and bureaucratic operations must be as simple, flexible and responsive as possible, and designed in direct support of the primary activities. This, in turn, means attention to the effectiveness of overall organization culture, and individual, professional and occupational career paths, especially those provided by head and regional offices (see Box 25.8).

Box 25.8: Middle managers

At present, many staff shakeouts and redundancy programmes concentrate on middle managers. In general and in personal terms, middle managers are seen as an expense (both necessary and also unnecessary) which organizations have to carry. They therefore become an easy target when, in general, redundancy and lay-off programmes are being considered.

In some cases, this is clearly a fair approach. As long ago as 1986, Tom Peters stated:

> One of the problems that I have always found as I go around companies and organizations is that large corporations are over-staffed in their managerial ranks between 400–800 per cent. On the rare occasions when somebody challenges this, they always state that I am under-estimating and not over-estimating.

So, again in general terms, the problem has long since been recognized. However, it is important to address the following:

- middle managers have extensive and substantive roles to perform in the context in which they are operating;
- organizations must have originally decided that these managerial positions were indeed required. There is therefore a body of work that has to be carried out even after lay-offs have been effected.

Additionally, with all lay-off and redundancy programmes, it is essential to address the presumption and assumption that the work will nevertheless continue to be done. This is invariably not the case; work has to be reorganized and re-prioritized alongside any programme of lay-offs in middle management ranks (or indeed in any other ranks).

continued . . .

> **Box 25.8: Middle managers ... *continued***
>
> It is also the case that redundancy programmes look neat and tidy on corporate balance sheets, and in top management and boardroom meetings. Particular activities and functions are removed; the organization looks leaner, fitter and more stream-lined. However, as well as being damaging to morale if not conducted properly, such programmes remove the perceived and understood career paths that people who joined the organizations expected to be able to follow. There is therefore the potential for a longer-term malaise, decline in morale and therefore performance to follow if such programmes aimed at middle managers are undertaken without the full under-standing of the context.

Structures and cultures

The demand here is that top managers take a continuous, positive interest in the ways in which activities are carried out, in order to ensure that the organization of staff continues to fit operational demands. Problems are caused when ranks and hierarchies work in favour of individuals and groups, but cause blockages in operations and activities. It is therefore essential that questions of culture and structure change are addressed as part of any wider staff management strategy, and that these elements are related directly to organizational policy, priority, direction and performance.

A starting point for this is to look at structures and cultures from the point of view of the extent of fit. The initial enquiry is to establish whether:

- structure, culture, strategy and staff management style clearly fit and match;
- structure, culture, strategy and staff management style fit in some parts but not others;
- structure, culture and staff management style do not match and fit with strategy direction at all.

One clear indicator of this is to assess what is rewarded and punished, and what is not. This enquiry causes attention to be drawn to the whole relationship between behaviour, operations, activities and direction. It is often not considered or not addressed fully because:

- its importance is not fully understood by directors and shareholders' representatives;
- there is a history of paying attention to 'the bottom line' rather than how the bottom line is achieved;
- it is not fully understood conceptually by top managers; or it is assumed that once direction is established, everything else will automatically fall into place;
- top managers take the easy way out, preferring to rely on consultants' prescriptions, rather than tackling critical issues for themselves (see Box 25.9).

Management and organization development

The present view of management and organization development is that in order to professionalize and make expert practice of management, and develop the expertise of

Box 25.9: Consultants

There still exists a large propensity for organizations to call in external consultants when faced with any difficulty whatsoever.

Specialist and expert consultancies quite legitimately exist in order to provide specific services when organizations are faced with particular issues.

However, in many cases, consultancies have come to exist as a kind of corporate crutch on which top and senior managers can, and do, lean whenever they are faced with something that is a little bit difficult or uncomfortable.

This has led to consultancies in turn prescribing overtly comfortable, neat and tidy, and off-the-shelf (rather than targeted) solutions to problems. Some of these solutions have been branded as follows.

- Business process re-engineering, which is overwhelmingly taken to mean reductions in head count, delayering and increases in workload for the front line.
- Downsizing, right-sizing, re-sizing, the outcome of which is normally a structured design suitable for the present rather than the future.
- Empowerment, normally resulting in pushing further responsibilities onto often overstretched frontline staff.
- Synergies and economies of scale – concentrating again on a narrow economic rather than broader context of behavioural aspects.
- Facilitation – guiding companies through extended programmes of change.

In many cases, this leads to a long-term relationship between consultants and client organizations. One way of looking at this is to consider 'the circular flow of consultancy'. This works as follows (Figure 25.1):

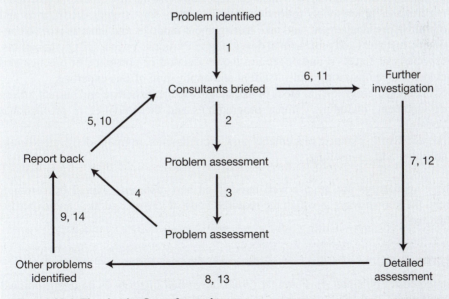

Figure 25.1 The circular flow of consultancy

continued . . .

Box 25.9: Consultants . . . *continued*

Fee levels charged by top-brand consultancies make it behaviourally very difficult to turn down their recommendations. There is also a collective perception that if fee levels are very high, then the consultants must necessarily know what is best for the organization. Many organizations and their top managers come, therefore, to depend on the consultants that they have hired.

Effectively, consultants are asked to come in. They provide an initial organizational assessment leading to the conclusion that 'the organization needs some work doing'. Consultants then produce further investigations and a report to the effect that 'you need some more work doing'.

---

individual managers, there is a body of skills, knowledge, attributes and qualities that must be learned about and put into action.

In essence this consists of each of the areas covered in this book, together with a commitment to take an active interest in keeping abreast of future developments. Beyond this, management training and development is addressed from the point of view of:

- Further and higher education: syllabus-based management teaching and learning programmes, ranging from Higher National Diploma certificates through to undergraduate programmes; the main standard management education remains the MBA;
- On and off the job balance: in which those in supervisory and junior managerial positions, or those coming into managerial positions for the first time from functional expertise or practitioner, follow courses in supervisory studies, certificates and diplomas in management, and take management modules and units as part of con-tinuing technical and professional development. National Vocational Qualifications, especially at Levels 4 and 5, require the production of portfolios of practice and evidence demonstrating understanding and application of this expertise.
- Short-course provisions in areas of skills, knowledge, expertise and current affairs development, including seminar programmes and the activities of professional bodies.
- Project work, planned placements and secondments, supported by mentoring, coaching and counselling.

These approaches are largely well understood and represent, almost by common consent, the known ways in which the required body of knowledge, skill and expertise is imparted.

Integrity

As stated above (Chapter 4), Pettinger (2000) identified integrity as an organizational and managerial skill. The great pressures on organizations to prevaricate, to tell a part of the truth only and in some cases to lie has led to a wider general consensus that the truth does not matter.

To get over this problem, the following is required for the effective future of management and organizational practice.

- Common standards of integrity in all dealings. This is an active, collective responsibility as well as one placed on individual managers and supervisors. Moreover, while this may stand to reason in theory, in practice, many managers do not approach all their dealings from the point of view of this absolute standard. It needs to be clearly understood that customers, clients, suppliers and staff all come to know very quickly when the person or organization with whom they are dealing is trustworthy, and when they are not. When the person or organization is proved to be untrustworthy, given any choice in the matter, they will move elsewhere if they possibly can.
- The need to develop a distinctive, positive and collective management style. This reinforces culture, values, attitudes and behaviour, and is reinforced by the approaches and activities of individual managers. It matters much less whether this is autocratic, participative or anything in between, than that it is common, open, honest and universally delivered.

The need to develop the style, attitudes and behaviour of individual managers along the above lines is vital. Key priorities have to be:

- visibility;
- openness of communications;
- the building of the personal, as well as occupational and professional, aspects of relationships;
- and the ability to develop suitable long-term work group cohesion, expertise and performance.

There is a critical need for continuous professional development. Many professional and occupational bodies now demand this as a condition of continued membership. In any case, part of the professional and personal responsibility of all managers is to keep abreast of developments in the whole field, to learn lessons as they become available and to study and evaluate practice in other organization sectors and locations. For example:

- one supermarket chain requires all its staff to go into competitors on a regular basis and to return with at least one example of what the competitor does better than them; to return and say 'there is nothing we can learn from them' is not acceptable;
- a dot.com travel agent, despairing at the lack of real customers, at last sent its staff into its high street competitors to study the real demands of customers; it consequently redesigned its approach and website to take account of these factors;
- a hospital reduced attacks on, and abuse of, its staff in its accident and emergency department by studying the management of long-stay customers and clients in airport lounges;
- a single-location grocery store quadrupled its turnover in six months as the result of studying the range available at Tesco and Asda and increasing the perceived choice available to customers as well as convenience.

Each of the actions indicated above represents a particular way in which the organizations concerned opened themselves up to their staff, and created the foundations for a greater mutuality of interest founded on a fundamental integrity of relationships (see Box 25.10).

Conclusions

As stated above, the key drive is towards managerial expertise in delivering performance and coping with whatever change and uncertainty the context presents. Organizations and their managers that blame environmental conditions for failings and shortcomings in their own expertise are therefore increasingly certain to get left behind by those that do not. All managers need to know and understand the effects of the following conditions, and be able to operate effectively when they change.

* Fluctuations in interest rates, inflation, retail prices indexes, currency values and other economic factors that 'simply could not be predicted or foreseen'.

Box 25.10: The future at Cadbury

In February 2010, Cadbury, the English chocolate company, was taken over by Kraft, the US food manufacturer and retailer. The takeover attracted a great deal of controversy.

When Kraft made its initial approach, it valued Cadbury at £6 billion. The response of Cadbury was instant – the company was worth at least £25 billion, and in any case it was not for sale at any price.

Kraft came back with a further offer of £7 billion, and this again was turned down. At this point Kraft issued further guarantees related especially to the enduring quality of the products, the independence that Cadbury would continue to enjoy and, above all, the working culture. This last was especially important, for Cadbury had been a beacon of employment excellence as well as a producer of good quality chocolate for over 150 years.

Kraft now came back with an offer of £8.5 billion, and restated that there would be no job losses or factory closures. Again the Cadbury board turned this down, but 24 hours later they changed their mind and accepted it. The deal therefore went through; and a further 24 hours later, Kraft announced the closure of a Cadbury factory at Bristol and the relocation of this work to Poland. There would be 700 immediate job losses from the closure.

In many ways, therefore, this example shows that, despite a much deeper understanding of how organizations work, and work effectively, very little sometimes changes in practice. In this case, a remote and distant management has used its financial size to get its own way, while promises made have simply been broken. The future of Cadbury is far from certain, and this uncertainty will inevitably affect the company culture, identity and ethos, as well as long-term management and work team performance.

- Currency collapses or surges making activities either too expensive to complete, or too expensive to contemplate.
- Turbulence in the global economy, especially competitive surges from different parts of the world.
- Changes in consumer demand and confidence caused by unfair trading practices on the part of manufacturers and service producers in areas of perceived cheap activities. (It should always be remembered that the first countries to be accused of this were Japan on manufacturing; the Gulf States and Norway on oil production; and Switzerland on banking and finance industry practices.)
- Resorting to public relations campaigns, rather than managerial enquiry, to counter the commentaries by media on organization and sectoral shortfalls.
- The practice of taking refuge in perceived sectoral league tables; this leads to the excuse that 'We are doing no worse than anyone else in our sector', or 'We are all beset by difficult trading conditions', as a substitute for active managerial responsibility (see Box 25.11).

Box 25.11: Bone idle

Reference has been made throughout the text above to the phenomenon of 'managerial laziness'. To date, there exists a large body of managerial practice which fails to attend to details, or else loses interest the minute that problems and difficulties arise.

This should be compared and contrasted with the following statement. It was made by Nicholas Hayek, the chief executive of SMH, the holding company for the entire Swiss watch industry. Speaking in 1994, he stated:

> I will not employ anyone – operative, engineer, designer, manager or executive – who refuses to take an active interest in the business. In particular, all executives need to know everything that is going on in their business. Anyone who simply wishes to turn up and collect a salary is not welcome here. Where I find this going on, I will dismiss them.

Of course, laziness is a behavioural trait. From a managerial perspective, laziness means:

- refusing to address difficult issues;
- unwillingness to learn how people collectively or individually think, behave and react;
- unwillingness to set standards, and ensure that people meet them;
- unwillingness to confront difficult or contentious issues or people.

In practice, managerial laziness is not always easy to observe or define. After all, anyone who is working anything up to 16 hours per day is clearly not 'lazy', at least in one-dimensional terms. However, by keeping their hands full, many people in this position are indeed being 'lazy', in that they are keeping themselves busy with what they are willing to do, while actually refusing to do what is necessary.

In practice, there is enough management literature, training, development, under-standing and awareness in all sectors, as well as overall, to ensure that each of these factors can be understood and accommodated. The most successful organizations in the long-term are those that accept the constraints under which they have to operate, accept the potential for competitive and operational turbulence, and understand the factors outside their control within which they have to operate. In the future, the best managers are going to be those who take active responsibility for this, and continue to deliver high-quality, high-value, profitable and effective products and services, rather than those who take refuge in a ready-made list of excuses.

The most important lesson for all managers to accept is that coping with change and uncertainty, and achieving things through people, comes with a wide range of active responsibilities. It is essential that those who seek and aspire to be effective and successful managers in the future learn and understand that the key to this is becoming expert in organizational, collective and individual behaviour, so as to be able to respond to anything that occurs in human, as well as professional, terms.

Bibliography and references

Abodaher D. (1986) *Iacocca* Star Books
ACAS (2007) *Flexible Working: an employers' guide* ACAS
Adair J.H. (1975) *Action-Centred Leadership* Cambridge University Press
Adair J.H. (1986) *Effective Team Building* Gower
Adair J.H. (2005) *Leadership* Gower
Adair J.H (2007) *Effective Group Leadership* Arrow
Adams I., S. Hamil and A. Carruthers (1994) *The Future of Organisations* Free Press
Adams S. (1999) *The Joy of Work* Boxtree
Adams S. (2003) *The Dilbert Principle* Boxtree
Argyle M. (1989) *The Social Psychology of Work* Penguin
Argyris C. (1957) *Personality and Organisations* Harper & Row
Armstrong M. (1993) *Personnel Management* Prentice-Hall
Armstrong M. (ed) (1995) *Strategic Human Resource Management* Kogan Page
Arnold J. (1997) *Work Psychology* Pitman
Ash M.K. (1985) *On People Management*, McDonald
Baron R. (1987) 'Workplace aggression as a consequence of negative performance feedback' *Management Communication Quarterly*, Vol. 10, No. 4, 433–454
Bartlett C., S. Ghoshal and J. Birkinshaw (2004) *Transnational Management* McGraw Hill
Beevor A. (2007) *Stalingrad* Faber and Faber
Belbin R.M. (1986; 2002) *Superteams* Prentice-Hall
Belbin R M. (1992) *Creating Effective Workplace Teams* Prentice-Hall
Berne E.H. (1984) *Games People Play* Penguin.
Bevan J. (2008) *The Rise and Fall (and Rise Again) of Marks and Spencer* Harper Business
Biddle D. and C. Evenden (1989) *Human Aspects of Management* IPM
Blake R. and J. Mouton (1996) *The New Managerial Grid* Gulf
de Bono E. (1984) *Lateral Thinking for Managers* Pelican
Bower T. (2000) *Virgin King: the unauthorised biography of Richard Branson* Harper
Branson R. (1996) *Losing my Virginity* Virgin Publishing
Braun E. (1999) *Futile Progress* Earthscan
Burnes B. (2007) *Organisational Change* Pearson
Burns T. and G.M. Stalker (1956) *Local Government and Central Control* Routledge
Burns T. and G.M. Stalker (1961) *The Management of Innovation* Tavistock
Cairncross F. (1999) *Technology's Empty Promise* Abacus
Cairncross F. (2003) *Green Inc* Earthscan
Carnegie D. (1936; 2004) *How to Win Friends and Influence People* Simon & Schuster
Cartwright R. (2000) *Mastering Customer Relations* Palgrave
Cartwright R. (2001) *Mastering the Business Environment* Palgrave
Caulkin S. (1995) *Hooked on High Tech* Business International
Champoux J. (2003) *Organizational Behaviour* Thomson
Charkin R. (2009) *So You Want to be a CEO?* Creative Content
Chartered Management Institute (2006) *Pressure at Work* CMI
Cheatle K. (2001) *Mastering Human Resource Management* Palgrave

Christensen C.R. (1980) *Business Policy* Irwin
Churchill, W. (1950) *The War Diaries* Allan & Unwin
CIPD (2008) *Equality and Diversity* CIPD
Clark A. (1998) *Barbarossa* Penguin
Clark E. (1988) *The Want Makers* Orion
Clark P. (1991) *Beyond the Deal* Harper
Cole G.A. (1994) *Management Theory and Practice* DPP
Cooper C. (2002) *Stress at Work* Hodder and Stoughton
Cornelius N. (2004) *Human Resource Management* Thomson Press
Creaton S. (2006) *Ryanair: the Story of an Airline* Abacus
Cruver B. (2003) *Enron: Anatomy of Greed* Harper
Daft R. (2007) *Management* Free Press
Deal T. and A. Kennedy (1973; 2001) *Corporate Cultures* Perseus Books
Donaldson B. and T. O'Toole (2002) *Strategic Market Relationships* Wiley
Donovan G. (1967) *Royal Commission on Trades Unions and Industrial Relations* HMSO
Drennan D. (1992) *Transforming Company Culture* McGraw-Hill
Drucker P.F. (1955) *Management by Objectives* Prentice-Hall
Drucker P.F. (1986a) *Drucker on Management* Prentice-Hall
Drucker P.F. (1986b) *The Practice of Management* Prentice-Hall
Drucker P.F. (1988) *The Effective Executive* Fontana
Drucker P.F. (1990) *Frontiers of Management* Heinemann
Drucker P.F. (1993a) *The Ecological Vision* Transaction
Drucker P.F. (1993b) *The Post-Capitalist Society* HarperCollins
Drucker P.F. (1999) *Management Challenges for the Twenty First Century* HarperCollins
Egan G. (1994) 'Cultivate your Culture' *Management Today* (April)
Etzioni A. (1964) *Power in Organisations* Free Press
Fiedler F.E. (1967) *A Theory of Leadership Effectiveness* McGraw-Hill
Fontana D. (1989) *Managing Stress* Excel Books
Fontana D. (2001) *Managing Stress: problems and practice* Routledge
French J. and B. Raven (1959) 'The Bases of Social Power', in D. Cartwright (ed.), *Studies in Social Power* University of Michigan
Frith R. (2008) *Communicating in Comfort* UCL
Furnham A. and A. Schaeffer (1984) 'Person-environment: fit, job satisfaction and mental health' *Journal of Occupational Psychology*, Vol. 57, 295–307
Goldsmith W. and D. Clutterbuck (1990) *The Winning Streak* Penguin
Goldthorpe J.H. *et al.* (1961) *The Affluent Worker, Vol. 1* Cambridge University Press
Goldthorpe J.H. *et al.* (1968) *The Affluent Worker, Vol. 3* Cambridge University Press
Gratton L. (2006) *Living Strategy* FTPearson
Greenberg J. and R. Baron (2007) *Behaviour in Organisations* Prentice-Hall International
Griseri P. (1998) *Managing Values* Macmillan
Griseri P. (2004) *Management Knowledge* Macmillan
Handy C.B. (1984) *The Future of Work* Penguin
Handy C.B. (1988) *The Age of Unreason* Penguin
Handy C.B. (1991) *The Gods of Management* Arrow
Handy C.B. (1992) *The Empty Raincoat* Arrow
Handy C.B. (1995) *Beyond Certainty* Macmillan
Handy C.B. (1970; 1996) *Understanding Organisations* Penguin
Handy C.B. (2006) *Understanding Organisations* Penguin
Handy C.B. and R. Harrison (1973; 2004) *Organisation Cultures* Wiley
Handy C.B. *et al.* (1981) *Making Managers* Penguin
Harris P. and R. Moran (1991) *Managing Cultural Differences* Gulf
Harvey Jones J. (1992) *Making it Happen* Harper
Heller R. (1996) *In Search of European Excellence* HarperCollins

Henry J. (1995) *Creative Management* Open University Press
Herz N. (2001) *The Silent Takeover* Arrow
Herzberg F. (1960, 1974) *Work and the Nature of Man* Granada
Herzberg F. *et al.* (1959) *The Motivation to Work* Chapman & Hall
Hofstede G. (1980; 2004) *Culture's Consequences* Sage
Hofstede G. (1996) *Culture and Organisations* Sage
Holmes T. and R. Rahe (1967) 'The Social Adjustment Rating Scale' *Journal of Psychosomatic Research*, Vol. 11, No. 2, 213–8
Honey P. and A. Mumford (2006) *Preferred Learning Styles* Peter Honey Publications
Huczynski D. and A. Buchanan (2006*) Organisational Behaviour* Pearson
Jay A. (1967) *Management and Machiavelli* Holt, Rinehart & Winston
Jay A. and J. Lynn (1999) *The Complete 'Yes Minister'* BBC
Johnson G., K. Scholes and R. Whittington (2007) *Exploring Corporate Strategy* Pearson
Kanter R.M. (1988) *When Giants Learn to Dance* Harvard
Kanter R.M. (1991) *The Change Masters* Harvard
Katz D. and R.L. Kahn (1978) *The Social Psychology of Organisations* Wiley
Kessler S. and F. Bayliss (1995) *Contemporary Industrial Relations* Macmillan
Klein N. (2001) *No Logo* HarperCollins
Kolb D. (1985) *Experiential Learning: experience as a source of learning and development* Prentice-Hall
Lessem R.S. (1987) *Intrapreneurship* Wildwood/Gower
Lessem R.S. (1991) *Global Management Principles* Prentice-Hall
Likert R. (1961) *New Patterns of Management* McGraw-Hill
Likert R. (1967) *The Human Organisation* McGraw-Hill
Livy B. (1987) *Corporate Personnel Management* Pitman
Luthans F. (1986) *Organisational Behaviour* McGraw-Hill
McAlpine A. (1999) *The New Machiavelli* Harper Business
McClelland D.C. (1988) *Human Motivation* Cambridge University Press
McGregor D. (1960) *The Human Side of Enterprise* Harper & Row
McSweeney B. (2002) 'Hofstede's model of national cultures and their consequences: a triumph of faith, a failure of analysis' *Journal of Human Relations*, Vol. 55, No. 1, 89–98
Machiavelli N. (1993) *The Prince* Penguin Classics
Maslow A. (1960; 1987) *Motivation and Personality* Harper & Row
Metcalfe R. (1980) *Computers and the Ethernet* Xerox publications
Metcalfe S. (1980) *The Economics of Technological Progress* Macmillan
Mintzberg H. (1979) *The Structuring of Organisations* Wiley
Mintzberg H. *et al.* (2005) *The Strategy Process* Prentice-Hall
Montgomery B. (1957) *Montgomery of Alamein* Weidenfeld and Nicolson
Moore J. (1988) *Writers on Strategy* Penguin
Moore J. (2001) *Writers on Strategy and Strategic Management* Penguin
Morita A. (1987) *Made in Japan: The Sony Story* Collins
Mullins L. (2008) *Management and Organisational Behaviour* FTPearson
Nicholl P. (2005) *Leading and Directing in the Central Banking Sector* Central Banking Publications
Ohmae K. (1990) *The Mind of the Strategist* Harper and Row
Ouchi W.G. (1981) *Theory Z* Avon
Owen H. (1985) *Myth Transformation and Change* Collins
Owen J. (2003) *Hard Core Management* Pearson
Owen J. (2006) *Inspirational Leadership* Pearson
Owen J. (2009) *Great Leadership* FTPearson
Parsons R. (2002) *The Heart of Success* Hodder and Stoughton
Pascal R. and A. Athos (1990) *The Art of Japanese Management* Free Press
Payne D. and D. Pugh (1970) *Organisations* Penguin
Payne D. and D. Pugh (2004) *Organisation Theory* Penguin

Peters T. (1986) *The World Turned Upside Down* Channel Four
Peters T. (1990) *Thriving on Chaos* Pan
Peters T. (1992) *Liberation Management* Pan
Peters T. (2000) *The Tom Peters Seminar* Dorling Kindersley
Peters T. and N. Austin (1986) *A Passion for Excellence* Collins
Peters T. and R. Waterman (1982) *In Search of Excellence* Harper Business
Pettinger R. (1998) *Managing the Flexible Workforce* Cassell
Pettinger R. (1999) *Investment Appraisal: a Managerial Approach* Macmillan
Pettinger R. (2002) *Mastering Employee Development* Palgrave
Pettinger R. (2005) *Contemporary Strategic Management* Palgrave
Pettinger R. (2007) *Introduction to Management 4th Edition* Palgrave
Pfeffer J. (1999) *Power in Organisations* Harvard
Pile S. (2000) *The Book of Heroic Failures* Harper
Porter M. (1980) *Competitive Strategy* Free Press
Porter M. (1985) *Competitive Advantage* Free Press
Price L. (2006) *The Spin Doctor's Diary* Hodder and Stoughton
Pugh D. (2004) *Writers on Organisations* Penguin
Reddin W. (1968) *Effective Management by Objectives: the 3D approach* Elsevier
Revans R. (1967) *Action Learning* McGraw Hill
Rice J. (1990) *Doing Business in Japan* BBC
Rogers C. (1947) *Freedom to Learn* Merrill Publishing
Roddick A. (1992) *Body and Soul: the Body Shop Story* Ebury Press
Schein E. (1988) *Organisational Psychology* Prentice-Hall
Semler R. (1992) *Maverick* Century
Semler R. (2003) *The Seven Day Weekend* Century
Senge P. (1992) *The Fifth Discipline* Century
Simon H. (1962) *Administrative Behaviour* Free Press
Statt D. (1994; 2006) *Psychology and the World of Work* Macmillan
Sternberg E. (2006) *Just Business* Warner
Stiglitz J. (2000) *Globalization and its Discontents* Penguin
Taylor A. (1969) *Bismarck: the man and the statesman* Knopf
Thomas K. and R. Kilmann (1974) *The Thomas/Kilmann Conflict Mode Instrument* CPP
Tibballs G. (2001) *Business Blunders* Robinson Publishing
Torrington D. and L. Hall (1995) *Employee Resourcing* CIPD
Torrington D. and J. Weightman (2007) *People Resourcing* CIPD
Tubbs W. (1993) 'Karoushi: stress-death and the meaning of work' *Journal of Business Ethics*, Vol. 12, 869–877
Tuckman B. (1965) 'Developmental sequence in small groups' *Psychological Bulletin*, Vol. 63, 384–399
Turner G. (2008) *The Credit Crunch* Pluto Press
Vroom (1964) *Work and Motivation* Wiley
Walton R.E. and R.B. McKersie (1965) *A Behavioural Theory of Labour Negotiations* McGraw-Hill
Weightman J. (2006) *Managing People* CIPD
Wheeler D. and M. Silanpaa (2002) *The Stakeholder Corporation* Pitman
Whittington R. (2004) *What is Strategy and Does it Matter?* Thomson
Wickens P. (1992) *The Road to Nissan* Collins
Wilkinson R. (1992) *Inequalities in Society* Penguin
Williamson D. (2002) 'Forward from a critique of Hofstede's model of national cultures' *Journal of Human Relations*, Vol. 55, No.11, 1373–1395
Woodward J. (1960) *Industry and Organisation* Oxford University Press
Woodward J. (1970) *Industrial Organisations: Behaviour and Control* Oxford University Press
Ye J.J. (2009) *The Effects of Cultural Background on Perception* UCL
Zimbardo P. (1973) *The Psychology of Imprisonment* Stanford University Press

Index